# THE TAPESTRY OF REASON

In recent years coherence theories of law and adjudication have been extremely influential in legal scholarship. These theories significantly advance the case for coherentism in law. Nonetheless, there remain a number of problems in the coherence theory in law. This ambitious new work makes the first concerted attempt to develop a coherence-based theory of legal reasoning, and in so doing addresses, or at least mitigates these problems. The book is organized in three parts. The first part provides a critical analysis of the main coherentist approaches to both normative and factual reasoning in law. The second part investigates the coherence theory in a number of fields that are relevant to law: coherence theories of epistemic justification, coherentist approaches to belief revision and theory-choice in science, coherence theories of practical and moral reasoning and coherence-based approaches to discourse interpretation. Taking this interdisciplinary analysis as a starting point, the third part develops a coherence-based model of legal reasoning. While this model builds upon the standard theory of legal reasoning, it also leads to rethinking some of the basic assumptions that characterize this theory, and suggests some lines along which it may be further developed. Thus, ultimately, the book not only improves upon the current state of coherence theory in law, but also contributes to the larger debate about how to articulate a theory of legal reasoning that results in better decision-making.

**European Academy of Legal Theory Series: Volume 12**

EUROPEAN ACADEMY OF LEGAL THEORY
MONOGRAPH SERIES

**General Editors**
Professor Mark Van Hoecke
Professor François Ost

**Titles in this Series**

Moral Conflict and Legal Reasoning
*Scott Veitch*

The Harmonisation of European Private Law
*edited by Mark Van Hoecke & Francois Ost*

On Law and Legal Reasoning
*Fernando Atria*

Law as Communication
*Mark Van Hoecke*

Legisprudence
*edited by Luc Wintgens*

Epistemology and Methodology of Comparative Law
*edited by Mark van Hoecke*

Making the Law Explicit
The Normativity of Legal Argumentation
*Matthias Klatt*

The Policy of Law
A Legal Theoretical Framework
*Mauro Zamboni*

Methodologies of Legal Research
Which Kind of Method for What Kind of Discipline?
*edited by Mark van Hoecke*

Objectivity in Law and Legal Reasoning
*edited by Jaakko Husa and Mark van Hoecke*

An Introduction to Comparative Law Theory and Method
*Geoffrey Samuel*

# The Tapestry of Reason

## An Inquiry into the Nature of Coherence and its Role in Legal Argument

Amalia Amaya

•HART•
PUBLISHING
OXFORD AND PORTLAND, OREGON
2017

**Hart Publishing**
An imprint of Bloomsbury Publishing Plc

Hart Publishing Ltd
Kemp House
Chawley Park
Cumnor Hill
Oxford OX2 9PH
UK

Bloomsbury Publishing Plc
50 Bedford Square
London
WC1B 3DP
UK

**www.hartpub.co.uk**
**www.bloomsbury.com**

Published in North America (US and Canada) by
Hart Publishing
c/o International Specialized Book Services
920 NE 58th Avenue, Suite 300
Portland, OR 97213-3786
USA

**www.isbs.com**



First published in hardback, 2015
Paperback edition, 2017



**British Library Cataloguing-in-Publication Data**
A catalogue record for this book is available from the British Library.

ISBN: PB: 978-1-50991-546-0
HB: 978-1-84946-070-5

Typeset by Compuscript Ltd, Shannon
Printed and bound in Great Britain by
Lightning Source UK Ltd

To find out more about our authors and books visit www.hartpublishing.co.uk. Here you will find extracts, author information, details of forthcoming events and the option to sign up for our newsletters.

A mis padres

# Acknowledgements

This book is based on my PhD dissertation, which I was privileged to do at the European University Institute. I am deeply grateful to Massimo La Torre, my PhD supervisor at the European University Institute, for his unwavering confidence and support through the many years it took me to write the dissertation of which this book is a descendant. To Manuel Atienza I owe a great personal and intellectual debt. He first led my way into philosophy of law when I was law student at the University of Alicante and, afterwards, as PhD supervisor, worked indefatigably on the dissertation, providing me with vigorous, but respectful, direction. The feedback given by Robert Alexy and Giovanni Sartor, as members of the PhD examining board, was precious for turning the dissertation into a book. This work would be very different had I not had the opportunity to spend some years at Harvard University. I am most grateful to Philippe Alston for his inestimable help in facilitating the transition from Florence to Cambridge as well as for his encouragement thorough the whole project.

Some of the ideas first elaborated in the PhD dissertation migrated and grew in my SJD dissertation, to finally return to this manuscript. I am greatly indebted to my SJD supervisor, Frederick Schauer, for his sustained guidance and support over the years I have been engaged in this project. I have learnt a lot – and this manuscript has greatly benefited—from his to-the-point criticisms and insight. I am also very grateful to Noam Chomsky and Robert Stalnaker who, as field supervisors of the SJD, devoted much time and energy in helping me to grasp many of the philosophical and linguistic problems discussed here and provided exceedingly valuable comments on several chapters of this book. For extensive discussion on some of the topics covered in this book I should thank Catherine Elgin, who also provided very helpful suggestions as member of the SJD examining board. The criticism received from Barbara Spellman, also a member of the SJD examining board, was very useful for improving on the psychological dimensions of the argument developed here.

This book is deeply interdisciplinary, and it would have been impossible for me to undertake a project of this nature without the generous help of many people. For useful discussion, I should thank Josep Aguiló, Arthur Applbaum, Jason Baehr, Scott Brewer, John Deigh, Michael Glanzberg, Peter Godfrey-Smith, Daniel González, Susan Haack, Irene Heim, Christine Korsgaard, Richard Moran, Charles Nesson, Robert Nozick, Vlad Perju, Hilary Putnam, Larry Sager, Dan Simon, Paul Thagard, Peter Tillers, William Twining and Mark Van Hoecke. I am very grateful to Ronald

Allen, Floris Bex, Jorge Cerdio, Juan Antonio Cruz, Marcelo Ferrante, Hendrik Kaptein, Henry Prakken, Rosella Rubino, David Sosa, Alex Stein, Walter Sinnott-Armstrong, German Súcar and Bart Verheij for valuable comments on writing material that have been incorporated, some way or another, into this manuscript. Special thanks to Atocha Aliseda, Michal Araszkiewicz, Carmen Curcó, Maksymilian del Mar, Maite Ezcurdia, Miguel Angel Fernández, Richard Heck, Ho Hock Lai, Juliano Maranhão, Gustavo Ortiz, James Pryor, Victoria Roca, Aldo Schiavello and Moises Vaca for their suggestions and comments on previous drafts of several chapters. For enjoyable discussions and sound advice on coherence and beyond, I am very grateful to Larry Laudan, who commented on several portions of the manuscript as well. I am also much obliged to Pablo Navarro, for his extremely kind invitation to devote an issue of *Discusiones* to the discussion of my work on legal coherentism. The criticisms raised by the contributors to that volume, namely, Manuel Atienza, Guillermo Lariguet, Juliano Maranhão, Claudio Michelon, Cristina Redondo and Aldo Schiavello, force me to clarify my views on coherence and law and to revise them in significant ways.

Some parts of this work were discussed at the Philosophy of Law Seminar at the University of Alicante, the SJD colloquium at Harvard Law School, the Graduate Fellows' Seminar at the Edmund J. Safra Center for Ethics at Harvard University, the XXIII World Congress of Philosophy of Law and Social Philosophy at Cracow, the Conference on Evidence and Law at Darmouth College, the *Noûs* Group at the University of Costa Rica, the Practical Philosophy Seminar and the Research Fellows Seminar at the Institute for Philosophical Research of the National Autonomous University of Mexico, the First Latin American Conference on Legal Epistemology at the University of Los Andes and the University of Texas School of Law at Austin. The suggestions and discussions with the participants in these forums greatly aided me to develop the ideas presented here. I benefited a great deal from discussion with the participants of a Byse Workshop that I gave on coherence in evidential reasoning at Harvard Law School as well as from discussion with students at a number of graduate seminars I taught on coherentism while writing this manuscript at the National Autonomous University of Mexico, the University of Costa Rica, the National University of Costa Rica, the National University of the South and the European Academy of Legal Theory.

For research support I am very grateful to The Gil Albert Institute, La Caixa Foundation, Harvard Law School, the Edmund J. Safra Center for Ethics, the Spanish Ministry of Education and the European University Institute. The Institute for Philosophical Research at the National Autonomous University of Mexico, my home institution, has been a wonderful place to be at the last stages of this project. Not only has it provided a friendly and stimulating working environment but it has also supported the process of writing this book by granting me a leave of absence to spend a semester at the University of Texas at Austin, where the manuscript was completed. For research assistance I thank my students Salvador Delgado, Eduardo Lapatí, Leoncio Monroy, Paola Recendiz and, especially, Ricardo Miranda. I am also very grateful to Pedro Espinosa, librarian at the Institute of Philosophical Research, for his efficient help thorough the final stages. Alicia Cabrera and Javier Blesa provided much needed technical assistance, which was vital for finalizing the manuscript.

Finally, I would like to express my gratitude to my (big) family, for their love and care during the process of writing this manuscript. They are the emotional pillar without which it would not have been possible for me to engage in any intellectual pursuit. To Maje, my dearest friend, I owe a continuous support through this book, as through all things in life. Pablo has been engaged in this project with unparalleled commitment, fortitude and enthusiasm. We have walked together all the way and for that I feel most fortunate and immensely grateful. My two children, Amalia Guadalupe and Pablo Antonio, were born during the process of writing this book, which made completing the book much more challenging, but also filled it with indescribable joy. It is to their grandparents, Amalia and Manuel, who taught me to take delight in effort and nurtured a curiosity for learning, that this book is dedicated.

# Contents

# Introduction

COHERENCE FIGURES PROMINENTLY in contemporary approaches to reasoning and rationality across different disciplines. Coherentism is a central position in the longstanding debate about the structure of epistemic justification. Coherence is also a main topic in the new, emerging, field of formal epistemology. In philosophy of science, explanatory coherentism has been advocated as a main alternative to the dominant Bayesian approach to theory choice. Coherentist views of the nature of truth are far more controversial than coherentist approaches to the justification of empirical and scientific beliefs. However, in the last decades, new forms of the coherence theory of truth have been developed and this theory is still advanced as a main competitor to the traditional view of truth as correspondence. In the domain of practical, rather than theoretical reason, coherence also plays a prevalent role. Important accounts of practical deliberation give coherence a place of privilege and moral reasoning is widely regarded as a coherentist kind of reasoning. Coherence features not only in philosophical approaches to reasoning and rationality but also in psychological approaches to the subject. Cognitive psychologists and linguists have used the concept of coherence to give an account of problems as diverse as impression formation, decision-making, discourse processing and analogical mapping.

In law, coherentism has been a very popular position as well. Coherence theories of law and adjudication have been extremely influential in contemporary legal theory. There are a number of reasons that make legal coherentism initially attractive. Coherentist standards of legal justification enjoy a high degree of psychological plausibility; they are particularly amenable to dynamic and emotional aspects of legal justification; they are instrumental to a number of central values in law; they bring about important social benefits; and they significantly contribute to the constitution of political identities and, in so doing, to the advancement of law's objective of resolving conflict rationally. These reasons make legal coherentism an appealing alternative, as I argue in this book, to both formalistic and sceptical approaches to legal reasoning.

Coherentism, however, faces formidable challenges. First, coherence is an elusive notion, and there is a need to further clarify how coherence should be understood for the purposes of legal justification. Secondly, the process whereby coherence is constructed in the course of legal decision-making remains largely mysterious. Thirdly, a coherence theory faces the challenge of showing that coherentist justification is neither viciously circular nor unduly conservative. Fourthly, there is a need to develop legal coherentism in a way that avoids its allegiance with an unrestricted version of holism that is the source of a number of serious problems. Last, legal coherentism should provide a thorough defence of the value of coherence in law. Despite the significant progress made by proponents of coherence theories of law and adjudication, these critical issues remain open, to a great extent, in the present literature on legal coherentism.

This book aims to improve on the current state of the coherence theory in law by developing a coherence theory of legal reasoning that has the resources to address (or, at least, mitigate) the foregoing problems. With a view to furthering this aim, the book brings together different perspectives on coherence and law. Reflection on coherence and law has been undertaken from within different bodies of legal scholarship. Legal theorists have mostly focused on the role that coherence plays with regard to normative issues, to the detriment of factual issues. Broadly coherentist positions have been developed by some evidence lawyers and narrative theorists. In the field of law and psychology, important work has been done on the relevance of coherence to both judicial and jury decision-making. There has been, however, little intersection between these varied literatures. As a result, theories of normative and factual coherence have been developed independently of one another; both kinds of theories, moreover, have largely unacknowledged current empirical work on the role that coherence plays in both normative and evidential reasoning in law. This book attempts to cross the disciplinary boundaries that have segmented the study of coherence in law by providing a theory of coherence that is meant to be applicable to both reasoning about facts and norms and that, in light of psychological research, has a good claim to psychological plausibility.

The main tenet of the theory of coherence defended in this book is that a belief about the facts under dispute or about what the law requires is justified if and only if it could be the outcome of epistemically responsible coherence-based reasoning, that is to say, if it is 'optimally coherent'. Coherence-based reasoning is taken to be an explanatory kind of reasoning: legal decision-makers reach optimally coherent beliefs about the facts and the law by means of an inference to the best explanation. According to this theory, coherence (both factual and normative) is a matter of satisfying a number of positive and negative constraints and a standard of legal justification that is highly sensitive to contextual factors. Optimal coherence, ie coherence against the background of epistemically responsible action, results, on this view, in legal justification.

This book falls into three parts. The first part, containing chapters one and two, provides a critical analysis of the current state of the coherence theory in law. The second part, containing chapters three through nine, investigates the coherence theory in a number of disciplines that are relevant to law. The third part, chapter ten, returns to law and aims to identify the main coherentist ideas across the examined domains and to put them to use in order to build a coherence theory of legal reasoning. Thus, the strategy followed is deeply interdisciplinary. The guiding idea is that an analysis of coherence theories proposed in different disciplines may decisively help us to better understand the concept of coherence and the nature of the problems that coherentism in law confronts as well as to identify the resources available, within the coherence theory, to successfully address these problems. While the coherence model that results from this work builds upon the standard theory of legal reasoning, it also leads us to rethink some of the basic assumptions which characterize this theory and suggests some lines along which it may be further developed. Thus, ultimately, this work is not only meant to improve upon the current state of the coherence theory in law, but also to contribute to the larger debate about how to articulate a theory of legal reasoning that results in better decision-making.

The discussions of the different topics in coherentism covered in this book converge in a particular vision about the nature of coherence and its role in legal argument. However, I have tried to make all chapters of the book self-contained so as to allow readers to select specific chapters depending on their interests. Readers interested mostly in epistemological issues are advised to read chapters two, three and four. Formal work on coherence may be found in chapters five and six. Those with an interest in practical philosophy might find one, seven and eight useful. Chapter nine is for readers interested in linguistics; philosophy of language is discussed in chapter six. My own approach to coherence and justification in law is provided in chapter ten. Although this chapter draws on the rest of the chapters, it is also meant to be a self-standing piece. Ample cross-references among chapters have been provided with a view to connecting the threads of argument that link ideas about coherence across disciplines, enabling the inclined reader to engage in a transdisciplinary analysis of coherentism and track its common trends, challenges and motivations.

There follows a brief sketch of the contents of each of the chapters. Chapter one provides a survey of the coherence theory as has been developed in legal theory. Three main coherentist approaches to legal reasoning are examined: MacCormick's views on normative coherence; Dworkin's theory of law as integrity; and Peczenik's weight and balance model of coherence. After stating the main objections that may be raised against these theories, I evaluate the extent to which they advance the objective of offering an alternative (and broader) view about the scope of reason in law than the one endorsed by formal legal positivism, which, it is argued, is the chief motivation driving the proposal of coherence theories in law.

Chapter two examines the main coherence-based approaches to legal reasoning about facts, which are the main alternative to the dominant probabilistic theories of legal proof, more specifically, the Bayesian model. After exposing the main problems of Bayesian approaches to evidence and proof, I discuss some proposals by evidence scholars that give coherence a prominent role in factual reasoning in law. Then, I analyse some jurisprudential views which take narrative coherence to be a crucial standard for the justification of conclusions about disputed questions of fact in law. Next, I explore the implications for coherentist approaches to legal reasoning of psychological research about how judges and juries reason about facts in law. This research provides the coherence theory with a solid empirical basis. However, it also reveals the risks inherent in coherence-based reasoning. Thus, for the coherence theory to provide a plausible alternative to the Bayesian model, it is necessary to show that it is not only psychologically plausible, but also normatively appealing. Several problems with current coherentist approaches to evidence and proof are identified, and some strategies for overcoming them are suggested.

Once the survey of coherence theories of law is completed, in chapter three, I begin to explore how coherence operates in argumentative contexts other than law. This chapter discusses the role of coherence in current work in epistemology. I focus on two main coherence theories of justification, namely, Lehrer's and BonJour's. These theories significantly advance the coherence theory on two fronts. On the one hand, they provide a cogent defence of the coherentist project against well-known objections, thereby showing the plausibility of the coherentist alternative to the traditional foundationalist picture of epistemic justification. On the other hand, they succeed in presenting a very detailed coherentist account of epistemic justification. Nonetheless, both theories may be criticized on the grounds that they put forward a model of justification that is beyond the capacities of most epistemic agents. I argue that this problem is to be taken seriously, for, ultimately, BonJour's and Leher's replies to the traditional objections against coherentism crucially depend on whether a solution to the problem of psychological plausibility is available. I claim that a contextualist version of coherentism is psychologically plausible and in a better position to respond to the objections that are raised against coherentism.

Chapter four examines the theory of explanatory coherence. According to this theory, whether a belief is justified depends on the way in which it fits into the best explanation. After examining a number of assumptions that characterize the theories of explanatory coherence, I focus on Thagard's version. Thagard has presented a computational theory that gives a precise account of coherence and of how it may be computed. I argue that this theory, suitably modified to account for the peculiarities of legal reasoning, provides a starting point for developing a theory of coherence that is precise enough to be usable in the legal context. The analysis of the theories of explanatory coherence further aids the project of developing a coherence-based theory of legal reasoning in two respects. Firstly, it brings to light the crucial role that explanations play in coherence-based legal reasoning. And, secondly, it provides a model of inference, to wit, inference to the best explanation, on the basis of which an account of coherence-driven inference in law may be articulated.

In chapter five, I deal with the issue of how, according to the coherence theory, we may rationally revise our beliefs. The basic tenet of coherence theories of belief revision is that we should change our beliefs in a way that maximizes coherence while minimizing change. Several formalisms have been proposed to model rational processes of belief revision. First, I introduce the most influential of these formalisms, the AGM model, and argue that a coherentist interpretation of this model is very problematical. Then, I discuss Olsson's generalized version of Hansson's theory of semi-revision. I conclude by arguing that, although Olsson's theory falls short of formalizing important aspects of the coherentist epistemology, it provides us with an extremely valuable array of coherence-based strategies of belief change upon which a detailed account of the different mechanisms whereby coherence emerges in the course of decision-making may be developed.

One of the main objections against coherence theories of epistemic justification is that there seems to be no compelling reason to believe that coherence is truth-conducive. Unless such a reason is given—so the argument goes—coherentist standards of epistemic justification cannot themselves be justified. In chapter six, I explore the relation between coherence and truth. After briefly examining some of the main realist and anti-realist arguments to the effect that coherence is truth-conducive, I focus on Davidson's views on truth and coherence. Then, I examine some recent attempts to connect coherence and truth by using probability theory. I conclude that none of the arguments for the truth-conduciveness of coherence seems conclusive. However, this is not a reason for despair, for, contrary to what is generally assumed, the meta-justification of coherentist standards of justification does not exclusively depend on whether those standards may be shown to be truth-conducive, but also on the extent to which they promote the achievement of goals other than truth that are taken to be important in a given domain.

While the preceding chapters explore the role of coherence in epistemic justification, the next two chapters move from the domain of theoretical reason to that of practical reason. Chapter seven examines the role of coherence in practical reasoning. The current debate in practical reasoning focuses on the question of what inference patterns are legitimate methods for arriving at decisions, plans, policies and judgements about what one ought to do. Some philosophers have answered this question by appealing to coherence. That is, they claim that coherence is the crucial standard against which the legitimacy of our practical inferences should be assessed. What this suggestion amounts to depends on one's views about the structure of practical inference. Specificationism holds that practical reasoning partly consists in specifying our conflicting ends and norms so as to render them coherent. According to case-based weighing models, our practical deliberations importantly proceed case by case, and their rationality is largely a matter of how well they preserve coherence across analogous cases. Other philosophers claim that practical reasoning amounts to choosing the most coherent plan, that is, the subset of goals, actions, emotions and values that best cohere with one another. This chapter examines the foregoing views on practical coherence, and argues that these proposals, taken together, provide an attractive alternative to the instrumentalist conception of practical reasoning.

In Chapter eight I explore the role of coherence in moral reasoning. I start by examining Rawls' method of reflective equilibrium, which is the most influential form of coherentism in ethics. I proceed then to analyse some prominent coherence-based accounts of moral reasoning, namely, DePaul's method of balance and refinement, Goldman's method of analogy and difference and Thagard's theory of ethical coherence. Several objections have been raised against the method of reflective equilibrium, eg that this method cannot guarantee anything more than a systematization of our moral prejudices, that it is at bottom a version of intuitionism, and that it fails to guide the agent's choice of moral views. It has been argued that, in order to meet these objections, it is required that the notion of reflective equilibrium be extended so as to incorporate the crucial role that emotions and perception play in moral reasoning. I examine the extent to which an 'extended reflective equilibrium' has the resources for meeting the main objections that have been raised against the use of coherence methods in ethics. The final section discusses the controversial issue of whether endorsing a coherence method of moral reasoning commits one to either moral realism or constructivism.

Chapter nine addresses the question of what role coherence plays in interpretation. Such an analysis is crucial for developing an account of legal reasoning that is responsive to the interpretative nature of legal argument. In this chapter, I review the most important views about discourse coherence, namely, topic-based theories of coherence, coherence relations approach, accounts of coherence in terms of mental models, and hermeneutic and intentional approaches, and argue that these views should not be seen as alternative theories of discourse coherence, but rather as complementary. I proceed then to examine the relevance theorists' critique to coherence-based theories of discourse interpretation. I contend that this critique does not show coherence theories to be untenable, but it does point out some problems that the coherence theory of discourse interpretation needs to face. Most importantly, such a theory should give an account of how coherence relates to other important notions in discourse theory such as acceptability and intelligibility; it ought to explicate the process of contextualization whereby discourse coherence is construed; and it needs to make explicit the implications of the coherence theory of discourse for a theory of discourse rationality. I conclude this chapter by suggesting some lines along which a coherence theory of discourse could be developed so as to deal with those issues.

After this long interdisciplinary journey through coherence's domain, I return to law in chapter ten. First, I redraw a map of problems of current coherence theories in law, emphasizing the structural similarity of these problems in relation to both reasoning about facts and reasoning about norms. Then, I identify some of the tools that the analysis undertaken in the previous chapters has put at our disposal for improving upon the current state of the coherence theory in law. I pick among the diverse perspectives on coherence that have been studied some of the elements and themes which I take to be valuable in thinking about coherence and law. I argue that these elements constitute the building blocks for constructing a coherence-based model of legal reasoning that has the resources to address the main objections that may be raised against current coherence theories in law.

The model that I develop has the following four components: a concept of legal coherence in terms of constraint satisfaction; an account of coherence-based legal inference as inference to the best explanation; a view of legal justification as optimal coherence; and a contextualist approach to the coherentist standards of justification. Next, I consider how the proposed theory deals with the main problems of coherentism in law. Most prominent amongst these critiques is that coherence theories of law fail to effect the appropriate connection between coherence and truth. I reject the assumption according to which it is required to conclusively show that such connection obtains for coherentist standards of legal justification to be justified. Different lines of argument are suggested to defend the value of coherence in legal reasoning and the plausibility of the model of coherence proposed.

From this model emerges a view of legal justification that has the following features: (i) it is non-foundationalist, for it takes the justification of any normative or factual proposition in law to be a matter of its relations with other propositions; (ii) it is contextualist, in that it claims that standards of legal justification are subjected to contextual variation; (iii) it is responsibilist, in that it takes the epistemic behavior of legal decision-makers to have a bearing on the justificatory status of their decisions; (iv) it is naturalist, for it is based on the assumption that psychological evidence about how legal decision-makers reason is relevant for answering questions about how they should reason; (v) it is explanationist, in that it takes explanatory merit to be pivotal to assessments of legal justification; and (vi) it endorses a non-instrumentalist view of legal reasoning according to which deliberation in law is also about ends. I conclude this chapter, and this book, by exploring the implications of this model for the received view on legal reasoning and by pointing out some of the problems that the coherence theory articulated and defended in this work opens up. These problems suggest some directions for future research on both the coherence theory and the broader theory of legal reasoning to which it pertains.

# Part I

# Legal Coherentism

# 1

# *Normative Coherence, Justification and Interpretation*

THIS CHAPTER PROVIDES a survey of coherence theories of legal justification. More specifically, it examines a number of coherentist approaches to the justification of disputed questions of law—I defer the discussion of coherence theories of the justification of disputed questions of fact to the next chapter. Two versions of the coherence theory, namely, a 'weak' version and a 'strong' one, may be distinguished. While 'weak' coherence theories claim that normative coherence is a necessary but not a sufficient condition of legal justification, 'strong' coherence theories claim that normative coherence is both a necessary and sufficient condition of legal justification. Thus, whereas some coherence theories of legal justification explain all there is to the justification of normative judgements in terms of coherence, other (more moderate) theories take coherence to be a central contributor, albeit not the only one, to legal justification.

The proposal of coherence theories, both weak and strong, is motivated by dissatisfaction with some aspects of classical legal positivism. Classical legal positivism constructs law and legal reasoning on a 'model of rules', thereby reducing legal reasoning to rule-application and legal justification to derivability from the applicable rules.[1] On this view, when rules fail to provide determinate guidance, judges enjoy discretion, as the reasons of law reach only as far as legal rules do. In contrast, coherence theories claim that there are constraints on what judges may do in these cases, namely, coherence constraints. The law does not run out when legal rules are not dispositive of the case, for there are reasons for coherence by which legal decisions may be justified. Thus, coherence theories aim at enlarging the scope of reason in law beyond the limits imposed by classical legal positivism. Ultimately, the objective of these theories is to provide a non-sceptical account of legal reasoning and rationality broader than the one defended by classical versions of legal positivism.

Keeping in mind the objective that coherence theories aim at achieving, let us now examine some of the main coherence theories proposed in the

[1] The phrase, as is well known, is Dworkin's. See Dworkin (1977) chs 2 and 3.

field of legal theory.[2] I shall discuss three versions of the coherence theory, namely, MacCormick's, Peczenik's and Dworkin's.[3] The discussion of each of these theories has the same structure. First, I examine the concept of legal coherence defended in each theory. Then, I focus on the role that, according to the theory under analysis, coherence plays in legal justification.[4] Last, I consider how each theory justifies the use of coherentist standards of legal justification, that is, I examine the issue of what are the reasons why coherence is a value worth pursuing in law. After completing this survey of coherence theories, I shall state some objections that may be raised against coherence theories in law. I shall conclude this chapter by suggesting some strategies for attacking these problems and, thus, for improving upon the current state of the coherence theory in law.

## I. COHERENCE AND RATIONALITY IN LEGAL REASONING

MacCormick has developed a theory of legal reasoning in which arguments from coherence play a prominent role.[5] In contrast to most coherence theories, MacCormick pays attention to the role that coherence plays in legal reasoning about both facts and norms. He distinguishes between two kinds of coherence that are relevant to legal argument, namely, normative coherence and narrative coherence. While the former has to do with the justification of normative propositions in the context of the legal system, the latter has to do with the justification of factual propositions in the

[2] One may examine coherence in law from two different perspectives: a systemic one—according to which coherence is a feature of the system—and an argumentative one—according to which the coherence of a particular ruling or interpretation works as a justification of the ruling or interpretation in question. In this chapter, I will mainly focus on normative coherence as a standard of justification. For analyses of coherence from a systemic perspective, see Alonso (2006); Pastore (1991); Pérez-Bermejo ((2006) and (2007)); Ratti (2007); and Schröter (2006). On the distinction between systemic and argumentative coherence, see Moral (2003) and Bertea 'The Argument from Coherence' *IVR Encyclopaedia of Jurisprudence, Legal Theory and Philosophy of Law*, available at ivr-enc.info/index.php?title=The_Argument_from_Coherence.

[3] These three authors have played a particularly important role in establishing coherentism as an alternative theory of legal justification. For some earlier coherence theories of legal justification, see Sartorious ((1968) and (1971)); and Hoffmaster (1980). Other important coherentist approaches in law include Günther ((1989), (1993) and (1995)); Moore (1987); Wintgens ((1992), (1993) and (2000)); and Hage ((2001), (2004), (2005) and (2013)). For a discussion of these theories, see Araszkiewicz (2010a).

[4] I will focus exclusively on the role that coherence plays in the justification of judicial decisions. This is the dominant perspective in contemporary approaches to legal coherence. However, it is worth noticing here that, unlike other theories, Dworkin gives some thought to the place of coherence within a theory of legislation. See Dworkin (1986) esp chs 6 and 8. On the role of coherence in a theory of legislation, see also Bobbio (1971: 243–49); Ost (1985: 191–204); and Wintgens ((2000: 547–50) and (2012)).

[5] See N MacCormick (1994).

context of legal fact-finding.[6] Since this chapter is devoted to analysing the role that coherence plays in reasoning about disputed questions of law, I shall focus on the notion and role of normative coherence in MacCormick's theory of legal reasoning. MacCormick's views on narrative coherence will be discussed in the next chapter, which examines the place of coherence in reasoning about facts in law.

## A. The Concept of Normative Coherence

Normative coherence, says MacCormick, is the property of a set of normative propositions which, taken together, 'makes sense' in its entirety. To be sure, more needs to be said about what 'making sense' means in order to make the concept of coherence more precise. MacCormick starts investigating the notion of 'making sense' by distinguishing 'coherence' from 'consistency'. A set of normative propositions is consistent if 'each can without contradiction be asserted in conjunction with every other and with their conjunction'.[7] MacCormick does not regard consistency as a necessary condition of coherence. A set of norms may make sense as a whole though it contains some internal inconsistencies.[8] Neither is consistency, in his view, a sufficient condition of coherence, for one can imagine a set of norms none of which contradict each other but that taken together involve the pursuit of no intelligible value. MacCormick gives the following example of such a set: a statute that lays down different speed limits for different cars according to the colour they are painted.[9] Such statute, although consistent, is not coherent. Now, asks MacCormick, why does such statute fail to make sense? That is, what is coherence, once the temptation to explain it in terms of the much clearer notion of consistency is resisted?

MacCormick claims that there are three crucial requirements of coherence. First, the normative coherence of a set of norms is a matter of their being rationally related to the realization of a common value or values. For instance, a colour-based statute regulating driving speeds is incoherent insofar as it does not serve the relevant common value, eg the goal of road

[6] MacCormick introduces the distinction between normative and narrative coherence in (1984: 37). On this distinction, see Comanducci and Guastini (1987: 273–75). The distinction between normative and narrative coherence has been criticized by some scholars on the grounds that it is based on an artificial separation between facts and norms; see Zaccaria (1990: 270ff); Van Roermund (1997: 38–39); Nerhot (1990: 205 and 215); and Van Dunné ((1996) and (1998)). For MacCormick's reply, see N MacCormick (2005: 233–36).

[7] N MacCormick (1984: 38).

[8] In MacCormick's view, although some inconsistency is compatible with coherence, 'perfect' coherence does require that all inconsistency be eliminated. See N MacCormick (2005: 190). This is also, as will be shown below, Peczenik's view. See also Wintgens (1993). *Cf* Pethick (2008).

[9] N MacCormick ((1984: 39) and (1994: 106–07)).

safety. Secondly, the coherence of a set of norms is also determined by the extent to which such set is oriented towards the fulfilment of some common principle or principles. To continue with the example of the colour-based speed limits driving laws, one might say that such laws are incoherent because they fail to satisfy or be instances of a single more general principle. That is, judged by reference to the principle according to which human life must not be unduly endangered by motor traffic on the roads, car-colour differential speed limits are arbitrary, in that the differential treatment of differently coloured, but otherwise identical, cars cannot be justified or explained by appealing to the relevant principle. Hence, according to MacCormick, we may express the coherence of a set of norms in terms of either common values or common principles. In fact, these two aspects of coherence are the two sides of the same coin, for, says MacCormick, there is an extensional equivalence between values and principles.[10] To these two requirements of coherence, MacCormick adds a third one, to wit, the relevant principle or values that justify a set of norms must express in their totality a 'satisfactory form of life'.

MacCormick defines the concept of normative coherence that results from putting together the foregoing requirements of coherence as follows:

> [T]he coherence of a set of norms is a function of its justifiability under higher order principles or values, principles and values being extensionally equivalent; provided that the higher or highest-order principles and values seem acceptable as delineating a satisfactory form of life, when taken together.[11]

Thus, MacCormick makes more specific the concept of normative coherence by distinguishing it from consistency and by positively linking it with the notions of common value/s, common principle/s and satisfactory form of life.

## B. The Role of Normative Coherence in Legal Justification

MacCormick takes coherence to be an important contributor of legal justification in hard cases. According to MacCormick, there is a crucial difference between the way in which legal decisions are justified in 'easy' as opposed to 'hard' cases.[12] In the former, decisions are justified by simple deduction

[10] On the relationship between principles and values in law, see Atienza and Ruiz (1998: 120–35).

[11] N MacCormick (1984: 43). See also N MacCormick (2005: 193).

[12] N MacCormick (1994: 197 and 227–28). The distinction between hard cases and easy cases although important is not, notes MacCormick, absolute. There is no dividing line, he says, between clear cases and hard cases. Instead, there is a spectrum of cases along which it is not possible to discern when easy cases stop and hard ones start.

from clearly established rules and the undisputed facts of the case.[13] In the latter, deductive justification does not suffice for we face problems related to either the normative premise of the normative syllogism or the factual premise. In these cases, we need to resort to 'second-order justification' to justify the acceptance of the premises from which the normative syllogism proceeds. MacCormick distinguishes four kinds of problems that arise in hard cases: the problem of interpretation, the problem of relevancy, the problem of classification and the problem of proof.[14] The 'problem of interpretation' occurs when there are different possible versions of the applicable rule and a choice must be made in order to resolve the ambiguity. Once the choice is made, a simple deductive justification of the particular decision follows. The 'problem of relevancy' also concerns the major premise of the normative syllogism. In this case, the problem is whether it is justifiable in law to assert some rule that is applicable to the case at stake. The 'problem of classification' arises when it is unclear whether some proven facts count as an instance of the conditional part of the applicable rule.[15] When it is controversial whether those facts obtained in the first place, we face the 'problem of proof'. Unlike problems of interpretation and relevancy, the problems of classification and proof concern the minor premise, rather than the major premise, of the normative syllogism. In all four kinds of hard cases, it is required to go beyond deductive justification and engage into 'second-order justification', that is, to justify the premises of the normative syllogism on the basis of which we ultimately justify the decision in the particular case. We may set aside for now the problems concerning the factual premise of the normative syllogism, and focus on those related to the major premise.[16]

According to MacCormick, in problems of both interpretation and relevancy, second-order justification involves checking rival possible rulings against two tests that are concerned with 'what makes sense in the world' and 'what makes sense in the context of the system'.[17] The former test involves using 'consequentialist arguments', which are essentially evaluative

[13] MacCormick's claim that in easy cases decisions are deductively justified has been harshly criticized in the literature. See the debate between MacCormick and Jackson in: N MacCormick (1991); B Jackson ((1991), (1992) and (1996a: 245–55)); and N MacCormick (1992). See also A Wilson (1982: 269–85) and MacCormick's reply to Wilson's critique in (1982).

[14] See N MacCormick (1994: 65–97) and ch V.

[15] The problem of classification is logically equivalent, MacCormick says, to the problem of interpretation. However, given the procedural differences between questions of law and questions of fact, we rather treat problems of classification as being different, although closely related, to problems of interpretation. N MacCormick (1994: 94–96). It is worth noticing that even if most problems of interpretation can be recast as problems of classification, there are some problems of interpretation—such as problems of constitutional interpretation, which cannot be rephrased as problems of classification; see Lifante (1999).

[16] For MacCormick's views on coherence and factual reasoning in law, see ch 2.

[17] N MacCormick (1994: 103).

and subjective.[18] The second test involves using 'arguments from consistency' and 'arguments from coherence'. Hence, it is at the second level of legal justification, ie second-order justification, more specifically, in relation with the requirement that legal decisions 'make sense in the context of the system', that, in MacCormick's view, normative coherence plays a role in legal justification.

How may it be established that a particular ruling 'makes sense in the context of the system'? That is, how do we show that it coheres with the legal normative order? According to MacCormick, normative coherence works as a justificatory mechanism by means of two types of arguments, namely, arguments from principle and arguments from analogy.[19] These arguments are used to justify a particular ruling in a hard case in a two-fold process. First, judges must inquire as to which principles or values make sense of the relevant set of legal norms. Then, these are applied in the present case as an analogous application of the same principle or value and, thus, as coherent with the pre-established body of law.[20] The question arises as to whether resort to arguments from coherence is sufficient for justifying the actual ruling in a case under consideration. To recall, MacCormick distinguishes between three types of arguments that may be used to justify decisions in hard cases: arguments of consistency, arguments of coherence and consequentialist arguments. Thus, an answer to the question of whether coherence is a sufficient condition of legal justification requires determining the relation of arguments from coherence vis-à-vis arguments from consistency and consequentialist arguments. Let us consider the relations between coherence arguments and each of these other kinds of arguments in turn.

MacCormick quite clearly states that for a legal decision to be justified it must be consistent with established rules. Thus, coherence alone does not suffice to justify a decision in a hard case, but it is also necessary that such decision be consistent with the settled law. Coherence and consistency seem then to be two distinct requirements of justified legal decisions. However, the relationship between arguments from consistency and arguments from coherence is more intricate than it might appear at first. The reason why this is so is that whether a decision is inconsistent with established rules depends, according to MacCormick, upon the interpretation of the

[18] See ibid, 108–19 and ch VI.

[19] See N MacCormick ((1984) and (1994: 157–61)). On the relationship between arguments from principles and coherence, see Michelon (2011b). Other arguments that carry a significant weight in legal reasoning because of the relevance of an ideal of coherence are the argument from contextual harmonization, the argument from precedent, the logical-conceptual argument and the argument from history. See N MacCormick and Summers (1991). See also N MacCormick (1993). For an analysis of the general structure of the various kinds of arguments that bring the idea of coherence into play to justify a legal decision, see Bertea ((2005a) and (2005b)).

[20] N MacCormick (1984: 45).

established rule. Prima facie, MacCormick claims, the interpretation supported by 'linguistic arguments'—that is, the interpretation of the text according to its literal and technical meaning—is accepted as justified, *unless* there are either reasons from coherence or consequentialist reasons for interpreting the text in less obvious senses. Thus, although it is plain that the requirement of consistency needs to be satisfied for a decision to be justified, whether this is so is, at least in some cases, a matter of coherence. Prima facie, whether the consistency requirement is justified is independent from considerations of coherence (as well as from consequentialist considerations), for whether a particular decision is consistent with established rules is determined by linguistic arguments. However, arguments from coherence (together with consequentialist arguments) may give us good reason to favour a less literal interpretation in some cases. In these cases, whether the requirement of consistency is satisfied depends, ultimately, on reasons from coherence (and consequentialist reasons).

The interaction between arguments from coherence and arguments from consequences is also quite complex. MacCormick emphasizes that the two kinds of arguments overlap in real life cases, given that consequentialist arguments are evaluative, and that coherence involves a reflection on the values of the system.[21] Nonetheless, in MacCormick's view, arguments from coherence and arguments from consequences are not identical. How do they interact in legal justification? What is their relative contribution to the justification of legal decisions in hard cases? The division of labour between arguments from coherence and arguments from consequences in legal justification may be stated in terms of a distinction between legally 'justifiable' decisions and 'justified' decisions. MacCormick claims that reasons from coherence are decisive in determining whether a legal decision is 'justifiable', but that, in order to show a legal decision to be 'justified' and not merely justifiable, we must look to consequentialist arguments. That is, arguments from coherence are pivotal in legal justification, for a decision unsupported by such arguments would lack any distinctive legal warrant. Thus, coherence considerations crucially delimit the decisions that may legitimately be given in a particular case. However, they do not suffice to justify a legal decision. Instead, arguments from consequences need to be used for singling out as justified one decision amongst the set of alternative decisions that satisfy the coherence test.[22] Coherence determines the permissibility of a legal decision, but it is only on the basis of arguments from consequences that such a decision may be positively justified.

The foregoing view about the weight of arguments from coherence vis-à-vis arguments from consequences in law might be called into question

[21] N MacCormick (1994: 107 and 112).

[22] See N MacCormick (1994: 126–27) and ch VII, throughout. See also N MacCormick (1984: 46–47).

in light of MacCormick's later work on legal interpretation, and, more specifically, on the relationship between different categories of interpretative arguments. When describing the general lines of a model of interaction for different interpretative arguments in law, MacCormick (with Summers) contends that we should accept as prima facie justified a clear interpretation based on arguments from coherence, unless there is some reason to take what he refers to as the category of teleological/deontological argument into consideration.[23] As he defines the latter category, it comprises the kind of arguments that, in other works, fall under the common heading of consequentialist arguments. Hence, apparently, one needs to resort to consequentialist arguments only when arguments from coherence fail to yield an unequivocal result. If so, then it seems that, contrary to what has been stated above, coherence may fully justify, at least in those cases in which it yields a clear decision. However, MacCormick claims that teleological/deontological arguments retain their capacity to defeat coherentist justification even in those cases in which arguments from coherence yield an unequivocal result. He writes,

> [I]t would not be correct to say that the category of teleological/deontological argument comes into play only if the other two categories [linguistic arguments and arguments from coherence] fail to yield an unequivocal result. Consideration of arguments in that category may show up such an absurdity as will displace a *prima facie* conclusion about the meaning of the legislative words in their (fully contextualized) 'ordinary signification.'[24]

Thus, consequentialist arguments are, ultimately, the basis upon which the justification of all legal decisions relies. They are needed in many cases to positively justify a particular ruling, in addition to coherence considerations. And, even in those cases in which it may appear at first that recourse to such arguments is not needed, they work in the background as a yardstick against which the decision justified on the basis of coherence must be checked.

To sum up, in MacCormick's model of legal justification, normative coherence plays an important although limited role in the justification of decisions about disputed questions of law in two kinds of hard cases, to wit, cases that involve problems of interpretation and problems of relevancy. On the one hand, a consistency requirement needs to be satisfied, in addition to the requirement of coherence, for a legal decision to be justified. On the other hand, arguments from consequences are also necessary to fully justify a legal decision. However, even if limited, coherence is an essential contributor to legal justification, for it importantly delimits the range of decisions

[23] N MacCormick and Summers (1991: 531).
[24] N MacCormick (1993: 27).

that the judiciary may legitimately make. Now, why does coherence justify? Whereof does it derive its force as an instrument of legal justification?

## C. Coherence and Reason in Law

MacCormick gives several reasons why coherence is relevant to legal justification.[25] First, coherence is agreeable to a certain conception of practical life that requires universality and the greatest possible degree of generality in practical principles. Secondly, legal rules are relatively detailed, and they would be arbitrary if they were not also instances of more general principles. Thirdly, the law is more cognizable and predictable if it instantiates a small number of general principles. And last, insofar as a legal order is an ideal order, it does not seem enough that it should constitute a mere aggregate of non-contradictory norms.[26] All the foregoing reasons why coherence enjoys justificatory force point towards the relationship between a coherent legal order and a legal order that satisfies the demands of justice. The coherence of a set of legal norms is related to its formal justice—ie universality and generality; a coherent set of norms is claimed to be less arbitrary; and, to the extent that such a set is more cognizable and predictable, coherence can contribute to the establishment of just relations between citizens and the state. Hence, according to MacCormick, an argument from justice may be used to answer the question of why coherence justifies in the legal setting.[27]

The kind of justice to which coherence is related is, however, 'formal' justice, as opposed to 'substantive justice'. Universality, generality in practical principles, non-arbitrariness, cognizability and predictability all contribute to enhance the degree to which our legal systems live up to a formal conception of justice. But these attributes say nothing about the actual content of such systems. According to MacCormick, because of the foregoing reasons, it is preferable that a legal system be conceptualized as instantiating some general principles that are coherent in the sense that they subserve a possible set of mutually compatible values. However, the coherence of a legal system does not say anything about whether such a system satisfies the demands of substantive justice. To take the point to the extremes: in MacCormick's theory, nothing prevents a coherent legal system from being an aberrant one from the moral point of view. He writes,

> 'Coherence' can then be satisfied by a system which does subserve what those responsible for determining its content do suppose to be values (eg racial purity

[25] N MacCormick ((1984: 46) and (2005: 201–05)).

[26] On MacCormick's characterization of the legal order as an ideal order, see N MacCormick (1999: 124ff).

[27] See Raz (1992: 301–02).

> under various elements of National Socialist law), even although from another point of view—let us say bluntly a better one—these supposed values are truly evils.[28]

Thus, according to MacCormick, coherence only provides a justification of a formal and relativistic kind.[29] It only determines what MacCormick calls 'weak derivability' but it does not provide the ultimate 'defensibility' of a legal ruling from a moral point of view. The latter is established by consequentialist reasoning. In contrast, claims MacCormick, coherence reasoning only imposes a negative constraint,

> unless by the coherence test some ruling or decision is at least 'weakly derivable' from existing law, it is not permissible for judges in their judicial capacity to make such a ruling or decision, however desirable on other grounds it may be.[30]

This constraint is an important one, for it determines the set of legally admissible decisions as well as the scope of legitimate judicial decisions (that is, the limits of judicial discretion). But it remains, in an important sense, a negative constraint. The positive justification of any legal ruling, that is, its defensibility, is ultimately established by arguments from consequences, and not by arguments from coherence.

MacCormick's understanding of coherentist justification as formal and relativistic, as opposed to the substantive justification that consequentialist reasoning provides, may be traced back to his views about the relationship between coherence and rationality as well as about the nature and limits of the latter. Rationality is, contends MacCormick, the first virtue in practical systems. However, it is a 'technical' and 'formal' virtue as well as a 'limited' one.[31] Rationality is a limited virtue in that

> even though it excludes many putative principles as 'discursively impossible', it yet leaves open the possibility that there may be a plurality of equally rational systems of practical reasoning, different in their practical substance though not in their rational form.[32]

[28] ibid, 47. See also N MacCormick (2005: 202).

[29] It is at least doubtful that coherence is as dramatically severed from ideals of substantive justice as MacCormick suggests, given the way in which MacCormick defines normative coherence. To recall, it is a requirement of coherence that the set of principles and values that structure a particular normative order express a satisfactory form of life. Hence, it seems that MacCormick incorporates some requirement of substantive justice into the ideal of coherence, given that, arguably (although not uncontroversially), some degree of substantive justice is needed for a normative order to express a satisfactory form of life. Nonetheless, MacCormick does not specify how the concept of satisfactory form of life should be understood. Hence, it is difficult to determine whether it amounts to including some requirement of substantive justice within a conception of coherence; see Atienza (1991: 146) fn 13.

[30] ibid.

[31] N MacCormick (1985).

[32] N MacCormick (1985: 171). Another limit of rationality is related to the fact that, in order to conduct ourselves as rational agents, we need virtues other than rationality, such as patience, courage, self-command or the will to pursue careful inquiry (intellectual pertinacity). See ibid, 170.

Thus, rationality does narrow down the number of acceptable systems, but it is limited in that it fails to determine the choice among equally rational possibilities.[33] In short, rationality is a fundamental yet limited virtue in the sphere of practical reasoning.[34]

The same conclusion holds as regards legal reasoning insofar as the latter is, in MacCormick's view, a highly institutionalized form of practical reasoning.[35] In the context of legal reasoning, rationality is exhibited by means of arguments from coherence. Thus, it is natural that coherence—being a manifestation of rationality—plays a fundamental role in law, but also that it inherits the formal and limited nature that MacCormick attributes to rationality. He writes,

> An examination of the models of legal reasoning both confirms and reveals the meaning of saying that reason can play, and in law appears to play, an indispensable role in the governance of practical affairs, but that there are limits to practical reason. Arguments from consistency and coherence reveal the former, the evaluative element of consequentialist arguments, the latter.[36]

Hence, coherence plays an important role in legal justification insofar as it contributes to the establishment of a rational normative legal order. However, rationality is only one among the goods disclosed within a legal system. Beyond coherence, we also strive for a normative legal order that satisfies other ideals, such as that of substantive justice.[37] Reason alone cannot determine the legal system that is substantively just, but it does limit the sets of norms that may make sense as a whole. The limited, although pivotal, position that, in MacCormick's view, reason occupies in law explains the formal nature of coherentist justification, and the limited, though crucial, role that, according to MacCormick, it plays in legal reasoning.

## D. Conclusions

MacCormick's theory significantly advances the coherence theory in three fronts, to wit, what coherence is, what role it plays in legal justification and why coherence is a value worth pursuing in law. However, there are problems with MacCormick's response to these three questions. First, MacCormick takes coherence to be distinct from consistency. In his view,

[33] Virtues other than rationality furnish us, according to MacCormick, with rational but not conclusive grounds of choice among equally rational systems. Such virtues include wisdom, far-sightedness, a sense of justice, compassion and courage. See ibid, 171 and 177.

[34] For a critique of MacCormick's claim that the scope of rationality in practical and legal reasoning is so limited, see Haakonssen (1981). For MacCormick's response, see (1981).

[35] See N MacCormick (1994: 272). See also N MacCormick (1985: 177).

[36] N MacCormick (1994: 271).

[37] N MacCormick (1984: 47).

the coherence of a set of norms is a matter of their being explained by more general principles that delineate a satisfactory form of life. While this conception of coherence brings to light the essential link that holds between coherence and legal principles, it is too imprecise to be a usable standard of legal justification. Some criteria of coherence are required for determining when a particular decision coheres with a set of norms to a degree sufficient for legal justification as well as for comparing the relative coherence of a number of alternative decisions.

Secondly, MacCormick gives coherence an important role in the justification of decisions in hard cases. By means of arguments from principle and arguments from analogy, coherence allows us to select some decisions as 'justifiable', provided that they have been shown to be consistent with the settled law. Among those justifiable decisions, decision-makers are bound to choose on grounds of the relative desirability of their consequences. It is only on the basis of arguments from consequences that legal decisions may be fully justified. MacCormick's coherence theory is thus a 'weak' theory, in that he claims that coherence is a necessary condition of justification (in hard cases) but an insufficient one. This picture of justification advances the coherentist project of providing a wider scope to reason in law to a very limited extent. Indeed, MacCormick gives a wider role to reason in law than the role accorded to it by (formal) positivist views. In his view, when linguistic arguments ran out, and there are several alternative rulings that are consistent with the legal rules, there are still arguments from coherence on the basis of which one may justify legal decisions. But, among equally coherent rulings, one is bound to decide on the grounds of arguments from consequences, which—according to MacCormick—are subjective in nature. Thus, in all cases in which coherence with the settled law does not yield a unique decision, reason leaves off, and decision upon personal preferences takes over. These cases are likely to be numerous in systems that, like ours, are responsive to the facts of value pluralism. Thus, while MacCormick extends the role of reason in law beyond its positivist boundaries, it leads us to yield, in a significant class of cases, to the sceptical challenge according to which legal decision-making is a matter of fiat rather than reason.

Thirdly, MacCormick provides a defence of the value of coherence on the grounds that it advances an ideal of formal justice. In his view, coherence is valuable because it contributes to the establishment of a rational normative order that satisfies the demands of formal justice. In this sense, the kind of justification that coherence provides is of a formal and relativistic kind. It never provides the ultimate defensibility of a ruling or a system on moral grounds. As argued, this view about the value of coherence in law follows from MacCormick's conception of legal (and practical) rationality as a formal and limited virtue. According to MacCormick, the virtues of rationality and coherence, although pivotal, are limited in that they cannot provide us with grounds for choice among equally rational systems which serve a number of different (and competing) visions of substantive justice. This view of rationality leads MacCormick to reduce the value of coherence to a formal ideal of our legal systems.

By taking coherence to be a formal value that allows us to restrict the number of possible rulings but that does not provide the ultimate defensibility of any legal decision, MacCormick's theory—as will be shown below—avoids a number of serious objections which stronger versions of the coherence theory must face. However, it falls short of fulfilling the coherentist aspirations towards enlarging the domain of reason within law. To be sure, this theory recognizes, in a way in which classical positivism does not, the relevance of coherence in legal justification, and it broadens the space of reason within law beyond the limits of deductive argument. However, to the extent that it gives a very limited role to coherence, and insofar as it takes consequentialist considerations to be the final clincher of justification, the degree to which it expands the space of reason in law—which is, to recall, the main driving force of the coherentist project—is very modest.

## II. A WEIGH AND BALANCE MODEL FOR LEGAL COHERENCE

In a number of works, Peczenik has defended the view according to which a method of weigh and balance is the main means to create coherence in law.[38] The general lines of Peczenik's weigh and balance model of coherence will be explained in three steps. I shall first describe the main criteria of coherence elaborated by Peczenik in a joint paper with Alexy.[39] Next, I shall consider Peczenik's coherentist theory of legal justification. Last, I will examine the relation between Peczenik's conception of justification as coherence and the notions of correctness and truth in law.

### A. The Concept and Criteria of Coherence

According to Alexy and Peczenik, the main idea of coherence may be stated as follows: 'the more statements belonging to a given theory approximate a perfect supportive structure, the more coherent the theory'.[40] Thus, the

[38] See Peczenik ((2009) esp ch 4, (1990), (1994), (1995), (1997a: 150–60), (1997b), (1998a), (1998b), (1999), (2000a), (2000b: 291–94) and (2004)).

[39] Alexy and Peczenik (1990).

[40] Alexy and Peczenik, (1990: 131). Alexy defines coherence in terms of consistency, comprehensiveness and connection in Alexy (1998: 41–42). In both works, consistency is taken to be a minimal presupposition of coherence. Peczenik argued later that while consistency is required for 'perfect' coherence, it is not necessary for 'reasonable' coherence. In addition, he claims, logical consistency is required only for sets of all-things-considered statements to be coherent, but a set of prima facie statements may be coherent, even if it is not logically consistent. See Peczenik (1997a: 161–63).

degree of coherence of a theory is a matter of the degree of perfection of its supportive structure. This structure depends on supportive relations between the statements belonging to the theory in question. They define the relation of support as follows: 'the statement *p1 supports* the statement *p2* if, and only if, *p1* belongs to a set of premises, *S*, from which *p2* follows logically'.[41] The degree of perfection of the supportive structure depends on the extent to which a number of criteria of coherence are fulfilled. Alexy and Peczenik distinguish ten criteria of coherence, which are divided in three classes: (i) criteria that determine the properties of the supportive structure constituted by the theory, which include the number and strength of supportive relations between the statements belonging to a theory, the length and connections of the justificatory chains that support these statements, the number of priority orders between the principles and the number of reciprocal relations between the statements belonging to the theory; (ii) criteria that determine the properties of the concepts applied by the theory, such as the generality of the concepts used by a theory and the conceptual cross-connections between these concepts and those used by other theory; and (iii) criteria that determine the properties of the scope of the theory, ie the number of cases covered by a theory and the diversity of fields of life to which a theory applies.

Alexy and Peczenik claim that the degree of coherence of a theory is determined by weighing and balancing the foregoing criteria of coherence. None of these criteria in isolation is sufficient for coherence, but they must be weighed and balanced against each other. Moreover, in some cases, the higher the fulfilment of one criterion, the lower is that of another. Hence, it is only through weighing and balancing the diverse criteria that we may determine the degree of coherence of a given theory. It is a problem of this theory that it does not provide any guidance as to how legal decision-makers can weigh and balance the different criteria of coherence so as to arrive at the best decision.[42] Most coherence theories remain very vague as to what coherence—as distinct from consistency—requires. In this sense, Alexy and Peczenik have importantly contributed to the coherence theory by providing a list of clear criteria against which the coherence of a particular set of normative propositions may be tested.[43] However, without an account of how the different criteria may be balanced against each other in legal decision-making, the theory remains, in an important sense, incomplete. Now, putting this problem aside, and granting that we are able

[41] ibid, 132.

[42] Peczenik claims that 'weighing and balancing of criteria of coherence must be as coherent as possible, which invokes the same criteria of coherence'. This is, however, poor guidance to legal decision-makers, and one that involves, despite Peczenik's claims to the contrary, a vicious circularity. See Peczenik (2000a: 162).

[43] For another effort to make the notion of legal coherence more precise, see Hage (2001: 22–31).

to determine the degree of coherence of a theory, what would this tell us about the truth of the theory? What about its correctness? Are we justified in accepting a theory just because it is, according to the foregoing criteria, coherent?

## B. Coherence, Defeasibility and Legal Justification

Peczenik has put forward a conception of legal justification that is structured around the notions of 'coherence' and 'weighing'. Here, I shall not attempt to offer a complete account of Peczenik's theory of justification. Instead, I shall focus exclusively on the role that the foregoing notions play into this theory.[44] It is important to notice at the outset that Peczenik, as is customary in legal theory, distinguishes between two kinds of cases, 'easy cases' and 'hard cases'.[45] In 'easy cases' the decision of the case follows from an established legal rule together with a description of the case. No appeal to coherence and no operation of weighing need to be performed in order to arrive at justified decisions in these cases. It is only in 'hard cases' that the foregoing notions need to be put to work in order to justify the legal decision.[46] In these cases, the solution of the case follows from a set of statements consisting of a legal rule, the description of the case and a reasonable additional premise. That is, in 'hard cases', there is a 'jump' between the premises one has and the legal conclusion.[47] As opposed to easy cases, in hard cases the inference that one needs to draw in order to arrive at a justified decision is not conclusive, but 'defeasible'.[48] In other words, the set of reasons that support a legal decision in a hard case may be defeated on the basis of new reasons against the decision. The justification of the legal decision in these cases consists, in Peczenik's view, in a coherent weighing and balancing of the reasons for and against this decision.[49]

What is the nature of the reasons that constitute the input to the operation of weigh and balance? According to Peczenik, the reasons that are 'weighed' in the process of legal reasoning have a prima facie character, that is, they

[44] For a brief and extremely clear summary of Peczenik's theory of legal justification, see Feteris (1999) ch X.

[45] See Peczenik ((1994: 147) and (2000b: 290–291)).

[46] In this sense, Peczenik's theory is similar to MacCormick's. To recall, MacCormick also restricts the role of coherence to hard cases.

[47] Peczenik (1997a: 144).

[48] See ibid, throughout. The literature on the defeasible character of legal reasoning is extensive. See, among others, Prakken (1997); Prakken and Sartor (2004); Bayón (2001); N MacCormick (1995); Sartor (1995); Schauer (1998); Bayón (2002); Hage (2003); and Ferrer and Ratti (2012).

[49] Peczenik (1992: 137).

do not determine definite duties.[50] Two kinds of prima facie reasons need to be weighed and balanced in order to arrive at a justified legal decision, to wit, legal and moral reasons. Moral reasons enter into the process of weigh and balance in law in two different ways: by outweighing reasons based on legal principles and by making exceptions to legal rules.[51] Ultimately, 'all-things-considered judgements', in hard cases, result from weighing and balancing all reasons for and against the application of legal provisions.[52] Such a weighing and balancing of reasons is rational, and thus the resulting all-things-considered judgement justified, if it is coherent; where the degree of coherence is to be determined by yet another kind of weighing, to recall, the balancing and weighing of the different criteria of coherence.

Now, what is it that should be made coherent? What constitutes the set of reasons the coherence of which yields justified all-things-considered judgements? So far, this much is clear: they are prima facie reasons and they include both legal and moral reasons. However, we still need some account of how such reasons are to be identified, and hence, of how the 'base' of coherence is to be determined.[53] Here, the key notions seem to be those of 'relevance' and 'comprehensiveness'. Peczenik writes, '*ceteris paribus,* a definite weighing and balancing is better, the greater number of relevant *prima facie* reasons is considered'.[54] And elsewhere, 'definite duties ... result from weighing and balancing of *all* morally and legally *relevant* values, principles, and rules in a particular case'.[55] Hence, in Peczenik's view, all-things-considered judgements are justified if they result from a coherent weighing of all relevant reasons.

Which reasons are relevant in a particular context of argumentation is, says Peczenik, a matter of convention.[56] In legal reasoning, as explained, two kinds of reasons are relevant, to wit, legal and moral reasons. The relevance of legal reasons is 'taken for granted' when reasoning in law:

> There is no need to argue that the sources of law are relevant. Relevance of the sources is taken for granted in legal justification, once and for all, as soon as one decides to assume the role of a jurist, ie to argue from a legal point of view.[57]

[50] 'Prima facie' is the term that Peczenik has been using in most of his writings. However, after a commentary by Rabinowicz, he came to recognize that reasons in legal reasoning are best understood as 'pro tanto' rather than 'prima facie'; see Rabinowicz (1998: 21). Peczenik conceded the point in (1998b: 57). On the distinction between *prima facie* and *pro tanto* reasons as drawn by Hurley, see ch 7.

[51] Hage and Peczenik (2000).

[52] Even though both rules and principles are defeasible there still remains, Peczenik says, an important difference between these kinds of norms. Whereas principles are always defeasible, rules are only defeasible in hard cases. See Peczenik ((1998b: 56) and (2000b: 291)).

[53] The term is Raz's, see Raz (1992: 284).

[54] Peczenik (1997a: 141).

[55] Peczenik (1998a: 10). Emphasis added.

[56] Peczenik (1997a: 165).

[57] Peczenik (1992: 146).

The relevance of moral reasons results from the fact that legal reasoning is defeasible. Legal reasoning, at least in hard cases, involves taking evaluative steps the justification of which depends, ultimately, on a balance between moral and legal reasons. Thus, moral reasons need to be included in the 'base' of coherence in order to arrive at justified decisions in these cases. But, which are those moral reasons the consideration of which is required for legal justification? Here, again, Peczenik appeals to social conventions. More specifically, 'a prima facie norm or value-statement is morally *relevant* if our moral culture compels us to consider it within moral weighing and balancing'.[58] Thus, our cultural heritage determines which moral and legal reasons are relevant in legal argumentation. All-things-considered statements are legally justified if they result from the coherent weigh and balance of the relevant reasons so identified. In such weighing, 'the weight of any considered reason is affected by all other reasons'.[59] Nonetheless, legal reasons, because of their relevance (as indicated by our background beliefs) have a privileged position in that 'their weight in the law is so great that only particularly substantive reasons are sufficient to override them'.[60]

The peculiar role that legal reasons play in legal reasoning, as opposed to other contexts of argumentation, eg moral reasoning, may shed some doubts about whether Peczenik's theory of justification is a coherentist theory after all. In principle, it seems quite clear that Peczenik's theory of justification is coherentist in the following sense. Whether a particular all-things-considered legal judgment is justified is a matter of coherence, more specifically, is a matter of whether it results from a coherent weighing, where the justificatory force or weight of any reason depends on the set of reasons to which it belongs. That is, it seems that, according to Peczenik, one cannot appreciate the weight of a reason in isolation but that, in a truly coherentist spirit, the weight of any reason is a matter of its relations to other reasons. However (and here it comes the trouble with the label 'coherentist'), some reasons, to wit, legal reasons, do seem to enjoy some independent weight. Is this not a foundationalist move after all? That is, one might argue that, by conceding that, when reasoning in law, the weight of legal reasons does not entirely depend on the coherence of the set to which they belong, but that these reasons have some justificatory force on their own, Peczenik is sneaking a foundationalist element into his apparently coherentist picture of legal justification.

Peczenik does not acknowledge this problem, but his theory, I would argue, has the resources for addressing it. There are two ways in which Peczenik's theory of justification may be defended against the objection that it betrays its coherentist commitments. First, according to Peczenik,

[58] ibid, 141.
[59] Peczenik (1997a: 143).
[60] Peczenik (1994: 155). See also Peczenik (1998a: 13).

legal reasons, no matter how weighty, may be defeated on the basis of other reasons. Thus, one could argue that these reasons provide at most 'provisional' starting points for legal reasoning, and that, in this sense, they are far from being the kind of 'unshakable' foundations that foundationalism seems to require.[61]

Secondly, and most importantly, ultimately, which reasons have a special weight in legal reasoning is determined by a theory about how law and morals relate to each other, and the justification of which is a matter of coherence. In this sense, whatever special force legal reasons enjoy in the legal context derives from the fact that the best theory of the law assigns them this status.[62] This line of reply is available to Peczenik insofar as he endorses a 'coherentist theory of law' according to which 'the law is what the most coherent theory of everything says it is'.[63] We shall later examine in further detail Peczenik's coherence theory of law. Here, it suffices to mention that crucial amongst the things that 'the most coherent theory of everything' should include is an answer to the question of how law and morality should be mutually harmonized. Therefore, given Peczenik's views about what the law is, it is open to him to argue that, at the end of the day, it is coherence that justifies whatever special position legal reasons enjoy in the process of weigh and balance that leads to justified legal judgments about what one ought to do all-things-considered.

To recapitulate, according to Peczenik, legal justification, as much as moral justification, is a matter of coherence. However, legal justification is to be distinguished from moral justification in that the 'base' of coherence is structured so as to give legal reasons a privileged place. In law, an all-things-considered judgement is justified if it results from a coherent weighing of both moral and legal reasons, where the latter have already a 'weight' that does not derive from their relationship with other reasons. It has been argued that this, however, does not make Peczenik's view a foundationalist one for, in accordance with Peczenik's coherence theory of law, one may claim that the justificatory force of legal reasons stems from the status that the most coherent theory of everything assigns to them. Thus, despite the fact that Peczenik attributes a prior weight to legal reasons, his theory is a

[61] This reply to the charge of foundationalism will not be effective as soon as one introduces the distinction between 'strong' and 'weak' versions of foundationalism. For 'unshakable foundations' are required only by strong, but not by weak, versions of foundationalism. On this distinction, see ch 3. The real work in the reply to the charge of foundationalism is done by the second reason.

[62] Hage distinguishes between 'broad coherence theories' and 'strict coherence theories'. He claims that an acceptance set that includes reasons why some acceptances should have a privileged status may be properly justified from the point of view of broad coherentism; see Hage (2004: 89–90). See also Hage (2013), where he similarly distinguishes between 'integrated' coherentism and 'narrow' coherentism.

[63] Peczenik and Hage (2004: 340).

coherentist one in that it ultimately explicates all there is to legal justification in terms of coherence.

So far, we have examined the distinctive way in which the base of coherence is constructed in legal reasoning, as opposed to moral reasoning. Assuming the role of a jurist implies that the relevance of legal reasons is taken for granted.[64] Moreover, such reasons must enjoy a special status if one is to perform 'legal' reasoning at all. According to Peczenik, there are also important differences as regards the base of coherence *within* legal argumentation.[65] First, the base of coherence varies from one context of legal argumentation to another, in that which reasons and which weight should be attributed to them depends on context. And secondly, the size of the base of coherence is also context-sensitive. Whereas legal scholars aim at establishing coherence in the legal system as a whole, within a total system of acceptances and preferences, judges only aim at establishing coherence to the extent that is required to solve the case at hand.

There is an important debate in the coherentist literature about whether a 'local' or a 'global' approach to coherence is more appropriate to understand the role that coherence plays in legal reasoning. According to 'local' models of coherence, coherence with a particular area of the law yields legal justification. In contrast, 'global' models of coherence contend that coherence with the legal system as a whole is a condition of legal justification. Unlike theorists who defend the relevance of either local or global coherence to legal argument, Peczenik seems to be holding the view according to which both kinds of coherence are necessary to give an account of legal argumentation. Before a court of law, he writes,

> what matters is, so to say, *local coherence*. Attention must be paid to the legal provisions and circumstances directly relevant to the solution of the case, and, in some cases to the effect the solution may have upon similar future cases.

To the contrary, 'legal scholars attempt at presenting the legal system *as a whole* as coherent'.[66] Hence, it seems that, according to Peczenik, whereas doctrinal legal reasoning aims at a kind of global coherence; judicial legal reasoning aims at building coherence among a narrower set of reasons, that is, it seeks, more modestly, local rather than global coherence.

Peczenik's insight that what the appropriate base of coherence is depends upon the context of argumentation is extremely interesting. However, some doubts may be raised about whether the distinction between the kinds of coherence that judges and legal scholars aim at holds once it is placed within Peczenik's broader theory of argumentation. For, despite his

[64] See Peczenik (1992: 147).

[65] Peczenik has argued for this point in a variety of places; see Peczenik ((1994: 157–58), (1995: 753–55), (1997a: 141), (1998a: 14), (1999: 214–16)).

[66] Peczenik (1997a: 150). Emphasis added.

apparently restrictive view on what has to be made coherent in concrete cases, the way in which Peczenik understands the operation of weighing and legal decision-making leads to a much broader view of what it is that judges should make coherent than it at first appears. To start with, Peczenik claims that 'weighs more' in juristic contexts works analogously to Lehrer's expression 'is more reasonable than'.[67] The trouble is that, according to Lehrer, judgements of comparative reasonableness are made by reference to the *complete* system of beliefs of the believer. That is, whether it is more reasonable for me to believe that *p* rather than, say, not-*p*, depends on whether, in light of my background system of beliefs, this is so.[68] Hence, if weighing in law is an operation analogous to that of determining what is more reasonable (as defined by Lehrer), then it seems that judges, far from being required to take into consideration only the norms and values that are relevant to the case at hand, are expected to bring in their whole system of beliefs. Thus, given the way in which Peczenik understands 'weighing', the search for local coherence ends up being a much less modest enterprise than it seemed to be at first.

Secondly, Peczenik contends that 'in decision-making, when one must determine the contents of the law, one cannot do better than come up with the best available theory of the law'.[69] And 'what is the best theory of the law, the thing that matters for legal decision making, is a part of the most coherent theory of everything'.[70] But, then, the task of judges really looks no different in any significant respect from the task of legal scholars. Both judges and legal scholars are required to come up with the interpretation that makes best sense of the law as a whole, and further, that best fits with one's overall system of beliefs. Hence, it turns out that the base of coherence that is relevant to legal decision-making is, as much as in legal dogmatics, extremely broad, and thus, that the purported distinction between the way in which coherence works in doctrinal and judicial reasoning evaporates. Ultimately, in both legal dogmatics and legal decision-making, legal justification is a matter of global, rather than local, coherence. This is highly problematic, for, as will be argued later, global models of coherence give rise to a number of serious objections.[71]

To sum up, in Peczenik's view, legal justification results from the coherent weighing and balancing of both moral and legal reasons. The latter enjoy some priority in the coherence calculation, but this priority, arguably, is compatible with Peczenik's coherentist commitments. It has been contended that Peczenik's coherentist theory, despite appearances to the contrary,

[67] Peczenik (1998a: 12).
[68] On Lehrer's theory of coherence, see ch 3.
[69] Peczenik and Hage (2004: 338).
[70] ibid, 339.
[71] See s IV of this chapter.

embodies a problematical commitment to a global model of coherence for the justification of any legal proposition. Now, the question arises, how does legal justification so conceived connect up with truth and correctness? What reason do we have to believe that legal propositions that are justified by virtue of their coherence are also likely to be true or correct?

## C. Coherence, Correctness and Truth

Peczenik addresses the problem of how coherence relates to truth and correctness by distinguishing between 'theoretical statements' and 'practical statements'. He accepts a correspondence theory of truth for theoretical statements, according to which 'a proposition p is true if and only if the facts are such as p describes them'.[72] Even if a coherence theory of truth should be rejected as a theory of the *meaning* of truth of theoretical statements, coherence remains, claims Peczenik, a valuable *criterion* of the truth of these statements. As regards practical statements, Peczenik distinguishes between two kinds of such statements, to wit, prima facie statements and 'definite' or 'all-things-considered' statements. He claims his theory to be 'cognitivist' as regards the former, and 'non-cognitivist' as regards the latter.[73] Prima facie legal interpretative statements are true, he contends, if they correspond to the cultural heritage of the society. Hence, Peczenik's theory is realist as regards prima facie values.

In contrast, all-things-considered practical statements, Peczenik claims, lack truth-value and cannot be object of knowledge. To recall, all-things-considered statements are the result of an operation of weigh and balance. Critically, 'the ultimate step of weighing is ultimately based on personal and intuitive preferences'.[74] Thus, there is no unique preference relation between values that yields one right answer to the case at hand, but there are several ways in which one may weigh and balance the relevant considerations. He writes,

> [W]e do not expect the same objectivity in the practical sphere as in the theoretical. If a theoretical proposition is true, it makes no sense to ask the question: 'True, for whom?' But a person or an action can be good for some and evil for others. An interpretation of the law can be correct for some and incorrect for others. If the competing interpretations are justified coherently, both sides can be right, both from his own point of view.[75]

[72] Peczenik (1990: 309). On the correspondence theory of truth, see ch 6.
[73] See Peczenik (2000a: 157).
[74] Peczenik (1992: 144 and 151). See also Peczenik ((1997b: 318) and (1998b: 62–66)).
[75] Peczenik (1992: 151–52).

Now, the question is, how does coherence relate to the 'correctness' of all-things-considered value-statements so defined?

Peczenik's views about how coherence connects up with correctness seem to have significantly evolved in the course of his writings. In earlier writings, Peczenik has defended the view that coherence is a criterion of correctness.[76] The more coherent a value-system is, he claimed, the more closely it approximates the ideal of correctness. With Alexy, he argued that even though coherence is a central element of a full-blown concept of correctness, there is another component of correctness that also plays a decisive role, to wit, the procedure of rational discourse.[77] In later writings, Peczenik, in contrast to Alexy, has denied that the procedure of rational discourse is a component of a theory of practical rationality distinct from the requirement of coherence.[78] According to Peczenik, the 'rules of rational discourse and the procedures—actual or hypothetical—emerging from the implementation of these rules have no privilege position. They are just a component of the belief system of the subject'.[79] It is coherence with the belief system of the subject—which includes beliefs about the procedures of rational discourse—that yields correct all-things-considered judgements. As Peczenik clearly puts it, 'in my opinion, correctness results from coherence'.[80] Hence, while Peczenik initially took coherence to be one criterion of correctness, which had to be supplemented by a theory of rational discourse, he later held a conception of correctness as coherence. Moreover, in a joint article with Hage, Peczenik has gone one step further and claimed that coherence is not only the standard against which the correctness of interpretative legal statements is to be evaluated, but also (under some ideal conditions) constitutive of 'legal truth'.

Peczenik (with Hage) has defended a 'coherence theory of law' according to which 'the law is what the most coherent theory of everything says that it is'.[81] Most importantly, the latter includes a conventionalist *cum* institutional theory of the law (CI) and personal morality. However, they say, it is required to complement the CI theory with the idea that the law should be coherent.[82] This idea not only comprises the requirement that the law

[76] Peczenik ((1989: 187) and (1994: 173)).

[77] Alexy and Peczenik (1990: 145–46).

[78] Alexy has further argued for the view that coherence together with the procedure of rational discourse constitutes a genuine twin-supercriterion in practical argumentation in (1998), throughout.

[79] Peczenik (1998b: 61).

[80] Peczenik (2000a: 158).

[81] Peczenik and Hage (2004: 343).

[82] The postulate that the law should be coherent should not be understood, argues Peczenik, as an absolute requirement. Coherence competes with other values, such as the value of subsidiarity and the value of dynamic adaptation. Nonetheless, the foregoing values can only be justified, he says, within a coherent moral and political theory. Hence, it is only coherence at a higher level that justifies incoherence at a lower level. Ultimately, it is coherence that determines the best blend of coherence and other values in law; see Peczenik ((1994: 157–58), (1998a: 14) and (2000a: 167–70)).

should be internally coherent, but also the claim that it should be harmonized with morality.[83] In this view, 'law exists as a rational reconstruction based upon, among other things, the law according to CI, and the personal morality of the person who conducts the reconstruction'.[84] That is, CI provides the starting point of a process whereby we mutually adapt CI with one's moral views, so as to arrive at a theory of 'what legally ought to be done'.[85] Hence, according to Hage and Peczenik, the contents of the law are determined by the best theory of the law, which is a part of what the best theory of everything says that it is. In practice, they admit, the most coherent theory of everything is not available. The best that can be achieved is an approximation. They claim that legal dialogues are the best means that we have available to construct such partial coherent theories:

> If such a dialogue is conducted under ideal circumstances ... the resulting partial theory is the best that is attainable in practice. The theory of the law that is a part of it is also the best that is attainable in practice. The individual beliefs that are part of it are therefore the best possible approximation to *legal truth*.[86]

What Hage and Peczenik seem to be getting at is a coherence theory of legal truth for law according to which statements about what ought to be legally done are true if they cohere with the best theory of the law that one may construct under ideal conditions. In a nutshell, they seem to be defending the view that truth in law is ideal justification, where such justification is a matter of coherence. They write, 'if the personal interpretation of the law is as perfectly justified as possible, the jurist can justifiably say that this interpretation *is* the law'.[87] Hence, Peczenik, in his more recent writings, seems to be endorsing not only a coherence theory of legal justification, but also a coherence theory of legal truth.

Thus, there is an important terminological change: while legal interpretative statements were first claimed to be 'correct' or 'incorrect', but not 'true' or 'false', later Peczenik was willing to label interpretative legal statements that belong to the most coherent theory of the law 'true'. However, this terminological change, I believe, does not spring from any substantial change in Peczenik's views about the kind of objectivity that one may reasonably expect legal interpretative statements to enjoy.[88] The coherence theory of truth that Peczenik seems to be arguing for is compatible with his earlier views about the non-cognitivist nature of all-things-considered

[83] Peczenik and Hage (2004: 334).
[84] ibid, 327.
[85] ibid, 343.
[86] ibid, 340. Emphasis added.
[87] ibid, 337.
[88] In fact, in his latest papers, Peczenik wavers between speaking of 'legal truth' (in the joint article with Hage) and claiming that legal interpretative statements 'may be more or less coherent, but not true' (2000a: 157).

legal statements, for the 'truth' that Peczenik now talks about is relative to one's personal morality. To recall, the main reason why Peczenik defended non-cognitivism about all-things-considered legal statements is the role that personal preferences play in the ultimate step of weighing. Similarly, because the contents of the law depend on the harmonization of the law (as identified by CI) and the person's morality, the law shares the subjectivity of personal morality. As a consequence, it might be the case that an all-things-considered legal statement is true, from my own perspective, but false, from yours. It is only in this subjective and relativistic sense that, according to Peczenik, legal statements may be said to be true. So understood, the truth-value of legal statements is fully compatible with Peczenik's non-cognitivism (or better subjectivism). In addition, it is worth noticing that appealing to ideal dialogues does not, in Peczenik's view, make the subjectivity inherent in all-things-considered judgements disappear, for there are many possible outcomes of rational discourse. Hence, there might be several incompatible but best justified, and thus, true, interpretative legal statements.

That Peczenik, by talking of 'truth', rather than 'correctedness', does not aim at injecting any kind of objectivity into his theory is also clear as soon as one notices that, according to Peczenik, the law is not always 'the end of the matter', but that even legal rules must sometimes be balanced against considerations such as morality or efficiency.[89] Hence, what the law is (according to the best theory of the law) does not always give us a response to the question of how we are to decide the legal case at stake. In some cases, moral reasons (and reasons from efficiency) will have to be balanced against legal reasons. Thus, what ought to be done all-things-considered might differ (albeit seldom) from what ought to be done according to the best interpretation of the law. And, again, there is no fact of the matter that determines how to best balance the various considerations. Criteria of coherence will guide legal decision-makers in rationally balancing the several conflicting reasons, but, ultimately, personal preferences will play a role as to which, among those equally justified all-things-considered judgements, one may pick as the basis for one's decision. According to Peczenik, this is as it should be, given that 'morality and law are subjected to reason, but, ultimately, governed by passion'.[90] Hence, like MacCormick, Peczenik finds in the passions the limits to reason, and thus, to coherence, in law. Passions determine, at the end of the day, the boundaries of coherence's empire in the practical sphere.

[89] Peczenik (1998b: 57).
[90] Peczenik (1999: 318).

## D. Conclusions

Peczenik's views on law and interpretation give coherence a most prominent place. As is apparent from the foregoing discussion, Peczenik defends a 'strong' theory of coherence, for he takes coherence to be a necessary and sufficient condition for legal justification. Several features of Peczenik's theory of coherence are particularly attractive. First, Peczenik, together with Alexy, has developed a number of criteria of coherence that do much in the way of making the concept of legal coherence more precise. Secondly, a main objection against coherence theories of legal justification, as we will see, is that they fail to take into account the authoritative character of law. In this sense, Peczenik's claim that, in contrast to moral reasoning, reasons from authority enjoy a privileged position among the set of reasons that a legal decision-maker ought to make coherent may prove to be very useful in developing a coherence theory of legal justification that successfully deals with this objection. Thirdly, as I will argue later, a theory of coherence that gives context its due in justification is the most promising version of coherentism in law. Some elements in Peczenik's theory of coherence hint towards a contextualized version of a coherence theory of legal justification.[91] Most importantly, the aforementioned distinction between moral and legal coherence, or the claim that coherence operates in a different way in different kinds of legal reasoning are, I shall claim, extremely valuable insights that point towards some contextual themes that a theory of legal coherence needs to incorporate. Last, Peczenik's theory interestingly draws to attention the connection that holds between a coherence-based approach to legal justification and discussions about what the proper logic for modelling legal argument is. Peczenik's work is very suggestive in that it links the role of coherence in legal justification with the defeasible nature of legal argument, and thus, with efforts to model legal argument by means of a defeasible logic.

Despite its virtues, there are some problems with Peczenik's theory of coherence. First, Peczenik and Alexy fail to give an account of how the different criteria of coherence may be weighed and balanced against each other. Such an account is necessary in order to have a concept of coherence precise enough for the purposes of legal justification.

Secondly, Peczenik's view that, ultimately, the last step of the weigh and balance operation is a matter of 'personal feeling', or 'individual preference', falls short of the kind of objectivity that, I would argue, one may reasonably expect our legal judgments to have. Peczenik correctly rejects any view that takes legal statements to possess the kind of objectivity that is characteristic of empirical statements. The reason is the familiar one that

[91] See chs 3 and 10.

while it is reasonable to assume that there is one world, common to all of us, it is highly implausible that there exists a 'world of all-things-considered goodness'[92] that we all share. However, one would say, between claiming that all-things-considered statements are true in the sense that they correspond to a world of all-things-considered goodness, and claiming that they are, ultimately, based on personal feeling or individual preference, there is a vast array of intermediate options. The viability of these options needs to be explored before concluding, as Peczenik does, that the ultimate steps of weighing are just a matter of personal choice.

This concession to the sceptic is very problematic, in light of what is—as argued—the main motivation of coherence theories, to wit, to provide a broader scope for the role of reason in law. Peczenik's theory goes one step further than MacCormick's in the project of expanding the role of reason in law. Unlike MacCormick, Peczenik makes rules 'the servants of reason' for they do not impose a limit to the set of decisions that may be justified by virtue of coherence.[93] Quite the contrary, rules might be defeated on grounds of their incoherence with a broader set of reasons that includes moral reasons alongside other legal reasons. In addition, Peczenik does not reduce the role of coherence to restricting the set of justifiable decisions, but rather, he claims that coherence (with both moral and legal reasons) may provide the grounds for taking as justified the best among a number of alternatives. In this sense, he importantly narrows down the number of cases in which reason leaves off, and decision on the grounds of personal preferences takes over. In MacCormick's view, subjective evaluations enter as soon as there are two decisions that equally cohere with the settled law. In contrast, for Peczenik, evaluative concerns enter only when there are two decisions that equally cohere with *both* the set of moral and legal reasons. By broadening the base of coherence, Peczenik imposes more stringent conditions of coherence over legal decision-making than MacCormick does. Still, Peczenik, by granting—like MacCormick—that the last step of deliberation is a matter of subjective preferences, importantly limits the coherentist ambition to expand the space of reason within law. At some point, reason leaves off, and legal decision-makers are at the mercy of their passions.

Thirdly, Peczenik takes the base of coherence to be constituted by all the moral and legal reasons that are relevant in the particular case. However, it has been claimed that, given his views about weighing and about what is involved in legal decision-making, the base of coherence is much broader than it appears at first. As argued, the base of coherence, far from being

[92] Peczenik (1992: 152).

[93] The expression is based on Schauer's discussion of Dworkin's theory of coherence. In Schauer's view, Dworkin defends a theory in which 'rules ... serve as the endlessly defeasible servants of their underlying reasons' (1986–87: 865).

restricted to the set of relevant reasons, is constituted by the whole system of beliefs. Moreover, in light of the coherence-based concept of law that Hage and Peczenik have articulated, it is not only the whole of one's beliefs about the law that one must engage when solving a particular legal case, but rather, all our beliefs. The 'most coherent theory of everything', as they say, rather than a limited set of reasons, ends up determining the all-things-considered judgement that is best justified. This globalizing tendency is even most explicitly endorsed by Hage's integrative version of coherence.[94] Such unrestricted holism gives rise to a number of serious problems, some of which will be explored later in this chapter.

Fourthly, while Peczenik, with Alexy, in earlier works was well aware of the limits of coherence methods in law, and more importantly, of the need to complement these methods with a theory of rational discourse, in his latter writings Peczenik has surrendered to the temptation of explaining all there is to legal reasoning on the basis of coherence. This is unfortunate, for, as I shall argue, while a theory of coherence is an extremely important part of a theory of legal reasoning, it is more than doubtful that the latter can be reduced to the former. Hence, there is a need to insert the coherence theory of legal justification within a full theory of argumentation. It is a further question whether coherence methods need to be supplemented by a procedural level, as Alexy claims, or whether, instead, we need a theory of legal argumentation that includes components other than idealized procedures, alongside coherence.

Last, it is highly unsatisfactory that Peczenik simply assumes coherence to be truth-conducive. Why should coherence lead to truth? Similarly, even though Peczenik offers some remarks as to the virtues of a practical system that is organized around the notion of coherence, he does not provide any argument to the effect that coherence fosters correctness or, as he has come to defend later, that correctness results from coherence. We need some argument that connects coherence, truth and correctness in a plausible way.

To conclude, Peczenik's theory embodies some valuable insights about how a contextualist theory of coherence may be further developed. In addition, he has contributed much to making the coherence theory in law more precise by providing, with Alexy, a number of criteria of coherence, and by suggesting some ways in which a 'logic' for modelling coherence-based legal argument can be found in current work on defeasible reasoning. Still, there remain some open problems in the theory as is currently defended. Most importantly, doubts may be raised about whether Peczenik succeeds in superseding the classical positivist view about the space of reason in law given Peczenik's subjectivism about moral value.

[94] See Hage ((2004) and (2013)).

## III. INTEGRITY, HOLISM AND INTERPRETATION

Dworkin has articulated what is probably the most influential approach to legal theory in the last decades.[95] His interpretative theory of law has been broadly interpreted as coherentist.[96] This section explores the coherentist aspects of Dworkin's theory. More specifically, I shall focus on Dworkin's conception of coherence as integrity, its role in his interpretative theory of law, and his arguments to the effect that coherence is a pivotal value in law, most importantly, the so-called argument from community.

### A. Coherence as Integrity

The notion of coherence has always played a central role in Dworkin's theory of law. Dworkin introduces a first conception of coherence, which he refers to as 'articulate consistency', in *Taking Rights Seriously*.[97] Articulated consistency requires, says Dworkin, that political decisions be brought within some comprehensive political theory that best justifies other decisions also thought right. Articulate consistency is 'consistency in the application of principle'. A legal decision is justified if it may be shown to be consistent with the principles relied upon in precedent cases and embodied in statutory and constitutional provisions, and not merely with the rules announced in the name of these principles. Thus, the demands of articulate consistency extend beyond the rules, to reach the principles upon which such rules may be justified. On the other hand, the scope of the requirement of articulate consistency is restricted in that it only requires consistency in principle, but its demands are relatively weak when policies, as opposed to principles, are in play.[98] This intimate link between articulate consistency and principle is the key feature around which Dworkin's mature conception of coherence, ie coherence as integrity, is structured.

Dworkin's conception of coherence as integrity is a more meticulous and detailed elaboration of the concept of coherence than the model of articulate consistency. However, the general lines of the concept of coherence as integrity

[95] See Dworkin ((1977), (1983b), (1985), (1986), (1993), (1996), (2002) and (2011)). For a brief and clear introduction to Dworkin's interpretative theory of law, see Bix (2003) ch VII. The most significant discussions of Dworkin's theory include: the Jurisprudence Symposium published in (1977) 11 *Georgia Law Review*; M Cohen (1983); Coleman (1987); Marmor (1992) esp chs 3, 4 and 6; Burley (2004); Ripstein (2007); Hershovitz (2008); and Guest (2012).

[96] Hurley (1989) and (1990); Marmor (1992); and Kress (1984). However, some authors are reluctant to discuss Dworkin's view as a coherence-based approach. See Raz (1992: 273) and (2004) and Shiner (1988: 95ff).

[97] Dworkin (1977: 88 and 162).

[98] See Dworkin (1977: 90).

were already depicted in his model of articulate consistency.[99] Integrity—like articulate consistency—is a matter of 'consistency in principle'.[100] According to Dworkin, consistency of principle is both more and less than 'bare consistency', that is, it requires both more and less of a political institution than that 'it repeats its own past decisions most closely or precisely in point'.[101] First, integrity calls for fidelity to the fundamental principles that justify the law as a whole. This demand is not satisfied by simply following the particular rules laid down in previous cases. Quite the contrary, integrity may demand that we depart from a line of past decisions to live up to our commitment to principles viewed as fundamental to the body of the law as a whole. Secondly, integrity requires less than consistency in that it does not require any simple form of consistency in policy.[102]

Hence, Dworkin defends a conception of coherence that is based on the notion of principle, as opposed, on the one hand, to rules and, on the other hand, to policies. This is hardly surprising given that Dworkin's main goal is that of providing an alternative to both conventionalism and pragmatism, which are the interpretative versions of legal positivism and legal realism, respectively. Conventionalism would require what we may refer to as 'consistency of rule', while pragmatism would insist on 'consistency of policy' for strategic reasons. Thus, Dworkin's principle-based conception of coherence is of a piece with his project of developing a theory of law that provides a third way between legal positivist and legal realist approaches to law and adjudication. I turn now to examine the role that coherence plays in Dworkin's theory of law and adjudication.

## B. Coherence, Interpretation and Justification

According to Dworkin, legal interpretation, like any other kind of interpretation, is a constructive enterprise. Under this view, legal interpretation aims to show the legal practice as a whole in its best light. To explain what the constructive model requires of legal interpreters Dworkin appeals to a comparison between law and literature. He invents a literary genre that he calls 'the chain novel', and claims that the role of judges deciding hard cases

[99] Thus, I take it that Dworkin's theory of coherence in *Law's Empire* is a development of Dworkin's views of coherence as defended in *Taking Rights Seriously* and *A Matter of Principle*. *Cf* Schiavello (2001: 239– 42).

[100] Dworkin (1986: 94–96; 132–35; 167; and 219–24).

[101] ibid, 219.

[102] This is not to say that integrity allows any kind of inconsistency in policy. It does require, says Dworkin, that the 'government pursue some coherent conception of what treating people as equals means' (1986: 223). For a discussion of the argument to the effect that integrity has, at least, some diffuse force in decisions of policy, see ch VIII of *Law's Empire*.

is rather like this literary exercise.[103] In this imaginary enterprise a group of novelists writes a novel *seriatim;* each of them has the job of interpreting the chapters he has been given and writes a new chapter, which is then added to what the next novelist receives. Each novelist has the job of writing his part so as to make the novel the best it can be. The novelist's task, Dworkin claims, may be fruitfully compared to the judge's task of deciding a hard case. A judge deciding a hard case is like an author in the chain of common law:

> He knows that other judges have decided cases that, although not exactly like his case, deal with related problems; he must think of their decisions as part of a long story he must interpret and then continue, according to his own judgment of how to make the developing story as good as it can be. (Of course the best story for him means best from the standpoint of political morality, not aesthetics).[104]

Thus, judges aim at constructing the interpretation that shows the law to be the best it can be in light of background political theory.

Dworkin distinguishes between two dimensions in the judges' interpretative judgments, ie the dimension of fit and the substantive dimension or the dimension of justification.[105] The former dimension provides a threshold requirement that an interpretation of some part of the law must meet in order to be eligible at all. The latter provides the ground for choosing, among eligible interpretations, the interpretation which seems best from the standpoint of political morality. The two dimensions of legal interpretation, claims Dworkin, are interconnected, for questions of fit also arise when testing an interpretation along the dimension of justification. The reason is that any deficiencies of fit will count against an interpretation, even if it has been shown to satisfactorily pass the threshold requirement. A judge not only will have to engage his substantive judgments about what makes an interpretation best from the perspective of political morality, but he will also have to engage his higher-order convictions about how he should trade off an interpretation success on one type of standard against its failure in another.

Three main stages may be distinguished in the process of judicial interpretation, namely, the preinterpretative stage, the interpretative stage and the postinterpretative stage. At the preinterpretative stage, the judge identifies the practices that count as legal practices in his community. At the interpretative stage, he articulates an interpretation of the practice and tests it

[103] Dworkin's narrative conception of legal practice—which the chain novel illustrates—is very close to hermeneutics' views on legal reasoning. For an analysis of the relationship between Dworkin's views and hermeneutics, see Honeyball and Walter (1998: 142–57); Nerhot (1990); Villa (1990); Zaccaria ((1990) and (1995)); and Lenoble (1998).

[104] Dworkin (1986: 239).

[105] Dworkin's distinction between fit and justification has received many criticisms. See Raz (1986a) and Finnis (1992).

against the dimension of fit. Last, at the postinterpretative stage, he refines his interpretation and adjusts his sense of what the practice requires in its light. The judge's working theory of interpretation will comprise three sets of convictions, which correspond to each of the different stages of interpretation, to wit, convictions about identity, about fit and more substantive convictions.[106] The judge's decision will be drawn from the interpretation that best fits and justifies the legal practice—as identified in the preinterpretative stage—as a whole.

Now, what is the place of coherence in this interpretative structure? What role does it play in the justification of judicial decisions? As will be shown later, coherence plays a crucial role in the identification of what the law in a given community is. Thus, a coherentist standard is already at work at the preinterpretative stage. For now, let us focus on the role of coherence in the two latter stages of interpretation, that is, the interpretative and the postinterpretative stage. One could identify 'coherence' with 'fit' and thus restrict the role that coherence plays in legal interpretation to the interpretative stage. Under this view, coherence is only a threshold requirement. It plays a negative role in ruling out as ineligible those interpretations that do not fit enough with the settled law. However, I would argue, the coherentist commitments of Dworkin's theory run far much deeper than the notion of coherence as a constraint of fit suggests. My claim is that, in Dworkin's theory, coherence is relevant to both the standard of fit and the standard of justification, and thus that it plays a role not only in the interpretative stage but also in the postinterpretative stage. That is, coherence not only allows us to rule out some interpretations as ineligible, but it also provides the tools for picking out the best alternative among those that satisfy the fit requirement. In order to see why this is so, let us return for a moment to the chain novel exercise.

A novelist working in a chain novel has, as has been explained, a number of structural as well as more substantive convictions. For the purposes of clarifying the role that coherence plays in Dworkin's theory of justification, it is crucial to notice the way in which Dworkin understands the contrast between the structural and the substantive convictions that the interpreter brings to bear while working in a chain novel and that the judge employs while (analogously) deciding a hard case. According to Dworkin, the contrast between the chain novelists' structural and substantive convictions is not a contrast between convictions that are dependent on an interpreter's aesthetic theory and those that are independent. On the contrary, 'both major types of convictions any interpreter has—about which reading fit

[106] Several authors have objected to Dworkin's use of the term 'conviction'. See Finnis (1987: 366) fn 11 and Simmonds (1987: 478). However, the use of the term 'conviction' is indeed most appropriate if, as argued, Dworkin's theory is a coherentist one. For it is coherence among beliefs (convictions) that—Dworkin claims—yields justification.

the text better or worse and about which of two readings makes the novel substantively better—are internal to his overall scheme of beliefs and attitudes, neither is independent in some way that the other is not'.[107] Similarly, Dworkin insists that, 'the different aspects and dimensions of a judge's working approach—the dimensions of fit and substance and the different aspects of substance—are in the last analysis all responsive to political judgment'.[108] Hence, in both law and literature, the interpreter starts up his task equipped with a number of structural and substantive convictions that depend upon the relevant background theory—either aesthetic or political. Both structural and substantive convictions in law and literature are but different kinds of political and aesthetic convictions, respectively. Thus, the judge (and the novelist in a chain) is to seek the interpretation that best coheres with a theory that comprises political (or aesthetic) convictions of different sorts.

It is now clear that, in Dworkin's theory, the role of coherence cannot be restricted to a formal dimension but that it is pervasive through the whole process of interpretation. Judges are not to check whether our interpretative beliefs satisfy a criterion of coherence with the settled law, and then select on non-coherence grounds the best among those that satisfy the fit requirement. Rather, they are urged to search for the interpretation that best coheres with their beliefs about fit as well as about substantive political morality. In this model, coherence does not function as *a* criterion of justification that allows us to reduce the number of plausible candidates. On the contrary, coherence works as *the* criterion of justification, for it is coherence with a number of both structural and substantive beliefs that leads judges to select one decision—the one that best coheres—as justified. Unlike theories, such as MacCormick's, that give coherence an important albeit negative role in legal justification, Dworkin takes legal justification to be a matter of coherence. In short, Dworkin is proposing a 'strong' coherence theory of legal justification according to which justification is a matter of coherence between the legal practice and a structure of principles that best fits and justifies such practice, in the light of background political theory.

According to this coherence theory of justification, judges try to achieve 'an equilibrium between the legal practice as they find it and the best justification of this practice'.[109] On the one hand, a judge will modify his views about what the legal practice requires in light of his political convictions—about both fit and substance. On the other, he will refine his political theory so as to make it cohere with his firm convictions about what the law in his community requires. In hard cases, judges would then 'develop his conception

[107] Dworkin (1986: 235).
[108] ibid, 257.
[109] ibid, 90.

of law and his political morality in a mutually supporting way'.[110] Thus, a judge's belief about what is the best interpretation will be justified if it coheres with the theory that best fits and justifies the legal practice as a whole. Legal justification does not result from picking out the best candidate (from the standpoint of political morality) among a set of alternatives that cohere with the settled law. Rather, it is coherence of the set of beliefs about the law and beliefs about political morality—including convictions about fit and substantive convictions—that yields legal justification.[111]

Does coherence provide merely a formal kind of justification or does it, to the contrary, lead us to accept as justified decisions which are also claimed to be defensible from the standpoint of political morality? The coherence of a legal decision would say nothing in the way of its substantive appeal if the test of coherence could be satisfied only by demonstrating that the decision is satisfactory along the dimension of fit. If that were the case, then, to use again MacCormick's example, a set of racist laws could be coherent. This is not so much of a problem for MacCormick, given that—in his view—the fact that a set of laws is coherent (or fails to be coherent) does not answer the question of whether we are justified in accepting them as the basis of our decisions. The issue, however, is more pressing in the case of Dworkin theory for, in contrast to MacCormick, he claims justification to be a matter of coherence. Thus, it seems that Dworkin is committed to the implausible view that a decision may be justified by virtue of its coherence with a set of morally abhorrent laws. However, no conclusion of this sort follows from Dworkin's theory of justification for, as argued, the role of coherence is not exhausted by the dimension of fit. On the contrary, legal decisions are coherent, and thus justified, only if they also fit with a number of more substantive political convictions. Integrity is not irrelevant once the threshold requirement of fit has been satisfied, for it is coherence among one's convictions about what the legal practice requires and convictions of political morality that yields legal justification.[112] Hence, by saying that a

[110] ibid, 258. Several commentators have emphasized the connection between Dworkin's views on coherence and Rawls' method of reflective equilibrium. See Kress (1984: 379); Levenbaum (1984: 365–369); and Marmor (1991: 389–96). For an approach to judicial reasoning built upon the notion of reflective equilibrium, see Maniaci (2008).

[111] Recently, Dworkin has argued that law is itself a part of political morality; see Dworkin (2011: 405). Thus, more precisely, it is coherence with a set of beliefs about political morality, which includes beliefs about the law, that yields legal justification.

[112] But then the problem arises as to why, when the law is not clear on a particular point, should we not simply decide on the basis of justice. This worry is raised and discussed at length by Raz (1992: 300ff). Dworkin's defence of the claim that judges ought to decide on the basis of the best interpretation of the settled law even when, apparently, the law (as embodied in the authoritative texts) fails to provide an answer lies in his views about the responsibilities of judges. This responsibility is ultimately rooted in the view that integrity is a substantive political ideal, which requires a judge to construct 'his overall theory of the law so that it reflects, as far as possible, coherent principles of political fairness, substantive justice, and procedural due process' (Dworkin, 1986, 405). In contrast to what Dworkin refers

particular legal decision is required by integrity, we are already factoring in substantive considerations.[113]

The question arises as to what the scope of coherence in Dworkin's model of justification is. As explained above, there are two main views on what is the appropriate size of the domain within which legal coherence ought to be sought. Under a 'local' model of coherence, a legal decision is justified if it coheres with the principles that best explain a particular area of law. In contrast, according to a 'global' model, the justification of a legal decision depends upon its coherence with the legal system as a whole.[114] A particular feature of judicial reasoning, as exemplified by Hercules (ie a philosophical judge Dworkin invents to illustrate how judges should work) is crucial for determining whether Dworkin's theory embodies a global model of coherence or rather a local one. When deciding hard cases, Hercules uses what Dworkin calls a 'principle of local priority'. This principle requires that Hercules' 'judgments of fit expand out from the immediate case before him in a series of concentric circles'.[115] This procedure, says Dworkin, 'gives a kind of local priority to what we might call 'departments of law'.'[116]

At first, in light of the principle of local priority, it might seem that Dworkin is endorsing here a 'local' model of coherence. Despite appearances, Dworkin's model of coherence, like Peczenik's, is global rather than local. The local priority that Dworkin envisages is not 'absolute', for it is up to Hercules not to defer to local priority should he have substantive reasons not to do so. Hercules, says Dworkin, may override the doctrine of local priority if the boundaries between traditional departments of law do not track widely held distinctions between principles of political morality.[117] Thus, it turns out that, ultimately, the legal materials that Dworkin takes to be relevant to the justification of a particular legal decision are not—as the principle of local priority would have it—the most immediate legal materials (ie those that pertain to a particular department of law), but reasons from political morality are also relevant. Thus, coherence is being sought not within a particular department of law—as it may seem at first—but in the wider domain of the set of principles of political morality that structure the legal system as a whole. It is coherence with the system as a whole that

as 'inclusive' integrity, 'pure' integrity 'consists in the principles of justice that offer the best justification of the present law ... abstracting from all the constraints of fairness and process' (ibid, 407). But it is critical to note that integrity, whether inclusive or pure, is a substantive political ideal. Thus, whether we are seeking either pure or inclusive integrity, we are still following a coherence method and one that leads to substantive results.

[113] Dworkin is quite explicit on this point. See Dworkin (1986: 262–63).

[114] See the previous section of this chapter.

[115] Dworkin (1986: 250).

[116] ibid. According to Wintgens, Dworkin's theory of concentric circles is too ambitious, if not impossible, insofar as it assumes that the law is the product of the expansion of a unique set of principles. See Wintgens (1993: 509–10 and 515–16).

[117] Dworkin (1986: 253).

yields legal justification, and not merely coherence with a particular branch, or area, of law. Any part of the legal system is relevant to the justification of any single decision. In consequence, any decision may be challenged on the basis that it does not cohere with the principles of political morality reflected in some other part of the law. The kind of justification that one achieves when the principle of local priority is deferred to is, I would suggest, merely a 'partial' kind of justification.[118] It is only when we are able to show that an interpretative belief coheres with the whole system of beliefs about the law and political morality that such a belief is 'fully', or 'completely', justified. Therefore, despite Dworkin's appeal to a principle of local priority, his model of justification is global, for it is the whole system of beliefs about the law that is, ultimately, justification-conferring. This commitment to holism about justification is problematical, for as will be argued below, it gives rise to a number of serious objections.[119]

To sum up, it has been suggested that in Dworkin's theory, coherence plays a fundamental role throughout the whole process of justification, from the selection of a handful of alternatives on the grounds of fit to the selection (among those that satisfy the threshold requirement) of the best candidate from the standpoint of political morality. Hence, the coherentist standard of justification that Dworkin employs is a substantive one rather than merely a formal standard. This coherentist account, I have claimed, is a holistic one, in that the justification of a single decision depends on whether the system of principles that best explains and justifies the whole body of the law is coherent. In Dworkin's theory, coherence, in addition to conferring justification to the legal decisions, also contributes to the identification of the law. That is to say, coherence does not only provide an answer to the question of how judges should decide cases, but also to the question of what the law is. Dworkin defends—I would argue—not only a coherence theory of legal justification but also a coherentist account of the truth conditions of legal propositions. I turn now to examine Dworkin's approach to the relation between coherence and truth in law.

### C. Coherence, Objectivity and Truth

Dworkin's conception of law is structured around the claim that law is an interpretative concept. The question of what the law is cannot be answered, he claims, by pointing to a set of semantic criteria of identification.[120]

[118] In fact, Dworkin seems to accept this point; see Dworkin (1993: 144).

[119] See s IV of this chapter.

[120] There are, says Dworkin, no shared criteria for identifying the conditions under which propositions of law are true. This, however, does not imply that there can be no genuine disagreement or agreement about what the law is. For a discussion of what Dworkin refers to as the 'semantic sting' argument, see Stavropoulos (1996); Coleman (2001: 155–58); Endicott (1998); and Himma (2002).

But answering this question requires that we engage in an interpretative enterprise of a rather peculiar sort. First and foremost, it requires that we develop towards the law an 'interpretative attitude'. This attitude has two main components. The first is the assumption that the practice that is object of interpretation, ie the legal practice, has a value that can be stated independently of the rules that make up the practice. The second is the assumption that the requirements of the practice are sensitive to its point or value, ie values of political morality, so that rules may be understood, applied, modified or extended by that point.[121] The identification of the law is the result of a process of constructive interpretation that is characterized by the interpretative attitude just described. Under this view, what the law is depends on what the best interpretation of the legal practice says that it is. This interpretation, as argued, results from mutually adjusting our beliefs about the law and our beliefs about political morality—including convictions about fit and more substantive convictions—so that they form a coherent whole.

Now, what are the implications of this interpretative conception of law for a theory of legal truth?[122] Dworkin's interpretative theory of law, I would argue, involves a commitment to a 'coherence theory of truth' according to which whether a particular proposition of law is true depends on whether it belongs to the most coherent theory that fits and justifies the settled law.[123] On this view, the truth of legal propositions does not depend on their correspondence with social or moral facts, but it is matter of coherence with other propositions, which include propositions about the legal practice as well as propositions about the values of political morality that such practice is meant to serve. Thus, Dworkin's version of the coherence theory of truth makes truth dependent upon legal practice and institutional history as well as moral and political theory. It is coherence with a set of interpretative beliefs about both law and political morality that yields legal truth.[124]

Dworkin's account of the truth conditions of legal propositions—which, as suggested, is best interpreted as a coherentist account—is claimed to apply to both very abstract legal propositions and very concrete legal

[121] Dworkin (1986: 46–49).

[122] The Fish-Dworkin debate is particularly relevant to this issue. See Fish ((1982), (1983) and (1987)) as well as Dworkin (1983b). On this debate, see Shelley (1985: 158–80); Glass (1988: 443–61); and Marmor (1991: 398–409).

[123] See Dworkin ((1977: 283), (1985: 70–76) and (1986: 225)). For a similar suggestion, see Hanen (1983: 89) and Pintore (2000: 156–60).

[124] This coherence theory of legal truth sharply contrasts with the legal positivist conception of the truth conditions for propositions of law, whether in its stronger versions (ie exclusive legal positivism), such as Raz's (see Raz (1979)), or in weaker versions (ie inclusive legal positivism) such as Coleman's (see Coleman ((1982) and (1998))). On the relationship between Dworkin's views on truth and the legal positivist's view, see Raz (1985); Coleman (2001); and Dworkin (2002).

propositions. For example, it is meant to explain when the proposition that 'the law forbids states to deny anyone equal protection within the meaning of the Fourteenth Amendment' is true and when a proposition such as 'the law requires Acme Corporation to compensate John Smith for the injury he suffered in its employ last February' is true.[125] Thus, Dworkin establishes a unitary account for the truth conditions of both propositions about what the law is and propositions about what the law requires on a given issue. On this view, an answer to the question of whether a particular proposition of law is true also yields an answer to the question of whether judges ought to take that proposition as the basis for their decisions.[126] Hence, in Dworkin's theory, coherence has the last word about what the law is and how judges ought to decide.

As is well known, coherence theories of truth suffer from a number of important problems.[127] However, these problems affect the different versions of the coherence theory to varying degrees. Thus, in order to assess the plausibility of Dworkin's coherentist account of the truth conditions of legal propositions, it is critical to determine which version of the coherence theory Dworkin advocates. There is a variety of coherence theories of truth. For our purposes, the most relevant dimension along which coherence theories of truth differ is the constitution of the set of beliefs such that coherence with it yields truth. Two main proposals may be distinguished. According to some theories, the specified set of beliefs is the set that is currently believed by actual people. Other theories claim that the relevant set is the set of propositions that would be believed at some limit of inquiry. Where does Dworkin's theory fall into this categorization? Is Dworkin committed to the view that an interpretative belief about the law is true if it belongs to the most coherent set of beliefs about the law and political morality that are shared at present in a particular community? Or does he, to the contrary, claim that a legal belief is true if it belongs to the most coherent set of beliefs about the law and political morality which would be held under idealized conditions? The question is important for these positions involve different views about the objectivity of legal judgments.

It might be helpful to distinguish here, following Coleman and Leiter, three conceptions of objectivity, to wit, minimal, modest and strong.[128] A 'minimal' conception of objectivity says that objectivity in law is a matter

[125] Dworkin (1986: 4).

[126] However, there are some extreme cases, Dworkin says, in which the question of how judges ought to decide is not settled by answering the question of what the law is on a given issue; see Dworkin (1986: 219).

[127] For a discussion of coherence theories of truth, see ch 6.

[128] Coleman and Leiter (1993: 594–635). For a very interesting analysis of the relationship between Coleman and Leiter's distinction between minimal, modest and strong objectivity and alternative accounts of the nature of legal facts, see Rosati (2004). For a critique, see Schiavello (2013).

of what the majority of the members of a relevant community believe to be right. According to a 'modest' conception of objectivity, objective legal judgments are those that would be held under ideal epistemic conditions. Last, a 'strong' version of objectivism says that legal judgments are objective insofar as they correspond to belief-independent facts. Given Dworkin's rejection of moral realism, it is clear that Dworkin's coherence theory of truth is at odds with any strong view about legal objectivity. The question is whether Dworkin's coherence theory of truth is based on a minimal or a modest view of legal objectivity. The answer depends on which version of the coherence theory of legal truth Dworkin advocates. While a minimal conception of objectivity would be involved in a theory of legal truth that took legal truth to be coherence with currently held beliefs in the relevant community, a theory of truth according to which truth is a matter of coherence with the set of beliefs that would be held under ideal conditions involves a commitment to a modest conception of objectivity.

There seem to be elements in Dworkin's theory that lend support to an interpretation according to which Dworkin endorses either one of the foregoing views. On the one hand, Dworkin's appeal to 'popular opinion' and 'popular morality', among the elements that judges ought to factor into their coherence calculations, may lead one to interpret Dworkin as claiming that a particular proposition of law is true if it belongs to a coherent set of beliefs about the law and political morality that are shared in a particular community.[129] Under this view, Dworkin would be endorsing a 'minimal' conception of objectivity in law. On the other hand, the role that Hercules plays in Dworkin's theory may suggest that he is advancing the view according to which propositions of law are true if they cohere with the set of beliefs that an ideal observer (ie Hercules) would held under idealized conditions.[130] According to this view, Dworkin would be advocating a 'modest' view of legal objectivity.

However, Dworkin's coherence theory of truth does not seem to me to fully square with any of these views. Despite references to 'popular morality', the view according to which Dworkin is endorsing a relativist version of a coherence theory of truth that makes the truth of legal propositions depend on matters of popular conviction is quite implausible, given Dworkin's views about morality and about how morality and law relate to each other. To recall, Dworkin's coherence account of the truth conditions for legal propositions makes legal truth at least partially dependent upon the truth of moral propositions. If moral propositions were true by virtue of their coherence with a set of shared beliefs about what is best in a society, then legal propositions could be objective only in a 'minimal'

[129] See Dworkin (1986: 250 and 252–53).

[130] This view was defended by Coleman and Leiter (1993: 633–35). Coleman later rejected this interpretation of the role of Hercules in Dworkin's theory in (2001: 165).

sense. Accordingly, Dworkin's coherence theory of legal truth would be best interpreted as stating that legal propositions are true if they best cohere with a set of shared beliefs about the law and political morality in a particular community. However, Dworkin rejects any relativistic view of moral truth as agreement within a particular community. Thus, it does not seem appropriate to interpret Dworkin as endorsing a view according to which coherence with currently held beliefs amounts to legal truth.[131]

Likewise, despite the prominent place that Hercules occupies in Dworkin's theory, a close reading of Dworkin's writings brings to light that he is not willing to endorse any view of legal truth according to which propositions of law are true if they cohere with the beliefs that would be held under idealized conditions. Dworkin quite explicitly averts against any interpretation of Hercules' answer to legal problems as defining what law as integrity requires.[132] Hercules, claims Dworkin, merely illustrates how a judge approaching a legal problem as law as integrity demands would proceed, but his judgments are not meant to be constitutive of the truth of the answer at which he arrives.

Thus, I have argued that Dworkin's views on legal truth do not quite fit into the two main kinds of coherence theories of truth that are defended in the literature, and that they cannot be properly interpreted as involving a commitment to either a minimal or a modest view of objectivity. Which is, under Dworkin's view, the set such that coherence with it yields legal truth? What is then the kind of objectivity that Dworkin's coherence theory of truth promises to deliver? Dworkin's conception of legal truth, I would argue, is best characterized as follows. According to Dworkin, truth-values of legal and moral propositions can only be assigned from within an enterprise. Legal and moral propositions are true (or false) whose assertion (or denial) is licensed by the ground rules of the practice. From this point of view, truth in law and morals amounts to warrant by the ground rules of the enterprise. There is no further truth to be established beyond determining what one may be warranted in claiming while engaging in a particular enterprise.[133]

Law (and morality for that matter), claims Dworkin, is an argumentative enterprise.[134] We justify propositions about law by way of argument oriented towards showing them to cohere with our best theories about what law and political morality require. If a particular proposition of law *p* coheres with what, as of now, is the best theory of law and political morality that we have available, then we may claim that proposition to be true. Of course, we might be wrong and after further thought we may come to

131 For a discussion of Dworkin's position in the debate between liberalism and communitarianism, see Honeyball and Walter (1998: 130–42).

132 Dworkin (1986: 239).

133 See Dworkin ((1972: 76) and (1983a: 275--78)).

134 Dworkin (1986: 13).

the conclusion that the case for *not-p* is stronger, in that it better coheres with the best theory we may develop. Alternatively, someone may challenge that *p* is true, and claim that it is *not-p* rather than *p* that is true, but he should do so by showing that it is not-*p*, rather than *p*, that is best warranted by the ground rules of the legal practice. The important point to notice is that, according to Dworkin, there is no argument that may establish what the true proposition—the right answer—is or that there is no right answer in the particular case, which is different from an argument to the effect that one, rather than another, is better grounded. Any conclusion about the truth-value of a proposition of law—including sceptical conclusions—has to be earned by way of argument.[135]

As suggested, in Dworkin's view, legal and moral arguments seek to construe coherence among a set of beliefs. It is by combining Dworkin's claim that truth is always truth within an enterprise—that is, warrant by the ground rules of the enterprise—with his claim that warrant within law—as an argumentative enterprise—is a matter of coherence that, I contend, we may come to see what version of the coherence theory of truth Dworkin defends as well as what kind of objectivity it involves. My suggestion is that Dworkin is advancing the view according to which truth and objectivity in law result from our best efforts to articulate the theories that make best moral sense of our legal practice. Thus, Dworkin's coherence theory of truth makes legal truth depend upon the best theories that we may develop in the course of legal deliberation—understood as an argumentative practice that aims at maximizing coherence among our different legal and moral convictions. The kind of objectivity that is involved in this version of the coherence theory of truth is, certainly, distinct from 'minimal' objectivity. For, obvious enough, the best theory needs not be the one upon which members of the community agree. It is not 'modest' objectivity either, in that idealization devices play virtually no role in identifying the best theory. It is objectivity as 'responsiveness to reasons', as Leiter has suggested, that best characterizes the kind of objectivity that Dworkin endorses.[136] And, I have argued, it is, more specifically, reasons from coherence that, in the Dworkinian framework, allow us to support (or challenge) any particular claim to objectivity or truth in the legal context.[137]

[135] See Dworkin ((1983a: 278–80), (1985: 171–74), (1996: 89) and (2011: 11)).

[136] Leiter (2001: 84).

[137] A similar account of legal and moral objectivity is splendidly articulated and defended by Hurley. For a brief description and discussion of Hurley's proposal, see ch 7.

### D. The Normative Value of Integrity

What reasons does Dworkin provide for putting coherence at the centre of a conception of law and legal justification? Why is coherence a value worth pursuing in law? In the course of his writings, Dworkin has developed the view according to which the best defence of coherence is to be found in the ground of political morality. Coherence is required, he argues, for independent reasons of political morality.

Dworkin's first step towards justifying a requirement of coherence on the basis of political morality may be found in *Taking Rights Seriously*. There, he argued that we may ground the requirement of coherence (then referred to as, to recall, articulate consistency) in a doctrine of political responsibility:

> This doctrine states, in its more general form, that political officials must make only such political decisions as they can justify within a political theory that also justifies the other decisions they propose to make ... It condemns the practice of making decisions that seem right in isolation, but cannot be brought within some comprehensive theory of general principles and policies that is consistent with other decisions also thought right.[138]

This doctrine of political responsibility thus requires that officials fit their decisions into a coherent program of action.[139] In *Law's Empire* Dworkin further grounds the requirement of coherence in the terrain of political morality.[140] Most importantly, he crucially adds a communitarian dimension to his defence of the value of coherence in law on the basis of political morality. In this work, Dworkin offers several arguments why coherence is worth pursuing, but the so-called 'argument from community' is the one that he develops in more detail. Before examining in some detail this argument, I shall briefly mention some additional reasons why, in Dworkin's view, coherence as integrity has a normative value in law.

Dworkin provides several reasons why integrity should be valued as a political ideal. First, integrity provides protection against different forms of official corruption. The reason is that there is more room for favouritism or vindictiveness in a system that permits decisions to be made on the basis of arbitrary distinctions. Secondly, integrity also contributes to the efficiency of law. For if people accept that they are governed not only by explicit rules laid down in past political decisions but also by the standards that flow from the principles embodied in those decisions, then the recognized set of public standards can expand or contract 'organically' without the need for detailed legislative or judicial decisions whenever new problematic cases

[138] Dworkin (1977: 87).

[139] That grounding of a requirement of coherence in a theory of (moral) responsibility is further developed in Dworkin (2011: 99–122).

[140] See Dworkin (1986) ch VI.

arise. These two arguments—the argument from corruption and the argument from efficiency—point towards the beneficial practical consequences of endorsing coherence as a political ideal. However, says Dworkin, there is also a moral and expressive reason, in addition to these practical reasons, to wit, that integrity is instrumental to the ideal of self-legislation. The ideal of self-legislation needs integrity because a citizen cannot treat himself as the author of a collection of laws that are inconsistent in principle. Particularly, argues Dworkin, there is one aspect of self-legislation that integrity promotes directly. As he puts it, 'Integrity expands and deepens the role individual citizens can play in developing public standards of their community because it requires them to treat relations among themselves as characteristically, not just spasmodically, governed by these standards'.[141] In so doing, integrity 'fuses citizens' moral and political lives' for it requires that citizens treat each other on the basis of the best interpretation of the common scheme of justice to which they are all committed by virtue of citizenship.

Besides its practical and expressive value, integrity is to be pursued because—and this is Dworkin's main argument for coherence—it promotes the moral legitimacy of legal systems. Dworkin claims that 'a political society that accepts integrity as a political virtue thereby becomes a special form of community, special in a way that promotes its moral authority to assume and deploy a monopoly of coercive force'.[142] This is what the 'argument from community' seeks to establish. This argument is long and difficult to disentangle. We may reconstruct Dworkin's argument from community to the effect that integrity is to be valued because it promotes the moral authority of the law as follows:

i. a state is legitimate if its constitutional structure and practices are such that its citizens have a general obligation to obey political decisions that purport to impose duties on them;
ii. political obligations (including the obligation to obey the law) are a case of communal or associative obligations (obligations of role);
iii. there are four conditions that associative obligations must satisfy in order to be genuine fraternal obligations, to wit, they must be special, personal, they must flow from a more general responsibility each member of the group has of concern for the well-being of others, and such concern must be equal for all members of the group;
iv. unlike other models of community, a community of principle—one that accepts integrity as a political ideal—satisfies the conditions of true associative obligations;

[141] Dworkin (1986: 189).
[142] ibid, 188.

v. a community that accepts integrity has a better case for claiming the authority of a genuine associative community, and can therefore claim moral legitimacy in the name of fraternity.

This argument gives rise to an obvious concern: how can a community that accepts integrity have a better case for legitimacy given the possibility—which Dworkin acknowledges—of conflict between the demands of integrity and the demands of justice?[143] The direct connection between integrity and moral legitimacy that the argument from community establishes is called into question once we notice that justice, fairness and integrity are distinct and sometimes conflicting ideals. Given that this is so, one may better achieve legitimacy by following the demands of morality and justice, as opposed to those of integrity—some have claimed.[144] But we may put these worries to rest if we get clear about what the argument actually seeks to establish. Dworkin does not purport to show that a community of principle *is* morally legitimate. He states:

> An association of principle is not automatically a just community; its conception of equal concern may be defective or it may violate rights of its citizens or citizens of other nations ... But the model of principle satisfies the conditions of true community better than any other model of community that it is possible for people who disagree about justice and fairness to adopt.[145]

Thus, a model of principle is not a just model *simpliciter*. However, it does satisfy the conditions of a true community better than alternative models and, in this sense, it may *claim* the moral authority of a genuine associative community. This claim, Dworkin crucially notes, may be defeated, for 'even true associative obligations may conflict with, and must sometimes yield to, demands of justice'.[146] Hence, the argument from community only establishes a presumptive link between moral legitimacy and integrity, in the name of fraternity, and one that may be rebutted.

In addition, the force of the objection that integrity in the hands of Dworkin may end up legitimizing 'wicked' legal systems is also downplayed once we notice what it is that the ideal of integrity, vis-à-vis justice and fairness, requires. Dworkin distinguishes two branches of integrity, the adjudicative principle and the legislative principle.[147] But none of these principles requires that decisions be always made as integrity mandates. For neither in legislation nor in adjudication, according to Dworkin, is integrity always sovereign over other virtues. A community that systematically abandons its general commitment to integrity could not claim moral legitimacy

[143] Dworkin (1986: 188).
[144] See Kress (1996: 349–51). See also Alexander and Kress (1995: 308–26).
[145] Dworkin (1986: 214).
[146] ibid.
[147] ibid, 167.

under the name of fraternity. But nothing in the way in which the argument is formulated requires that integrity be always chosen over justice. Hence, the reason to strive for integrity, both in its legislative and adjudicative dimensions, is not to automatically gain access to moral legitimacy. The relationship between integrity and morality is much more complicated than that. Integrity is strived for because doing so is necessary to have a true community at all, and, thus, necessary to claim moral legitimacy on the grounds of fraternity.

The relevance of accepting the ideal of integrity for having a true associative community points towards yet another reason why coherence is to be striven for. Not only does a general abandonment of the ideal of political integrity forfeit the argument from community, and thus denies a political community its claim to moral legitimacy on the grounds of fraternity, but it also seems to deny that any such community could be a genuine community at all. Thus, political integrity seems to play in Dworkin's theory a constitutive role of political communities. Interestingly, the constitutive dimension of coherence in relation to political identity is analogous to the constitutive role that coherence has been claimed to play in relation to individual identity. Hurley has persuasively argued that coherence plays such a constitutive role in individual self-determination.[148] She starts her discussion of coherence and self-determination by asking why, given that conflict is ineliminable, should we as individuals seek a coherent way of resolving it. Her response appeals to the constitutive role of coherence in personal identity. She claims that qualities of agency are not entirely fixed, but that they are in part the result of self-interpretation, an interpretation which, like any other interpretative activity, is guided by various constitutive constraints, most importantly, a constraint of coherence. In seeking coherence we seek our very identities, we are trying to determine who we really are. The reason why there is a point in seeking a coherent way of proceeding in the face of conflict, even though we cannot eliminate conflict, is now apparent. The concern with personal coherence is not something that we are free to disown entirely, for in so doing we would be giving up our own agency. We seek coherence in the face of ineliminable conflict because this is the only way that we have to proceed, if we are to proceed as persons, as unified agents, at all.

[148] Hurley (1989: 260–63). See ch 7 for a discussion of Hurley's views on the constitutive value of coherence.

Similarly, Dworkin claims that, even though it would not be possible to bring all the discrete rules and other standards enacted by our legislatures into a coherent scheme of principle,

> we must report this fact as a defect, not as a desirable result of a fair division of political power between different bodies of opinion, and that we must strive to remedy whatever inconsistencies in principle we are forced to confront.[149]

That is, even though, given the differences between political forces, conflict is an unavoidable feature of the life of the law, we should nevertheless strive for coherence in the face of such conflict. But, why—one may ask—should this be so? Why not accept the conflictual nature of law and meet the demands of the group that seem more legitimate on the particular case? Again, the reason why this is so has to do with the constitutive role that coherence plays, this time, in community self-determination. Officials, and citizens—we may say—are not entirely free to give up the ambition of coherence, for in doing so they would be refusing to determine their own identity as a community. Accepting conflict as inevitable and abandoning the search for coherence is only possible if the aspiration of being a true community is given up in the first place.

## E. Conclusions

Dworkin articulates a theory of law and adjudication that takes coherence to be a standard far more reaching than the coherence theories that have been previously examined. From *Taking Rights Seriously* to *Law's Empire*, Dworkin has refined and elaborated a theory of law as coherence that constitutes a very sophisticated alternative to legal positivism. However, despite the fact that coherence is of fundamental importance to Dworkin's legal theory, he leaves the concept of coherence mostly undefined. Beyond the idea that coherence is 'consistency in principle', Dworkin provides us with no criteria for comparing the relative coherence of alternative interpretations and for selecting one of them as justified.[150]

As explained, Dworkin takes coherence to be a necessary and sufficient condition for legal justification. Thus, he defends a 'strong' version of the coherence theory. I have argued that, in this theory, coherence allows us to restrict the number of plausible alternatives as well as to select one of them as justified. The kind of justification that coherence provides—I have contended—is 'substantive' rather than 'formal'. In this sense, legal decisions justified by virtue of their coherence are not only, in Dworkin's view,

[149] Dworkin (1986: 217).
[150] See Finnis (1987: 373).

justifiable, but also defensible from the standpoint of political morality. I have argued that Dworkin's model of justification is based, despite appearances to the contrary, on a 'global' conception of coherence, and as such it is vulnerable to the objections which, as I will argue below, may be raised against global models of coherence.

Not only does Dworkin endorse a coherence theory of legal justification, but also—I have argued—a coherence theory for the truth of legal propositions. More specifically, I have suggested that he advocates a version of the coherence theory of truth according to which truth in law results from coherence with the best theory of law and morality that we are able to articulate. This version of the coherence theory embodies a view of legal objectivity as 'responsiveness from reasons to coherence', in contrast to some alternative versions of the coherence theory of truth that are based on either minimal or modest conceptions of objectivity.

Dworkin's theory may be seen as advancing a truly alternative framework for thinking about law and legal reasoning. As opposed to the 'jurisprudence of rules', which characterizes legal positivism, he has put forward, what Schauer has termed a 'jurisprudence of reasons'.[151] Indeed, Dworkin has pushed to the extremes the coherentist project of enlarging the domain of reason in law by claiming that, except in rare cases, reasons from coherence allow us to pick a uniquely best decision as justified. The right answer thesis has been harshly criticized in the literature. In a nutshell, the critique is that, as Finnis puts it, Dworkin 'overestimates practical reasoning's power to identify options as the best and the right'.[152] In other words, Dworkin's theory involves, as MacCormick succinctly says, 'an untenable form of ultra rationalism'.[153] As I have argued, MacCormick and Peczenik seem to be far too aware of the limits of reason in law, and this leads them to concede too much to the sceptic. This is troubling in light of the motivation of coherence theories to provide a non-sceptical alternative to (strong) legal positivism. Dworkin, to the contrary, does provide such an alternative, but by underestimating the limits of practical reason and minimizing, rather than confronting, the import of the sceptical challenge. What would be desirable is to have a coherentist account of law and adjudication that, unlike positivism, accords a broad space to reason in law, while acknowledging and undermining (to the extent that this is possible) the force of the sceptical claims.

[151] Schauer (1986–87).
[152] Finnis (1987: 357).
[153] N MacCormick (1994: 265).

## IV. OBJECTIONS AGAINST COHERENCE THEORIES OF LEGAL REASONING ABOUT NORMS

I shall now examine some of the main objections that may be directed against coherence theories of law and adjudication.[154] Some of these objections have already been touched upon in the course of our survey of coherence theories in law. However, I think that it is convenient to have a clear and complete account of the main challenges that coherence theories in law ought to face, even if this makes for occasional repetition.

### A. The Vagueness Problem

Coherentist accounts of legal justification are too vague in two important respects. The notion of 'coherence' is too imprecise to provide usable standards of legal justification. A coherence theory must specify in detail what it means for a legal decision to cohere with a body of legal rules and standards as well as the conditions of coherence that a set of norms must satisfy for it to be justification-conferring. MacCormick's and Dworkin's principle-based concept of coherence leaves the foregoing questions unanswered. The most important effort at determining precisely what coherence requires is Alexy and Peczenik's list of criteria of coherence. Their proposal is very suggestive as regards the different ingredients of coherence, but it says little about how one ought to combine them in a coherence calculation. In their view, in order to determine whether a particular theory is coherent or more coherent than alternatives, we need to weigh and balance the different criteria of coherence. But when criteria conflict, how are we to proceed? Some account is needed of how the different criteria of coherence may be balanced against each other when reasoning about norms in law.

Coherence theories in law are vague in another respect as well. Not only do they lack an account of the conditions under which the outcome of a coherence calculation is coherent (and justified), but they also fail to explain how the process of coherentist justification works. In other words, coherence theories do not specify the process of reasoning whereby we may arrive at the legal decision that is best justified. If all that the coherence theory has to say about how to reason in law is that one should search for the most coherent alternative -but it provides no guidelines as to how one should do so- then it amounts to little more than a recommendation to pick

[154] There is another objection that has been raised in the coherentist literature but that I shall not deal with here, to wit, 'the retroactivity objection'. The objection is that coherence theories are path-dependent and that this leads to retroactive application of the law. See Kress (1984: 377–388). For responses to Kress' retroactivity objection, see Hurley (1990: 235–251) and Habermas (1996: 219–220).

the decision that seems intuitively best. Hence, it is imperative for coherence theories that they give a full account of the reasoning patterns whereby coherence may be established over the course of legal decision-making.

## B. Coherence and Legal Conservatism

Against coherence theories, it has been argued that they have a tendency to favour the status quo and that they prevent genuine revisions of one's beliefs. Faced with a decision as to whether to believe or disregard, for example, a piece of evidence that fails to cohere with one's accepted views, one may take (and justifiably so by the coherentist standards) the decision not to accept the belief in such a piece of evidence as justified. Similarly, coherence theories of law—so the objection goes—urge legal decision-makers to stick to previously held views and decide cases accordingly. In short, the charge is that coherence theories, insofar as they take justification to be a matter of coherence with the settled law, are a roadblock to legal change. That this objection is a serious one becomes clear as soon as one considers the implications of coherence-based legal decision-making in morally wicked legal systems, if such theories—as the objector claims—have an in-built conservative tendency. In such systems, coherence theories, as Raz puts it, 'require further injustices to be perpetuated in 'hard cases' in the name of coherence'.[155]

Dworkin has given a response to the objection from conservatism by arguing that once 'we grasp the difference between integrity and narrow consistency' we may come to see that 'integrity is a more dynamic and radical standard than it first seemed, because it encourages a judge to be wide-ranging and imaginative in his search for coherence with fundamental principle'.[156] That is, coherence theories enable judges to justify their decisions by virtue of their coherence with fundamental principles that are necessary to justify the law as a whole. The problem, however, is that there are no clear criteria for determining what coherence, once it is distinguished from consistency, requires. Thus, this line of response is successful only if a solution to the problem of vagueness is available. Even with a good account of coherence in hand, this reply would fail to avoid the undesirable conservative implications in systems in which even fundamental principles are morally outrageous. For consistency in principle, as opposed to bare consistency, would still prevent judges from mitigating, rather than propagating, the injustices of such regimes.

[155] Raz (1986a: 111). Raz's critique is directed specifically against Dworkin's theory of coherence; see also Wacks (1984).

[156] Dworkin (1986: 220).

Another response to the problem of conservatism, I would argue, is available for (strong) coherence theories in law. A coherence theory of legal justification—such as Dworkin's or Peczenik's—which incorporates moral reasons into the base of coherence, properly developed, has the resources for meeting this objection. It is possible to downplay the impact of unjust source-based law in the outcome of a coherence calculation (that is, in the result of applying a test of coherence to a particular base) by requiring that a justified legal decision must cohere as well with sound moral principles. Hence, a coherence theory will not perpetuate injustice in systems in which fundamental principles of law are morally indefensible if it takes the kind of coherence that is relevant to legal justification to be coherence among both legal reasons and moral reasons. In such a theory, a decision may cohere with the set of legal and moral reasons, even if it fails to cohere with (morally wicked) fundamental principles of the settled law.[157]

However, there must be limits to the foregoing coherentist strategy for meeting the objection from conservatism. Otherwise, decisions that are justified according to a coherentist standard of justification could not be regarded, in any sense, as the result of interpreting the legal materials rather than simply as a result of following the requirements of morality. That is to say, to use Dworkin's terminology, one cannot make the set of beliefs about fit with settled law and political morality coherent by loosening the requirement of fit in such a dramatic way as to make a legal decision, which is justified by virtue of its coherence with such a set, unrecognizable as a 'legal' decision, rather than a moral one. After all, as Peczenik says, what distinguishes 'legal' reasoning from other kinds of reasoning is that the relevance of reasons from authority is taken for granted. Thus, a coherence theory of legal justification (as distinct from a coherence theory of moral justification) must ensure that reasons of authority play the role that they ought to play in the legal domain. Otherwise, requiring coherence with both moral and legal reasons for legal justification would solve the problem of conservatism only at the cost of making the coherence theory fall pray of the isolation objection, that is, the objection that coherence theories may yield justified beliefs that are not properly connected with the reasons of legal authorities—which I will discuss shortly.

## C. The Circularity Objection

A problem with a coherence-based view of legal inference is that, it is claimed, it involves a vicious circularity. Coherence theories seemingly

[157] This line of response is not available, however, to weak coherence theories insofar as these theories take coherence with the settled law to be a necessary condition of justification.

license an inference from *p* to *q*, on grounds of coherence, and then from *q* to *p*. If nothing but coherence generates justification, then any chain of arguments that one may construct would eventually bite its tail. Following a coherentist approach, we may justify, for instance, a particular principle because it properly coheres with a body of precedent, and eventually justify a decision because it coheres with such a body of precedent, which we accepted as justified by virtue of its coherence with this very same principle. Most coherence theorists in law accept rather than address the objection of circularity.[158] There is, in fact, no reason why they should do so. There is a well-known response among advocates of coherentist theories of epistemic justification that is easily available.

The circularity objection—so the reply goes—is based on the wrong assumption that inference is linear in the sense that justification involves a chain of beliefs along which justification is transferred from one element to another down the chain. As soon as one replaces a linear view of justification by a holistic one, according to which justification is a property of a coherent set of elements each of which is justified by virtue of its belonging to such a set, one may put worries about circularity to rest.[159] Of course, the justification-conferring set must satisfy some additional constraints to meet the circularity objection. That it be sufficiently big is one common consideration. I would like to suggest, though, that it is not so much the size of the set as the complexity of its structure that is crucial for a successful response to the circularity objection.[160] Insofar as the justification-conferring system is divided up into several subsystems that also exhibit a sophisticated sub-structure of their own, the risks of a chain of justification 'biting up' its tail are minimal. For the justification of any element of the system depends on its coherence with sets of elements the coherence of which depends, on their turn, on their connections with yet other sets of elements. A highly structured set of beliefs is thus necessary for coherentist justification's circularity to be a benign one.[161]

[158] See Moral (2003: 319); and Peczenik (1998a: 11–12). When legal theorists claim that circularity cannot but be accepted, however, they seem to have in mind not the problem of circularity but rather the problem of isolation—which is a related but different problem. See Peczenik ((1997a: 167–68), (1997b: 316–17), and (1999: 198–99)). See also Weinrib (1988: 974 and 1010).

[159] For a full account of this line of reply, see ch 3.

[160] This point has been also argued for by Rabinowicz (1998: 19–20).

[161] Dworkin's reply to the so-called objection from 'theory-dependence', which is, at bottom, a version of the problem of circularity, also appeals to the relevance of complexity. On the relation between the objection from circularity and the objection from theory-dependence, see Marmor (1992: 79). For a statement of the objection from theory-dependence, see Dworkin (1985: 169). For Dworkin's response, see Dworkin (1983b: 293). See also ch 10.

### D. Coherence vs Authority

Coherence theories are inconsistent with the authoritative nature of law, as they fail to give an account of the pivotal role that legal sources ought to play in determining what the law is and how cases should be decided.[162] If, as the coherence theory has it, the law is what the most coherent theory of law and morality says that it is, what ensures that the resulting view about the content of the law is not severed from the reasons of legal authorities? And, if legal decision-makers ought to decide on the basis of such a theory, what prevents them from taking decisions which, while warranted by the best theory about law and morality, are not warranted by the class of legal reasons alone?

A first step towards meeting this objection is to require that the base of coherence include acts of legislation and adjudication. The introduction of such a requirement is problematic in that, arguably, it infiltrates a non-coherentist element into the theory. For now, I shall set aside the worry of whether introducing this requirement amounts to a relapse into foundationalism, or whether instead one may provide a coherentist justification for the requirement that the base contain authority acts.[163] In any event, requiring that the base include reasons from authority only helps meet the objection from authority if these reasons effectively constrain theory construction in law. In other words, to meet the objection, coherence theories need not only show that the input to coherentist reasoning includes reasons from authority, but also ensure that the output, ie the theory about the content of the law, is not isolated from the set of authoritative rules and standards. What have current coherence theories offered by way of a response to this objection?

As explained above, Hage and Peczenik have argued that 'the law is part of what the most coherent theory of everything says that it is'.[164] This 'coherent theory of everything' includes beliefs about how different parts of the theory ought to cohere with each other, as well as beliefs about the relative weights of different kinds of reasons within the theory.[165] Now, what are the implications of this view for the objection that coherence theories of law fail to take due notice of the role of authority reasons? Hage and Peczenik argue that whether the content of the law is, according to the coherence theory, more or less dependent upon personal morality depends on one's views on the relation between what they refer to as the 'social' and the 'practical' nature of law. That is, it depends on whether one takes it

[162] See Raz (1985) esp 305–10. For a discussion of Raz's critique, see Michelon (2011b) and Rodriguez-Blanco (2001).

[163] See chs 3, 4 and 10.

[164] Peczenik and Hage (2004: 337).

[165] See Hage (2004: 97–99).

that legal norms are those that are generally accepted as such, or whether, instead, norms may be accepted as legal only if one is prepared to act upon them. Thus, in their view, it is one's theory about how law and morality relate to each other that determines what the content of the law is, and, ultimately, how far removed it may be from the norms generally accepted as authoritative. In a similar vein, Hage contends that coherentism is compatible with different views about what the proper role of legal authorities in the construction of the law is. Coherentism only requires that one's views about the relation between law and state authorities and between law and politics cohere with one's views about how much leeway legal decision-makers have to make the law cohere.[166]

Dworkin's response to Michaels' objection to the effect that Dworkin's theory of interpretation allows us to accept as justified an interpretation of a literary text which is utterly severed from the textual facts—which is a literary version of the 'isolation objection'—gives us a hint as to how Dworkin would address the 'isolation objection' against coherence theories of law.[167] According to Dworkin, no theory of interpretation about the point of reading a text would allow us to make an interpretation that had nothing in common with the work that is the object of interpretation.[168] Similarly, one might say, in Dworkin's view, the danger of endorsing a coherence theory of the law that allows us to underplay the relevance of reasons from authority in legal justification is averted because we cannot accept (on pain of incoherence) a theory about the point of the legal practice that would permit this. Dworkin insists that the theory on the basis of which the reader or the legal decision-maker interprets a text comprises different parts—including parts about how closely the interpretation ought to fit the textual facts, or, we might say, about how much a legal interpretation may depart from the law that is authoritatively binding—which are sufficiently disjoint as to supervise and constrain each other.

Hage's, Peczenik's and Dworkin's coherentist views may be seen as pointing, in different ways, towards the relevance of second-order beliefs (ie beliefs about our beliefs about the content of the law) in a coherence-based approach to theory construction in law. The suggestion seems to be the following one: whatever theory of the law we may construct results from our efforts at making cohere a set of beliefs that includes beliefs about the law, beliefs about political morality *and* beliefs about how the different parts of our belief structure relate to each other. To elaborate the point, the base of coherence includes not only first-order beliefs about law and political morality, but also beliefs about the relative weight and relevance of first-order beliefs and about how these different beliefs constrain each

[166] ibid, 102.
[167] Michaels (1983: 337).
[168] Dworkin (1983b: 312).

other. Most importantly, a base of coherence is structured so as to include beliefs about the relative weight and relevance of authority reasons as well as beliefs about how beliefs about what legal authorities have enacted relate to beliefs about political morality. The claim is that Hage, Peczenik and Dworkin seem to suggest—but do not articulate—a response to the objection that says that coherence theories in law are incompatible with the authoritative character of law that appeals to the relevance of second-order beliefs in legal justification.[169] A theory about what the law requires that is unconnected to the authoritative sources will be ruled out as unjustified because it fails to cohere with one's beliefs about the proper role of authoritative sources in theory construction in law. Hence, in order to meet the challenge that coherentist standards of legal justification are incompatible with law's authoritative nature, coherence theories need to give a detailed account of the role of second-order beliefs in legal justification.

### E. Legal Dilemmas

The coherentist approach to legal justification gives rise, the objector says, to 'legal dilemmas'. Different decisions may cohere with the settled law equally well. In these cases, coherence does not provide courts with determinate guidance.[170] Coherence theories fail to supply a criterion for choosing among decisions that equally fit with the settled law.[171] The force of this objection varies depending on the kind of coherence theory that is proposed. This objection has no force against coherence theories, such as MacCormick's, which take coherence to be a necessary, albeit insufficient, condition for legal justification. These theories are ready to admit that there may be cases in which coherence does not decide, and among which one should choose on the basis of moral considerations.[172] Under this view, moral merit acts as a tiebreaker between equally coherent theories. But the need to appeal to moral considerations does not show any flaw in this version of the coherence theory, for they never claimed that coherence was a sufficient condition for justification in the first place.

[169] An alternative response to the isolation objection is provided by Peczenik. He claims, following Lehrer, that the isolation objection is just a skeptical claim that, like any other challenge, ought to be beaten on the basis of one's system of acceptances and preferences (see Peczenik ((1998a: 12), (2000a: 163), (1999: 199) and (2000b: 293))). For a detailed exposition of Lehrer's response to the isolation objection, see ch 3.

[170] Some authors have given yet other reasons why coherence theories undermine the determinacy of law. See Edmunson (1996) and Mackie (1983: 168–69).

[171] For statements of this objection, see Kress (1996: 538–39); and Raz (1992: 299 and 309) fn 64.

[172] Dworkin would also be holding such a view, according to some commentators who take the requirement of fit to be the coherence requirement.

The objection mainly affects those coherence theories that claim that coherence with the settled law is only one among other conditions of legal justification, but do not give coherence lexical priority over other values. Under this view, the justified decision is the one that results from the best combination of coherentist and other considerations. This version of the coherence theory gives rise to legal indeterminacy for, as Raz puts it, 'there is no way of deciding which mix of coherence and other values is best'.[173] Several 'mixes' of coherence and other values may be equally good—so the objection goes—and coherence theories leave us with no guidance as to how to select one as best.

Two (controversial) assumptions are critical for this objection to get off the ground: first, that moral and legal values are incommensurable and, secondly, that value commensurability is a prerequisite of rational choice. Finnis claims—against Dworkin's version of the coherence theory—that the suggestion that legal decision-makers ought to decide on the basis of the interpretation that seems best in the 'general balance of political virtues' (that is, that seems best along the dimension of fit and substance) in 'the absence of any metric which could commensurate the different criteria (the dimension of fit and inherent moral merit) ... can legitimately mean no more than bear in mind, conscientiously, all the relevant factors and choose'.[174] And he adds that the problem is even more intense 'for there is not just one dimension of soundness or substantive political justifiability, but many incommensurable dimensions'.[175] Similarly, Mackie writes that Dworkin's right answer thesis assumes 'too simple a metric for the strength of considerations, that such strengths are commensurable on a linear scale ... but in fact considerations may be imperfectly commensurable'.[176] And Raz writes that 'on many occasions there is a whole range of ways of mixing the different values, none of which is superior to the others',[177] and it is because of 'pervasive incommensurabilities among values'[178] that he takes coherence theories to fail to provide a determinate guide for legal decision-making. Thus, the objection is that coherence theories give rise to indeterminacy because they take as justified the decision that results from the best combination of coherence and other values, but given value incommensurability, there will be cases in which there are several equally good mixes. In these cases, the objector says, the coherence theory leaves the decision-maker with no grounds for choice.

[173] Raz (1992: 299).
[174] Finnis (1987: 374).
[175] ibid, 374 and 375.
[176] Mackie (1983: 165).
[177] Raz (1992: 312).
[178] ibid, 309.

Before examining what the coherence theories have to say against this objection, it is important to notice that the objection so stated misrepresents the coherence theories that are defended in legal scholarship in an important respect. For the conflict among the purportedly incommensurable values is not one between coherence and moral value/s but one, as Alexy puts it, 'inside coherence'.[179] Coherence theories, such as Dworkin's or Peczenik's, do not take coherence to be one value among many. They do not ask legal decision-makers to balance coherence with the settled law against other values, most importantly, moral values. Instead, what they propose is that we broaden the base of coherence so as to include not only authoritative reasons, but also moral reasons. These coherentist views are best described as urging decision-makers to take the decision that coheres best with a base broadened in this way. In other words, what is the 'best' mix is pretty clear for coherence theories, namely, the 'most coherent' one. The problem that the objection correctly understood raises is whether there may be different 'mixes' that are equally coherent, so that the coherence theory fails to provide guidance for choosing among two decisions which equally cohere with a set of beliefs which comprises both beliefs about the law and beliefs about morality.

Now, what are the responses to this objection available in the current state of the coherence theory in law? The responses heavily depend on the different views that coherence theories have on the scope of reason within the domain of morality. Peczenik defends, to recall, non-cognitivism about all-things-considered moral judgements. In his view, we achieve coherence by means of weighing and balancing the relevant values, but the last step of this operation is a matter of 'personal feeling' or 'individual preference'. Given that individuals have different preferences, a weighing operation may yield different justified outcomes. Thus, it seems that, according to Peczenik, the fact that coherence methods yield different but equally justified decisions in hard cases is only a natural consequence of the subjective nature of moral values. Thus, under Peczenik's view, legal dilemmas are not 'dilemmas' at all, for it is only if we assume that there need to be only 'one' correct answer that dilemmas should arise in the first place. To the question of how we should decide among equally coherent lines of reasoning the answer is clear: just pick what seems best from your point of view. This position, as argued, is deeply unsatisfactory. It just disposes of the problem by endorsing a highly implausible subjectivist view of moral and legal values.

Dworkin's response to the objection we are considering is (unsurprisingly) different from the one given by Peczenik. As is well known, Dworkin has argued at length against the view according to which there are no right

[179] Alexy (1998: 46).

answers in hard cases. According to Dworkin, if law is an enterprise—as he claims—in which propositions are assertable as true if they provide a better fit than their negation with propositions already established, then the question of whether the judge ought to decide for one or other side in a hard case almost certainly has a right answer. For it is very unlikely that, in modern legal systems, one answer will not provide a better fit than the other does.[180] Dworkin concedes that there is a theoretical possibility of a tie in cases in which the argument from one side may be as good as the argument from another. However, he claims that in complex legal systems such ties must be rare. Thus, Dworkin's reply to the objection that coherence fails to provide guidance in cases in which there are equally coherent decisions is that the situation that the objector envisages is just too rare to have any relevance for practical purposes. That it is unlikely that in modern legal systems such ties occur presupposes, he admits, 'a conception of morality other than some conception according to which different moral theories are frequently incommensurate'.[181] Thus, Dworkin's response to the objection is based on the assumption that values are commensurable (or at least that incommensurability is a rare possibility). In a similar vein, Alexy claims that a coherence approach is based on a non-sceptical view about the possibility of weighing values and on some kind of commensurability among values.[182]

This response does not solve the problem of legal dilemmas, but it does mitigate the force of the objection by diminishing its practical import. However, whatever success this line of response has depends on the (controversial) view that values are in some sense commensurable.[183] Given that the claim that moral and legal values are commensurable is a highly contentious one, it would be convenient for coherence theories to meet the objection in a way that does not rely on value commensurability. That is, it is incumbent on coherence theories to show how one may reason about conflicting values in law in a coherentist fashion, without assuming value commensurability.[184]

## F. Coherence and Truth in Law

We come now to the main problem for coherence theories of legal justification, to wit, the problem of whether coherence is truth-conducive. Do we have any reason to believe that coherentist standards of justification

[180] See Dworkin (1972) esp 75–76 and 83–84.

[181] Dworkin (1983a: 272).

[182] Alexy (1998: 46–48).

[183] For the current debate on this issue, see Raz (1986b) and Chang (1997).

[184] For some coherentist approaches to practical reasoning that do not rely on the assumption that values are commensurable, see ch 7.

conduce us to legal truth? Do coherence methods lead us to accept as justified propositions about the law that are likely to be true? The problem of how coherence and truth connect up is one that all coherence theories of justification need to address. For coherence theories of empirical justification the problem, as we will see, is particularly acute, given the plausibility of the correspondence theory of truth (in some sophisticated version).[185] Since coherence is an internal property of propositions, the issue of how it is appropriately connected with the external world is a serious one. In contrast, coherence theories in ethics are in a better position to meet the objection because non-realist theories of moral truth are initially more attractive.[186]

Truth in law, unlike in the empirical domain, is not exclusively a matter of correspondence with an external reality, ie the rules and standards accepted as authoritative in a particular society. But, as opposed to ethics, the view that there are facts that are mind-independent and that constrain the kinds of theories of law one may possibly advance is a plausible one. In short, because of the dual nature of law as both a conventional and a normative enterprise, the problem of the truth-conduciveness of coherence is an extremely knotty one. Ultimately, whether a particular version of the coherence theory of legal justification succeeds in meeting the 'truth objection' critically depends on which notion of truth one takes to be more adequate for the legal domain.

Needless to say, I cannot go here into an exploration of the different theories of truth in law.[187] Rather, I shall focus on the problem of how different combinations of coherence theories of legal justification and theories of legal truth address the truth objection. To begin with, it is important to notice that the problem of how coherence and truth connect up does not arise if one holds, as MacCormick does, a weak coherence theory of legal justification. Because weak versions of the coherence theory do not claim that coherence is all that there is to legal justification, they do not need to address the issue of how endorsing as justified beliefs about the law by virtue of their coherence leads one to accept true propositions about the law. The connection between justification and truth in law is established by means other than coherence. The problem arises for 'strong' theories of legal justification according to which coherence is both a necessary and sufficient condition of justification.

Among (strong) coherence theories of justification we may distinguish between two different positions. One may hold a coherence theory of

[185] See chs 3 and 6.
[186] See ch 8.
[187] For a survey of theories of truth in law, see Pintore (2000) and Patterson (1996).

legal justification while endorsing a realist view about legal truth.[188] Alternatively, one may hold a coherence theory of legal justification while endorsing a non-realist view of legal truth. The truth objection is a strong one against the former kind of views, that is, against views that aim at combining a coherence theory of legal justification with a correspondence theory of legal truth. Moore's version of natural law theory provides an example of such a view.[189] The question of what reason we have to believe that coherence theories of legal justification yield beliefs that are likely to be true, in the sense that they correspond with a realm of mind-independent legal facts, is an extremely difficult one to answer.[190] For such theories need to show that coherence, which is a matter of internal relations, is connected with truth as correspondence with an external reality in the right way.

A second kind of view within the camp of strong versions of coherence theories take an anti-realist stance towards legal truth. Truth in this view is not discovered but constructed through a process of coherentist justification. It is coherence with a specified set of beliefs that yields legal truth. To be sure, these theories succeed in addressing the truth objection, for they forge a conceptual relation between coherence and truth. Under this view, revising one's beliefs so as to maximize their coherence necessarily brings one closer to the truth. This direct response to the truth objection, however, is fraught with problems. There are different forms that a coherence theory of legal truth may take, and each of these comes with its particular set of problems.

As I mentioned above, there are many different views that may be brought together under the heading of the 'coherence theory of truth'. In law, the most relevant difference lies in the diverse ways in which the base of coherence is identified. The difference among these theories lies in the diverse moral reasons which, alongside authority reasons, comprise the base of coherence. We may distinguish three versions. A first version claims that whether propositions about the law are true is a matter that partially depends on personal morality. In this sense, the content of the law is relative to one's views about morality. This is the view that, as I argued before, Hage and Peczenik endorse. The problem with this position is that it injects a subjectivist element into the theory of legal truth, which is, to my mind, deeply unsatisfactory. A similar objection may be raised against coherence

[188] It is crucial to note that by 'realism' about truth, I am referring to any theory of truth that claims that truth-makers are mind-independent facts. This is a kind of 'metaphysical' realism, which is importantly distinguished from 'legal' realism, as a theory of legal decision-making. In fact, legal realists typically reject realism about truth (at least in the normative domain).

[189] See Moore ((1985) and (2004)). See also Brink (1988).

[190] For an analysis of the problems that arise from combining a coherence theory of legal justification and a realist view about legal facts, see Coleman and Leiter (1993: 612–16).

theories of truth in law that claim that legal truth is partially dependent on moral truth understood as coherence with the mores or social conventions.

A second version claims that it is coherence among the beliefs about the law and morality that would be held under ideal conditions that yields legal truth. This is the view which, according to some interpretations, Dworkin may be seen as defending. This view would have to face severe objections against 'ideal' views about what morality requires, the most significant of which is their seeming inability to guide conduct in a less-than-ideal world.[191]

Last, one may claim legal truth to be coherence with the best theory of law and political morality that one may devise under real life constraints—as distinct from the one that we would elaborate under ideal conditions. As I have argued, Dworkin's writings on truth and objectivity in law are best interpreted as arguing for this view. A problem for this version of the coherence theory of truth is that it is uncertain whether it articulates a sufficiently stringent standard for assessing the truth of legal claims. MacCormick writes,

> For the decision to be justified in the full, strong sense which Dworkin demands, it is necessary that the theory which authorizes it is the best possible theory of the legal system in question at the time in question. This seems a tall order … But Dworkin does not claim that we can be sure that we have achieved the best possible theory. He claims only that the best possible theory is what we must try our best to achieve.[192]

But are 'good intentions' enough for 'truth'? It seems that some constraints ought to be imposed upon the relevant set of alternative theories so as to ensure that the best out of this set has some legitimate claim to truth.

Setting aside the different problems that the diverse versions of the coherence theory of truth in law face, there is yet one more problem that is common to all of them. All these views meet the truth objection by conflating justification with truth, since they define truth in law (variously conceived) as justification. In short, coherentist *cum* anti-realist views, like coherentist *cum* realist views, face important difficulties in showing that the right connection obtains between coherence and legal truth (variously conceived). The problem of the truth-conduciveness of coherence thus remains an important one for current coherence theories in law, in both its realist and anti-realist varieties.

[191] This problem is closely related to the 'problem of access', as Coleman and Leiter term it, see (1993: 629). The problem of access is as follows. If, according to views of legal truth as 'ideal' justification, true propositions about the law are those that one would justifiably hold under ideal conditions, and given that ideal conditions do not obtain (by definition), then it follows that legal truth would be inaccessible to real judges operating in less-than-ideal conditions. Such a theory fails to guide judges in their task of decision-making for it makes legal justification and legal truth unattainable by real judges.

[192] N MacCormick (1983: 188).

## G. Value Pluralism, Conflict and Coherence

Coherence theories, some scholars have argued, are based on the wrong assumption that legal systems are coherent (or that they may be reconstructed so as to be coherent in a way that is compatible with their authoritative nature).[193] This assumption is untenable given the impact of political contest in the shaping and development of the law as well as the pluralism of values that the law is likely to reflect. This objection has been most forcefully stated by Raz.[194] According to Raz, while we may expect the law to be coherent 'in bits—in areas relatively unaffected by continuous political struggles', there is no reason to expect the law as a whole to be coherent.[195] Raz's argument is that (i) the content of the law must be determined by reference to the intentions of legal authorities; (ii) there is a plurality of intentions, as he puts it, 'there is no spirit to the law, only different spirits';[196] therefore, (iii) there is no reason to expect the law to be coherent. By assuming that the law is coherent (or by imposing coherence on the whole of the law) global coherence accounts err in two ways. First, they underestimate the degree and implications of value pluralism. And secondly, they wrongly attempt to idealize the law out of the concreteness of politics. But in countries with decent constitutions the untidiness of politics is sanctioned by the morality of authoritative institutions, and thus there is no reason why the effects of politics ought to be minimized.[197]

To what extent does this critique undermine coherence theories? First, one should notice that the critique is directed against global versions of coherence, and thus that it leaves non-global accounts intact. Hence, whatever the force of the objection is, a properly developed local version of the coherence theory is immune to this objection. In addition, it is worth pointing out that Raz's critique is most effective if coherence is understood, as he suggests, as 'unity'.[198] However, there is no reason why coherence should be so defined. In fact, most coherence theories in law (as much as everywhere else I should say) do not endorse such a view of coherence.[199] Raz saddles the coherence theory with a conception of coherence that makes these theories more vulnerable to the objection we are considering.

193 This is the problem of authority, which I have discussed above.

194 This objection has also been raised by critical legal studies, specifically, against Dworkin's version of the coherence theory. See Kennedy (1997). For a discussion of the critical legal studies' critique, see Waldron (2008).

195 Raz (1992: 295).

196 ibid, 302.

197 ibid, 309ff.

198 ibid, 286.

199 See Kress (1996: 539–46), for an analysis of the different ways in which coherence and unity relate to each other in various conceptions of coherence. Most versions of the coherence theory in law do not define coherence as unity. Weinrib's theory is a notable exception. See Weinrib ((1988) and (1994)). For a critique, see Kress (1994).

This said, the most important line of response to Raz's critique—and one which coherence theories in law have thus far failed to articulate—is to deny the assumption from which it proceeds, to wit, that coherence methods aim at explaining away the value conflict that is inherent in law. In contrast, it could be argued that coherence rather than explaining conflict away provides a way to proceed in the face of conflict.[200] It is precisely because 'morality is a plurality of irreducibly independent principles' and because 'the reality of politics leaves the law untidy' that we need coherence methods in the first place. Thus, coherence accounts, far from being incompatible with the value pluralism that pervades our legal systems, can arguably be seen as providing a method for guiding legal decision-making, given such value pluralism. Of course, coherence can provide such a method only if it is granted that one may rationally deliberate among the different values that inform laws in democratic societies, and articulate a coherent theory about how these values relate to each other. At the bottom of Raz's argument to the effect that coherence accounts underestimate the implications of value pluralism and the extent to which law reflects the 'vagaries of politics' there is (again) a sceptical attitude towards the possibility of weighing and balancing the different values to which the law is responsive in a rational way.[201] Hence, doubts may be raised about whether Raz's critique to coherence accounts would still hold under the assumption that it is possible to rationally weigh and balance the conflicting values that are at stake in hard cases. This is the assumption which coherence theories must—but do not—argue for in order to meet the objection from value pluralism (as well as the objection from legal dilemmas, as was explained above). Further, they need not only show that legal decision-makers may rationally weigh and balance conflicting values, but also that coherence methods provide a most valuable guide as to how they may do so.

## H. Herculean Ideals and the Base of Coherence

What is the domain of coherence in law? What is the set of norms that is relevant for determining the coherence, and thus the justificatory status, of a legal decision? As explained before, two main alternatives are on the table. One may claim that it is the whole body of the law that a legal decision ought to cohere with for it to be justified. Under this view, the kind of coherence that yields legal justification is 'global' coherence. One may even argue for yet a more comprehensive view of the 'base' of coherence

[200] For an extremely illuminating account of the relationship between coherence and conflict in moral deliberation, see Hurley (1989) pt III, to whom this response to Raz's critique owes much. I discuss Hurley's views in ch 7.

[201] See Alexy (1998: 46).

according to which it is not only legal norms, but also moral norms that comprise the base of coherence. Alternatively, one may restrict the domain within which coherence is to be sought to an area of the law, and defend a 'local' model of coherence.

Current coherence theories, as argued, embrace a 'global' version of the coherence theory. By endorsing a global model of coherence, coherence theories in law commit themselves to a wholesale holistic view of legal justification that is very problematic. There are three main problems with holism about legal justification. First, it is psychologically implausible. No judge—save Hercules—has the memory resources and cognitive capacities required to establish coherence within the whole domain of the law—let alone within the whole domain of law and morality.[202] Secondly, holistic models of justification offer a poor description of the processes whereby legal decision-makers justify their decisions, for judges and other decision-makers do not typically engage in the kind of global justification that holism requires. And, last, holistic models of legal justification have undesirable normative consequences in that they make the justification of any single decision defeasible on grounds of the incoherence of any part of the legal system. While it is highly plausible that this is so if the incoherence arises between beliefs that are in the 'near neighborhood',[203] it is problematical that we should rule out as unjustified decisions that fail to cohere with largely unrelated areas of law.[204]

The foregoing battery of objections brings to light some of the weaknesses of current theories of coherence in law. These objections, as we will see, are not unique to coherence accounts of law, but rather analogous objections have been raised against coherence accounts of epistemic as well as moral justification.[205] I suggest that some of the strategies that have been developed by advocates of coherence theories of epistemic and moral justification, adequately modified to suit the legal context, may prove to be useful for improving upon current coherence theories in law so as to make them less vulnerable to these objections. Thus, it is instructive to examine (and this is what I propose to do in the next chapters) what coherence theories of justification in both the empirical and the practical domain have to offer by way of a response to these objections. An analysis of these responses will provide some tools to further develop the coherence theory in law and, more specifically, to remedy the problems that afflict current coherence theories in law.

[202] In fact, Dworkin seems well aware of this problem. See Dworkin ((1986: 245) and (1993: 144)).

[203] The phrase is Plantinga's. See Plantinga (1993: 112).

[204] The point is persuasively argued for by Schauer (1986–87: 858).

[205] See chs 3, 4 and 8.

## V. CONCLUSIONS

This chapter has surveyed some of the main coherentist approaches to law and adjudication. More specifically, it has provided a discussion of MacCormick's theory of normative coherence, Peczenik's weigh and balance approach to coherence and Dworkin's theory of law as integrity. As argued, several objections may be raised against these theories. These objections are serious enough to raise doubts about the viability of coherence theories. Most importantly, they call into question whether coherence theories are in a position to deliver what they promised us, namely, a non-sceptical account of law and legal reasoning that gives a larger role to reason than the role accorded to it by classical legal positivism.

The study of coherence theories that have been proposed in areas other than law may prove useful, I have argued, to address these problems. The notion of coherence figures prominently in different theories that address broadly normative questions in a variety of disciplines. The suggestion is that an inquiry into the concept and role that coherence plays in justification in a variety of disciplines may help us develop a coherence-based model of legal justification that deals with the foregoing problems and, thus, that improves upon the current state of the coherence theory in law.

I advance that the coherence theory of legal justification that I shall argue for (in chapter ten) has the following components: (i) a conception of normative coherence as constraint satisfaction; (ii) an explanatory account of coherence-based inference in law; (iii) a view of the justification of normative propositions in law as 'optimal coherence', which embodies a responsibilist conception of legal justification; and (iv) a contextualist approach to the coherentist standards for the justification of normative propositions in law. An examination of the different ways in which coherence operates in realms other than law is required before we are in a position to develop in detail this theory and examine the extent to which it may overcome the objections raised against legal coherentism. However, before launching ourselves into this interdisciplinary analysis, beyond law's domain, we still need to consider the place of coherence in the 'other part' of legal reasoning, that is, legal reasoning about facts, which is the topic of the next chapter.

# 2

# *Coherence, Evidence and Proof*

THE MAIN PURPOSE of this chapter is to review and assess the current state of coherence-based theories of legal reasoning about facts. By 'coherence-based theories of legal reasoning about facts' I refer to any theory of evidential reasoning in law that gives coherence a prominent role.[1] Evidence is a truly multidisciplinary subject.[2] Over the past decades, statisticians, philosophers, legal scholars and psychologists have devoted considerable attention to the issue of how to reason about facts in law. Coherence-based theories of legal reasoning about facts have also been proposed within a number of different disciplines. Here, I shall focus on the contributions to coherence studies in evidence and proof in law made by evidence scholars, cognitive psychologists and legal theorists.

The survey and discussion of coherence theories of evidence and proof will proceed as follows. First, I shall explain the main tenets and problems of the dominant model of evidence and factual inference in law, to wit, the Bayesian model. This model has been subjected to severe criticism. As we shall see, it is mainly the problems of the Bayesian paradigm that have motivated the search for coherence-based theories, the analysis of which will occupy us in the rest of the chapter. I shall start this analysis by examining the coherence-based theories of evidence and proof that have been proposed in evidence scholarship. Next, I will review the main coherentist proposals of legal decision-making about facts that have been developed in the field of psychology and law. Traditionally, the study of fact-reasoning in law has not been at the centre of legal theorists' research agenda.[3] Nevertheless, some legal theorists have paid some attention to the topic. Some of these jurisprudential theories also give coherence a pivotal role in legal reasoning about facts. I will briefly introduce them in the section that follows. Then, I will state the main objections that may be raised against coherence-based theories of fact-reasoning in law. I shall finish this chapter by drawing some conclusions about the current state of the coherence theory of legal reasoning about facts.

[1] I will use through this chapter the phrase 'coherence-based theory of legal reasoning about facts' and 'coherence theories of evidence and proof' interchangeably.

[2] See Twining and Stein (1992: xxi and xxiv). See also Twining ((1997: 18–21) and (2003)). For a discussion of different interdisciplinary trends in evidence scholarship, see Park and Saks (2006).

[3] Twining (2006: 306).

## I. PROBABILISM AND EVIDENTIAL REASONING IN LAW

In the preceding chapter I argued that it is in the context of a critique to strong versions of legal positivism that we may locate the emergence of coherence-based accounts of legal reasoning. Now, what motivates the proposal of coherentist theories of evidence and proof? Before launching into the analysis of the diverse coherence-based theories that have been proposed in a variety of disciplines, it might be convenient to put into context the emergence of coherence studies of evidence and proof. As will be shown, it is in the context of the debates over probabilities that have occupied much of the 'new evidence scholarship' that we may explain the advent of coherence-based theories of fact-reasoning in law.

### A. The New Evidence Scholarship

The last decades have witnessed a remarkable revitalization of evidence scholarship.[4] The 'revival' has been so dramatic that Lempert coined the term, which is now common currency in evidence circles, of 'new evidence scholarship'.[5] The most important development that marks the upsurge of the discipline is a shift of interest away from the rules of evidence towards the process of proof.[6] This move from evidentiary rules to principles of proof is not a novel one. The two giants of Anglo-American evidence theory, Bentham and Wigmore, already contributed significantly to the transition from rules of evidence to processes of proof.[7] After Bentham and Wigmore's steps, the 'new evidence scholarship' has definitely embraced the shift of focus from rules to reason.[8] Evidentiary rules are no longer the main object of evidence scholarship; rather, evidence scholars are primarily concerned with the nature of reasoning about facts, that is, the analysis of the processes of proof and the legitimate patterns of factual inference. More specifically, the most important topic in the agenda of the 'new evidence scholarship' has been the study of the nature and uses of probabilistic reasoning in law.[9] In fact, the phrase 'new evidence scholarship' has been equated with the debate on probabilities and proof in adjudication.[10] We may distinguish three stages, or waves, in the debate over probabilities in law.[11]

[4] Twining (2006: 72–73).
[5] Lempert (1986).
[6] See Twining and Stein (1992: xv).
[7] See Twining (2006: 41–45 and 63–65). See, also, Twining and Stein (1992: xix–xxi). On Wigmore's and Bentham's theories of evidence, see Twining (1985).
[8] Not all evidence scholars have been ready to embrace the change of focus in evidence scholarship from rules to reasons. See eg Park (1990–91).
[9] See Park and Saks (2006: 984–98).
[10] But see Twining (1997) (arguing for a broader conception of the new evidence scholarship).
[11] See Twining (1991: 297).

First, sparked off by a very controversial decision of the US Supreme Court, *People v Collins,* in which an erroneous attempt was made to use statistical reasoning to resolve problems of evidence, a lively debate took place about the scope, limitations and appropriateness of explicitly using mathematical reasoning about probabilities at trials.[12] Some evidence scholars argued for the potential of mathematical probability analysis to resolve problems of fact in litigation, provided that it is correctly used. Against this view, others argued that it is inappropriate and dangerous to use mathematical probability theory in forensic contexts for a number of reasons. First, as long as legal decision-makers can be assumed to be innumerate, they should be addressed in a language that they can understand. Secondly, mathematical arguments are likely to seduce triers of fact and lead them to give undue weight to statistical data over 'soft' variables. And thirdly, as a political matter, it is wrong to quantify certain issues, such as an acceptable risk of conviction of the innocent.[13] Despite disagreements on various points, all the participants in the debate agreed that reasoning about probabilities is a form of mathematical reasoning. This is precisely the assumption that is challenged in the second stage of the debate, which was initiated by Cohen.

Cohen advanced the thesis that not all reasoning about probabilities is mathematical (Pascalian), but that some judgements of probability are better justified on the basis of non-mathematical (Baconian) criteria. He further argued that a Baconian theory of probability provides the right model for reasoning about facts in law.[14] His main argument in favour of this theory is that a Baconian model does not encounter the various difficulties facing a Pascalian account of legal reasoning about facts. More specifically, Cohen argued that the application of Pascalian probability theory to law gives rise to, by now, well-known paradoxes, namely, the 'conjunction paradox'[15] and the 'gatecrasher's paradox'.[16] Cohen's theses provoked yet another important debate about whether there is a sensible distinction to be drawn between Baconian and Pascalian theories of probability, and if so, which is the most appropriate theory for modelling arguments about

[12] See Finkelstein and Fairley (1970); Cullison (1970); and Tribe (1971).

[13] See Twining (1997a: 13).

[14] LJ Cohen (1977).

[15] On the 'conjunction paradox', see s I.C.

[16] The 'gatecrasher's paradox' results from applying a principle of probability theory, namely, the complementational principle. According to this principle, on a scale ranging from 0 to 1, the cumulated probability value of a proposition and its negation must be one. Cohen illustrates this paradox by means of the following hypothetical. Suppose that 1000 people attend a rodeo of whom only 499 have paid admission and the rest are trespassers. If the rodeo owner sues all the 1000 who attended and introduces no evidence other than the fact that only 499 paid, the probability in each case that the defendant was a gatecrasher would be over 0.5, and thus, against our intuitions, the plaintiff should win; see LJ Cohen (1977: 74).

probabilities in forensic contexts.[17] While Baconian approaches to evidence and legal inference have been—and still are—advocated by prominent evidence scholars, the dominant theory of evidence and legal proof relies on Pascalian probabilities.[18] Within Pascalian approaches, a special place is given to one particular piece of probability theory, to wit, Bayes theorem. The last wave of the debate has turned on the issue of what role, if any, Bayes theorem should play in reasoning about facts in law.

This stage of the debate has brought to the surface a number of deep disagreements among evidence scholars that go beyond the potential use of Bayes theorem in legal contexts.[19] In a sense, the debate over Bayes theorem is a continuation of the previous debates over probabilities in law. Some of the issues that were contested in earlier phases of the debates over probabilities come up again in the current scholarly discussion. And some of the arguments that Cohen put forward against Pascalian views of legal inference also figure in current attacks to the use of bayesianism in law. However, the debate over Bayes also opens up a new phase of inquiry for evidence scholarship that is, in important respects, removed from the concerns that characterized most of the production of the 'new evidence scholarship'.

To start with, despite the enormous theoretical variety that characterizes the writings of evidence scholars in the last decades, there is a common thread that brings all these contributions together, to wit, a concern about probabilities and inference under uncertainty in law.[20] In contrast, Bayesian-sceptics are putting forward concepts other than those that feature in probabilistic accounts of inference, such as coherence or plausibility, and in doing so, they are moving the discipline away from the prominent interest in probability theory that dominated the 'new evidence scholarship'.

In addition, Bayesians are committed to 'atomism', that is, the view that probative force is attributed to individuated items of evidence and that factual determinations are made by aggregating these probative values.[21] A commitment to atomism is also one of the main assumptions that characterize the received tradition in evidence scholarship, ie the 'Rationalist Tradition'.[22]

[17] See G Williams (1979); LJ Cohen (1980) and G Williams (1980). On this debate, see Twining (1992). See also Schoeman (1987) and LJ Cohen (1987).

[18] For a defence of a Baconian view of legal reasoning about facts, see Taruffo (1992). Others, such as Twining or Schum, claim that while Baconian probabilities play an important role in reasoning about facts in law, we need different systems of probability to capture the richness of evidential reasoning in law. See Twining (1992: 169) and Schum (2001: 41).

[19] See Tillers and Green (1988); Allen et al (1994–95); and Allen and Redmayne (1997).

[20] See Tillers (1986b: 389).

[21] Atomistic models have also been called 'meter models' because they require the fact-finder to make an assessment of the guilt/innocence of the defendant after each single piece of evidence is evaluated on its own merits, so that the assessment changes every time a new piece of evidence is heard. 'The juror's state of belief can thus be likened to that of a 'mental meter' which continually adjusts as more evidence is heard'. See JD Jackson and Doran (1995: 214).

[22] Twining (2006: 309). On the main assumptions that characterize the so-called 'Rationalist Tradition', see Twining ((1985) ch 1 and (1994) ch 3).

In contrast, these alternatives to Bayesianism rest on a 'holistic' view of legal inference, according to which the mass of evidence and its probative force must be assessed as a whole.[23] Hence, the holistic proposals do not merely seem to question the relevance of probability theory to fact-reasoning in law, but, more fundamentally, pose a challenge to the received tradition.

I suggest that we pick up the debate in evidence scholarship at this third stage, in which we seem to have slowly moved from debating probabilities to rethinking, more broadly, the contrast between atomist and holist approaches to reasoning about facts in law. I shall now explore the main issues that are contested at the third stage of the debate. More specifically, I shall examine the main characteristics of the Bayesian model of fact-reasoning in law, identify its main problems and present some of the alternatives that give coherence a prominent role.

## B. The Bayesian Model of Legal Proof

The core problem that a theory of the justification of conclusions about facts in law has to address, as any other theory of non-deductive inference, is the so-called problem of confirmation. What is it for an observation to provide evidence for, or confirm, a theory? Many philosophers have tried to solve the problem of confirmation by using probability theory. The idea is that a piece of evidence confirms a hypothesis if it raises the probability of the hypothesis. Bayesianism is one version of this idea. Bayes theorem tells us how to measure the difference between the probability of a hypothesis and its probability in light of a new piece of evidence.[24] This theorem is a simple logical consequence of the axioms of probability theory:

$$P\ (h/e) = P\ (e/h)\ P\ (h)\ /\ P\ (e)$$

The form in which it is most generally used is as follows:

$$P\ (h/e) = P\ (e/h)\ P\ (h)\ /\ P\ (e/h)\ P\ (h) + P\ (e/not\text{-}h)\ P\ (not\text{-}h)$$

Here is how to read formulas of this kind: P $(h)$ is the probability of $h$. And P $(h/e)$ is the probability of $h$ conditional upon $e$, or the probability of $h$ *given e*. Bayes tells us how to compute this last value, P $(h/e)$, which is called the 'posterior' probability of $h$, that is the probability of a hypothesis $h$ in light of evidence $e$. Bayes theorem expresses P $(h/e)$ as a function of two different types of probability: probabilities of hypotheses of the form

[23] Damaška (1990: 91).

[24] For an introduction to Bayes theorem, see Hacking (2001: 69–78) and Joyce (2004). For an introduction to Bayesian epistemology, see Hájek and Hartmann (2010). For recent work in Bayesianism, see Corfield and Williamson (2001); Swiburne (2002); Bovens and Hartman (2003b); and Oaksford and Chater (2007). On the Bayesian approach to scientific inference, see Godfrey-Smith (2003) ch 14; Earman (1992); and Howson and Urbach (1993).

P (*h*)—and P (*not-h*)—which are called 'prior' probabilities, that is, the probability of *h*—and *not-h*—measured without regard for evidence *e*, and probabilities of the form P (*e*/*h*), which are called 'likelihoods', or the likelihood of evidence on theory. What Bayes gives us is a way of computing the impact of new pieces of evidence on the probability of a hypothesis, that is, how to 'update' probabilities in the light of new evidence.

The application of Bayes theorem to legal fact-finding is straightforward.[25] The fact-finder is expected to use evidence E to cast light on two hypotheses: G (the 'prosecution hypothesis', ie the hypothesis that the defendant is guilty) and not-G (the 'defence hypothesis', ie the hypothesis that asserts the falsity of G). The fact-finder's task is to update the prior probability of these hypotheses by considering E. At the end of this process, she should have arrived at a posterior probability of guilt given the evidence. If this final probability is sufficiently high to meet the applicable standard of proof, the verdict 'guilty' is appropriate.[26]

For example, suppose that at a murder trial the hypothesis that the defendant committed the crime (*h*) and several hypotheses that entail innocence are being considered. Then, evidence that the fingerprints found in the glass containing the poison that killed the victim matches the fingerprints of the defendant (*e*) is presented at trial. Suppose that before this piece of evidence was presented the fact-finder thinks that the probability that the defendant is guilty is 0.5. He also believes that the probability that the fingerprints found on the glass matches those of the defendant if the defendant had handed the glass over to the victim is 0.8, because fingerprint identification is a highly reliable method, while the probability of matching if the defendant *did not* hand over the glass to the victim is only 0.1. Then, the fact-finder may calculate the probability that the defendant is guilty in light of the new evidence by using Bayes theorem: P (*h*/*e*) = (.5) (.8)/ [(.5) (.8) + (.5) (.1)], which is almost 0.9. So the fingerprint evidence raises the probability of *h* from 0.5 to 0.9; and thus it strongly confirms the guilt-hypothesis. If a probability of 0.9 is taken to be sufficiently high to meet the standard of proof, then a finding against the defendant is in order.

[25] There is a large body of literature discussing the applications of Bayesianism to model legal inference. See Tillers and Green (1988); Tillers (1991); Allen and Redmayne (1997); Park (2010). Important monographs on this topic include: Aitken (1995); Eggleston (1983); Schum (2001); Robertson and Vignaux (1995); Kadane and Schum (1996); Gastwirth (2000); and Taroni et al (2006).

It is important to notice that Bayesianism is the prevailing approach in the United States, but there is no comparable 'Bayesian orthodoxy', as Taruffo likes to call it, in Europe. Nonetheless, the application of probabilistic models is discussed to a significant extent in the legal literature in some civil law countries as well. Generally, the use of probabilistic models of legal proof is considered with scepticism, even if there are some recent opinions supporting the application of these models. See Taruffo (2003: 662–64).

[26] For a detailed and clarifying example of how Bayesianism deals with the evidence in a particular legal case, see Dawid (2002: 72–78).

As is apparent, we can only use Bayes theorem to compute the posterior probability of a hypothesis, whether in law or in any other domain, if we have an interpretation of probability that enables us to assign a numerical value to the prior probability of *h* as well as to probabilities of the form P (*e*/*h*). The so-called 'subjectivist' interpretation of probability allows us to talk about the kind of probabilities that are necessary to use Bayes theorem. According to the subjectivist interpretation, probabilities are degrees of belief. In this view, a probability measures a person's degree of confidence in the truth of a proposition.[27] For example, if Anna says that the probability that it will rain tomorrow is 0.8, she is saying something about her degree of confidence that it will rain tomorrow. According to subjectivism, one may read off a person's degree of belief in a proposition from her gambling behaviour. To determine a person's degree of belief, we look for the odds on a given bet such that the person would be equally willing to take either side of the bet, ie the person's subjectively fair odds for that bet. On the basis of these odds, we can read off her degree of belief in the proposition that the bet is about. We may do this as follows. Suppose someone thinks that a bet on *h* at odds X:1 is a fair bet. That is, she is willing to risk losing X if *h* is false, in return for a gain of one coin if she is wrong. It is evident that the larger X is, the higher the confidence in *h* is. More specifically, if someone's subjectively fair odds for a bet on *h* are X:1, then her degree of belief in *h* is X/X+1. This is the way in which subjectivists read off degrees of beliefs from gambling behaviours. For example, suppose that Anna thinks that 4:1 is a fair bet on the truth of the proposition that it will rain tomorrow. That is, she will win one coin if it does rain, and lose four if it does not. Then, we may say that Anna's degree of belief in the proposition *p* that it will rain tomorrow is 0.8 (that is, 4/4+1).

Of course, Anna's degree of belief in *p* will be related to her degrees of belief in other propositions as well, such as *not-p*, or *p*&*q* etc. Again, to find out Anna's degree of belief in *p*&*q*, for instance, we should find her subjectively fair odds for a bet on *p*&*q*. And the same may be said with regard to the rest of Anna's beliefs. Hence, according to subjectivism, a person's belief system can be described as a set of subjective probabilities. Now, what are the conditions under which such a set of beliefs is rational? According to subjectivism, a person's system of degrees of belief is rational or 'coherent' if it does not violate the sets of axioms of probability. Since Bayes theorem is a logical consequence of these axioms, it follows that compliance with this theorem is a condition of rationality.[28] Moreover, many Bayesians claim that compliance with the rules of probability, including Bayes rule, is all that is needed in order to have a rational system of beliefs.

[27] For a brief and clear introduction to the different interpretations of probability, see Hacking (2001) ch 11.

[28] See Joyce (2004: 134).

Bayesians use the so-called 'Dutch-Book' argument in support of their view of rationality. This is an argument to the effect that if a person's degrees of belief do not conform to the principles of probability calculus, there are possible gambling situations in which she is guaranteed to lose.[29] Thus, the Dutch Book argument purports to show that anyone who does not keep his degrees of belief in line with the probability calculus is irrational. Only by updating our degrees of belief as Bayes theorem prescribes, can we ensure that no one can possibly make a Dutch book against us, and thus, can we properly be said to be rational agents.

Bayesianism is a very elegant and powerful tool for understanding how to make use of new evidence. Nonetheless, there are severe problems with Bayesianism that raise serious doubts about whether Bayesianism may work as a general approach to induction and confirmation, and more specifically, about whether it may provide us with a general framework for thinking about evidence in law.[30] I proceed now to examine in some detail the main objections that have been raised against Bayesian models of legal proof.

## C. Some Problems with Bayesianism and its Legal Applications

The application of Bayesianism to legal evidence faces two different kinds of problems. First, several challenges have been raised against the adequacy of Bayesianism as a general theory of evidence, which may also be directed against the legal applications of Bayesianism. Moreover, as we will see, some of these general objections are even more forceful against a Bayesian theory of legal evidence. And secondly, there are some problems with regard to the specific applications of Bayes theorem to the legal realm.

### *i. The General Problems of Bayesianism*

Four main problems figure prominently in the debate over the adequacy of Bayesianism as a general approach to induction and confirmation. Very briefly, these problems are as follows:

#### a. The Problem of the Priors

According to Bayesianism, the initial set of prior probabilities is a 'free choice'. No initial set is better than another as long as it conforms to the axioms of probability. What Bayesianism claims to offer is a rational way

[29] For an example of a Dutch Book argument, see Godfrey-Smith (2003: 207–08).

[30] The most representative works challenging the Bayesian paradigm, which correspond to the three stages distinguished above, are: Tribe (1971); LJ Cohen (1977); and Allen (1986). The debate over Bayes theorem is summarized in Allen and Redmayne (1997).

of updating the set of prior probabilities, but it says nothing about which initial assignment of probabilities one should endorse in the first place. Hence, Bayesianism cannot criticize any initial assignment of probabilities, no matter how strange. According to Bayesians, this is not a problem because, although prior probabilities are freely chosen and might be very weird initially, they get 'washed out' by incoming evidence, so long as the updating is done rationally. That is, they claim that it can be proved that for any amount of initial disagreement about the prior probability of *h*, there will be some amount of evidence that will get people to converge in the final probability of *h*. However, this argument from convergence fails to solve the problem for two reasons. First, the convergence could take a very long time. Hence, there is also the possibility that for some initial set of priors the evidence available will *not* wash out the initial disagreement. In addition, the convergence proofs assume that when two people have very different priors, they nonetheless agree about their likelihoods. This is required for disagreement about the priors to be 'washed out'. But there is, of course, no reason why people need to agree on the likelihoods.[31] Hence, Bayesianism leaves us without any base for criticizing any initial assignment of probabilities. Even worse, as long as these probabilities are coherent, even if totally outrageous, and one updates them properly, one can be said to be rational in accepting the final probabilities that result from the process.

### b. Data Unavailable

There is a great practical problem in attaching meaningful probabilities to the various propositions involved in a probability judgement in most domains. In light of the difficulties in coming up with such probabilistic information, some Bayesians have proposed that we interpret the probabilities required for running Bayesian calculations objectively.[32] That is, they have suggested that instead of interpreting probabilities subjectively, as degrees of belief, we should interpret them as involving frequencies in a population. The problem, though, is that, in many contexts, the relevant objective probabilities are unavailable.

### c. Computational Complexity

There is substantial psychological evidence that people's degrees of belief and reasoning processes are not in accord with probability rules.[33]

[31] Godfrey-Smith (2003: 209–10).

[32] For a brief introduction to objective Bayesianism, see Howson (1995: 12).

[33] For a summary of the main empirical findings to the effect that Bayesian models fail to accurately describe the inferences of human decision-makers, see Sacks and Thompson (2003: 338–39) and McAuliff, Nemeth, Borstein and Penrod (2003: 306–07).

Computing probabilities in the way that Bayes theorem prescribes would require a storage capacity and computational power that goes far beyond our cognitive resources. In order to update the probability of a proposition *p*, one would have to assign probabilities to various conjunctions of *p* together with one or more of the propositions describing the evidence. This leads to combinatorial explosion, since the number of such conjunctions is an exponential function of the number of possible relevant evidence propositions.

d. Incompleteness

Bayes theorem does not suffice to provide a comprehensive theory of evidence. Bayesianism gives us at best a rational way to update one's degrees of beliefs in propositions in light of new evidence. However, much more than this is surely involved in drawing inductive inferences and confirming or testing hypotheses. How do we set the values of prior probabilities? How do we attach the values to the required likelihoods? By which criteria do we determine the relevance of a particular piece of evidence? We need to appeal to something other than probability theory in order to successfully put Bayes theorem to use.[34]

### *ii. The General Problems of Bayesianism in the Legal Context*

All the foregoing objections may be addressed against the legal applications of Bayesianism. Moreover, some of them apply even in a stronger form.

1. The problem of the priors is more acute in the legal context for three reasons. First, the argument from convergence is much less likely to succeed in meeting the objection that Bayesianism licenses inferences from any coherent set of prior probabilities, no matter how bizarre, in the legal context than in other contexts. The reason is that the two problems with this argument are very serious in the legal realm. To start with, as stated earlier, convergence may take a very long time, something we certainly do not have in the legal context. Hence, for any amount of evidence that one may possibly have available at trial, there surely will be some initial set of priors such that this evidence will not get legal decision-makers to agree by the end. In addition, it would be most surprising if legal decision-makers agreed about the likelihoods (and such agreement is required for the argument from convergence to work), given the non-standard types of likelihoods that they need to assign.

Secondly, since there are no constraints on the initial assignments of probabilities other than those imposed by the rules of probability, there

[34] This point has been forcefully argued by Brown (1994).

is also no way in which one's set of degrees of beliefs (as they result from updating one's priors in a Bayesian fashion) can be 'closer to the real facts about probability', as Godfrey-Smith puts it, than another.[35] This strict subjectivism is at odds with the goal of our legal systems of maximizing accuracy in fact-finding.

And last, there is a need to assign a non-zero prior probability to the hypothesis whose probability we are updating in order to be able to use Bayes theorem. This has very troubling consequences in the legal context, given the presumption of innocence, for one would need to assign some prior probability to the hypothesis of guilt. 'In other words'—as the Connecticut Supreme Court put it in *State v Skipper*—'Bayes theorem can only work if the presumption of innocence disappears from consideration'.[36]

2. The lack of data is also a particularly serious problem in the context of legal fact-finding. The application of Bayes theorem in law requires making—in Allen's words, 'non-standard' probability assessments. That is, legal decision-makers are required to determine probability values that are not the sort of thing that even statisticians, let alone lay people, go around estimating. As a result, the risk of plugging in weird probability values in Bayes theorem is not a fanciful one. Stein refers to two different problems that legal decision-makers have to face when trying to determine the probability values necessary to calculate the degree of confirmation of a hypothesis in accordance with Bayes theorem.[37] To start with, legal decision-makers are left free to devise whatever criteria they please for attributing the initial probability values. If the distribution of probabilities violates the rules of probability calculus, then legal decision-makers are forced to revise these assessments. However, Bayesianism does not provide any criterion for conducting such revision, ie the 'problem of the criterion'. In addition, legal decision-makers must face the difficult task of converting or translating their evaluations of uncertain possibilities into numbers, ie the 'conversion problem'.

Hodgson, a judge of the Supreme Court of New South Wales, vividly illustrates the gravity of these problems. As an exercise, he wrote a judgement of a hypothetical case of his own design that applies Bayes theorem. He reported his experience as follows:

> It required two assumptions of prior probabilities of hypotheses, and twelve Bayesian steps, each involving two assumptions of numerical probabilities of evidence, given the truth or falsity of hypotheses: twenty-six guesses in all. In all twenty-six,

[35] Godfrey-Smith (2003: 208).

[36] 228 Conn. 610, 637 A. 2d 1101 (1994). For a discussion of this decision as it bears on the applicability of Bayes theorem to fact-reasoning in law, see Allen et al (1994–95). On the conflict between Bayesianism and the presumption of innocence, see, amongst others, Rawling (1999) and A Stein (1997a: 35–37).

[37] Stein (1997a: 38–41).

> I found I had virtually no confidence in the numbers I initially selected ...; and I felt that I had to check the numbers against the plausibility of the results, and then adjust (and re-adjust) the numbers, in order to arrive at numbers in which I had very slightly more confidence (That is, I had to cheat). Such little confidence as I ended up with depended heavily on my common sense assessment of the plausibility of the intermediate results and the conclusion.[38]

In light of these problems, one could advocate an objectivist interpretation of probability. However, such an approach is not applicable to the legal domain. Since legal trials are generally about a single event, the required frequencies are unavailable.[39]

3. The problems arising from computational complexity are even more severe in law than in other domains, given the complexity of the inferential task that legal decision-makers are engaged in.[40] Arguments about disputed questions of fact in law are based on a mass of evidence, which is often incomplete and unreliable. Moreover, in most cases, evidence is conditionally dependent. To deal with dependent evidence one must form $2^n$ probability assessments of all the possible conjunctions, where $n$ is the number of pieces of evidence. Even in a simple trial, there is a significant amount of evidence. Hence, the problem of combinatorial explosion is an actual and serious one in the legal domain.[41]

4. In law, as everywhere else, one must come up with a great deal of information before one is in a position to apply Bayes theorem. Hence, unless one is willing to leave to 'simple intuition' the determination of issues such as the value of prior probabilities, the value of likelihoods etc one will need to appeal to resources other than probability theory when reasoning about facts in law.[42] Moreover, the need to employ some rational method for determining these values is, in law, a more pressing issue than in other domains, for at least three reasons. First, as said before, one cannot rely on an objectivist interpretation of probability to provide the required values.[43] Secondly, given the objectives of the legal system, most importantly, the goal of factual accuracy, it is critical that a theory of evidence provide us with some criteria for assessing the rationality of all the determinations that fall beyond the scope of probability theory. Even more so, if, as argued, we cannot expect convergence results to clean up idiosyncratic assignments of

[38] Hodgson (1993: 56). See also Allen et al (1994–95: 297).

[39] Allen (1991: 373–76). See also Thagard (2004: 242–43).

[40] The problem of computational complexity as it applies to the legal context has been particularly emphasized by Callen; see Callen ((1982: 10–15) and (1991: 129)).

[41] See Thagard (2004a: 243), for an illustration of this problem in the *von Bülow* case.

[42] For a full defence of the claim that rules of probability are 'far from sufficient and that the most important and interesting aspects of satisfactory fact-finding lie elsewhere'; see Hodgson (1993).

[43] But see Goldman's proposal of 'quasi-objectivism', which posits the existence of objective likelihoods in AI Goldman (2002).

prior probabilities (which, besides, are very likely to occur given the non-standard kind of probability assessments that are involved in legal decision-making and the enormous complexity of the inferential task at hand). And last, Bayes leaves us with no guidance as to how to address some issues that are pivotal in legal reasoning about facts in law, such as the interpretation of legal criteria and the evaluative categorization of facts.[44]

### *iii. Problems Specific to the Legal Applications of Bayesianism*

In addition to the general problems, as they apply to law, the Bayesian approach to legal evidence also faces some problems that are specific to the legal domain.

5. Descriptive problems. As Allen has argued, the context of legal decision-making does not possess the necessary conditions for the application of Bayes theorem.[45] Typically, fact-finders do not know until the end of the trial either the legal elements or the possible alternatives. Moreover, they are not bound by closing arguments, and new theories of the case may emerge during deliberation. This has several implications. First, it is only at the stage of deliberation that fact-finders may assign probabilities to the several theories of the case. Thus, these assignments of probability will be made in light of all the trial evidence, with the result that all evidence is 'old evidence'. That is, there is nothing for Bayes theorem to operate on. Secondly, during deliberation, in some cases new theories will emerge. When they do, the probability space must be reconfigured, and there is no way to do so by means of probability calculus. And last, Bayes theorem conditions guilt on the evidence, but guilt is a legal conclusion. Hence, again, there is nothing for Bayes theorem to operate on.

6. Normative problems. The application of Bayes theorem to legal fact-finding has been also criticized on moral and political grounds.[46] I have already mentioned the conflict between Bayesianism and the presumption of innocence. By assigning a prior probability to the hypothesis of guilt, legal decision-makers would be disregarding this presumption. In addition, a Bayesian interpretation of the notion of 'proof beyond a reasonable doubt' involves the admission of a certain fraction of wrongful convictions. This would lead to the law losing much of its moral force and it would erode the citizen's confidence in the legal system.[47] Not only does Bayesianism violate moral values intrinsic to the criminal process, but it also posits a

[44] See Zuckerman (1986).

[45] Allen (1997a).

[46] See Twining and Stein (1992: xxii), for a summary of these criticisms. For a brief statement of these criticisms and some of its responses, see also Koehler (1992: 173–76).

[47] The classical article on the importance of not quantifying the standard of proof is Tribe (1971: 1372–75). See also Laudan (2003: 310–13).

similar threat in the context of civil trials. As the much discussed blue bus case illustrates,[48] within a Bayesian framework, we may allow cases to be won or lost on the ground of 'naked statistics' rather than 'individualized' evidence about the actual events.[49] This implies that people's rights and duties would be determined only on the basis of their association with some statistically significant class. And this seriously undermines the acceptability of verdicts.[50]

7. Problems with the Bayesian interpretation of the standards of proof. Probability theory cannot provide a satisfactory account of the standards of persuasion, either in civil or criminal law cases. As regards the standard of proof in civil cases Bayesians should face the 'the problem of conjunction'. The problem arises in cases in which one has to prove elements that are conditionally independent. If one such case has two elements, the fact-finder may assess the probability of each element to be greater than 0.5, say, 0.6, and yet assess the probability of their conjunction as being less than 0.5 (in this case, 0.36). Hence, the plaintiff's case would not have been proved by the preponderance of evidence despite the fact that he has succeeded in proving the probability of each of the elements to be over 0.5.[51] Bayesians so far have also failed to give a plausible interpretation of the standard of proof in criminal cases.[52] To start with, as was pointed out before, there is the concern that any quantification of the degree of belief necessary for a finding of guilt will seriously erode the legitimacy of the criminal system and the acceptability of the verdicts. But, even if we put these worries to one side, and endorse a quantification of the standard of proof, it is nevertheless very unclear what level of probability should be associated with this standard.

8. The problem of weight. Last, Bayesianism does not take into account the relevance of the quality and completeness of evidence to legal decision-making.[53] The problem is as follows. Under a Bayesian approach, cases are to be decided on the basis of probability calculus alone. But, in some cases,

[48] This case concerns a plaintiff who is injured by a bus that she cannot identify. The only information presented to help determine who should be liable is proof that a Blue Bus Company owns 85 per cent of the buses in town. Even if there is no specific evidence as to the colour of the bus that caused the accident, a Bayesian would have to grant a directed verdict to the plaintiff, for there is a much higher probability (and certainly much higher than the required probability of 0.5) that a blue bus was involved in the accident. Yet, it can be argued that a court should grant a directed verdict for the defendant in this hypothetical case.

[49] As is well known, the preference for particularized legal decision-making is generally seen as a moral imperative. For an argument against the widely shared preference for direct ('individualized') evidence as opposed to statistical evidence, see Schauer (2003) ch 3.

[50] See Nesson ((1985) and (1986)).

[51] On the Bayesian interpretation of the burden of persuasion in civil cases, see Kaye (1999). For a critique, see Allen (2000).

[52] For a critique to the Bayesian interpretation of the 'reasonable doubt' standard, see, amongst others, Nesson (1979); Rawling (1999); and Thagard (2004).

[53] See Redmayne (1998: 65–67) and Stein (1997a).

the evidence is so skimpy that, even if a case is proved to have a probability higher than 0.5, in a civil trial, or higher than the specified threshold required to satisfy the applicable standard of proof in a criminal trial, we feel reluctant to find against the defendant. Hypothetical cases such as the 'gatecrashers' case or the 'blue bus' case make the point very vivid. One reason why we may feel reluctant to grant relief to the plaintiff in these cases is that, despite the high probability, the evidence is very incomplete. Bayesianism seems to allow judges to proceed from any informational base, however weak it may be. Yet, factors such as the 'weight' of the evidence at trial are crucial to assess the merits of a case.

There has been an intense debate in legal scholarship about whether these objections might be met.[54] Indeed, these problems are very serious and the prospects of articulating a response within the Bayesian framework look bleak.[55] However, regardless of whether the Bayesian framework may ultimately be shown to have the resources to satisfactorily address these problems, I shall argue that there is a more fundamental problem with Bayesianism, which concerns the conception of rationality underwriting this model of legal fact-finding. The next section develops this critique of the Bayesian model of legal proof.

## D. Probability and Rationality in Juridical Fact-Finding

The examination of the debate over the role of Bayes theorem in legal reasoning about facts pushes one to consider a deeper problem, to which it is inextricably linked, namely, that of determining the nature and scope of rationality in legal fact-finding. The disagreement between Bayesians and Bayesioceptics does not merely concern the role of Bayes theorem in the legal context. Rather, the issue over which Bayesians and Bayesiosceptics disagree is, at bottom, that of determining the appropriate conception of rationality for legal fact-finding. Hence, the debate over Bayesianism is closely related to a wider debate about rationality and law; it is at this level, I would argue, that the real differences between opponents and defenders of a Bayesian approach to legal proof should be located and examined.[56]

[54] An important step towards putting an end to the so-called 'Bayes wars' is that of trying to reach agreement about the distinct purposes that Bayes theorem might serve in the context of legal fact-finding. For an account of the different ways in which one may use Bayesianism in evidence law, see Lempert (1986: 440–50) and Tillers (2011).

[55] For some Bayesian responses to these critiques, see Sacks and Thomspson (2003); Robertson and Vignaux ((1993) and (1997)); Koehler (1992); Carriquiry (1997); Fienberg (1997); Friedman ((1997a), (1997b) and (1996)); Donnelly (1997); AI Goldman (2002); Allen et al (1994–95); and Kaye ((1988), (1997) and (1999)).

[56] See Hodgson (1993).

What is it that makes Bayesianism so attractive amongst evidence lawyers? Bayesianism creates a sense of logic and certainty in conducting our legal affairs as well as the sense that the whole enterprise is a 'scientific' one.[57] This perception is, at least partly, due to the fact that there is a widespread belief that without 'formalism', 'algorithms' etc there is nothing left but whim, bias or irrationality.[58] So that, faced with a choice between scientific rationality/irrationality, Bayesians choose to be, understandably, on rationality's side.[59] The question is whether this assumption is granted. This question is not simply about whether Bayesians are right or wrong, or about who has won the debate at the end of the day. On the contrary, an answer to this question has important implications for the legitimacy of fact-finding institutions. For if sound reasoning is Bayesian reasoning, and, as stated before, there are serious doubts over whether Bayes theorem is applicable to the legal arena, then it follows that there is no sensible way in which legal decision-making may be said to be a rational process at all. Ultimately, the assumption that Bayesian rationality is the only possible standard for assessing legal fact-finding leads to a severe form of fact-scepticism.[60]

However, there is no need to give in to the sceptic as this assumption, I would argue, is not granted. In claiming that probability theory provides the only rational standard for legal fact-finding, Bayesians are committing the so-called 'irrationality fallacy'. This fallacy proceeds from the recognition that formal models have limited value in legal decision-making to the claim that legal decisions are not based on rational criteria.[61] But there is no reason why one should choose between logic or irrationality, between the 'absolute' and the 'arbitrary', as Elgin puts it,[62] at least not before one explores the feasibility of non-sceptical alternatives to formal models of legal proof. Furthermore, not only is the claim to uniqueness problematic, but there are also some serious problems with the formal conception of rationality embodied in the Bayesian model of legal proof.

First, the Bayesian standard of rationality, because of its high degree of idealization, fails to have any normative import in the context of legal fact-finding. To begin with, it is impossible for us, given our cognitive resources, to conform to the standard of probabilistic coherence. This being so, this

[57] See Taruffo (1992: 181).

[58] See Allen (1997a: 255).

[59] For quite uncompromising views about the extent to which Bayesianism provides the only logical way to reason about evidence, see Robertson and Vignaoux (1993); and Allen et al (1994–95: 288). See also Prof Donnelly's expert testimony in the *Adams* case as reported in [1996] 2 Cr App R 467, 470–71. For discussion of this controversial case, see Dawid (2002) and Redmayne (1997).

[60] That there is a route from Bayesianism to scepticism is also argued by Twinning (2006: 120).

[61] Wasserstron (1961).

[62] Elgin (1997).

standard cannot have direct normative relevance, in the sense of imposing on legal decision-makers an epistemic obligation to be probabilistically coherent, for no one can be obliged to do what one cannot.[63] The standard does not have indirect normative relevance either, that is to say, it does not define an epistemic ideal that legal decision-makers ought to strive to approximate.[64] While it may be rational for an 'ideal' fact-finder with more potent logical, reasoning, and memory capacities than we have to avoid probabilistic incoherence, this does not mean that this is an appropriate standard for real fact-finders.[65] Moreover, seeking probabilistic coherence might not even be the rational thing for fact-finders to do, insofar as it might deprive them of other more important epistemic goods.[66] Thus, the ideal of probabilistic coherence fails to provide a standard against which to judge the rationality of legal decision-makers' beliefs. In addition, this standard also fails to be a useful guide about how fact-finders ought to regulate their epistemic behaviour. The ideal of probabilistic coherence is so far removed from what fact-finders may be expected to achieve that it cannot play a substantial role in determining what they ought to believe.[67]

Secondly, the Bayesian standard of rationality is too narrow to serve as the appropriate standard for legal fact-finding. There are many aspects of factual inference in law that fall beyond the scope of application of Bayesianism.[68] Bayesianism tells us nothing about where the initial factual hypotheses come from; how fine-grained the hypotheses about the facts under dispute at trial ought to be; what evidence is relevant to assessing the hypotheses put forward at trial; whether one should expand the set of hypotheses under consideration; whether a hypothesis previously discarded should be re-considered in light of new evidence; whether one should, for the time being, suspend judgement and seek out more evidence; how one should assign an initial probability to the competing hypotheses; or whether one should accept a piece of evidence as reliable. All these questions (and yet many others) fall beyond the scope of the Bayesian theory. As a

[63] Normative principles of rational belief are governed by the constraint that 'ought implies can'; see Schimtt (2004: 877–78).

[64] *Cf* Zynda (1996).

[65] See Foley (1993: 159–60).

[66] See Plantinga (1993: 144).

[67] Another problem with the idealized conception of rationality put forward by Bayesianism is that it prevents us from addressing important questions concerning the rationality of belief revision; see Lance (2000).

[68] The point holds with regard not only to the rational evaluation of hypotheses in law but also in science; see Brown (1994: 355). Ligertwood (1997: 324) has persuasively argued that we need a broader logic to model the process of proof. The view that there is no scope of rationality beyond Bayesian analysis has been categorically rejected by Taruffo as well (1992: 192). This is not to say that Bayesianism plays no role in the evaluation of hypotheses at trial. Eg Bayesianism is critical in cases in which there is key statistical evidence (see eg Stein (1997a: 35) fn 17 and 45 and Allen (1997a: 258). And there is no denying either that it may be a useful heuristic device (see Stein (1997b: 339)).

consequence, a good deal of what is involved in reasoning about evidence is, at best, neither rational nor irrational. The Bayesian conception of rationality fails to provide a standard for assessing the rationality/irrationality of judgements about many important issues that arise in the course of legal decision-making as well as for regulating a substantial part of legal fact-finders' reasoning processes.

Last, Bayesianism embodies a subjectivist view of rationality that is untenable in the context of legal fact-finding.[69] As explained before, it is a main tenet of Bayesianism that rationality constraints are fulfilled as long as the axioms of probability are satisfied, regardless of which values are attached to prior distributions. The most popular strategies for grounding objectivity within the Bayesian framework are 'washing out' the priors and imposing objective constraints on either the priors or the likelihoods. However, as argued, it is doubtful whether these strategies succeed in rebutting the charge of subjectivism.[70] Alternatively, one could defend Bayesianism against the charge of subjectivism by appealing to an analogy with deductive logic. Just as we do not say that deductive logic is subjective despite the fact that it does not impose any constraint on the premises of deductive argument, it does not follow that Bayesianism is subjective, simply because it does not impose any constraint on the priors.[71] This defence of Bayesianism seems to me to be impeccable. On this view, Bayesianism, like deductive logic, is meant to provide an 'internal justification' of initial assignments of probability or premises. Just as deductive logic only declares that certain conclusions are the only consistent ones with some premises, but it does not tell us which premises one ought to believe, Bayesianism states that if one assigns certain degrees of belief to certain propositions one is bound in consistency to assign others. But, as branches of formal logic, neither deductive nor inductive logic evaluate premises or initial assignments of probability from the perspective of truth-seeking, that is to say, they say nothing about 'external justification', and thus about whether our beliefs are likely to be true.[72] Indeed, Bayesianism, understood as a theory of inductive logic, need not be in conflict with objectivity, any more than deductive logic is. The problem arises when one expects, as has been the case among many evidence scholars, Bayesianism to provide a theory of rational belief. As such, it founders as the consistency constraint on rational

[69] On the charge of subjectivism, see Earman (1992: 137–63) and Joyce (2004: 132 and 149–53). For replies, see Galavotti (1988) and Howson and Urbach (1993: 413–20).

[70] See the previous section.

[71] Howson and Urbach (1993: 418).

[72] Both deductive and inductive logic are branches of 'formal' logic, or the logic of consistency, as opposed to 'human' logic, or the logic of truth. See Ramsey (1926: 86–87).

belief imposed by this theory is merely an 'internalist' constraint, unrelated to the goal of truth which is paramount in adjudication.[73]

## E. Towards a Coherence Theory of Evidence and Legal Proof

So much for the debate over Bayesianism. As has been rightly suggested, 'the time has come to put this debate aside and move on to other matters'.[74] But, what other matters? What are the components of a broader view of inference and proof that can fulfil the promise to give us what Bayesianism fails to provide? The review of the debate over Bayes theorem has made it patent that we need a broader framework for thinking about evidence in law. Now, the question is: where should we turn to? There are several alternatives on the table, offered from quite different perspectives. Some have suggested that we focus on the role of stories and narratives in legal decision-making. Others, instead, have proposed that we turn to the question of the nature of plausibility arguments and plausible explanations in law. Yet others have proposed that we concentrate on the analysis of the reasoning patterns that are actually employed by legal decision-makers by using constraint satisfaction mechanisms.

Despite differences, all these proposals involve, in varying degrees, a commitment to holism. In addition to this commitment, all these views put the notion of coherence at the forefront. Very different positions are placed under the heading of 'holism'. Similarly, there is not a unique way in which these proposals are 'coherentist', for they embrace very different views about the concept of coherence and its role in legal fact-finding. But these proposals, taken together, put forward a picture—even if not a homogenous one—of how to reason about evidence in law that is remarkably different from the predominant atomistic and probabilistic view.

The rest of this chapter is devoted to examining the coherence-based alternatives that are proposed in different bodies of literature, to wit, evidence

[73] To be more precise, formal constraints on rational belief are *uninterestingly* related to the goal of truth. That is, there is a weak connection between these constraints and truth. If two propositions are logically inconsistent, then it follows that both of them cannot be true. Similarly, if two propositions are probabilistically inconsistent to a high degree, then it is reasonable to conclude that they cannot both be truth. However, the fact that two propositions are both logically consistent and probabilistically coherent says nothing about whether they are true. Thus, while there is a connection between formal constraints of rationality and truth, the connection is too weak to be an interesting one from the point of view of devising theories of rational belief that help us advance the goal of truth.

[74] The phrase is Michon's. See Michon (1997).

scholarship, the psychology of legal reasoning and legal theory.[75] I start the survey and discussion of these theories by examining the holistic models of evidence and proof that have been advanced by evidence scholars.

## II. HOLISTIC THEORIES OF EVIDENCE AND LEGAL PROOF

In this section, I shall analyse the main versions of holism about evidence evaluation that have been proposed in contemporary evidence scholarship.[76] The examination of these theories will allow us to have a better understanding of the sources, history and main tenets of evidentiary holism.[77]

### A. Abu-Hareira: Side-Stream Traditions

Abu-Hareira has developed a version of holism based on James Glassford's writings on judicial fact-finding.[78] Glassford was an important member of the Scottish School of Common Sense, who was particularly interested in evidence and procedure.[79] In *An Essay on the Principles of Evidence and Their Application to Subjects of Judicial Inquiry* (1820), Glassford applied the 'Common Sense' philosophy to judicial reasoning about facts. Abu-Hareira contends that Glassford embraced a holistic approach to juridical evidence. Taking this interpretation of Glassford's work as a starting point, Abu-Hareira argues for a version of holism and contrasts it with the atomistic approach. According to Abu-Hareira, three main objections may be raised against atomism. First, the evidence in any contested case consists of elements of, at least, two contradictory stories—one false and one true—that are intermixed. It is only when a final decision is made, that we may be able to identify the elements of the true story. Hence, it is 'illogical' to assign a truth or probability value to any single item of evidence *prior* to the decision, as atomism would have us do. Secondly, insofar as the elements of proof are linked together in a 'connected whole', one single element

[75] Theories of evidence and legal proof that give a prominent role to coherence have also been advanced as alternatives to Bayesian approaches by philosophers applying their own epistemological theories to the field of legal evidence. See ch 4 for a discussion of the application of Thagard's coherence theory of justification to law. See also Haack (2012), for a legal application of Haack's foundherentism.

[76] Not only has holism been embraced by evidence scholars, but it has also been sanctioned by courts. The Supreme Court of the United States endorsed a version of holism in the case of *Old Chief v United States* 519 U.S. 172 (1997). For a discussion of the Court's opinion as it bears on the atomist/holist debate, see Pardo (2000: 406–09); D Simon (2004: 564–69); Mnookin (2013: 1557–1562); and Ledwon (2003: 1145–47).

[77] For a brief and enlightening exposition and criticism of holistic approaches, see Twining (1985: 183–85); and (1994: 238–42).

[78] See Abu-Hareira (1986).

[79] ibid, 81–88.

should not be treated in isolation from the others, contrary to what atomism requires. Last, the atomistic approach undermines the factual nature of juridical proof by converting facts into propositions inferred from general experience. In so doing, it wrongly disregards the circumstances of the particular case.

As opposed to atomism, Abu-Hareira argues for a holistic view of evidence and proof according to which (i) the weight of evidence is a matter of its actual effect on the 'mind' of the particular fact-finder, more specifically, it is a function of the extent to which some of the relevant evidence may be viewed by the fact-finder as constituting a consistent story; (ii) no factual conclusions may be drawn on the basis of isolated pieces of evidence alone, however remarkable, but one ought to weigh the evidence and arrive at a factual conclusion only after the 'whole' evidence of the case has been heard; and (iii) factual judgements can only be formed on the basis of an 'examination of the particulars', and, thus, general knowledge, ie generalizations and probabilities, plays a very limited role in legal decision-making.

Abu-Hareira's work is extremely interesting in that it brings to light the extent to which holism draws from philosophical sources different from those of atomism. Furthermore, it shows that, alongside the mainstream atomistic tradition, holism existed as a side-stream in theoretical works on evidence as early as the 1800s. I turn now to examine a contemporary approach to evidence and proof, to wit, Tillers', which importantly advances the understanding of the inner workings of holistic inference and how it relates to atomistic inference.

## B. Tillers' Irenic Approach to Legal Inference

Tillers' approach to inference is generally taken to be a holistic one, as opposed to an atomistic one.[80] However, Tillers' primary interest is not so much to defend a version of holism as is to reconcile holism and atomism. According to Tillers, neither atomism nor holism allows us to give an accurate picture of factual reasoning in law.[81] To start with, an atomistic approach misses the important point that the meaning of evidence sometimes attaches to the whole of the evidence. In addition, atomistic attempts to 'dissect' evidence and to make explicit all the premises of our factual reasonings may severely distort the fact-finder's representation of the problem at hand.[82] However, according to Tillers, it does not follow from this that one should reject atomism and embrace straightforwardly a holistic view. For 'it is hard even to imagine what it means to take the evidence

80 See Pardo (2000: 422–24) and Twining (2006: 309).
81 Tillers (1989: 1253).
82 Wigmore (1983) §37.7, 1068, fn 36 and §30, 986, fn 5.

"as a whole"... Moreover, it is hard even to imagine how we can imbibe the evidence we "see" without performing some sort of mental analysis'.[83] Thus, according to Tillers, both atomistic analysis and holistic assessments play an important role in inference in legal contexts.[84]

Tillers' claim that rational inference involves the interaction of both atomistic and holistic analysis has important implications for the conceptualization of the relationship between evidence and theory. According to Tillers, theory and evidence are interdependent.[85] On the one hand, theory shapes and structures the evidence. On the other hand, theory is also dependent on evidence because the shaping of evidence by theory must be supported by events and state of affairs that are taken as genuine data. Tillers warns us that this interdependence thesis is to be distinguished from the claim that evidence lacks any independence and is merely a construct of the observer. Given that theory depends on facts, as much as facts depend on theory, this thesis about the relationship between theory and data does not lead to either 'epistemological solipsism' or 'fact scepticism'.[86]

According to Tillers, from the interdependence thesis it follows that 'neither theory nor evidence has primacy as an abstract matter. Moreover, whether uncertainty about theory or uncertainty about the inferential implications of data has primacy depends altogether on the contours of the particular problem of evidence'.[87] That is, the appropriateness of using a particular model of inference (either atomistic or holistic) is a function of the prominence of specific types of uncertainty in particular problems of evidence. Consequently, no single model of inference—either atomistic or holistic—can provide a complete description of legal inference. Rather, 'a portrait of rational inference requires the use of at least several logically disparate theories of evidence'.[88]

Tillers illustrates the thesis according to which different models of inference are fit for diverse inferential problems by examining some hypothetical problems in which a 'coherentist, story-based, and narrative method' for evaluating evidence is most appropriate.[89] First, coherentist methods are particularly well-suited for modelling how fact-finders face 'problems of factual interpretation'. In these cases, a coherentist analysis helps illuminate how fact-finders construct different stories (ie hypotheses, explanations or

[83] Tillers (1989: 1253).

[84] A similar point has been argued by Twining. See Twining ((1986: 399) and (2006: 311)). For a formal theory that combines both arguments and stories to model reasoning in the process of legal proof, see Bex et al (2010); Bex (2011); and Bex and Verheij ((2012) and (2013)).

[85] Tillers (1986a: 899ff).

[86] ibid, 903, and 904–07.

[87] ibid, 906.

[88] ibid, 889.

[89] ibid, 922.

interpretations) that explain the evidence, and weigh their relative plausibility, so as to arrive at a factual judgement. Other kinds of problems of evidence that involve a sort of coherentist reasoning are those in which the emphasis of the fact-finders is on trying to construct a story that irons out discrepancies and conflicts among various pieces of evidence. In these cases, the trier of fact has numerous strategies to preserve coherence at her disposal. She might suggest a different interpretation of a fact, reject the fact as mistaken or she might revise her hypothesis in light of conflicting evidence. The important thing to notice, in Tillers' view, is that the process of searching for the appropriate interpretation, or constructing a story that irons out discrepancies in the evidence is, *pace* Bayesians, a perfectly rational way of confronting an evidence problem. The right question to ask is not whether or not a given model of inference is correct, but rather, what the proper domain of any particular model is.[90] Thus, the aim of a general theory of evidence is to delimit and describe those domains, so as to regulate the use of lower order theories of inference.[91]

To be sure, a general theory of inference conceived in this way would depart in significant ways from the mainstream view about evidence and inference. To start with, it vindicates the relevance of kinds of inference other than probabilistic inference in reasoning about facts in law. In so doing, it challenges the atomistic assumptions of the received tradition by giving holism an important role in legal inference. In addition, it is based on a broader view of rationality than the conception of rationality as probabilistic coherence assumed by Bayesian models of inference. However, it is important not to exaggerate the extent to which Tillers questions the central tenets of the Rationalist Tradition for important realist assumptions about truth and the possibility of knowledge are kept untouched. A holistic view that lends itself more readily to a relativist interpretation is Pardo's, which I shall now proceed to examine.

## C. Pardo's Pragmatic Version of Holism

Pardo has proposed a version of a holistic theory of juridical evidence that is based on Quine's thesis about 'meaning holism', ie the thesis that the meaning of any statement is a function of the role that it plays in one's overall

[90] A similar view is defended by Thagard—see ch 4. Both Tillers and Thagard claim that probabilistic models are adequate for some but not all problems of reasoning about uncertainty. There is a main difference between Thagard's and Tillers' views though. Thagard takes probability theory to be useful in some domains, amongst which, he does not include law. In contrast, Tillers seems to defend the view according to which *within* the legal domain some problems are amenable to Bayesian approaches, while a coherentist analysis is most appropriate for attacking other evidential problems in law.

[91] Tillers (1986a: 889–90 and 934).

theory of language.[92] According to Pardo, the process of proof crucially involves the interpretation of a set of statements about the evidence presented at trial. These statements include 'all the given testimony, statements about the proffered real (or physical) evidence, statements the fact-finder articulates about demeanor, as well as statements made by the attorney about the proffered evidence'.[93] He claims that the process of interpretation of evidence basically consists in assigning pragmatic meaning to these statements by fact-finders.[94] Pardo's main contention is that Quine's theory of 'meaning holism' provides a framework for understanding the process by which fact-finders assign pragmatic meaning to evidentiary statements at trial. More specifically, Pardo claims that Quine's thesis of the 'indeterminacy of translation' illuminates how fact-finders choose among competing assignments of pragmatic meaning to statements about juridical evidence.

Very roughly, Quine's thesis of the indeterminacy of translation states that 'no semantic fact of the matter fixes the meaning of particular claims'.[95] Quine argues for this thesis by means of a thought experiment which involves 'radical translation'. 'Radical translation' is the process of translating the sentences of a formerly unknown language of a newly discovered people with a language and culture that has no links to any known language into English. In this context, claims Quine, there is no fact of the matter as to which propositional content is expressed by any particular assertion. Rather, linguistic behaviour fixes meaning relative only to a particular translation manual. Manuals for translating this language into English can be set up in divergent ways, which are compatible with the totality of speech dispositions, yet incompatible with one another. According to Quine, there is no fact of the matter as to which of these manuals is correct. Instead, the choice about which manual to adopt is determined by pragmatic considerations. In Quine's view, the example of radical translation reveals the indeterminacy that lurks in any interpretation. As he puts it: 'The resort to a remote language was not really essential. On deeper reflection, radical translation begins at home'.[96] Children learning a language for the first time are, in Quine's view, in the same position as the field linguist breaking into a native language of a hitherto unknown culture. Furthermore, Quine later accepted the thesis, stated by Davidson, according to which the indeterminacy of translation may be fully extended to interpretation. That is, any process of interpretation is indeterminate in

[92] On meaning holism, see ch 6.
[93] Pardo (2000: 434).
[94] By 'pragmatic meaning', Pardo refers to 'the extra-semantic meaning that a speaker adds to sentences (or how the speaker uses sentences)'; ibid, 429.
[95] ibid, 427.
[96] Quine (1969: 46).

that different meanings may be assigned in a way that is compatible with the evidence available.

Pardo claims that Quine's views on interpretation may be fully applicable to the interpretation of statements about juridical evidence. He draws an analogy between Quine's radical translation and the assignment of meanings in the courtroom:

> In Quine's thought experiment, we decide how to interpret the meaning of an utterance by choosing the meaning assigned to it to the best available conceptual scheme or holistic theory. Likewise, in the courtroom, fact-finders decide how to interpret the pragmatic meaning of a particular statement (including the *probandum*) by choosing the pragmatic meaning assigned to it by the best available narrative or holistic theory of the evidence.[97]

Thus, in Pardo's view, Quine's holistic theory of interpretation allows us to explain how fact-finders interpret evidentiary statements in law.

According to Pardo, the process of proof at trial may be described as follows. Fact-finders are, first and foremost, involved in a process of interpretation. The competing parties offer competing pragmatic interpretations of various evidentiary statements. For example, 'the defendant's blood at the crime scene' may pragmatically mean to one party 'the defendant committed the crime', and to the opposing party, 'the defendant was framed by the police'.[98] The fact-finder organizes these various statements in the form of narratives or evidentiary schemes. Next, he chooses the best available narrative that explains the various evidentiary statements. Such a choice, he claims, is governed by 'basic principles of rationality, such as coverage, coherence, and uniqueness'.[99] On the basis of this narrative, or holistic theory, the fact-finder assigns pragmatic meaning to the different statements. Only after this assignment has taken place, can the fact-finder determine the probative value of evidence. Such determination will be a function of the fact-finder's evidentiary scheme. That is, Pardo claims that the probative value of any particular piece of evidence depends on the role that it plays in the larger evidential scheme, developed by the fact-finder. In this way, says Pardo, this approach does not eliminate the need for an atomistic analysis, but it does show that such an analysis depends upon the holistic theory under which it proceeds.

What are the implications of the holistic view proposed by Pardo for evidence law, as well as for the conception of truth and objectivity on which it relies? Pardo explicitly argues that a holistic view suggests a shift towards a system of free proof.[100] The current view according to which

[97] ibid, 434.
[98] ibid, 429, fn 211. See also 424, fn 249; and 437, fn 264.
[99] ibid, 435.
[100] ibid, 399 and 441. But see Bilz (2010) (arguing that deliberate exclusion of evidence fits comfortably with the narrative model of judging).

judges play the role of 'gate-keeper' of evidence presupposes, says Pardo, an atomistic view of evidence. For, contrary to holism, it assumes that judges can evaluate the probative value of evidence *before* they know the whole story. In addition, the holistic perspective locates the evidence *within* the fact-finder, for meanings are assigned to evidentiary statements, and probative value is attributed to pieces of evidence based on the role they play within each juror's subjective evidentiary scheme. This, according to Pardo, does not entail that jurors will end up with wildly different subjective stories, for fact-finders are likely to adhere to one of the two opposing stories presented at trial. However, says Pardo, it does follow from this view that there is no algorithm that can explain how a fact-finder will organize the various evidentiary statements presented at trial. Even if Pardo explicitly warns us against overestimating the degree of indeterminacy that lurks in his framework, the implications of his views for objectivity and truth in adjudication are quite subversive of the conventional approach. He appeals to both contemporary narrative theory and, again, Quine's theory of meaning, to argue for the claim that the distinction between basic story/different versions disappears in a holistic model of judicial proof. Narrative analysis indicates that there is no 'single basic story' underneath the different versions. Similarly, he says, Quine's thesis suggests that there is no correct interpretational scheme that can be said to capture the basic story. In his view, this implies that in the courtroom 'there is not one correct story of the case in which both advocates are fighting to offer the "right" one'.[101] Consequently, Pardo concludes, 'what John Bart once wrote of (and in) fiction applies, *mutatis mutandis,* to the trial: truth must yield to plausibility'.[102] A holistic approach that also gives a pivotal role to 'plausibility', but that conceptualizes the relation between plausibility and truth in a rather more conventional way is Allen's, to which I turn now.

## D. The Relative Plausibility Theory

In a number of articles, Allen has developed what he calls the 'relative plausibility theory', which is, to date, the most articulated holistic theory of legal reasoning about facts.[103] The main claim of the relative plausibility theory (RPT) is that 'legal fact-finding involves a determination of the comparative plausibility of the parties' explanations offered at trial rather

[101] ibid, 438, fn 269.

[102] ibid, 439.

[103] See Allen ((1991), (1994) and (1997a: 271–75)) and Allen and Leiter (2001: 1527–37). For a useful summary of this theory as well as the main arguments that Allen has given to support it, see Pardo (2000: 415–22). For critiques of this theory, see Lempert (1986); Friedman (1992); La Rue (1992); and Nance (2001: 1563–85). See also Carriquiry and Allen (1997).

than a determination of whether discrete elements are found to a specific probability. In civil cases, the fact-finder must identify the most plausible account of the relevant events, whereas in criminal cases, the prosecution must provide a plausible account of guilt and show that there is no plausible account of innocence'.[104] As opposed to an 'elements approach', this theory implements an 'episode approach' which is inherently holistic. Under an 'elements approach', the task of the fact-finder is to determine liability by considering whether each of the formally necessary elements satisfy the requisite burden of persuasion. Instead, an 'episode approach' requires that fact-finders determine whether the episode that instantiates the formal requirements of the law is satisfactorily established, and so is each of its parts.[105] This approach is holistic in that the parties' theories are to be accepted or rejected as a whole, where such acceptance is determined by the applicable burden of persuasion.[106]

Allen has given a number of arguments in support of RPT. To start with, RPT avoids some problems inherent to the conventional—atomistic—approach to the structure of proof, such as the conjunction problem,[107] the problems relative to the allocation of ambiguity[108] and problems of computational complexity. Secondly, it satisfactorily explains what fact-finders actually do.[109] In contrast to Bayesian models, there is substantial empirical evidence that jurors proceed holistically when reasoning about evidence and that stories play a prominent role in the whole reasoning process.[110] Thirdly, RPT is well supported by case law[111] as well as being consistent with the rules of evidence.[112] Fourthly, RPT focuses on case-specific evidence, thereby maximizing the fact-finder's capacity to reach accurate factual determinations.[113] Last, RPT provides a theory of evidence that has greater explanatory power than the conventional view. The conventional theory claims that the rules of evidence provide the necessary and sufficient conditions of evidence. Accordingly, what the court admits in compliance with the rules of evidence provides the basis for determining liability. In contrast, Allen's holistic theory states that 'evidence is the result of the interaction of the intelligence and knowledge of the fact-finder with

[104] Allen and Leiter (2001: 1528). The relative plausibility theory is a development of Allen's 'equally well specified' proposal. For this proposal, see Allen (1991) s III.

[105] On the elements vs. episode approaches distinction, see Allen (1991: 383ff).

[106] Allen (1994: 609).

[107] See Allen (1994: 605–12). See also Allen and Stein (2013: 571–575).

[108] On the problem of allocation of ambiguity, see Allen (1994) s II.

[109] See Allen and Stein (2013: 575–577).

[110] See next section.

[111] For some of these examples, see Allen (1991: 414–17); Allen and Leiter (2001: 1528–30 and 1532–33); Allen (1994: 633–40); and Allen and Stein (2013: 569–570).

[112] See Allen and Leiter (2001: 1534–35) and Allen and Stein (2013: 569).

[113] Allen and Leiter (2013: 577–579).

the sum of the observations generated during trial'.[114] Crucially, this theory shifts the locus of a theory of evidence from the judge to the fact-finder. It is not the rules of evidence or a judge's ruling that determines what counts as evidence, instead, 'data become evidence if they influence a fact-finder'.[115] Fact-finders, it is claimed, engage in their task equipped with a store of 'stories', 'scripts' and 'scenarios'.[116] These knowledge-structures are fluid enough to permit a constant cycling back and forth between them and the data that get embedded into them. 'It is'—Allen says—'into this bubbling cauldron that the trial "evidence" must enter, and its effect is determined by the interaction of the data with prior knowledge stored in the related constituted stories'.[117] Given the complexity of the process of proof, we should give up the ambition to construct a formalized theory of evidence.[118] This is not to say, Allen emphasizes, that we should surrender to irrationality, for the dynamic process by which fact-finders come to conclusions about the past remains rational despite our inability to capture it in a set of necessary and sufficient rules.[119]

Despite its advantages, as Allen recognizes, there are still important questions that have to be answered for RPT to be a fully developed theory. Most importantly, the question remains of what 'plausibility' means.[120] According to Allen, what makes stories plausible 'seems to be determined by such variables as coherence, completeness, uniqueness, economy and (yes) probability'.[121] But, to be sure, a more precise understanding of this concept, as well as of how it relates to the notion of probability, is required. There is also the question of what it means to provide a plausible 'explanation' of the facts under dispute, and which type of argument patterns one may use to defend the plausibility of one explanation against another. These questions need to be seriously considered and answered before one is in a position to build up a solid enough explanation-based account of legal reasoning about facts in law.

The holistic approaches examined thus far, ie Abu-Hareira's, Pardo's, Tillers' and Allen's, put forward a picture of evidence evaluation which is significantly different from the atomistic one endorsed by both Bayesianism and the Rationalist Tradition. All these holistic approaches share a number of important features: (i) the claim that the probative value of a piece of

114 ibid, 630.

115 ibid, 627.

116 See ch 9 for a full explanation of these notions.

117 Allen (1994: 629).

118 ibid, 627. The point was already argued for in Allen (1991: 413).

119 ibid, 629. It is worth noticing that there is a theory of free proof implicit in Allen's theory of evidence; see ibid, 631, fn 82.

120 See Carriquiry's comments in Carriquiry and Allen (1997: 467). See also Nance (2001: 1569 and 1594).

121 See Allen (1997a: 273).

evidence depends on the evidential structure to which it belongs; (ii) the relevance of 'evidentiary schemes', 'narratives', 'stories', 'explanations' and 'hypotheses' for organizing the evidence at trial and determining the relative probative value of a single piece of evidence; (iii) the importance of coherence as a criterion for selecting the best among a number of alternative evidentiary schemes; (iv) an emphasis on the fact-finder who actively engages in constructing alternative narratives and selecting one of them as the basis for her decision; and, (v) a tendency to favour a system of free proof as opposed to a rule-based system.

Critically, these holistic approaches rest on a 'naturalized' conception of the kind of rationality that is engaged in legal fact-finding according to which facts about how legal fact-finders reason are relevant for answering questions about how they should reason.[122] It is a main advantage of holistic theories of evidence that, unlike probabilistic models, they do not impose upon jurors a way of reasoning that is alien to them, but that, on the contrary, build upon legal decision-makers' ordinary forms of inference.[123] Now, I would like to consider a number of psychological studies that show that the holistic approach to evidence that I have sketched above does, in fact, enjoy a high degree of psychological plausibility.

## III. COHERENCE AND THE PSYCHOLOGY OF LEGAL DECISION-MAKING

In the last decades, there has been an increasing interest amongst psychologists in the reasoning processes of both juries and judges. A substantial part of this research has suggested that much legal reasoning about facts is a top-down process in which legal decision-makers argue from hypotheses that take the form of stories, or narratives, to evidence. Hence, this research establishes that narrative coherence plays a significant role in fact-finding in adjudication. Here, I shall examine two bodies of research that are directed towards clarifying the role of stories in legal argument: Hastie and Pennington's story model of jurors' decision-making and Wagenaar, Koppen and Crombag's theory of anchored narratives, which explores the role of narrative coherence

[122] The trend towards naturalizing rationality can be tracked in several domains such as epistemology (see ch 3), philosophy of science (see ch 4) and ethics (see ch 8). There have also been recent attempts to 'naturalize' evidence law; see Allen and Leiter (2001) and Callen et al (2003). See also Lempert (1997). I discuss the relevance of naturalism to the development of a theory of legal reasoning and, specifically, a coherence theory of legal reasoning in ch 10.

[123] On the problems that derive from the clash between, on the one hand, the 'elements approach', which the law imposes and the Bayesian theory models, and, on the other, the natural reasoning processes of legal decision-makers, see Allen (1991) s II.

in the context of judicial decision-making.[124] More recently, an important body of psychological research has been conducted by Simon and collaborators which aims to illuminate the role of a different kind of coherence—coherence as constraint satisfaction—in legal decision-making about facts. I shall conclude this overview of the psychological literature on coherence in legal decision-making by introducing Simon's empirical findings.

## A. The Story Model

In a series of works, Hastie and Pennington have developed a story model for jurors' reasoning.[125] They claim that a central cognitive process in decision-making is the construction of 'causal models' to explain the available facts. The structure of these models, they argue, depends on the decision-domain. In the case of jurors' decision-making, they assert that jurors use 'narrative structures' to organize and interpret evidence. Among alternative explanatory structures, jurors accept the story that seems to best explain the evidence. The story model proposed by Hastie and Pennington has three component processes: (1) the construction of explanations that account for the evidence in the form of a story; (2) the representation of the decision alternatives by learning verdict category attributes; and (3) the reaching of a decision through the classification of the story into the best fitting verdict category.[126]

1. *Construction of the stories.* According to this model, jurors impose a narrative structure on legal evidence. Such a structure is a hierarchy of embedded episodes, or units. This organization enables the critical interpretative processing of the evidence and provides jurors with an index of importance and relevance of the different information presented and inferred. According to Hastie and Pennington, this narrative structure is constructed by reasoning from three types of knowledge: (i) case-specific information acquired during the trial, eg the testimony of a witness; (ii) knowledge about events similar to those that are

[124] Both the story model and the theory of anchored narratives owe much to Bennett and Feldman's pioneering work on legal decision-making, in the field of social psychology; see Bennett and Feldman (1981). Bennett and Feldman's work has also had an important influence on some legal theorists' approaches to issues of legal reasoning about facts, such as Jackson's (see s. IV.B of this ch).

[125] See Hastie and Pennington ((1986), (1991), (1992), (1993a), (1993b), (2000) and (2003)) and Hastie (2008).

[126] According to Hastie and Pennington, although the story model does not include stage interaction, it is possible that all three processes interact in legal decision-making. Further, in their view, to investigate whether a more cyclical view of decision-making has merit is a promising direction, since there is an indication in their data that one way jurors have of trying to understand verdict definitions is in terms of the stories they imply. Thus, story construction influences verdict understanding; see Hastie and Pennington (1993b: 533).

under dispute, eg information about similar crimes in the media; and (iii) generic expectations about the structure of stories, eg the knowledge that most human actions (eg a murder) are motivated by the achievement of certain goals (eg to inherit a substantial amount of money).
2. *Learning verdict definitions.* The second stage in the jurors' decision process consists in learning the decision alternatives, which are the definitions of the verdicts. As a result, jurors create a set of potential solutions, called the 'choice set', eg first degree murder, second degree murder and manslaughter.
3. *Story classification.* The final stage involves a classification process in which the best match between accepted stories and verdict categories is achieved, eg the story that best instantiates the elements of the legal definition of 'murder'. The story classification stage also involves the application of the procedural instructions on the presumption of innocence and the standard of proof. In this model, if the best story does not satisfy the verdict categories beyond a reasonable doubt, the juror should presume innocence.

Thus, according to this theory, jurors' decision-making consists of the acceptance of the story that, among alternative stories, best explains the evidence. Hastie and Pennington specify a number of principles, eg 'certainty principles', which determine the acceptability of a story as well as the resulting level of confidence in the story—the so-called 'global confidence'. Three certainty principles govern the acceptance of a story: coverage, coherence, and uniqueness. First, 'coverage' refers to the extent to which a story accounts for the evidence presented in a trial. Secondly, for Pennington and Hastie, 'coherence' is a criterion that has three components: consistency, plausibility and completeness. A story is 'consistent' if it lacks internal contradictions. The 'plausibility' of a story depends on the degree to which it corresponds to the decision-maker's world-knowledge. A story is 'complete' if its expected structure has all its parts. Last, according to the 'principle of uniqueness', if there are multiple coherent stories, belief in any of them will be decreased.[127]

Parameters similar to those used to establish the coherence of alternative stories are also employed to judge the acceptability of a particular proposition (the so-called 'local confidence'). In the story model, the final level of acceptability of any proposition is a function of its inferential support, its plausibility and its role in the larger story structure. Thus, it results from Hastie and Pennington's experiments that probability evaluation, both of

[127] Sloman's experiments about judgements of likelihood have yielded to a similar conclusion as regards the relevance of the number of alternative explanations for the levels of confidence in a decision. According to Sloman, alternative explanations compete with the effect of reducing each other's credibility; see Sloman (1994: 1ff).

alternative explanations and of particular propositions, has a secondary role in judgement under uncertainty in the legal context. On the contrary, Hastie and Pennington's work provides support for the view that fact-finders evaluate evidence in a holistic manner.

### B. The Theory of Anchored Narratives

In *Anchored Narratives: The Psychology of Criminal Evidence,* Wagenaar, Van Koppen and Crombag present a theory of how triers of fact reach their decisions in criminal cases, namely, the 'theory of anchored narratives' (TAN).[128] The authors tested their theory by analysing a corpus of 35 criminal cases tried in The Netherlands in which the verdict was anomalous, resulting in a 'dubious conviction'.[129] Even though this testing-by-anomaly strategy was restricted to Dutch cases, TAN is claimed to be applicable to any legal system. For, the authors claim, the psychological difficulties in decision-making in criminal cases are independent of the particular rules of evidence and procedure, and of whether the fact-finders are professional judges or lay jurors.

The result of this testing-by-anomaly strategy provided, they contend, strong evidence for the theory. In many of these cases there were errors of reasoning which can be explained by their theory. The authors claim that the TAN heuristic is quite successful in common cases (ie easy cases), but it often produces incorrect results in 'dubious cases' (ie hard cases), such as those examined. In their view, the lesson to be drawn from the analysis of these cases is not that we need to change the way in which courts reason. Instead, the remedy consists in identifying the pitfalls of the strategy of anchored narratives and providing adequate safeguards for its misuse.[130] Their claim is that, ultimately, the errors of reasoning identified in the corpus are due to the fact that rules of evidence do not provide sufficient safeguards in situations in which heuristics may produce mistaken results. They conclude their work by proposing a set of universal rules of evidence, the aim of which is to reduce errors of reasoning in difficult cases. I shall now explain in some detail the main tenet of TAN and introduce the set of rules of evidence that it prescribes.

[128] Wagenaar, van Koppen and Crombag (1993). For a brief statement of the main tenets of the theory, see Wagenaar (1996). For some discussions of this work, see Twining (2002); B Jackson (1996b); and den Boer (1995).

[129] A 'dubious conviction' is defined as follows: 'either the District Court's verdict was later reversed by the Court of Appeals because of a different evaluation of the evidence (...) or a defence attorney remained strongly convinced of his client's innocence, even after (repeated) conviction' (Wagenaar, van Koppen and Crombag (1993: 11)). Dubious cases are a much larger category, they say, than 'wrongful convictions'. Whereas in the latter, the outcome was wrong, in dubious cases it is the reasoning that went wrong, but the outcome of wrong reasoning may or may not be wrong (ibid, 13–14).

[130] ibid, 98.

The main tenet of TAN is that legal decision-makers reach their decisions in criminal cases on the basis of two judgements (i) a judgement assessing the plausibility of the prosecutor's narrative; and (ii) a judgement assessing the degree to which such a narrative is properly anchored.[131] Whereas the former judgement determines the 'goodness' of the story, the second determines the degree to which it is supported, or 'anchored', by facts. Together they result in an assessment of the credibility of the prosecutor's story on which the final decision depends. Now, what constitutes a good and well-anchored story? Following Bennett and Feldman, they claim that the 'goodness' or 'plausibility' of a story depends on two aspects: a readily identifiable central action and a context that provides a compelling explanation of the central action.[132] This account of 'goodness' provides us with the first test that a story should satisfy to be believable. However, they claim, 'stories told in a criminal court must not only be good, we want them to be true'.[133] This is why they require that a second test be satisfied for stories to be believable: they must be supported by facts. For, they claim, 'the truth of a story is established by means of evidence'.[134] Every piece of evidence, they argue, needs to be supported by generally accepted common sense rules, which they call 'anchors'. For instance, the belief in the testimony of an eyewitness is anchored to the common sense belief that eyewitnesses speak the truth most of the time.[135] In a safely anchored story, the evidence is ordered in such a way that it forms anchors between the story and a 'ground' of generally accepted common sense rules. Each piece of evidence forms a sub-story in itself, which needs an anchor in the form of further evidence which, in turn, forms a sub-sub-story in need of yet another anchor.

[131] ibid, 10. It is important to notice that the main thesis of TAN is importantly different from the thesis put forward by the story model. To recall, in the story model (and in some other theories such as Allen's), it is claimed that legal decision-makers assess the relative plausibility of the prosecutor's and the defence's stories. But, 'the theory of anchored narratives does not assume that a court considers two narratives, one from the prosecution and one from the defense, which then are required to retain equal prominence till the final choice is made. On the contrary, the theory predicts that mainly the prosecution version of what happened will be considered and verified on the basis of the evidence presented in both sides'; ibid, 210.

[132] ibid, 35–37 and 200.

[133] ibid, 37.

[134] ibid.

[135] Anchors are referred to as 'generally accepted rules', 'common sense beliefs', 'common sense presumptions' and 'general beliefs'. Twining has argued that the way in which these authors seem to equate the foregoing terms is a potential source of confusion. In ordinary usage, he says, the examples that they give of these rules would all be treated as 'empirical generalizations' rather than 'rules' (see Twining (2002: 430)). To be sure, the terminology is loose, but there is an important sense in which rules and presumptions might be related to generalizations. Schauer (2003) has argued that both rules and presumptions are particular cases of generalizations. If this is so, then anchors may be described as general beliefs, general rules, or presumptions, for independently of which term one uses one would still be emphasizing the important feature that all anchors share, to wit, that they are kinds of generalizations. On the role of generalizations in arguments about facts in law, see Schum (2001: 82–83 and 109–10); TJ Anderson (1995); and Twining ((1999a) and (1999b)).

Whether a sub-story is safely anchored depends on our willingness to accept as true the common sense rule of which the sub-story is an instance.[136] Anchoring structures must meet three requirements: (i) all relevant parts of the narrative must be anchored; (ii) only common sense rules that are generally accepted as safe, ie rules that sensible people would normally be unwilling to challenge, can serve as anchors; and (iii) the anchoring construction as a whole must prove guilt 'beyond a reasonable doubt'.[137]

The authors suggest that the following five criteria allow us to judge the quality of a legal decision about facts: (i) every piece of evidence used for the decision must be anchored; (ii) all critical episodes in the story need to be anchored; (iii) all anchoring should be based on legally obtained evidence; (iv) all evidence must be anchored to rules that are safe enough to pass the criterion of 'reasonable doubt'; and (v) the evidence should not be a biased selection from the available evidence.[138] Do legal decisions comply with these criteria? In practice, the authors say, legal decision-making does not uphold these principles. The authors submit that many of the errors of reasoning identified in the corpus resulted, in fact, from applying the heuristics of anchored narratives without checking the extent to which these five criteria had been satisfied.

The authors claim that the following 'universal rules of evidence' provide the required safeguards against the pitfalls of the anchored narratives heuristics: (i) the prosecution must present at least one well-shaped narrative; (ii) the prosecution must present a limited set of well-shaped narratives; (iii) essential components of the narrative must be anchored; (iv) anchors for different components of the charge should be independent of each other; (v) the trier of fact should give reasons for the decision by specifying the narrative and the accompanying anchoring; (vi) a fact-finder's decision as to the level of analysis of the evidence should be explained through an articulation of the general beliefs used as anchors; (vii) There should be no competing story with equally good or better anchoring; (viii) There should be no falsifications of the indictment's narrative and nested sub-narratives; (ix) There should be no anchoring onto obviously false beliefs; and (x) The indictment and the verdict should contain the same narrative.[139] These rules are not meant to be implemented, the authors claim, in all legal systems. But they do propose that legal systems be scrutinized in light of these rules.[140]

136 Wagenaar, van Koppen and Crombag (1993: 40).

137 ibid, ch 4.

138 ibid, 41.

139 ibid, ch 12.

140 Twining has objected that the authors jump too fast from establishing certain points to embodying them in legal rules. In Twining's view, some of the authors' rules might be acceptable as admonitory instructions, or rather as guidelines, but not as rules; see Twining (2002: 432–33).

TAN, together with the story model, is a psychological model of decision-making built around the notion of story. According to both TAN and the story model, the process of legal decision-making is best understood as one of story construction and story comparison. In this view, the key concepts in a theory of legal decision-making are those of narratives, plausibility and narrative coherence. As we saw before, these are the pivotal concepts in current holistic theories of evidence and proof as well. In addition, as will be shown below, these notions also feature in the most prominent jurisprudential accounts of legal reasoning about disputed questions of fact. Now, I would like to introduce an emerging body of research called 'coherence-based reasoning' which offers a different holistic view of legal decision-making and of the kind of coherence that is relevant to it. As will be explained shortly, in 'coherence-based reasoning', it is the notion of coherence as constraint satisfaction, rather than that of narrative coherence, that is taken to be of central importance in a descriptive theory of legal reasoning about facts. The bulk of this research has been conducted by Dan Simon, in collaboration with Keith Holyoak, Chadwick Snow and Stephen Read.[141] Let us now examine Simon, Holyoak, Snow and Read's experimental results.

## C. Coherence-based Reasoning

'Coherence-based reasoning' posits that legal decision-making is a process whereby decision-makers reconstruct the mental representation of the difficult and complex decision tasks that are involved in most legal cases into easy ones, yielding confident conclusions. More specifically, it is held that through the decision-making process, the decision-maker's mental representation of the decision task undergoes gradual change and ultimately shifts towards a state of coherence with one of the decision alternatives. At this point, the decision follows from the coherent representation with ease and confidence. Hence, in coherence-based reasoning, legal decision-making is no longer conceptualized in terms of story construction and comparison, but as the manipulation of the representation of the decision task so as to achieve a state of coherence that facilitates the making of the decision. In this view, the kind of coherence that is relevant to legal decision-making is not 'narrative coherence' but 'coherence as constraint satisfaction', that is, a state at which considerations—the so-called 'constraints'—that support the emerging decision are strongly endorsed, and those that support the

[141] See Holyoak and Simon (1999); Simon et al (2000); Simon and Holyoak (2002); Read, Snow, and Simon (2003); and Simon, Snow and Read (2004). For a summary of the experimental research, see D Simon (2004: 520–49). See also D Simon ((2011: 195–200) and (2012: 33–36 and 173–77)).

alternative decision are dismissed.[142] I shall now briefly explain the main tenets of the theory and its experimental support, as well as examine its implications for current views on legal decision-making.

Coherence-based reasoning is a general model of judgement and decision-making in conditions of complexity. Complex tasks are those in which the 'constitutive considerations are numerous, contradictory, ambiguous, and incommensurable'.[143] Most legal cases that are litigated and appealed are complex in this sense. The model has been applied to appellate judicial decision-making, as well as to decision-making at trial. Here I shall focus on the applications of this model of decision-making to the context of fact-finding.[144] The central tenet of coherence-based reasoning is that decision-making crucially involves a transformation of the representation of complex decision tasks into easy ones by amplifying one alternative and deflating the other. In the process of decision-making, the diverse and conflicting considerations that provide equivocal support for different decision alternatives are restructured until they fit into a 'coherent' representation, ie a representation in which the chosen alternative is supported by strong considerations and the rejected one is supported by weak considerations. At the end of the process, the decision-maker's representation of the task is skewed towards conformity with the emerging decision, which follows then confidently.

Coherence-based reasoning assumes a 'connectionist architecture' of mental representations and proposes that the process of decision-making is governed by mechanisms of 'constraint satisfaction'.[145] In this view, the process of decision-making starts with a mental representation of the task variables, ie all the factors that need to be included in the decision. In connectionist systems, each variable is represented by a unit, which is then connected through the network to all the other units by means of excitatory (positive) and inhibitory (negative) links. Constraint satisfaction mechanisms handle mental tasks by a process in which the several variables interact with each other like an electrical network. In each processing cycle, the mental representation is modified until it settles into a state of equilibrium, ie a point of maximum coherence. At this stage, similarly linked variables are highly activated, and variables supporting the alternative decision become poorly activated. That is, when coherence is reached, the subset of the task variables that support the emerging decision is strongly endorsed, while the alternative subset is suppressed or rejected. In this way,

[142] For a full development of the notion of coherence as constraint satisfaction, see Thagard's theory of coherence reported in ch 4.

[143] D Simon (2004: 516).

[144] For applications of coherence-based reasoning to the domain of appellate adjudication, see D Simon ((1998) and (2002)).

[145] A more detailed introduction to connectionist representations and mechanisms of constraint satisfaction is provided in ch 4.

the representation drifts towards either one of two skewed mental representation. The initially complex and incoherent representation is thus spread, by a constraint satisfaction process, into two subsets, one which dominates the other, enabling an easy and confident decision.

The coherence-based reasoning model is empirically supported by a solid body of experimental research. This research comprises two series of experiments: one based on a civil case, ie *Quest v Smith,* and another based on the criminal case of *Jason Wells.*[146] In both cases, participants were presented with a pretest that contained a number of apparently unrelated vignettes, followed by a statement or two that could be inferred from the vignette. Participants were asked to rate their agreement with each inference. In the second phase of the experiment, participants were presented with the arguments of both sides, which pertained to inferences from the underlying evidence. Then, they were asked to render a verdict, rate their confidence in the decision, and rate their agreement with the inferences. The questions were virtually identical to those asked in the pretest. In both the *Smith* and the *Jason* experiments, the key measure is the comparison between the rating given on the vignettes and the subsequent stage of making the decision. Coherence-based reasoning would predict a shift in the ratings, from an initial state of incoherence to a state in which variables cohere with the decision and with the other variables that support the same decision. All the results were consistent with these predictions. Together, these experiments have revealed the following eight features of coherence-based reasoning:[147]

1. *The basic finding of coherence shifts.* The most important finding of the coherence-based research is that, in the course of making complex decisions, the mental representation of the task shifts towards coherence with the emerging decision. In the experiments, while the vignette ratings were mostly moderate, the ratings of the arguments and the facts shifted towards coherence with the chosen verdict. For instance, in the *Jason* case, there were no significant differences between the mean pretest ratings of the inculpating and exculpating items or between the mean ratings given by participants who ultimately decided against the defendant and the ratings given by participants who acquitted him. In contrast, in the ratings of the second phase of the experiment, there are large differences between participants who found Jason guilty and those who found him innocent. For the former, there is an increase in the ratings of inculpating items and a decrease in those of the exculpating

[146] For the reports of the Smith's sets of experiments, see Holyoak and Simon (1999) and Simon, Pham, Quang and Holyoak (2000). For the reports of the Jason's set of experiments, see Simon, Snow and Read (2004).

[147] These findings are summarized in D Simon (2004: 523–49).

items. The opposite pattern was observed for those who decided in his favour. As predicted, participants in both sets of experiments showed high levels of confidence in their decisions.

2. *Lack of awareness*. Coherence shifts are governed by automatic cognitive mechanisms that operate under the level of conscious awareness. This was shown by two studies based on *Quest* in which participants were asked to recall their ratings at the vignette phase. The ratings they reported approximated their post-coherence shift ratings, instead of their original ratings. That is, people feel that their current beliefs are the ones that they held all along, and are unaware of the changes that they have undergone throughout the decision-making process.
3. *The facilitative function of coherence shifts*. Coherence shifts play a functional role in the decision-making process in that spreading apart the variables creates a dominance of one alternative over the other which enables an easy and confident decision. This is supported by predecidisonal shifts that were observed in both the *Quest* and *Jason* cases. Hence, coherence shifts play an active role in the course of decision-making, rather than serving as a mere post hoc rationalization for decisions driven by other mechanisms.[148]
4. *The breadth and depth of coherence effects*. Coherence is a pervasive and powerful feature that spreads beyond the specific decision task at hand into the background knowledge-structures as well as from one decision task to another. The *Jason* experiments showed not only that factual inferences shifted towards coherence with the respective verdict, but that the background beliefs shifted as well. In one of the *Quest* experiments, participants were asked to decide a second unrelated case. Results showed that coherence effects spread from the first verdict to the verdict in the second case. These experiments suggest that coherence effects run deep and wide into the legal decision-maker's belief system.
5. *The effects of indirect influences*. A change on one variable triggers changes throughout the mental representation of the task: not only does it change the distribution of verdicts but also the ratings of variables that are unrelated to the manipulated variable. Such indirect influences, which are inherent in connectionist models of cognition, were found in studies based on both the *Quest* and the *Jason* cases. In the former, manipulating information about Smith's character had a strong influence in the distribution of verdicts as well as in the ratings of all the other variables. Similarly, the introduction of a piece of DNA evidence

[148] In this respect, coherence-based reasoning sharply contrasts with dissonance theory—ie the dominant variant of consistency theories. On the relation between cognitive consistency theories and coherence-based reasoning, see D Simon (1998: 45–54); Simon, Snow and Read (2004: 814–15 and 832–34); and Simon and Holyoak (2002), throughout.

in one of the variants of the *Jason* case resulted in changes in all the other pieces of unrelated evidence.

6. *The effect of predilections—motivations and attitudes*. Coherence effects interact with motivations and with the decision-maker's pre-existing attitudes, particularly those embedded in the person's enduring value-system. For example, in a study based on the *Jason* case, it was found that participants with strong pro-death penalty attitudes were more likely to convict than participants with anti-death penalty attitudes. Consistent with the predictions, the participants' mental representations of the task shifted to cohere with the corresponding verdicts. People with strong pro-death penalty attitudes or anti-death penalty attitudes interpreted all the evidence in a way that cohered with conviction and acquittal, respectively.
7. *The transitory nature of coherence*. A different set of experiments which elicited coherence shifts in a job choice task showed that coherence effects are transient: they reach the maximum value at the point of decision, but then recede when the decision task is completed. This suggests that our cognitive system is highly flexible and adaptive in that it enables representations to shift towards coherence in order to facilitate the task at hand without encumbering the decision-maker for future decisions.[149]
8. *Moderating (debiasing) coherence*. A version of the *Quest* case examined whether coherence effects can be moderated. Participants were assigned to one of three conditions: a condition in which participants were given an instruction urging them 'to be unbiased'; a condition in which they were instructed to 'take some time to consider seriously the possibility that the opposite side has a better case'; and a control condition in which no instruction was given. Results showed that the 'be unbiased' instruction was ineffective, but that inducing the participants to create a mental representation of the decision task in which they imagine alternative conclusions and consider their correctness had a moderating effect on coherence shifts. The 'consider the opposite' instruction reduced coherence shifts by one-half.[150] This said, it is important to notice that coherence shifts are nevertheless mediated by task-specific factors, as well as by idiosyncratic characteristics of

[149] Even if coherence is transitory, Simon claims that, under particular circumstances, coherence effects may be more permanent. Recurring coherence shifts, he says, may eventually modify the background system of beliefs. For example, a judge who repeatedly renders verdicts on criminal cases in which the rate of conviction is high might end up developing a guilt-prone attitudinal system. Further experimentation is needed, he claims, to test the endurance of coherence effects; see D Simon (2004: 547).

[150] See also Schweizer (2014) (showing that forcing subjects to assess the likelihoods for each individual item of evidence and integrating the obtained values using a Bayesian Network leads to reduced coherence shifts).

> the decision-makers. A higher degree of ambiguity of the task at hand makes it more likely that coherence shifts occur. Besides, individuals vary in their tolerance for inconsistency, which also affects the value of the coherence shifts.[151]

Now, what are the implications of these experimental results for legal decision-making? What is their bearing on the theory of legal reasoning, specifically, on the theory of legal reasoning about facts? In the context of legal fact-finding, the foregoing research has important implications for the debate between atomism vs holism. First, this body of research seriously questions the empirical validity of the atomist view on evidence evaluation. These experiments crucially show that legal decision-making is a 'bidirectional' process, that is, a process in which 'evidence influences the conclusions and, at the same time, the emerging conclusion affects the evaluation of the evidence'.[152] This finding is blatantly inconsistent with the atomist assumptions inherent in the Bayesian model of fact-finding. In this model, each piece of evidence is evaluated in its own terms and is not affected either by other pieces of evidence or by the conclusion. This assumption relies on a view of legal reasoning as 'unidirectional' in which inferences flow from the individual pieces of evidence towards a computed judgement, but the evaluation of the evidence is in no way affected in the reverse direction, ie by the emerging conclusion, and there are no interactions between the pieces of evidence.[153] Hence, coherence-based reasoning poses a strong challenge to the descriptive adequacy of the Bayesian model and, more generally, to any atomistic view of evidence evaluation.

Secondly, the research conducted by Simon and collaborators confirms and strengthens the empirical support for a holistic conception of legal inference, most notably, the story model. The empirical findings are consistent with the central features of the story model. The coherence-based reasoning research confirms that decisions are determined by constructions of representations, rather than by computing independent values of pieces of evidence; that the emerging representation plays a crucial role in the interpretation of evidence; and that confidence in the decision is determined by the coherence of the final representation. However, the story model is restrictive in that it contends that the representation of the evidence has a narrative structure. Although this undoubtedly fits the cases in which the model was based, ie a murder charge that hinged on a determination of the defendant's mental state, its relevance to some other kinds of legal cases is limited. Many legal cases do not involve intentional or causal schemes in

[151] Festinger referred to this characteristic as 'mental agility'; see ibid, 549, fn 115. See also D Simon (1998: 102).

[152] Simon, Snow and Read (2004: 814).

[153] ibid, 816.

which evidence lends itself to narrative structures. In contrast, coherence-based reasoning has a broader scope of application, for it also gives an account of coherence-driven processing in the absence of narrative structures. In addition, insofar as it relates coherence-based reasoning to constraint satisfaction mechanisms, it provides a deeper theoretical explanation of holistic processing, which may be extended to realms of reasoning other than legal reasoning.[154] This is interesting in that it enables a potentially enlightening comparison between legal reasoning and other kinds of complex reasoning which also involve the integration of multiple inferences.

It is important to emphasize that coherence reasoning is intended to be an empirical theory, and not a normative approach. Interestingly, even though Simon claims that coherence-based reasoning provides empirical support for holism, he holds that this research calls into question the normative adequacy of the holistic view. He writes,

> Precisely because the holistic account of human cognition is correct, its prescription is wrong. Due to the connectionist nature of the decision-making process, extra vigilance is needed to contain the adverse effect of potentially prejudicial evidence—a task best performed by an atomistic analysis.[155]

Hence, while coherence-based reasoning furnishes a coherence theory of legal justification with a solid empirical basis, it also sheds some doubts about whether this theory provides a sound normative model for the justification of legal decisions.

To conclude, the body of experimental research that I have discussed in this section—Hastie and Pennington's story model, the theory of anchored narratives and coherence—based reasoning—provides the view that fact-finders evaluate evidence in a holistic manner with solid empirical support. This research shows that decision-makers use global structures to organize and interpret the evidence and to reach decisions about facts in law. While narrative structures are crucial in the holistic processing of evidence, as the story model and the theory of anchored narratives suggest, coherence-based reasoning shows that holistic processing is not limited to cases in which the representation of the evidence lends itself to narrative structures, but that, in the absence of such structures, legal fact-finders also decide on the grounds of their representation of the evidence at trial. All these psychological studies show that it is by constructing and comparing alternative representations of the evidence—narrative or otherwise—that legal decision-makers reason about evidence in law rather than by computing independent values of pieces of evidence. Thus, the psychological literature tells against the descriptive adequacy of atomistic approaches to evidence evaluation in law, most importantly, the Bayesian approach. A common

[154] D Simon (2004: 564).
[155] ibid, 569.

feature of all these studies is that they take coherence—narrative coherence, and more recently, coherence as constraint-satisfaction—as a key criterion for assessing the relative plausibility of the representations that determine legal fact-finders' decisions about disputed questions of fact. Coherence, according to these studies, is thus crucial for facilitating the decision task in legal contexts. However, these studies also bring to light the serious risks involved in processing evidence by constructing and comparing the relative coherence of alternative representations. Thus, these psychological studies lend strong empirical support to holism about evidence evaluation, but also raise doubts about whether holism is an appropriate theory about how legal decision-makers ought to reason. It is, therefore, a main challenge of coherence-based theories of fact-reasoning in law to show that they are not only descriptively adequate, as the psychological evidence demonstrates, but also an attractive alternative to probabilism from a normative point of view.[156] The next section examines some efforts, drawn from the realm of jurisprudence, to elaborate coherence-based theories for the justification of conclusions about disputed questions of fact in law.

## IV. NARRATIVE COHERENCE IN LEGAL REASONING ABOUT FACTS

The discussion of coherentist approaches to evidential reasoning in law in legal theory focuses on two proposals: MacCormick's theory of narrative coherence and Jackson's semiotic model of legal proof. These theories are similar in that, in line with evidence scholars and legal psychologists, they vindicate the role that 'narrative coherence' plays in legal reasoning. However, there are notable differences between them. MacCormick's theory of narrative coherence is embedded in his own theory of legal reasoning, which is a main representative of the standard approach to legal reasoning. In contrast, Jackson's work in legal theory departs in significant ways from the mainstream view, and it may be better located within the field of 'legal hermeneutics'. Hence, MacCormick, on the one hand, and Jackson on the other, may be regarded as main representatives of coherence theories that have been developed within very different jurisprudential traditions.

### A. MacCormick's Theory of Narrative Coherence

As was explained in the previous chapter, MacCormick has articulated an influential theory of legal reasoning that gives an important role to coherence.

[156] I take up this challenge in ch 10.

To recall, MacCormick distinguishes between two kinds of coherence: normative coherence and narrative coherence. While the former contributes to the justification of conclusions about disputed questions of law, the latter contributes to the justification of conclusions about disputed questions of fact. We have already examined the notion and role of normative coherence in MacCormick's theory of legal reasoning. Let us now have a closer look at MacCormick's views on narrative coherence.[157]

MacCormick takes 'narrative coherence' to be 'a test of truth or probability in questions of fact and evidence upon which direct proof by immediate observation is unavailable'.[158] MacCormick endorses a correspondence theory of truth, which is the view that true statements are those that correspond with the actual state of affairs in the world.[159] The truth of certain present tense statements, says MacCormick, can be tested by checking whether they correspond with the facts. However, most legal disputes concern past events whose truth cannot be directly verified by immediate observation. MacCormick's suggestion is that the only type of test that we have available for verifying contested assertions about the past is a test of 'narrative coherence'. Hence, narrative coherence is of central importance to the justification of conclusions about disputed question of fact in law. Three questions need to be addressed in order to give a full account of the place of narrative coherence in MacCormick's theory of justification: 'What is narrative coherence?' 'What is its role in the justification of factual conclusions?' and 'Why does coherence have any justificatory force in making legal decisions about matters of fact?' I shall now take up MacCormick's answers to these questions in turn.

As stated earlier, according to MacCormick, coherence is the property of a set of propositions which, taken together, 'makes sense' in its entirety. Normative coherence, to recall, refers to the property of a set of normative propositions which 'hang together'. Analogously, narrative coherence is the property of a set of factual propositions which 'makes sense' as a

[157] For MacCormick's views on narrative coherence, see N MacCormick ((1980), (1984), (1994: 89–92) and (2005) ch 11).

[158] N MacCormick (1984: 48). Van Roermund has criticized this conception of narrative coherence as a test of probability, or plausibility, of factual statements on the grounds that such a concept is unduly restrictive. According to Van Roermund, 'narrative coherence' should be conceived as 'the very principle of the relation between facts and norms (case and decision), not—as professor MacCormick seems to do—only as the ordering principle of one of the terms of that relation' (Van Roermund (1988: 160)). Jackson has also proposed a theory of narrative coherence which does not restrict the role of this notion to the factual domain. In contrast to MacCormick, Jackson claims his theory of narrative coherence to be applicable to the construction of facts at trial as well as to the construction and application of law. I shall examine Jackson's alternative model of coherence below in this chapter.

[159] N MacCormick ((1980: 45), (1991: 166) and (1994: 90)). In the latter article, MacCormick defends the sustainability of the correspondence theory of truth against semiotic attacks. For Jackson's response to MacCormick, see B Jackson (1991). On Jackson's views on narrative coherence and truth, see s IV.B.

whole. But, what does such an elusive notion of 'making sense' mean? To gain a better understanding of the notion of narrative coherence, says MacCormick, we should first of all properly distinguish it from 'consistency', ie no contradiction. MacCormick does not regard consistency as a necessary condition of narrative coherence, for 'a story can be coherent on the whole and as a whole, though it contains some internal inconsistencies'.[160] Consistency does not suffice either for coherence, given that a story, 'though it may contain no proposition which directly contradicts or logically entails a contradiction of any other proposition in the story, yet in some way fails to make sense'.[161] What is then that makes a story 'coherent' if mere consistency is not enough? MacCormick's answer, like his response concerning normative coherence, appeals to the notion of 'principle'. As explained before, MacCormick takes the coherence of a set of norms to be a function of its justifiability under a common set of higher-order principles, or values. Similarly, according to MacCormick, a set of factual propositions is coherent if they can be all explicable in terms of a single set of explanatory principles of a causal and motivational kind.[162]

MacCormick illustrates how this notion of narrative coherence can be used as a test for the justification of factual conclusions in the legal setting by means of the following example: the case *R v Smith*.[163] The summary of the evidence in the headnote of the report of this case reads as follows:

> The appellant was indicted for the murder of M. who had been discovered in her bath after having gone through a ceremony of marriage with him. At the trial evidence was given that subsequently to the death of M. two other women had died in their baths in similar circumstances after having gone through marriage ceremonies with the appellant. Evidence was also given of a consultation between the appellant and a solicitor concerning, *inter alia,* the effect in law of a voluntary settlement made by M., and whether the trustees could buy an annuity without M's permission.[164]

MacCormick considers two possible factual conclusions which could be argued for on the basis of this evidence: 'All the Mrs. Smiths died by sheer accident' or 'Mr. Smith willfully killed all the Mrs. Smiths in their baths'. How can we be justified in accepting one or the other as the fact of the matter? MacCormick answers this question by comparing the relative coherence of two alternative stories in which these conclusions could be embedded.

160 N MacCormick (1984: 38).
161 ibid, 37.
162 ibid, 50.
163 ibid, 49–50. See also N MacCormick (2005: 220–24). For another illustration, see N MacCormick (1980: 46–47) (which is also discussed in N MacCormick (1994: 91–92)).
164 N MacCormick (1984: 49).

On the basis of the foregoing evidence we may assert that (1) 'The first Mrs. Smith died in her bath and Mr. Smith was at home at the time'; (2) 'The second Mrs. Smith died in her bath and Mr. Smith was at home at the time'; (3) 'The third Mrs. Smith died in her bath and Mr. Smith was at home at the time'; and (4) 'Before the first Mrs. Smith died, Mr. Smith checked up on the probability of his inheriting her money'. MacCormick claims that, although sentences (1)–(4) are not contradictory with either the statement that 'All the Mrs. Smiths died by sheer accident' (5) or with 'Mr. Smith willfully killed all the Mrs. Smiths in their baths' (6), (6) coheres with (1)–(4) in a way that (5) does not. More specifically, (6) plus (1)–(4) belongs to a single scheme of explanation whereas (5) plus (1)–(4) does not. The former set of sentences, unlike the latter, can be explained in terms of a single set of general principles of causation and motivation. According to these explanatory principles:

> Accidents which occur without human intervention have to be explained in a non-intentional and non-motivational causal or probabilistic way. The probability of the conjoint occurrence of the necessary causal conditions for any person's drowning in a bath is low. Even lower is the probability of these conditions recurring three times in the case of three persons successively enjoying the same relation-ship with a given fourth party. But the probability that a human agent can intentionally bring about the realization of these necessary conditions is so high as to amount to certainty. And the probability that someone who has a strong motive to do this intentionally will do so is high.[165]

Given these explanatory principles, we can 'weakly derive' (6) from the combination of (1)–(4), something which we could not do as regards (5) unless we suppose further auxiliary hypotheses and facts. Hence, we are justified, says MacCormick, in accepting (6) because it better coheres with (1)–(4) than (5) does. [166] [167]

But, why, MacCormick asks, should the test of narrative coherence have any justificatory force in decision-making about factual issues, such as the one described above? According to MacCormick,

> such a test justifies beliefs, and thus justifies decisions about matters of past fact because (a) it is a necessary condition of the intelligibility of the phenomenal world; and because (b) rationality requires us to make the phenomenal world intelligible.[168]

Hence, like in the case of normative coherence, it is again the intimate link which, according to MacCormick, holds between coherence and rationality

[165] ibid, 50.

[166] For a critique of MacCormick's claim that coherence plays a role in the justification of conclusions about disputed questions of fact, see Gianformaggio (1990).

[167] Of course, we may take (6) as the basis for our decision only if (6) meets the relevant standard of proof. See N MacCormick (1980: 50).

[168] N MacCormick (1984: 52).

that gives narrative coherence its justificatory force. Because we esteem rationality, we seek to construct various explanatory principles to make the world intelligible for us. Intelligibility, MacCormick says, has two conditions: one is the supposition that whatever we perceive is real; another is the supposition that what is real is related under some explanatory principles to whatever else is real. From this it follows that, in the legal setting, we are justified in believing that propositions about the past are true as long as they cohere with propositions considered to be true on the basis of perception, ie propositions describing the evidence in a case. That we cannot make the world intelligible unless we take our perceptual judgements and the judgements which cohere with those to be true does not mean that they *are* true. As MacCormick says, our explanatory schemes are revisable, our perceptual information incomplete and some of our perceptions delusive. But, he points out, acknowledging that our explanations are tentative should not be equated with scepticism. This is because 'the propositions which satisfy the truth conditions set within our schemes of explanation could be true' (in the sense of correspondence with reality), even if 'we could never be sure that they are'.[169] Hence, despite the fact that MacCormick is fully aware of the fallibility of our empirical knowledge, and specifically, of the fallibility of our procedures of proof in law, he explicitly cautions us against any interpretation of his views as involving a rejection of the correspondence theory of truth or a commitment to scepticism. I shall now discuss other jurisprudential views on coherence which, unlike MacCormick's, do pose a challenge to some of the main tenets of the traditional view of truth as correspondence.

## B. Jackson's Semiotic Model of Fact-construction

Narrative accounts of fact-reasoning in law have also been advanced from a semiotic perspective.[170] Semiotic approaches to narrative coherence differ importantly from other views on narrative coherence in their intended scope of application. Unlike MacCormick's theory of narrative coherence, semiotic views claim narrative coherence to be a pivotal concept in reasoning about both facts and norms. In this section, I shall only consider the applicability of these theories to fact-reasoning in law. Specifically, I will focus on Jackson's theory of narrative coherence, as a distinguished exponent of the semiotic approach.[171]

[169] N MacCormick (1984: 52).

[170] See 'Approaches du Discours de la Preuve en Droit', *International Journal for the Semiotics of Law*, vol I (3), 1988, and vol II (4), 1989; and Nerhot (1990).

[171] Jackson has developed his theory in a number of works, the most important of which are: B Jackson ((1988a), (1988b) and (1995)).

Jackson's theory of narrative coherence is inspired by Greimasian semiotics.[172] This theory is meant to provide a model of adjudication alternative to the traditional one, which explains adjudication in terms of the normative syllogism. The main tenets of Jackson's narrative model of adjudication are as follows: (i) the major premise of the normative syllogism conceals a narrative form; (ii) the minor premise is also constructed as a narrative; and (iii) the relationship between the major and minor premise should be conceived as one of coherence or pattern matching. Thus, in this view, the operation of adjudication involves mainly a comparison between the narrative construction of the facts and the narrative model underlying the rule of law to be applied.[173] Now, let us examine the main features of Jackson's narrative model of adjudication as it bears on the narrative construction of the facts under dispute.

Jackson's narrative model of fact-construction takes Bennett and Feldman's research as a starting point. According to Bennett and Feldman, the construction of truth in the courtroom is a matter of the overall plausibility of the story told at trial, where such plausibility is being assessed by comparing the content of the story told with other stories that form the stock of social knowledge of the jury. Although Jackson endorses the general approach of Bennett and Feldman, he points out some problems of this model.[174] Two criticisms are particularly important for understanding Jackson's appraisal of this model as well as for identifying the main elements of Jackson's theory of narrative coherence. The first problem with Bennett and Feldman's work is that it unduly reduces the whole trial process to a single semantic level, neglecting the pragmatic level. Bennett and Feldman, argues Jackson, view evidence in terms of its coherence with the story that is told *in* the trial. Bias, in their view, enters into the process of decision-making when it is relevant to the *content* of the particular narrative being told. According to Jackson, Bennett and Feldman fail to appreciate that narrative analysis needs to be applied not only at the semantic level, but also at the pragmatic one. Fact-construction, Jackson claims, requires two kinds of narrativization: that of the semantics told at trial and that of the pragmatics of those stories. In other words, the trial contains two types of stories: 'the story *in* the trial' and 'the story *of* the trial'. It is not merely the content of the evidence, or that of the story told at trial, that is relevant to juror's decision-making, but the process of giving evidence, or the way in which a story is told, plays a crucial role as well. Jackson claims that jurors' judgements about the truth of the claims made at trial

[172] For a brief introduction to Greimasian semiotics and the main claims of a legal semiotics inspired by Greimas, see B Jackson ((1988a: 27–32) and (1995: 141–63)). See also B Jackson (1985) pt II.

[173] B Jackson (1988a: 58–60).

[174] ibid, ch 3, and (1995: 158–63).

are based on two distinct judgements. First, they are based—as Bennett and Feldman rightly argued—on judgements about the plausibility and coherence of the story told by the witnesses. Such plausibility, Jackson claims, is a function of the narrative typification of action already internalized by the jurors. And, secondly, these judgements of plausibility are also determined by the jurors' narrative typifications of truth-telling, ie images of who tells the truth, how, and under what circumstances.[175] It is this pragmatic dimension that Bennett and Feldman, argues Jackson, overlooked. This pragmatic dimension, which Jackson refers to as the 'narrativization of pragmatics', is a pivotal element of Jackson's model of fact-construction, and one that distinguishes it from other narrative approaches to legal proof.[176]

The second problem of Bennett and Feldman's work, claims Jackson, results from an underlying ambivalence in their theory regarding the concept of truth. Bennett and Feldman want to give an account of fact-construction in the courtroom in terms of the coherence of the narratives told and its similarities with the jury's stock of social knowledge. It is this coherence and similarity that constitutes the basis for making the judgements of plausibility. However, juries are not supposed to be merely convinced of the plausibility of a story, but also of its truth. To account for this, Bennett and Feldman propose to distinguish between 'story' and 'evidence'. The latter, Jackson says, has a dual function in Bennett and Feldman's theory: 'On the one hand, it is the basis from which plausible stories may be inferred; on the other, it has an implied reference to the outside world, since it is only on the basis of true evidence that it is justifiable to infer such stories'.[177] Under this view, the evidence

> gives rise on the one hand to an 'intentional' account of narrative coherence; on the other it depends upon an extensional view of the relationship between the meaning of the words used in evidence, and the outside world to which those words refer.[178]

Hence, according to Jackson, Bennett and Feldman's distinction between story and evidence reveals the extent to which the authors waver between 'intensional, discursive frameworks, on the one hand, and referential, truth conditional concepts on the other'.[179] Unlike Bennett and Feldman, Jackson discards all remnants of the traditional view of truth as correspondence. In place of this concept of truth, Jackson puts forward a concept of 'integrity'. The focus of this approach, Jackson claims, is 'upon trust in people, not in the relationship between what they say and some external reality'.[180]

[175] B Jackson (1995: 392).
[176] On the relevance of pragmatic considerations to assessments of coherence, see ch 9.
[177] B Jackson (1988a: 73).
[178] ibid, 73–74.
[179] ibid, 74.
[180] ibid, 193.

According to Jackson, 'integrity' focuses upon 'truth-telling' rather than truth. A commitment to integrity in truth-telling requires that we seek to construct a 'whole' truth, one which takes account of all relevant data, and that we honestly communicate the state of our own feelings and opinions, as well as the force or importance of what we intend to say.[181] An individual has 'integrity' when 'he has the ability, both in thought and in action, to evaluate theories, policies, and strategies with the highest possible degree of self-awareness and criticism'.[182] It is at this level of 'integrity' that the justification and evaluation of claims in the courtroom, Jackson claims, needs to be sought.

The narrativization of pragmatics and the rejection of the correspondence theory of truth are the two main building blocks of Jackson's narrative model of fact-construction. In this model, truth claims at trial are assessed by reference to both the plausibility of the story told (which is determined by its similarity to the jurors' narrative typification of action) and the integrity of the claimant (which is determined by its similarity to the jurors' narrative typification of truth-telling). In this model, therefore, factual claims in law are evaluated in terms of their coherence with narrative structures that operate both at the semantic and pragmatic levels.

Jackson's theory departs in significant respects from other views on the nature and role of narrative coherence in fact-reasoning in law.[183] His emphasis on pragmatics and his endorsement of a non-correspondence view of truth sharply distinguishes Jackson's theory of coherence from MacCormick's as well as from some holistic theories of evidence and inference, such as Allen's and Tillers', and bring him closer to critical approaches to evidence and proof.[184] Moreover, as is apparent, this view poses a stark challenge to the main tenets of the Rationalist Tradition of evidence scholarship.[185] Thus, Jackson's model illustrates the extent to which coherence studies in evidence and proof may be developed in directions that challenge the main epistemological assumptions of the received tradition.[186]

The jurisprudential accounts of fact-reasoning in law that I have reviewed in this section (ie MacCormick's and Jackson's) put forward a

[181] ibid, 173.

[182] ibid, 189.

[183] For Jackson's evaluation and critique of other views on narrative coherence, see ibid, 18–27.

[184] In fact, Jackson locates his project in the same family as critical legal studies and deconstruction. See B Jackson (1988a) ch 7. For some critical approaches to issues of evidence and proof, see Nicolson (1994) and Seigel (1994).

[185] As a matter of fact, Jackson explicitly presents his semiotic model as an alternative to the Rationalist model of evidence (see B. Jackson (1995: 390–91)). For an analysis of the extent to which Jackson's theory poses a challenge to the Rationalist Tradition, see JD Jackson (1990).

[186] Another coherentist approach that also calls in question the epistemological framework assumed by the received tradition is Van Roermund's; see Van Roermund ((1988), (1990) and (1997)).

view of legal justification that gives narrative coherence a pivotal role. In these views, narrative coherence is a key criterion for justifying conclusions about disputed questions of fact in law. These theories defend diverse views about what narrative coherence means in the legal context. They also importantly differ on whether a coherence-based theory of justification should be combined with a correspondence theory of truth, like MacCormick does, or whether, instead, we should abandon the conception of truth as correspondence and embrace a coherence-based account of truth and fact-construction in law, as Jackson proposes. But despite differences, both contend that fact-reasoning in law involves first and foremost the construction and comparison of alternative stories. It is a main claim of these theories that legal decision-makers are justified in accepting the most coherent story of a number of alternatives as the basis for their decisions. Thus, according to these theories, justification of factual statements in law is not a matter of compliance with the main axioms of probability calculus, but rather, a matter of narrative coherence.

The examination of coherence studies in fact-reasoning in law is now complete. Coherence, as we have seen, is a pivotal concept in some theories of evidence evaluation, in psychological theories of decision-making in the context of legal argumentation about facts, and in jurisprudential accounts of evidential reasoning. The introduction of the notion of coherence in the study of evidence and proof has given rise to a number of objections. The next section states the main lines of criticism to coherence-based theories of fact-reasoning in law.

## V. CRITIQUES TO COHERENCE THEORIES OF FACT-REASONING IN LAW

Coherence-based theories of fact-reasoning in law are open to a number of objections, the most important of which are the following:

### A. The Proto-theory Critique

Perhaps, the most common complaint about coherence theories in fact-reasoning in law is that they are seriously underdeveloped. Quotes to the effect that holistic alternatives to atomism are far from constituting a complete theory of evidence and proof that is on an equal footing to the paradigm they are meant to replace abound in the literature. Interestingly, holists or sympathizers of holism have been those who have most seriously objected to coherence proposals on the grounds that they still are too sketchy to provide a sound normative theory of evidence and proof. Tillers has argued that 'if we are to believe that holistic assessments play a part in inference, we must have a more subtle version of "holism"'.[187] Pardo has complained that 'to date we do not have an articulated theory of evidentiary holism.'[188] And Twining has concluded that holistic approaches 'have yet to be presented in the form of rounded theories'.[189] It is also widely recognized that key concepts of holistic views, such as plausibility and coherence, are poorly understood or used rather loosely. As a consequence, holistic theories do not provide a clear criterion for choosing among alternative competing explanations of the facts.[190] Thus, a coherence-based theory for fact-reasoning in law needs to rest on a solid account of coherence and of how criteria of coherence operate to pick out the best explanation of the facts under dispute at trial.

## B. The Dangers of the Case-as-a-Whole Approach

A holistic approach to evidence and proof is risky because it does not provide enough safeguards against decisions being taken on factors other than the relevant evidence at trial. Twining has most forcefully argued that, while stories have a legitimate contribution to make to rational argument,[191] they may also be used in illegitimate or dubious ways. Specifically, narratives may be used to 'sneak in' irrelevant considerations, to conceal attention from weaknesses in argument, to appeal to emotion rather than reason, to resort to hidden prejudices or stereotypes, and to subvert legal principles such as 'judge the act not the actor; consider only relevant evidence; argue from evidence; do not invent or suppress facts; keep separate questions of fact, value, law, and disposition'.[192] In a nutshell, Twining claims that narratives are undoubtedly necessary, but dangerous.[193] Taruffo has also warned us against the perils of endorsing a holistic approach to evidence evaluation. He argues that a holistic view suggests that decisions be made on the basis of 'something other, even if not well precise, than proofs'. As a consequence, holistic theories ignore problems like the definition of fact, the relevance of proof, and the burden of proof, amongst others. Taruffo concludes that it is doubtful that holistic theories are legitimate, in light of the principles which govern legal decisions.[194]

[187] Tillers (1989: 1252).
[188] Pardo (2000: 401).
[189] Twining (2006: 309).
[190] Taruffo (1992: 285).
[191] See Bex (2011), for a proposal of a hybrid theory of evidence that combines stories with argument.
[192] Twining (1999b: 80).
[193] See Twining ( (1999a), (1999b) and (2006: 319)).
[194] Taruffo (1992 : 288–89). See also Menashe and Shamash (2005). *Cf* Allen (2005).

These dangers are quite real, if we are to take seriously, as we most certainly should, Simon's empirical findings. Simon alerts us of the risks inherent in holistic processing. The coherence experiments show that sufficiently strong pieces of evidence can affect the entire mental representation of the case through indirect influences on other variables; that judgements based on past conduct, character traits and group identity will be accompanied by coherence shifts in the perception of all evidence; and that affective dimensions can have a strong impact on putatively rational decision-making. In light of these results, it could be concluded, as Simon does, that a holistic account of inference, while empirically correct, is normatively inadequate. However, there are some reasons to keep holism as a normative theory, the problems involved in coherence processing notwithstanding. For models of evidence and legal proof to regulate practice, it is critical that they be psychologically plausible. Indeed, the objective of improving legal decision-makers' performance may be frustrated if we draw too sharp a distinction between descriptive and prescriptive theories of inference. More broadly, if one endorses a naturalist framework, one cannot simply bypass the requirement that 'ought implies can' when constructing a model of juridical proof. Therefore, rather than interpreting Simon's experimental results as an indication that we should abandon holism as a normative theory, I believe that they should be viewed as posing the challenge of designing a model of proof that, while being psychologically plausible, is nevertheless respectful of the principles and standards that regulate legal proof.[195]

## C. The Coherence Bias

The characterization of the process of fact-reasoning as one of coherence-seeking poses yet another grave hazard. If legal decision-makers' task is that of deciding on the basis of the most coherent story, what prevents them from unduly disregarding contradictory evidence so as to enhance coherence? Or what impedes them to augment the force of an argument that supports an alternative explanation of the facts under dispute so as to facilitate the decision? As Tillers explained, fact-finders may use several strategies for preserving coherence. He mentions, amongst others, that they may suggest a different characterization of the evidence, or treat a fact as a report of a fact, and conclude that it is false.[196] To be sure, the trier of fact may also revise his hypothesis as he receives new information. And

[195] I will argue in ch 10 that a moderate version of holism, or, better, a contextualist version of a coherence theory of justification may provide us with a model of legal proof that is not only descriptively adequate but also normatively sound.

[196] Tillers (1986a: 923–24). For a critique of Tiller's view, see Taruffo (1992: 291) fn 206.

Tillers also includes this strategy amongst those that the fact-finder has at his disposal. But the troubling feature of coherence reasoning is that he may also manipulate the new information so as to make it cohere with his hypothesis. In a nutshell, in their effort to maximize coherence, legal decision-makers may stick to their favoured explanations of the facts under dispute and either reinterpret all incoming evidence so that it fits with their hypotheses, or blatantly disregard conflicting evidence.

Again, there is substantial psychological evidence that shows that we do pursue these kinds of strategies in order to preserve coherence. As we saw, Hastie and Pennington suggested that the causal model constructed by jurors direct the inferences that they make.[197] I have also already discussed at length the empirical research conducted by Simon et al, which convincingly shows that the process of coherence seeking has both a facilitative and a biasing effect. This finding, Simon states, is consistent with an extensive previous body of research on evidence evaluation.[198] This research shows that people tend to evaluate new evidence in a biased way: they are likely to accept at face value any piece of evidence that confirms their preconceptions, while critically scrutinizing disconfirming evidence. Further, when people are faced with new incoherent evidence, they are likely to engage in an erroneous interpretation which helps eliminate the introduced inconsistency, or discount the conflicting piece of evidence as unbelievable or unacceptable, so as to maximize the coherence of their system of beliefs. Similar results were suggested by Wagenaar, van Koppen and Crombag in their studies about police investigation and the construction of proof at trial.[199]

Hence, coherence-driven reasoning importantly facilitates the task of decision-making, but the prize of coherence may be a high one. In their effort to preserve coherence, decision-makers may engage in a number of strategies that distort the evaluation of evidence. These strategies may go from the unconscious reconstruction of the decision variables in a variety of ways so as to make them cohere with the selected hypothesis, to a straightforward rejection of conflicting evidence. Empirical research shows that such reconstruction lies at the heart of the task of decision-making. We face difficult decision tasks by imposing coherence upon the decision elements. In this sense, a drive towards coherence is an unavoidable feature of our cognitive equipment. However, the conception of the process of decision-making as one of coherence seeking harbours problematic implications. Any normative theory that advocates a coherentist approach to fact-reasoning in law needs to be fully aware of these intricacies. Specifically, it must

[197] See s III.A.
[198] See D Simon (1998: 88–89).
[199] Wagenaar, van Koppen and Crombag (1993) ch 5.

provide the necessary safeguards to ensure that the prize of coherence is not the dismissal or distortion of potentially disturbing evidence.

## D. Circularity

It is a common feature of the coherence-based theories examined in the previous sections that they posit a reciprocal relationship between the evidence of the case and the hypotheses about the case. A central tenet of coherence-based reasoning, as investigated by Simon et al, is that decisions are the product of a cognitive mechanism that operates 'bidirectionally', between premises and facts on the one hand, and conclusions, on the other.[200] Similarly, Tillers argues that neither theory nor evidence has primacy when reasoning about facts. Instead, he claims that theory and evidence are 'interdependent'.[201] In an analogous fashion, the theory of anchored narratives predicts that courts select and reject evidence based on its fit with the accepted narrative, while at the same time they hold a narrative to be true on the basis of the evidence supporting it.[202] This way of characterizing factual inferences raises an obvious concern: is not this reasoning process circular? But if so, is coherence-based inference not patently fallacious? It is a main challenge to coherence-based theories of fact-reasoning in law to show how hypotheses and evidence may mutually support each other in a way that does not involve vicious circularity.

## E. Coherence is in the Mind's Eye

A main problem for coherence-based theories of evidence and proof is to ensure that evidence plays the crucial role that it ought to play in the justification of conclusions about disputed questions of fact. Since coherence is a matter of internal relations, a story may be perfectly coherent while lacking any connection with the actual events. Hence, if we take the coherence of a story to be the basis of our decisions, we may end up accepting as justified a factual conclusion which is not responsive to the evidence that we have. Within a coherentist framework, there is no way of distinguishing—so the objection goes—a fancy story from a story which is properly anchored to the evidence we have. It seems that, according to holism, fact-finders may, and justifiably so, decide on the basis of a story which is not supported by the evidence, as long as it is the most coherent and plausible of those considered.

[200] Simon (2004: 516).
[201] Tillers (1986a: 899ff).
[202] Wagenaar, van Koppen and Crombag (1993: 211).

Some holists have explicitly argued that they do not intend their theories to have any such implications.[203] Tillers has claimed that his views about the theory-dependence of evidence do not necessarily imply 'that we receive no objective information from the world', nor do they show that inferences are 'entirely a matter of the mind's eye'.[204] And it is a main theme of the theory of anchored narratives that stories should not be accepted without being anchored to particular evidence and background generalizations.[205] The problem is how to consistently defend a holistic approach to evidence and proof while giving evidence this anchoring function. For the bidirectional nature of holistic reasoning allows evidence to be restructured on the basis of theory so as to maximize coherence. Hence, a sophisticated version of holism should put some kind of constraints on these modifications if evidence is to provide the required point of contact between coherent stories and the events in the actual world.

## F. Coherence Ties

Yet another objection against holistic approaches to evidence is that they fail to guide legal decision-makers in cases in which there is a tie between equally coherent or plausible stories. In these cases—so the objection goes—legal decision-makers need to appeal to criteria other than plausibility or coherence in order to choose amongst the various decision alternatives.[206] That there may be, for any adjudicative event, several incompatible but coherent stories just shows that the coherence of a story does not provide a sufficient reason to believe such a story to be true.[207] For, obviously enough, two contradictory stories cannot both be true. Both the objection that coherence may be the product of a fact-finder's fantasizing mind and the objection that there may be equally coherent but incompatible stories point towards what is probably the main problem with coherence-based theories of fact-reasoning in law: the problem of showing that deciding on the basis of coherence promotes, rather than hinders, accurate fact-finding in adjudication.

[203] See Twining (2006: 328) fn 116.

[204] Tillers (1986a: 893, fn 26 and 905, fn 41).

[205] See s IV.B.

[206] Gianformaggio has addressed this objection against MacCormick's theory of narrative coherence in (1990: 425 and 430). Nance does not seem to think that the objection is one that we should worry about. He writes: 'The possibility that no single story is most plausible could be handled easily enough, at least in the most probable context of such an unlikely event, a two-way tie for the most plausible. Either both theories favor the same party and the decision is easy or they split between favoring the plaintiff and favoring the defendant, in which case the familiar default rule in favor of the defendant would presumably apply'; Nance (2001: 1586) fn 107.

[207] See Damaška (1998: 291–92).

## G. Coherent Stories and True Stories

It is generally acknowledged that the pursuit of truth is a primary goal of adjudication.[208] Hence, a main criterion for determining the adequacy of any theory of fact-reasoning in law is the extent to which it helps legal decision-makers reach accurate factual determinations. Certainly, there is always the possibility that conclusions accepted as justified on the basis of any theory could be false. No theory of inference will succeed in eliminating the uncertainty inherent in legal reasoning about facts. But, we do expect that theories of legal reasoning give us some reason to believe that conclusions accepted as justified in accordance with these theories are, at least, likely to be true. A main objection against coherence-based theories of fact-reasoning is that they fail to provide such a reason. That is, we have no reason to believe—so the objection goes, that coherent stories are likely to be true. There may be stories which are coherent and plausible, but not true. And there may be stories which are true, even if they fail to satisfy the criteria of plausibility and coherence.[209]

To be sure, there is an important distinction to be made between coherent stories and true stories.[210] Conclusions which are coherent, and thus justified, according to the coherence theory, may turn out to be false. However, in this respect, a coherence theory of fact-reasoning in law is not worse off than any other theory for the justification of factual conclusions in law. For, again, the establishment of the truth of factual statements in adjudication will always fall short of certainty. The urgent question is rather: do we have any reason to believe that by choosing the most coherent story as the basis of one's legal decision, one is also choosing the story that is more likely to be true? One may answer the question in the affirmative by claiming that truth is a matter of coherence, that is, by endorsing a coherence theory of truth. To recall, according to the 'coherence theory of truth' a statement is true if it belongs to a coherent set of statements.[211] From this point of view, using coherence as a criterion for selecting amongst alternative decisions will certainly lead one to accept the alternatives which are more likely to be true. That is, endorsing a coherence theory of truth ensures that the right

[208] The claim that the pursuit of truth is a primary goal of adjudication should not be interpreted in the sense that it is the *only* goal of adjudication. In fact, it is a main tenet of the Rationalist Tradition that trial procedures are meant to serve a number of goals other than truth such as the security of the state, the protection of family relations or the curbing of coercive methods of interrogation. See Twining (2006: 76). The problem arises of what the proper weight to be attributed to fact-finding accuracy in legal proceedings is. That is, a multipurpose legal system poses the problem of determining when it is justified to sacrifice accuracy in fact-finding at the expense of realizing values other than truth. On this issue, see Summers (1999) and Damaška (1998). I shall take up this issue in ch 10.

[209] See Taruffo (1992: 286).

[210] On the distinction between 'good' stories and 'true' stories, see Twining (2002).

[211] For a detailed exposition and discussion of this theory, see ch 6.

connection obtains between coherence and truth. A version of a coherence theory of truth has been defended by some of the leading proponents of coherence-based theories in law. For instance, Jackson has explicitly rejected the traditional view of truth as correspondence. And Pardo's claim that in law, as much as in literature, truth must yield to plausibility may also be interpreted as a defence of a version of the coherence theory of truth.

The attempt to meet the objection that a coherence theory does not help us achieve the goal of establishing the truth at trial by endorsing a coherence theory of truth is highly problematic. Besides the general objections that have been addressed against the coherence theory of truth, the defence of such a theory in the context of fact-finding in law raises additional problems.[212] To start with, many procedural and evidential institutions, including most legal remedies, depend for their intelligibility in the separation of truth from justification.[213] Thus, the coherence theory of truth, insofar as it conflates justification and truth, does not seem appropriate for modelling fact-reasoning in the legal institutional setting. In addition, a basic element of our ideals of justice is that legal consequences be imposed only if it has been established, in accordance with the applicable standard of proof, that the factual statements conform to the way the events actually happened. Hence, accepting a coherence theory of truth will not only require a substantial revision of our legal institutions, but it will also demand a dramatic change in our conceptions of what constitutes a just legal system. Specifically, it will call into question the belief, which is deeply entrenched in legal practice and legal theory, that legal fact-finding seeks to determine the truth of a set of factual statements in the sense that they correspond with an independent reality.

Even if the project of showing that a coherence theory of truth were a viable alternative to the correspondence theory of truth, and further, appropriate in the legal context, still the question of how to connect up coherence with truth would remain open for many advocates of holist theories of evidence and proof. Several authors who endorse a version of holism are, nonetheless, unwilling to replace a correspondence theory of truth with a coherence view of truth. For instance, Tillers has repeatedly protested against any interpretation of his views as implying a commitment to anti-realism.[214] MacCormick has explicitly claimed that while he endorses a coherence theory for the procedures of proof, it is the correspondence theory of truth that best explains the nature of truth.[215] Similarly, Allen

[212] On the general objections against the coherence theory of truth, see ch 6. For a critique of the coherence theory of truth in law, see Taruffo (1992: 148–50); Pintore (2000); and Damaška (1998: 291–92). For a defence of a theory that aims at combining a coherence theory of truth and a correspondence theory of truth for law, see Bankowski (1990).

[213] Damaška (1998: 295).

[214] See s II.B.

[215] See s IV.A.

has succinctly stated that 'the epistemology of juridical proof is coherentist; its metaphysics is realist'.[216] Hence, it is a main challenge to these holistic theories to show that coherence standards of justification may lead us to accept conclusions about the facts under dispute which are likely to be true in a way that does not involve a definition of truth in terms of coherence.

## VI. CONCLUSIONS

This chapter has provided an introduction to several theories of evidence and proof that give an important role to coherence. These proposals are meant to be an alternative to the dominant Bayesian paradigm, which is, as argued, very problematic. Coherence theories seek to provide a more encompassing framework for assessing the rationality of legal fact-finding, which goes beyond the mere probabilistic coherence of the fact finder's beliefs about the events at trial. They also have a distinctive advantage over probability models in that they have a good claim to psychological plausibility. Nonetheless, coherence approaches to evidence and proof face a number of severe objections, and this sheds serious doubts over the convenience of shifting from a probabilistic model of legal proof to a coherentist one. Thus, the coherence theory of evidence and proof needs to be shown to have the resources necessary to successfully address these objections for it to be a solid alternative to probabilistic models of proof.

The objections directed against coherentist approaches to evidence and legal proof are, on closer inspection, versions of the traditional objections against coherence theories of justification.[217] Thus, an examination of the different replies that advocates of coherentism have given to these objections may prove useful for the purposes of devising a coherentist theory of the justification of factual conclusions in law that has the resources to address the problems which remain open in the current state of the coherence theory of evidence and proof. The main elements of the coherence-based theory of evidence and legal proof that I shall argue for are the following: (i) a notion of factual coherence as constraint satisfaction; (ii) a conception of factual inference in law as inference to the best explanation; (iii) an account of the justification of factual conclusions in law in terms of optimal coherence; and (iv) a contextualist approach to the coherence-based standards for the justification of factual propositions in law.

Already at this stage, we may note that there is an important analogy between the structure of the model for reasoning about disputed questions of fact in law that has been suggested and the structure of the model for

[216] Allen (1991: 391).

[217] An analogous conclusion was reached as regards the objections against coherence theories of reasoning about disputed questions of law. See ch 1.

reasoning about disputed questions of law that I outlined in the previous chapter. To recall, the elements of this model are: (i) a notion of normative coherence as constraint satisfaction; (ii) an explanatory approach to legal inference; (iii) a view of the justification of normative propositions in law as optimal coherence; and (iv) a contextual analysis of the coherentist justification of conclusions about disputed questions of law. Hence, the coherentist view about fact-reasoning in law, I would argue, may be shown to have important parallels with a coherentist account of legal reasoning about normative questions. A further objective—which I will try to accomplish in the last chapter—is to integrate both the coherentist model of fact-reasoning in law and the model of normative reasoning in law into a unified coherence-based model of legal reasoning.

In order to develop such an integrated coherentist model, I shall examine the role that coherence plays in justification in contexts other than law. Let me advance that the unitary coherence-based model of legal reasoning that I shall attempt to develop has the following prominent features: (i) it is a non-foundationalist model, in that it takes the justification of any proposition in law to be a matter of its relations with the rest of propositions; (ii) it is naturalist, that is, it is based on the assumption that psychological facts about how legal decision-makers reason are relevant for answering normative questions about how they should reason; (iii) it is contextualist, for it takes the standards of legal justification to be context-dependent; (iv) it posits a responsibilist model of justification according to which the epistemic behaviour of legal decision-makers has a bearing on the justificatory status of their decisions; (v) it embodies an explanatory approach to legal inference; and (vi) it is grounded on a non-instrumentalist view of legal reasoning.

As is apparent, a thorough development of coherence theories in law along the foregoing lines leads us to question the validity of some of the basic assumptions of current theories of reasoning. Hence, coherence studies make us rethink the received tradition on legal reasoning in some important respects. More specifically, as I argued in the previous chapter, coherentism about normative reasoning poses a challenge to the legal positivist paradigm; and, as has been shown, coherentism about evidential reasoning poses a challenge to the probabilistic framework. With the objective of developing such a coherence-based model of legal reasoning, and with, indeed, the more ambitious objective of rethinking some of the assumptions about reasoning and rationality accepted by the standard view on legal reasoning about both facts and norms, let us now undertake the task of examining the diverse theories of coherence that have been proposed in a variety of disciplines. I shall start by analysing coherence studies in epistemology, where coherence theories of justification were first proposed.

# Part II

# Interdisciplinary Perspectives

# 3

# *Coherence, Knowledge and Justification*

THIS CHAPTER DISCUSSES the role of coherence in current work on epistemology.[1] More specifically, I shall investigate the role that coherence plays in epistemic justification. A main issue that has occupied much of the contemporary debate over the notion of epistemic justification is that of identifying what the best description of its structure is. The traditional account of the structure of justification is foundationalism. This view has been severely attacked for a number of reasons. It is the failure of foundationalism that has mainly motivated the proposal of coherence theories of justification. The first section of this chapter focuses on the foundationalist-coherentist debate; it briefly examines the main tenets and problems of foundationalism, presents the coherentist alternative and considers the main objections that have been addressed against coherence theories of justification. The following two sections examine BonJour's and Lehrer's theories of coherence, as representatives of the current state of the coherence theory. The next section contrasts BonJour's and Lehrer's models of coherence and evaluates the extent to which they advance the case for coherentism in epistemology. I shall conclude this chapter by introducing an account of the structure of epistemic justification alternative to both foundationalism and coherentism, to wit, contextualism. Some versions of contextualism give coherence a prominent role in epistemic justification. It is a contextualist approach to coherentist justification, I shall argue, that is the most promising account of epistemic justification.

## I. COHERENCE, FOUNDATIONS AND THE STRUCTURE OF EPISTEMIC JUSTIFICATION

One of the main tasks of epistemology is that of providing an account of the overall justificatory structure of an individual's system of justified beliefs.

[1] I will deal here with coherence theories developed within traditional analytic epistemology. Coherentist approaches in formal epistemology will be discussed in ch 5 (coherence theories of belief revision) and ch 6 (probabilistic approaches to coherence).

There are two main views about the structure of epistemic justification: foundationalism and coherentism.[2]

## A. Foundationalism and its Problems

Foundationalism is the view that the structure of our system of justified beliefs is divided into a 'foundation' and a 'superstructure', so that beliefs in the latter depend on the former for their justification but not vice versa.[3] Foundationalists distinguish between two kinds of justification: mediate (or indirect) justification and immediate (or indirect) justification.[4] A belief is mediately justified if it is justified by some appropriate relation to other justified beliefs, ie by being inferred from other justified beliefs that provide adequate support for it, or by being based on adequate reasons. For instance, if my reason for supposing that a witness is lying is that he is sweating, he looks pale, he seems to be nervous and he speaks in an unusually hesitant tone, then my belief that the witness is lying is justified by being adequately supported by my justified beliefs that he is sweating, he looks pale, he seems to be nervous and he speaks in an unusually hesitant tone. A belief is immediately justified if its justification is of a sort other than the relations that such a belief has to some other justified beliefs, ie if it is justified by being based on experience, or it is self-justified. For example, my belief that the witness looks pale may not be based on anything else that I am justified in believing, but just on the way he looks to me. Candidates for basic beliefs, ie immediately justified beliefs, include some perceptual beliefs[5] (eg the belief that there is a red book on the desk), beliefs about our own sensations (eg the belief that I am in pain) and beliefs about own sensory experiences[6] (eg the belief that it appears as though there is a red book on the desk).

A common metaphor for the foundationalist picture of the structure of justification is that of a pyramid, where immediately justified beliefs serve as the foundation that supports the body of mediately justified beliefs.[7] Turning the pyramid metaphor on its head, we may represent the foundationalist structure of justified belief as a multiple branching tree structure

[2] Hybrid theories, which result from combining both foundationalism and coherentism, have also been defended. See Haack ((1993) and (1997)). For a brief statement of Haack's foundherentism, see Haack (2000: 283–93). For an evaluation of Haack's hybrid alternative, see BonJour (1997); Tramel (2008); and Thagard (2000a: 41–48). See also Goldberg (2012) (for a defence of a version of reliabilism that combines foundationalist and coherentist elements).

[3] See Alston (1998: 144).

[4] This terminology is Alston's; see Alston (1989: 58–59).

[5] Quinton (1973).

[6] Lewis (1946).

[7] See Sosa (1980: 5).

at the tip of each branch of which is an immediately justified belief.[8] Thus, the central tenet of foundationalism is that there are some basic beliefs that possess a degree of non-inferential justification in virtue of which they constitute the ultimate foundation of our knowledge. We may divide the core of the foundationalist view into two claims: (i) there are immediately justified beliefs, that is, there are foundations; and (ii) a person has a set of basic beliefs that suffices to generate chains of justification that terminate in whatever justified beliefs he has, that is, the foundations suffice to hold up the building of justified belief.

There are different versions of foundationalism depending on (i) the degree of non-inferential justification that basic beliefs are held to possess; and (ii) the ways in which justification is transmitted from basic to non-basic beliefs. A main distinction is drawn between 'strong' (or 'classical') foundationalism and 'weak' ('moderate' or 'modest') foundationalism.[9] Historical forms of foundationalism are typically strong. They require that the foundations be 'infallible', 'indubitable', 'certain' or 'incorrigible'[10] and that the superstructure be deductively inferred from the foundations. In contrast, contemporary versions are of a weak kind in that they only require that basic beliefs be 'initially credible' or 'prima-facie justified' and allow non-basic beliefs to be justified by appeal to basic beliefs on the grounds of inferential relations other than deduction.[11]

Foundationalism is an epistemological view that has a long history. It has been the classical view in epistemology and, still today, it continues to attract many contemporary philosophers.[12] What drives philosophers towards accepting a foundationalist view? The main argument for foundationalism is the regress argument. Foundationalism, it is held, is the only plausible solution to the so-called 'regress problem'. The problem is as follows. The most obvious way to show that a belief that *p* is justified is by pointing out that *p* is inferable in some acceptable way from the belief that *q*. However, for *p* to be genuinely justified by virtue of such a justificatory argument, it must be shown that the belief that *q* is already justified. Here again, the way to show this is by appealing to inferential justification: the belief that *q* may be justified in virtue of being inferable from some further belief.

[8] See Alston (1976: 166).

[9] On the contrast between weak and strong varieties of foundationalism, see BonJour (1985: 26–30).

[10] For the distinction between infallibility, indubitability etc, see Alston (1971).

[11] But see DePaul (2001), for a contemporary defence of foundationalist positions that resurrects important tenets of classical foundationalism.

[12] Descartes' *Meditations* is the classical formulation of the foundationalist view. Traditional forms of foundationalism are defended in Russell (1912); Ayer (1955); and Lewis (1946). In contemporary epistemology, Chisholm (1982) and Moser (1985) are prominent defences of foundationalism. For an introduction to different versions of foundationalism (both classical and contemporary), see Dancy (1985a) chs 4 and 5 and Pollock (1986) ch 2. For a survey of work in foundationalism in the last decades, see Triplett (1990).

But then, the very same question may be raised about the justification of this latter belief, and so on, indefinitely. Thus, our knowledge seems to be threatened with an infinite regress of justification.[13] In order to avoid this regress, there seem to be only three alternatives:[14] (i) the regress may terminate in beliefs which are offered as justifying premises for earlier beliefs but for which there is no justification available; (ii) the justificatory chain may circle back upon itself, so that eventually beliefs which have appeared as premises earlier in the sequence of justificatory arguments and which were conditionally justified are again appealed to as justifying premises; and (iii) the regress might terminate because basic beliefs are reached, beliefs that have a degree of epistemic justification that is not dependent on other beliefs and thus raise no further issue of justification. The foundationalist opts for the last alternative. The 'regress argument' for foundationalism is that since option (i) leads to scepticism, and (ii) is viciously circular, (iii) provides the only plausible solution to the regress problem. Foundationalism allows us to avoid the threat of infinite regress—it is argued—by providing us with a secure foundation for our knowledge.

At first sight, foundationalism seems to offer quite an intuitive view of the structure of justification as well as an elegant solution to the regress problem. However, there are serious problems with the foundationalist picture.[15] The two main claims of foundationalism—to recall, (i) there are basic beliefs and (ii) basic beliefs suffice to confer justification to all non-basic beliefs—are subjected to severe criticism. Hence, the most important problems of foundationalism fall into two main groups: the first pertaining to the nature and justification of basic beliefs and the second pertaining to the relation between basic beliefs and beliefs the justification of which is conferred by basic beliefs.[16]

[13] The *locus classicus* of this argument is Aristotle's *Posterior Analytics*, bk II. However, Williams argues that though Aristotle brings in regress considerations, it is far from clear that he sees himself as raising and responding to sceptical issues at all. Williams prefers to think of the 'regress argument' as the 'Agrippan problem', after Agrippa, the ancient sceptic who, in his view, seems first to have given a clear articulation of the regress problem. See M Williams ((2001) ch 5 and (1999) afterword). For a clear statement of the regress problem, see BonJour (1999a: 118–19); Audi (1998: 187–88); and Alston (1976: 171–73). For a discussion of the regress argument, see Armstrong (1973) ch 11; M Williams (1999) ch 3; and BonJour (1985: 17–26).

[14] Instead, one may call into question that we need to avoid infinite regress at all. Sosa has argued that there are no compelling reasons for rejecting the infinite regress as vicious. Hence, an infinite regress of justification cannot be dismissed out of hand. See Sosa (1980: 9–13). For other discussions of the possibility of justification by infinite regress, see Harker (1984); Clark (1988); Klein (2005); and Ginet (2005).

[15] For critiques of foundationalism, see, among others, BonJour (1985) chs 2, 3 and 4; Lehrer (2000a) chs 3 and 4; and M Williams (1999).

[16] Yet another problem of foundationalism that I shall not deal with here is the problem of dogmatism. According to the argument from dogmatism, foundationalism is dogmatic insofar as it is committed to holding beliefs in the absence of any reasons for regarding them as acceptable. The charge of dogmatism has been brought up by Aune (1967: 41–43). For replies to this objection, see Alston (1976: 182–85) and Audi (1988) s V.

The first group of problems concerns the possibility that some beliefs be immediately justified. Following Williams we may refer to this problem as 'the problem of the basis' or the 'problem of security'.[17] Where do putative basic beliefs get their justification from? The most prominent general argument against immediate justification is a 'level ascent argument'.[18] According to this argument, when we consider any putative immediately justified belief, we find that such a belief really depends for its justification on some higher-level reasons that have to do with its epistemic status. More specifically, the argument shows that a putatively basic belief can only be justified if the subject is justified in supposing that the putative belief enjoys whatever properties make the belief basic. Hence, since the justification of the putative belief depends on the justification of a higher-level belief, the justification is not immediate after all.[19]

A second group of problems concerns the justificatory relation between basic beliefs and non-basic beliefs. Following again Williams' terminology, we may refer to this problem as the 'problem of the superstructure' or the 'problem of adequacy'.[20] The seriousness of this problem depends on just how much is included in the set of basic beliefs. A version of foundationalism according to which at least some beliefs about physical objects count as basic will have less difficulty in giving an account of the justification of non-basic beliefs than a more traditional version of foundationalism, which restricts the set of basic beliefs to beliefs about subjective states of experience, will.[21] The problem, though, is that beliefs about subjective states of experience are better candidates for basic beliefs than perceptual beliefs. For, even in the most modest versions of foundationalism, perceptual beliefs fall short of what is required for a belief to count as basic. Because of that, most current versions of foundationalism identify basic beliefs with beliefs about subjective states of experiences. Thus, foundationalists seem to face

[17] M Williams (2001: 85).

[18] Another argument against immediate justification that has been advanced in the literature goes as follows. It is argued that a belief can be immediately justified only if it does not depend on other beliefs, that is, only if it could be held without the subject holding any other belief. If this were so, then this would be a serious objection to the feasibility of foundationalism, for there are powerful reasons for denying the possibility that beliefs may be isolated to such an extent. For a discussion of this objection, see Alston (1989: 62–64) and Firth (1973: 546).

[19] Alston provides this argument against the possibility of immediate justification and calls it 'the second-level argument' in Alston (1976: 170). He refers to it as the 'level ascent argument' in Alston (1989:64). Sosa calls this argument the 'Doxastic Ascent' argument in Sosa (1980: 16). We owe to BonJour the most detailed statement of this argument; see BonJour ((1978: 5–6) and (1985: 30–33)). For an earlier, and very influential, version of the level ascent argument, see Sellars (1956: 168). For a critique of both BonJour's and Sellar's versions of the level ascent argument, see Alston (1989; 57–81). For another criticism to BonJour's anti-foundationalist argument, see Sosa (1980: 16–18); Steup (1989a: 178–81); AI Goldman (1989: 109); and Grundmann (1999).

[20] M Williams (2001: 85).

[21] *Cf* BonJour (1999a: 120–21).

the following dilemma. Our basic beliefs must have sufficient content to support the superstructure, but no belief with such content is likely to have the properties that distinguish basic beliefs from non-basic beliefs. If one includes perceptual beliefs within the set of basic beliefs, then one has less difficulty in showing non-basic beliefs to be justified, but then one has more difficulty in showing that the purported basic beliefs enjoy the properties that single out some beliefs as basic. If one, more plausibly, restricts the set of basic beliefs to beliefs about subjective experiences, then one has less trouble in showing that these beliefs have whatever is necessary to immediately justify a belief, but one has very serious trouble in showing that they suffice to confer justification to all mediately justified beliefs.

To sum up, the foundationalist is in a severe predicament. There are deep problems with the claim that some beliefs may be immediately justified, as well as with the claim that non-basic beliefs may ultimately depend on immediately justified beliefs. Moreover, it seems that a solution to the problem concerning the nature and justification of basic beliefs makes it even less likely that we reach a solution to the problem concerning the justification of non-basic beliefs.[22] The severe problems that foundationalism faces have motivated the proposal of coherence theories, as an alternative account of the structure of empirical justification.

## B. The Coherentist Alternative

Coherence theories of justification deny that there is an epistemically privileged class of beliefs, which provide a foundation for the structure of justified belief. Coherentists thus reject the foundationalist metaphor of the pyramid in favour of Neurath's metaphor according to which 'we are like sailors who must rebuild their ship upon the open sea'.[23] Sosa explicates this metaphor as follows:

> our body of knowledge is a raft that floats free of any anchor or tie. Repairs must be made afloat, and though no part is untouchable, we must stand on some in order to replace or repair others. Not every part can go at once.[24]

Hence, according to the coherentist, we cannot start anew the process of building the edifice of knowledge, as the foundationalist view seems to

[22] This point is stressed by M Williams (2001: 85). Admittedly, the problem concerning the justification of basic beliefs will not be encountered by reliabilist versions of foundationalism, such as that proposed in AI Goldman (2000). That is, in light of the problems of foundationalism, one might, as externalist theories have done, reject the internalist commitments of traditional foundationalism. There are, however, as will be argued below, several reasons why an externalist approach to justification (and knowledge) is unappealing.

[23] Neurath (1959). Cited in Pollock (1986: 4).

[24] Sosa (1980: 6).

advocate. Instead, we must start with the beliefs that we have, and 'repair' them from within as best as we can. As the metaphor vividly pictures it, justification—coherentists hold—cannot be built from a privileged set of beliefs, but it is a matter of our body of beliefs hanging together in a coherent fashion.[25] According to coherentism, all our beliefs are justified in virtue of their relations with other beliefs, specifically, in virtue of belonging to a coherent system of beliefs.[26] The main historical proponents of the coherence theory of justification include positivists—Neurath and Hempel—as well as idealists—Bradley, Bosanquet and Blanshard.[27] Aune, Sellars, Harman, Lehrer, Rescher, BonJour and Dancy are amongst the most influential defenders of coherentism in contemporary epistemology.[28]

Coherence theories are mainly motivated by failure of foundationalism.[29] However, these theories also have a number of serious problems. The following objections are traditionally raised against coherence theories:[30]

(i) *Vagueness.* A main problem for coherence theories is that of developing a plausible conception of coherence. Intuitively, coherence is a matter of how well a set of beliefs hangs together, but a more concrete account of this notion needs to be offered. It is claimed that without a more precise concept of coherence, these theories cannot even be considered as a serious alternative to foundationalism.[31]

(ii) *Circularity.* Another standard objection against coherence theories is that they are viciously circular, licensing an inference of *p* from *q*, and then of *q* from *p*.

(iii) *Conservatism.* The coherentists' claim that for a belief to be justified it must cohere with one's system of beliefs, or their emphasis on minimizing change in our antecedent views, has led some to charge

[25] Other common metaphors in the coherentist literature include: the net, the jigsaw, the crossword, the spiral and the chain novel. For a discussion of these metaphors and their potential to illuminate the concept of coherence, see Pérez-Bermejo (2013).

[26] The core thesis of coherentism admits of different versions. For a discussion of different kinds of coherentism, see Pollock (1986: 71–77); Haack (2000); and Firth (1973).

[27] See Neurath (1959); Hempel (1934–35); Bradley (1914); Bosanquet (1920); and Blanshard (1939). A survey of these theories can be found in BonJour (1985) app B. *Cf* Stern (2004) (arguing that early proponents of coherentism were not advancing coherentism as a theory of justification but rather as a test for truth).

[28] Aune (1967); Harman (1973) and (1986); Sellars (1963); Lehrer (1974); Rescher (1973) and (1979); BonJour ((1976) and (1985)); and Dancy ((1984) and (1985a)).

[29] In addition, a positive motivation results from cases where beliefs seem to be justified by their coherence. For a discussion of these cases, see Shogenji (2001).

[30] Other objections include: (i) the problem of basing; (ii) the problem of feasibility; (iii) the problem of justified inconsistent beliefs; (iv) the regress problem; and (v) the problem of necessary falsehoods. I shall deal with the feasibility objection and the regress problem below in this chapter. On the 'problem of basing' for coherentism, see Pollock (1986: 81–83). For a reply to this objection, see Kvanvig (1997). On the (related) problems of 'justified inconsistent beliefs' and 'necessary falsehoods', see Roche (2011); Kvanvig (2012); and Lycan (2012).

[31] See Fumerton (1999: 247–50) and Olsson (2005: 13).

coherentism with a built-in tendency to favour received views. For example, coherence theories, so the objection goes, encourage us to disregard observational beliefs which incohere with accepted bodies of scientific beliefs. Such conservatism, it is argued, is a roadblock to inquiry and must be removed.[32]

(iv) *The isolation objection.* It is argued that since coherence is exclusively a matter of internal relations within a system of beliefs, it cannot allow for any input from the external reality and, therefore, it cuts off justification from reality. For example, a coherent system of beliefs that were the product of a visionary mad man or literary fiction would be, according to this theory, justified.[33]

(v) *The alternative coherent systems objection.* It seems possible to invent indefinitely many different and incompatible systems of belief that are equally coherent. Thus, each of these systems would be equally justified, so that only a purely arbitrary choice between such systems can be made.[34]

(vi) *The problem of truth.* It is argued that only by identifying truth with coherence, can coherentist standards of justification be shown to be truth-conducive. Thus, the price of endorsing a coherentist theory of justification is embracing a coherentist theory of truth. To recall, according to the coherence theory of truth, the nature of truth is constituted by a relation of coherence between the belief being assessed and other beliefs.[35] Since such anti-realist views of truth are highly implausible, coherence theories of justification cannot be considered a viable alternative.

Several attempts have been made to show how a theory of coherence can be developed so as to meet these objections. Here, I will focus on the work of two leading proponents of coherentism in contemporary epistemology: Laurence BonJour and Keith Lehrer, whose theories will be discussed in the next two sections.

[32] For a statement and reply to this objection, see M Williams (1980: 249).

[33] For a presentation of the isolation objection, see Pollock (1974: 27–28). Pollock replies to this very same objection in Pollock (1986: 76–77).

[34] For a discussion of these objections, see Tersman (1992). It is important to notice that not everyone sees this line of thought as an objection. The so-called 'alternate coherent systems of objection' (or 'many systems objection') can also be interpreted as an argument for relativism. Hence, coherence theorists who are committed to relativist views are not troubled by this objection. See M Williams (2001: 118).

[35] For a brief discussion of this theory in the legal context, see chs 1 and 2. I examine in detail the problem of coherence and truth in ch 6.

## II. BONJOUR'S EPISTEMIC COHERENTISM

Laurence BonJour's *The Structure of Empirical Knowledge* is one of the most influential defences of the coherence theory of epistemic justification.[36] I will organize the presentation of BonJour's views as follows. First, I will give an account of the elements that, according to BonJour, are essential to a viable coherence theory. Then, I will examine BonJour's response to the traditional objections that have been raised against coherentism. I shall conclude this section by pointing out some of the problems that this theory of coherence faces.

### A. Elements of BonJour's Coherence Theory

BonJour proposes a theory of coherence that consists of the following elements: (i) the idea of non-linear justification; (ii) the concept of coherence; (iii) the doxastic presumption; and (iv) a coherentist conception of observation.

#### *i. The Idea of Non-Linear Justification*

According to BonJour, the tacit assumption that underlies the epistemic regress problem is that justification is linear in the sense that it involves a sequence of beliefs ordered by epistemic priority, along which epistemic justification is transferred. If this is a correct account of the structure of justification, then, coherentism is not even a possibility worth considering. A linear view of justification would imply that any coherence theory is viciously circular. That coherence theories lead to vicious circularity is, as we have seen, a main objection against these theories. Thus, the first step towards developing a plausible coherence theory of knowledge is to challenge the linear conception of justification that gives rise to the objection in the first place. BonJour claims that justification is holistic, or systematic, in character, despite its linear appearance. He distinguishes two levels at which issues of empirical justification can be raised: the local level of justification and the global level of justification.

The local level of justification refers to the justification of a single belief or small set of beliefs, within the context of a cognitive system whose overall justification is taken for granted. The global level of justification refers to the overall justification of the entire system of beliefs. In practice, only issues of the local sort are explicitly raised. It is at this level that inferential justification *appears* lineal. However, BonJour argues that such linearity

[36] BonJour ((1976), (1978) and (1985)). Later, BonJour came to reject coherentism; now, he advocates a version of foundationalism, see BonJour ((1999a: 117–42), (1999b) and (2001)).

is illusory. A fully explicit justification of a particular belief would make it patent that the relation between beliefs is not one of linear dependence, but rather one of mutual or reciprocal support.[37] BonJour claims that the following four steps are involved in the justification of a particular belief:[38]

1. the inferability of that particular belief from other beliefs and further relations among particular beliefs;
2. the coherence of the overall system of beliefs;
3. the justification of the overall system of beliefs; and
4. the justification of the particular belief in question by virtue of its membership in the system.

Thus, the justification of a belief is derived from the justification of the whole system of beliefs to which it belongs. It is neglecting steps (2) and (3) that lends plausibility to the linear conception of justification, and thus generates the regress problem. Hence, by replacing a holistic view of justification by a linear one, BonJour claims to make coherentism a plausible solution to the epistemic regress problem.[39]

### *ii. The Concept of Coherence*

BonJour sets up the following list of conditions for coherence:[40]

1. A system of beliefs is coherent only if it is logically consistent.
2. A system of beliefs is coherent in proportion to its degree of probabilistic consistency.
3. The coherence of a system of beliefs is increased by the presence of inferential connections between its component beliefs and increased in proportion to the number and strength of such connections.
4. The coherence of a system of beliefs is diminished to the extent to which it is divided into subsystems of beliefs that are relatively unconnected to each other by inferential connections.
5. The coherence of a system of beliefs is decreased in proportion to the presence of unexplained anomalies in the believed content of the system.

The first two conditions refer to the controversial relation between consistency and coherence. BonJour distinguishes two kinds of consistency: logical and probabilistic. He understands 'logical consistency' as the absence of explicit contradiction and 'probabilistic inconsistency' as the relation between a

[37] BonJour's distinction between local and global is quite different from the contextualists' take on this issue. See M Williams (1996: 287–291). On contextualism, see s V below.

[38] BonJour (1985: 92).

[39] For an argument to the effect that coherentists need not replace a linear view of inference by a non-linear (ie holistic) one in order to successfully respond to the regress problem; see Day (1989).

[40] BonJour (1985: 93–100).

belief that $p$ and the belief that it is extremely improbable that $p$. According to condition (1), logical probability is a necessary, although not a sufficient, condition of coherence.[41] Condition (2) states that the coherence of a system of beliefs is proportional to its degree of probabilistic consistency. Such degree depends on how many conflicts of this probabilistic sort the system contains and the degree of probability involved in each case. These two requirements are not enough for coherence. As BonJour says, one could imagine a set of beliefs, each member of which is entirely irrelevant to each other; though the set is both logically and probabilistically consistent by ruling out any possibility of conflict, it will also fail to hang together in any significant way. Thus, BonJour concludes, along with the coherentist tradition, that coherence must involve some sort of positive connection among beliefs.

The fact that coherence has to do with the positive relations that link beliefs within a system is captured in condition (3). According to BonJour, coherence is a matter of mutual inferability of beliefs. The relevant inferential relations are 'any sort of relation of content which would allow one belief or set of beliefs, if justified, to serve as the premise(s) of a cogent epistemic-justificatory argument for a further belief'.[42] BonJour endorses the standard view according to which the distinguishing characteristic of epistemic justification is its essential relation to the cognitive goal of truth. Consequently, he holds that any sort of relation that is, to some degree, truth-preserving serves as an appropriate positive connection. In addition to this requirement, BonJour claims that inferential relations must be reciprocal. Allowing for one-way relations

> creates the possibility that a system of beliefs could count as coherent to as high a degree as one likes by being composed by several subsystems, each internally connected by strong inferential relations but none having a significant connection with the others.[43]

The relevance of positive connections between subsystems of beliefs for assessments of coherence leads to the addition of condition (4).

As noted, in BonJour's view, any kind of inferential relation, as long as it is truth-conducive and reciprocal, contributes to the coherence of a system of beliefs. Unlike certain proponents of coherentist theories, he does not reduce the kind of inferential relations that determine coherence to explanatory relations.[44] However, BonJour considers these relations to be a central

[41] As will be explained below, BonJour later changed his mind about the relation between coherence and consistency.

[42] BonJour (1985: 96).

[43] BonJour (1985: 97).

[44] According to the theories of explanatory coherence, the coherence of a set of beliefs depends entirely on explanatory connections. I will examine these proposals in the next chapter.

ingredient of coherence. In his view, explanatory connections are not just one more kind of inferential connections, but relations of a particularly pervasive kind. He accounts for this fact by adding condition (5) to the list of conditions of coherence. The significant way in which the coherence of a system is enhanced by the presence of explanatory relations is accounted for by introducing the notion of 'anomaly' into the account of coherence. BonJour defines 'anomaly' as follows:

> For my purposes, an anomaly is a fact or event, specially one involving some sort of recurring pattern, which is claimed to obtain by one or more of the beliefs in the system, but which is incapable of being explained (or would have been incapable of being predicted) by appeal to other beliefs in the system.[45]

According to BonJour, the presence of anomalies detracts from the coherence of the system in a way that cannot be accounted for in terms of having fewer inferential connections. The distinctive significance of anomalies lies in the fact that they undermine the claim that basic explanatory principles unify the system of beliefs, and thus, pose a more serious threat to its overall coherence.

### *iii. The Doxastic Presumption*

BonJour's coherentism is committed to internalism, ie the view that all the factors needed for a belief to be epistemically justified should be 'internally available' (or 'cognitively accessible') to the believer, ie knowable on the basis of introspection and reflection. In contrast to internalism, externalist theories of justification claim that justifying factors need not be so available, but that they can be external to the believer's cognitive perspective. In this view, a belief is justified if the appropriate relation obtains between such a belief and an appropriate set of facts, regardless of the believer's conception of the situation.[46] The most prominent externalist views are versions of reliabilism, ie the view that a belief is justified if it is produced in a way or via a process that makes it objectively likely that the belief is true.[47]

An externalist version of coherentism would hold that the person whose belief is justified need himself have no cognitive access to the facts upon which justification depends, ie to the fact of coherence, but his belief would be justified if it in fact coheres with his system of beliefs.[48] BonJour

[45] BonJour (1985: 99).

[46] For an introduction to the internalist/externalist distinction, see BonJour (1998b). On the externalist/internalist controversy, see Steup (1999a); Fumerton (1988); Kim (1993); Kornblith (2001); Greco (2005); and Feldman (2005). For a very interesting discussion of the internalism/externalism debate and its relation to the ethics of belief, see Pryor (2001: 103ff).

[47] For a defence of externalist theories of knowledge and justification, see Armstrong (1973); AI Goldman ((1976), (1979) and (1986)) chs 4 and 5; and Nozick (1981) ch 3.

[48] Kornblith takes Harman to provide an example of externalist coherentism. See Kornblith (1989: 210–11).

considers this view implausible, given the formidable problems that beset externalism about justification, and argues instead for an internalist version of coherentism, which requires that the fact that a belief coheres with the believer's system of beliefs be cognitively accessible to the believer, so that it can give *him* a reason for accepting the belief.[49] Now, if the believer is to have cognitive access to the facts of coherence, he must also have a grasp of his own system of beliefs, relative to which assessments of coherence must be made. But, what does this grasp consists of? According to BonJour, it cannot be but a set of metabeliefs to the effect that one has such specific beliefs. But then the problem arises: how are these metabeliefs justified? If a return to foundationalism is precluded, the answer apparently must be that they are also justified in virtue of their coherence with the rest of the system of beliefs. However, as BonJour says, such a solution is viciously circular. BonJour responds to this problem by introducing a third element into his theory of coherence, to wit, the 'doxastic presumption'.

According to the doxastic presumption, one's reflective grasp of one's system of beliefs is approximately correct, that is, one 'approximately' holds the system of beliefs which one believes oneself to hold.[50] BonJour describes this presumption as follows:

> It [the doxastic presumption] is (...) a characterization of something which is, from the standpoint of a coherence theory, a basic and unavoidable feature of our cognitive practice. Epistemic reflection, according to such a theory, *begins* from a (perhaps tacit) representation of myself as having (approximately) such and such specific system of beliefs: only relative to such a representation can questions of justification be meaningfully raised and answered.[51]

Thus, the doxastic presumption is, according to BonJour, unavoidable, if the process of justification, understood along internalist coherentist lines, is even to get started.

### *iv. Coherence and Observation*

According to BonJour, it is extremely important, for coherentism to be a plausible theory of justification, that a coherentist account of observation be provided. Only on the basis of such an account, argues BonJour, can coherentism successfully meet the traditional objections. The basic claim of BonJour's coherentist account of observation is that 'my observational beliefs are epistemically justified or warranted only in virtue of background empirical knowledge which tells me that cognitively spontaneous beliefs

[49] For a discussion of the main problems confronting externalism, see BonJour (1980) and (1985) ch 3; Lehrer and Cohen (1983); Pollock (1984); and S Cohen (1984).

[50] BonJour (1985: 128).

[51] ibid, 104.

of that specific sort are epistemically reliable ... under the conditions then satisfied'.[52] Two concepts are in need of clarification: cognitive spontaneity and reliability. A belief is 'cognitively spontaneous' when it simply occurs to the observer, strikes her, in a manner which is both involuntary and quite coercive, that is, when it is not the result of a discursive process of reasoning (either explicit or tacit). For example, the belief that there is a red book on the desk is such kind of belief. It is cognitive spontaneity that marks a belief as putatively observational. Cognitively spontaneous beliefs are reliable if they are very likely to be true when they occur.[53]

BonJour's argument for the justification of observational knowledge goes as follows:

(1) I have a cognitively spontaneous belief that P which is of kind K.
(2) Conditions C obtain.
(3) Cognitively spontaneous beliefs of kind K in conditions C are very likely to be true.

Therefore, my belief that P is very likely to be true.
Therefore, (probably) P.[54]

BonJour offers a detailed account of how these premises may be justified while still remaining within a coherentist framework. In this account, both introspection and the doxastic presumption play a major role in the justification of observational knowledge.[55] First, introspection is needed for the justification of claims of cognitive spontaneity, of some claims involved in specifying the conditions of observation, as well as for the justification of some aspects of the claim that an observational belief is a belief of the appropriate kind. Secondly, BonJour argues that, on the basis of the doxastic presumption, the believer is able to identify certain beliefs as cognitively spontaneous, and to determine that certain kinds of those beliefs, under certain conditions, are reliable, as judged from within the believer's system and thus, likely to be true. It is agreement among the various observational beliefs that determines their internal reliability and, ultimately, their being likely to be true. It is also primarily with these observational beliefs that other beliefs must cohere in order to be justified. So much for the elements

[52] ibid, 122.

[53] BonJour distinguishes reliability from 'converse reliability', which attaches to beliefs that are very likely to occur in situations in which they would be true (1985: 121). These two senses of reliability allow for a distinction between two kinds of observational knowledge: positive and negative knowledge, respectively. My discussion of BonJour's justification of observational knowledge focuses—as BonJour does—on positive knowledge, but an analogous justification may be provided for negative knowledge.

[54] BonJour (1985: 123).

[55] BonJour provides an account of how introspective knowledge may also be justified within a coherence theory that follows, in the main, the arguments presented for the justification of observational knowledge in BonJour (1985: 132–38).

of BonJour's coherentism. I turn now to examine BonJour's replies to the traditional objections against coherentism.

## B. BonJour on Coherence and the Truth-Connection

BonJour examines in detail the extent to which his theory is able to meet some of the standard objections to coherentism. Some of these objections, to wit, the isolation objection, the alternative coherent systems objection and the truth objection raise, in different ways, the problem of how coherence and truth relate to each other. In what follows I will review BonJour's response to these traditional objections, more specifically, his views on coherence and truth.

### *i. The Isolation Objection*

BonJour's reply to the isolation objection (which, to recall, alleges that coherentist justification involves no input from the extra theoretic world) consists in the introduction of what he calls the 'Observation Requirement'. This requirement states that a cognitive system must contain laws attributing a high degree of reliability to a reasonable variety of cognitively spontaneous beliefs. It is thus required that a cognitive system contain beliefs to the effect that enough kinds of cognitively spontaneous beliefs are likely to be true. These beliefs constitute the input against which any claim within the system is tested. New observational beliefs that conflict with other parts of the system force a choice between, at least, two alternative ways of revising the system: the alteration, or abandonment, of parts of the system, and the rejection of observational beliefs. The primary basis for making this choice is the relative coherence of the alternatives, under the constraints imposed by the Observation Requirement. Thus, this requirement effectively guarantees that a system that satisfies it receives input from the world and that empirical justification does not depend exclusively on internal relations among beliefs.

### *ii. The Alternative Coherent Systems Objection*

The Observation Requirement also provides the answer to the alternative coherence systems objection that says that multiple equally coherent systems could be constructed arbitrarily. As BonJour puts it, the objection cannot merely state that at a given time there may be equally justified systems, for this claim also holds for any theory of justification. On any account of the standards of epistemic justification, it is likely that there will be competing sets of empirical claims that are justified at a particular time and between which those standards do not offer at that time a basis for a decision. The objection should be interpreted as meaning that, in the long run, there could be multiple equally coherent systems between which the coherence theory provides no grounds for choice. BonJour's reply to the objection so stated is as follows: an arbitrarily constructed system will not in general satisfy the Observation Requirement, and even if it initially does, there is no reason to think that it will remain coherent as observations accumulate.

### *iii. The Problem of Truth*

A theory of justification must not only give an account of the standards of epistemic justification, but it must also provide an argument to the effect that adhering to these standards is truth-conducive. BonJour refers to such an argument as the 'metajustificatory argument'. A traditional objection to coherence theories of justification is that such a metajustification can be provided only by endorsing a coherence theory of truth. BonJour replies to this objection by advancing a different sort of metajustificatory argument, one that allows for a combination of a coherence theory of justification with a correspondence theory of truth. BonJour argues that:

> A system of beliefs which (a) remains coherent (and stable) over the long run and (b) continues to satisfy the Observation Requirement is likely, to a degree which is proportional to the degree of coherence (and stability) and the longness of the run, to correspond closely to independent reality.[56]

BonJour defends this thesis by appeal to an inference to the best explanation. He argues that the best explanation, the likeliest to be true, of a system of beliefs remaining coherent (and stable) over the long run while continuing to satisfy the Observation Requirement is that (i) the cognitively spontaneous beliefs which are claimed to be reliable are systematically caused by the world; and (ii) the entire system corresponds approximately to an independent reality. This correspondence hypothesis is claimed to be more likely to be true than alternative explanations of coherence-cum-stability such as alternatives that envision a world in which our observational beliefs are caused in a regular way by the world, but in which the system of beliefs presents a picture of the world that is in some important way incomplete or distorted as well as sceptical hypotheses (eg Cartesian demons or brains in a vat).[57] Thus, BonJour concludes that it is reasonable to accept the correspondence hypothesis and, therefore, that the truth objection can be successfully met.

To sum up, according to BonJour, in order for a belief to be justified, the following conditions must be satisfied. First, it must belong to a system of beliefs that is actually held by someone, since it is only long run coherence that provides a reason for thinking that the beliefs of a system are likely to

[56] BonJour (1985: 171).
[57] See BonJour (1985: 173–88).

be true, and the idea of long run coherence is only applicable to a system that is actually held by someone. Secondly, the system must satisfy the Observation Requirement. Thirdly, it must be coherent to a high degree and more coherent than any alternative that also satisfies such a requirement. Last, the person must have a reflective grasp, which relies on the doxastic presumption, of the fact that the system satisfies the third condition. Indeed, this account of justification is a very articulate alternative to the foundationalist view of justification and knowledge. Moreover, it significantly contributes to the coherence theory by showing how the traditional objections against coherentism may be overcome while remaining within a coherentist framework. However, as I shall argue, there are several problems with BonJour's coherence theory of justification.

## C. BonJour's Coherentism Examined

BonJour's *Structure of Empirical Knowledge* is a subtle and detailed defence of a coherence theory of epistemic justification. However, BonJour's coherentist approach to epistemic justification faces a number of problems.

### *i. BonJour's Concept of Coherence*

To start with, BonJour fails to successfully meet the vagueness objection against coherence theories. His notion of coherence is too vague for the purposes of justification as well as problematic in several respects.[58] First, BonJour takes consistency to be a necessary condition of coherence, and this seriously undermines the plausibility of his coherentist approach to justification.[59] In some cases, a complex system of beliefs, even if it contains some trivial inconsistencies, may be preferable to a much less rich system that is perfectly consistent. Already in *The Structure of Empirical Knowledge*, BonJour acknowledged the problems deriving from regarding logical consistency as a necessary condition of coherence,[60] but it was later when he came to recognize that, in light of general human logical fallibility and more specific problems such as the paradox of the preface, it is a mistake to view logical consistency as a necessary requirement for coherence.[61]

[58] That BonJour's notion of coherence is too vague is also pointed out by Swain. See Swain (1989: 116).

[59] That logical consistency cannot be a necessary condition for coherence is also argued by AI Goldman (1989: 112). Swain also doubts that logical consistency is a necessary condition for coherence in Swain (1989: 116). See Olsson (2005: 15–16 and 190) for a critique of BonJour's position concerning the relation between coherence and probabilistic, rather than logical, consistency.

[60] Bonjour (1985: 240) fn 7.

[61] BonJour (1999a: 124).

His suggestion is that not all sorts of inconsistency are equally inimical to coherence and thus to justification. While any sort of inconsistency detracts to some degree from the coherence, and hence, justification, of a system of beliefs, perhaps some of them do not do so enough to make them fail to satisfy the level of justification required for knowledge. Hence, a system of beliefs could have a high degree of coherence, and thus be justified, despite of the presence of some sorts of inconsistency.[62]

Secondly, very little is said in relation to which kinds of inferential relations contribute to coherence, other than requiring that such relations be, to some degree, truth-preserving. Unfortunately, it is far from obvious what relations satisfy BonJour's requirement (do, for instance, inferences to the best explanation meet BonJour's condition?) In addition, while inferential connections are surely important to coherence and justification, it is not clear that the number of them matters—as BonJour's account of the conditions of coherence states.[63]

Thirdly, it is a virtue of BonJour's approach that it emphasizes the relevance of one kind of inferential relations, eg explanatory relations, without claiming that these relations are the only kind of inferential relations that contribute to coherence. However, BonJour does not provide any account of the nature of explanatory relations or of the relation between coherence and explanation. If, as BonJour argues, explanatory relations are crucial to coherence, then such an account is indispensable for explicating how justification works within a coherentist framework.

### *ii. Problems with Holism*

BonJour makes the justification of any belief depend on the coherence of the entire system of beliefs; justification, he argues, despite its linear appearance, is holistic. This conception of justification does indeed provide a solution to the epistemic regress problem. We do not need to postulate basic beliefs in order to stop the regress, but we may allow justificatory chains to loop upon themselves. Once we replace a linear by a holistic view of justification, we may come to see that the coherentist solution does not involve vicious circularity. However, serious objections may be raised against this holistic view of epistemic justification.[64]

First, it seems to be psychologically implausible for human beings to draw the inferences that such a view of justification requires. To start with, as will be argued below, it is doubtful that we have a complete representation of our system of beliefs. But, even if we grant that we have such a

[62] BonJour (1989: 284).

[63] Swain (1989: 116).

[64] Parallel problems were also noted with regard to holistic views of legal justification (see ch 1).

representation, it is very unlikely that we are able to determine whether, by BonJour's standards of coherence, a set of beliefs is actually coherent.[65] One such criterion is consistency; but, as is well known, the difficulty that human beings have in determining consistency is non-trivial. Another of BonJour's criteria of coherence has to do with explanatory relations among beliefs. But there can be little doubt that inference to the best explanation can be astoundingly difficult. Drawing inferences to the best explanation may require that we deal with huge bodies of data and theory, and, on BonJour's account, such inferences would indirectly involve all of an agent's beliefs. In short, the inferential tasks that BonJour wants us to perform in order to establish coherence seem to be far beyond human capacities.[66] In order to possess a minimum degree of psychological plausibility, a theory of justification must ensure that inferential mechanisms operate at a local level, that is, over small fields of belief, rather than over the whole system of beliefs.[67]

Secondly, setting psychological worries aside, a holistic view of justification is also unsatisfactory from a normative point of view. For, in a holistic approach, anyone's beliefs would be unjustified as soon as there is some part of one's belief system—no matter how irrelevant to the belief the justification of which is at stake—that is incoherent, eg a botanist's belief that she is looking at a pine tree would be unjustified, if she happens to have absurd beliefs about, say, astronomy. To avoid this unpalatable consequence, we should make the justification of a belief depend not on the coherence of the entire system of beliefs, but rather, on the coherence of a subset of it, more specifically, on the set of beliefs that are in the 'near neighbourhood' of the belief in question.[68] This amounts to replacing a holistic model of justification by what Olsson calls a 'modular' model. In this model, justification would still be primarily a property of a set of beliefs that is sufficiently coherent, but such set need not (and typically does not) coincide with the whole system of beliefs of a person.[69]

Thirdly, BonJour's holistic coherentism does not allow different degrees of justification to be attached to different beliefs in the system.[70] If what

[65] Kornblith (1989). This problem is also posed by AI Goldman (1989: 112) and Bogen (1989: 146–47).

[66] Furthermore, the problem of determining coherence, argues Kornblith, is not limited to human beings. But, insofar as coherence requires consistency, to determine the consistency of a large set of sentences is beyond the powers of any possible computational device. See Kornblith (1989: 210–11).

[67] As suggested by Kornblith (1989).

[68] The phrase is Plantinga's. See Plantinga (1993: 112).

[69] See Olsson (1997b) and Roche (2011: 189–190). For Williams, a commitment to holism is a definitory feature of a coherentist epistemology. Hence, to give up holism would amount to replacing coherentism by another epistemology, ie a contextualist one. See M Williams (1996) ch 7.

[70] Plantinga (1993: 110).

confers justification on a belief is that it is an element of a coherent system of beliefs, then all beliefs within a system are either justified or unjustified: justified if the system is sufficiently coherent and unjustified otherwise.[71] Plantinga suggests a way in which such difficulties may be overcome:

> Perhaps there are ways of partitioning my system of beliefs into subsystems, some of which display more coherence (and thus confer more warrant) than others; or perhaps a particularly large and impressive subsystem could be identified as a central core, other beliefs having warrant in proportion to their probability with respect to that central core.[72]

Hence, there seems to be a need to qualify the unrestricted holism endorsed by Bonjour's coherentism by partitioning the system of beliefs into distinct subsystems and distinguishing between a core and a periphery so as to allow for the possibility that some beliefs be more or less justified than others.

Last, BonJour's commitment to holism, when put together with his views about the conditions of coherence, would have the troubling consequence that nobody ever has any justified belief. For, as claimed, it is unlikely that anyone's whole system of beliefs satisfies BonJour's conditions of coherence, eg logical consistency. Two possible solutions may be proposed: either we give up the idea that the coherence of the whole system of beliefs is required for the justification of any belief, or we weaken the conditions of coherence. My claim is that a viable coherentist theory of justification should pursue both strategies simultaneously, since, as we have seen, there are independent reasons to deny such a holistic approach to justification as well as to give up the idea that coherence requires consistency.

### *iii. The Doxastic Presumption: Problems with Internalist Coherentism*

As explained before, BonJour's coherence theory of justification is internalist. According to this theory, it is not enough for a belief to be justified that it belongs to a system of beliefs that is in fact coherent. It is further required that the believer have access to the fact that the belief in question coheres with one's overall system of beliefs. Hence, the believer must have an adequate grasp, or representation, of his system of beliefs, since it is with respect to this system that issues of coherence and justification should be decided. This grasp consists of a set of metabeliefs to the effect that the believer has such and such specific beliefs, and these metabeliefs must be themselves justified. The problem arises, as noted, as to how these metabeliefs can be justified. A possible solution would be to justify these metabeliefs by appealing to coherence with the rest of the system. However, BonJour claims that such a solution is unacceptable because 'such a justification would be

[71] This point is brought up by Goldman in AI Goldman (1989: 111).
[72] Plantinga (1993: 110).

hopelessly and unavoidable circular dependent on the acceptability of the very representation of my system of beliefs whose justification is at issue'.[73] In addition, a coherentist justification of one's metabeliefs that I have such-and-such system of beliefs threatens to generate an infinite regress.[74] For *S* to be justified in believing that *p*, he must be justified in believing that *p* coheres with other beliefs in the belief system of which it is a member (*p'*). Now, *p'* is justified for *S* only if *S* is justified in believing that it coheres with *S*'s other beliefs in the belief system in which it is a member, and so on.

As argued, BonJour introduces the doxastic presumption to solve the problems concerning the epistemic status of the representation of one's system of beliefs. He treats the set of metabeliefs as an unjustified hypothesis in relation to which issues of justification are conditionally assessed. His suggestion is that all empirical justification must be relativized to, or conditional upon, the presumption that my representation of beliefs is at least approximately correct. This solution avoids the circularity involved in postulating that the metabeliefs to the effect that I hold such a system of beliefs may be justified by virtue of their coherence with the rest of the system. This presumption can also short-circuit the regress just noted (although the regress is not BonJour's reason for introducing the doxastic presumption).[75] However, this solution to the regress that internalist coherentism's commitments generate gives rise, in its turn, to a number of problems.

First, a main concern with the doxastic presumption is again related to the issue of whether the view of justification that BonJour advances is applicable to actual human believers. Even though BonJour claims that the grasp of one's system of beliefs is possibly tacit and only approximately correct, it seems implausible that humans have such a grasp. Most of a person's beliefs are stored in long-term memory, and it is doubtful that one has, even implicitly, anything like a complete grasp of *all* of them. In fact, many stored beliefs are quite difficult to access, and it is certainly impossible to retrieve all of them simultaneously.[76]

Secondly, as BonJour claims, from the doxastic presumption follows a certain version of scepticism, according to which no one has any justification *simpliciter* for any empirical belief but only, at best, for the conditional claim that if a certain presumption is correct, then various empirical beliefs are justified.[77] Given BonJour's commitment to internalism, this would have

[73] BonJour (1985: 283). See also BonJour (1985: 102).

[74] Bruecker (1988). Moser has also argued that BonJour's internalism leaves us with an infinite regress, in Moser (1988). BonJour's has replied to Bruecker in BonJour (1989: 282–84) and to Moser in BonJour (1988).

[75] BonJour (1988: 165).

[76] AI Goldman (1989: 112).

[77] On the charge that the doxastic presumption leads to a form of scepticism, see BonJour ((1985: 105–06), (1989: 283–284) and (1999a: 129)).

the result that all empirical beliefs are ultimately unjustified. The problem seems to be as follows. It is open to the sceptic to push the objection further, and either deny or question the truth of the metabeliefs which fall under the presumption, with the result that all empirical beliefs would be unjustified. It is clear that all empirical beliefs would be unjustified if the metabeliefs which fall under the presumption are false. But, one could argue, the fact that justification is always relative to the presumption that the representation of one's system of beliefs is correct, does not mean that one has no justified beliefs. For if this presumption is, in fact, true, then the various empirical beliefs are justified, since there is a reason why they are likely to be true. However, according to BonJour, this is a mistake, because though such a reason would exist in the abstract, it would be inaccessible to the believer—or to anyone else.[78] Hence, for this presumption to actually meet this version of scepticism without compromising internalism what is required is not that one's metabeliefs be true, but that the believer be justified in holding them.[79] But, does this not lead BonJour's coherentism to collapse into a kind of foundationalism in which basic beliefs are the metabeliefs that fall under this presumption?

That the doxastic presumption introduces a foundationalist element into BonJour's coherentism is an objection—the last one to be considered here—which has been raised by a number of authors.[80] BonJour's coherence theory, it is argued, is a version of foundationalism in which the foundational beliefs are the person's metabeliefs about the composition of his own system of beliefs, that is, those beliefs specified by the doxastic presumption. It follows from the doxastic presumption that not for every justified empirical belief, the believer must justifiably believe some propositions that make his belief likely to be true. For the metabeliefs specified by the doxastic presumption seem to be an exception to this general claim. These beliefs, it is argued, satisfy the characterization of basic empirical beliefs: they have justification immediately and in themselves. Against this charge, it may be argued that, even though the doxastic presumption does function as a 'foundation' in that it is a presupposition without which empirical justification cannot even get started, this foundation is very different from the kind of foundations postulated by the standard foundationalist view. As BonJour has clearly stated, in a reply to this objection, the difference between his theory and foundationalism is that the metabeliefs that fall under the doxastic presumption are not claimed to

[78] BonJour (1999a: 141) fn 26.

[79] This is argued by Plantinga in (1993: 108).

[80] See Plantinga (1993: 109); Bruecker (1988: 158); AI Goldman (1989: 109-111); Swain (1989: 118); and Lemos (1989: 181–84). For BonJour's reply to the charge that his theory is a version of foundationalism in which foundational beliefs are the person's metabeliefs about the composition of his own system of beliefs, that is, those beliefs specified by the doxastic presumption, see BonJour ((1985: 146–47) and (1989: 283)).

be epistemically justified. Rather, they provide a background presumption against which issues of epistemic justification are meaningfully raised.[81]

*iv. BonJour's Coherentist Account of Observation*

BonJour's coherentist account of observational input is an extremely interesting effort to provide a solution to the isolation objection and the alternative coherent systems objection. Once it is guaranteed that any empirical beliefs should be capable of being checked against the set of observational beliefs if it is to be justified, the force of these objections seems to be seriously undermined. For this solution to work, however, it is necessary to provide an account of how the system of beliefs is supposed to be checked against the observational beliefs, that is, of how the system should be revised in the light of the observational input. As I shall argue, BonJour's explanation of this process, although very suggestive, presents several problems.

BonJour claims that there are, at least, two alternative ways of revising the system of beliefs: by modifying the system or by rejecting the observational beliefs. This revision should be done under two constraints: the Observation Requirement and the relative coherence of the alternatives.[82] The problems of BonJour's proposal concern the question of how the relative coherence of the alternatives and the Observation Requirement constrain the revision of the system. I will address the issue of the relative coherence of alternatives in the next section. Here I will focus on the question of whether the Observation Requirement satisfactorily constrains the revision of our systems of beliefs. The main problem with this requirement is that it is too vague.[83] For the requirement to be met, the system must contain laws attributing a 'high degree of reliability' to a 'reasonable variety of cognitively spontaneous beliefs'. So stated, it may be difficult to actually determine whether such a condition has been satisfied by the several cognitive systems that can be candidates for empirical justification.[84]

In addition, as BonJour says, the Observation Requirement was introduced 'with an eye toward the sort of case in which a person persistently rejects apparent observations in order to preserve some favoured view or

[81] This reply to the charge of foundationalism has given rise to still another objection against BonJour's doxastic presumption: if the metabeliefs are not justified, how can they serve to justify the beliefs that are their subject? See Bruecker (1988: 159) fn 10; and Moser ((1986: 672) and (1988: 162)).

[82] BonJour (1985: 140).

[83] For an examination of other objections to BonJour's account of observation, see Silvers (1989: 168–75).

[84] In addition, the vagueness of this requirement poses problems with regard to the relation between coherence and truth. This point is noted by Moser (1986: 674).

theory'.[85] However, the systematic rejection of apparent observations is only one way in which epistemic agents might reach a coherent system of beliefs that is, nevertheless, isolated from experience. Often coherence is reached not by blatantly discarding conflicting observational beliefs but by seriously misinterpreting them so as to preserve (or even enhance) the coherence of some favoured view.[86] This tendency to fabricate coherence, which the observational input might upset, poses a serious problem to coherence accounts of justification, and it does not seem that BonJour's Observation Requirement prevents this tendency from running wild.[87]

### *v. The Search for the Most Coherent Alternative*

Let us grant, for the sake of the argument, that we do have a representation of our system of beliefs and that such a system satisfactorily meets the Observation Requirement. There is still a third condition that our systems of belief must meet—according to BonJour—in order to be justification-conferring. For a belief to be justified the system to which it belongs must be coherent to a high degree and more coherent than any alternative. BonJour does not give a satisfactory account of how the process of evaluating the relative coherence of the alternatives, with a view to selecting the most coherent one as justified, works.

First, we are not told how these different alternatives are generated. In addition, nothing is said about how the construction of the alternatives is related to the task of selecting the most coherent of the alternative systems. What strategies are we supposed to employ for generating and choosing among those alternatives? Do we generate all of them first, and choose after, or do we use an item-by-item strategy? BonJour's coherentist theory of epistemic justification needs to be complemented with an account of these issues.

Secondly, BonJour tells us that one should choose the most coherent of the alternatives. But, given the vagueness of his notion of coherence, it seems difficult to determine how these judgements of comparative coherence should be made. In most cases, the conditions of coherence that he proposes are not precise enough to enable such a comparison. Furthermore, he does not address the issue of how these different criteria of coherence

[85] BonJour (1985: 153).

[86] Consider, eg, religious beliefs. Those who hold religious beliefs rarely reject apparent observations that conflict with their religious beliefs. Rather, they interpret observational beliefs so as to make them cohere with their religious beliefs. Furthermore, such beliefs can even increase the coherence of the belief system by providing explanations of phenomena which current scientific knowledge cannot account for. For a related discussion of the problems that religious beliefs pose to BonJour's coherentism, see Swain (1989: 122) and BonJour (1989: 289).

[87] For a discussion of this problem, see ch 10.

should be balanced against each other. When conflicts among these criteria arise, BonJour's coherence theory of justification does not provide any guidance for choosing among several alternatives.

Last, according to BonJour, only those alternatives that are coherent to a high degree are potential candidates. In other words, only the systems that meet a 'threshold level of coherence' (and that we may refer to as 'minimally coherent') may be adequately justified for knowledge. BonJour acknowledges that this requirement is too vague, but he concludes that this is unlikely to pose a serious problem in practice. According to BonJour, in most cases, there will be systems available which clearly exceed the threshold of coherence, so that the decision of which of them to accept will normally need to be made on the basis of comparative coherence, rather than by appeal to such a threshold level.[88] However, BonJour seems to underestimate the practical significance of having a clear account of how the choice of the alternatives is constrained. Indeed in some justificatory contexts, it may well be the case that none of the explanations under consideration satisfy the threshold of coherence required for knowledge. Thus, it is a desirable feature of a coherence theory of justification that it rule out as unjustified alternatives that are not minimally coherent.

To sum up, BonJour's theory of justification shows that the traditional objections against coherentism are less compelling that is usually thought, and thus, that the coherence theory may be a plausible alternative to foundationalism. However, as has been argued, BonJour's coherentism faces several problems. More specifically, there are three aspects of BonJour's theory of coherence that are not satisfactorily dealt with and that need to be further developed. First, a better understanding of the criteria of coherence and of how the different criteria may be balanced against each other is called for. Secondly, the unit of justification—the base of coherence—cannot be, as BonJour's holistic coherentism requires, the entire system of beliefs. We need to define a unit of justification that is psychologically plausible and that allows us to give an account of how relevance considerations affect our judgements of coherence. Last, it is necessary to further develop a picture of how justification works in a coherentist framework, namely, how the system of beliefs is revised, the different alternatives generated, and the best one selected.

[88] BonJour (1985: 154).

## III. LEHRER'S COHERENCE THEORY OF KNOWLEDGE

Lehrer's theory of knowledge and justification is one of the most influential coherentist epistemologies.[89] His analysis of knowledge builds on the traditional definition of knowledge according to which a subject *S* knows that *p* if and only if (i) *S* believes that *p*; (ii) *p* is true; and (iii) the belief that *p* is epistemically justified. Lehrer's analysis of knowledge develops the traditional scheme in three respects. First, the belief condition is replaced by an 'acceptance condition'. Only a special kind of belief, namely, the acceptance of something for the purpose of attaining truth and avoiding error is a condition of knowledge. Secondly, the justification condition is explained entirely in terms of coherence. Coherence with a background system of acceptances yields justification. Last, the notion of knowledge is also given in terms of coherence: it is coherence with a corrected version of the system of acceptances that yields knowledge. Lehrer's theory of knowledge, as we shall see, is a very refined version of a coherence theory that incorporates some features of both internalist and externalist epistemologies.

### A. Belief, Acceptance and Truth

Lehrer's proposal starts by distinguishing 'belief' from 'acceptance'.[90] Acceptance is a special kind of belief: belief aimed at truth, that is, it is the acceptance of something for the purpose of obtaining truth and avoiding error.[91] Lehrer claims that sometimes we may believe things that we do not accept for this epistemic purpose. For example, we may believe that God exists for the sake of felicity, rather than for the regard for truth. It is acceptance in the quest of truth rather than belief that is the requisite of knowledge. Thus, what is needed for knowledge is to accept that *p* only if it is true that *p*. It is only this kind of belief that is a condition for knowledge.

The difference between belief and acceptance is but a particular case of a more fundamental difference that exists between two kinds of mental

[89] Lehrer originally proposed his theory of knowledge in (1974). This theory was revised in (1986b) as well as in (1988). A complete exposition of his version of a coherence theory was given in (1990a). Lehrer has further refined his proposal in (1997) and (1999). Still some modifications have been introduced in (2000a). For a discussion of Lehrer's theory of coherence, at different stages of its development, see Bogdan (1981); Bender (1989a); Brandl, Gombocz, and Piller (1991); and Olsson (2003).

[90] For Lehrer's distinction between belief and acceptance, see Lehrer ((1979), (1982), (1983), (1988), (1990), (2000a), and (2000c)). For a critique of Lehrer's version of the belief/acceptance distinction, see Manning (1994) and Piller (1991). Lehrer's replies may be found in Lehrer (1991a) and Nine and Lehrer (2001).

[91] Different accounts of the belief/acceptance distinction have been proposed in the literature. See S. Cohen (1992); Van Fraassen ((1989) and (2002)); Stalnaker (1984); Bratman (1992); Engel (2000); Tuomela (2000); and Cresto (2010).

states: 'first order states' and 'evaluated states'.[92] According to Lehrer, there are states of our first order mind, namely, beliefs, desires and inferences, which arise in us unreflectively. These states can be raised to the level of criticism and evaluation, and when we do so, we may accept some but not all of what we believe, prefer to satisfy some of our desires and reason in accord to some of our inferences. The resulting states of acceptance, preference, and reasoning are the evaluated states of the metamind. Thus, whereas we may believe something uncritically, the acceptance of something results from evaluation in terms of the interest in obtaining truth. It is coherence with the metamental states that yields justification and, ultimately, knowledge.[93]

## B. Coherence and Personal Justification

Lehrer defines justification as coherence with a background system. The relevant background system is the 'acceptance system', that is, the system of information that we accept in the interest of obtaining truth. Lehrer defines the 'acceptance system' as follows:

> *Acceptance system.* The acceptance system of *S* at *t* may be defined as the set of statements of the form '*S* accepts that *p*' attributing to *S* just those things *S* accepts at *t* with the objective of obtaining truth and avoiding error with respect to the content accepted, that is, with respect to the content that *p*.[94]

Thus, the acceptance system of a person is a set of statements of the form, *S* accepts that *p*, *S* accepts that *q*, and so forth. Lately, Lehrer has expanded this background system into an 'evaluation system', which contains not only acceptances but also the other states of the metamind, namely, preferences and reasonings.[95] Coherence with the evaluation system yields 'personal justification':

> *Personal justification. S* is personally justified in accepting that *p* if and only if *p* coheres with the evaluation system of *S* at *t*.

[92] See Lehrer (1997) ch 1.

[93] A qualification is needed here. Lehrer distinguishes between 'primitive knowledge' and 'discursive knowledge'. This distinction parallels Lehrer's distinction between first-order mind and second-order mind or metamind. Whereas primitive knowledge consists of belief that originates in some specific way, discursive knowledge amounts to undefeated justified acceptance. Hence, acceptance and not belief is a condition of knowledge, if by knowledge we mean 'discursive knowledge'. For this distinction, see Lehrer (2000b). For commentary, see Craig (2000: 656–57).

[94] Lehrer (1990a: 117).

[95] See Lehrer (1999: 245). For a discussion of the acceptance system and the related systems concerned with acceptance which form the evaluation system, see Lehrer ((2000b: 651) and (1990a: 126–28, 130 and 170)).

It is important to notice that, according to Lehrer, the kind of coherence that is relevant to justification is 'relational' coherence. It is the relation of coherence between an acceptance and a system of evaluation that provides the basis for defining personal justification. Coherence with such a system suffices for personal justification. No further constraint is imposed on the system of evaluation of the person. Lehrer does not even require that the system be consistent in order for it to justify an acceptance. Inconsistent systems, as long as they are not deductively closed, may justify beliefs. He illustrates this possibility with the following example:

> Consider Bertrand Russell's beliefs when he believed an axiom about the existence of sets that was inconsistent. Surely, the fact that Russell's system contained that inconsistency did not have the result that he was not justified in believing anything, for example, that he was a Russell.[96]

Thus, the central notion in Lehrer's theory of justification is the relation of coherence with an evaluation system. What does this relation of coherence consist of? Lehrer gives a rather singular notion of coherence:

> *Coherence.* An acceptance of *p* coheres with an evaluation system if all objections to the acceptance of *p* are met on the basis of an evaluation system.

Hence, according to Lehrer, coherence is the positive capacity, or resource, of an evaluation system to resolve conflicts or meet objections to a given acceptance. Justification requires that one be in a position to meet all objections to this acceptance on the basis of one's evaluation system. Lehrer defines an objection as follows:

> *Objection.* An objection o to the acceptance of *p* is such that it is more reasonable to accept that *p* on the assumption that o is false than on the assumption that o is true.[97]

Objections are not only claims that contradict a given claim, but they may be such that, even though they are logically consistent with the proposition accepted, they shed doubts on the reasonableness of such an acceptance. For example, consider the accepted proposition 'John saw Alice killing George'. A critic might raise an objection that contradicts this claim such as 'Sandra is the murderer of George'. An objection that does not contradict the claim may be: 'John was hallucinating'. The claim that 'John saw Alice killing George' is not contradicted by the claim that 'John was hallucinating', for it is logically possible for a person to witness a murder, even though he is hallucinating.[98] However, it is less reasonable for me to accept that John saw Alice killing George if John was hallucinating than if John was

[96] Lehrer (1999: 252).

[97] Lehrer (1999: 247). In previous works, Lehrer call 'objections', 'competitors'. See Lehrer (1990: 117ff).

[98] Cases of 'veridical hallucinations' are to the point here. See Lewis (1980).

not. These objections pose a threat of incoherence, because what the critic says conflicts with what is accepted. Coherence results when the objections are met and all threat of incoherence is removed.

There are two ways in which objections can be met on the basis of an evaluation system: they can be either beaten (or answered) or neutralized. These notions are defined as follows:

> *Beating*. An objection *o* is beaten if it is more reasonable to reject *o* than to accept *o* on the basis of the evaluation system.[99]
>
> *Neutralization*. The objection *o* is neutralized by *n* when the conjunction of *o* and *n* is not an objection, and the conjunction is as reasonable to accept as the objection *o* alone on the basis of the evaluation system.

Thus, an objection is met when the evaluation system of a person implies that it is more reasonable to accept a claim than competing claims. How are we to decide whether this is so? Lehrer suggests that one may determine whether an objection is beaten or neutralized by imagining how a person would respond to the questions of the critic or the sceptic. He invites us to imagine a 'justification game', in which a claimant plays to show that she is personally justified in accepting what she does.[100] The justification game is played as follows. The claimant presents something she accepts as true. The critic may then raise any objection to what the claimant presents. If such an objection can be either beaten or neutralized, then the claimant wins the round. If all the objections are met, then the claimant wins the game, and she is personally justified in accepting what she presented; if not, she is not personally justified. For example, imagine that I am a member of a jury listening to a witness testimony. The witness, John, says, 'I saw Alice killing George'. On the basis of this testimony, I come to accept that 'John saw Alice killing George'. So I enter that as the claimant in the justification game.

> *Claimant*: John saw Alice killing George.
>
> *Critic*: Sandra is the murderer of George.
>
> *Claimant*: It is more reasonable for me to reject that Sandra is the murderer of George than to accept that Sandra is the murderer of George. (I have no reason to believe that Sandra killed George. John is known for his honesty. So his testimony is trustworthy evidence that John did see Alice killing George).
>
> *Critic*: John was hallucinating that Alice killed George.

[99] Lehrer (1999: 246).

[100] See Lehrer (1990a: 119ff). Actually, Lehrer conceives the game as one that is played between a claimant and the sceptic. However, it seems natural to use the same heuristics to show how a claimant is personally justified when the objections that are raised against his claim are not the traditional sceptical objections.

> *Claimant*: It is more reasonable for me to accept that John saw Alice killing George than to accept that John was hallucinating. (There is no evidence that would lead me to think that John was hallucinating. There is no indication that he took any drug that may have caused him hallucinations and there is trustworthy evidence that he was not hallucinating).

Thus, in these two rounds, the claimant beats both objections and she wins the rounds. Now, there are some objections that cannot be beaten, in cases in which a person is, nonetheless, personally justified. The reason is that some objections may be more reasonable to accept than to reject, and as reasonable to accept as the claim itself. It is to account for these cases that Lehrer introduces the notion of neutralization. An objection of this kind may be met as follows:

> *Claimant*: John saw Alice killing George.
>
> *Critic*: People sometimes hallucinate.
>
> *Claimant*: John was not hallucinating.

On the basis of my evaluation system, it is as reasonable for me to accept that 'people sometimes hallucinate' together with the neutralizer, 'John was not hallucinating', as to accept that people sometimes hallucinate. Thus, even though I cannot beat the objection (for it is certainly more reasonable for me to accept that people sometimes hallucinate than to reject it), I should be allowed to use the neutralizer as a reply to the critic. Thus, in this example of the justification game, I am able to meet all the objections presented, either by beating them or by neutralizing them. Each challenge to my claim is rejected on the grounds that it does not cohere with what I accept, as the parenthetical remarks indicate, while my claim does cohere with my evaluation system. These remarks are the part of my evaluation system that is relevant to the justification of my claim. Since, on the basis of this system, it is more reasonable for me to accept that 'John saw Alice killing George' than any conflicting claim, I win the justification game, and, thus, I am personally justified in accepting that 'John saw Alice killing George'.

As the justification game brings to light, Lehrer's basic idea is that a person is justified in accepting a proposition if it coheres with an evaluation system; and a proposition coheres with an evaluation system provided that, on the basis of this system, it is more reasonable for the subject to accept this proposition than to accept competing propositions. The concept of coherence, and that of personal justification, is thus defined in terms of comparative reasonableness. But, how should this notion be understood? Lehrer takes 'reasonableness' as a primitive. This has, according to Lehrer, two constructive advantages. First, it acknowledges the normative aspect of justification, by stating that an epistemically rational agent ought not to accept something if it is more reasonable to accept its denial, while leaving open the question of whether this notion of reasonableness can be reduced to some non-normative conception. Secondly, it allows a plurality of factors to influence the normative evaluation, that is, it leaves open which considerations might make it more reasonable to accept one's claim over competing claims on the basis of one's evaluation system.[101]

One acceptance of the evaluation system is, in Lehrer's view, pivotal to judgements of comparative reasonableness: the acceptance of my own trustworthiness. When I have no reason to trust some source of information, my evaluation system fails to provide any basis for considering it more reasonable to accept the information that I receive from one source than to reject it. Lehrer claims that it is not enough that one accepts something for it to be more reasonable than competing claims on the basis of one's evaluation system. It is required that one has some information to the effect that such an acceptance is a trustworthy guide to truth. If the person does not accept that she is trustworthy in what she accepts, then there is an objection to anything she accepts that cannot be met, namely that she is not trustworthy in what she accepts, eg that I cannot tell a trustworthy witness from one that is not trustworthy. Thus, the keystone acceptance of my own trustworthiness is what yields the reasonableness of what I accept. Lehrer accounts for the primary role of such an acceptance by introducing the 'principle of trustworthiness'. He formulates this principle as follows:

> *T.* Whatever I accept with the objective of accepting something just in case it is true, I accept in a trustworthy manner.[102]

Therefore, there is one special principle of my acceptance system, to wit, that I am trustworthy in matters of obtaining truth and avoiding error. On the basis of this principle, if I accept that I am trustworthy, then my accepting something will be a reason to accept it. Self-trust works, in this view, in a way similar to the way in which we trust other people. If someone else accepts that I am trustworthy when accepting something, then my accepting something will be a reason for her to accept it. For example, if I accept that John is trustworthy in telling Alice from, say, Sandra, then his accepting that he saw Alice is a reason for me to accept that he did see her. Similarly, given that I consider myself to be trustworthy in telling trustworthy witnesses from untrustworthy witnesses, my accepting John's testimony is a reason for accepting it.

A main consequence of adding principle (T) to the evaluation system is that whatever I accept is more reasonable for me to accept than its denial. The principle of trustworthiness has thus the primary effect of permitting to detach the content of what the person accepts from her acceptance of

[101] Lehrer (1990a: 127).

[102] Lehrer (1990a: 122). In the second edition of this book, Lehrer introduces analogous principles in relation to both reasonings and preferences. See Lehrer (2000a: 140–41).

the content. For example, John's acceptance system tells him that he accepts that Alice killed George. The information that he accepts that Alice killed George does not justify him in accepting the conclusion that, indeed, Alice killed George. How can John detach this conclusion from his acceptance of it? He needs the additional information that his accepting it is a trustworthy guide to obtain truth and avoid error. The principle of trustworthiness, according to Lehrer, supplies this information, and therefore functions as a principle of detachment. It enables one to reason from it and the acceptance of some target acceptance to the conclusion that the target acceptance is reasonable. Let *p* be Alice killed John. According to Lehrer, such reasoning would be as follows:

> T. I am trustworthy in what I accept with the objective of accepting something just in case it is true.
>
> I accept that *p* with the objective of accepting that *p* just in case it is true.
>
> Therefore, I am trustworthy in accepting that *p* with the objective of accepting that *p* just in case it is true.
>
> Therefore, I am reasonable in accepting that *p* with the objective of accepting that *p* just in case it is true.

Lehrer refers to this argument from trustworthiness to reasonableness as the 'trustworthiness argument'.[103] This argument assumes that my trustworthiness explains why it is reasonable for me to accept what I do. Hence, a person may appeal to principle *T* to defend the reasonableness of accepting what she does, but what defence can she offer in favour of *T* itself? How is the principle of trustworthiness justified?

The justification of the principle of trustworthiness is two-fold. On the one hand, it is justified on the basis of its coherence with other things that I accept; ie the principle must cohere with what I accept about my successes and failures in reaching the truth in the past. Thus, the reasonableness of accepting this principle is supported by the acceptances, preferences and reasonings of my evaluation system, as it supports the reasonableness of them. On the other hand, the principle of trustworthiness provides in part its own justification. We are, at least in part, personally justified in accepting that we are trustworthy precisely because we accept that we are. That is, the principle of trustworthiness applies to itself, and provides its own detachment. Thus, the consequence of adding this principle to an evaluation system is that whatever I accept, including this principle, is more reasonable for me to accept than its denial. In this way, self-trust is the keystone notion on which Lehrer's account of personal justification relies.

[103] See Lehrer (2000a: 139). Analogous arguments are available for reasonings and preferences. See ibid, 140–42. See also Lehrer (1997: 12–14), for the trustworthiness argument as regards preference and (1997: 20–22), for the reasoning argument.

## C. Knowledge as Undefeated Justification

As we have seen, an acceptance that coheres with the evaluation system of a person is personally justified. Personal justification is not, however, sufficient for knowledge. To start with, as the traditional account of knowledge states, one may have justified beliefs that are, nevertheless, false. For example, I may be personally justified in accepting that John saw Alice killing George, even though it is not true that he did. Moreover, a person may be personally justified in accepting something that is true but, because other things that she accepts which are necessary for justifying it are false, she does not know it. For example, even if I am personally justified in accepting that John saw Alice killing George, and it happens to be true that he did, I may not know that he did if the acceptances that I need for meeting the objections to my knowledge (eg that he is a trustworthy witness, that the conditions under which he saw the crime were normal) are not true. In this case, my personal justification of this acceptance is defeated by the falsity of other things that I accept and that are essential for justifying the claim, and thus, I do not know it. Knowledge is obtained when personal justification does not depend on any false proposition, ie when the justification is undefeated.

Like personal justification, undefeated justification is a matter of coherence with a system. The difference lies in the system that is relevant to each kind of justification. While personal justification results from coherence with the evaluation system, undefeated justification requires coherence with a modified version of such a system: the 'ultrasystem'. Undefeated justification may be thus defined as follows:

> *Undefeated justification.* S is justified in accepting *p* in a way that is undefeated if and only if *p* coheres with the ultrasystem of *S* at *t*.

The ultrasystem is the system consisting of the elements of the evaluation system that are true (the t-system), while acknowledging the states of the original evaluation system.[104] The t-system is a subset of the original acceptances, reasonings and preferences of the evaluation system. It consists of t-acceptances, t-reasonings and t-preferences. T-acceptances are all acceptances of propositions that are true; t-reasonings are the subset of original reasonings that contain true premises; and t-preferences are the set of preferences for accepting *p* rather than *q* in which it is not the case that *p* is false and *q* is true.

As explained above, an acceptance coheres with an evaluation system (and is thus personally justified) if there are no objections that can successfully

[104] This notion of ultrasystem was introduced by Lehrer in (1999), which is substantially different from the earlier conception as stated in Lehrer (1990a: 149). Lehrer has included the revised view in Lehrer (2000a: 153ff).

undermine such an acceptance on the basis of this system. The same notion of coherence is employed for analysing undefeated justification. Hence, a person is justified in a way that is undefeated when she can meet all objections to her knowledge claim on the basis of her ultrasystem. Even though all states of the evaluation system are acknowledged, only t-acceptances, t-reasonings and t-preferences can be used to meet objections. If such a restriction does not result in the person being unable to meeting an objection to her claim, her personal justification is undefeated and converts into knowledge.

Lehrer suggests that a modified version of the justification game, the 'ultrajustification game', be used as a heuristic device for evaluating knowledge claims.[105] In the ultrajustification game, the sceptic or critic is allowed a new sort of move. She may disqualify a claimant's move by indicating that the person's justification depends on a false claim. Consider again how the justification game deals with John's example:

*Claimant*: John saw Alice killing George.

*Critic*: John was hallucinating that Alice killed George.

*Claimant*: It is more reasonable for me to accept that John saw Alice killing George than to accept that John was hallucinating. (John has said that he saw Alice killing George. John is known by his honesty. There is no evidence that would lead me to think that John was hallucinating. There is no indication that he took any drug that may have caused him hallucinations, and there is trustworthy evidence that he was not hallucinating).

In this round, the claimant wins the justification game, and she is personally justified. Now, suppose that John took a medicine that, unbeknown to him, may cause hallucinations as a side effect. When it seemed to John that he saw Alice killing George, John was under the effects of this medicine. As it turns out, though, he did see Alice killing George. Although the claimant wins the original justification game, she loses the ultrajustification game because the critic can disqualify the claimant's move:

*Critic*: John did take a drug that may have caused him hallucinations!

The claimant's personal justification is defeated because it depends on a false statement and, thus, she lacks knowledge. On the basis of her acceptance system, which includes the principle of trustworthiness, she took herself to be a trustworthy evaluator of her sources of information, when she was not. The falsity of this assumption prevents her personal justification from being undefeated. Thus, victory in the ultrajustification game requires that a person be trustworthy as she takes herself to be. For another example,

[105] The ultrajustification game, as presented in Lehrer (1990a), was meant to be a tool for the evaluation of knowledge claims on the basis of their coherence with the ultrasystem, as was defined by Lehrer until its modification in Lehrer (1999). I have modified the game so that it reflects the later version of the notions of ultrasystem and undefeated justification.

consider John's justification for accepting that he saw Alice killing George. John's personal justification depends on the acceptance that perception is a trustworthy source of information in general as well as in the special circumstances at stake. For such personal justification to be undefeated, this assumption about his own trustworthiness must also be true. Hence, for personal justification to transform into knowledge, there is a requirement for a 'match between what one accepts as a trustworthy guide to truth, and what really is a trustworthy guide to truth'.[106] As we shall see now, Lehrer claims this match to provide the truth-connection between a person's evaluation system and the external world.

## D. Lehrer on Coherence and the Truth-Connection

The most troubling criticism to coherence theories of justification is that there is no apparent connection between coherence and truth. As we have seen, this is the problem that motivates one of the main traditional objections against coherence theories, namely, the isolation objection. According to this objection, coherence theories cut off justification from the world, for a set of beliefs may satisfy the coherentist conditions of justification, even though it is totally isolated from the world. Lehrer distinguishes between two forms that this objection may take: the 'positive isolation argument' and the 'negative isolation argument'.[107] The former is an argument to the effect that coherentist standards of justification may fail to be truth-conducive because they may ignore input from the external world. The argument amounts to the traditional objection that coherence theories cannot give a satisfactory account of the role of perception and sensation in justification. Lehrer's response to this objection is formulated as a dilemma. Either sensations are representational, or they are not. If they are, then the evaluation of the representation will become part of the evaluation system, and may, as a result, influence justification. If they are not representational, then they are uninformative, and will not be part of our evidence, or of our evaluation system. Thus, claims Lehrer, sensations, when they are informative, do play a role in the process of justification by being integrated into the evaluation system.

According to the negative isolation argument, justification in terms of internal coherence might fail to provide any connection with reality. Lehrer replies to the negative version of the isolation objection by means of the 'transformation argument'. The crucial point of Lehrer's response is that

[106] Lehrer (1974: 144).

[107] Lehrer (1999: 254). What Lehrer refers to as 'positive isolation argument' corresponds to what BonJour calls the 'input or isolation objection'; and the 'negative isolation argument' corresponds to BonJour's 'truth objection'.

the isolation objection is an objection that, as any other objection, must be met by accepting the denial of isolation. If such an acceptance is correct because the person is not isolated, then personal justification will transform into knowledge. If, on the contrary, the person wrongly accepts that she is justified in accepting the denial of the objection, then, her personal justification is defeated, and she lacks knowledge. Thus, Lehrer claims, either way the theory gives the adequate results. The justification game illustrates how, according to Lehrer, the isolation problem can be solved:

> *Claimant*: I see a book in front of me.
>
> *Sceptic*: You are isolated from the external world.
>
> *Claimant*: It is more reasonable for me to accept that I see a book in front of me than that I am isolated from the external world. (I am visually connected with the external world and not isolated from it.)

In this example of the justification game, the claimant is personally justified in accepting that she sees a book in front of her. Her evaluation system enables her to meet the isolation objection by informing her that she accepts that she is appropriately connected with the world. If she is right in accepting this, then her personal justification will be undefeated, and she knows that she sees a book in front of her. If, on the other hand, she is wrong in accepting this, her personal justification will be defeated, and it will fail to transform into knowledge. In this case, she will lose the ultrajustification game, for the objection cannot be met on the basis of her ultrasystem:

> *Claimant*: I see a book in front of me.
>
> *Sceptic*: You are isolated from the external world.
>
> *Claimant*: It is more reasonable for me to accept that I see a book in front of me than that I am isolated from the external world. (I am visually connected with the external world and not isolated from it.)
>
> *Sceptic*: You are not visually connected with the external world!

Thus, according to Lehrer, victory in the ultrajustification game ensures that the appropriate connection obtains between internal coherence and the external world. In any of its forms the isolation argument, says Lehrer, is satisfactorily replied, and the right relation between coherentist standards of justification and truth effected.[108]

[108] The extent to which Lehrer's theory satisfactorily meets the isolation objection is a very much discussed issue in the literature. Among others, see Moser (1989: 29ff); Mattey (1989); and Halbach (1999). For Lehrer's reply, see Lehrer (1989).

## E. Coherence, Externalism and Self-Trust

Lehrer's theory of knowledge and justification is a very innovative version of the coherence theory that departs in some respects from traditional coherence theories. First, Lehrer does not use a standard notion of coherence. Second, whereas coherence theories are typically internalist, Lehrer's theory consists of a combination of internalist and externalist components. Last, it incorporates self-trust as a main ingredient of a coherentist epistemology.

### *i. Lehrer's Conception of Coherence*

Lehrer's theory of knowledge and justification is based on a notion of coherence that differs in several respects from the standard conception that characterizes most coherentist epistemologies. First, the coherence that is relevant to justification, according to Lehrer, is not systemic coherence, but relational coherence. Most coherence theories, such as BonJour's, have attempted to define, first, what is required for a system to be coherent, and then consider as justified the beliefs that belong to such a system. In contrast, according to Lehrer, what is crucial for justification is the relation of coherence that a belief has with a system, where such a relation consists of the invincibility of a knowledge claim on the basis of the system. Thus, the standard talk of simplicity, explanatory power and inferential connectedness of a system is replaced by an account of coherence in terms of the positive capacity of a system to meet objections to a particular knowledge claim.

This relational theory of coherence has some advantages over systemic accounts of justification. First, it puts forward a dynamic picture of justification that is more akin to the way in which we actually justify our claims. Emphasizing the way in which a knowledge claim is defended against competitors seems a more accurate description of our justificatory practices than highlighting the properties that a system must satisfy in order to be justification-conferring. Secondly, as argued, systemic theories are psychologically unrealistic, for it is far beyond human capacities to perform the task that these theories require for justification, eg to compute the degree of coherence of a whole system of beliefs. In contrast, since Lehrer does not impose any constraint on the belief system, there is no need to go through the Herculean task of computing the coherence of the whole system, and thus, these psychological worries may be put to rest. Last, theories that require system coherence for justification have the undesirable result of making a belief unjustified if some of the beliefs of the system are incoherent, even if they are totally unrelated to the belief whose justification is at stake. Instead, Lehrer avoids this result for, according to his theory, only some claims, ie the objections, are relevant to the justification of a belief.

Despite these advantages, there are serious problems with Lehrer's relational theory of coherence. To being with, it is doubtful whether such a notion of relational coherence suffices for justification. For suppose that all objections to an acceptance are met on the basis of an evaluation system that is incoherent, or further, inconsistent. In this case, Lehrer's theory implies the counterintuitive result that such an acceptance will be justified. Since, in Lehrer's theory, justification does not depend in any way on the overall coherence of a person's system of evaluation, nothing prevents a person who accepts a lot of strange and divergent things from being personally justified.[109] To avoid this result, further conditions of coherence must be imposed on the system, besides its capacity to meet all objections.

In addition, the core notion that is behind this theory of relational coherence is that of comparative reasonableness. An acceptance coheres with a system, if all objections are met, that is, if it is more reasonable to accept such a claim than to accept competing claims. Such an analysis of coherence in terms of reasonableness is, indeed, very suggestive. The problem is, though, that Lehrer employs a rather obscure notion of reasonableness.[110] As argued, one of the main criticisms to coherence theories is that they rely on a notion of coherence that is, in most cases, poorly defined. Appealing to a notion such as that of reasonableness, whose prospects of being clearly defined are not better off than those of defining coherence itself, does not help to solve this problem. Not until we have a more detailed explanation of Lehrer's notion of reasonableness, can the extent to which his theory yields adequate results be determined.

### *ii. Externalism, Internalism and Lehrer's Coherentism*

Typically, coherence theories are internalist, since they require that the agent have access to the facts of coherence on which justification depends. Lehrer departs from the coherentist tradition in that his coherence theory is a combination of internalist and externalist elements.[111] On the one hand, personal justification is entirely an internal matter. For a person to be justified in accepting something, all objections to such acceptance must be met. It is not required, however, that a person reflects on these objections. It is enough, in order for a person to be justified, that her acceptance system implies that it is more reasonable to accept a claim than the competitors. These judgements of comparative reasonableness are based on a

[109] The point has been forcefully argued by Brendel (1999: 293–307). For Lehrer's reply to the objection that the notion of relational coherence does not suffice to justify what a person accepts when the system is incoherent, see Lehrer (1999: 252–54) and (2000b: 644).

[110] Feldman (1989: 69–76).

[111] Lehrer explicitly denies that his coherence theory of knowledge is an instance of either internalism or externalism. See Lehrer (2000b: 651).

keystone acceptance, ie the acceptance that our sources of information are trustworthy. One is justified in accepting something because one's evaluation system says that such an acceptance is a trustworthy guide to truth. Thus, in Lehrer's view, as opposed to externalist theories, it is not sufficient for justification that our beliefs arise from a trustworthy source, we must also accept that this is so.[112]

On the other hand, the notion of undefeated justification adds an externalist dimension to Lehrer's coherentism. Lehrer requires that for personal justification to be undefeated, and thus, convert into knowledge, what we accept about the trustworthiness of our sources of information must be true. This requirement incorporates the externalist insight that the reliability of our belief-forming process is a condition of knowledge, that is, that there must be a proper connection between our beliefs and the truth of what we accept. For Lehrer, the principle of trustworthiness provides the truth-connection that is required by externalism. It is the correctness about our own trustworthiness that supplies this connection. Hence, Lehrer's theory is a combination of both internalist and externalist conditions. First, it is internalist in that it is not enough for justification that we are reliable, but it is also required that we accept our own trustworthiness. And, secondly, it is externalist in that, in addition to our acceptance of our own trustworthiness, there must be an adequate connection between our beliefs and their truth. This externalist condition is established by the requirement that what we accept about our own trustworthiness be true.

Now, the question arises as to whether Lehrer's hybrid theory has the virtues of both internalism and externalism, and the vices of none of them. It is a main virtue of internalism that it allows justification to perform the guiding role that it is meant to. Doubts may be raised, however, about the extent to which internalism is psychologically plausible, for it requires that for someone to be justified he should know that the conditions of justification are satisfied, and it seems psychologically unrealistic to include such a requirement into the analysis of justification. In contrast, externalism is psychologically attractive; children and animals can be said to know, as long as their belief-forming processes are reliable. This conception of justification as reliability also provides a connection between standards of justification and truth, which is quite problematic to establish within an internalist framework, once foundationalism is rejected. However, this truth-connection comes with a price, for it is difficult to see how justification (as reliability) can guide action. The problem, thus, is that of determining whether: (i) the internalist dimension of Lehrer's hybrid theory suffices

[112] According to Lehrer, externalist theories cannot account for the kind of knowledge that has a role in critical reasoning and justification (ie discursive knowledge), but merely for the possession of information (ie primitive or informational knowledge). For Lehrer's critique of externalism, see (2000a) ch 8, esp 185–88.

to guarantee that justification can guide action; and (ii) its externalist component succeeds in guaranteeing that the standards of justification are truth-conducive. I shall leave the consideration of the second question for the next section, and consider now the first one.

If justification is to perform its essential role in guiding action, it is necessary that a person be able to know whether the conditions of justification obtain. Indeed, this insight is one of the main motivations of internalist theories. There are, however, reasons to doubt that Lehrer's coherentist notion of justification is up to this guiding task. To recall, according to Lehrer, an acceptance is justified provided that all objections are met on the basis of an evaluation system. Such an acceptance will be undefeated, and thus, will transform into knowledge, as long as such a justification is not taken away by allowing only part of the system (the t-system) to be used for meeting the objections. It seems, thus, that in order to know that one is personally justified one would need to (i) identify all objections; and (ii) determine whether they are met. In addition, since personal justification does not suffice for knowledge, one will know that one knows only if one knows that such a justification is undefeated. The trouble is that these are conditions that seem to be rarely, if ever, satisfied.

To begin with, the key role that the notion of reasonableness plays in the account of justification is a first source of problems. As explained, according to Lehrer, objections are claims whose truth-value has an influence on the reasonableness of accepting something. An objection is beaten if it is more reasonable to reject it than to accept it. Given the obscurity of the notion of reasonableness, it would be difficult to determine whether a putative objection is, in fact, so, let alone know whether it may be met on the basis of the evaluation system. In addition, it is important to notice that, according to Lehrer, justification is achieved only once *all* objections are met. It is unclear how one is supposed to know that these conditions obtain, for there can always be claims that are relevant to one's justification and that one has not even conceived. Thus, Lehrer's conditions of justification are such that it is virtually impossible that a person knows that she is personally justified.[113] To know, moreover, that such justification is undefeated, ie to know that the part of my evaluation system that is true suffices to meet all objections is, surely, beyond our reach.

### *iii. Self-Trust, Coherence and Truth*

The incorporation of self-trust, as a main ingredient of a coherentist epistemology is a very original feature of Lehrer's theory. Self-trust, in the form

[113] Peterson has argued at length that Lehrer's theory is such that one could never know that one knows anything in (1989: 77–93). For Lehrer's reply, see Lehrer ((1989: 265) and (1990a: 147)).

of the principle of trustworthiness, plays a key role in Lehrer's solution to the problem of coherence and truth. To recall, this principle states that I am trustworthy in what I accept with the objective of accepting something just in case it is true. However, on Lehrer's view, it is not enough for justification to go undefeated and thus convert into knowledge, that we accept that we are trustworthy, but we must in fact be trustworthy, as we take ourselves to be. If it is true that the appropriate connection obtains between trustworthiness and reliability, as the person accepts, then she would be justified in a way that is undefeated, and have knowledge. Hence, self-trust is meant to be a bridge-notion that provides the link between internal conditions of justification and external conditions of reliability.[114]

This externalist strategy, however, does not seem to work as a solution to the problem of the truth-conduciveness of coherence. As Lehrer recognizes, it does not follow from the principle of trustworthiness that one's acceptances are an infallible guide to truth or even a reliable guide to truth.[115] All that the principle allows one to infer is that one's acceptances are reasonable.[116] Furthermore, that one's acceptances are reasonable, says Lehrer, does not imply that they are justified in a way that is undefeated: for them to be so the person must accept that if she is trustworthy, then she is reliable, and such an acceptance must be true.[117] But then that an acceptance is justified because of its coherence with one's acceptance system says nothing about whether such an acceptance is reliable, let alone, true. In short, in the acknowledged gap between 'trustworthiness' and 'reliability' as well as between 'reasonableness' and 'justification' lies an unwanted gap between 'justification' and 'truth', that is, between coherence and truth.[118]

Thus, the principle of trustworthiness does not seem to satisfactorily show coherence to be truth-conducive. Moreover, as a matter of fact, there are serious difficulties with this principle. As explained earlier, according to Lehrer, principle *T* is justified as a result of applying the trustworthiness argument to *T* itself. In addition, principle *T* is justified on the basis of other things one accepts, and the reasonability of which is supported by *T*. However, there are two problems with this two-fold-justification. First, this justification introduces a foundationalist element into Lehrer's coherence theory, as the principle of trustworthiness seems to have the

[114] See Lehrer (2005: 421–23).

[115] Trustworthiness, says Lehrer, is to be understood as a capacity or disposition to be worthy of my trust in what I accept, as opposed to an infallible guide to truth or a reliable indicator of truth. See Lehrer (1997: 15ff). See also Lehrer (2000a: 139). So understood, self-trust is very much like an intellectual virtue. On the relation between trustworthiness and intellectual virtue, see Lehrer ((2000a: 140 and 209–12) and (2000b: 648–50)).

[116] Some critics have raised doubts as to whether this more modest conclusion, ie that one's acceptances are reasonable, may be inferred from the principle of trustworthiness. See David (1991) and S Cohen (1999).

[117] Lehrer (1997: 35).

[118] For a similar line of criticism, see Craig (2000: 659–60).

kind of self-justificatory status that is distinctive of basic beliefs.[119] And, second, there is a vicious circularity in the trustworthiness argument, for we use principle T as a premise to support the conclusion that the other acceptances are reasonable, and then use those acceptances and the principle itself to conclude that it is reasonable to accept it. Thus, it is at least doubtful whether Lehrer's principle of trustworthiness can be justified in a way that does not seriously compromise Lehrer's coherentism, while avoiding vicious circularity.[120]

To sum up, self-trust, as embodied in a presumption of trustworthiness, is a core element in a coherentist epistemology. Despite its advantages, this principle cannot solve the problem of connecting up coherence and truth. I may be worthy of my own trust, as the presumption states, and thus reasonable in accepting what I do. I may even be able to answer all objections to my acceptance on the basis of my evaluation system. And yet, I may be wrong about whether I am, in fact, trustworthy in what I accept. Since, as Lehrer acknowledges, my trustworthiness is no guarantee of success. To be sure, if it happens that my ultrasystem does indeed sustain what I accept, including the acceptance of my own trustworthiness, then I am justified in a way that is undefeated, and attain knowledge. The connection between justification and truth arises thus when we turn from personal justification to undefeated justification. But, since the facts upon which undefeated justification depends are unavailable to us, we are left without a reason for thinking that any of the beliefs that we justify on the basis of its coherence with our acceptance system is even likely to be true.

## IV. THE CURRENT STATE OF THE COHERENCE THEORY OF EPISTEMIC JUSTIFICATION

As I explained earlier, the coherence theory of epistemic justification was originally proposed as an alternative to foundationalism. However, for this theory to be a plausible alternative, it needs to be advanced in two fronts. On the one hand, there is a need to provide a cogent defence of the coherentist project against well-known objections. On the other, in order to move from mere 'theory sketch' to 'actual theory', as Bender puts it, it is necessary to work out in detail a coherentist account of epistemic justification.[121] The coherence theories of Lehrer and BonJour that I have discussed in the previous two sections are the most significant efforts to date to advance

[119] For a formulation of this problem, see Davis and Bender (1989: 64–66).

[120] For Lehrer's reply to the charge of foundationalism, see Lehrer ( (1997: 9), (1989: 274) and (2000a: 143)). For Lehrer's reply to the charge of circularity, see Lehrer ((1986a: 188), (2000a: 143ff) and (1997: 23)).

[121] Bender (1989b: 1).

the coherence theory in both directions. Here, I shall briefly contrast both theories and examine their similarities. This comparison may help appreciate the extent to which the coherence theory may be seen as a plausible alternative theory of epistemic justification, as well as to identify the main problems that still remain open and await further research.[122]

## A. The Role of Coherence in Justification

BonJour's and Lehrer's epistemologies give coherence a different role. According to Lehrer, justification and knowledge are a matter of coherence with one's evaluation system, and one's t-system, respectively. Thus, in his view, coherence is sufficient for both justification and knowledge. In contrast, BonJour's theory is best understood as a theory of justification, rather than as a theory of knowledge. Most importantly for the purposes of this chapter, his views on the role of coherence in epistemic justification importantly diverge from Lehrer's. Unlike Lehrer, he does not take coherence to provide a sufficient condition for epistemic justification. In BonJour's view, coherence is a paramount condition of justification, but he adds to it a number of substantive additional constraints. To recall, according to BonJour, for a belief to be justified, it must belong to a system that is coherent, and for that system to be a justification-conferring system, in addition to being coherent, it must satisfy the following conditions: (i) it must be a system held by someone; (ii) it must meet the Observation Requirement; (iii) it must remain coherent and stable over time; and (iv) the person must have a reflective grasp, ensured by the doxastic presumption, that the system satisfies the required conditions. As BonJour recognizes, this theory is not a 'pure' coherence theory, since justification is constrained by criteria other than coherence and coherence is not claimed to be 'the sole basis of justification'.[123] An examination of both BonJour's and Lehrer's views has brought to light the formidable difficulties that an attempt to explain all justification in terms of coherence faces. 'While—as says BonJour—it is plausible that coherence or something like it is *one* important ingredient in empirical justification, it is initially very implausible that it is the whole story'.[124] Thus, it seems sensible to supplement the appeal to coherence with other elements in order to meet the objections against coherentism. It is an open question though whether supplementing coherence with other relevant criteria helps meet the objections against coherentism but at the

[122] For an insightful discussion of the coherence theory that focuses on the work of Lehrer and BonJour, see Bender (1989b: 1–14).

[123] BonJour (1985: 148).

[124] BonJour (1999a: 122).

price of leading the coherence view to a relapse into foundationalism—on this issue see section IV.I.

## B. Coherentism, Externalism and Internalism

The internalist-externalist divide is one of the most important debates in current epistemology, and it also extends over the design of the coherence theory. BonJour and Lehrer's views importantly diverge on how accessible the facts of coherence must be. BonJour's commitment to internalism leads him to require that for a belief to be justified, the believer must have a grasp of his overall system of beliefs as well as access to the facts of coherence on which justification depends. In contrast, Lehrer's theory has both internalist and externalist components. On the one hand, personal justification requires that the believer's system of acceptances include metabeliefs about one's trustworthiness. On the other hand, undefeated justification is a matter of coherence with a corrected system, which includes those metabeliefs. Since we have no access to the corrected system (for surely a person does not know which among her acceptances are false), the facts of coherence required for undefeated justification, and thus knowledge, are not available to the subject. Arguments in favour and against internalism and externalism may be extrapolated to the discussion over whether coherentism must be wedded with internalism, as BonJour does, or whether, instead, a hybrid coherence theory, such as Lehrer's, is a more plausible alternative. On the one hand, internalist coherentism faces the plausibility objection in a particular strong form—see section IV.G below. On the other, by allowing externalist elements into the coherentist picture, we make it harder, if not impossible, for coherentist justification to play the regulative role in thought and action that it ought to play.

## C. The Role of Second-Order Beliefs in Coherentist Justification

An important lesson to be drawn from both BonJour's and Lehrer's accounts of coherence regards the issue of what should be included in the base of coherence, ie the system of beliefs coherence with which yields justification. Both BonJour and Lehrer give a prominent role to second-order beliefs in their coherentist accounts of justification. According to BonJour, one needs to have metabeliefs to the effect that one holds such and such beliefs, that one's system of belief is coherent, that one's system of beliefs has remained so in the long run and that it contains laws attributing a high degree of reliability to a reasonable variety of cognitively spontaneous beliefs. Lehrer requires that one's evaluation system contain meta-acceptances to the effect that the person is trustworthy in accepting a certain proposition, where such meta-acceptances are inductively inferred from the meta-acceptance that one accepts that *p* and one's acceptance that one is a trustworthy evaluator of truth.[125] Hence, the base of coherence should include both first-order and second-order beliefs. Moreover, these second-order beliefs are crucial for responding to some of the most serious objections against coherentism. In what follows, I shall briefly consider the extent to which Lehrer and BonJour's theories succeed in meeting the objections that have been raised against coherentism.

## D. Systemic vs Relational Coherence

The first objection against coherentism that we listed at the beginning of this chapter was the 'vagueness objection'. According to this objection, the coherence theory relies on a notion of coherence that is poorly specified. Both BonJour and Lehrer make a significant contribution towards clarifying this notion, but their views on coherence importantly differ. In fact, BonJour's and Lehrer's theory may be seen as advancing two different models of coherence: a 'systemic' model and a 'relational' one, respectively.[126] According to the former, coherence is a property ascribable to systems of beliefs. In the latter, coherence is a relation between a given belief and a system of other beliefs, rather than a property of the whole system. Whether systemic or relational coherence is more fundamental is an open question, as is the question of how these two kinds of coherence relate to each other.[127]

As an account of system coherence, BonJour's list of conditions of coherence does clarify some of the main factors that contribute to the coherence of a system of beliefs. Nevertheless, as argued, BonJour's analysis of the notion of coherence is somewhat wanting. Some aspects of this notion need to be further developed, such as the relation between coherence and consistency as well as the kind of inferential relations that are relevant to coherence. Lehrer's relational theory of coherence in terms of reasonableness is quite innovative. However, as claimed, it would be desirable to have a fuller account of reasonableness to plug into the notion of coherence. This said, it must be noticed that the notion of coherence is closely related to other

[125] This appeal to second-order beliefs which Lehrer and BonJour share is also prominent in other coherentist accounts of justification. See eg M Williams (1980: 248).

[126] In addition, whereas Lehrer's theory is more amenable to model the dynamic aspects of coherence, BonJour's theory seems to embody a synchronic, rather than a diachronic, model of coherence. The role of coherence in the dynamics of epistemic justification will be the focus of the next two chapters.

[127] On the distinction between systemic and relational coherence, as well as on the relations between them, see Bender (1989b: 2–3); Bartelborth (1999); M Williams (1996: 279); Olsson (1999); U Wiedemann, 'Michael William's Concepts of Systematical and Relational Coherence' available at www.pyrrhon.de/cohere/williams.htm; and Hansson (2006: 96–99).

notions, such as that of explanation, probabilistic relations etc the elucidation of which are among the most important, and yet unsolved, problems in epistemology. Hence, one should not blame the coherence theory for not providing solutions to these longstanding problems. As the theory of explanation, the canons of induction, or the theory of probability evolve, coherence theories would also be in a better position to articulate a precise conception of coherence.

## E. Problems of Coherentist Justification: Circularity, Conservatism and Regress

The battery of objections addressed against coherence theory includes the charge that coherentist justification is viciously circular and unduly conservative. BonJour's remarks on the holistic nature of justification, according to which the unit of justification is the whole system of beliefs, as well as Lehrer's metaphoric picture of our evaluation system as a loop in which a circular keystone supports and connects the arches of acceptance and preference which, in turn, lean against the keystone and hold it in place, replace the linear view of justification, which gives rise to the problem of circularity in the first place, by one in which justification is a matter of mutual support.

As regards conservatism, BonJour's and Lehrer's appeal to second-order beliefs suggest a way in which coherence theories need not be interpreted as favouring received views, even in the face of conflicting evidence.[128] Lehrer's appeal to the acceptance of our own trustworthiness provides a *rationale* for the kind of conservatism that is inherent to coherentist views. According to epistemic conservatism, our actual system of beliefs provides the basis of justification. But this is as it should be if, as Lehrer says, we consider our beliefs as worthy of our trust.[129] BonJour's appeal to our second-order beliefs to the effect that our system of beliefs satisfies the Observation Requirement puts a limit to the conservative policy involved in coherentism. We cannot protect our views against contrary evidence if this results in our system of beliefs failing to satisfy the Observation Requirement. Hence, there are elements in both BonJour's and Lehrer's theory that prevent coherentist justification from being both circular and unduly conservative.

As soon as some answers are given to some objections, other objections are addressed against coherence theories. More recently, two objections

[128] That the conservative objection has no force against a coherence theory which includes not only first-order beliefs but also second-order beliefs has also been argued by Williams; see M Williams (1980: 249).

[129] Lehrer (1997: 26).

have been added to the list of traditional objections against coherentism: the regress objection and the feasibility objection. I shall discuss the latter shortly (see section IV.G). As for the objection that a coherentist justification of one's beliefs that one has such-and-such system of beliefs generates an infinite regress, it is, again, appeal to second-order beliefs (more specifically, metabeliefs to the effect that one approximately holds the beliefs that one takes oneself to hold) that provide the defence for coherentism. These metabeliefs fall within what BonJour calls, to recall, the doxastic presumption, which functions as a regress stopper. Even though, as argued, there are many problems with the doxastic presumption, it is indeed a very interesting way of dealing with the issue of the believer's representation of his own system of belief, which internalist coherentism requires, in a way that avoids falling back into an infinite regress.

### F. Coherence and Truth

Most important among the objections against coherentism are those that challenge that the appropriate connection obtains between the coherence of a system of beliefs and the goal of truth. There are three objections that have to do with the relation, or purported lack of relation, between coherence and truth: the isolation objection, the alternative coherent systems objection and the truth objection. BonJour and Lehrer effect the truth-connection, and thus, answer these objections, in quite a different way. Crucial to BonJour's response to the isolation or input objection is the appeal to the Observation Requirement. Hence, BonJour adds some material constraints on coherentist justification to ensure that one's system of beliefs takes good notice of empirical input, and is thus properly connected with the external world. In contrast, Lehrer does not directly impose any material constraints on the justification-conferring system. His suggestion is that these constraints indirectly follow from his conception of justification. For a person to be justified all objections to one's claim must be either beaten or neutralized, including the objection that one is not properly connected with the external world. Thus, what is needed for meeting the objections against one's claims also suffices, in Lehrer's view, to meet the isolation (and input) objections against coherentism.

With regard to the truth objection, BonJour's strategy is to connect coherence with truth *via* the justificatory argument. According to this argument, the best explanation of a system of beliefs that remains coherent and stable in the long run while satisfying the Observation Requirement is that it is approximately true. In contrast, Lehrer draws the truth-connection conceptually: undefeated justification results from coherence with one's ultrasystem, ie one's true acceptances. Nonetheless, from the believer perspective, there is no reason to believe that what she accepts on the basis of coherence is likely to be true. The person must accept that she is trustworthy, and that her trustworthiness is connected with her reliability; however, in addition to that, such an acceptance must be true, if it is to pass into the ultrasystem. And whether this is so is, after all, inaccessible to the believer. Thus, it is only when the externalist component of justification comes into the picture that the connection between coherence and truth gets effected.

## G. The Plausibility Objection

Another objection against coherence theories is the 'psychological plausibility objection', or the 'feasibility objection'. The problem, as explained before, is that the coherentist model of justification requires us to perform inferential tasks which are well beyond the capacity of most epistemic agents. More specifically, it is psychologically implausible, so the objection goes, that people have the beliefs they would need to achieve coherence and, therefore, knowledge. Both BonJour and Lehrer are charged with objections along these lines.[130] We typically lack the second-order beliefs about the contents of our belief system, its degree of coherence and the number and kinds of beliefs about which of our beliefs are reliable that BonJour's coherence theory requires. Similarly, it is psychologically implausible that epistemic agents hold meta-acceptances to the effect that one's acceptances follow from one's evidence and that one's acceptances are a trustworthy guide to truth. The objection is one that needs to be taken seriously. For notice that these second-order beliefs the plausibility of which is challenged are crucial to responding to other objections against coherentism. Hence, ultimately, the success of BonJour's and Lehrer's theory in responding to the traditional objections against coherentism may be seriously undermined if the plausibility objection is not, at least, mitigated.

Lehrer's answer to this objection appeals to the functional role of acceptance. According to Lehrer, the functional mental state of acceptance may arise without reflective judgement. Thus, acceptances need not be explicit believings. Because of that, we may posit acceptances of certain sorts where positing an analogous belief would be controversial. As has been argued, a clearer account is needed of the conditions of acceptance than the one that is available so far, for this response to be successful.[131]

BonJour's strategy against the plausibility objection is similar to Lehrer's in that he also claims that the relevant metabeliefs need only be tacit. However, ultimately, BonJour disposes of the objection by accepting that the conditions of coherence he postulates are not applicable to real epistemic

[130] For a discussion of this objection as it applies to BonJour's and Lehrer's coherence theories, see Greco (1993).

[131] See Bender (1989: 12).

agents, and by suggesting that they are an ideal which human beings may only approximate.[132] The trouble is that BonJour's ideal seems to be just too far removed from what we can reasonably be expected to accomplish for it to provide us with any guidance in our epistemic inquiries.[133] Hence, what we need is a coherentist model of justification that, while being normatively appealing—and this will surely involve an element of idealization—is also psychologically plausible.

## H. Coherence and Holism

The psychological implausibly of both BonJour's and Lehrer's models is seriously aggravated by the fact that they put the whole system of beliefs at work in order to justify any single belief. I have already indicated, while discussing BonJour's views, the problems that derive from BonJour's commitment to holism. In BonJour's theory, the 'systemic coherence' of the whole system of beliefs is relevant to the justification of any single belief. Lehrer's view is also holistic, albeit in a different sense. In Lehrer's theory, the 'relational coherence' of any single belief, and thus its justification, is a function of its reasonableness in comparison to competing propositions, given the person's *whole* system of evaluation.

The holistic element that exists in both BonJour and Lehrer's theory dramatically diminishes their adequacy as theories of justification that can be put to work in a real setting. BonJour has recently come to recognize the need to construe the unit of justification in a way that does not involve the whole system of a person's beliefs.[134] Lehrer also seems to be sensitive to the problem of the large size of the unit of justification, when he restricts the number of objections that an agent must consider to those that are relevant.[135] Nonetheless, neither Lehrer, nor BonJour, have actually worked out in detail an account of coherence and justification in which the unit of justification can be put to actual functioning. In such an account, context is likely to play a pivotal role in individuating the unit of justification in a given instance of a process of justification. This is, as a matter of fact, a main tenet of the contextualist theories of epistemic justification, which I shall discuss in the next section. Thus, the development of a psychologically

[132] BonJour (1989: 284).

[133] See Bender (1989:12).

[134] BonJour later came to accept that the justification of individual beliefs is partially a function of the particular inferential connections that pertain directly to those beliefs; see BonJour (1989: 290).

[135] Originally, Lehrer introduced the notion of 'epistemic field' with regard to the notion of 'epistemic competitor'. Epistemic agents are expected to restrict their consideration to some set of statements that they believe to be germane to the statement in question, ie the epistemic field; see Lehrer (1974: 195).

plausible model of coherentist justification goes hand-in-hand with the development of a contextualized one.[136]

## I. Coherentism and Foundationalism

Lehrer and BonJour do provide some answers to the main objections that have been addressed against coherence theories. As noted, the responses of both of them rely on metabeliefs of diverse kinds. Now, the question arises of whether their strategies for meeting these objections, in particular, their reliance on a set of metabeliefs, are serious concessions to foundationalism. Are BonJour's Observation Requirement and the doxastic presumption, as well as Lehrer's principle of trustworthiness, significant qualifications to their coherence theories? As argued before, despite appearances to the contrary, BonJour and Lehrer do provide genuine alternatives to foundationalism. As regards BonJour, the Observation Requirement should not be interpreted as requiring that some initial credibility be attached to cognitively spontaneous beliefs. Thus, nothing supports the view that his coherence theory is, at bottom, a kind of moderate foundationalism. In addition, BonJour does not claim that the beliefs specified by the doxastic presumption possess any sort of independent justification. In his view, they are not in need of justification, coherentist or otherwise. Rather, they are a presupposition in relation to which any question of justification is to be addressed. On this point, BonJour's view about the metabeliefs required for coherentist justification markedly differs from Lehrer's. According to Lehrer, the metabeliefs to the effect that one is trustworthy do stand in need of justification. However, such justification is also a matter of coherence with the rest of the evaluation system. Hence, BonJour and Lehrer do seem to avoid a relapse into foundationalism.

To conclude, Lehrer and BonJour must be given credit for having articulated in detail a coherence theory of epistemic justification and taken up the task of addressing the well-known objections against this view. Most important among these objections is the objection from psychological plausibility, particularly, the objection that BonJour and Lehrer's theories appeal to second-order beliefs that are psychologically unrealistic. Because BonJour and Lehrer's responses to several objections against coherentism importantly rely on these beliefs, the charge that these are psychologically unrealistic sheds serious doubts upon the capability of these theories to successfully deal with these objections.

[136] For a proposal about how the process of epistemic justification could be developed in a coherentist, contextualized and naturalized way, see Duran ((1986) and (1993)).

As argued, the charge of psychological implausibility is aggravated by the fact that both BonJour and Lehrer's theories involve a commitment to holism. A theory of epistemic justification which, while giving coherence a role in justification, does not take it that it is the whole system of beliefs that is relevant for assessing the justificatory status of a belief would be in a much better position to solve the problem of psychological plausibility, and thus, to mitigate the force of the rest of the objections. A theory along these lines has been proposed by some advocates of contextualist theories of epistemic justification, the analysis of which is the objective of the next section.

## V. CONTEXUALISM, COHERENCE AND EPISTEMIC JUSTIFICATION

Contextualism is the view that standards of justification and knowledge vary with context. Contextualism is a newcomer in the epistemological landscape. The traditional foundationalist view of knowledge and justification, as well as the relatively recent coherence theory, are based on the assumption that epistemic standards are fixed across contexts. That is, both foundationalism and coherentism take it that the conditions under which beliefs are justified are not context-dependent. Thus, contextualism diverges in an important respect from the epistemological tradition in which the foundationalism-coherentism debate takes place.

As may be clear from the previous discussion, the debate over the structure of justification is in a kind of impasse. The problems of foundationalism—as argued—if not insurmountable, are serious enough to prompt the consideration of alternative accounts of epistemic justification. Coherentism is the most important alternative to foundationalism. However, coherentism comes along with a number of equally daunting problems. The force of the objections against coherentism is importantly diminished against current versions of the coherence theory, such as BonJour's and Lehrer's theory. These theories significantly advance the case for coherentism in epistemology, but, as I have just claimed, there are still a number of problems that remain open in the current state of the coherence theory. Most importantly, both BonJour's and Lehrer's coherence theories are committed to an unrestricted version of holism which seriously undermines the psychological plausibility of these theories and sheds doubts about whether these theories are ultimately capable of meeting the traditional objections that have been raised against coherentism.

There is a wide variety of contextualist positions.[137] For our purposes, the most interesting kinds of contextualism are structural versions of

[137] There is a wide variety of more or less closely related contextualist positions. For a useful discussion of contextualist views, see Timmons (1999: 182–90) and DeRose (2009: 1–46).

contextualism.[138] Structural contextualism claims to provide a third theory about the structure of epistemic justification.[139] Under this contextualist view, the unit of justification is neither the single belief—as foundationalism has it—nor the whole system of beliefs—as coherentism affirms—but rather the subset of the system of beliefs that is relevant for justification in a particular context. In what follows, I shall focus on some contextualist proposals of this structural variety and contrast them with the foundationalist and coherentist views about the structure of epistemic justification which they purport to replace.

## A. Contextualism and the Structure of Epistemic Justification

'Structural contextualism' is the thesis that regresses of justification may legitimately terminate with beliefs, which, in the context in question, are not in need of justification.[140] Structural contextualism (hereinafter 'contextualism') has its roots in the writings of pragmatists like Peirce and Dewey, in Austin, and the later writings of Wittgenstein. According to contextualism, the set of recognized responses to the regress problem is too restrictive. To recall, the solutions to the regress problem that are generally considered are: the regress stops with a set of foundational beliefs, which are non-inferentially justified and provide the epistemic basis for inferentially justified beliefs; there are no regress stoppers, rather, all justification is inferential; the regress ends with beliefs that are unjustified; and the chain of justifying beliefs continues infinitely. Given the implausibility of the last two options, we seem to have two kinds of solutions available: foundationalism

[138] I am using here Timmons' label, who distinguishes between semantic, structural, circumstantial and normative contextualism (Timmons: 1999: 187). An important distinction is that between 'subject' contextualism and 'attributor' contextualism. While the former makes epistemic standards relative to the context of the putative subject knowledge, the latter makes them sensitive to features of the context of the attributor, ie the person who appraises the epistemic status of the subject's belief. See DeRose (1999: 190–91). Structural contextualism is a species of subject contextualism. In addition, it is important to distinguish between contextualist views which are concerned with making substantive claims about knowledge or justification itself and views the focus of which is not knowledge/justification per se, but rather the linguistic mechanisms we use when speaking about knowledge and justification. See P Rysiew, 'Epistemic Contextualism', *The Stanford Encyclopedia of Philosophy* (Winter 2011 edn), EN Zalta (ed), http://plato.stanford.edu/archives/win2011/entries/contextualism-epistemology/. Structural contextualism falls in the substantive side of the substantive/semantic divide.

[139] Other versions of contextualism are not a thesis about the structure of knowledge or justification and are claimed to be, in fact, consistent with both foundationalism and coherentism; see DeRose ((1999:190) and ((2009: 21)).

[140] Timmons defends a version of structural contextualism about justified moral belief (1999) ch 5. For a defence of structural contextualism about practical rationality, see Heath (1997). On structural contextualism about epistemic justification, see Annis (1978); M Williams ((1980), (1999) Afterword and (2001)); and Henderson (1994).

embraces the first one, while coherentism favours the second option. Contextualists dispute that the regress argument so stated correctly defines the space of possible epistemological theories. According to contextualism, there is another way to solve the regress problem, namely, the regress of justification may terminate with beliefs that are not in need of justification, ie 'contextually basic beliefs'.

Different analyses of the notion of 'contextually basic belief' yield different versions of structural contextualism. Here I shall very briefly introduce three versions of structural contextualism: Annis' pioneering work on contextualism; Timmons' contextualism; and Williams' contextualist model. According to Annis, 'a belief is *contextually* basic if given an issue-context the appropriate objector-group does not require the person to have reasons for the belief in order to be in a position to have knowledge'.[141] The 'issue-context' is the specific issue someone raises about a belief. And the 'objector-group' is the group of people qualified to raise objections about a particular belief. For Annis, a person is justified in holding a belief if she has responded to all challenges to that belief coming from the objector-group in a way that satisfies its practices and norms of justification.

Timmons' brand of contextualism—unlike Annis'—does not rely on a 'challenge-response model of justification'. Timmons holds that whether one's belief needs justification varies in ways that depend upon one's goals and purposes. He claims that an individual is justified in holding a belief 'when she has adequately dealt with those counterpossibilities whose seriousness is indicated by her own background beliefs and with those indicated by relevant information widely shared by a relevant community'.[142] Shifts in goals or in their relative importance determine the range of relevant counterpossibilities that bear on the justificatory status of one's belief. Timmons refers to things like expertise in some area of inquiry, one's occupation, and the importance of being right in one's belief about a certain matter as factors that affect the range of counterpossibilities which in a context one needs to check in order to be justified.

As Williams construes contextualism, it is the view that justification always takes place in a context of inquiry in which inquirers take some things for granted. He writes: 'justification is a matter of accommodating beliefs that are being questioned to a body of accepted beliefs'.[143] Williams claims that justification has what Brandom calls a 'default and challenge' structure.[144] In this model, says Williams, 'questions of justification always arise in a definite justificational context, constituted by a complex

[141] Annis (1978: 216).
[142] Timmons (1999: 212).
[143] M Williams (1999: 112).
[144] See Brandom (1994) ch 4.

and largely tacit background of entitlements, some of which will be default'.[145] Now, what beliefs are those that need to be accommodated, that is, those that are open to challenge? Williams' reply is that '[w]hat is to be accommodated to what depends on what questions are being asked. Contextualization of the notion of justification brings with it contextualization of the notion of doubt'.[146] Hence, according to Williams, the set of contextually basic beliefs is determined by the nature of the inquiry we are engaged in. Williams mentions five different factors that influence the epistemic status of claims and challenges, that is, that determine whether a belief is contextually basic in a particular context of inquiry. First, there are semantic constraints. Many beliefs must be taken for granted, for a question to be intelligible at all. Secondly, methodological constraints exclude some propositions from doubt when raising questions of some specific kind and determine the direction of inquiry. Thirdly, there are dialectical constraints. Claims which face standing objections may not enjoy default status. Fourthly, economic issues are also relevant here. A defeater does not come into play simply by virtue of being mentioned: there has to be a reason to think that it might obtain. Analysis of costs and benefits prominently figure here. For instance, if it is important to reach some decision, and if the costs of error are low, then, argues Williams, it is reasonable to have a relaxed attitude towards justificatory standards. Last, situational factors, that is, facts about the actual situation in which claims are entered, come into play as well.[147]

Despite differences, all versions of structural contextualism embrace the same strategy for stopping the regress of justification, to wit, they appeal to contextually basic beliefs, that is, beliefs that need not be justified in a given context. Hence, structural contextualism provides a solution to the regress problem that is alternative to the more traditional foundationalist and coherentist solutions. I shall now conclude this (admittedly brief) discussion of contextualism by exploring the relationship between contextualism and the two main competing accounts of the structure of epistemic justification, namely, foundationalism and coherentism.

### B. Contextualism and the Foundationalism vs Coherentism Debate

As explained, contextualism, in its structural variety, purports to offer an alternative account of the structure of epistemic justification. From a contextualist perspective, both foundationalism and coherentism endorse an

[145] M Williams (2001: 159).
[146] M Williams (1980: 253).
[147] M Williams (2001: 159–62).

implausible view of the structure of justification. Williams expresses the point very clearly:

> From a contextualist point of view, both foundationalist and the coherence theory are overreactions. Seeing the need for fixed points to block the indefinite repetition of requests for evidence, the foundationalist postulates a stratum of intrinsically credible or self-justifying beliefs. The coherence theorist sees the problems that the demand for intrinsic credibility gives rise to. In particular, he notices that individual beliefs owe their justificatory status and significance to relations with further beliefs. But he goes from this reasonable anti-atomism to radical holism, with its own serious difficulties. Contextualism, because it allows both fixed points and epistemic interdependence, has a good claim to incorporate the best features of its traditionalist rivals.[148]

As this passage states, contextualism rejects both foundationalists' 'atomistic' view of justification, as embodied in the linear model of justification, and coherentists' 'holistic' view of justification.

As opposed to foundationalism, contextualists reject that there is a homogeneous class of beliefs with a distinct characteristic that gives them a measure of non-inferential justification so that they serve as regress stoppers in all contexts of justification. Contextualists grant to coherentists that relations of mutual support are crucial for justification. However, they deny that the kind of systemic relations of mutual support featured in coherentist accounts is sufficient for justification. For, along with the foundationalists, they require that some beliefs serve as regress stoppers, ie beliefs that are not in the particular context open to challenge. These beliefs, it is hold, properly form the foundation for the beliefs the justificatory status of which is called into question in a specific context. Hence, contextualists reject the holistic view of justification, which coherentism typically endorses, according to which the justification of any belief ultimately depends on the justification of our whole system of beliefs. More specifically, they reject a strictly global application of the coherentist standards of justification. To start with, contextualism alleges that such an application is not feasible for human beings. The coherentist justificatory schema seems to require that agents have an explicit grasp of their full system of beliefs and be able to survey them and check them for coherence. This task, contend the contextualists, is far beyond the power of human cognitive endowment.[149] Moreover, the coherentist standard of justification is not even an ideal for contextualists. It is not as if contextualism is merely a kind of unambitious coherentism, that is, a modest approximation to other ideals, ie the coherentist ideal. Rather,

[148] M Williams (2001: 168).

[149] Henderson (1994: 633, 635 and 637). On the 'feasibility objection' against coherentism, see Kornblith (1989); Cherniak (1986) ch 3; and M Williams (2001: 136–37). See also Timmons (1993) (on this objection as it applies to coherentism about the justification of moral, rather than empirical, beliefs).

contextualists insist that coherentist standards are holistic in a seriously problematic manner. Holistic coherentism, in their view, is not only psychologically unrealistic, but also epistemologically troubling.[150] In short, from a contextualist perspective, coherentist standards of justification are not desirable at the level of ideals, not just unworkable in practice.[151]

In short, contextualism advocates a view of justification that is meant to be an alternative to both foundationalists' atomism and coherentists' holism. Still, one could insist that in contextualism there are 'basic beliefs', even if which beliefs are basic varies with context. Thus, it may be argued that contextualism is, at bottom, a kind of foundationalism. Similarly, one could stress the fact that contextualism makes justification a matter of inferential relations, even if the set of beliefs that are relevant to justification is contextually determined. Thus, it might be argued that contextualism is, properly understood, a kind of coherentism. Surely, one could view contextualism as foundationalism with changing and heterogonous foundations, or as coherentism with a changing base. But the fact remains that the conception of justification that it embodies is different from both foundationalism and coherentism.

Contextualism represents a significant departure from the epistemological tradition that both foundationalism and coherentism represent. First, as opposed to the context-free notion of justification that foundationalism and coherentism embrace, contextualists take contextual parameters to be pivotal to justification. Secondly, foundationalists and coherentists have looked for universal and a priori principles of justification that are applicable to the whole system of belief of an individual. In contrast to the tradition's epistemic individualism, contextualists emphasize the social dimension of epistemic justification. Last, foundationalism and coherentism aim at rebutting the sceptical conclusion that the regress argument entails by offering a view about the structure of the individual's whole system of justified belief. This conception of the epistemological enterprise is indeed very different from the sort of inquiry in which contextualists engage. Contextualists take justification to be a social, local and contextualized notion. Just as they contextualize the notion of justification, they contextualize the notion of doubt. Hence, not only do they refuse to talk of the structure of justification at the level of our total view, but they also refuse to take answering the global sceptic, who asks what reason we have for

[150] Coherentists' commitment to holism gives rise, argues Williams, to a dilemma. If coherentists take their commitment seriously, then they open an infinite regress. The only way to avoid the regress is to exclude the criteria of coherence themselves from thorough revisability. But then coherentism ends up being a kind of foundationalism in which criteria of coherence enjoy a foundational status; see M Williams (2001: 134–35). That coherentism is a species of foundationalism is also argued by Fritzman (1992); Plantinga (1993: 77–80); and Fumerton (1999).

[151] This point is pressed with particular force by Henderson (1994: 634–35).

thinking that any of the beliefs we hold are justified, as the primary goal of epistemological inquiry.[152] Thus, the contextualist's picture of justification is very far removed from the traditional view of justification that both foundationalism and coherentism embrace.

Regardless of whether one takes contextualism to be a kind of either foundationalism or coherentism, or rather, a distinctive alternative, the important thing to note here is that it suggests a very interesting way in which coherence may be claimed to play a role in epistemic justification. As the brief examination of the contextualists views brings to light, coherence may operate not only at the level of the whole system of beliefs, but also at a more local level, ie at the level of a subset of beliefs. The identification of such a subset of beliefs is, in the contextualist view, a matter of context, where the 'context' may be fixed in different ways. It may be determined by individuating which beliefs go unchallenged by a particular group (eg Annis), by identifying the beliefs that are presupposed in a particular context of inquiry (eg Williams) as well as by reference to the goals and purposes of those who are engaged in the activity of justification (eg Timmons). Moreover, the degree of coherence that such a set of beliefs must exhibit for it to be justified may also be claimed to depend on contextual parameters. For instance, when the issue at stake is really important, it seems reasonable to require that beliefs strongly cohere with one another for them to be justified. This contextualized approach to coherentist justification avoids the serious problems that coherence theories of justification face because of their commitment to *tout court* holism, and thus may present a plausible alternative to the foundationalist view of epistemic justification. It is within a contextualist framework, I would contend, that issues of coherence and justification may be most profitably addressed.

## VI. CONCLUSIONS

This chapter has examined the role of coherence in epistemic justification. There are two main competing accounts of the structure of epistemic justification, to wit, foundationalism and coherentism. It is mainly the failure of foundationalism to cope with a number of enduring problems that has motivated the proposal of coherence theories of justification. Here, I have examined two main coherence theories of justification in contemporary epistemology, namely, BonJour's and Lehrer's. These theories, I have argued, significantly advance the project of articulating a detailed account of coherentist justification that has the resources for meeting the main objections that have been traditionally raised against coherentism.

[152] See Annis (1978: 214) and M Williams ((1980: 253–54, 262 and 272), (1996) and (2001: 150–52 and 168–70), throughout).

Nonetheless, I have claimed that there are still serious problems in the current state of the coherence theory. Most importantly, these theories are committed to holism about justification. This commitment seriously compromises the psychological plausibility of these theories. More specifically, it undermines the psychological plausibility of the second-order beliefs posited by these theories, which play a crucial role in BonJour's and Lehrer's response to the traditional objections that have been raised against coherentism. Thus, it is crucial that the coherence theory be free of its holistic commitments for it to provide a plausible account of the structure of epistemic justification.

In short, I have argued that the coherence theory needs to abandon the holistic assumption according to which it is the whole system of beliefs that is relevant to epistemic justification. Instead, the coherence theory may, more plausibly, contend that only a subset of one's beliefs is relevant for making the coherence judgements that are necessary to assess the justificatory status of a belief. The problem is, of course, that of individuating the subset that is relevant to justification. Some versions of contextualism, that is, the view that standards of justification (and knowledge) vary with context, indicate an interesting way in which this problem may be addressed. The crucial contextualist insight is that 'context' provides a valuable guidance as to how to identify the relevant set. According to (some versions of) contextualism, contextual features (such as one's goals and purposes, the stakes in a particular context of justification, background assumptions which go unchallenged in a specific context etc) fix the severity of our epistemic standards. This contextualist tenet when embedded in a coherentist epistemology implies that contextual factors determine the severity of the coherentist standards, that is, the domain within which coherence ought to be sought as well as the degree of coherence that such a base ought to exhibit in order to be justification-conferring. It is—I suggest—a contextualized version of coherentism that provides the most promising account of how coherence contributes to epistemic justification.

# 4

# *Explanatory Coherentism*

THIS CHAPTER FOCUSES on theories of explanatory coherence. According to these theories, whether a belief is justified depends on the way in which it fits into the best explanation of some puzzling facts. Thus, from this perspective, explanatory relations are the key for understanding the concept of coherence and its role in justification. This view, which was first propounded by Sellars,[1] has been defended, among others, by Harman,[2] Lycan,[3] Bartelborth[4] and Thagard.[5] Theories of explanatory coherence continue the tradition of explanationism, according to which 'explanation' is the core notion in a theory of reasoning and rationality.[6] I shall begin the examination of the theories of explanatory coherence by characterizing the explanationist view, within which these theories should be located, by a number of assumptions. After introducing the theories of explanatory coherence and placing them within the explanationist framework, the rest of the chapter concentrates on Thagard's version of the theory of explanatory coherence. In the discussion of Thagard's views on coherence, I will proceed as follows. First, I will present Thagard's notion of coherence and his proposal as to how it can be computed. Next, I will introduce Thagard's theory of explanatory coherence, together with its computational implementation. Then, I will give an account of the non-explanatory kinds of coherence that figure in Thagard's explanatory coherentism. After having described these several kinds of coherence and their computational implementations, I will illustrate how this approach can be applied to the solution of one coherence problem, to wit, epistemic justification.

[1] See Sellars (1963).

[2] See Harman ((1973), (1980), (1986) and (1995)).

[3] See Lycan ((1988), (1996) and (2012)).

[4] See Bartelborth (1999).

[5] See Thagard (1989). An improved version of Thagard's theory of explanatory coherence was presented in (1992a). See also Thagard (2000a) for a concise statement of Thagard's theory of coherence and applications to a number of different problems.

[6] For a brief summary and discussion of the main accounts of explanation, see Newton-Smith (2000) and J Woodward, "Scientific Explanation", *The Stanford Encyclopedia of Philosophy* (Winter 2011 edn), EN Zalta (ed), http://plato.stanford.edu/archives/win2011/entries/scientific-explanation/. For an excellent critical survey of models of scientific explanation, see Salmon (1990). For anthologies that contain a number of influential articles on explanation, see Ruben (1993) and Pitt (1988). For a detailed survey of research on explanation, see Kitcher and Salmon (1989).

## I. EXPLANATIONISM

### A. The Common Framework

The distinctive characteristic of theories of explanatory coherence is their emphasis on the role that explanatory relations play in justification and their significance for understanding the notion of coherence. This emphasis usually comes together with a number of claims and assumptions:

i. Most proponents of explanatory coherence theories of justification endorse a cognitive naturalistic framework, very broadly understood as the view that psychological facts are relevant to epistemological issues, so that there is no sharp distinction between the normative and the descriptive.[7]
ii. Explanationists do not usually make a sharp distinction between practical and theoretical reasoning, and they claim that explanatory coherence is crucial in both realms.[8]
iii. They consider conservatism, in addition to explanatory coherence, as a pivotal factor in theory change and belief revision.[9]
iv. Most of them advocate a holistic view of justification according to which the whole system of beliefs is relevant to the justification of any single belief.[10]
v. They take inference to the best explanation to be the basic kind of non-deductive reasoning (if not the only legitimate kind).
vi. In contrast to Bayesian approaches to scientific inference,[11] explanationists consider probability to be at best incidental to belief revision and theory choice in most domains.[12]

Whereas assumptions (iii) and (iv) are also shared by advocates of non-explanatory kinds of coherentist theories of justification, the rest of the

[7] For a very clear introduction to naturalism, see Godfrey-Smith (2003) ch 11. For the history of naturalism, see Kitcher (1992). For a collection of papers on naturalism, see Kornblith (1993). Thagard has explicitly placed his work in the framework of cognitive naturalism in (2000) ch 1. Lycan defends that scientific and philosophical method is one and the same method in (1988) ch 6. See also Harman ((1986: 7) and (1995: 177–79 and 187–89)).

[8] See Harman ((1980: 155), (1995: 186–87) and (2004)); Lycan (1988: 125–26); and Thagard (2000a: 20–25).

[9] See Harman ((1986: 46–47) and (1995: 189–93)) and Lycan (1988) ch 8. According to Thagard, conservatism is a consequence of the theory of explanatory coherence rather than a separate factor in belief revision and theory choice. See Thagard ((1988: 152–55), (1989: 465–66), and (2000a: 75)).

[10] Harman ((1973) ch 10 and (1986: 33)).

[11] I have briefly discussed Bayesianism in ch 2. For an introduction to Bayesianism and its relevance to theory choice in science, see Godfrey-Smith (2003). See also Earman (1992) and Howson and Urbach (1993).

[12] See Harman ((1973) ch 7, (1980: 154–55) and (1986) ch 3); Thagard ((2000b) ch 8 and (2004)); and Eliasmith and Thagard (1997).

assumptions are typically embraced by the explanationist versions of coherentism. Assumption (v) is particularly important for the purposes of developing a coherence theory of legal justification, for, as will be argued in chapter ten, inference to the best explanation is a pivotal element in such a theory. Because of the relevance of this form of inference to legal coherentism, it is convenient to investigate in some detail the structure of inference to the best explanation as well as the main problems around which the current debate over this form of inference revolves.

### B. Inference to the Best Explanation

Explanationists assign a prominent role to explanatory reasoning, ie reasoning whereby explanatory hypotheses are formulated and evaluated. Discussions on explanatory reasoning take Peirce's classification of types of arguments into deductive, inductive and 'hypothesis' (or 'abduction') as their point of departure. Peirce's views on this classification of forms of reasoning considerably changed over time.[13] At an earlier stage, he distinguished between deductive reasoning, inductive reasoning and a kind of reasoning which he called 'hypothesis'. He characterizes 'hypothesis' as follows: 'Hypothesis is where we find some very curious circumstance which would be explained by the supposition that it was the case of a certain general rule, and thereupon adopt that supposition'.[14] Peirce holds that induction and hypothesis are two ways of inverting deductive arguments. Deduction is an inference of a result (conclusion) from two premises: a rule and a case. Induction results from exchanging the result with the major premise (the rule). Abduction results from exchanging the result with the minor premise (the case). He illustrated these forms of reasoning by means of the following example:

> All the beans from this bag are white. (rule)
>
> These beans are from this bag. (case)
>
> Therefore, these beans are white. (result)

Induction is the inference of the rule from the case and the result:

> These beans are from this bag. (case)
>
> These beans are white. (result)
>
> Therefore, all the beans from this bag are white. (rule)

[13] See D Anderson (1986) and Campos (2011: 421–31). For an attempt to reconstruct Peirce's notion of abduction and an analysis of the problems that it gives rise to, see Rescher (1978) and Kapitan (1997).

[14] Peirce (1932–58) vol 2, para 624.

Abduction is the inference of the case from the rule and the result:

All the beans from this bag are white. (rule)

These beans are white. (result)

Therefore, these beans are from this bag. (case)

In this early characterization, abduction has thus the following modern logical form:

Given the law $\forall x\ (Fx \rightarrow Gx)$

From Ga infer Fa.[15]

At a later stage, Peirce replaced 'hypothesis' in his classification with 'abduction'. In this new classification, abduction 'furnishes the reasoner with the problematic theory which induction verifies'.[16] Thus, abduction is the coming up with a hypothesis, which is then tested by induction. Peirce defines the abductive operation as follows:

The surprising fact C is observed;
But if A were true, C would be a matter of course;
Hence, there is reason to suspect that A is true.[17]

This schema is different from the previous one in two important respects. First, there is a shift from the belief that abduction can be a pattern of reasoning that gives us reasons for accepting a certain proposition, to the weaker view that it is only a form of discovery. In addition, and closely related to the previous point, there is a different understanding of the relation between induction and abduction. Whereas in the earlier schema abduction and induction are distinguished on the basis of their syllogistic form, in the latter, they are regarded as different phases in explanatory reasoning. The contrast between Peirce's characterizations of abduction identifies two major issues that are still today the subject of a lively debate: (i) the scope of the role of abduction in explanatory reasoning, that is, whether it plays a role only in the generation of hypotheses, or whether it also plays a role in their evaluation; and (ii) the relation between induction and abduction. In Peirce's thought we also find the basic contours of another problem that is at the centre of the current debate on abduction, namely, the issue of whether abduction is a legitimate form of inference. If, as Peirce suggested, abduction is an autonomous kind of reasoning, different from induction and deduction, what does abductive correctness come up to? According to Peirce, the legitimacy of abduction 'depends upon altogether different

[15] Niiniluoto (1999: 436).

[16] Peirce (1932–58), vol 2, para 776.

[17] ibid, vol 2, para 189. It is important to note that this formulation makes up the explanatory aspect of abduction. According to Peirce, there are two additional aspects of an explanatory hypothesis that ought to be considered: it should be testable and economic. See Aliseda (2006: 172) and Kapitan (1992: 10).

principles from those of other kinds of inference'.[18] The problem is: what are those 'altogether different principles'? The difficulties and ambiguities that permeate Peirce's writings on abduction carry over into the contemporary research on this topic, which revolves around three main problems: the nature of abduction, its relationship with induction, and the issue of whether abduction is a legitimate form of inference.

### *i. The Nature of Abduction*

We may distinguish two main conceptions of abduction, a weak conception and a stronger one.[19] According to the weak conception, abduction is an inference pattern the role of which is restricted to the hypothesis-generation phase. In this view, abduction gives reasons for suggesting and entertaining a hypothesis, as distinguished from reasons for accepting a hypothesis.[20] Abduction thus refers to the two-fold process of discovery and pre-testing the hypotheses one should further examine. Abduction in this weak sense only gives us reasons for pursuing a hypothesis, and eventually to test it by deriving observable predictions from it. According to this interpretation, abduction provides us with a 'logic of discovery' as distinct from a 'logic of justification'.[21] This conceptualization of abduction follows the traditional distinction between 'context of discovery' and 'context of justification'.[22] But it significantly departs from the tradition in that it holds that discovery also involves a rational process, albeit a different one from the kind of process involved in justification.

In contrast, in the strong interpretation, abduction is not only a method of discovery, but it also provides a way of justifying an explanation. In this view, abduction should be interpreted as 'inference to the best explanation' (IBE), that is, as a pattern of reasoning whereby explanatory hypotheses

[18] Peirce (1932–58) vol 6, para 525.

[19] The distinction between weak and strong interpretations of abduction is Niiniluoto's, see Niiniluoto (1999). Paavola (2006) draws a related distinction between two varieties of abduction: Harmanian—which is concerned with both the generation and the selection of explanatory hypotheses—and Hansonian—which concerns the logic of discovery.

[20] Hanson proposed that Peircean abduction gives reasons for suggesting a hypothesis, as distinguished from reasons for accepting a hypothesis. See Hanson (1961). On Peirce's view on the kind of reasons that might be used for selecting hypotheses for further test, see Kapitan (1992: 10).

[21] See Schurz (2008) and Aliseda (2004), for a classification of patterns of abduction as means of discovery. Thagard distinguishes the following kinds of abduction as a mechanism for discovery: simple, existential, rule-forming and analogical abduction (1988: 54). Magnani studies what he calls 'manipulative abduction', the kind of abduction that results in the generation of hypotheses through the manipulation of external objects; see Magnani (2001) ch 3. Images often play an important role in creative thinking. 'Visual' abduction refers to the process whereby we generate explanatory hypotheses that are more parsimoniously captured visually. On visual abduction, see Magnani (2001) ch 4 and Thagard and Shelley (1997).

[22] See Reichenbach (1938).

are formed and evaluated.[23] A crucial assumption of this model is that the process of hypothesis generation and the process of hypothesis evaluation cannot be neatly separated. As Josephson has explained, either type of process will sometimes need the other one as a subprocess.[24] On the one hand, there is an evaluative dimension in the generation process. We are not interested in generating hypotheses that are irrelevant or highly implausible. Given limitations of attention, memory and other cognitive resources, we cannot possibly generate and consider all possible alternatives. Thus, a pre-screening process is required in order to remove those alternatives that are implausible or irrelevant. The need for pre-testing, or pre-screening, is also recognized by those who defend abduction in a weak sense. The crucial difference is that philosophers who endorse a strong interpretation of abduction claim that there is no sharp distinction between reasons or methods employed in selecting hypotheses for further test and those used in evaluating hypotheses.[25] Justification, in this view, depends in part on evaluating the quality of the discovery process. For evaluating an explanatory hypothesis may require that alternative explanations be generated and considered, and that a judgement concerning the quality of the search for alternative explanations be made. The view that methods of generation have a bearing on the justification of a hypothesis is clearly non-congenial to a clear distinction between generation and evaluation, such as the one endorsed by advocates of weak abduction.

Now, what is the pattern of abductive reasoning as IBE? According to Lycan, inference to the best explanation follows this pattern:[26]

> $F_1$, ... $F_n$ are facts.
>
> Hypothesis H explains $F_1$... $F_n$ ('explains' here is to be read in its non-success sense, as 'would explain if true'.)
>
> No available competing hypothesis explains the $F_i$ as well as H does.
>
> Therefore, (probably) H is true.

That is, IBE proceeds from observations to a hypothesis that explains those observations better than any alternative hypothesis.[27] As Lipton puts it,

[23] It was Harman in his landmark article 'Inference to the Best Explanation', who baptized this pattern of inference. See Harman (1965). *Cf* Minnameier (2004) and Campos (2011) (arguing that abduction and inference to the best explanation ought to be kept as distinct). See also Mackonis (2013) (arguing that abduction is neither conceptually distinct from IBE nor identifiable with IBE but rather that both forms of inference overlap to some degree).

[24] See Josephson ((2000: 34) and (1994: 8–9)).

[25] This is what Nickles refers to as the 'divorce thesis'; see Nickles (1980: 183).

[26] Lycan (1988: 129). See also Josephson (1994: 5).

[27] There are several accounts in the literature of what makes an explanation better than another. Josephson mentions the following criteria: consistency, simplicity, explanatory power, predictive power, precision, specificity and theoretical promise. See Josephson (2000: 36). Hendrik and Fayek (1999) speak about correctness, empirical adequacy, simplicity, unification, consistency, practical usability and economy. Others put many of these criteria together under the heading of 'explanatory coherence'. See Thagard (1989) and Harman (1986).

the governing idea of the IBE model is that 'explanatory considerations are a guide to inference, that scientists infer from the available evidence to the hypotheses that would, if correct, best explain that evidence'.[28] These explanatory considerations apply to both generation and selection.[29] This is suggested by what Lipton calls the 'two-filter' procedure. IBE includes two filters, one that selects plausible candidates, and a second one that selects among them.[30] The mechanism of selection depends on explanatory considerations: we prefer differences that allow explanations that specify a causal mechanism, that are precise and that contribute to the unification of our overall explanatory scheme. Background beliefs about, for instance, the sorts of causal mechanisms that are relevant to the case at hand are crucial in selecting among the candidate explanations. The mechanism of generation depends on explanatory considerations as well. For the generation of a shortlist of plausible candidates depends on judgements of plausibility that rest on explanatory grounds insofar as the background beliefs that generate them (and which are themselves the result of explanatory inferences whose function was to explain different evidence) are so based. Hence, IBE can account for both the process of generation and that of selection of competing hypotheses.

IBE has the advantage of giving a natural account of many inferences in different domains. Many inferences in a vast array of contexts are naturally described in terms of inferences to the best explanation. IBE is a common pattern in scientific reasoning.[31] For example, Darwin inferred the hypothesis of natural selection because, although it was not entailed by the biological evidence, natural selection would provide the best explanation of that evidence.[32] A detective infers that it was Peterson who committed the crime because this hypothesis best explains the fingerprints, blood stains and other forensic evidence.[33] Harman claims that when we infer that a witness is telling the truth, our confidence in his testimony is based on our conclusion about the most plausible explanation for that testimony.[34] Medical diagnosis, natural language understanding and fault diagnosis are among other tasks that are also characterized as abduction (as IBE).[35] And,

[28] Lipton (2000: 184). For a complete statement of Lipton's views on inference to the best explanation, see Lipton (2004).

[29] Lipton (1991: 117ff).

[30] ibid, 60.

[31] *Cf* Hintikka (1998: 509–10).

[32] Lipton (2000: 184).

[33] The characteristic reasoning process of detectives has been characterized as abduction (as IBE); see Sebeok and Eco (1983).

[34] Harman (1965: 89). On the application of IBE to testimony, see, among others, Lipton (2007) and Gelfert (2010).

[35] On abduction and medical diagnostic reasoning, see Magnani (2001) ch 4. Fault diagnosis in AI is taken to be a prototypical abductive task, see Peng and Reggia (1990). Language understanding has also been seen as an abductive process, see Hobbs, Stickel, Appelt and Martin (1993).

as will be argued later, many legal inferences may also be best characterized as instances of IBE.[36]

### *ii. The Autonomy of Abduction*

A second problem that has attracted much attention in both philosophy of science and artificial intelligence (AI) is the issue of whether abduction is an autonomous form of reasoning and, if so, how it is related to deduction and induction.[37] It seems uncontroversial that deduction should be singled out as a kind of reasoning that is fundamentally different from both induction and abduction.[38] Whereas deductive arguments are non-defeasible (or monotonic), non-deductive arguments are defeasible (or non-monotonic). The question is how non-deductive arguments should be mapped out. There are different views on how the domain of defeasible reasoning should be divided up. Some hold that no further categorization is needed, whereas others insist in keeping both induction and abduction as distinct. Among the former, some take all non-deductive reasoning to be inductive, that is, they claim that abduction is a case of induction.[39] Others advocate the opposite view that all non-deductive reasoning is abductive, with induction being a case of abduction.[40] Among those who advocate a further division of non-deductive reasoning into induction and abduction there are also important differences concerning the criterion that they choose for distinguishing between them. Some follow Peirce's earlier views, and distinguish abduction and induction on the basis of their syllogistic form.[41] In contrast, others follow Peirce's later views, and claim that they are distinct forms of reasoning insofar as they are concerned with different phases of inquiry, generation of hypotheses, in the case of abduction, and evaluation, in the case of induction. Yet others appeal to the different way in which abduction and induction, as forms of ampliative reasoning, extend our knowledge, whereas induction provides inductive generalizations, abduction provides

[36] See ch 10.

[37] There is comparatively little psychological research done on abduction, but see Thagard (2007b), arguing for a neurocomputational theory of abductive inference.

[38] But *cf* Hintikka, who draws interesting similarities between abduction and deduction; see Hintikka (1998: 524–28).

[39] Fumerton has argued for the view that abduction (as inference to the best explanation) is a case of induction in (1980). See also Fumerton (1992). According to Fumerton, inferences to the best explanation are enthymematic, and when we make explicit the suppressed premise, we can see that they are really disguised inductive arguments.

[40] This was first proposed by Harman in (1965). For a critique to Harman's view, see Ennis (1968). Harman responded to Ennis in Harman (1968). That all non-deductive reasoning is abductive and, thus, that induction should be considered as a case of abduction is also argued by Josephson ((1994: 19–22) and (2000)); Lycan (1988) ch 9; and Weintraub (2013).

[41] Flach and Kakas (2001: 6 and 11) notice that the distinction between abduction and induction in logic programming follows Peirce's syllogistic classification to a large extent.

explanations.[42] Given this state of affairs, it has been even proposed that we shift our terminology, and speak instead of 'explanatory reasoning', trying to describe its fundamental aspects without having to decide first if they are instances of abduction or induction.[43] At bottom, the debate over the classification of forms of reasoning is parasitic on the debate over the nature of abductive reasoning. A clarification of the latter issue will shed light on the issue of how the domain of non-deductive reasoning may be more adequately mapped out.

### *iii. The Legitimacy of Abduction*

Finally, the issue of whether abduction is a legitimate form of inference is a critical one in current discussions on the subject. Does abduction yield justified beliefs? This question may be broken down into two different questions, depending on what concept of abduction (weak or strong) we endorse. For abduction-generation: Is there any sense in which we may be said to be justified in accepting a hypothesis for further examination? In other words, is there a logic of discovery? And, for abduction as IBE: Is there any sense in which we may be justified in believing a hypothesis on the basis of IBE? That is, do we have any reason to believe that the best explanation is also likely to be true? Hence, the justification of abductive inferences involves two distinct problems: 'the problem of control', ie the problem of whether our discovery processes are subjected to rational control; and the 'problem of the legitimacy of IBE', ie the problem of whether there is a rationale for IBE that allows us to distinguish between rational and irrational applications of IBE. Let us examine these two issues in turn.

The problem of the justification of abduction as discovery—the problem of control—is already present in Peirce's writings. For Peirce, abduction is both 'an act of insight' and an 'inference'. He speaks of our abductive hypotheses-forming power as a 'mysterious guessing power', but he also speaks of abduction as a 'method of making good conjectures'. Hence, the problem is whether abductive inferences in a weak sense are under our rational control, and can thus be rationally evaluated. Hintikka and Kapitan have given two interesting solutions to this problem. In both cases, the justification of abductive conclusions is claimed to be different from the kind of epistemic warrant that conclusions of inductions and deductions

[42] See Flach and Kakas (2001: 1–27).

[43] Aliseda argues for the new term 'explanatory reasoning' in Aliseda ((1997) and (2006: 34)). Psillos also takes 'explanatory reasoning' to be the basic type of ampliative reasoning, irrespective of the logical form that it may admit. Despite his use of the term 'explanatory reasoning', he is better located among those who take induction to be a case of abduction, as he describes abduction as the basic type of 'explanatory reasoning', and suggests that induction and hypothesis (ie Peirce's earlier view on abduction) are cases of abduction as inference to the best explanation. See Psillos (2001: 59–77).

enjoy. According to Hintikka, the justification of an abductive inference is a strategic one: abductive conclusions are justified insofar as they serve the overall aims of inquiry, for instance, by opening up the possibility of new questions.[44] For Kapitan, abductive conclusions should be understood as practical directives that recommend a course of action, ie to further examine a hypothesis and, as such, their justification depends on whether they are positively sanctioned by the standards that govern practical reasoning.[45] Hence, Hintikka's and Kapitan's analyses on abduction suggest that there may be ways for justifying abductive conclusions, while restricting abduction to the generation of hypotheses.

The problem of the legitimacy of abduction as IBE has given rise to a hot debate in the literature on philosophy of science. Part of the reason why it has been so controversial a topic is that IBE has been used as a main argument for scientific realism, and hence those who seek to argue against scientific realism, have attempted to do so by undermining the legitimacy of IBE.[46] In the context of the debate over scientific realism, the most vigorous critic of IBE is Van Fraassen. Van Fraassen gives two arguments against the legitimacy of IBE: the argument from underconsideration and the argument from incoherence.[47] The 'argument from underconsideration' (also called the argument from the bad lot) is this: any IBE works only given some hypotheses to choose from. However, unless we know that the set of hypotheses under consideration contains the truth, we have no reason to suppose that inferring to the best explanation would make it likely that we pick the true one.[48] The 'argument from incoherence' seeks to establish that IBE leads to incoherent belief. Imagine that we are updating our beliefs in accordance with Bayes theorem. We know that beliefs sets that violate probability calculus lead to incoherence, for we may make a Dutch book argument—that is, bets that cannot fail to win—against anyone who assigns probabilities in non-standard ways. But this is what IBE asks us to

[44] See Hintikka (1998).

[45] See Kapitan (1992).

[46] The best well-known example of the application of IBE in defence of scientific realism is Putnam's 'no-miracles argument'. See Putnam (1978: 18–22). For a clear statement of this argument, see Lipton (2000: 191). A prominent defender of scientific realism on the basis of an application of IBE is Boyd; see Boyd (1985: 2–34).

[47] See Van Fraassen ((1989: 161–70) (for the argument from incoherence) and (1989: 142–50) (for the argument from underconsideration)).

[48] Two other problems which focus on the 'best' of the inference to the best explanation slogan are the 'problem of weak evidence' and the 'problem of the multiplicity of explanations'. The problem of weak evidence arises in cases in which there is only one explanation and it does not seem good enough. On this problem, see Salmon (2001a). A similar problem arises when there are several explanations but none of them is clearly superior, on the evidence we have, to the others. See Niiniluoto (1999: 447). The problem of the multiplicity of explanations challenges the claim to uniqueness that seems to be involved in IBE, for there are sometimes several legitimate explanations of a single phenomenon. See Salmon (2001a: 67). For a reply to these objections, see Lipton (2001: 102–04).

do. We gather hypotheses, assess their conditional probability on all our other beliefs and evidence, and then give bonus points to the hypothesis that best explains. Hence, IBE has us add extra credence to the hypothesis that best explains, credence that is above what we would assign it by conditionalizing on the totality of our evidence. In so doing, we violate the probability calculus. Hence, Van Fraassen claims that IBE does not take us to the truth, and, moreover, makes us incoherent. I will not attempt to analyse the extent to which Van Fraassen's critique is successful, let alone to examine whether IBE does provide a justification for realism, or whether, as Van Fraassen and others have claimed, IBE arguments for realism are flawed or too weak to establish the desired conclusion.[49] As Ben-Menahem argues, we do well in distinguishing between the general question of the legitimacy of IBE and the more restricted question of the legitimacy of IBE in debates over realism.[50] Hence, I shall set aside the problem of IBE and realism, and focus instead on the former issue.

There are different positions regarding the issue of whether IBE yields justified beliefs. Some, like Lipton, argue that, despite the fact that IBE provides an illuminating description of our inferential practices, we lack any ground for taking it to provide a solution to the problem of justification, that is, there is no way to show that accepting a hypothesis on the basis of IBE leads us to accept a true hypothesis and reject false ones. Hume's sceptical argument displays all its force against the justification of IBE, as much as it does against induction. For, he claims, the argument 'seems to depend on little more that the undeniable fact that inductive arguments are not deductively valid'. Hence,

> reports of past observations will never entail that future inferences to the best explanation will in fact select true hypotheses; and any argument that the reliability of inference to the best explanation would itself be the best explanation of what we have observed begs the question.[51]

Others are less pessimistic with regard to the prospects of providing a justification for IBE, and even though they recognize that IBE cannot respond to the sceptical challenge, they hold that there is still a sense in which IBE can

[49] The literature on this topic is extensive. For a reply to Van Fraassen's argument from underconsideration, see Lipton (1993) and Psillos (1996). For a reply to Psillos' arguments to the effect that Van Fraassen's arguments fail to undermine IBE, see Ladyman, Douven, Horsten and Van Fraassen (1997). Psillos responds in Psillos (1997). For a discussion of Lipton's and Psillos' critique to Van Fraassen's argument from underconsideration, see Iranzo (2001) and Khalifa (2010). For a reply to Van Fraassen's argument from incoherence, see Douven (1999). Richmond has argued that Van Fraassen's critique of IBE is at odds with Van Fraassen's owns epistemological views in Richmond (1999).

[50] Ben-Menahem (1990).

[51] Lipton (2000: 190–91). For a detailed account of Lipton's views on IBE as a solution to the problem of justification, see (1991) ch 9. On the prospects of providing a solution to Hume's problem on the basis of IBE, see Papinau (1993) ch 5.

yield justified hypotheses, that is, hypotheses that we should regard as likely to be true.[52] This is what contextual construals of IBE advocate.[53] Under the contextual approach, it is possible to provide a rationale for IBE, and hence to distinguish between justified and unjustified inferences to the best explanation. But such a rationale is a contextual one, and hence whether IBE is warranted will vary with context. More specifically, the justification of a particular application of an IBE depends on whether the standards of explanatory merit that are used to assess it are properly informed by broad empirical considerations that are largely domain-specific. Hence, the force of IBE depends on background assumptions about explanation in general and more specific empirical assumptions. Ultimately, this contextualist approach justifies applications of IBE by appealing to the coherence of a body of background beliefs, which critically includes beliefs about explanation in general and more specific empirical beliefs. Indeed, for the coherentist, applications of IBE would be justified insofar as they maximize the (explanatory) coherence of our belief system. In other words, it is the coherence-enhancing role of IBE that confers justification to its conclusions.[54] Thus, if the 'best' of the 'inference to the best explanation' slogan is understood as best on a test of coherence,[55] we may put worries about the legitimacy of IBE to rest, provided, of course, that one has satisfactorily

[52] Alternatively, it has been argued that IBE is justified not because we can assume that the best available theory is likely to be true but because we ought to accept it, ie we ought to take it as a premise in our theoretical and practical reasoning. That is to say, IBE does not warrant belief, but it does warrant acceptance (Dawes: 2013).

[53] See Ben-Menahem (1990) and Day and Kincaid (1994). An alternative way to justify IBE has been suggested by Betz (2012). On Betz's view, IBE can be justified insofar as accepting the best explanation as true furthers the epistemic aim of maximizing the robustness of one's position. Thus, on Betz's account, the rationale underlying IBE is a practical—rather than a contextual—one.

[54] For the claim that inferences to the best explanation are justified insofar as they lead to an increase on explanatory coherence, see Fumerton (1992); Harman (1986) ch 7; Thagard, (1989); Psillos (2002); and Mackonis (2013). A closely related account of 'best' is defended by Lipton. According to Lipton, IBE should be construed as inference to the 'loveliest' explanation, which is the explanation that would, if true, provide the greatest degree of understanding. See Lipton ((1991: 54–64) and (2001: 105–09)). For a critique of Lipton's thesis, see Barnes (1995). Glass ((2007) and (2012)) also argues that the 'best' of the 'inference to the best explanation' slogan should be understood in terms of coherence, but advocates a probabilistic account of coherence, rather than an explanatory one, to determine the goodness of explanations.

[55] Alternatively, one could understand 'best' by using probability theory. Most importantly, there are some important attempts to cast inference to the best explanation into a Bayesian framework. See Niinuluoto (2003); Iranzo ((2007: 342–45) and (2008)); and Salmon (2001b). See also Lipton ((2001) and (2004: 103–21)) (arguing that inference to the best explanation and Bayesianism are complementary models) and Weisberg (2009) (arguing that if Bayesianism and IBE are to be fit together, an objective Bayesianism is to be preferred). For a critique of attempts to bring together inference to the best explanation and Bayesianism, see Psillos ((2004) and (2007)).

addressed the issue of whether a coherence-based criterion for justification is truth-conducive.[56]

Now, granted that what we infer on the basis of IBE may be justified, how can we measure the strength of such justification? In induction, it is common to consider the degree of confirmation of a hypothesis by evidence (as formalized by probability theory) as a measure of the strength of the inductive argument, 'E, therefore H', but what criteria may help us determine the degree of strength of an IBE? Qualitative criteria, as opposed to quantitative ones, are called for here. Josephson has provided a number of (very intuitive) qualitative criteria for measuring the strength of an abductive conclusion (as a conclusion of an IBE argument).[57] According to Josephson, the strength of an abductive justification depends on: (i) how decisively a hypothesis H surpasses the alternatives; (ii) how good H is by itself, independently of considering the alternatives; (iii) how confident we are in the accuracy of the data; (iv) how thorough the search for alternative explanations was;[58] and (v) pragmatic considerations, such as the cost of error and the benefits of being right, and how strong the need is to come to a conclusion, especially considering the possibility of gathering further evidence. Thus, on Josephson's criteria, the justification of abductive conclusions is a combination of both epistemic and non-epistemic reasons (ie practical reasons).[59]

### C. Weak vs Strong Explanationism

IBE figures prominently in all explanationists approaches to knowledge and justification. However, there are different views as to the proper scope of explanatory reasoning. Lycan has distinguished between two versions of explanationism: strong and weak explanationism.[60] Strong explanationists hold that explanatory coherence is the only kind of coherence, and inference to the best explanation, the only legitimate form of inference. Thus, all justified reasoning yields an increase of the explanatory coherence of one's system of beliefs. Lycan himself has held a strong version of explanationism. Harman can also be considered as a strong explanationist, even

[56] For a discussion of the problem of the truth conduciveness of coherence, see ch 6.

[57] See Josephson ((1994: 14) and (1998: 10–12)).

[58] In evaluating the thoroughness of the search for alternative explanations, two distinguished classes of explanations deserve special attention: what Josephson refers to as the 'noise' hypothesis (which considers the data to be explained) and the 'new' hypothesis (which raises the possibility that a new possibility obtains); see Josephson (2002: 293).

[59] Magnani seems to suggest that the relevance of epistemic and non-epistemic reasons is context-dependent. For instance, whereas in selecting the best diagnosis epistemic reasons are dominant, in selecting the best therapy, other reasons—ie pragmatic, ethical and motivational criteria—also play an important role; see Magnani (2001: 27).

[60] Lycan (1989: 480).

though he seems to endorse such a view in a more cautious way than Lycan does. According to Harman, 'explanatory coherence is an important sort of coherence, perhaps the only sort'.[61]

As opposed to strong explanationists, Bartelborth does not claim explanatory coherence to be all that there is to justification. Nonetheless, he attributes to non-explanatory relations a peripheral role. He writes, 'Besides deductive and statistical relations (which can of course also contribute to the coherence of a belief system), it is mainly explanatory relations which bring about coherence'.[62] And somewhere else, 'most of the local inferential connections responsible for coherence are explanatory relations'.[63] Thagard clearly holds a weak version of explanationism. Already in the first statement of his theory, Thagard explicitly rejected the strong version of explanationism. He wrote, 'I am not trying to give a general account of epistemic justification: I hold that there are other legitimate forms of inference besides inference to the best explanation'.[64] And, in a later work, he claimed that he was not offering 'a general account of coherence', and made it clear that his characterization of explanatory coherence 'leaves open the possibility that two propositions can cohere for non explanatory reasons ... explanation is thus sufficient but not necessary for coherence'.[65] In a series of works, Thagard has developed a complete theory of coherence that includes a characterization of five kinds of coherence (analogical, deductive, conceptual, perceptual and deliberative), in addition to explanatory coherence, which is, nevertheless, he says, 'the most important contributor to epistemic justification'.[66]

Weak explanationism, such as Thagard's, seems to be a more plausible version of explanationism than stronger varieties. It overcomes a main objection that has been raised against the explanationist tradition, namely, that it cannot account for cases of justified beliefs whose justification does not seem to depend on explanatory relations to other beliefs. Weak explanationism, while acknowledging the pivotal role of explanatory relations to coherence, also accounts for cases in which justification arises from non-explanatory reasons. In addition to providing a theory of justification that is able to deal with cases in which there is justification without explanation, Thagard's theory, as opposed to most theories of explanatory coherence (both weak and strong), gives a precise definition of the notion of explanatory coherence (as well as of the non-explanatory kinds of coherence). Because

[61] Harman (1986: 75).
[62] Bartelborth (1999: 212).
[63] Bartelborth (1996: 24).
[64] Thagard (1989: 464).
[65] Thagard (1992a: 65).
[66] Thagard (2000a). See, also, Thagard, Eliasmith, Rusnock and Shelley (2002).

of that, in the rest of this chapter, I shall focus on Thagard's theory, as a representative of explanatory coherentism.[67]

## II. COHERENCE AS CONSTRAINT SATISFACTION

### A. The Notion of Coherence

Paul Thagard and Karsten Verbeurgt have provided a general characterization of coherence according to which, given a set of elements, maximizing coherence is a matter of maximizing the satisfaction of a set of positive and negative constraints. They informally summarize this notion of coherence as follows:[68]

1. Elements are representations such as concepts, propositions, parts of images, goals, actions and so on.
2. Elements can cohere (fit together) or incohere (resist fitting together). Coherence relations include explanation, deduction, facilitation, association and so on. Incoherence relations include inconsistency, incompatibility and negative association.
3. If two elements cohere, there is a positive constraint between them. If two elements incohere, there is a negative constraint between them.
4. Elements are to be divided into ones that are accepted and ones that are rejected.
5. A positive constraint between two elements can be satisfied either by accepting both of the elements or by rejecting both of the elements.
6. A negative constraint between two elements can be satisfied only by accepting one element and rejecting the other.
7. The coherence problem consists of dividing a set of elements into accepted and rejected sets in a way that satisfies the most constraints.

The idea is the following one. We start with a set *E* of elements, which may be propositions or other representations. The problem is how we can accept some elements and reject others in a way that maximizes the coherence of *E*. The claim is that we turn *E* into as coherent a whole as possible by taking into account the coherence and incoherence relations

[67] Thagard presented his theory of explanatory coherence in Thagard (1989). Some modifications were introduced in Thagard (1992a). From this theory, emerged the idea of providing a general characterization of coherence in terms of constraint satisfaction, described in Thagard and Verbeurgt (1998). This general theory was later applied to different coherence problems, see Thagard (2000a). My exposition of Thagard's coherence theory proceeds in reverse chronological order. I will first present the general account of coherence, ie Thagard's constraint satisfaction approach to coherence, and then I will discuss Thagard's views on one specific kind of coherence, ie explanatory coherence.

[68] Thagard and Verbeurgt (1998: 2–3).

that hold between pairs of elements of *E*. These relations put constraints on what can be accepted or rejected. To maximize coherence, we partition *E* into two disjoint subsets *A*, which contains the accepted elements, and *R*, which contains the rejected elements in a way that takes into account the local coherence and incoherence relations. For example, if a hypothesis *h1* explains *e1*, we want to ensure that if *h1* is accepted, so is *e1*. On the other hand, if *h1* is inconsistent with *h2*, then we will make sure that if *h1* is accepted, then *h2* is rejected. The coherence problem is thus that of dividing up *E* into *A* and *R* in a way that best satisfies the most constraints. Thagard and Verbeurgt characterize formally the *coherence problem* as follows:

> Let *E* be a finite set of elements $\{e_i\}$ and C be a set of constraints on *E* understood as a set $\{(e_i, e_j)\}$ of pairs of elements of *E*. *C* divides into *C*+, the positive constraints on *E*, and *C*-, the negative constraints on *E*. Each constraint is associated with a number *w*, which is the weight (strength) of the constraint. The [coherence] problem is to partition *E* into two sets *A* and *R*, in a way that maximizes compliance with the following two *coherence conditions*:
>
> 1. if $(e_i, e_j)$ is in *C* +, then $e_i$ is in *A* if and only if $e_j$ is in *A*.
> 2. if $(e_i, e_j)$ is in *C* -, then $e_i$ is in *A* if and only if $e_j$ is in *R*.
>
> Let *W* be the weight of the partition, that is, the sum of the weights of the satisfied constraints. The coherence problem is then to partition *E* into *A* and *R* in a way that maximizes *W*.[69]

The coherence of a partition of *E* is *W*, the sum of the weights of the constraints that satisfy the above conditions. Coherence is maximized if there is no other partition of *E* that has greater total weight. Thagard and Verbeurgt claim that this abstract characterization of coherence applies to a wide variety of problems, among others, epistemic justification, moral and legal justification and discourse comprehension. In their view, to show that a given problem is a coherence problem, as defined above, it is necessary to specify the elements and constraints, provide an interpretation of acceptance and rejection, and show that solutions to the problem do in fact involve the satisfaction of the specified constraints. Consider, for example, epistemic justification. Here, the elements are propositions, and the positive constraints can be a variety of relations, including entailment and explanation. Negative constraints can include inconsistency, but also weaker constraints such as competition. Propositions that are accepted are justified, while others are rejected as unjustified. Now, the question arises of how, once the elements and the constraints are specified, can the elements be accepted and rejected in a way that maximizes compliance with the two coherence conditions. According to Thagard and Verbeurgt, this notion of coherence is precise enough for addressing the problem of computing coherence.

[69] ibid, 3.

### B. Computing Coherence

Coherence problems are inherently intractable computationally.[70] There exists, however, a number of approximation algorithms available for solving coherence problems. Thagard and Verbeurgt have examined the applicability of five algorithms, namely, exhaustive, incremental, connectionist, greedy and semidefinite programming, to the problem of computing coherence:

i. *Exhaustive algorithms* consider all possible ways of dividing elements into accepted and rejected, evaluate the coherence of each of them and pick the one with highest value of *W*. This approach seems inadequate to deal with computationally intractable problems, such as the coherence problem. For a set of *n* elements, there are $2^n$ possible acceptance sets. A small coherence problem involving 100 propositions would require considering $2^{100}$ = 1,267,650,600,228,229,401,496,703,205,376 solutions. It is apparent that no computer, and no mind, is able to compute coherence in this way.
ii. *Incremental algorithms* consider elements in an arbitrary order. Then, each element in the ordering is added to *A* if it increases the total weight of the satisfied constraints more than adding it to *R*. The problem with this algorithm is that it seriously depends on the order of the elements. Nonetheless, it may well describe people's limited rationality. Cognitive limitations may lead people to adopt suboptimal ways of computing coherence, such as the one implemented by incremental algorithms.
iii. *Connectionist algorithms* use artificial neural networks, and they provide a partition of *E* by virtue of a network settling in such a way that some units of the network that represent the elements of *E* are activated—accepted—while others are deactivated—and thus, rejected.
iv. *Greedy algorithms* randomly assign elements of *E* into *A* and *R*, then, for each element, they calculate the gain in the weight from moving an element from *A* to *R*, and produce a new solution by flipping the element that most increases coherence. This procedure is repeated until there is no flip that increases coherence. Greedy algorithms usually produce the same acceptances and rejections as the connectionist algorithms. However, they are psychologically less plausible, in that they use random solutions and a great many coherence calculations.
v. *Semidefinite programming* is an approximation algorithm for MAX CUT, a difficult graph theory problem that, until very recently, had no good approximation. Verbeurgt has proved that the semidefinite

[70] Coherence problems are computationally intractable for there are no polynomial-time procedures for solving them, ie the amount of time necessary to solve a coherence problem increases at a faster than polynomial time as the problem grows in size.

programming technique applied to MAX CUT can also be used for coherence problems. It has also been shown that this algorithm yields equivalent results to the connectionist one.

According to Thagard and Verbeurgt, connectionist networks give a natural solution to the problem of computing coherence. They have been applied to computationally implement Thagard's theory of explanatory coherence, as well as some other kinds of coherence, as will be shown in detail below.

### C. Measuring Coherence

As Thagard and Verbeurgt point out, the formal characterization of coherence, together with the various algorithms for computing it, suggest various means by which coherence can be measured. They distinguish three measures of coherence: the degree of coherence of an entire set of elements, the degree of coherence of a particular element, and the degree of coherence of a subset of elements.

i. *The coherence of the entire set of elements.* The goodness-of-fit (harmony) measure of a neural network can be interpreted as the coherence of an entire set of elements. The harmony of a network is defined by $H(t)= \sum_i \sum_j w_{ij} a_i(t) a_j(t)$. In this equation, $w_{ij}$ is the weight from unit $i$ to unit $j$, and $a_i(t)$ is the activation of the unit $i$ at time $t$.[71] This measure is of limited use since it is very sensitive to the number of elements, as well as to the particular equations used to update activation in the networks. Thagard and Verbeurgt have offered two network-independent measures of coherence. First, an ideal measure of the coherence of a system will be the ratio of the coherence $W$ (the sum of the weights of the satisfied constraints) to coherence $W\_opt$ of the optimal solution. Since the value of the optimal solution is generally unknown, they suggest an alternative measure: the ratio $W/W^*$, where $W^*$ is the sum of all constraints.[72] The higher this ratio, the closer the solution is to optimal.
ii. *The coherence of an element.* The connectionist algorithms provide a useful way to measure the degree of coherence of a particular element, since the activation of a unit represents the degree of acceptability of an element.
iii. *The coherence of a subset of elements.* None of the foregoing measures provides a way of defining the degree of coherence of a subset of

[71] Thagard (1989: 443).
[72] See Thagard and Verbeurgt (1998: 14).

elements. Nonetheless, such a measure of coherence could be roughly defined as the mean activation of the elements of a subset.

According to Thagard and Verbeurgt, these measures are useful for both philosophical and psychological purposes. Normative judgements often bear on questions about the degree of coherence of an element or a system. And the degree of coherence is often correlated with the degree of confidence that people have in their own judgements.

### D. Kinds of Coherence

The application of this abstract characterization of coherence as constraint satisfaction requires, as explained, the specification of the elements and the constraints that are relevant in a particular domain. Thagard has claimed that the solution of a particular coherence problem involves the interaction of different kinds of coherence. He distinguishes six kinds of coherence: explanatory, analogical, deductive, perceptual, conceptual and deliberative. Each kind requires different sorts of elements and constraints. Thagard has proposed theories for all these six kinds of coherence, eg the theory of explanatory coherence for the first kind. These theories are supposed to supplement the abstract characterization of coherence as constraint satisfaction so that it can be applied to the solution of a coherence problem. I will present in detail Thagard's theory of explanatory coherence and its computational implementation. As stated above, Thagard considers explanatory coherence to be the most important contributor to epistemic justification. In addition, the theory of explanatory coherence was the first theory of coherence that Thagard proposed, and the one that he has elaborated in more detail. In fact, the theories of all the other kinds of coherence, together with their computational implementations, have been generated by analogy with the theory of explanatory coherence. Among the non-explanatory kinds of coherence, I will also pay particular attention (even if in a later chapter) to deliberative coherence, given its prominent role in legal reasoning.[73]

## III. THE THEORY OF EXPLANATORY COHERENCE

According to Thagard, explanatory coherence is one of the main criteria for selecting among competing theories. More specifically, explanatory relations, claims Thagard, are crucial for understanding the kind of theory-choice that is involved in scientific revolutions. In scientific revolutions,

[73] See ch 7.

an existing theory that exhibits a lower degree of explanatory coherence is superseded when a theory comes along with a higher degree of explanatory coherence. In Thagard's view, legal decision-making may be equally captured by the concept of explanatory coherence. From this perspective, a verdict is the result of assessing the relative explanatory coherence of the prosecutor's and the defence's views of what happened. Thus, Thagard's theory of explanatory coherence is intended to account for a wide range of explanatory inferences, from the evaluation of scientific theories to the acceptance of factual hypotheses in law.[74]

## A. Explanatory Coherence

Explanatory coherence is the holding together because of explanatory relations. This concept may be understood in several ways:

a. as a relation between two propositions;
b. as a property of a whole of related propositions;
c. as a property of a single proposition within a set of propositions.

Thagard claims that (a) is fundamental, with (b) depending on (a) and (c) depending on (b). That is to say, explanatory coherence is primarily a relation between two propositions, but we can derivatively speak of the explanatory coherence of a set of propositions or of a proposition that belongs to such a set. Hence, in Thagard's view, the most important kind of coherence is relational coherence, more specifically, 'pairwise' relational coherence. Relational coherence as is generally understood in the coherentist literature, ie as a relation between a proposition and a set of propositions, plays no role in Thagard's theory.[75] The other main kind of coherence that is distinguished by coherence theorists, to wit, systematic coherence, is taken to be a function of this specific kind of relational coherence. In Thagard's theory of explanatory coherence, elements are propositions that describe hypotheses or pieces of evidence. Positive and negative constraints are established by means of a number of principles that constitute what Thagard calls TEC, which stands for Theory of Explanatory Coherence.

[74] See Thagard (1989) and (1992a).
[75] See ch 3.

## B. Principles of Explanatory Coherence

Thagard proposes seven principles that establish relations of explanatory coherence between elements and make possible the evaluation of the coherence of a particular theory. These principles are as follows:[76]

*Principle E1: Symmetry.*
(a) If $P$ and $Q$ cohere, then $Q$ and $P$ cohere.
(b) If $P$ and $Q$ incohere, then $Q$ and $P$ incohere.

According to this principle, pairwise coherence and incoherence, unlike probability or logical entailment, are symmetrical relations. In other words, two propositions $p$ and $q$ cohere (or incohere) with each other equally.

*Principle E2: Explanation.*
If $P_1 \ldots P_m$ explain $Q$, then:
(a) For each $P_i$ in $P_1 \ldots P_m$, $P_i$ and $Q$ cohere.
(b) For each $P_i$ and $P_j$ in $P_1 \ldots P_m$, $P_i$ and $P_j$ cohere.
(c) In (a) and (b) the degree of coherence is inversely proportional to the number of propositions $P_1 \ldots P_m$.

This principle establishes the most important positive constraint for assessing explanatory coherence. Part (a) of principle 2 embodies the claim that hypotheses cohere with what they explain, which can be either evidence or another hypothesis. Principle (b) states that hypotheses also cohere with their cohypotheses—hypotheses that together explain some other proposition.[77] Part (c) of principle 2 says that the more hypotheses it takes to explain something, the lower their degree of coherence. This principle subsumes two important criteria of theory choice: explanatory breath (or consilience) and simplicity. In a previous work, Thagard claimed explanatory breath or consilience to be the most important criterion for selecting the best explanation.[78] It follows from this principle that the more a hypothesis explains, the more coherent it is and, hence, the more acceptable. This principle also embodies another relevant standard for theory choice, namely, simplicity. According to this criterion, we should prefer theories that generate explanations with a unified core of hypotheses to explanations that require a myriad of *ad hoc* hypotheses.[79]

[76] I present here the principles of explanatory coherence with the modifications to their first formulation (in Thagard (1989)) that were introduced in Thagard (1992a) ch IV.

[77] Thagard offers the following definition of cohypothesis: 'H1 and H2 are cohypotheses if both must be formed together in order to accomplish an explanation' (1988: 89–90).

[78] See Thagard (1978).

[79] It is important to notice that simplicity is an important constraint on consilience, since we do not want to achieve maximally consilient theories by dramatically decreasing their simplicity. On simplicity and consilience, see Thagard (1988: 78–86).

*Principle E3: Analogy.*
If $P_1$ explains $Q_1$, $P_2$ explains $Q_2$, $P_1$ is analogous to $P_2$, and $Q_1$ is analogous to $Q_2$, then $P_1$ and $P_2$ cohere, and $Q_1$ and $Q_2$ cohere.

This principle does not simply state that analogous hypotheses cohere. There must be an explanatory analogy, with two analogous propositions occurring in explanations of two other propositions that are analogous to each other. That is, this principle establishes a positive constraint between similar hypotheses that explain similar pieces of evidence.

*Principle E4: Data priority.*
Propositions that describe the result of observations have a degree of acceptability on their own.

According to this principle, propositions that describe the results of observations are given priority in being chosen for the set of accepted elements. However, as Thagard emphasizes, a proposition may have some independent acceptability and still not be accepted if it is only coherent with propositions that are not themselves acceptable. Thagard, together with Eliasmith, Rusnock and Shelley, has proposed a classification of coherence problems that is relevant here. They have distinguished between pure coherence problems, foundational coherence problems and discriminating coherence problems.[80] A 'pure' coherence problem does not favour the acceptance of any particular set of elements. A 'foundational' one selects a set of elements as self-justified. A 'discriminating' coherence problem favours a set of elements, but their acceptance still depends on their coherence with other elements. Even though the abstract definition of coherence in terms of constraint satisfaction is non-discriminating, in the sense that all elements are treated equally, principle 4 makes Thagard's notion of explanatory coherence discriminating. As will be explained below, all of Thagard's non-explanatory kinds of coherence are discriminating as well. Understood in this way, principle 4 captures important features of the everyday experimental practice in which evidence is treated more seriously than other kinds of information, but it is also often discarded. A theory is not typically rejected because it has some empirical problems until a better theory, that explains the discarded evidence, is fully developed.

*Principle E5: Contradiction.*
If $P$ contradicts $Q$, then $P$ and $Q$ incohere.

Therefore, contradiction amounts to incoherence. This principle, together with principle 6, establishes the negative constraints required for the assessment of explanatory coherence.

[80] Thagard, Eliasmith, Rusnock and Shelley (2002).

*Principle E6: Competition.*
If $P$ and $Q$ both explain a proposition $P_i$, and if $P$ and $Q$ are not explanatorily connected, then $P$ and $Q$ incohere. Here P and Q are explanatorily connected if any of the following conditions holds:
(a) $P$ is part of the explanation of $Q$,
(b) $Q$ is part of the explanation of $P$,
(c) $P$ and $Q$ are together part of the explanation of some proposition $P_j$.

According to this principle, hypotheses that explain the same evidence and are not explanatorily related compete, and are thus incoherent with each other. Two propositions are explanatorily related if one explains the other or if together they explain some other proposition.

*Principle E7: Acceptability.*
(a) The acceptability of a proposition $P$ in a system $S$ depends on its coherence with the propositions in $S$.
(b) If many results of relevant experimental observations are unexplained, then the acceptability of a proposition $P$ that explains only a few of them is reduced.

According to the first part of this principle, the acceptability of a proposition in a system of propositions depends on its coherence with them. Thus, acceptability judgements are holistic, and are based solely on pairwise coherence relations. The second part of this principle is intended to handle cases in which the best available hypothesis is still not very good in that it accounts for only a fraction of the relevant evidence. By 'relevant evidence', Thagard understands any piece of evidence that is explained by a hypothesis or by one of its competitors.

All these criteria operate simultaneously in order to select the theory that possesses greatest explanatory coherence. This comparative degree of system coherence is derived from particular coherence relations. As stated before, the constraint satisfaction approach provides a method for integrating these criteria of coherence, and connectionist algorithms allow us to derive general coherence from holistic judgements of acceptability of particular propositions. The theory of explanatory coherence has been computationally implemented by one such connectionist program, which is described below.

## C. ECHO, Connectionism and Explanatory Coherence

The principles of explanatory coherence have been implemented in a connectionist program called ECHO.[81] Connectionist algorithms use artificial

[81] This computational implementation is interesting in that it allows for a more precise comparison between explanationist and probabilistic approaches to scientific reasoning. For such comparison, see Thagard (2000b) and Thagard (2000a) ch 8. For a comparison between probabilism and explanationism in the legal domain, see Thagard (2004).

neural networks and are holistic in that the acceptability of an element potentially depends on its relation with a whole complex of elements. Because of that, they provide a natural solution to the problem of computing coherence. Connectionist networks consist of units, crudely analogous to neurons, connected by excitatory and inhibitory links. A coherence problem can be translated into a connectionist network as follows:[82]

1. For every element $e_1$ of the set of elements $E$, construct a unit $u_1$ which is a node in a network of units.
2. For every positive constraint (coherence relation) between elements $e_1$ and $e_2$, construct a symmetric excitatory link between the corresponding units $u_1$ and $u_2$.
3. Construct an excitatory link between those elements whose acceptance is favoured and a special unit whose activation has a fixed maximum activation.
4. For every negative constraint (incoherence relation) between elements $e_1$ and $e_2$, construct a symmetric inhibitory link between the corresponding units $u_1$ and $u_2$.
5. Assign every unit an equal initial activation, and then update the activation of all units in parallel. The updated activation of a unit is calculated on the basis of its current activation, the weights on links to other units and the activation of the units to which it is linked.
6. Continue updating of activation until all units have settled. If a unit $u_1$ has a final activation above a specific threshold, then the element $e_1$ is accepted. Otherwise, it is rejected.

Similarly, in ECHO, coherence and incoherence relations, as established by the seven principles of explanatory coherence, are encoded by excitatory and inhibitory links, so that units—propositions describing both hypotheses and evidence—can have varying degrees of activation. The activation level of a unit depends on the activations of the units to which it is linked. For example, if the hypothesis H1 explains two pieces of evidence—E1 and E2—whereas the alternative hypothesis H2 explains only one—E1—ECHO will be given the following formulas as input:

(EXPLAIN (H1) E1)

(EXPLAIN (H1) E2)

(EXPLAIN (H2) E2)

(CONTRADICT (H1 H2))

(DATA (E1 E2))

[82] Thagard and Verbeurgt (1998: 9).

These formulas will generate a network, with excitatory links between H1–E1, H1– E2 and H2–E2, and an inhibitory link between H1 and H2. Excitatory links will also be generated between each data unit and a special evidence unit. Because H1 explains more than H2, it becomes more active, while H2 will be deactivated. Thus, in a simulation, ECHO will accept hypothesis H1, and reject H2. Input to ECHO can optionally reflect the fact that not all data and explanations are of equal merit. For example, a data statement can have the form:

(DATA (E1 (E2. 8))).

This formula indicates that E2 is not as reliable a piece of evidence as E1. In ECHO's applications to date, these parameters have not been used, because they are difficult to determine. But it is important that ECHO can use them if they are available.

It may be worth noticing that ECHO has numerous degrees of freedom, some of which are epistemologically interesting and highly relevant for assessing the possible applications of Thagard's computational theory of explanatory coherence:

1. *Tolerance*: The tolerance of a system is the absolute value of the ratio of excitatory weight to inhibitory weight. With high tolerance, the system will entertain competing hypotheses. With low tolerance, winning hypotheses deactivate the losers.
2. *Simplicity impact*: The importance of simplicity in theory choice may be changed by increasing the number of cohypotheses to an exponent that represents the simplicity impact of the system. The greater the simplicity impact is, the more the weights will be diminished by having more cohypotheses.
3. *Analogy impact*: Similarly, the weights established by analogy can be affected by a factor representing analogy impact.
4. *Scepticism*: Another important parameter of the system is decay rate; the higher it is, the more excitation from the data will be needed to activate hypotheses.
5. *Data excitation*: It is also possible to set the initial activations for each data unit separately.

ECHO has been applied to important cases from the history of science, such as Darwin's theory of evolution as opposed to creationism.[83] It has also been used to model jurors' reasoning in murder trials in which the explanations

[83] Thagard (1992a) has applied the theory of explanatory coherence to model reasoning in the main scientific revolutions. Other applications of the theory of explanatory coherence include: contemporary debates about why the dinosaurs become extinct (1991); adversarial problem-solving, where one has to infer an opponent's intentions (1992b); psychological investigations of how people perceive relationships (Miller and Read (1991)); and the debate between the reticular theory and the neuron theory in neurology (Toombs (2003)).

of the evidence supporting the defendant's innocence and the defendant's guilt were evaluated.[84] Although the simulation is not claimed to handle all the factors that go into real jurors' decisions, it successfully handled a large part of the evidence and hypotheses in these complex cases of legal reasoning. After briefly examining the non-explanatory kinds of coherence that Thagard has proposed, I will describe in detail one such application.

## IV. NON-EXPLANATORY KINDS OF COHERENCE

Thagard, by analogy to the principles of explanatory coherence, has proposed principles for five other kinds of coherence: deductive, analogical, perceptual, conceptual and deliberative. All these kinds of coherence are construed in terms of constraint satisfaction and have been implemented using connectionists programs similar to ECHO.

### A. Deductive Coherence

Thagard discusses deductive coherence in the context of mathematics. Nonetheless, as he points out, this kind of coherence is also relevant to other domains, such as ethics. In deductive coherence, the elements are mathematical propositions, that is, axioms and theorems. The positive and negative constraints are specified by the following set of principles:[85]

> *Principle D1: Symmetry.* Deductive coherence is a symmetric relation among propositions, unlike, say, deductive entailment.
> *Principle D2: Deduction.* (a) An axiom or other proposition coheres with propositions that are deducible from it. (b) Propositions that together are used to deduce some other proposition cohere with each other. (c) The more hypotheses it takes to deduce something, the less the degree of coherence.
> *Principle D3: Intuitive priority.* Propositions that are intuitively obvious have a degree of acceptability on their own. Propositions that are obviously false have a degree of rejectability on their own.
> *Principle D4: Contradiction.* Contradictory propositions are incoherent with each other.
> *Principle D5: Acceptance.* The acceptability of a proposition in a system of propositions depends on its coherence with them.

[84] See Thagard (1989: 449ff), where Thagard applies ECHO to two murder trials, to wit, the *Meyer* and *Chambers* cases. The same cases have been also analysed by another program, PEIRCE-IGTT, which is an abductive problem-solving machine. See JR Josephson and S Josephson (1994: 216ff). See also Thagard (2003).
[85] Thagard (2000a: 53).

Like relations of explanatory coherence, relations of deductive coherence are symmetrical (principle 1). The coherence-producing relation of deduction is the source of a number of positive constraints (principle 2). For example, if an axiom coheres with a theorem because of the deductive relations that hold between them, there is a positive constraint, and they will be either accepted or rejected together. Principle 3 accounts for the intuitiveness of mathematical propositions, so that they tend to be accepted. Negative constraints prevent the acceptance of contradictory propositions simultaneously (principle 4). In this account, as the last principle states, axioms are accepted on the basis of the theorems they yield, while at the same time, theorems are accepted on the basis of their derivation from axioms (principle 5).

### B. Analogical Coherence

Holyoak and Thagard have proposed that the use of analogy can be understood in terms of coherence.[86] Using analogies requires the ability to map between two analogues, the target problem to be solved and the source that is intended to provide a solution. According to Holyoak and Thagard, such mapping is a matter of satisfying various constraints. The elements are hypotheses concerning what maps to what, that is, which objects and concepts correlate to each other. The main constraints are similarity, structure, and purpose. Thagard has proposed to capture this theory of analogy by means of the following principles:[87]

*Principle A1: Symmetry*. Analogical Coherence is a symmetric relation among mapping hypotheses.
*Principle A2: Structure*. A mapping hypothesis that connects two propositions, *R (a, b)* and *S (c, d)*, coheres with mapping hypotheses that connect *R* with *S*, *a* with *c* and *b* with *d*. And all those mapping hypotheses cohere with each other.
*Principle A3: Similarity*. Mapping hypotheses that connect elements that are semantically or visually similar have a degree of acceptability on their own.
*Principle A4: Purpose*. Mapping hypotheses that provide possible contributions to the purpose of the analogy have a degree of acceptability on their own.
*Principle A5: Competition*. Mapping hypotheses that offer different mappings for the same object or concept are incoherent with each other.
*Principle A6: Acceptance*. The acceptability of a mapping hypothesis in a system of mapping hypotheses depends on its coherence with them.

[86] See Holyoak and Thagard (1989). They have presented their general theory of analogical thinking in (1995).
[87] Thagard (2000a: 49).

In analogical coherence, the terms of the coherence relation are mapping hypotheses. Like any other kind of coherence, these relations are symmetrical. There are three kinds of positive constraints: structure, similarity and purpose. The first constraint is that we should maintain the structure when mapping hypotheses. For example, if we have the following two representations: (circle (electron nucleus)) and (revolve (planet sun)), then, mapping circle to revolve requires that we map electron to planet and nucleus to sun. The second positive constraint, similarity, requires that we favour hypotheses that relate similar objects and concepts. Similarity can be either semantic or visual. Darwin's analogy between natural and artificial selection is an example of semantic analogy. We draw a visual analogy when, for example, we pictorially compare the atomic structure with the solar system. The last positive constraint is pragmatic: we should favour mappings that can accomplish the purpose of the analogy, such as problem-solving or explanation. In addition to positive constraints, there is also a negative constraint: competition. Such constraint arises between hypotheses representing incompatible mappings, for example, between the hypothesis that the electron corresponds to the planet and the hypothesis that it corresponds to the sun.

### C. Perceptual Coherence

Thagard has claimed that coherence produces not only propositional knowledge, but also perceptual knowledge. Such knowledge arises from accepting the perceptual representation that satisfies the most of a number of constraints. In this kind of coherence, the elements are non-verbal representations of sensory input and full-blown perceptual interpretations. Our perceptual knowledge includes visual, auditory, olfactory and tactile representations, but Thagard has focused exclusively on one kind of perceptual knowledge, ie visual knowledge. Thagard proposes the following principles for visual coherence:[88]

> *Principle V1: Symmetry.* Visual coherence is a symmetric relation between a visual interpretation and a low-level representation of sensory input.
> *Principle V2: Interpretation.* A visual interpretation coheres with a representation of sensory input if they are connected by perceptual principles such as proximity, similarity and continuity.
> *Principle V3: Sensory priority.* Sensory input representations are acceptable on their own.
> *Principle V4: Incompatibility.* Incompatible visual interpretations are incoherent with each other.

[88] ibid, 59.

*Principle V5: Acceptance.* The acceptability of a visual interpretation depends on its coherence with sensory inputs, other visual interpretations and background knowledge.

Principle 2 establishes a positive constraint: visual representations tend to be accepted along with the sensory inputs with which they cohere. Such coherence relations are governed by innate perceptual principles, such as the Gestalt principles. For example, an interpretation that joins two visual parts together in a pattern will cohere with the sensory input that has the two parts close to each other. Other kinds of perceptual knowledge would have a different version of this principle, based on the innate perceptual system for that modality. Principle 3 establishes another positive constraint by taking the sensory input as a given. Nonetheless, these inputs may fit with multiple visual interpretations that are incompatible with each other. These interpretations are incoherent, and thus the source of negative constraints (principle 4). Visual knowledge arises when we accept the visual interpretation that satisfies the most positive and negative constraints.

### D. Conceptual Coherence

In conceptual coherence, the elements are concepts, and the positive and negative constraints arise from positive and negative associations between concepts. Thagard proposes the following principles for conceptual coherence:[89]

*Principle C1: Symmetry.* Conceptual coherence is a symmetric relation between pairs of concepts.
*Principle C2: Association.* A concept coheres with another concept if they are positively associated, ie if there are objects to which both apply.
*Principle C3: Given concepts.* The applicability of a concept to an object, for example, of the concept *woman* to a particular person, may be given perceptually or by some other reliable source.
*Principle C4: Negative association.* A concept incoheres with another concept if they are negatively associated, ie if an object falling under one concept tends not to fall under the other concept.
*Principle C5: Acceptance.* The applicability of a concept to an object depends on the applicability of other concepts.

The foregoing principles are claimed to explain how concepts are applied to a particular object. As principles 3 states, some applications are given by perception or by another reliable source. But others result from negative and positive associations between concepts. These associations between

[89] ibid, 61.

concepts can be understood in terms of social stereotypes. For example, the stereotype that some people have of gypsies includes positive associations with other concepts, such as drug dealer and pickpocket; and negative associations with others, such as honest and hard worker. Thagard and Kunda have shown that applying such stereotypes can be explained in terms of conceptual constraint satisfaction.[90] Within this framework, they have been able to give an account of many of the phenomena discussed in the literature on how people form impressions of others.[91]

### E. Deliberative Coherence

Deliberative coherence concerns how decisions are made on the basis of coherence among actions and goals. This kind of coherence is relevant to practical inference, from decision-making to ethical, political, and legal issues, and it will be discussed at length in the chapters devoted to practical reasoning and moral reasoning.[92] Here, in order to give a complete overview of Thagard's theory of coherence, I shall mention the basic lines of this theory. In deliberative coherence, elements are actions and goals. Factors cohere with each other according to the following principles:[93]

> *Principle L1: Symmetry*. Coherence and incoherence are symmetrical relations: if factor (action or goal) $F_1$ coheres with factor $F_2$, then $F_2$ coheres with $F_1$.
>
> *Principle L2: Facilitation. Consider* factors $F_1$, ....... , $F_n$, that together facilitate the accomplishment of factor $F_G$. Then
>
> (a) each $F_1$ coheres with $F_G$,
>
> (b) each $F_i$ coheres with each other $F_j$, and
>
> (c) the greater the number of actions required, the less the coherence among the actions and goals.
>
> *Principle L3: Incompatibility*.
>
> (a) If two factors cannot both be performed or achieved, then they are strongly incoherent.
>
> (b) If two factors are difficult to perform or achieve together, then they are weakly incoherent.

[90] Kunda and Thagard (1996).

[91] Thagard has also applied his theory of conceptual coherence to explain conceptual combinations, see Thagard (1997).

[92] See chs 7 and 8.

[93] Thagard and Millgram (1995: 441–42). Thagard and Millgram have further developed the theory of deliberative coherence (TDC) in Thagard and Millgram (1996). See also Thagard (2000a: 127–32).

*Principle L4: Goal priority.* Some goals are desirable for intrinsic or other non-coherence reasons.

*Principle L5: Judgement.* Facilitation and competition relations can depend on coherence with judgements about the acceptability of factual beliefs.

*Principle L6: Decision.* Decisions are made on the basis of an assessment of the overall coherence of a set of actions and goals.

The main positive constraint is established by facilitation relations between actions and goals, as well as between actions that jointly contribute to achieving the same goal. Coherence relations, as opposed to facilitation relations, are symmetrical. The principle of incompatibility establishes relations of incoherence between pairs of factors. The principle of goal priority acknowledges the fact that some things are simply desired for their own sake. The principle of judgement expresses the idea that coherence between actions and goals depends on one's beliefs about what facilitates what, which in turn is a matter of coherence. Finally, principle 6 states that decisions are made by holistically assessing various competing goals and actions.

As is apparent, the principles of deliberative coherence have essentially the same structure as the principles of explanatory coherence. Just as the acceptability of beliefs depends on their explanatory coherence with a complex set of data and hypotheses, the desirability of actions and goals is determined on the basis of judgements of deliberative coherence. If theory evaluation—theoretical inference—is seen as an inference to the best explanation, decision-making—practical inference—is best viewed, in Thagard's and Millgram's words, as an 'inference to the best plan'. Coherence is, under this view, the main factor in determining both what to believe and what to do. Thagard's theory thus embodies a unified account of coherence-based inference.

## V. A UNIFIED ACCOUNT OF COHERENCE-BASED INFERENCE

### A. Coherence Problems

The six kinds of coherence that Thagard distinguishes share a basic common structure. All six kinds are specified in terms of elements and constraints, and there are similar connectionist algorithms for implementing them. According to Thagard, this suggests a unified view of coherence-based inference. From this perspective, 'the only rule of inference is this: accept a conclusion if its acceptance maximizes coherence'.[94] One and the same kind of inference is at work in both theoretical and practical reasoning. In a

[94] Thagard (2000a: 66).

particular coherence problem, different kinds of coherence will be involved, with different kinds of elements and constraints, but inference is performed by exactly the same kind of constraint-satisfaction algorithm. Thagard has defended the view according to which the justification of ethical judgements and ethical principles can be accomplished by taking into account four kinds of coherence: deductive, explanatory, analogical and deliberative coherence. Similarly, epistemic justification requires the interaction of diverse kinds of coherence: deductive, explanatory, analogical, perceptual and conceptual. In chapters seven and eight, I shall examine how these different kinds of coherence interact to give an account of justification in the practical domain. Let us now see how this unified theory of coherence accounts for epistemic justification.[95]

## B. Epistemic Justification

Thagard, together with Eliasmith, Rusnock and Shelley, has proposed that five kinds of coherence are relevant to the assessment of knowledge claims: explanatory, analogical, deductive, perceptual and conceptual. The integration of these kinds of coherence leads to a 'comprehensive, computable, naturalistic theory of epistemic coherence'.[96] It is also claimed that this theory can handle some of the standard objections that have been raised against coherence theories of knowledge and justification.[97] First, this theory gives a clear notion of coherence and of how the coherence of a set of elements may be computed.

Secondly, the connectionist algorithms involve a global and parallel way of assessing coherence and show how coherentist justification may be non-viciously circular. In addition, since coherence relations are taken to be symmetric, this approach to coherence-based inference also overcomes the regress problem.

Thirdly, Thagard claims that his theory is not conservative in a way that prevents genuine changes in view. If new elements are sufficiently coherent with other elements, they can dislodge previously accepted ones. In fact, the computational implementation of this theory has successfully modelled dramatic changes in view, such as those that are involved in scientific revolutions.

Fourthly, all the kinds of coherence that interact in epistemic justification are discriminating, ie some elements are given priority in being accepted. Thus, this coherentist theory of justification allows for some kinds of

[95] Thagard (2000a) has dealt with other examples of complex inference, ie the problem of other minds (ch 4) and decisions to trust someone (ch 6).

[96] Thagard, Eliasmith, Rusnock and Shelley (2002: 120). See also Thagard (2000a) ch 3.

[97] See ch 3 for a statement of these objections.

beliefs, eg perceptual beliefs, to enjoy a special status in the network of beliefs. By giving perceptual beliefs such a status, this coherence theory aims at meeting the charge that coherentist accounts of justification do not give observational knowledge the role that it ought to have in epistemic justification, ie the input objection.

Fifthly, Thagard argues that his theory provides two ways of overcoming the isolation objection. To start with, it gives some priority to empirical evidence and other reliable information. Because of that, we can have some confidence that hypotheses that are adopted on the basis of their coherence with these elements, ie the results of observation, correspond to the world, and are not merely isolated beliefs that are internally coherent. In addition, the existence of negative constraints, eg inconsistency, makes it unlikely that an isolated body of beliefs could turn out to be justified. For example, this theory will prevent astrological beliefs from being accepted, since they lack coherence with empirical evidence and often conflict with psychological and astronomical explanations.

Last, it is claimed that this theory of epistemic coherence shows how coherence-based inference can yield true conclusions. Again, it is the fact that Thagard's coherence theories are discriminating that provides a way of overcoming the truth-objection. Since these theories give priority to some elements, ie empirical evidence, we have a reason to believe that theories that cohere with them are true. This is not to say that, Thagard points out, the coherentist method guarantees the avoidance of falsehood. For example, this method does not prevent that two inconsistent elements end up being accepted. One would be justified in accepting both elements even though, of course, both cannot be true. However, according to Thagard, we had better leave open the possibility that coherence is temporarily maximized by adopting inconsistent sets of beliefs, for sometimes it may be more reasonable to live with an inconsistency than to reject one of two inconsistent propositions. For example, quantum theory and general relativity are incompatible, but given their independent evidential support, it will not be reasonable that we reject one of them. According to Thagard, the most we can expect of a theory of coherence is that it be generally reliable in accepting the truth and rejecting the false. And temporary tolerance of contradictions may be a useful strategy of accomplishing this long-term objective. Thagard claims his theory to provide this sort of truth-connection.[98]

In addition to the fact that these theories of coherence are discriminating, and this helps effect the connection between truth and coherence, Thagard claims that coherentist standards can be defended on the grounds of their

[98] For a criticism of Thagard's views on coherence and truth, see Millgram (2000) and Olsson (2005: 166–67). See Thagard (2012) for reply to Millgram.

fitting our practices of justification. He gives the following argument to the effect that explanatory coherence is truth-conducive:

1. scientists have achieved theories that are at least approximately true;[99]
2. scientists use explanatory coherence;
3. Therefore, explanatory coherence leads to theories that are at least approximately true.[100]

The first premise depends on the acceptability of scientific realism. Thagard has defended this view primarily on the basis of the successful technological applications of scientific theories.[101] The second premise is supported by a number of computational experiments. ECHO simulations have shown that many important historical cases of scientific reasoning are best understood in terms of explanatory coherence.[102] Thus, Thagard's justification of the use of coherentist standards of justification is, in its turn, a coherentist one: 'There is no foundational justification of coherentism, only the coherentist justification that coherentist principles fit well with what we believe and what we do'.[103] For example, principles of explanatory coherence fit well with scientific practice. Then, given that we have reason to believe that scientific theorizing produces true conclusions, we also have reason to believe that coherentist standards of justification are truth-conducive.[104]

## C. An Illustration: The Chemical Revolution

As explained, according to Thagard's theory, epistemic justification results from the interaction of several kinds of coherence. However, the most detailed applications of this theory have focused on one kind of coherence, ie explanatory coherence. Hence, for the purposes of illustrating how Thagard's theory of epistemic justification applies to actual cases, I shall describe Thagard's application of TEC and ECHO to a case from the history of science: the chemical revolution.[105] The dominant chemical theory

[99] It should be noticed that the notion of 'approximate truth' that this argument assumes is far from being an uncontroversial notion. The anti-realist philosophers of science have denied that there is any respectable notion of approximate truth. For a classical critique to the notion of approximate truth, more specifically, to Popper's theory of verisimilitude, which is the best formal account of this notion, see Miller (1974). For contemporary work on the notion of approximate truth, see Kuipers (2000) and Festa, Aliseda and Peijnenburg (2005).

[100] See Thagard (2012: 46). Thagard (2007a) has argued that a scientific theory is progressively approximating the truth if it is the best explanation of the evidence and satisfies two conditions: it broadens its evidence base over time and is deepened by explanations of why the theory works.

[101] See Thagard (1988: 145–49).

[102] See Thagard (1992a).

[103] Thagard (2000a: 80).

[104] For a critique to this line of reasoning, see Olsson (2005: 167–70).

[105] See Thagard ((1989: 444–46) and (1992a: 82–88)).

in the middle of the eighteen century was the phlogiston theory of Stahl. This theory provided explanations of important phenomena of combustion, respiration and calcination. According to this theory, combustion takes place when phlogiston in burning bodies is given off. In the 1770s Lavoisier developed the alternative theory that combustion takes place when bodies combine rapidly with oxygen from the air. By 1789, the vast majority of chemists had gone over Lavoisier's oxygen theory. Table 1 and 2 presents the input given to ECHO to represent Lavoisier's argument against phlogiston.[106] Table 1 shows the propositions used to represent the evidence to be explained and the competing theories. Table 2 shows the part of the input that sets up the network used to judge explanatory coherence.

**Table 1: Input Propositions for Lavoisier Example.**

Evidence:
E1 In combustion, heat and light are given off.
E2 Infammability is transmittable from one body to another.
E3 Combustion only occurs in the presence of pure air.
E4 Increase in the weight of a burned body is exactly equal to weight of air absorbed.
E5 Metals undergo calcination.
E6 In calcination, bodies increase weight.
E7 In calcination, volume of air diminishes.
E8 In reduction, effervescence appears.

Oxygen hypotheses:
OH1 Pure air contains oxygen principle.
OH2 Pure air contains matter of fire and heat.
OH3 In combustion, oxygen from the air combines with the burning body.
OH4 Oxygen has weight.
OH5 In calcination, metals add oxygen to become calxes.
OH6 In reduction, oxygen is given off.

Phlogiston hypotheses:
PH1 Combustible bodies contain phlogiston.
PH2 Combustible bodies contain matter of heat.
PH3 In combustion, phlogiston is given off.
PH4 Phlogiston can pass from one body to another.
PH5 Metals contain phlogiston.
PH6 In calcination, phlogiston is given off.

[106] In order to keep this illustration simple, I present the simulation presented by Thagard in (1989) in which incoherence relations are restricted to two contradictions. In the simulation presented in (1992) Thagard does not specify any contradictions between the phlogiston hypotheses and oxygen hypotheses, since, he explains, the hypothesis that burning objects give off phlogiston does not appear to strictly contradict the hypothesis that burning objects absorb oxygen. Instead, ECHO detects numerous competitions among the hypotheses of both theories.

**Table 2: Input Explanations for Lavoisier Example.**

Oxygen explanations:
(explain (OH1 OH2 OH3) E1)
(explain (OH1 OH3) E3)
(explain (OH1 OH3 OH4) E4)
(explain (OH1 OH5) E5)
(explain (OH1 OH4 OH5) E6)
(explain (OH1 OH5) E7)
(explain (OH1 OH6) E8)

Phlogiston explanations:
(explain (PH1 PH2 PH3) E1)
(explain (PH1 PH3 PH4) E2)
(explain (PH5 PH6) E5)

Contradictions:
(contradict PH3 OH3)
(contradict PH6 OH5)

Data:
(data (E1 E2 E3 E4 E5 E6 E7 E8))

These explanations and contradictions generate the network partially represented in Figure 1. E1–E8 are evidence units; OH1–OH6 are units representing hypotheses of the oxygen theory; and PH1–PH6 represent the phlogiston hypothesis. Solid lines are excitatory links, and dotted lines are inhibitory links:

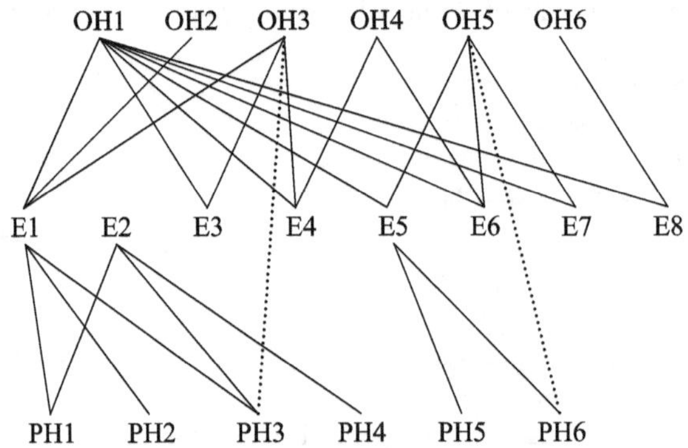


**Figure 1: Network Representing Lavoisier's Argument.**

When ECHO runs this network, starting all hypotheses with activation .01, it favours the oxygen hypotheses, giving them activation greater than 0. In contrast, all the phlogiston hypotheses become deactivated. Hence, the implementation of TEC in ECHO successfully models the chemical revolution, which resulted in the rejection of the phlogiston theory and the acceptance of the oxygen theory.

## D. Emotional Coherence

Social psychologists distinguish between 'cold' and 'hot' cognition. While the former, refers to intellectual, information-driven processes, the latter involve motivations, emotions and desires.[107] The theory of explanatory coherence models scientific theory choice as if it involved only cold cognition. However, emotions and motivations are also involved in scientific reasoning.[108] Similarly, inferences about what to believe in forensic contexts rely on the production of emotional judgements too.[109] Therefore, the theory of explanatory coherence insofar as it involves exclusively cold cognition neglects a crucial dimension of our practices of theory evaluation. The same holds for probabilistic accounts of theory choice, which obviously do not account either for the role that hot cognition may play in our decisions about what to believe. However, coherence-based approaches to theory choice, unlike the probabilistic ones, may be easily modified to make room for emotions. A very interesting effort towards integrating the role of emotion within a coherence-based approach to theory choice is that of Thagard's. Thagard has suggested that we complement his theory of coherence with a theory of emotional coherence. The resulting model tightly integrates hot and cold cognition by showing how emotional assessment can be linked with explanatory coherence and other kinds of coherence to produce judgements about what to believe.[110]

Emotional coherence is not an additional kind of coherence, but an expanded way of considering the different elements and constraints that are involved in computing the six kinds of coherence already described. On the theory of emotional coherence and its computational implementation (HOTCO, which stands for 'hot coherence') elements have, in addition to the cognitive status of being accepted or rejected, an emotional status called 'valence', which can be positive or negative, depending on one's emotional attitude towards the element. Just as elements in the different kinds of coherence are related to each other by positive and negative constraints, so they can also be related by positive and negative valence constraints. Some elements have intrinsic positive and negative valences, while others acquire valences in virtue of their connections with other elements. These connections can be valence constraints or epistemic constraints, ie any of the constraints posited by the theories of coherence. The valence of an element is determined by the valences and the acceptability of all the elements to which it is connected. The valence calculation can be affected by all the kinds of coherence. However, given the important place of explanatory coherence in Thagard's model, I shall illustrate Thagard's theory of emotional coherence by means of an example of his in which only the contribution of this kind of coherence is taken into account, ie the OJ Simpson case.[111] This

[107] See Kunda (1999) ch 6 and Thagard (2006).
[108] Thagard (2002).
[109] On the role of emotion in legal judgment, see Bandes (1999); Bornstein and Wiener ((2006) and (2010)); and Abrams and Keren (2010).
[110] For Thagard's detailed description of the theory of emotional coherence, see (2000a) ch 6.
[111] Thagard (2003).

example is particularly interesting in that it brings to light an acute problem that Thagard's theory of emotional coherence (as much as any theory that brings together hot and cold cognition) must face. While to neglect emotions seriously undermines the descriptive adequacy of any theory that purports to explain our factual inferences, including them threatens the normative adequacy of such a theory.

## E. An Illustration: The OJ Simpson Case

OJ Simpson was tried for the murder of his ex-wife, Nicole Brown Simpson, and her friend Ron Goldman. At first glance, evidence that OJ Simpson was the murderer of this ex-wife was overwhelming. Police who came to Simpson's house found drops of blood in his car that matched his own blood and that of Ron Goldman. In Simpson's back yard, the police found a bloody glove that was of a pair with one found at the scene of the crime, and they found a bloody sock in his bedroom. Simpson had a cut on his hand that might have been caused by a struggle with the victims. Simpson's blood was found on a gate near the crime scene. Moreover, there was a plausible motive for the murder, as Simpson had been physically abusive of his wife and was reported to have been jealous of other men who saw Nicole after their divorce.

The defence lawyers set out to generate hypotheses that explained the deaths and other evidence and that would compete with the hypothesis of Simpson's guilt. Based on Nicole's known story of cocaine use, they hypothesized that she was killed by drug dealers. In order to explain the circumstantial evidence linking OJ Simpson to the crime scene, the defence contended that the items had been planted by LA Police Department officers determined to frame Simpson for the crime. The lawyers were able to identify irregularities in the conduct of the investigation. They found evidence that Fuhrman, the detective who had allegedly found the bloody glove in Simpson's yard, was a racist who frequently had bragged in the past about framing blacks, especially those involved with white women.

The lawyers were unsuccessful in finding any substantial evidence for the hypothesis that Nicole was killed by drug dealers, but they were very effective in offering alternative explanations of the blood evidence. The glove that Simpson had supposedly used in the murder did not appear to fit his hand when he tried to put it on in court. One of the detectives had carried a sample of Simpson's blood around with him for hours, and some of the blood taken from Simpson was unaccounted for. Blood had not been noticed on the sock until weeks after it had been held by the police. The blood on the glove and the sock showed traces of EDTA, a chemical used as an anticoagulant in samples taken from OJ Simpson and Ron Goldman. Fuhrman and other detectives had ample opportunity to plan the evidence that implicated Simpson, and Fuhrman had a racist motivation to do so.

An analysis of the Simpson case in terms of the theory of explanatory coherence requires that we specify the input and the constraints, as shown below:

**Table 3: Input Propositions for the OJ Simpson Case.**

Evidence:
E1 Nicole Simpson and Ron Brown are dead.
E2 Simpson's blood was found on a gate at the crime scene.
E3 There was blood on Simpson's car.
E4 A bloody glove was found in Simpson's car.
E5 Simpson's sock had blood on it.
E6 Simpson beat Nicole.
E7 Furhman lied.
E8 EDTA was found in Simpson's sock.

Hypotheses that OJ Simpson is guilty:
G1 OJ Simpson killed Nicole Simpson and Ron Brown.
G2 OJ was abusive and jealous.

Hypotheses that OJ Simpson is innocent:
I1 Nicole was killed by drug dealers.
I2 The LA police department framed OJ

**Table 4: Input Explanations in the OJ Simpson Case.**

The case for OJ Simpson's guilt:
(explain (G1) E1)
(explain (G1) E2)
(explain (G1) E3)
(explain (G1) E4)
(explain (G1) E5)
(explain (G1) E6)
(explain (G2) G1)

The case for OJ Simpson's innocence:
(explain (I1) E1)
(explain (I2) E2)
(explain (I2) E3)
(explain (I2) E4)
(explain (I2) E5)
(explain (I2) E7)
(explain (I2) E8)

Competitions:
(compete (I1) G1)
(compete (I2) G1)

The following figures show the explanatory coherence analysis of the competing stories in the Simpson case. Solid lines are excitatory links and dotted lines are inhibitory links:

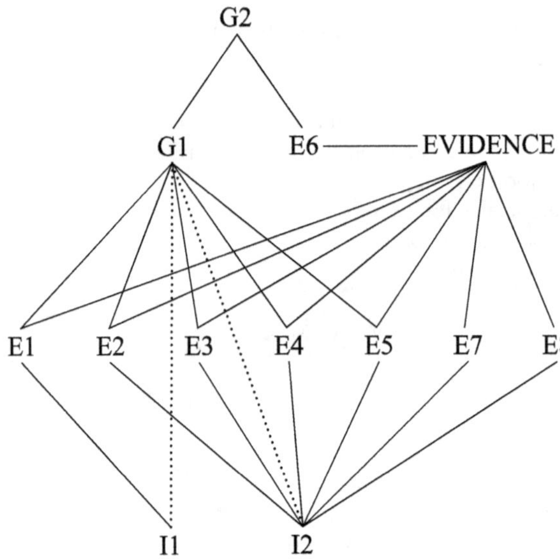


**Figure 2: Explanatory Coherence Analysis of the OJ Simpson Case.**

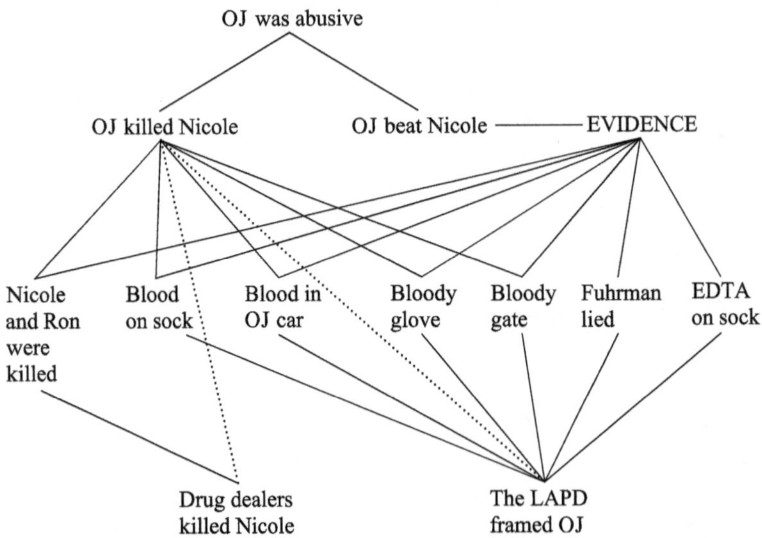


**Figure 3: Expanded Explanatory Coherence Analysis of the OJ Simpson Case.**

In the theory of explanatory coherence, the claim that Simpson killed Nicole is accepted if so doing maximizes the overall coherence among pieces of evidence and conflicting hypotheses. That is, if it belongs to the accepted subset that results from partitioning the set of all elements (evidence and hypotheses) in a way that maximizes the satisfaction of the constraints, as established by the principles of explanatory coherence. In the Simpson case, ECHO, unlike the jury, finds Simpson guilty. From this result, Thagard concludes that the jury's decision in this case was not based solely on explanatory considerations, but that emotional assessments were also crucial to the decision. These emotional judgements may be taken into account by expanding ECHO to allow the units that stand for propositions to have valences as well as activations. This is what HOTCO does. For instance, just as the hypothesis that Simpson is the murderer can have a positive or a negative activation, in HOTCO one can also attach a positive or negative valence to it, depending on whether one thinks that this is good or bad. Can HOTCO provide a more adequate account of a juror's judgement about what to believe?

According to Thagard, HOTCO still embodies an overly rational theory of emotional coherence. In HOTCO, valences are partly determined by activations, but not vice versa. As a result, it allows explanatory considerations to influence emotional judgements but does not allow valences to influence activations. Thagard has altered HOTCO to allow a kind of biasing of activations by valences. The resulting amended program is called HOTCO2. Figure 4 shows an expanded network, with the addition of 'evaluation units' which correspond to representations that have both a cognitive and an affective dimension. In the case under consideration, Thagard included units corresponding to 'OJ is good' and 'LAPD is good'. Depending on a person's emotional bias, these units may have positive or negative valences. For instance, given that many black jurors had a positive emotional attitude towards Simpson, and a negative one towards the LA police, 'OJ is good' has a positive link to the valence unit, and 'LAPD is good' has a negative link. The activation of these units is a function both of the activation input to them but also of the valence input. Hence, 'OJ is good' tends to be activated, while 'LAPD is good' tends to be deactivated. Then, these units can influence the activations of hypotheses, such as that OJ was the murderer, or that the LAPD framed him. There is a negative link between 'OJ is good', and 'OJ killed Nicole', so that a positive evaluation of Simpson tends to suppress acceptance of the hypothesis that he killed Nicole. Similarly, a negative evaluation of the LAPD tends to support the hypothesis that Simpson was framed. The next figure shows the expanded network. As before, solid lines are excitatory links and dotted lines are inhibitory links; thick lines are valence constraints:

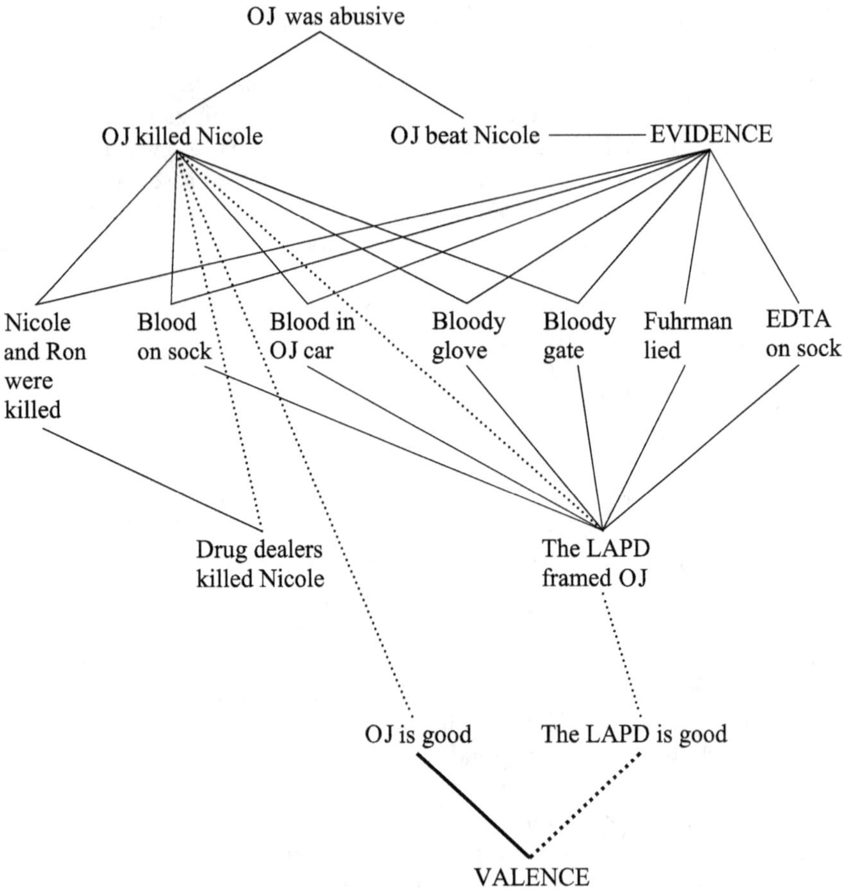


**Figure 4: Emotional Coherence Analysis of the OJ Simpson Case.**

When HOTCO2 is run on the foregoing network, it rejects the conclusion that OJ killed Nicole, just as the jury did. This shows, argues Thagard, that the jurors in the Simpson case made their decisions based on emotional coherence, which combines an emotional bias with an assessment of competing explanations of the evidence.[112] In addition, several empirical studies

[112] In contrast, some analysts of this case have argued that reasonable doubt considerations were determinant of the decision of the jury. See Hastie and Pennington (1996) and Dershowitz (1996). As I will argue in ch 10, in order to apply Thagard's theory of explanatory coherence (and its computational implementation) to the legal context, it is necessary to include a number of institutional constraints, most prominently, the presumption of innocence

have shown that people's inferences actually involve the kind of cognitive and emotional constraints implemented in HOTCO2.[113] Now, even if we grant the descriptive adequacy of this model, there are considerable doubts as to its normative adequacy. The HOTCO model, by allowing activations to influence valences, shows how emotional and cognitive judgements may be smoothly integrated. But HOTCO2 by also allowing valences to influence activations is obviously dangerous. This model does not simply legitimize wishful thinking (eg it does not allow us to accept that OJ Simpson killed Nicole just because it makes us happy to do so) for it requires that factual judgements be partially based on cognitive considerations. But, nevertheless, it does allow emotions to have a strong influence on factual inferences. Having emotions influence the assessment of evidence and hypotheses seems to hamper the success of our explanatory practices, in law, science and other contexts, as tools for the acquisition of true beliefs.

Despite the danger that emotions may undermine our factual inferences, it does not seem reasonable to expect scientists or jurors to shut down their emotional reactions. Moreover, there are good reasons to doubt that such emotion-free judgements, even if possible, are at all desirable. As some studies have shown, emotion-free decision-making is highly defective.[114] And it seems to be part of our concept of an ideal scientist or an ideal judge or detective, that he has the 'appropriate' emotions.[115] Hence, it seems that any theory of hypothesis selection must give some account of how cognition and emotion should be related to each other. Admittedly, Thagard does not provide a solution to the problem of how this interaction should be understood. As he himself recognizes, from a descriptive point of view, the theory of emotional coherence is far too simplistic, in that it considers only positive and negative emotions, among the incredibly rich range of emotions experienced by people. And, as argued, it is also far from satisfactory from a normative point of view. Given that we cannot do without emotions and, more importantly, that emotions figure prominently in our views about what good factual inferences should look like, it is desirable that a model of theory evaluation, rather than simply modelling a kind of biased reasoning,

and the standards of proof. My hypothesis is that the outcome of applying such expanded theory (and its computation implementation) to the OJ Simpson case would be the rejection of the conclusion that OJ killed Nicole. That institutional constraints on the maximization of coherence—rather than emotional bias—played a prevalent role in this case is argued in Amaya (2009).

[113] Thagard (2003: 376–79).

[114] See Damasio (1994).

[115] Indeed, virtues, according to Aristotle, are both a way of acting and a way of feeling. Thus, the virtuous scientist, judge or detective does not only act in a way that is appropriate to the circumstances of the case but also has the right sort of emotional response. On virtue and emotion in Aristotle, see Hursthouse (1999) ch 5; Sherman (1989) ch 2; and Stark (2001).

show us how to improve our epistemic practices with the aid of the right emotions. Despite these limitations, Thagard's theory importantly advances the project of constructing coherentist models of factual inference that give emotions their due.

## VI. CHALLENGES TO EXPLANATORY COHERENTISM

Thagard's version of explanatory coherentism is attractive for a number of reasons. First, it provides a unified coherentist approach to practical and theoretical reasoning which is, nonetheless, sensitive to the differences between both domains. Secondly, it does not restrict all justification to explanatory coherence, but it more plausibly allows for other kinds of coherence to play a role in justification. Thirdly, it gives a precise notion of coherence and how it may be computed. Last, this theory may easily account for the role that emotions plays in theory evaluation.

Besides, Thagard's theory gives reasonable solutions to the longstanding problems of coherentism: (i) the constraint satisfaction conception of coherence and its computational implementation succeeds in meeting the vagueness objection; (ii) the symmetry of the relations of coherence allows to clearly distinguish between circular chains of inference and mutually supporting inferences; (iii) while Thagard's theory exhibits a modest kind of conservatism, it is capable of modelling even large-scale changes of views; (iv) this theory is committed only to a kind of local holism and thus avoids the problems of global versions of holism; (v) Thagard's treatment of epistemic justification as a discriminating problem provides a way of overcoming the input and isolation objections; and (vi) his defence of the truth-conduciveness of coherence-based inferences on the grounds that it provides the best explanation of the success of scientific theories is a very appealing approach to the problem of truth.

To be sure, Thagard's theory does not solve the problems of coherentism once and for all. Moreover, this theory, in an important respect, does not address the same problems that other coherentist theories of coherence set themselves to solve. Unlike BonJour's and Lehrer's theories, Thagard's theory does not provide us with a picture of the structure of our whole body of empirical belief. And in the same way, it can hardly be seen as providing a solution to the problem of how such a body of belief, if coherent, manages to connect up with the world. His theory of justification has a more local, down to earth, character. The driving questions of his research seem to be questions such as how we can justify adherence to a particular scientific theory, belief in a given mathematical theorem, or acceptance of a guilt-hypothesis in a courtroom, on the basis of coherence. And within these domains of application, this theory does seem to successfully address the main objections raised against coherentist theories of justification.

Now, notwithstanding its attractiveness, several problems remain open. Some aspects of this theory await further development:

1. *The selection and the generation stages.* The process of justification involves two stages: the generation of alternatives and the selection of the best one. Thagard's theory, as Thagard recognizes, is limited in that it is concerned exclusively with the latter stage. In addition, the generation of alternatives, their comparison and the selection of the best one are not separate stages, but we typically move back and forth from one stage to another. The selection of the best theory takes place in the same process of elaborating and dismissing alternatives. The incorporation of evaluation into the stage of hypothesis generation does not only increase the descriptive adequacy of a model of theory choice, but it is also convenient from a normative standpoint. For the sake of efficacy, it is necessary to introduce evaluation in the process of hypothesis construction in order to reduce the number of explanations generated. Thus, it would be desirable to complement Thagard's theory with an account of how the base of coherence, eg the set of elements over which the coherence calculation is performed, is generated, as well as with an account of how the generation and the selection stage relate to each other. At the level of computational implementation, this could be done by combining ECHO, as well as the other programs modelled after ECHO, with discovery programs that are able to generate their own hypotheses, such as GLAUBER, STAHL and PI (an acronym meaning 'Process of Induction').[116] At the level of the coherence theory, it is particularly interesting to explore the role of coherence in the generation stage. Thagard has suggested that the generation of new elements is sometimes driven by 'incoherence'. That is, failure to achieve a coherent interpretation prompts the generation of elements that reestablish the desired coherence.[117] While examining the role of coherence in generation it is important to keep in mind some psychological findings that may cast doubt on the legitimacy of these coherence-based mechanisms. For instance, an important observation in the psychology of belief is that people often interpret ambiguous events in a manner consistent with their existing beliefs; research on memory suggests that memory for information congruent with prior beliefs is better than memory for information irrelevant to prior beliefs; we also tend to drive our attention to encode information which is consistent with our expectations; and we are prone to seek information that supports our beliefs rather

[116] The automatization of ECHO input is, in fact, a further goal of Thagard's research; see Thagard (1989: 454). A full account of how PI invents its own hypotheses is given by Thagard in (1988) ch IV. About STAHL and GLAUBER, see Langley, Simon, Bradshaw and Zytkow (1987).

[117] Thagard (2000a: 67–69). According to Thagard, new elements are not always incoherence-driven. Other generation mechanisms include serendipity, curiosity and motivation. As regards constraints, he claims some of them to be innate, while others result from empirically discovered relations among elements.

than disconfirm them. This evidence suggests that the information that is entered into the set E is itself determined by using methods that promote coherence among certain elements.[118] If the set of elements over which the coherence calculation is performed is biased in some of these ways, then we do not seem to have a good reason for accepting as justified the elements that end up in the A (acceptance) set that results from computing coherence.[119] Thus, it is crucial to include a theory of generation into a coherence theory of evaluation. Only by clearly distinguishing the different forces that drive element-generation, and examining the extent to which they succeed in including all the relevant elements within the set, can the outcome of the coherence computation be regarded as epistemically justified.

2. *Problems with the input.* One of the main problems of Thagard's theory of coherence and its computational implementation concerns the input.[120] Many questions must be addressed before Thagard's ECHO (and related programs) starts running its search for the best solution to a coherence problem. When are two hypotheses explanatorily analogous? When are they contradictory? What are the criteria for individuating hypotheses and evidence? Which propositions are intuitively obvious? How are weights to links assigned? How are their comparative values fixed? What evidence is relevant? What evidence supports what hypothesis? What are the conditions under which two concepts are positively associated? In most difficult cases, in science, in law, or in ordinary contexts of justification, these questions are very controversial. It suffices to mention, for example, disagreements among scientists over the relevance of evidence, arguments in the courtroom to establish which facts may be considered as proven in a given case, problems concerning the reliability of evidence in forensic, scientific and ordinary contexts, as well as disputes over the acceptability of a proposed analogy. Despite the seriousness of these problems, it would be unfair to charge coherence theories with the task of providing adequate solutions to the diverse and difficult issues with which the notion of coherence is closely intertwined. What these problems make patent, in my view, is the need to locate a theory of coherence within a general theory of reasoning and rationality that successfully deals with these issues.

3. *Foundationalism in disguise?* The problem of input is particularly important in relation to the discriminating constraints that figure in the different kinds of coherence. Elements of the subset D (discriminating elements) of E are favoured to be members of A (accepted elements). Hence, one may

[118] For the implications of these empirical findings to the adequacy of Thagard's model, see Markman (2002).

[119] On this problem as it applies to legal reasoning, see ch 10.

[120] Many of the peer reviews of Thagard (1989) discuss the problem of the input as one of the main problems that Thagard's theory faces. See, among others, Klayman and Hogarth (1989: 478); Dietrich (1989: 473); and McCauley (1989: 482). For Thagard's reply to this objection, see Thagard ((1989: 490ff and (1992a: 89)).

wonder whether by introducing these kind of constraints Thagard is not conceding too much to the foundationalist. Since Thagard's purported solutions to endemic problems of coherentism, eg isolation, input and truth objections, heavily rely on principles of discriminateness, one may also question whether he has provided genuine solutions to these problems, or whether, in fact, he has only apparently solved them by sneaking a foundationalist element into the theory. Thagard says that his theory is not foundationalist because there is no guarantee that the elements of D will be accepted.[121] However, weak versions of foundationalism give basic beliefs only an a priori justification. In this regard, Thagard's theory is not different from weak foundationalism. What makes Thagard's theory non-foundationalist is his justification of the coherentist principles, the discriminateness principle included. These principles are adopted because they fit with our beliefs. There is, hence, no appeal to foundations to determine why there should be a principle of discriminateness or why a particular set of beliefs should fall within the scope of such principle. But, it is only coherence among our beliefs that provides the ultimate court of appeal. In this sense, Thagard's theory of justification may be properly characterized as a coherentist one.

4. *The plausibility objection.* We have seen how Thagard's theory copes with traditional objections against coherentism. In previous chapters, I introduced an additional objection that has been raised against current coherence theories, the so-called 'psychological plausibility objection' or 'feasibility objection'.[122] The charge is that coherence theories of justification require performing operations that are far beyond humans' cognitive capacities. As a cognitive naturalist, Thagard is well aware of the need to take into account facts about our cognitive endowment when designing theories of justification. In fact, he wants his computational theory of coherence to be both 'a powerful theory of important cognitive mechanisms and a non-foundational solution to philosophical problems about justification"[123] Now, the question arises of whether Thagard's model of coherentist justification succeeds in meeting the 'psychological plausibility objection'. As argued, problems of feasibility are more severe when wedding (internalist) coherentism with holism.[124] We cannot possibly have access to our whole system of belief, let alone to the facts of coherence on which justification—according to the holist model—depends. Insofar as Thagard's theory exhibits only a kind of moderate holism, it is in a much better position to overcome the feasibility problem than holistic coherentism is. As the base of coherence is reduced, the possibilities for accessing the relevant beliefs and the connections among them sensibly improve.

[121] Thagard (2000a: 71).
[122] See esp ch 3.
[123] ibid, 13.
[124] See ch 3.

In addition, this coherence theory is consistent with evidence showing that processes of parallel constraint satisfaction are important in human cognition. In particular, the ECHO computer model of coherence has proven useful as a model of human reasoning.[125]

Nonetheless, there are still some issues that have to be dealt with before certifying the adequacy of Thagard's model as a psychologically plausible model of justification. To start with, even if Thagard's moderate holism substantially reduces the complexities of the tasks involved in coherentist justification, it still risks going beyond human processing limitations. People are unlikely to consider all the interdependences activated by ECHO, and similar programs.[126] Limitations of short-term memory prevent the retrieval of all relevant hypotheses and data at once. Humans can only do limited coherence-seeking. In addition, Thagard's model assumes that evidence, hypotheses, concepts and other elements are all available at the same time. However, in most domains, these elements become available sequentially. Hence, people's beliefs typically develop incrementally, with coherence calculations being performed over smaller sets of elements, as they become available. There are, at least, two ways in which Thagard's model may be revised so as to lower the demands on epistemic agents and bring the model closer to people's real performance: (i) it could focus on one kind of coherence and then on another; and (ii) it could concentrate on some elements and then on others. The latter strategy has been pursued by Hoadly, Ranney and Schank.[127] They have designed WanderECHO, a variation of the ECHO model, which simulates attentional and memorial limitations with a stochastic updating algorithm that is based on a travelling focus of attention. Rather than updating every unit in the network at every cycle, WanderECHO updates one unit—the model's focus of attention—at a time. The next node to be updated is determined by reference to weight links with the former one. In addition, WanderECHO has a local stopping criterion, and thus it does not require the calculation of the energy change of the entire system in order to determine whether to stop. Hence, the development of variations on Thagard's model, such as WanderECHO, may help to increase the psychological plausibility of this model.

5. *The problem of integration.* As Thagard recognizes, a main problem of this coherence-based theory of inference concerns how the different kinds

[125] For applications of ECHO and TEC to psychological experiments, see Ranney (1991) and Miller and Read (1991). Hastie and Pennington have shown the relevance of coherence mechanisms to jurors' decision-making (1991). Byrne has modelled the stories that were generated by the subjects in Pennington and Hastie's experiments with ECHO. ECHO reached in those cases the same verdicts as humans did (1995).

[126] Peng and Keane (1989: 469). Thagard also recognizes that his theory expects too much of people, given their psychological resources, see (2000a: 140–142, 163 and 278).

[127] Hoadley, Ranney and Schank (1994).

of coherence can be integrated with each other.[128] We need a more detailed account of how the different kinds of coherence interplay in order to give an optimal solution to a coherence problem. The problem is not an easy one. In difficult cases, opposite conclusions may follow from the different kinds of coherence. In addition, the relations among some of these kinds are particularly problematical. For instance, while it is clear that explanatory coherence must influence deliberative coherence, it is controversial whether deliberative coherence should also influence explanatory coherence. Despite difficulties, the prospects of simulating the integration among the different kinds of coherence are good. All the different programs use the same connectionist algorithm for maximizing coherence. Hence, it is possible to run all the programs together so as to reach a conclusion based simultaneously on all the considerations that the different kinds of coherence bring to bear on a particular issue.[129] Recently, computational implementations of the diverse kinds of coherence have been integrated in a computer program COHERE.[130] Computational experiments may shed light on which constraints among the different relations that may hold among kinds of coherence yield the desired results.

## VII. CONCLUSIONS

This chapter has examined theories of explanatory coherence. Unlike other coherentist accounts of epistemic justification, these theories regard explanatory relations as pivotal to coherence and justification. Theories of explanatory coherence should be located within a broader explanationist framework, which may be characterized by means of the following claims: (i) the defence of a cognitive naturalist framework that closely ties philosophy with cognitive science; (ii) the view that there are important connections between theoretical and practical reasoning; (iii) the relevance of conservatism when changing views; (iv) a holistic view of justification; (v) the importance of inference to the best explanation within a theory of justification; and (vi) the view that probabilities play a minor role in reasoning. All theories of explanatory coherence are committed to some version of the foregoing claims.

Among the different versions of explanatory coherentism, I have focused on Thagard's theory of explanatory coherence. This theory provides a

[128] Thagard (2000a: 63–64, and 169).

[129] Thagard has run a computer simulation using together ECHO, ACME and DECO of the problem of whether capital punishment is morally justified. See Thagard (2000a: 142–44) as well as the last section of ch 8.

[130] The software COHERE is available at http://cogsci.uwaterloo.ca/#software. To my knowledge, no results from computer simulations that integrate all the different kinds of coherence have been published so far.

precise characterization of coherence that is applicable to a number of different domains and gives a satisfactory response to the traditional problems that have been raised against coherentism. Nonetheless, there are several aspects of this theory that need to be further developed. More specifically, this theory does not give an account of the process of discovery and how it relates to the process of evaluation; it can only be put to work once the input to the theory and its computational implementation is already generated; some have raised doubts about the extent to which this theory is a genuine alternative to foundationalism; it is also controversial whether it satisfactorily meets the feasibility objection; and it does not provide a definite solution to the problem of how different kinds of coherence may be integrated with each other.

Despite these problems, Thagard's coherence theory is a psychologically quite plausible, descriptively accurate and normatively appealing theory about how one may be justified in accepting a particular scientific theory (as opposed to a competing one) and change one's views accordingly. I shall now examine other theories that also purport to explain the role of coherence in the dynamics of justification, to wit, the coherence theories of belief revision. Unlike theories of explanatory coherence, which deal with conceptual change, these coherence theories are concerned with explaining small-scale belief changes, such as those that occur in belief revision.[131]

[131] There are, nonetheless, interesting connections between theories of belief revision and theory change in science, which only recently have been explored. For a discussion of possible applications of theories of belief revision to analyse the mechanics of theory change in science, see Olsson and Enqvist (2011) and Aliseda (2006: 179–201).

# 5

# *Coherence and Belief Dynamics*

OUR SYSTEM OF beliefs is not static but, as time passes, new information is acquired, and beliefs change accordingly. Thus, a central problem for a theory of justification is to give an account of what constitutes justified changes of belief. In this chapter, I propose to consider this problem; more specifically, given that the main subject of this book is the notion of coherence, I propose to investigate the role of coherence in the dynamics of belief. Two competing theories of belief revision or belief change may be distinguished: the foundations theory and the coherence theory.[1]

The key issue that sets apart the foundationalist theory of belief revision from the coherentist one is whether one needs to keep track of one's original justification for one's beliefs. According to the foundations theory, it is necessary to keep track of the reasons for one's beliefs. That is, according to the foundations theory, a rational agent should give up a belief that *p* as soon as one does not associate one's belief in *p* with adequate justification. Furthermore, if one is not justified in continuing to believe that *p* in this way, one has to abandon as well all beliefs whose justifications depend on *p*. As opposed to the foundations theory, the coherence theory states that one may not (justifiably) give up a belief that *p* simply because one has no reasons for such a belief; one needs to have the positive belief that one's reasons for *p* are not good. Hence, the coherence theory of belief revision is conservative in a way that the foundations theory is not. From a coherentist perspective, one's present beliefs are justified just as they are, and changes are allowed only to the extent that they increase the overall coherence of one's system of beliefs. Moreover, those changes should be the minimal ones that are necessary to eliminate the incoherence. Thus, from a coherentist perspective, there are two competing aims of reasoned revision: to maximize coherence and to minimize change.

There seem to be good reasons for favouring the coherence theory of belief revision over the foundationalist one. Some experiments designed to explore the phenomenon of belief perseverance in the face of evidential discrediting seem to give support to the thesis that people do not keep

[1] Harman (1986: 29–39).

track of all the justifications for their beliefs.[2] In addition, as Harman and Gärdenfors argue, the coherence theory is not only more adequate from a descriptive point of view, but it is also to be preferred on normative grounds. People ought not to keep track of all the justifications of their beliefs because it is 'intellectually extremely costly' to do so. There is a practical reason to avoid 'cluttering' one's mind with all the reasons for one's beliefs. It is more efficient not to try to remember those justifications and the justifying beliefs. Thus, a 'principle of intellectual economy', in Gärdenfors' words, or 'clutter avoidance', as Harman says, entails that it is rational to neglect the pedigree of one's beliefs.[3]

Several formalisms for modelling belief revision have been proposed in different areas of philosophy, computer science, psychology and linguistics; eg belief sets, Ellis' belief systems, models based on possible worlds, Doyle's Truth Maintenance System and Bayesian models.[4] According to Gärdenfors, with the exception of Dolye's theory, most models of belief revision are in accordance with the coherence theory.[5] The most influential of such models is the AGM theory, whose change operations are applied to belief sets.[6] I shall start the discussion of the place of coherence within a theory of belief revision by introducing the AGM theory and examining the extent to which it appropriately formalizes the basic tenets of the coherentist epistemology. Then, I shall give an account of the different coherence-based strategies of belief revision that have been proposed in the literature. I shall conclude this chapter by considering the extent to which belief revision formalisms contribute to the development of a coherentist approach to epistemic justification.

[2] Ross and Anderson have shown that beliefs typically survive potent logical and empirical challenges. They can even survive 'the total destruction of their original evidential basis' (1982: 129–52). Harman argues that these studies strongly support the claim that the coherence theory is in line with the way in which people actually reason. *Cf* Tennant (2012: 322–28).

[3] The normative adequacy of the coherence theory is defended by Harman and Gärdenfors. See Harman (1986: 35–42) and Gärdenfors (1990: 30–32).

[4] For a brief and clear introduction to belief revision formalisms, see Peppas (2008) and Gärdenfors (2003). For a more detailed description of the several models, see Gärdenfors (1988) ch 2.

[5] Gärdenfors (1988: 35).

[6] The most detailed argument for the interpretation of the AGM theory as a coherentist theory and for preferring the coherence approach, which AGM is claimed to exemplify, to the foundations approach, which Doyle's theory exemplifies, is provided by Gärdenfors (1990: 25ff). For a critique, see Hansson and Olsson (1999) and Shaffer (2002). For an examination of Gärdenfors' criticism of the foundations approach, and a defence of this framework, see Doyle (1992). Under some interpretations, formalisms that use 'belief bases' instead of 'belief sets' are in accordance with a foundational approach to belief revision. For a defence of one such model, and a comparison with the coherence approach that AGM embodies, see Bochman ((1999) and (2000)).

## I. THE AGM MODEL

The standard model of belief revision is the AGM theory (so called after its three originators, Carlos Alchourrón, Peter Gärdenfors and David Makinson).[7] Before getting into the details of the theory, I shall give a brief introduction to the main elements of theories of belief revision as well as explain the way in which these elements are understood in the AGM model.

### A. Elements of the Formal Theories of Belief Revision

Gärdenfors suggests that four epistemic factors form the core of theories of belief revision. First, central elements of these theories are the 'epistemic states'. These entities are used for representing a person's knowledge at a given point of time. The AGM theory models the epistemic state of an individual by representing it as a set of sentences. Such a set consists of those sentences that the individual accepts, that is, treats as true. Epistemic states are intended to be idealizations of psychological states. For example, AGM assumes the sets of sentences that an individual accepts to be consistent and closed under logical consequences. In this model, idealized epistemic states are supposed to be in reflective equilibrium. To explain what this means, Gärdenfors distinguishes two kinds of epistemic forces: on the one hand, the 'internal forces' pushing an epistemic state toward an equilibrium and, on the other, the epistemic inputs that serve as 'external forces' taking a state from one equilibrium to another. To give an example, if a set of beliefs is not consistent, then the individual should, if she is to be rational, adjust her state of belief until she reaches a rational state of belief. Such equilibrium may be disrupted by new inputs, in which case, the individual should make the changes necessary for establishing the equilibrium again. In this view, 'a rational state of belief is one that is in equilibrium under all forces of internal criticism'.[8]

In addition to epistemic states, theories of belief revision also have an account of 'epistemic inputs', which can be thought of as 'the deliverances of experience or as linguistic (or other symbolic) information provided

[7] Alchourrón, Gärdenfors and Makinson (1985). This article has set the foundations for what is now the dominant paradigm for research in belief revision. For detailed surveys of the current state of this research, see Fermé and Hansson (2011); Hansson (1999a); and Gärdenfors and Rott (1995). Research on belief revision is closely connected with another important area of research, ie non-monotonic reasoning. For a discussion of the connections between belief revision and non-monotonic reasoning, see Makinson and Gärdenfors (1991); Fermé and Hansson (2011: 314); H Rott (2001); and Makinson (2005: 141–48). Useful references on work on the relationship between non-monotonic reasoning and belief revision are provided in Peppas (2008: 8). The connection between the logic of belief revision and non-monotonic logic is, however, not uncontroversial. See Maranhão ((2012a) and (2013)).

[8] Gärdenfors (1988: 9).

by other individuals'.[9] In the AGM theory, inputs are confined to single sentences.

The third element is a classification of 'epistemic attitudes' that describe the status of various elements of belief that are contained in an epistemic state. For example, a person may accept or may not accept a particular fact, judge it to be certain, find it extremely likely or possible. Different models allow for expressing different kinds of attitudes towards the same fact. In the AGM model, three different kinds of attitudes are expressible: a proposition *A* may be accepted; rejected, which is to say that its negation (–*A*) is in the belief state; or it may be indetermined, which means that neither *A* nor –*A* is an element of the epistemic state. In this model, there is no way of expressing any degree of plausibility of different propositions. In contrast, a richer typology of attitudes can be expressed in probabilistic models. Another way of introducing degrees of acceptance or plausibility, different from probabilities, is Spohn's generalized possible worlds model. In this model, inputs are not only propositions, but propositions together with a degree of plausibility, which makes it possible to introduce more interesting epistemic attitudes, to wit, 'more plausible than' or 'believed more firmly than', besides the standard 'accepted', 'rejected' or 'kept in suspense'.[10]

Fourthly, 'epistemic changes' form the core of the theories of belief revision. The two kinds of epistemic forces that Gärdenfors distinguishes, to recall, internal and external forces, correspond to two different kinds of belief change: changes necessary to move from a non-equilibrium state to a state of equilibrium and changes necessary to incorporate new input. Since AGM assumes that epistemic states are states in equilibrium, it requires that all changes of belief be accounted for by some external forces. That is, in the AGM model, belief revision always occurs in response to epistemic inputs. Thus, AGM is mainly a theory about how to rationally change our beliefs in the light of new information. Much of the structure of this theory results from distinguishing between three kinds of belief change: 'expansion', 'contraction' and 'revision'. The first kind of change, ie expansion, consists in adding the sentence *A*, which encodes the new piece of information to the belief set, *K*. This is the simplest way of modelling the changes induced by the results of observations or of accepting a testimony, when they do not contradict the beliefs previously held. The expansion of *K* by *A* is denoted $K^{+}A$, which corresponds to the logical closure of the set KUA.

A 'contraction' occurs when one gives up a belief. This kind of change can be made in order to open up for an investigation some proposition that contradicts what the agent previously believed. In a debate a belief that *A* (–*A*) may also be hypothetically retracted to give the belief that –*A* (or *A*)

[9] Gärdenfors (1988: 7).

[10] On Spohn's model, see Gärdenfors (1988: 30–32).

a hearing without begging the question. The task of the disputants is to find arguments that support either *A* or –*A* from the rest of their beliefs. Gärdenfors argues that a similar argumentative strategy is followed when someone gives an explanation, and thus, that contractions play an essential role in explanatory reasoning. The contraction of a belief set *K* with respect to the sentence *A* is denoted by $K^{-}A$.

The last kind of change, ie 'revision', is when a sentence *A* contradicts the beliefs that are already in *K*. In this case, it becomes necessary to give up some old beliefs in order to accept *A* while maintaining consistency. Revisions are also made when someone, for the sake of the argument, hypothetically accepts a proposition, although she presently believes in its negation. The new belief set that results from revising *K* by adding *A* and making whatever other changes that requires is denoted $K^{*}A$.

Last, models of belief revision are governed by a number of 'criteria of rationality' for belief changes, which are meant to guarantee that the resulting belief state is coherent. Two important rationality criteria governing the AGM theory are 'consistency' and 'logical omniscience'. The former criterion requires that the set of accepted sentences must be consistent. The latter requires that the logical consequences of what is accepted should also be accepted. Sets of sentences that satisfy these criteria are called 'belief sets', and they represent rational epistemic states. Thus, in the AGM model, coherence amounts to consistency and closure under logical entailment. In addition to coherence, another criterion is pivotal for specifying what constitutes a rational belief change: the criterion of 'informational economy' or 'conservativity principle'.[11] The key idea is that 'when we change our beliefs, we want to retain as much as possible of our old beliefs—information is in general not gratuitous, and unnecessary losses of information are therefore to be avoided'.[12] This criterion, thus, demands that the change should be the minimal one required to accommodate the input while preserving the coherence of the belief set.[13]

Theories of belief revision aim at characterizing rational changes of belief. To do this, belief sets models, such as AGM, follow two complementary strategies. The first strategy consists in formulating various 'rationality postulates'

[11] But *cf* H Rott (2000) (challenging the importance of this principle for AGM). It is important to note that the criterion of informational economy and the conservativity principle coincide only when one deals with logically closed sets. See Maranhão (2009).

[12] Gärdenfors (1988: 49).

[13] The principle of conservatism is traditionally opposed to the principle of coherence. A different view on the relation between coherence and conservatism is suggested by Rott. He distinguishes between synchronic (or inferential) coherence and diachronic coherence. While the idea of synchronic coherence applies to belief states, the idea of diachronic coherence applies to sequences of belief states by requiring that prior and posterior belief states somehow 'hang together'. Diachronic coherence comes down to the principle of minimal change. Hence, in Rott's view, conservatism may be interpreted as a strategy aiming at a certain kind of coherence. See H Rott ((1999: 401–04) and (2001: 67–75)).

that should be satisfied by the appropriate belief changes. Secondly, the goal is to present an 'epistemic commitment function', which is a rule for determining how an epistemic state would rationally change as a result of various inputs, in a way that satisfies the rationality postulates. Let us first examine the rationality postulates that are proposed in the AGM framework.

## B. Rationality Postulates for Belief Changes

The postulates advocated within the AGM theory are motivated to a large extent, as will be shown, by the economic side of rationality, to wit, the criterion of informational economy. For expansions, the following postulates are proposed:

($K^+1$) $K^+A$ is a belief set
($K^+2$) $A \in K^+A$
($K^+3$) $K \subseteq K^+A$
($K^+4$) If $A \in K$, then $K^+A = K$
($K^+5$) If $K \subseteq H$, then $K^+A \subseteq H^+A$
($K^+6$) For all beliefs sets K and all sentences A, $K^+A$ is the smallest belief set that satisfies ($K^+1$) – ($K^+5$)

The first postulate expresses the idea that expansion is a function from belief sets and sentences to belief sets. The second requires that the input be accepted in the expanded set of beliefs. The third postulate is motivated by the principle of conservatism: all old beliefs should be retained in the expansion of K by A. Of course, if A is already accepted in K, then the expansion of K by A should have no effect, as the fourth postulate states. If K is a subset of H, then it is natural that the expansion of K by A should not have any beliefs that are also not included in the expansion of H by A. This is the motivation for the fifth postulate. Last, ($K^+1$) – ($K^+5$) do not exclude the possibility that the expanded set contain a lot of beliefs not included in K, which have no connection with A. Because we want to avoid endorsing beliefs that are not justified, we should require that the expanded set does not have any beliefs that are not required by the other postulates. Technically, this idea is formulated in the last postulate.

According to the AGM theory, an expansion is rational if the resulting set meets the conditions required by these postulates. But, which is this set? Alchourrón, Gärdenfors and Makinson show that the set of all logical consequences of the old beliefs together with the new belief A is the smallest set that satisfies ($K^+1$ – $K^+5$). They prove the following theorem:

*Representation Theorem for Expansion.* The expansion function + satisfies ($K^+1$ – $K^+6$) iff $K^+A = Cn(K \cup \{A\})$,

where Cn (K) denotes the set of all logical consequences of a set K.

Hence, the rationality postulates uniquely determine the expansion of a set K by A as the set of all logical consequences of K together with A. Only if an expansion process has such a set as a result, can it be said to be a rational change of belief. It is not possible to give a similar explicit definition of contractions and revisions. The reason why this is so is that, from a logical point of view, there are several ways of specifying the revision or contraction of a belief set. To illustrate this, Gärdenfors gives the following example:

> I may now believe that all philosophers are scatterbrained, that Wittgenstein was a philosopher, and consequently that Wittgenstein was scatterbrained. If I then, somehow, receive compelling evidence that Wittgenstein was *not* scatterbrained, I will be forced to revise my earlier beliefs, on pain of inconsistency. The revision can be made by giving up either my belief that all philosophers are scatterbrained or my belief that Wittgenstein is a philosopher. So long as *logic* is considered, both of these ways will do.[14]

Thus, an important problem concerning revisions and contractions is how one selects the beliefs that are to be retained and those that should be given up. The rationality postulates proposed within the AGM theory do not give a unique solution to this problem; instead they are claimed to circumscribe the set of rational solutions. The rationality postulates for revisions are the following:

($K^*1$) For any sentence A and a belief set K, $K^*A$ is a belief set
($K^*2$) $A \in K^*A$
($K^*3$) $K^*A \subseteq K^+A$
($K^*4$) If $-A \notin K$, then $K^+A \subseteq K^*A$
($K^*5$) $K^*A = K\bot$ if and only if $\vdash -A$
($K^*6$) If $\vdash A \leftrightarrow B$, then $K^*A = K^*B$
($K^*7$) $K^*\ A \,\&\, B \subseteq (K^*A)^+B$
($K^*8$) If $-B \notin K^*A$, then $(K^*A)^+B \subseteq K^*A \,\&\, B$

The first postulate requires that the output of the revision process be a belief state. The second postulate, in line with ($K^+2$), is the postulate of 'success', and it guarantees that the epistemic input A is accepted in the revised state. The third and fourth postulates entail that expansion is a special case of revision. According to ($K^*5$), the revision of K by A yields the absurd state of belief $K\bot$ (the set of all sentences) if $-A$ is logically necessary. In this case, logical closure forces an inconsistency, and, since inconsistent belief sets entail everything, the resulting revised set is the absurd state of belief $K\bot$. In the rest of the cases, the revision of K by A is a consistent state. The sixth postulate states that logically equivalent sentences should lead

[14] Gärdenfors (1988: 53).

to identical changes. The last two postulates generalize ($K^*3$) and ($K^*4$) to iterated changes of belief. The idea is that the minimal change of K that is necessary to include both A and B ought to be the same as the expansion of $K^*A$ by B, so long as B does not contradict the beliefs in $K^*A$.

In relation to contraction, the following postulates are proposed:

($K^-1$) For any sentence A and any belief set K, $K^-A$ is a belief set
($K^-2$) $K^-A \subseteq K$
($K^-3$) If $A \notin K$, then $K^-A = K$
($K^-4$) If not $\vdash A$, then $A \notin K^-A$
($K^-5$) If $A \in K$, then $K \subseteq (K^-A)^+A$
($K^-6$) If $\vdash A \leftrightarrow B$, then $K^-A = K^-B$
($K^-7$) $K^-A \cap K^-B \subseteq K^-A \,\&\, B$
($K^-8$) If $A \notin K^-A \,\&\, B$ then $K^-A \,\&\, B \subseteq K^-A$

The first postulate is of a familiar kind: the contracted set should be a belief set. The second one requires that no new belief occur in $K^-A$. According to ($K^-3$), if A is not in K, then the contraction of K by A should have no effect. The fourth postulate states that the contraction be successful, that is, that the sentence to be contracted must not be a logical consequence of the beliefs retained in $K^-A$ (unless A is logically valid). ($K^-5$) postulates that all beliefs in K are recovered after first contracting and then expanding by the same belief.[15] The sixth postulate ensures that the contraction of a set by logically equivalent sentences yields the same result. ($K^-7$) requires that the beliefs that are both in the contracted set $K^-A$ and $K^-B$, are also in the contraction of K by A and B. The last postulate is motivated by the idea that the minimal change of K necessary to give up A and B is closely related to the minimal change necessary to give up A, if it is the case that in the contraction of K by A and B, A is rejected because it is epistemologically less entrenched (this idea will be expanded later). With these postulates in mind, let us now examine how AGM constructs the functions for revising belief sets.

## C. The Construction of a Contraction Function

The main goal of AGM is to provide an epistemic commitment function, to recall, a rule for determining how an epistemic state would rationally change in the light of new information. For this purpose, the AGM strategy is to formulate several postulates that must be satisfied for a belief change

[15] This postulate is the most controversial of the AGM contraction postulates. See Hansson (1999a: 72–74) and Tennant (2012: 296–98). An important attempt to construct an operation of contraction on belief sets that does not satisfy recovery may be found in Rott and Pagnucco (2000).

to be rational. In the case of expansion, the axioms lead to an explicit definition of the belief change process. In contrast, it is not possible to give definitions in the same way for revisions and contractions. The postulates for revision and contraction are claimed to cover all logical properties that characterize these processes of belief change. However, as was argued, there is logically a multitude of ways to revise and contract a belief set. Thus, these postulates do not suffice to determine a revision or contraction function; other epistemic factors play a role as well.

Now, the problem is how to determine the epistemic commitment function for a belief set, that is, how the exact content of the set that results from all three processes of belief change can be specified. This task is greatly simplified by the fact that such a function is completely determined by a contraction function. The reason why this is so is that revisions (which include expansions as a special case) can be defined in terms of contractions. The 'Levi Identity', proposed by Levi and endorsed by AGM, gives us such a definition. According to this identity, belief revision can be regarded as a sequence of contractions and expansions. That is, in order to construct the revision $K^*A$, one first eliminates –A as well as all other beliefs that entail –A, and then expands the contracted set by A. Formally, Levi's thesis can be expressed by the following definition:

*Definition of Revision.* $K^*A = (K^- \text{-}A)\ {}^+A$[16]

Thus, a contraction function suffices to fully characterize the process of belief change. The general idea in AGM is to start from $K^-A$ and then give some recipe for choosing which propositions to delete from K so that $K^-A$ does not contain A as a logical consequence. Because of the criterion of informational economy, it seems natural to require that $K^-A$ be as large a subset of K as possible. For this reason, according to AGM, we should focus on the subsets of K that do not contain A and then search among these for the 'largest', that is, those that contain as much information as possible (without deriving A). Such subsets are defined as follows: A belief set K' is a maximal subset of K that fails to imply A if and only if: (i) K' is a subset of K; (ii) $A \not\in K$; and (iii) for any proposition B that is in K, but not in K', $B \rightarrow A$ is in K', that is, if K' were expanded by B, it would entail A. That is, K' is a maximal subset of K that does not contain A and such that no member of K that is not in K' can be added without entailing A. In general, there are several such subsets. The set of all beliefs sets K' that are

[16] Levi advances the thesis that revisions can be analysed as the composition of a contraction and an expansion in Levi (1977). It is worth noticing that contractions can be also defined in terms of revisions, assuming expansions as given. The idea here, first presented by Harper, is that a sentence B is accepted in a contracted set $K^-A$, if and only if B is accepted both in K and $K^*$-A. Thus, in the terminology of AGM, 'contraction' may be defined as follows: $K^-A = K \cap K^*\text{-}A$ (see Harper (1976)). For the interpretation of these identities in the terminology of AGM, see Gärdenfors (1988: 69–71).

maximal subsets of K that fail to imply A is denoted K ⊥ A. Now, the AGM's strategy for defining a contraction function is to determine the contraction of a belief set K with respect to A by means of a selection function Σ that picks out some elements of the set of all belief sets K' that are maximal subsets of K that fail to imply A. Such function is called a 'partial meet contraction function', and it can be defined as follows:

*Partial Meet Contraction.* $K^{-}A = \cap\, \Sigma\, (K \perp A)$

The contraction function is defined as the intersection of all the subsets selected by Σ among the members of K ⊥ A. The selection function Σ picks out the 'most important' members of K ⊥ A. Since several members of K ⊥ A may be picked out by Σ as the best way of contracting K by A, the contracted set is the intersection of those selected members of K ⊥ A. Alchourrón, Gärdenfors and Makinson further prove that the set that results from applying the partial meet contraction function satisfies the rationality postulates.

Now, the question arises of how these 'most important' members should be selected when contracting a belief set.[17] Such selection, as we have seen, is not determined on logical grounds, but other epistemic factors also play a role. Thus, the problem is that of specifying which epistemic factors determine which members of K ⊥ A ought to be preferred. Gärdenfors has proposed that the contracted set should be the intersection of those members of K ⊥ A that are 'epistemologically most entrenched'. He has shown that for any contraction function satisfying the rationality postulates, there is some ordering in terms of epistemic entrenchment of the maximal subsets in K ⊥ A. This ordering, denoted by ≤, can be used to define a selection function:

(*Selection Function*) $\Sigma\, (K \perp A) = \{K' \in K \perp A: K' \leq K'' \text{ for all } K'' \in K \perp A\}$

Thus, the selection function picks out, among the maximal subsets of K that fail to imply A, those that are epistemologically most entrenched. Gärdenfors explains the notion of epistemic entrenchment as follows:

> The fundamental criterion for determining the epistemic entrenchment of a sentence is *how useful it is in inquiry and deliberation*. Certain pieces of our knowledge and beliefs about the world are more important than others when planning future actions, conducting scientific investigations, or reasoning in general. To give an example of the scientific case, in modern chemical theory, knowledge about the combining weights is much more important for chemical experiments than knowledge about the color or taste of the substances. This difference in entrenchment is reflected in that, if chemists for some reason changed their opinion concerning the

[17] It is critical to note that this issue was not one AGM aimed to address; it became a question only in subsequent research. See Levi (1991) and Gärdenfors (1988), whose approach is discussed below.

> combining weights of two substances, this would have much more radical effects on chemical theory than if they changed their opinion concerning the tastes of the two substances.
>
> This example also shows that, in general, the epistemic entrenchment of different sentences is *not* connected with probabilities ... Rather than being connected with probabilities, the epistemic entrenchment of a sentence is tied to its *explanatory value* and its *overall informational value.*[18]

Thus, the notion of epistemic entrenchment in terms of usefulness in inquiry and deliberation can be seen as closely related to some modern theories of scientific change. Kuhn's 'symbolic generalizations', which form part of a paradigm, or Lakatos' distinction between the 'core' of a research program and the 'protective belt', present a rudimentary hierarchy among the sentences of a scientific theory according to their relative epistemic importance. This hierarchy can be interpreted as a rough ranking of sentences into degrees of epistemic entrenchment, so that the sentences with a higher degree are included in the core part of the theory. Like the ordering of epistemic entrenchment, which determines the result of contraction, this hierarchy is also claimed to play a crucial role in the revision of scientific theories. In fact, changes of an ordering of epistemic entrenchment are closely related with processes of theory change in science. As Gärdenfors points out:

> a change of paradigm typically involves a radical change of the ordering of epistemic entrenchment and, vice versa, a substantial change of the degrees of epistemic entrenchment of the theses in a scientific field is a strong indication of what Kuhn calls a 'scientific revolution.'[19]

We can illustrate this, again, with the aid of the chemistry example. According to the phlogiston theory, qualitative facts (eg facts about colour and taste of substances) were regarded as more 'important' than quantitative facts (eg facts about combining weights). After the Lavoisier revolution took place, the quantitative properties of substances were thought of as more fundamental than the qualitative properties; that is, they had a higher degree of epistemic entrenchment. A change in the hierarchy, or ordering of epistemic entrenchment, characterizes a major scientific change.[20]

[18] Gärdenfors (1988: 87). Emphasis added. Relations of epistemic entrenchment have become one of the most important tools in the modelling of belief revision. On this notion, and its role in determining what to retract and what to retain in the process of revision, see Gärdenfors and Makinson (1988); Cantwell (2001); Nayak, Nelson and Polansky (1996); Bochman (2002); and H Rott ((1992b) and (2001) ch 8).

[19] Gärdenfors (1988: 89).

[20] Despite the natural interpretation of these theories of scientific change in terms of epistemic entrenchment, Gärdenfors considers that, in many cases, these metascientific considerations are of little help when determining the finer structure of the ordering of epistemic entrenchment. Instead, in these cases one must rely on pragmatic factors in order to specify which one of two sentences is the most entrenched; see Gärdenfors (1988: 93).

This qualitative approach to the notion of epistemic entrenchment contrasts with the more quantitative approach to the relative informational value of the sentences based on probabilities. In this view, the epistemic entrenchment of a sentence could be identified with the quantity of information that is lost when it is retracted, where such information is measured with the aid of Bayesian statistics.[21] On the contrary, Gärdenfors does not assume that one can quantitatively measure degrees of epistemic entrenchment. Instead, he formulates some postulates for the qualitative properties of epistemic entrenchment. The postulates are the following:

(EE1) For any A, B, and C, if A $\leqslant$ B, and B $\leqslant$ C, then A $\leqslant$ C (Transitivity)
(EE2) For any A and B, if A $\vdash$ B, then A $\leqslant$ B (Dominance)
(EE3) For all A and B in K, A $\leqslant$ A & B or B $\leqslant$ A & B (Conjunctiveness)
(EE4) When $K \neq K_{\perp}$, A $\notin$ K iff A $\leqslant$ B for all B (Minimality)
(EE5) If B $\leqslant$ A for all B, then $\vdash$ A

The first postulate requires that $\leqslant$ satisfy transitivity, a minimal requirement of an ordering relation, so that if A is at most as entrenched as B and B is at most as entrenched as C, then A is at most as entrenched as C. 'Dominance' states that if a sentence A entails B, and either A or B must be retracted from K, then it will be a smaller change to give up A and retain B rather than to give up B, because then A must be retracted as well if we want the revised set to be closed under logical consequences. According to the third postulate, if we want to retract A & B from K, this can only be achieved by giving up either A or B and, consequently, the informational loss incurred by giving up A & B will be the same as the loss incurred by giving up A or that incurred by giving up B. The 'minimality' postulate says that if a sentence is not in K, then it is minimal in the ordering. Conversely, the last postulate establishes that the most entrenched sentences are those that are logically valid, because they will never be given up.

It is thus the epistemic entrenchment that determines the sentence's fate when a state is contracted or revised. Moreover, Gärdenfors argues that the ordering of epistemic entrenchment can be used to give a formal definition of a contraction function. The central idea is that when contracting K with respect to A, the sentences that should be retained in the contracted state are those which have a higher degree of epistemic entrenchment than A. The definition is the following:[22]

(C-) B $\in$ $K^{-}A$ if and only if B $\in$ K and
(i) A is logically valid (in which case $K^{-}A$ = K) or
(ii) A $\leqslant$ A v B

[21] For a survey of this approach see PM Williams (1980). A fundamental assumption of this approach is that belief states should not be represented by belief sets, but by a probability measure defined over the relevant sentences. For an introduction to this representation, see Gärdenfors (1988) ch 5.

[22] Gärdenfors (1990: 37).

Gärdenfors and Makinson have shown that if the ordering of epistemic entrenchment satisfies the postulates (EE1-EE5), the contraction function defined above satisfies all the rationality postulates for contraction.[23] Therefore, there seem to be two basically equivalent proposals for constructing an epistemic commitment function for a belief state: one based on maximal subsets of K and another based on an ordering of epistemic entrenchment.[24] These proposals are claimed to answer the question of how we should rationally change our beliefs in the light of new information.

## II. AGM AS A COHERENCE THEORY OF BELIEF REVISION

The AGM theory has been interpreted as being in accordance with the coherence theory of belief revision.[25] Three main features may seem to favour this interpretation: its focus on logical structure rather than on inferential pedigree; the fact that its rationality postulates are basically motivated by the objective of making minimal changes while maintaining the coherence of the belief state; and the lack of a formal distinction between a set of basic beliefs and non-basic beliefs. However, there are reasons to doubt that one may adequately formalize the basic tenets of coherence theories of belief revision by means of AGM. To start with, this theory relies on a notion of coherence that does not correspond with the intuitive notion that characterizes the coherentist tradition. The AGM, and all the literature in belief revision that it has given rise to, holds that a set of beliefs is coherent if it is consistent and logically closed. This conception of coherence is quite problematic. To start with, it disregards the network dimension of the notion of coherence, presumably because the positive criteria of coherence are 'less precise'.[26] But, it is well known that consistency is not a sufficient condition of coherence; perhaps, as has been suggested, it is not even a necessary condition.[27] To reduce coherence to consistency is to trivialize the notion of coherence. The requirement that a coherent set be closed under logical consequence can be interpreted as an attempt to formalize the positive connections that must hold between the members of

[23] Gärdenfors and Makinson (1988). *Cf* Hansson (1999a: 101–03).

[24] An alternative proposal consists in using 'safe contraction' or 'Kernel contraction', which is a generalization of safe contraction. Instead of choosing among maximal sets that do not imply the sentence to be contracted (as in partial meet contraction), these operators are based on a selection among the elements of minimal subsets that imply the sentence to be contracted. On safe contraction, see Alchourrón and Makinson (1985). On Kernel contraction, see Hansson (1994b).

[25] It is important to note that coherentist interpretations of AGM were subsequent to the development of this theory. Originally, AGM was not proposed with a view to providing a formalization of the coherence theory of justification.

[26] Gärdenfors (1990: 28).

[27] See ch 3.

a consistent set of beliefs for it to be coherent.[28] However, as Olsson and Hansson have forcefully argued, it is far from clear that logical closure is a reasonable condition of coherence.

Olsson and Hansson have claimed that the basic criteria of coherence are incompatible with a representation of states of beliefs as logically closed sets, which the AGM theory postulates.[29] They give two arguments for this claim. First, they propose four formal principles that are claimed to capture the essential features of the coherentist epistemology as it is traditionally conceived. These principles are as follows:

(*Residual support*) If, for all $\alpha \in K$, $K \setminus \{\alpha\}$ supports $\alpha$, then K satisfies mutual support.[30]
(*Supraclassicality*) If $K \vdash \alpha$, then K supports $\alpha$.
(*Classical coherence*) If K is consistent and satisfies mutual support, then K is coherent.
(*Non-Triviality*) There is some K such that K is consistent but incoherent.

The first postulate formalizes the traditional condition of coherence according to which in a coherent belief system it must be possible to justify each belief in terms of the rest of the beliefs of the system, that is, they must mutually support each other. If the support relation is understood as an inference relation, then 'supraclassicality holds'. This condition says that a set supports a sentence if it can be logically derived from that set. The third condition postulates that consistency and mutual support are sufficient conditions for coherence.[31] Last, 'non-triviality' is required to guarantee that coherence is not reduced to mere consistency. Hansson and Olsson show that the addition to these conditions of the AGM's assumption that belief states are deductively closed yields a contradiction.[32]

It might be argued that the foregoing postulates deviate from the traditional coherentist thesis in that they characterize the notion of coherence as an all-or-nothing matter. Hansson and Olsson give a second argument to support the untenability of the coherentist interpretation of AGM. They show that this theory is not compatible either with the comparative notion of coherence that has been traditionally employed. One such gradational analysis is BonJour's. As explained in chapter three, according to BonJour, a set A is more coherent than B if (i) it contains more contradictions, or contradictions of a greater severity; (ii) it has a higher degree of probabilistic coherence; (iii) its elements are connected by a larger number of inferential

[28] According to Doyle, 'A deductively closed set represents the extreme case in which each belief follows from all others' (1992: 30). That AGM defines the positive aspect of coherence in terms of deductive closure has also been argued by Olsson (1998).

[29] Hansson and Olsson (1999). See also Hansson (2006).

[30] The sign '\' stands for set-subtraction. Eg if $K = \{\alpha, \beta, \chi\}$, then, $K \setminus \{\alpha\} = \{\beta, \chi\}$.

[31] Hansson and Olsson leave open whether these conditions are necessary or not.

[32] For the proof of incompatibility, see Hansson and Olsson (1999: 247–48).

connections, or if the connections are of greater strengths; (iv) it contains fewer subsystems that are unconnected by inferential connections; and (v) it contains fewer unexplained anomalies.

Hansson and Olsson show that two of BonJour's criteria, to wit, the criteria according to which the degree of coherence of a set depends on its degree of probabilistic consistency (ii) and the number of unexplained anomalies (v) cannot be captured by AGM. This theory, it is argued, lacks the formal resources that are necessary to represent both the notion of probability and the notion of explanation. In addition, this theory blurs the distinctions relevant for evaluating the relative coherence of a state of belief by the other three criteria. In relation to the consistency dimension (i), there is only one set that is both inconsistent and logically closed, namely, the set of all sentences. Thus, in AGM, only a binary distinction can be made in relation to this criterion. Then, as regards criterion (iii), in the AGM theory, there can be no distinction between degrees of inferential connectedness, since all logically closed sets satisfy this criterion to a maximum degree. Last, in connection with (iv), the mass of spurious deductive relations introduced through logical closure connects all subsystems of a belief system in a way that cannot be distinguished from the significant inferential relations in terms of which the coherence of a system must be determined.

Thus, on the basis of the two preceding arguments, Hansson and Olsson conclude that the requirement that belief bases be deductively closed should be given up. Ultimately, the main problem with combining AGM with coherentism is that AGM does not pay sufficient attention to the distinction between derived and non-derived beliefs. Only the coherence of non-derived beliefs, they argue, is relevant to epistemic justification. Since AGM does not make a distinction between real beliefs and its logical consequences, it fails to model a concept of coherence adequate to work as a standard of justification. They illustrate the point as follows:

> Suppose that you believe that Paris is the capital of France ($\alpha$). Exercising your skills in elementary logic, you also come to believe (1) either Paris or Quito is the capital of France ($\beta$), and (2) that if Quito is the capital of France, then so is Paris ($\beta \rightarrow \alpha$). Clearly, $\alpha \vee \beta$ and $\beta \rightarrow \alpha$ together imply $\alpha$. However it makes no sense to say that $\alpha \vee \beta$ and $\beta \rightarrow \alpha$ contribute to your belief in $\alpha$, or indeed that they contribute to any other belief whatsoever. Each of the two sentences $\alpha \vee \beta$ and $\beta \rightarrow \alpha$ is believed only because $\alpha$ is believed ... The sort of support that $\alpha$ receives from $\alpha \vee \beta$ and $\beta \rightarrow \alpha$, in the situation described in the previous paragraph, has nothing to do with the sort of support that makes a belief state coherent and capable of justifying beliefs.[33]

Hence, AGM, by embracing a representation of epistemic states as logically closed sets of sentences, blurs the distinction between cases in which

[33] Hansson and Olsson (1999: 259).

inferential connections contribute to the kind of coherence that is relevant to epistemic justification and those in which they do not.

Besides the inadequacy of the notion of coherence that figures in the AGM theory, this theory falls short of adequately formalizing the coherentist mechanisms of justification in another respect. The AGM model formalizes changes where the input is accepted. This is guaranteed by the 'success postulate', according to which the sentence that encodes the input must be a member of the revised belief set. However, it is a common feature of coherentist theories of knowledge and justification that input is not always accepted; instead it is evaluated in the light of the background system of beliefs.[34] Closely related to this point, the coherentist interpretation of AGM suffers from a third problem. The field of application of this theory is restricted to changes of belief that are mediated by external input. Thus, internal changes of belief fall beyond the scope of application of this theory. However, coherentist standards of justification play a role in both external and internal changes. In fact, as will be argued later, no distinct line can be drawn between changes of beliefs that are necessary to push a state toward an equilibrium, and those that, by incorporating input, take a state from one equilibrium to another. Because of this, despite the extraordinary progress that AGM has made towards formally representing rational belief changes, it cannot be used to give a coherentist account of these changes.

In light of the foregoing remarks, it can be concluded that an appropriate coherentist model of belief revision must satisfy the following conditions: (i) it should not formally represent the network aspect of coherence by requiring that belief states be logically closed; (ii) it should also model epistemic movements where new information is evaluated but not necessarily accepted; and (iii) it must give an account of both external and internal changes of belief. Fortunately, some formal models that have the resources to implement these conditions are available.

First, some theories of belief revision do not represent belief states as belief sets, ie as logically closed sets of sentences, but by means of 'belief bases'. A belief base is a set of sentences that is not closed under logical consequence so that its elements represent non-derived beliefs.[35] Changes are performed on the belief base, and derived beliefs are changed only as a result of changes of the base. These non-derived beliefs may include not

[34] In fact, one of the most forceful objections to coherence theories is that, because they are not input-assimilating, they can cut off justification from the world. That is, since input is always evaluated in terms of its coherence with the old system of beliefs, coherentist standards of justification may end up 'isolating' the system of beliefs from external input. To recall, this is the so-called 'isolation objection'. On this objection, see ch 3.

[35] The principle of 'clutter avoidance' mentioned above provides an important motivation to work with belief bases rather than with belief sets. It implies that one should not believe explicitly in the logical consequences of one's beliefs and thereby introduces a distinction between explicit (basic) and implicit (derived) beliefs. See Maranhão (2009: 467) and Hansson (1999a) ch 1.

only observational beliefs, but also beliefs of an explanatory or general nature—as long as these beliefs are held independently of the others. Thus, these beliefs should not be identified with the 'basic beliefs' that foundationalists postulate.[36] Secondly, the so-called non-prioritized models of belief revision reflect the fact that new information is not always accepted, but rather weighted against old information.[37] In these models, no special priority is assigned to new information owing to its novelty.[38] And lastly, unlike AGM, these models have introduced operations that formalize not only external changes of belief but also internal changes.

Hansson's theory of 'semi-revision' is a non-prioritized model of belief revision that uses belief bases for representing epistemic states.[39] Moreover, Hansson's theory not only allows for operations of change induced by epistemic input, but it also introduces an operation of 'consolidation' that models internal changes of belief. Thus, this theory seems to be more in line with the coherentist ideas than the AGM framework. To this theory, I turn now.

## III. HANSSON'S THEORY OF SEMI-REVISION

Operations in Hansson's theory are largely modelled after operations in the AGM model. The same three types of changes are distinguished: expansion, contraction and revision. Partial meet contraction is defined in the same way, but partial meet semi-revision is adjusted so that the outcome is not logically closed. Hansson constructs the operator of partial meet semi-revision on the basis of the following two suboperations:

[36] See Hansson (1994a) and (1999a). That belief bases should not be taken to be a component of a foundationalist theory is argued by Hansson and Olsson (1999: 264). In contrast, some belief revision theorists have considered belief base models as providing a foundationalist picture of belief revision. The argument is that in these models, as opposed to belief sets models, not all beliefs are equally fundamental, but those that are in the base provide the foundation for the derived beliefs. See Fuhrmann (1991: 210); H. Rott (1992a: 23); and Bochman (2002: 3). However, as we have seen, a coherentist approach to justification must differentiate between the coherence of non-derived beliefs and that of derived beliefs, since only the former is epistemically relevant. A natural way to draw this distinction is by adopting a belief base model of belief revision. In addition, belief sets, as Olsson and Hansson have extensively argued, are incompatible with basic coherentist postulates.

[37] Non-prioritized belief revision is also called 'autonomous belief revision', since it allows for an autonomous agent who decides herself whether or not to accept an input; see Galliers (1992).

[38] For a very brief introduction to non-prioritized belief revision models, see Hansson (1997a). Hansson summarizes and systematizes work in this area of belief revision in (1999b).

[39] It is important to notice that the motivation to use belief bases—and thereby drop the requirement of logical closure—and the motivation to use non-prioritized models—and thereby refuse to assign a special priority to new information—are independent from each other. Hansson's theory is a non-prioritized belief base model, but there are also non-prioritized models of belief revision that employ forms of representing belief states other than belief bases, such as belief sets models or propositional models. For an overview, see Hansson (1997a).

1. Expand by $\alpha$
2. Consolidate the belief base

In the first step the input sentence is added to the belief base. In the second step, the belief base is 'consolidated', which is the operation by which a belief base is made consistent. Consolidation takes us from a belief base, to a consistent subset of itself.[40] This function is also of a partial meet kind. Hansson defines consolidation as follows:

> An operation > is an operation of partial meet consolidation if and only if $K> = \cap\gamma\,(K\perp^{\perp})$,

where $K\perp^{\perp}$ is the set of all maximally-inclusive consistent subsets of K, and $\gamma$ is a function which for each K selects a subset of $K\perp^{\perp}$. Thus, the consolidation of a set is the intersection of some of the maximally-inclusive consistent subsets of K. Hansson has proved that consolidation can be axiomatically characterized as follows:

> An operation > is an operation of partial meet consolidation if and only if, for all K:
>
> (i) K> is consistent
> (ii) $K> \subseteq K$
> (iii) If $\alpha \in K \backslash K>$ then there is some K' with $K> \subseteq K' \subseteq K$ such that K' is consistent and $K' \cup \{\alpha\}$ is inconsistent.

Thus, according to the two first postulates, the result of consolidating K is a consistent subset of K. The third postulate says that whatever is excluded when a belief base is consolidated must have contributed to making the original base inconsistent. Hansson then uses consolidation to define semi-revision:

> An operation ? is an operation of partial meet semi-revision if and only if $K ? \alpha = (K \cup \{\alpha\}) >$, where > is an operation of partial meet consolidation.

That is, the result of semi-revising K is that of consolidating the set that results from adding set-theoretically $\alpha$ to K. Hansson has proved the following representation theorem for partial semi-revision:[41]

> An operation ? is an operation of partial meet semi-revision if and only if, for all K and $\alpha$:
>
> (i) $K?\alpha$ is consistent (consistency)
> (ii) $K?\alpha \subseteq K \cup \{\alpha\}$ (inclusion)
> (iii) If $\beta \in K \backslash K?\alpha$, then there is some K' such that $K?\alpha \subseteq K' \subseteq K \cup \{\alpha\}$, K' is consistent, and $K' \cup \beta$ is inconsistent (relevance)
> (iv) $(K \cup \{\alpha\})?\alpha = K?\alpha$ (pre-expansion)
> (v) If $\alpha, \beta \in K$, then $K?\alpha = K?\beta$ (internal exchange)

[40] Hansson (1994a).
[41] Hansson (1997b).

'Consistency' says that the result after semi-revision is consistent. According to 'inclusion' such result is included in the set-theoretical addition of $\alpha$ to K. The 'relevance' postulate says that only beliefs that are to be blamed for inducing inconsistency can be given up. According to 'pre-expansion' whether $\alpha$ is already believed or not is irrelevant to the result of semi-revising by $\alpha$. The last postulate states that if $\alpha$ ad $\beta$ are both believed, then it does not matter which of them we semi-revise: the result of semi-revision will be the same.

From this brief introduction to Hansson's model of belief revision, it is already apparent what the main problem that it faces as a formalization of a coherence theory of belief revision is: it reduces the coherence of a belief state to its consistency. Hansson noted the possibility of a version of his theory in which the positive dimension of coherence could be incorporated. However, he remarked that such a version is problematic because 'it is difficult to make the notion of coherence operative in a formal setting'.[42] Olsson has taken up the challenge of formalizing a positive notion of coherence. He has developed a generalized version of Hansson's theory in which the consistency requirement is replaced by a requirement of coherence.[43] I turn now to examine Olsson's proposal.

## IV. OLSSON ON COHERENCE AND BELIEF REVISION

I will introduce Olsson's coherentist approach to belief revision in some detail, for it is the most articulated attempt to bring together belief revision formalisms and a coherentist epistemology. The exposition of the theory will be as follows. First, I will show how, according to Olsson, coherence can be formally represented. Then, I shall introduce Olsson's coherentist interpretation of consolidation and semi-revision. Next, I will present Olsson's analysis of the notion of relational coherence. Last, I shall examine how Olsson generalizes his theory so as to include cases in which the input is not a single sentence, but a set, by using a 'merge' operation. This operation, argues Olsson, adequately models the coherentist picture of justification.

### A. Olsson's Notion of Coherence

Instead of equating coherence with consistency, Olsson views coherence as involving consistency as well as some other kind of stability. The con-

[42] ibid.

[43] Olsson (1998) presents a generalized version of Hansson's theory of consolidation. He has also developed a coherentist version of Hansson's semi-revision in Olsson (1997a). The presentation of Olsson's coherentist version of the operations or consolidation and semi-revision is based on these two articles.

sistency part of coherence is captured by using a consequence operation.[44] Olsson introduces a 'stability set' to serve as the formal counterpart of the preferred concept of stability. Olsson does not specify whether 'stability' should be defined in terms of derivability, probability, explanation or other concepts. He is not interested in studying the qualitative nature of coherence, but coherence-making in belief change. For this purpose, he claims, nothing has to be assumed about conditions of coherence, except that there is a stability set *S* of consistent sets of sentences such that any set of sentences is coherent if and only if it is an element of *S*.[45] Let L be a standard propositional language, built up from the usual connectives. More precisely, Olsson defines coherence as follows:

> *Coherence*. Let $S \subseteq$ P (L). A set A $\subseteq$ L is coherent with respect to *S* if and only if (i) A $\in$ *S*, and (ii) A is consistent.

Stability, and thus, coherence, is seen as a matter of all or nothing. Any consistent set that does not belong to *S* is said to be incoherent. With this definition of coherence, Olsson explores the extent to which it is possible to develop a coherentist interpretation of the main operations of Hansson's theory. Let us start with consolidation.

## B. The Coherentist Interpretation of Consolidation

As opposed to Hansson's theory, in Olsson's approach, to 'consolidate' is not to make a belief state coherent, in the narrow sense of making it consistent, but to change it so that it is also stable. Perhaps, from an internal point of view, the most obvious reason to revise is the presence of some inconsistency. However, there are more subtle forms of epistemic conflict than inconsistency, for example, when one belief is very implausible given other beliefs, or when we cannot explain why some beliefs should be held true. In these cases, it would be irrational to settle with having merely consistent beliefs. Thus, Olsson argues, consolidation must be understood as the process of internally changing one's system of beliefs so as to achieve stability, in a way that cannot be reduced to consistency. Olsson's approach to consolidation differs from Hansson's in another respect. Whereas Hansson only considers that a system can be consolidated by subtracting beliefs, Olsson argues that this is only one type of consolidation. Klein and Warfield have argued that coherence can be achieved by subtracting beliefs

[44] On this operation, see Olsson (1998: 145–46).

[45] Nevertheless, Olsson makes some assumptions regarding the concept of coherence. The first is that it is coherent not to hold any non-derived beliefs at all. Next, it is also assumed that, for any consistent set, there is always some coherent superset. Olsson (1998: 144–45).

as well as by adding beliefs.[46] Following Klein and Warfield, Olsson has distinguished between two kinds of consolidation: 'subtractive consolidation' and 'additive consolidation'.

The subtractive strategy amounts to subtracting a belief (and perhaps with it many more) from an incoherent set, thereby rendering it coherent. Let K> be the result of applying subtractive consolidation to a set K. Closely following Hansson, Olsson formulates the following postulates for *subtractive consolidation*:

i. $K> \subseteq K$ (Inclusion)
ii. K> is consistent (Consistency)
iii. K> is coherent (Coherence)
iv. If K> = K, then K> is coherent (Coherence for Identity)
v. If $\alpha \in K \backslash K>$ then there is some K' with $K> \subseteq K' \subseteq K$ such that
   a. K' is coherent, and
   b. K" is incoherent for all K" such that $K' \cup \{\alpha\} \subseteq K'' \subseteq K$ (Strong Coherent Relevance)

The first postulate says that a set that has been consolidated by a subtractive strategy is a subset of the original set. The consistency postulate says that the result of consolidation should be a consistent set. The third postulate requires that the result of consolidation must be not only consistent, but also coherent. The next postulate expresses the idea that if consolidation has no effect on the belief base then such a base was already internally coherent. The intuitive meaning of the last postulate is that any element that is excluded when a belief base is consolidated must have contributed to making the original base incoherent, and there is no way of repairing the incoherence made by such element simply by considering more conservative subsets of K.[47]

After formulating these postulates, the next step is to construct a function for subtractive consolidation. This operation is also modelled after Hansson's theory. The crucial change in the formalism is that the set of maximal consistent subsets of a belief base that Hansson used for constructing the consolidation operation is replaced by $K\bot^{\bot}_{S}$, the set of all maximal coherent subsets of K, ie the set of all maxiconsistent subsets of K that are members of the stability set. Then, Olsson introduces a selection function

[46] See Klein and Warfield (1994). Like Klein and Warfield, Olsson assumes that there is a clear-cut line between these two approaches and considers each of them separately.

[47] These postulates closely resemble Hansson's postulates for consolidation. Both the 'inclusion' postulate and the 'consistency' postulate are the same as the ones that Hansson formulates. The coherence postulate does not figure in Hansson's axiomatic characterization of consolidation. There is no analogous postulate either for 'coherence by identity' in Hansson's proposal. The last postulate substitutes the consistency requirement by the coherence one, and it adds the idea that if the lack of coherence caused by a given element can be easily overcome, then there is no reason to delete such element. This idea has to be added because even if a set is incoherent, some appropriate superset may well be coherent. In contrast, there is no consistent superset of an inconsistent set.

that picks out some elements among the maximal coherent subsets of K. More formally, (subtractive) partial meet consolidation is defined as follows:

> An operation> is an operation of partial meet consolidation if and only if K> = $\cap\gamma K\,(K\bot^{\bot}{}_{S})$.

Olsson shows that Coherence for Identity, Inclusion and Strong Coherent Relevance are satisfied by the foregoing definition of subtractive consolidation. However, the coherence of the consolidated set is not guaranteed. The postulate of Coherence is only satisfied by a particular class of stability sets: the intersective sets. A set *S* is intersective with respect to a property P if this property is preserved by the operation of intersection on it. For example, let $S_{dis}$ = {A ⊂ L| A is disjunctively closed}.[48] The set $S_{dis}$ is intersective: the intersection of a family of disjunctively closed sets is also disjunctively closed. According to Olsson, performing partial meet consolidation relative to an intersective stability set always leads to a coherent result.[49] An interesting class of stability sets that are intersective are those sets that are 'robust' in the sense that if a given set is stable, then so is every subset of that set. All stability sets that make a set of sentences stable just in case those sentences have some property in common (eg belonging to the same topic, having a probability above a certain threshold) are robust.[50] Thus, the coherence of the belief state that results from consolidating belief bases relative to a stability set that is defined in this way is also guaranteed.[51]

[48] A set of sentences A is disjunctively closed (closed under disjunction) if and only if for all sentences α and β: if α € A, and β € A, then α v β € A.

[49] The question arises of whether the fact that only consolidation relative to intersective stability sets leads to coherent results imposes some constraints on the way in which stability should be conceived. Hansson gives an argument in support of the claim that rational belief bases should be closed under disjunction; see Hansson (1996a: 232).

[50] Consolidations that are based on robust stability sets are interesting in that the postulate of 'Strong Coherent Relevance' reduces to the weaker postulate 'Coherent Relevance'. The latter postulate only says that if a sentence is excluded when consolidating, then it must have contributed to incoherence, without requiring that there must be no way of overcoming such incoherence by considering more conservative sets of K.

[51] However, as we will see, stability sets that formalize a positive notion of coherence cannot plausibly be taken to be either intersective or robust. Thus, subtractive and stable partial meet consolidation cannot model coherentist belief revision unless coherence is interpreted as negative coherence. Hence, it is a main drawback of Olsson's theory that one of its pivotal operations—substractive consolidation—cannot guarantee the coherence of the result if coherence is defined by reference to a stability set which corresponds to the positive, connectivity, aspect of coherence.

The addition strategy consists of adding one or more beliefs to a consistent set of beliefs in order to render it coherent.[52] Olsson presents the following postulates for the operation of *additive consolidation* ($<$):

i. $K \subseteq K<$ (Reversed Inclusion)
ii. If K is consistent, then $K<$ is coherent (Conditional Coherence)
iii. If K is consistent, then $K<$ is consistent (C1)
iv. If K is consistent and $K< = K$, then K is stable (C2)
v. If K is inconsistent, then $K< = K$ (C3)
vi. If $\beta \in K< \setminus K$ then there is some K' with $K \subseteq K< \subseteq K'$ such that
    a. K' is coherent, and
    b. K" is incoherent for all K" such that $K \subseteq K'' \subseteq K' \setminus \{\beta\}$ (Strong Reversed Relevance)

The first postulate is the reverse of the familiar inclusion postulate: the original set must be a subset of the set consolidated by addition. The second, third and fourth postulates correspond respectively to the Coherence, Consistency and Coherence for Identity postulates for subtractive consolidation, but on the assumption that the original set is consistent. This assumption is needed because of a structural difference between these two kinds of consolidation. Whereas there is always a consistent subset of a given set, an inconsistent set lacks consistent supersets.[53] If the original set is inconsistent, then it is assumed, as C3 says, that additive consolidation has no effect.[54] Like the analogous Strong Coherent Relevance for subtractive consolidation, the last postulate is also motivated by a principle of conservatism. This postulate requires that no belief be added unless it makes a set coherent which would otherwise be incoherent, and there is no way to get the coherence back by considering supersets that are closer to K.

Olsson aims at constructing an operation of additive consolidation that satisfies the foregoing postulates. He constructs a function of additive partial meet consolidation in exact analogy to the construction of its subtractive version except that instead of looking at maximal coherent subsets, he focuses on the minimal coherent supersets of K, denoted by $K{\Uparrow}{\perp}_S$. The best supersets of K are then selected by an additive selection function $\gamma K$. Formally:

> An operation $<$ is an operation of additive partial meet consolidation if and only if $K< = \cap\gamma K(K{\Uparrow}{\perp}_S)$.

[52] Olsson points out that we can also think of additive consolidation as an operation that adds explanations to beliefs already entertained in order to achieve explanatory coherence. In this case, the selection function will pick out the best explanation. Thus, there is an interesting link between additive consolidation and inference to the best explanation; see Olsson (1998: 157). Olsson (1997c: 48–52) provides a proposal for making beliefs coherent by adding explanatory beliefs. On abductive belief revision, see also Aliseda (2006) and Schurz (2008).

[53] See Olsson (1998: 153).

[54] Olsson points out that there are other alternatives to this postulate. For example, one could require that if K is inconsistent, then subtractive consolidation must be performed. It could also be postulated that, even if the inconsistency cannot be removed, additive consolidation should at least stabilize the belief state.

Olsson shows that an operation of additive partial meet consolidation so defined satisfies Reversed Inclusion. However, the rest of the postulates are satisfied only given certain restrictions on the class of selection functions that are used. It is argued that only 'minichoice consolidators' may satisfy all these postulates. An operation of consolidation can be said to be a 'minichoice consolidator' if the selection function is 'opinionated', that is, if it returns a singleton subset when applied to the set of all minimal coherent supersets of K. Thus, the partial meet approach simplifies in the case of additive consolidation.

## C. The Coherentist Interpretation of Semi-Revision

Using the generalized partial meet consolidation, Olsson proposes a coherence interpretation of semi-revision.[55] To recall, semi-revision is an externally motivated change of belief in which new information is not necessarily accepted. Semi-revision is a two-step operation: the first step consists of adding new information and the second of consolidating the new system. Olsson presents the following postulates for generalized partial meet semi-revision:

i. $K?\alpha$ is coherent (Coherence)
ii. If $K?\alpha = K \cup \{\alpha\}$, then $K?\alpha$ is coherent (Coherence for Identity)
iii. If $K?\alpha \subset K \cup \{\alpha\}$ (Inclusion)
iv. If $\beta \in K \backslash K?\alpha$, then there is some K' such that $K?\alpha \subseteq K' \subseteq K \cup \{\alpha\}$ such that
    a. K' is coherent, and
    b. K" is incoherent for all K" such that $K' \cup \{\beta\} \subseteq K'' \subseteq K \cup \{\alpha\}$ (Strong Coherence Relevance)
v. $(K \cup \{\alpha\})?\alpha = K?\alpha$ (Pre-Expansion)
vi. If $\alpha, \beta \in K$, then $K?\alpha = K?\beta$ (Internal Exchange)

The first postulate requires that the result of semi-revision be, not only consistent, as Hansson required, but also coherent. The second postulate says that if the semi-revision of a set is the set-theoretical union of the original set and the new information, then the semi-revised set must be coherent. The third postulate is the same as Hansson's inclusion postulate. However, Olsson notes that such postulate will be valid only for semi-revision that uses subtractive consolidation, and not for the kind of semi-revision in which additive strategies are employed. Strong Coherence Relevance imposes on semi-revision the same condition as the analogous postulate for consolidation, and it differs in the same respects from the analogous postulate in Hansson's model. The last two postulates are identical to those proposed by Hansson for, as Olsson argues, these two postulates are well in line with coherentism. Pre-expansion says that when we semi-revise by $\alpha$, it

[55] See Olsson (1997a).

is irrelevant whether such a sentence is already believed or not, as it should be if, as coherentism claims, the only factor that matters to justification is whether or not a belief fits together with the rest of the beliefs. Internal exchange says that the effect of considering the effect of a particular belief is the same as the effect on K of considering any other belief. Olsson shows that this postulate, given the relation between consolidation and semi-revision, implies the holistic principle according to which the effect of considering one single belief is the same as the effect of considering all beliefs at once.[56]

Olsson constructs an operation of partial meet semi-revision that parallels Hansson's definition of partial meet semi-revision in terms of partial meet consolidation except that both operations are coherence-oriented, as opposed to consistency-oriented. Let $\div^{\perp}S$ denote the operation of partial meet consolidation arising from using $S$ as the stability set, that is $K\div^{\perp}_{S} = \cap\gamma K(K^{\perp} \div^{\perp}_{S})$. The generalized version of partial meet semi-revision can be defined as follows:

> An operation ? is an operation of partial meet semi-revision if and only if $A?\alpha = (A \cup \{\alpha\})\div^{\perp}_{S}$.

Thus, the coherence version of an operation of partial meet semi-revision amounts to consolidating (in the sense of making it both consistent and stable) the set theoretical union of the original set and the new information. The operation of partial meet semi-revision satisfies all postulates, except for the 'Coherence' postulate. Like the generalized version of subtractive partial meet consolidation, the result after semi-revising is coherent only if the underlying stability set is intersective. Stability sets corresponding to negative coherence can be assumed to be intersective. For instance, if both A and B are probabilistically inconsistent, then so is $A \cap B$.[57] However, stability sets corresponding to the positive dimension of coherence cannot plausibly be assumed to be intersective. As Olsson argues, it is easy to construct a counterexample using a traditional definition of mutual support. Let $S_{Mut}$ be a stability set such that $A \in S_{Mut}$ if and only if, for all $\alpha \in A$, $A\backslash\{\alpha\} \vdash \alpha$. Even if two sets A and B are both stable with respect to this stability set, their intersection need not be stable. Thus, it cannot be guaranteed that performing the operation of partial meet semi-revision, which involves the intersection of stable sets, will yield a coherent set as a result.

56 See Olsson (1997a: 110–11).

57 According to Olsson, BonJour's notion of probabilistic consistency and logical consistency, as well as Lehrer's competition-based concept, are all negative concepts of coherence and, thus, correspond to intersective stability sets (Olsson (1997a: 121)). However, it is at least doubtful that a stability set that serves as the formal counterpart of Lehrer's notion of coherence is intersective. For even if I can meet all objections to a particular claim on the basis of the set A as well as on the basis of the set B, it seems that it need not be so on the basis of the intersection of A and B.

As Olsson recognizes, this result suggests that generalized partial meet semi-revision can plausibly model coherentist belief revision, only if coherence is interpreted as negative coherence.

## D. The Notion of Relational Coherence

Olsson argues that this generalized theory of semi-revision not only helps to model, to a limited extent, as pointed out, the coherentist approach to belief change, but it can also be of use in order to answer two questions that have been raised in the coherentist literature: how the notion of relational coherence may be conceptualized and how it relates to the notion of systemic coherence.[58] Hansson suggested the following weak-success postulate for relational coherence: 'If $\alpha$ coheres with K, then $\alpha \in K?\ \alpha$', that is, a sentence coheres with a set only if it belongs to the set that results from semi-revising this set by the sentence.[59] Taking this postulate as a starting point, Olsson defines 'relational coherence' as follows:

> $\alpha$ ?-coheres with K, if and only if $\alpha \in K?\alpha$.

Olsson argues that 'systemic coherence' can be defined in terms of relational coherence: a system is coherent just in case each of its members coheres in its turn with the remaining members. Thus, the relation between relational and systemic coherence can be formally stated as follows:

> Let ? be an operation of partial meet semi-revision. K is coherent if and only if, for each $\alpha \in K$, $\alpha$ ?-coheres with $K \setminus \{\alpha\}$.[60]

In a later work, Olsson has further studied the notion of relational coherence from the perspective of belief change formalisms.[61] He has taken relational coherence to be a relation between two sets of propositions, rather than a relation between a proposition and a set. He has defined relational coherence as follows:

> A coheres with B is and only if $A \cup B \in COH$,

[58] See chs 3 and 4 for a discussion of these problems. For a discussion of the problem of how systemic and relational coherence relate to each other that employs the resources of belief revision, see Hansson (2006).

[59] Hansson (1997b).

[60] Olsson (1997a: 120).

[61] Olsson (1999).

where COH is the class of all coherent sets of sentences.[62] This notion of relational coherence satisfies the following principles, which are prima facie quite plausible, given our intuitions about coherence:

(Symmetry) If A coheres with B, then B coheres with A.
(Irrelevant addition) If A coheres with B, then A coheres with $A \cup B$.
(Irrelevant subtraction) If A coheres with B, then A coheres with $B \setminus A$.
(Irrelevance) If $A \cup B = C \cup D$, then A coheres with B if and only if C coheres with D.

The relation between relational and systemic coherence is captured by the 'Residual Coherence' principle:

$A \in COH$ if and only if, for each $\alpha \in A$, $\alpha$ coheres with $A \setminus \{\alpha\}$.

How do these notions of relational and systemic coherence enter into the process of justification? According to Olsson, we do not statically compare whether our new information coheres with a system and then decide whether we are justified in accepting it or not. Instead, justification is a dynamic process in which new information is merged with old information in order to arrive at the best system given our total information.[63] He describes the process as follows:

> Let us take a common situation in which we may ask for epistemic justification. Suppose that I see a tree over there, in the sense that my visual system reports a tree to be present at a particular location. Am I justified in believing that there is actually a tree? It seems to me that the processing of the new information about the tree can be seen as proceeding in the following steps. First, the sight report is added to my information system, which contains information about the light conditions, about whether there is evidence of hallucination, among other things. Second, I try to reinterpret my total information state in the light of the new information. This may lead to a number of candidate interpretations, all satisfying the minimum requirement of being coherent. Finally, I select (at least ideally) one of these candidates as the best interpretation, corresponding to my new state of belief, which may or may not contain the belief that there is actually a tree.[64]

Olsson has suggested that we use a 'merge operation' to model this coherentist approach to justification. Let us see how this operation formally models this picture of justification.

[62] Olsson hardly connects these later views about relational coherence with his previous work on the coherentist interpretation of semi-revision and consolidation. Presumably, COH would be the class of sentences that are consistent and stable, in relation to a particular stability set.

[63] See Olsson (1999: 280–83).

[64] Olsson (1999: 284).

## E. Merge Operations

Merge operations, as opposed to semi-revision, do not take the input to be a single sentence.[65] Fuhrman has defined a merge operation ° in which two belief bases are combined into a consistent one.[66] According to Fuhrman, these operations are, like semi-revision, of a partial meet variety. Like semi-revision, these operations which model externally motivated changes of belief can also be defined in terms of internal changes, eg consolidation. Let ! be the consolidator operator:

$$A \circ B = (A \cup B)!$$

Olsson's definition of merge differs from Fuhrman's in two important respects: the result of merge is required to be coherent, and not merely consistent, and it is not a partial meet function. Let $K\nabla$ be the set of largest coherent subsets of K and $\gamma$ a selection function. The elements of $K\nabla$ are the candidate interpretations of the total information—old and new. Among those elements, the selection function will select the best candidate system. Olsson defines the merge of two sets A and B as follows:

$$A \circ B = \gamma\ ((A \cup B)\nabla)$$

That is, merging A and B results in the best system among the maximally inclusive coherent subsystems of $A \cup B$. Olsson shows that this merge operation exhibits formal properties that parallel the foregoing principles of relational coherence. Thus, it seems to be an appropriate way of formalizing the role of systemic and relational coherence in a dynamic theory of justification. The result of merging is a coherent set, indeed a maximally inclusive one.[67] This system is the most justified one, given our information. Then, A will (relationally) cohere with B if the merging of A and B is the union of these sets. The question of whether we are justified in accepting a new piece of information can be read off from the system: if it belongs to the system that results from merging, then we are justified in accepting it.

[65] Semi-revision could be considered as a merge operation of a set with a singleton. There seem to be no reason though why the input should be reduced to single sentences. On the contrary, a conception of coherence as a relation between sets better squares with our intuitions about justification. Hence, merge operations are better suited for modelling coherentist epistemology than the operator of semi-revision.

[66] Fuhrman (1997: 80–85).

[67] The fact that Olsson's function for merge does not use intersection makes the requirement that the result of the merge operation be a coherent set non-problematic. It is not necessary to postulate that stability sets be intersective (a condition that only negative coherence can meet) to guarantee the coherence of the result.

V. BELIEF REVISION AND COHERENTIST EPISTEMOLOGY

The formal coherence-based approaches to belief revision that I have reviewed in the previous sections take up many of the central issues that coherentist epistemologies aim at explaining. Now, I would like to consider the issue of whether these formalisms help answer some of the problems posed by coherence theories of epistemic justification.

### A. The Concept of Coherence

What is the notion of coherence that lies behind these formalisms? Do they contribute to a better understanding of this notion? As we have seen, the more widespread notion of coherence that is used in these formalisms is the AGM conception of coherence as consistency plus logical closure. As has been argued, logical closure cannot adequately capture the positive aspect of coherence. Belief revision formalisms that represent states of belief by means of belief bases, such as Hansson's theory of semi-revision, drop the requirement of logical closure, thereby equating consistency with coherence. It is however well known that such identification does not correspond with our basic intuitions of coherence. The most developed notion of coherence that has been presented in this brief introduction to the belief revision literature is Olsson's conception of coherence as consistency plus stability. The positive dimension of coherence is captured by means of a stability set, which can be defined as derivability, or in terms of more interesting epistemic concepts. Olsson's notion of coherence is a significant step towards the formalization of coherence. It helps meet one of the main objections that have been addressed against coherence theories, namely, that they rely on a notion of coherence that is not susceptible of being precisely defined and formalized. However, Olsson's notion of coherence suffers from a number of problems.

First, it is far from clear that consistency must be required for coherence. Despite appearances, consistency, as argued in chapter three, does not seem to be a necessary condition of coherence. To begin with, it is psychologically implausible to require that one's system of belief be consistent. Moreover, giving up this condition does not only allow us to define a notion of coherence that is more in accord with our cognitive capacities, but it is also desirable from a normative point of view.[68] Sometimes, it may be reasonable and rational to be inconsistent.[69] This being the case, it is not even a normative

[68] *Cf* Olsson (1999: 283).

[69] See Harman (1995: 178 and 183–86) and Nozick (1993: 85 and 89–93). For a proposal of a theory of belief revision that endorses the view that it can be rational to hold contradictions, see Mares (2002) and Wassermann (1999b).

ideal that we should always avoid inconsistencies. Thus, a theory of belief revision that proceeds on the assumption that consistency is a requirement of coherence is not only descriptively inadequate, but also normatively flawed. Next, the other factor of coherence which figures in Olsson's analysis of this concept, 'stability', is left undefined. Thus, the lack of precision is transferred from the notion of coherence to that of stability. In addition, Olsson's theory does not guarantee the coherence of the result unless the stability set is interpreted as negative coherence.[70] This is a main problem for the theory, given that it is the positive aspects of coherence that makes coherence an interesting standard of justification. Last, Olsson formalizes an all-or-nothing notion of coherence. However, the kind of coherence that seems to be crucial to justification is rather a comparative one.[71]

## B. The Dynamic View of Justification

Both formal and informal theories of belief revision see justification from a novel point of view. Whereas the foundationalism-coherentism debate focuses on the structure of justification, belief revision theories put the emphasis on the processes of justification, that is, on the issue of what constitutes a justified change of belief.[72] This dynamic approach to justification is attractive in that it reflects more accurately the problems of justification that we encounter in ordinary life as well as in science than the abstract structures of justification that coherentists and foundationalists dispute over. As far as the coherence theory of justification is concerned, this change of perspective also means a shift on the way in which the notion of coherence and its role in justification is to be studied. The objective now is not to see whether an element belongs to a coherent set (membership model) or coheres with such a set (relational model) in order to determine its justificational status. Instead, the aim is to determine how, given my system of beliefs, and in the light of new information, I can achieve a coherent state of belief, one that can be said to be justified. Thus, the problem is how the

[70] It seems that if 'merge' is used, then the coherence of the result can be guaranteed, no matter how coherence is defined.

[71] However, a non-gradational notion of coherence can also be regarded as pivotal for justification in the sense that one can say that what matters is that the resulting state of beliefs is coherent *enough* for the purposes of justification. A problem arises, though, when there are several sets that meet this minimum of coherence. Olsson suggests that more refined models of coherence, which give an account of degrees of coherence, may be developed based on the work of Rabinowicz ((1989) and (1996)) and Hansson (1996b). See Olsson (1998: 147).

[72] The focus of belief revision formalisms on dynamic aspects of justification is criticized by Cantwell. In his view, belief revision formalisms neglect the concept of static justification, which also plays a role in the dynamics of belief. See Cantwell (1999).

acceptance of new information changes one's original state of belief and whether the resulting state is better justified than the original one.

These dynamic theories of justification have some advantages over those that adopt a static stance towards justification and coherence. First, static approaches to justification fail to consider the crucial issue of how a coherent state of belief is achieved and how its coherence is preserved in the light of new information. Secondly, in these approaches, the system of beliefs is taken as a given against which all incoming information is to be tested. This leads to an extremely conservative view of justification.[73] If one were justified in believing only what coheres with one's original beliefs, then no 'genuine revision' could take place.[74] In fact, it is a valuable insight of dynamic approaches to justification that they have clarified the way in which coherence is linked to conservatism in a way that is not to be blamed. The economic side of rationality justifies that we minimize the loss of information when merging new information in our system of beliefs. However, this sane conservatism does not prevent us from modifying our system of beliefs so as to accommodate new information if this is required for reaching yet a more coherent set of beliefs. Thirdly, and closely related to the previous point, static views of justification make the coherence theory more vulnerable to severe forms of the isolation objection and related objections.

## C. The Mechanics of Coherentist Justification

Probably, the most important contribution of theories of belief revision to a coherentist epistemology is that of working out in detail of a number of coherence-making mechanisms. Belief revision formalisms provide the tools necessary to better specify the process that leads to a state of coherence. In particular, they help us think about how different epistemic alternatives are generated and the best one selected. The classification of two kinds of changes: external and internal, and its corresponding operations: semi-revision (or, better, merge) and consolidation (additive and subtractive), respectively, are extremely useful for characterizing the different mechanisms whereby we render our beliefs coherent and, therefore, justified. The fact that external and internal changes can be interdefined in these formal theories also sheds some light on the way in which internal and external coherence relate to each other. It is also remarkable that these formalisms give an answer to the question of how relational coherence is related to systemic coherence.

[73] See ch 3 for a discussion of the problem of conservatism.

[74] Similarly, Olsson has pointed out that a relational theory of coherence according to which one is justified in accepting a sentence if it coheres with one's system of beliefs excludes the possibility of genuine belief revision in Olsson (1998: 283).

Nevertheless, regarding both the generation of epistemic alternatives and the selection of the best one, these formalisms have severe limitations. As far as the generation stage of the justification process is concerned, it has to be noticed that, since the epistemic alternatives are taken to be the maximal coherent subsets of the set of beliefs under consideration, only the coherence (as an all-or-nothing property) and the size of the sets is taken into account when determining whether a particular subset should belong to the pool of alternatives or not.[75] No comparative notion of coherence is involved.[76] However, one might want to say that a set is more coherent than another, even if it is a smaller set. That is, consilience does not seem to be the only criterion of coherence that is relevant to justification.

With regard to the selection stage, the selection mechanism employed by these formalisms is not very helpful. It is unclear how the selection function picks out the 'best candidates'. The order of epistemic entrenchment that has been proposed by Gärdenfors is extremely interesting in this regard: the most entrenched elements are those that are selected. However, we need a more thorough explanation of how the relative epistemic entrenchment of the sentences in a belief system can be determined independently of what happens to such a system when it is revised. In addition, the selection function is again based on an all-or-nothing notion of coherence. However, according to coherentism, for a system to be justification-conferring it has to be the most coherent one among a number of plausible alternatives. Olsson points out that it should be possible to construe a selection mechanism that is based on a gradational notion of coherence.[77] Given the relevance of a comparative notion of coherence to justification, it is indeed necessary that such a construction be developed if these selection mechanisms are to adequately model our processes of justification.

In short, these formalisms help improve the structure of the coherence theory of justification. They give valuable insights as to how coherence and justification may be conceptualized; how relational and systemic coherence relate to each other; what is the relation between coherence and conservatism; and how the coherentist process of justification may be modelled. All these improvements contribute to the project of making the coherence theory

[75] But see Levi (1991) and Rott (1992b).

[76] This raises the question of the psychological plausibility of these formalisms. It is a well-known fact that we should pre-select a manageable number of candidates. There is, however, no control over the number of elements that the set of maximal coherent subsets of a set can have. This is just one respect in which belief revision formalisms depart from the reasoning capacities of non-ideal agents. Others include: the requirement that agents hold only consistent beliefs; that their system of beliefs be closed under logical consequence; or the assumption that they have infinite memory. For a theory of belief revision that takes into consideration human limited cognitive resources, see Wassermann (1999a) and Tennant (2012).

[77] Olsson ((1997a: 122) fn 15 and (1999: 285)).

of epistemic justification a plausible alternative to foundationalism. In addition, if, as claimed, coherence theories of belief revision are psychologically more plausible than foundationalist theories, then this provides us with yet a further reason for taking coherentism seriously.

Nevertheless, as has been argued, these formal theories of belief revision are limited in several respects. Most importantly, they fall short of formalizing a substantive notion of coherence and they simplify the actual process by which we render our views coherent. As regards the notion of coherence, it would be desirable to further investigate how a positive notion of stability can be defined and formalized, as well as to model a gradational concept of coherence. This concept could provide the basis for defining operations of belief change that better capture the complexities of our actual processes of justification. With the aid of a gradational and positive notion of coherence we can devise the mechanisms for making up a pool of candidate belief systems on the base of more interesting notions than the all-or-nothing coherence of sets and their size. In this regard, it would be helpful to have a richer representation of the system of beliefs, ie the base or unit of coherence, upon which belief revision operations are performed.[78] As Stalnaker has pointed out:

> the choice [between alternative revisions] will depend on assumptions about epistemic and causal dependence and independence, on the reasons one has for one's beliefs as well as on the beliefs themselves ... we will need to impose *additional structure* on our notion of a belief state before we can say much about the way beliefs change or ought to change in response to new information.[79]

There are several complementary ways of imposing this additional structure. First, further investigations on the notion of epistemic entrenchment are likely to provide important insights as to how to develop richer representations of belief states. Secondly, we may attach degrees of plausibility to each element, maybe along the lines suggested by Spohn. Thirdly, and related to the previous point, it may be interesting to allow for both real beliefs and hypothetical beliefs within the belief base. This would allow us to give an account of the process of selection as one in which the subject hypothetically adds several beliefs (by building up alternative belief bases), then manipulates these bases through revision and contraction, and finally chooses among them the most coherent one. Fourthly, it may be convenient to devise a way of dividing up the belief set into relatively isolated subsets, for our judgements of coherence seem to be sensitive to this kind of internal

[78] Pollock and Gillies also point out that a richer characterization of epistemological states is needed in order to take into account the complexity of the dynamics of belief. See Pollock and Gillies (2000: 86 and 90).

[79] Stalnaker (1984: 96–97). Emphasis added.

organization.[80] Last, we must give an account of how the structure of reasons can be represented.[81] Further work on the various ways in which we may impose an additional structure on the base, together with research about how a positive and gradational account of coherence can be formally represented, will shed some light on the way in which the several candidates are generated and the most coherent of such set of alternatives chosen.

Hence, richer formal representations of the dynamics of belief have to be developed in order to model the complex aspects of coherentist justification. Current formalisms are not rich enough for this purpose. This is not a reason for dismissing these models. On the contrary, the relationship between epistemology and belief revision formalisms seems to me to be very fruitful, in both directions.[82] On the one hand, as has been argued, current formalisms are very useful in constructing a well-structured coherentist epistemology.[83] Thus, it is to be expected that new developments in the area of belief revision will help further devise the details of coherentist justification. On the other hand, to the extent that epistemology comprises a detailed theory of the dynamics of coherentist justification, it will be an extraordinarily useful guide for doing formal research in this area.

## VI. CONCLUSIONS

This chapter has reviewed and assessed some attempts to formalize coherence theories of belief revision. According to these theories, we should revise our beliefs in a way that maximizes the coherence of our belief states while minimizing change. The AGM theory, the most influential belief revision formalism, has been claimed to adequately model the coherence approach to belief revision. However, the AGM theory does not seem appropriate as a formalization of coherentism because of two reasons. First, this theory relies on a notion of coherence as consistency plus logical closure, which does not seem to be in accordance with the traditional concept of coherence.

[80] It is a problem of most belief revision formalisms that the domain of the different operators is the whole system of beliefs. This problem has been acknowledged by Hansson (1999a: 370). For a proposal that develops local versions of the operations of belief change, see Wassermann (1999b) and Hansson and Wassermann (2002).

[81] For a proposal, see Gärdenfors (1990: 39–44). Pollock and Gillies also point out the need to represent the structure of reasons in the characterization of the epistemological states (2000: 86). Recent attempts to complement belief revision theory with argumentation theory provide a promising way of addressing this problem. See Falappa, Kern-Isberner and Simari (2009).

[82] See Hansson (2003) for a useful list of problems the solution of which requires inputs from both logic and philosophy. For a defence of the thesis that there is a symbiotic relationship between epistemology and belief revision, see H Rott (2001) ch 2. For a strong criticism of the utility of belief revision formalisms for developing an epistemological theory, see Pollock and Gillies (2000).

[83] See Hansson (2006) (showing how the formalization provided by belief revision theory yields new insights that have important implications for the development of a coherentist epistemology).

And secondly, it requires that new information be always accepted, a requirement that clearly conflicts with coherentist views of justification according to which it is only coherence with a belief system that determines whether or not we are justified in accepting new information. Thus, it is necessary to seek out an alternative formal theory of belief revision that better squares with the coherentist ideas.

Hansson's theory of semi-revision seems to provide a plausible framework for formalizing a coherentist approach to belief revision. Semi-revision is an operation that has two steps: first, the new information is added, and then the resulting set is consolidated, that is, made consistent. Hansson's theory differs in two important respects from the AGM theory: first, it is a non-prioritized form of belief revision, so that input is not always accepted, and secondly, it represents belief states not as belief sets, but as belief bases, so that logical closure is given up. These two features bring semi-revision more into line with coherentism than AGM.

Taking this theory as a starting point, Olsson has developed a coherentist interpretation of both semi-revision and consolidation. He has further proposed that there are two kinds of consolidation (and, therefore, of semi-revision): subtractive and additive. In addition to these two operations, Olsson has suggested that we use a 'merge' operator to model rational changes of belief in the light of new information. 'Merge', as defined by Fuhrman, is an operation whereby one may combine two sets into a consistent one. Thus, this operation, as opposed to semi-revision, does not take the new input to be single sentences, but sets of sentences. Olsson's 'merge' operator differs from Fuhrman's in that it is not of a partial meet kind, and in that the result of merging is not merely consistent sets, but coherent sets. These sets represent, according to Olsson, the most justified systems of belief, given our current state of information. Olsson's proposal importantly advances the project of formalizing a coherentist epistemology. Nevertheless, there are some serious problems with Olsson's proposal. Most importantly, Olsson implausibly makes consistency a condition of coherence, leaves 'stability', which is a condition that is meant to capture the positive aspect of coherence, undefined, and he does not provide a gradational notion of coherence, which is critical to give an adequate account of the dynamics of coherentist justification.

To conclude, belief revision formalisms, as they stand, still fall short of formalizing relevant aspects of coherentism. However, they do provide us with the tools for thinking more precisely about coherence and its role in epistemic justification. A cross-fertilization between the literature on belief revision and coherentists approaches to epistemology is likely to be beneficial to both fields. While formal research in belief revision may contribute to the development of a more detailed coherentist epistemology, epistemologists' work on the role of coherence in the dynamics of belief may inspire the construction of more complex belief revision formalisms.

# 6

# *Is Coherence Truth-Conducive?*

IN PREVIOUS CHAPTERS, I have examined the role of coherence in epistemic justification from both a structural and a dynamic perspective. As we have seen, one of the traditional objections against coherence theories of justification is that there seems to be no compelling reason to believe that coherence is truth-conducive. Unless such a reason is provided, so the argument goes, coherentists standards of justification are not themselves justified.[1] There are many different kinds of arguments that purport to show that there is an appropriate connection between truth and coherence in the coherentist literature. We can divide coherentist approaches to knowledge and justification into three groups. First, some defend coherence theories of justification, but do not claim that coherence provides a definition of truth as well. In these views, coherence is a criterion of truth, as opposed to a theory about the nature of truth.[2] The nature of truth, in these approaches, is explained along the lines provided by the traditional realist view on truth, to wit, the correspondence theory of truth. This is the kind of coherence theory of justification on which I have focused in the discussion of coherentist approaches to justification in previous chapters. In contrast, other coherentists reject realist accounts of truth, and defend both coherence theories of truth as well as coherence theories of justification. Last, some authors, most importantly Davidson, defend a version of the coherence theory that does not easily fit in the realist/anti-realist dichotomy.

In this chapter, my aim is to deal with the issue of how coherentist justification may be shown to connect up with truth. My discussion of the relation between coherence and truth will be as follows. First, I shall briefly

[1] According to Williams, the challenge to connect coherence with truth is just a variant of the familiar sceptical challenge to show how knowledge is possible, given that 'appearances' could be just what they are even if the world were not at all what we take it to be. The difference between the worry that our beliefs might be coherent and yet be comprehensively false and the traditional Cartesian demon and brain in a vat hypotheses is that whereas in the latter appearances tend to be identified with sensory experiences, the challenge to show the truth-conduciveness of coherentist justification involves generalizing the notion of appearance to cover all beliefs about the world. See Williams (1996: 248 and 267ff).

[2] The distinction between criterial theories of truth—which establish criteria of truth, and definitional theories of truth—which explain the meaning of truth, is proposed by Rescher (1973).

rehearse the realists' arguments.[3] Then, I will briefly touch upon the anti-realists' account of coherence and truth. Next, I will explain Davidson's views on truth and coherence in some detail, and this will occupy us for a substantial part of this chapter. Davidson's take on the problem of the truth-conduciveness of coherence is extremely interesting because it calls into question the very same terms in which the debate over the relationship between coherence and truth has been traditionally conducted. Thus, I believe that it is indeed worthy to analyse thoroughly Davidson's original way of tackling this issue. I will conclude this chapter by discussing some recent work, in formal epistemology, that attempts to relate coherence and truth by using probability theory.

## I. COHERENCE, REALISM AND ANTI-REALISM

### A. Realism and Coherentist Epistemology

Prominent coherentists, such as BonJour, Lehrer and Thagard—whose theories of justification we have examined in detail in chapters three and four—hold a realist view about truth and the external world. That is, according to these philosophers, there is an objective world that is independent of our thinking of it. And a proposition is true if it corresponds with such an objective world. As shown, different arguments are given to the effect that coherence yields such correspondence. To recall, BonJour appeals to an inference to the best explanation. In this view, the best explanation of coherence plus stability of a system of beliefs that meets the observation requirement (which guarantees that the belief system attributes high reliability to a reasonable variety of cognitively spontaneous beliefs) is that it corresponds (in the long run and approximately) to the external world.[4] Lehrer's externalist coherentism ensures that a justified belief is also true. He claims that for a belief to be justified in a way that is undefeated, and thus, for it to be knowledge, it must be more reasonable for the believer to hold that belief than to reject it on the basis of her ultrasystem of beliefs, where such ultrasystem is a modified version—one that includes only true beliefs—of her system of beliefs.[5] And Thagard gives the following indirect argument for the truth-conduciveness of coherence: scientific theories are at least approximately true, and scientists do use coherence-based reasoning, therefore, coherence is truth-conducive.[6]

[3] For a detailed account of these arguments, see chs 3 and 4.
[4] BonJour (1985: 171). On BonJour's views on coherence and truth, see ch 3.
[5] On Lehrer's views on coherence and truth, see ch 3.
[6] See ch 4, for a discussion of Thagard's view on this topic.

None of the foregoing arguments are taken to be conclusive. Thus, to a great extent, the problem of how coherence is appropriately connected with truth as correspondence is still open. In addition, coherentist theories that adopt a realist stance have to face the objections that have been addressed against correspondence theories of truth. A main problem with realist approaches is that they entail a debilitating form of global scepticism. Since we cannot step outside of our beliefs, we can never check to see if they correspond to the world or not. Thus, concludes the sceptic, we can never know whether our beliefs are true. As Putnam puts it, truth understood as correspondence is 'radically non-epistemic'.[7] A related problem with realist approaches to truth is pointed out by Dummett. If truth transcends what we can verify, as realists claim, then we cannot recognize whether a statement has the property of truth. And since understanding and truth are closely linked, it is mysterious how meaning and understanding are even possible.[8] The need to avoid these problems has driven some defenders of coherentist theories of justification to embrace a version of the coherence theory of truth.

## B. The Coherence Theory of Truth

The coherence theory of truth is a theory about the nature of truth. It holds that for a proposition to be true is for it to cohere with a certain system of beliefs. There are different versions of the coherence theory of truth. These versions differ in two main respects. First, coherence theories of truth give different accounts of the coherence relation. Some take it to be simple consistency,[9] others require mutual entailment.[10] Still others explain it in terms of notions such as agreement or social consensus.[11] Secondly, different versions of the coherence theory differ in the answers they give to the question of what system is the intended one. Coherentists generally agree that the relevant system must be a set that consists of propositions believed or held to be true. They disagree, though, about which system of beliefs is the relevant one. Some claim that truth amounts to coherence with the largest consistent set of propositions currently believed.[12] Others appeal to coherence with the system of beliefs that human beings would hold at the

[7] Putnam (1978: 125).
[8] See Dummett (2001: 229–51).
[9] Eg Davidson. See Davidson (2001a: 155).
[10] Eg Blanshard (2001: 107).
[11] Most postmodernist coherence theories hold some version of this thesis. For an overview, see Alcoff (1996).
[12] See Young (1995).

limit of inquiry.[13] Still others regard truth as coherence with the system of propositions that would be believed by an omniscient being.[14]

In addition to the differences that result from the different positions on how coherence and the intended system should be characterized, a further distinction between versions of the coherence theory of truth can be made based on the scope that the theory is intended to have. Walker has distinguished between 'pure' and 'impure' coherence theories.[15] Whereas the former explains all kinds of truth in terms of coherence, the latter gives a coherentist account of some kinds of truth and a correspondence account of others. For example, Blackburn's theory of coherence is an example of this mixed view, for he combines a correspondence account of fact-stating discourse with a coherentist account of the truth of moral statements.[16]

Coherence theories of truth have been regarded as attractive alternatives to correspondence theories for two main reasons. One is the desire to avoid an extreme form of global scepticism. In its coherentist version, the sceptical challenge is that of showing that coherence is appropriately connected with truth. By defining truth in terms of coherence, coherence theories of truth directly provide a connection between truth and coherence, and thus, offer an escape from Cartesian scepticism. Another main force that motivates coherence theories comes from verificationism. In this view, our statements cannot have truth conditions (on which the meaning of the sentences depends) that transcend our capacity to verify them. Coherence conditions, as opposed to the kind of objective conditions postulated by correspondence theories, can be known, and thus, make understanding possible. In contrast to correspondence theories, the different versions of coherence theories of truth hold an epistemic notion of truth and reject the realist assumptions on which such theories rely. The rejection of these assumptions leads to quite different positions, and to different coherence theories of truth, which cannot easily be put under a single label. Among those who have defended—or have been attributed—some version of a coherence of truth are absolute idealists, irrealists, pragmatic idealists, anti-realists, global anti-realists, internal realists and a similarly different number of views in continental philosophy.

[13] Eg Putnam. See n 25 below.

[14] In some versions of idealism, see n 17.

[15] Walker (1989a: 6).

[16] Blackburn (1984) ch 6. According to Walker, Kant and Quine also hold an impure coherence theory of truth. Kant takes truth in the everyday world—the world of appearances—to be a matter of coherence, and truth about how the things are in themselves to be a matter of correspondence. Quine's coherence theory is of an impure type, because it allows the truth of observation statements to be determined by correspondence. See Walker (1989a), chs 4 and 10 and 210–17.

Absolute idealists such as Joachim, Blanshard and Bradley, are among the first precursors of coherence theories of truth.[17] Goodman's irrealism leads him to defend a version of a coherence theory of truth in *Ways of World Making*.[18] For Goodman, truth is better understood in terms of 'fit'. As he puts it, 'the truth of statements and rightness of descriptions, representations, exemplifications, expressions ... is primarily a matter of fit: fit to what is referred to in one way or another, or to other renderings, or to modes and manners of organization'.[19] Within the framework of pragmatic idealism, Rescher has defended the view according to which truth is tantamount to ideal coherence. In his view, if one considers coherence from an idealized perspective—that is, as optimal coherence with a perfected data base—then an essential link between truth and coherence emerges, and it becomes evident that coherence is suited not only as a criterion of truth, but also as a definitional standard of truth.[20]

Certain modern forms of verificationism have also been claimed to involve a commitment to some form of coherentism, eg Dummett's anti-realism and Putnam's internal realism.[21] Anti-realism is a theory about meaning and understanding according to which to understand the meaning of a sentence is to understand the conditions under which it is warrantedly assertible. According to Dummett, truth conditions that we could never know about cannot enter into the understanding of a sentence, because there is no way we could either learn or manifest understanding of them.[22] That is, truth, as opposed to what realists hold, cannot transcend what a speaker can verify.[23] Dummett's anti-realist stance leads—in some interpretations—to

[17] See Bradley (1914); Blanshard (1939); and Joachim (1906). Early logical positivists are also sometimes identified as proponents of the coherence theory of truth. See Neurath (1959) and Hempel (1934–35). Walker has attributed coherence theories of truth to philosophers such as Kant or Spinoza, tracing coherentism further back in the history of philosophy, see Walker (1989a). *Cf* Damnjanovic and Candish (2013) (arguing that the attribution of a coherence theory of truth to the idealists as well as to the logical positivists is mistaken and that it is at least highly controversial that this theory may be retrospectively attributed to earlier philosophers as Spinoza).

[18] See Goodman (1978), esp chs 1 and 7. For a discussion of Goodman's views, see PJ MacCormick (1996).

[19] Goodman (1978: 138).

[20] See Rescher (1985). For a discussion of Rescher's views on truth and coherence, see Puntel (1998).

[21] Walker argues at length that certain modern forms of verificationism involve a commitment to a coherence theory of truth (1989a), esp. chs II and X. That contemporary versions of anti-realism, like Dummett's and Putnam's, are versions of the coherence theory of truth is also argued by Horwich and Fumerton. See Horwich (1990: 10) and Fumerton (1994). Wright objects to Walker's coherentist reading of anti-realism (1995: 288–92). BonJour (1994) argues against Fumerton's coherentist interpretation of anti-realism. See also Damnajanovic and Candlish (2013), for an argument to the effect that neither Dummett nor Putnam may be held as proponents of the coherence theory of truth.

[22] On the so-called 'acquisition argument' and 'manifestation argument', see Young (1995: 70ff).

[23] See Dummett (1978).

a coherence theory of truth. For warrantedness cannot be but a matter of coherence with other beliefs, and truth is a matter of what can, through coherence, be recognized as true. An explicit defence of a coherence theory of truth based on a particular version of anti-realism, to wit, 'global anti-realism', is provided by Young.[24] Global anti-realism can be characterized as the view that sentences have 'coherence truth conditions', that is, as the view that the conditions under which a sentence is true are the conditions under which it coheres with the speaker's beliefs. This is so because, argues Young, the only conditions that a speaker can detect are, as the coherence theory of knowledge entails, the conditions under which sentences cohere with a system of beliefs. A version of verificationism also leads Putnam—or so it is argued—to defend a coherence theory of truth. Putnam distinguishes between metaphysical realism and internal realism. Unlike metaphysical realism, internal realism—the view that Putnam advocates—asserts that the totality of objects is not fixed, because objects themselves exist only relative to conceptual schemes. According to Putnam's internal realism, a proposition is true when it would be rationally acceptable in ideal epistemic conditions.[25] This view, as Walker argues, amounts to taking truth to be a matter of coherence with idealized standards of justification.[26] From this point of view, to understand a sentence is to know when it would be rationally acceptable to assert it, that is, to know the conditions under which it coheres with these standards.[27]

Some philosophers in the continental tradition have also claimed that coherence is all that we have when inquiring about truth. In particular, Linda Alcoff has defended the view according to which both justification and truth are a matter of coherence.[28] According to Alcoff, the best conception of truth is not correspondence, but 'the achievement of coherence among the multiple and diverse elements involved in the process or flow

[24] See Young (1995).

[25] Putnam's views on truth have evolved in the course of his writings. The view that is presented here is the one that he holds in (1981).

[26] See Walker (1989a: 185–92). For a different coherentist interpretation of Putnam's views, see Alcoff ((2001: 170–73) and (1996) ch 6).

[27] Another pragmatist who, from a different perspective, has also been interpreted as defending both a coherence theory of truth and a coherence theory of justification is Richard Rorty. Rorty states his position as follows: 'nothing counts as justification unless by reference to what we already accept, and there is no way to get outside our beliefs and language as to find some test other than coherence' (1979: 178). Despite this endorsement of coherence as the ultimate test to which we can aspire, it does not seem appropriate to include Rorty among those who defend a coherence theory of truth, if only because Rorty has repeatedly stated that the notion of truth does not play any explanatory role in a sensible epistemology.

[28] Alcoff states her coherentist views on truth and justification in (1996) and (2001). In addition to her own proposal, Alcoff has also suggested an alternative reading of Foucault and Gadamer according to which these authors should be seen as holding a version of a coherence theory of truth. See (1996), chs I, II and V. For a discussion of Alcoff's work on coherence, see Lynch (1998).

of knowing practices'.[29] In Alcoff's view, this coherence theory is aligned with what she calls 'immanent realism'.[30] This form of realism is one that eschews the 'Cartesian bifurcations between man and world, culture and nature, mind and reality'.[31] Instead of this binary picture, Alcoff proposes an immanent account of knowledge in which we are not severed from the world, but are always engaged with it. In this alternative picture, truth is neither seen as completely subjective, nor as completely objective. For truth requires coherence not only among beliefs, but also with 'non-subjective aspects of lived reality'.[32]

Several objections have been addressed against the coherence theory of truth.[33] A main objection, first raised by Russell,[34] is that it allows any proposition to be true, since any proposition can be a member of some coherent set. However, as Walker argues, this objection misses the point because coherence theorists do not say that membership of any arbitrary coherent set of propositions is sufficient for truth. What they say is that truth is coherence with some specific set of beliefs that is actually held or would be held.[35] This line of argument, however, gives rise to a more sophisticated version of the specification objection. Coherence theories of truth fail to identify the specified set of beliefs without contradicting their position. They need to give a non-coherentist account of the truth conditions of second-order beliefs such as the belief that belief *b* is actually held in order to specify the system of beliefs in relation to which the truth of a particular belief is to be determined.[36]

A different way of effecting the connection between coherence and truth is proposed by Davidson. As I mentioned before, Davidson's views on truth are not easily classified under the realist or the anti-realist sides of the debate. On the contrary, Davidson attempts to question the very terms in which this debate is framed. Davidson's argument for the truth-conduciveness of coherence is based on his theory of interpretation, as we will see in a moment.

[29] Alcoff (2001: 164).

[30] On Alcoff's immanent realism, see Alcoff (1996: 208–20) and (2001: 159–82).

[31] Alcoff (1996: 213).

[32] Lynch (2001: 100).

[33] For a discussion of the several objections that have been raised against the coherence theory of truth, see Walker (1989a: 25–34) and Young (1995: 58–67).

[34] Russell (1906–07).

[35] That the base of coherence consists of a set of beliefs, and not of any set of propositions, is explicitly argued by, among others, Davidson and BonJour.

[36] According to Walker, a parallel objection can be addressed against coherence theories of justification. Ultimately, coherence theories of justification, contrary to their own theory, must assign beliefs about what our beliefs are a foundational status. For a discussion of Walker's objection, see Wright (1995) and Young (2001).

## II. COHERENCE, TRUTH AND INTERPRETATION

Davidson has embraced a coherentist view of justification according to which the only reason to hold a belief is another belief.[37] As Davidson explicitly recognizes, this view of justification requires—in order for it to meet the sceptical challenge—that one give a reason for thinking that any belief that is coherent with a body a beliefs is likely to be true. According to Davidson, the reason why the fact that a belief coheres with a system of beliefs is a reason for believing that such a belief is true is that our system of beliefs is mostly true. Thus, argues Davidson, there is a presumption in favour of the truth of a belief that coheres with a system of beliefs. This response is grounded on Davidson's views about belief, meaning and interpretation. Davidson's take on these issues is informed by a general view on meaning and belief ascription that, following Quine's steps, has been highly influential in philosophy of mind and philosophy of language. Before getting into the details of Davidson's theory, I would like to introduce some of the main lines of the general picture of interpretation that lies behind Davidson's theory.

### A. A Neo-Rationalist Framework

The 'neo-rationalist' approach to interpretation—borrowing Cooper's term—may be characterized by means of the following three theses: 'holism', 'normativity' and 'congruence'.[38] Different versions of these theses form the basis of a prominent picture of interpretation that has been, most notably, developed by Quine, Davidson, Lewis and Dennett.

'Holism', very roughly, is the thesis that it is impossible to assign meanings (meaning holism) or belief contents (mental holism) except in the context of the whole language and network of beliefs. This thesis is interpreted in many ways. Block writes:

> Even if we restrict ourselves to holism of meaning and content, we have many different holisms. Some take holism about meaning to be the doctrine that if you've got one meaning, you've got lots of them. On other views, to say meaning is holistic is to say that the meaning of each term depends on the meanings of all

[37] For Davidson's objections to foundationalism, see Davidson (2001a: 137–53 and 159–75).

[38] These theses characterize an important view in the philosophy of social science that David Cooper has called 'neo-rationalism' (Cooper (1985–86: 51–68)). These theses and the 'neo-rationalism' label are very useful, I believe, for characterizing a prominent view on interpretation that has been defended, among others, by Davidson. Not surprisingly, a main line of argumentation within this tradition draws heavily on Davidson's ideas (see M Rott (1986: 272–304)). For a discussion of this approach to social science in the context of coherentism, see Risjord (1993: 247–58).

> or most other terms. Others take meaning holism to be the doctrine that there is no real distinction between language and theory or between the 'dictionary' and the 'encyclopedia.'[39]

Fodor and Lepore take 'meaning holism' to be the thesis that 'only whole languages or whole theories or whole belief systems *really* have meanings, so that the meanings of smaller units—words, sentences, hypotheses, prediction, discourses, dialogues, texts, thoughts, and the like—are merely derivative'.[40] In this view, thus, the basic tenet of meaning holism is that the unit of meaning is the whole language.[41] It may be useful to distinguish between two kinds of holism: methodological holism and constitutive holism.[42] Whereas the former requires that certain theoretical constraints should apply to the body of data as a whole, the latter states that the identity of the object of interpretation is constituted by the connections that obtain between the beliefs/sentences comprising a whole theory. While methodological holism constrains theory construction, constitutive holism constrains that which the theory is about.

Holism about interpretation is a very widespread doctrine in analytic philosophy as well as in continental philosophy and literary criticism.[43] Different motivations have led these diverse approaches to interpretation to accept some version of meaning holism: reflections on the holistic nature of the confirmation and learning of scientific theories,[44] arguments from the functional nature of the mind, or from 'inferential role semantics',[45] and arguments that turn on the conditions under which radical interpretation and intentional explanation are possible.[46] These arguments, as Fodor and Lepore have forcefully argued, do not seem to conclusively make the case for holism.[47] And even if they did, holism still raises several problems: it threatens the possibility of making generalizations in psychology, for if the content of any state depends on all others, then it is unlikely that two believers can share a state with the same content. It also seems to jeopardize a standard picture of communication and learning according to which speakers' meanings and beliefs can overlap partially to varying degrees, that is, one can understand part of a language without having learned all of it,

[39] Block (1995: 151).

[40] Fodor and Lepore (1992: x).

[41] It is worth noticing the parallelism between meaning holism, understood in this way, and coherentist justification, in which the 'unit of justification' is the whole system of beliefs.

[42] Malpas (1992: 53–57).

[43] A holistic view of interpretation characterizes the hermeneutic tradition, from Schleiermacher to Heidegger and Gadamer. Some weak version of meaning holism is also assumed in most literary criticism. For a critical survey of developments in both the analytic and continental philosophy as well as literary theory, see Norris (1999).

[44] See Quine (1953).

[45] See Block (1986: 615–78).

[46] Davidson (1984: 123–41); Lewis (1983: 108–21); and Dennett (1981: 2–22).

[47] Fodor and Lepore (1992).

or two speakers' beliefs can be only partially in agreement. For much the same reason, holism also makes the possibility of translation problematic.

In view of these problems, some philosophers refuse to 'convert' to holism and endorse an atomistic view of meaning. In this view, which has a long tradition, meaning and content are not characterized in terms of a web; that is, sentences and beliefs have meaning or content independently of their relations to other sentences or beliefs. Still others refuse to adopt either a holist or an atomistic theory of meaning and accept a 'molecularist' approach. Molecularism characterizes meaning and content in terms of relatively small parts of the web in a way that allows many different theories to share those parts.[48] Molecularism may be difficult to distinguish from some versions of holism that appeal to some kind of 'locality condition', which restricts the context relevant to the assignment of meanings and propositional attitudes.[49] Molecularism and 'local-holism' are attempts to find a difficult middle ground between straight atomism and radical holism. If successful, this irenic account would certainly bear more resemblance to our actual practices of interpretation.

In addition to the holistic thesis, the second element that characterizes the neo-rationalist approach to interpretation is the thesis that interpretation is normative.[50] Normative principles, it is claimed, constrain the process of interpretation, that is, the process of assigning propositional attitudes to speakers and meanings to utterances. Following Fodor and Lepore, we may characterize the normative picture of the constraints on interpretation by means of the following principles: 'the truth-principle', 'the coherence principle', the 'closure principle' and the 'probity principle'.[51] According to these principles, intentional ascriptions necessarily represent a speaker's beliefs as mostly true, coherent and logically closed. Furthermore, they necessarily attribute to speakers those desires that are good for them to have. As is apparent, these principles may be roughly subsumed under an assumption of rationality that, in this view, would govern the interpretative activity. Dennett explicitly claims that interpretation (from the intentional

[48] See Block (1998: 488).

[49] Several holistic theorists have argued in favour of a more local approach to meaning and belief. Eg Bilgrami (1994) introduces a local level of content attribution ('locality condition'). Malpas appeals to the hermeneutic notion of 'horizon' to account for the local character of interpretation (see (1992), II (4), esp 112–14). A motivation to find an intermediate position between semantic atomism and holism also seems to lie behind some notions of structural semantics, such as 'frames' and 'semantic fields'. See Feder (1992: 229–52).

[50] The relation between the holistic and the normative theses is unclear. Fodor and Lepore argue that from the premise that certain (intrinsically holistic) normative principles are essentially involved in content attribution, it is inferred the holism of the psychological (1992: 155). In contrast, that interpretation is normative is generally presented as a necessary consequence of the fact that meaning and belief are holistically constituted. Eg Davidson introduces the principle of charity as a solution to the problem posed by the holistic thesis of the interdependence of meaning and belief.

[51] Fodor and Lepore (1992: 142–43).

stance) requires that we use an 'assumption of rationality or cognitive/conative optimality'.[52] Lewis, Quine and Davidson endorse different versions of the principles that encode this rationality constraint—broadly understood—on interpretation.

Lewis understands interpretation in terms of constraint satisfaction, and proposes six constraining principles on interpretation. For example, the 'rationalization principle', which requires that the interpretee be represented as a rational agent, or the 'principle of charity', which requires that the ascribed propositional attitudes be the same as our own. The best interpretation would be the one that better fits all six principles overall.[53] Normative principles, in Quine's and Davidson's theories of interpretation, also include, most importantly, a 'principle of charity'. Quine's version of this principle says that 'assertions that are startingly false on the face of them are likely to turn on hidden differences of language'.[54] The rationale behind this principle, in Quine's words, is that 'one's interlocutor's silliness, beyond a certain point, is less likely than bad translation—or, in the domestic case, linguistic divergence'.[55] In Davidson's theory, the principle of charity directs the interpreter to treat the speaker as having mostly true and consistent beliefs. As Davidson puts it, interpreters must try for a theory that finds the speaker 'consistent, a believer of truths, and a lover of the good (all by our own lights, it goes without saying)'.[56]

What has just been said in relation to the normative character of interpretation should make it clear what the third thesis that characterizes the neo-rationalist tradition, to recall, 'congruence', means. It is a common feature of these approaches to interpretation, that the interpreter necessarily maximizes agreement with the interpretee. The interpreter is supposed to read off her own standards of rationality and truth into the speaker's utterances. Thus, correct interpretations ensure that there is congruence or agreement between the interpreter's and the interpretee's views. The theses of holism, normativity and congruence find their most developed expression in Davidson's theory of interpretation, which I shall now examine.[57]

[52] Dennett (1990: 187).

[53] It is worth noticing the similarities between this approach to interpretation and Thagard's notion of coherence as constraint satisfaction (Thagard (2000a)). Lewis' approach could be then easily interpreted as a coherentist approach to interpretation.

[54] Quine (1960: 59).

[55] ibid.

[56] Davidson (2001b: 222).

[57] Another shared feature of these approaches, which I shall not attempt to explain here, is the 'indeterminacy of interpretation'.

### B. Radical Interpretation

Davidson responds to the sceptical challenge that our beliefs may hang together and still be false by arguing that belief is intrinsically veridical. It is not possible, claims Davidson, for our system of beliefs to be mostly wrong. This gives us a reason to believe that a belief that coheres with such a system is likely to be true. Hence, from this perspective, what is essential for the truth-conduciveness of coherence is to show that the notions of belief and truth are connected in the right way. Davidson effects the link between truth and belief by means of two pairings: truth and meaning, and meaning and belief. Thus, the connection between truth and belief is mediated by the notion of meaning. The first pairing results from adopting a Tarskian theory of truth, relativized to speaker and time, as a theory of interpretation for natural languages.[58] Such theory of truth, argues Davidson, is a theory of meaning in the sense that explicit knowledge of the theory suffices to understand the utterances of a speaker.

The second pairing—that of meaning and belief—appears as the claim that belief and meaning are interdependent. According to Davidson, belief and meaning play interlocking and complementary roles in interpretation. We cannot interpret a speaker's utterances without identifying his beliefs, nor is it possible to attribute those beliefs without knowing what his utterances mean. As Davidson says:

> The interdependence of meaning and belief is evident in this way: a speaker holds a sentence to be true because of what the sentence (in his language) means, and because of what he believes. Knowing that he holds a sentence to be true, and knowing the meaning, we can infer his belief; given enough information about his beliefs, we could perhaps infer the meaning.[59]

The interdependence of meaning and belief makes patent Davidson's commitment to methodological holism. Nonetheless, Davidson's holism is not only methodological, but also constitutive. In Davidson's view, there are no such things as isolated meanings and beliefs. As he puts it, 'it is the pattern of belief that allows us to identify any thought, and it is the pattern of sentences held truth that gives sentences their meaning'.[60]

The pairings of truth and meaning, on the one hand, and meaning and belief, on the other hand, constrain the actual task of constructing and testing a theory of interpretation. First, given the first pairing, such theory aims at producing a Tarski style characterization of truth for a speaker's language. Secondly, given the interdependence of meaning and belief, such

[58] Davidson defends the claim that a theory of truth, modified to be applied to natural languages, can be used as a theory of interpretation in (1984: 126–139). See also ibid, 28–35 and 149–150.

[59] ibid, 134–35.

[60] ibid, 162–63.

characterization must go hand-to-hand with the production of a theory of the speaker's beliefs. This is the complex task that 'radical interpretation' consists in. As Davidson writes, 'in interpreting utterances from scratch -in radical interpretation- we must somehow deliver simultaneously a theory of belief and a theory of meaning'.[61]

Now, the question arises, what evidence can be used for constructing and testing a theory of radical interpretation? Because of the interdependence of meaning and belief, according to Davidson, the evidence for such a theory must be neutral between these two notions. That is, in order not to beg the question, the evidential basis for a theory of interpretation should not assume knowledge of meanings or detailed knowledge of beliefs. Davidson claims the attitude of holding a sentence true to provide such an evidential basis. For it seems plausible, in Davidson's view, that we can tell under what external circumstances a speaker holds a sentence to be true without knowing either what he means or what he believes about its unknown subject matter. Thus, the problem of radical interpretation is how, given this evidence, the interpreter can work out what the speaker's beliefs are, and what his words mean. In other words, the problem is how to disentangle the interlocking roles of belief and meaning in the interpretation of speech.

To solve the problem of the radical interpreter, Davidson appeals to the second thesis that characterizes the so-called 'neo-rationalist' framework: the claim that interpretation is normative. The interpreter must separate out meaning from belief on normative grounds by deciding what, in her view, optimizes intelligibility. In so doing, she will make use of the 'principle of charity'. It is this principle that provides the solution to the problem of radical interpretation, by holding belief steady while allowing meaning to be assigned. Belief is held constant by assigning truth conditions to the speaker's sentences that make him right (in the interpreter's opinion) whenever possible.[62] Thus, Davidson's solution is that we begin interpretation by assuming beliefs and, on that basis, develop a tentative theory of meaning. This initial theory can then be used to revise our initial assumptions about beliefs, which could, in their turn, be used to revise our theory of meaning. The interpreter would be moving then back and forth between interpretation of meanings and attributions of beliefs until she reaches a state of 'interpretative reflective equilibrium'.[63]

[61] ibid, 144.

[62] ibid, 137.

[63] See Malpas (1992: 44–45). That coming up with a theory of interpretation, as Davidson conceives it, amounts to something like achieving a Rawlsian reflective equilibrium was first suggested by Rorty (1986: 342). The parallelism between Davidson's account of interpretation and an account of justification in terms of the coherence-based idea of reflective equilibrium suggests that Davidson's views on interpretation are congenial to a coherence-based account of interpretation.

Charity, as a normative constraint on interpretation, ensures agreement between the speaker and the interpreter's beliefs.[64] Here, we have Davidson's commitment to the third basic tenet of the neo-rationalist framework: the thesis that interpretation yields 'congruence' between the speaker's and the interpreter's beliefs. The interpreter will read off, whenever she can, her own standards of rationality on the speaker's behaviour, so that the speaker's norms of rationality will necessarily be in agreement with the interpreter's norms of rationality.[65] Davidson's justification of the introduction of the principle of charity as a device for solving the problem of radical interpretation seems to be two-fold. First, Davidson has repeatedly claimed that what justifies this procedure of interpretation is the fact that disagreement is intelligible only against a background of massive agreement.[66] From this point of view, charity is not an option, but a condition on the same possibility of interpretation. Davidson's writings may be interpreted as providing another kind of justification for the principle of charity, to wit, a moral one. Charity is required on moral grounds because only when we interpret the speakers' utterances and other behaviour as revealing a set of beliefs that is largely true and coherent (by our own standards), are we treating them as creatures endowed with reason, as persons, that is, as moral agents.[67]

Davidson's theory of interpretation provides the resources—he claims—for showing how coherence is truth-conducive. It follows from Davidson's neo-rationalist theory of interpretation that most of anyone's beliefs are mostly true, at least by the interpreter's light. If this is so, then, we have at last a reason for believing that a belief that coheres with an individual's system of beliefs is true. More precisely, Davidson's claim is that there is a 'presumption' in favour of the truth of such a belief. In Davidson's view, every belief in a coherent total set of beliefs is justified in the light of such presumption.[68] Davidson's argument for the truth-conduciveness of coherence can be stated more explicitly as follows:

i. The belief that *p* coheres with *S*' system of beliefs;
ii. Most of *S*' beliefs are true;

Therefore, there is a presumption that *p* is true.

[64] The requirement of agreement is an aspect of charity, together with the requirement that the interpreter treat the speaker as having mostly coherent and true beliefs. See Pagin (2013: 233).

[65] It also follows from the principle of charity that interpretation must depict the speaker as largely sharing the interpreter's own values. See Rescorla (2013: 477).

[66] See Davidson ((1984: 137, 153, 169, and 197) and (1990: 321)).

[67] Eg Davidson writes, 'To the extent that we fail to discover a coherent and plausible pattern of attitudes and actions of others we simply forego the chance of treating them as *persons*' (2001b: 221–22). Emphasis added.

[68] Davidson (2001a: 138–39).

The soundness of this argument crucially depends on the justification of premise (ii), which depends in its turn on the acceptance of Davidson's theory of interpretation. Still, even if it is granted that Davidson's theory of interpretation is right in the main, the question remains, how can it be shown that most of our beliefs are objectively true? For all that, apparently, Davidson has shown so far is that most of anyone's beliefs are true by the interpreter's lights. It may well be the case that speaker and interpreter understand each other on the basis of shared but false beliefs. Davidson gives an argument—the so-called 'omniscient interpreter argument'—to the effect that most of our beliefs are objectively true, and thus, that there is a presumption in favour of the objective truth of any belief that coheres with a system of beliefs.

## C. The Omniscient Interpreter Argument

The sceptical challenge amounts to the claim that our beliefs may hang together and still be comprehensively false. Obvious enough, to claim that this situation cannot obtain, from the interpreter's point of view, given what it is that interpretation consists in, does not satisfactorily answer the sceptic. Only if the case can be made for the impossibility that a system of beliefs be coherent, but false, from an objective point of view, can the sceptical challenge be refuted. That is, in order to show that coherence is truth-conducive, it does not suffice to ensure that there is subjective agreement between the beliefs of speakers in a linguistic community—what may be called, following Genova, the 'agreement thesis'—, but it is also required that the picture of the world that speakers share is largely true—what Genova calls the 'objectivity thesis'.[69] The link between the weaker claim (agreement thesis) and the stronger one (objectivity thesis), that is, between sentences held true and the truth of these sentences, between coherence and truth, is provided by means of the 'omniscient interpreter argument'.[70] Davidson's basic idea is as follows. Suppose that there is an omniscient interpreter, a being who knows all that is relevant to interpretation, but who is, nevertheless, subject to the same method of interpretation as the rest of us. Interpretation by such an infallible being must involve revealing a set of beliefs that are largely true, by the omniscient interpreter's standards. But these standards, by definition, are true. Since the beliefs attributed to the speaker must necessarily be in agreement with the omniscient interpreter's beliefs, and these are true, the speaker's beliefs must also be mostly true.

[69] See Genova (1999: 174).

[70] Davidson invokes the 'omniscient interpreter argument' in (2001a: 150–51) and (1984: 201).

Therefore, we cannot be massively mistaken, and the relation between coherence and truth—in an objective sense—is guaranteed.

Davidson's omniscient interpreter argument has been very much contested in the literature. The various objections that have been addressed against this argument may be classified under three heads.[71] First, the 'anti-theist objections' say that Davidson's omniscient interpreter argument depends on the unsupported premise that there is such a being.[72] Second, the 'limitations to interpretation objections' turn on Davidson's apparent assumption that the omniscient interpreter will always succeed in interpreting any belief system, no matter how mistaken it may be.[73] Last, the 'belief-content scepticism objections' contend that, even granting that we cannot be massively mistaken, we might be systematically wrong about the contents of our beliefs.[74] A different kind of objection that is relevant here is raised by Dalmiya. Dalmiya presents a counter-argument to Davidson's omniscient interpreter argument which starts from the idea of a 'deluded interpreter', defined as a being with mostly false beliefs. In Dalmiya's view, the omniscient interpreter argument is not a convincing argument for the coherentist, but a viciously circular one, because it requires the prior identification of our beliefs as true, rather than false.[75] Thus, as it turns out, Davidson's response to the truth objection ultimately depends on an argument the validity of which is, to say the least, doubtful.

A way out of the sceptical problem could still be found, within the Davidsonian framework, if the case for the impossibility of massive error could be made on other bases. In fact, this is what Davidson came to defend later. He argued that the thesis that belief is veridical (in an objective way), and thus that coherence is truth-conducive, can be defended without appealing to the Omniscient Interpreter Argument. Davidson stated his position as follows:

> I regret these sorties into science fiction and what a number of critics have taken to be theology. If the case can be made with an omniscient interpreter, it can be made without. But how can it be made? ... what I think should 'defuse the skeptical challenge' is the 'dependence of belief-content on the causes of belief.'[76]

Thus, in Davidson's view, we cannot be massively mistaken because interpreters should identify the object of the speakers' beliefs with the causes of those beliefs. Davidson has emphasized the thesis according to which

[71] See Genova (1999: 177).
[72] See Foley and Fumerton (1985: 83–89).
[73] Rasmussen (1987: 315–319).
[74] Bruecker (1986: 264–368) and Craig (1990: 213–14).
[75] See Dalmiya (1990: 86–94).
[76] Davidson (1999: 193).

what ensures that most of our beliefs are true is that the content of beliefs is determined by its causes in a number of places.[77]

Hence, there seem to be two arguments available, within the Davidsonian framework, which support the thesis that our picture of the world is largely correct: the omniscient interpreter argument and the argument that arises from Davidson's theory of content, which might be called the 'argument from the causal dependence of belief-content'.[78] Under this interpretation of Davidson's views, the plausibility of the claim that massive error is not possible would not depend on the controversial omniscient interpreter argument, but also (or even exclusively, as Davidson claims) on the argument from the causal dependence of belief-content. However, it is doubtful that the latter argument properly supports the thesis of the unintelligibility of massive error. To start with, this argument seems to be defective for a number of reasons. Klein has claimed that Davidson's argument is circular, since it assumes that the interpreter already knows that there are external events that are causally connected with belief states, and thus, that global scepticism is false.[79] Genova has argued that it fails to meet the sceptical challenge because the threat of scepticism may emerge within the context of radical interpretation itself—what he calls 'internalized semantic skepticism'. In this view, it is perfectly intelligible to suppose that the construal of what the interpreter takes to be the causal conditions of belief and the resultant specifications of belief content are mostly false.[80] McGinn has also argued, on the grounds of our ability to think of sceptical scenarios, that belief-contents cannot be read off from the world in the way in which Davidson suggests and thus that the premises of the argument fail to establish the desired conclusion.[81]

Besides, even if the argument from the causal dependence of belief-content were sound, it seems that it does not provide any reason for the thesis that belief is veridical that is independent from the one provided by the omnisicent interpreter argument. The reason is that, ultimately, it is the principle of charity that lies behind both arguments. This principle requires, among other things, that the interpreter take the causes of beliefs that she identifies as the content of those beliefs. The claim is that, since these causes determine what the speaker means as well as the content of his beliefs, it is not possible that the speaker's beliefs be mostly false. Thus, it is the nature of interpretation, as constrained by charity, that ensures that the interpretee's view of the world is in the main correct. But if this is

[77] See Davidson ((2001a: 213 and 189) and (1990: 325)).

[78] Eg Sosa and Evnine say that Davidson attempts to show the truth-conduciveness of coherence in two different ways: the omniscient interpreter argument and reflections on how belief-contents are determined. See Sosa (1986a: 395) and Evnine (1991: 141–43).

[79] Klein (1986: 368–86).

[80] Genova (1999: 175).

[81] McGinn (1986: 357–68).

so, then, it seems that the argument from the causal dependence of belief-content cannot independently justify the thesis of the veridical nature of belief. The reason is that, as we have seen, charity among flesh and blood interpreters does not exclude massive error in content-attribution, from an objective point of view, but it only ensures intersubjective agreement. It was this fact that required invoking the omniscient interpreter argument in the first place. Thus, *pace* Davidson, there are reasons for thinking that the case for the massive truth of our beliefs cannot be made without appealing to the omniscient interpreter argument. And, if this is so, then, Davidson's argument for the truth-conduciveness of coherence ultimately depends on the omniscient interpreter argument, the plausibility of which is, as argued, highly controversial.

## D. Davidson, Realism and Anti-Realism

Whatever the merits of Davidson's sophisticated argument for the truth-conduciveness of coherence, it has the main virtue of having shifted the discussion about the relation between truth and coherence to a new terrain. The terms in which the problem has been traditionally framed present it as a straight choice between endorsing a realist view of truth, which seems incapable of bridging the gap between the truth and the coherence of our beliefs, and accepting an epistemic view of truth, in which truth and coherence are directly linked. Davidson has shown how an a priori connection between truth and coherence can be indirectly effected by endorsing an interpretative framework that is beyond both realism and anti-realism. Davidson does not accept—as he has repeatedly claimed—any version of either realism or anti-realism, explained in terms of the radically non-epistemic or epistemic character of truth, respectively.[82] According to Davidson, truth is 'beautifully transparent',[83] and all attempts (anti-realist or realist) to define, or explain, it that go beyond giving empirical content to a structure of a Tarskian sort are empty or wrong.[84]

Hence, Davidson's views on truth cannot be located within a realist or anti-realist position.[85] On the one hand, Davidson explicitly rejects two

[82] See Davidson (1990), esp 298 and 309 and (2001a: 177–91).

[83] Davidson (2001a: 139).

[84] In (1984), essay 3, Davidson argued that Tarski's theory is a version of the correspondence theory of truth. Davidson has later rejected this interpretation of Tarki's theory in (1990: 304) and (2001a: 182–83).

[85] There is no agreement in the literature about the location of Davidson's views within the contemporary dispute between realism and anti-realism. Rorty has argued that Davidson is 'beyond realism, and anti-realism' (Rorty (1986: 354)). Smart sees nothing in Davidson's views that might be incompatible with realism (Smart (1999: 109–25)). Glanzberg says that 'Davidson takes a different approach to truth than many in the traditional and current debates' (2013: 169). For a discussion of the realists/anti-realists interpretations of Davidson's theory, see Malpas (1992) ch 7.

basic tenets of realist theories of truth: (i) he rejects that truth is correspondence because, in his view, the idea of confrontation does not make sense, and, more importantly, because there is nothing for true sentences to correspond to; and (ii) he denies that it is possible for all our beliefs to be false, as the realist view on truth entails. On the other hand, Davidson also rejects the anti-realist view according to which truth is dependent on our methods of verification. The mistake of anti-realism, in Davidson's view, is that of making a connection between truth and justified belief by linking the notion of justification with that of truth. As we have seen, Davidson's strategy is that of making this connection through the notion of belief, which is claimed to be in its nature veridical. As Davidson puts it:

> Truth emerges not as wholly undetached from belief (as a correspondence theory would make it) nor as dependent on human methods and powers of discovery (as epistemic theories of truth would make it). What saves truth from being 'radically non-epistemic' (in Putnam's words) is not that truth is epistemic, but that belief, through its ties with meaning is intrinsically veridical.[86]

Davidson's arguments for the truth-conduciveness of coherence are, thus, originally located within a framework that is neither realist, nor anti-realist. It is because our shared picture of the world is largely true, as Davidson's picture of interpretation implies, that we can safely conclude—if Davidson's arguments are granted—that there is a reason for thinking that coherentist methods of justification are truth-conducive.

## III. PROBABILITY, COHERENCE AND TRUTH

Recently, there have been a number of important efforts that attempt to relate coherence and truth by using probability theory. This body of work, in formal epistemology, is highly technical and its relevance to traditional epistemology is contested. Nevertheless, it has significantly raised the level of the discussion over coherence and truth in terms of precision and it has notably revitalized the debate over the epistemic value of coherence. I will not provide here a detailed exposition and discussion of this research, which is by now fairly extensive. But I would like to highlight some of the main findings of this body of research as well as examine their bearing on the problem of the truth-conduciveness of coherence.

[86] Davidson (2001a: 156).

### A. Probabilistic Measures of Coherence

Consider the following propositions:

$A_1$= 'June died a natural death last night'
$A_2$= 'June was murdered last night"
$A_3$= 'Someone violently broke into June's house last night'

Why intuitively does $A_2$ cohere better with $A_3$ than with $A_1$? Because, one might argue, the probability that June was murdered, given that someone violently broke into her house, exceeds the probability that June died of natural death, given that someone broke violently into her house. These kinds of considerations have motivated some philosophers to develop probabilistic approaches to the concept of coherence. These approaches take Lewis' definition of 'congruence' as their starting point. According to Lewis:

> A set of statements, or a set of supposed facts asserted, will be said to be congruent if and only if they are so related that the antecedent probability of any of them will be increased if the remainder of the set can be assumed as given premises.[87]

Thus, a set is coherent, or congruent, in Lewis' sense when each individual proposition is made more probable by assuming the others to be true. After Lewis, several proposals have been put forward that attempt to make the notion of coherence precise in probabilistic terms. More specifically, over the past years a number of probabilistic measures of coherence have been proposed. These measures consist in functions that give each set of propositions a number that represents its degree of coherence. The first such quantitative measure was proposed by Shogenji.[88] According to Shogenji, a straightforward way to capture the idea that coherent beliefs 'hang together' is that they are either true together or false together. Since coherence is a matter of degree, we want to say that the more coherent beliefs are, the more likely they are true together. Formally, in the case of two beliefs, this may be expressed by saying that the degree of coherence between beliefs $B_1$ and $B_2$ should be proportional to the conditional probability of $B_1$ given $B_2$ or Prob $(B_1|B_2)$. That is to say, the more coherent two beliefs are, the stronger is the positive impact of the truth of one on the truth of the other. Next, Shogenji determines the neutral point at which beliefs are neither coherent nor incoherent. Two beliefs, says Shogenji, are neutrally related just in case they are probabilistically independent, ie Prob $(B_1|B_2)$ = Prob $(B_1)$. This means that the truth of $B_2$ does not affect the likelihood of $B_1$. Once we adopt probabilistic independence as the point of neutrality we may use the ratio Prob $(B_1|B_2)$/Prob $(B_1)$ as a measure of

[87] Lewis (1946: 338).
[88] Shogenji (1999).

pairwise coherence, so that two beliefs are coherent/incoherent if and only if this ratio is higher/lower than one. Replacing the conditional probability Prob ($B_1$ | $B_2$) with its definiens Prob ($B_1$ & $B_2$)/Prob ($B_2$) yields the following definition of pairwise coherence:

C ($B_1$, $B_2$) = Prob ($B_1$ & $B_2$)/Prob ($B_1$) × Prob ($B_2$)[89]

Hence, C ($B_1$, $B_2$) measures the degree to which two beliefs are more likely to be true together than they would be if they were neutrally related. Shogenji offers the following generalization of this measure for sets of beliefs greater than two:

C ($B_1$, …, $B_n$) = Prob ($B_1$ & … & $B_n$)/Prob ($B_1$) × … × … Prob ($B_n$)[90]

As in the case of pairwise coherence, C ($B_1$, …, $B_n$) compares the joint probability of the beliefs with the value that this joint probability would take if they were probabilistically independent. That is to say, this function allows us to measure the degree by which the beliefs are more likely to be true together than they would be if they were related neutrally. The beliefs are coherent/incoherent if and only if the ratio is higher/lower than one. In short, the main idea behind Shogenji's proposal is that the coherence of a set of beliefs is represented by the positive relevance among the members of that set.

Shogenji's seminal proposal has been the target of numerous critiques and a number of alternative measures of coherence (and variations of them) has been advanced over recent years. Olsson has proposed to measure the degree of coherence of a set by measuring the extent of agreement among the statements in the set.[91] Bovens and Hartmann construct a probabilistic theory of coherence based on the idea that coherence is a property of an information set with the role of boosting our confidence in that information set.[92] Fitelson's coherence measure aims to reflect the level of mutual support of the members of a set.[93] Douven and Meijs propose a general schema for generating measures of coherence the starting point of which is the claim that system coherence depends on the degree of confirmation its elements provide to each other.[94] Roche has developed a coherence measure based on Douven and Meijs' schema but which involves a different measure of confirmation.[95] For the purposes of this chapter, there is no need

[89] ibid, 339.

[90] ibid, 340.

[91] Olsson (2002: 250). See also Olsson (2005: 96–101).

[92] Bovens and Hartmann (2003a) and (2003b). Strictly speaking, Bovens and Hartmann do not provide a measure of coherence, in the sense that each information set is assigned a specific value of coherence. Rather they provide a definition of the relation of 'being no less coherent than', which induces a quasi-ordering on the set of all information sets.

[93] Fitelson (2003).

[94] Douven and Meijs (2007).

[95] Roche (2013).

to go into the details of each of these probabilistic measures of coherence, let alone examine their respective merits.[96] The important issue is whether these attempts to render precise the notion of coherence by using probability theory help us advance the investigation of the relationship between coherence and truth. To this issue I turn now.

## B. Impossibility Results

Is a system that is *more* coherent than another system thereby *more* likely to be true? Suppose we have received information $A_1, \ldots, A_n$ from some sources and another competing account of the situation, in the form of reports $B_1, \ldots, B_m$, from other sources. Thus, we may have two sets S = $\{A_1, \ldots A_n\}$ and S' = $\{ B_1, \ldots, B_m\}$. Suppose, for example, that S is more coherent than S'. Are we allowed to conclude that S is more likely to be true than S' as a whole? Most proponents of probabilistic approaches to coherence have focused on this comparative question, that is, on the question of whether more coherence implies a higher likelihood of truth.[97] In light of the coherence measures described above, this comparative aspect of the problem of the truth-conduciveness of coherence boils down to the question of whether the fact that a set of items of information S is more coherent, according to a particular measure, than another set of items of information

[96] For a discussion of the pros and cons of these measures, see Akiba (2000); Bovens and Hartmann (2003a) and (2003b); Douven and Meijs (2007); Fitelson (2003); Meijs and Douven (2005); Meijs (2007); Schupbach (2011); Siebel (2004) and (2005); and Siebel and Wolff (2008).

[97] The question of whether a system that is more coherent than another system is thereby more likely to be true is the issue that has received more attention in the literature. Alternatively, one could examine the question of whether the fact that a system is coherent implies that the system is highly likely to be true. This issue has been examined in formal epistemology by investigating cases of witness agreement as cases of coherence. The point of departure of this work is again Lewis. According to Lewis, congruence among witness reports cannot by itself assure even the lowest degree of probability of what is reported; however, given some degree of individual credibility, even a slight one, agreement may provide a very high probability of the truth of the story agreed upon. See Lewis (1946). *Cf* BonJour (1985: 147–48). Huemer, Olsson, and Shogenji have formally shown Lewis' point. They have established that coherence by itself does not imply truth: witness agreement does not establish a high probability of what is agreed upon unless the witnesses have some individual credibility. See Huemer (1997); Olsson (2005); and Shogenji (2005). This has been taken to be an argument in favour of the claim that coherence may amplify justification but it cannot by itself generate justification where there is none—and thus as an argument in favour of weak foundationalism and against coherentism. For a discussion of the implications of these formal results for the foundationalist-coherentism debate, see Van Cleve (2011) (arguing that an investigation into the problem of witness agreement in probability theory shows that coherence may amplify, but not generate warrant and thus that weak foundationalism is well-motivated) and Roche (2012) (arguing that these results do not undermine coherentism because though coherentists deny that there can be non-inferential justification they need not deny that there can be individual credibility).

S' implies that S is more likely to be true than S'. Bovens and Hartmann and Olsson have answered this question in the negative: they have shown that there cannot be any coherence measure that is truth-conducive in the comparative sense.[98]

Before presenting Bovens and Hartmann and Olsson's so called 'impossibility results', it is convenient to note that there are important features that they share.[99] First, both Bovens and Hartman and Olsson claim to assess the truth-conduciveness of coherence not when sets of propositions per se are at stake, but rather they seek to evaluate the claim that more coherence implies higher likelihood of truth with respect to belief systems, that is, sets of propositions that are believed by a particular person. Secondly, they propose to analyse belief systems as sets of propositions each of which is supposed to be reported by relatively unreliable witnesses and independent from all other witnesses. The idea is to study witness scenarios with a view to carrying over the results obtained to belief systems, on the assumption that an individual may view her beliefs as 'reports' from her belief system analogous to the witness reports in court. Thus, witness reports are used to model other kind of reports, in a wide sense, such as reports from the senses, reports from memory, etc. Thirdly, they argue that one should translate likelihood of truth into posterior probability, that is, the probability that the conjunction of the propositions in the set is true given that independent and relatively unreliable sources have claimed them to be true. Fourthly, they argue that there is a need to add a *ceteris paribus* clause. Specifically, the reliability of the sources should be assumed to be equal across scenarios. Witness reliability is, however, spelled out differently by Bovens and Hartmann, on the one hand, and by Olsson, on the other. Another important difference between the two impossibility results is that Bovens and Hartmann, but not Olsson, add another *ceteris paribus* condition, namely, equal prior probability, ie the unconditional probability that the conjunction of the propositions in the set is true. Last, both Bovens and Hartmann' and Olsson' theorems work by showing that whatever measure of coherence we pick, counterexamples to their truth-conduciveness can be found.

Bovens and Hartmann start their investigation into the truth-conduciveness of coherence by characterizing 'Bayesian Coherentism', ie the claim that our confidence in information gathered from independent and relative

[98] See Olsson (2005: 134–40) and Bovens and Hartmann (2003b: 19–22). A previous negative result was also obtained by Klein and Warfield (1994). In a seminal paper, Klein and Warfield presented a case in which intuitively coherence increases but probability does not. For discussion of Klein and Warfield's argument, see Merricks (1995); Shogenji (1999); Cross (1999); Akiba (2000); Olsson (2001) and (2005: 105–08); and Bovens and Olsson (2002).

[99] See Meijs and Douven (2007: 2) and Angere (2007: 322).

unreliable sources is positively affected by its coherence. In their view, the following two tenets are the core of Bayesian Coherentism:

> ($BC_1$) For all information sets S, S' ∈ S, if S is no less coherent than S', then our degree of confidence that the content of S (i.e., the conjunction of the propositions in S) is true is no less than our degree of confidence that the content of S' is true, *ceteris paribus*.
>
> ($BC_2$) A coherence ordering over S is fully determined by the probabilistic features of the information sets contained in S.[100]

Bovens and Hartmann present an impossibility result to the effect that these two theses cannot jointly be true. They prove this result by constructing examples in which the reliability of the sources changes which information set will merit the greater degree of confidence. Hence, a coherence measure, which, by ($BC_2$), should be defined exclusively in terms of a probability distribution, cannot tell us which set is more likely to be true (in violation of ($BC_1$)).

Olsson's impossibility theorem reads as follows:

> There are no informative coherence measures that are truth conducive *ceteris paribus* in a basic Lewis scenario (given independence and individual credibility).[101]

In the proof of this theorem, Olsson shows that in cases of full agreement between independent reports that are individually credible (ie basic Lewis-type scenarios) no function C on the probability distribution can be truth-conducive under circumstances of equal reliability of the sources, but where the prior probability is allowed to vary.[102] His reasoning is as follows. In order for coherence to be truth-conducive, more coherence must imply a higher posterior probability. Now, the height of the posterior probability depends not only on the prior probability of what the reports say but also on the prior probability of reliability. However, coherence is a property on the level of report contents and, by its very nature, cannot make reference to reliability, which is a mixed-level property that concerns the relations between contents and reports. Hence, considerations of coherence alone do not allow us to make comparative assessments of the height of the posterior, which is what truth-conduciveness precisely involves.

In sum, what the impossibility results, independently reached by Bovens and Hartman and Olsson, establish is that, given independence and relative unreliability, there is no measure of coherence guaranteeing that more coherence implies higher posterior probability in a *ceteris paribus* sense. In other words, the impossibility results show that not even under 'fortunate'

[100] Bovens and Hartmann (2003b: 11–12).

[101] Olsson (2005: 135).

[102] See Olsson (2005) app B, for the proof of the theorem.

circumstances, as Olsson puts it,[103] can there be any measure of coherence that is truth-conducive.

### C. Discussion

What are the implications of these results for the problem that occupies us, that is, for the problem of showing that there is an appropriate connection between the coherence of an agent's beliefs and their truth? To be sure, these results ought to be taken seriously. Nonetheless, there are various responses to these results that limit the extent to which probabilistic analyses of coherence and truth-conduciveness might undermine the coherence theory of justification.

First, a number of authors have criticized these impossibility theorems from within the formal probabilistic framework that underwrites them. For instance, Schupbach, Meijs and Douven and Huemer have called into question some of the background assumptions that lie at the basis of these results (eg the *ceteris paribus* conditions, the explanation of witness reliability, the claim that coherence should be defined as a property of information sets, etc).[104] Wheeler has claimed that Hartmann and Bovens and Olsson select a specific class of probabilistic models that is not representative of the range of options available to the coherence theorist.[105] And Schubert and Olsson have argued that extending the formal treatment of coherence to second-order beliefs, which play an important role in coherentist epistemology but that do not figure in probabilistic models of coherence, sheds doubts on the generality of the impossibility results.[106]

Secondly, there have been some important efforts to regain the truth-connection notwithstanding the validity of these results. Bovens and Hartmann have argued that while the impossibility results show that there is no measure of coherence that imposes an ordering over information sets, it is still possible to construct a coherence measure that induces a quasi-ordering over information such that the more coherent a body of information is the greater our degree of confidence should be that the information is true.[107] And Shogenji has argued that more coherence—according to his own measure of coherence—does imply a higher joint likelihood of truth, provided that we keep strength fixed, ie provided that the two sets under

[103] Olsson (2005: 135).
[104] Huemer (2007) and (2011); Schupbach (2008); and Meijs and Douven (2007).
[105] Wheeler (2012).
[106] Schubert and Olsson (2012).
[107] See Bovens and Hartmann (2003b). For a critique, see Olsson (2005: 152–55).

comparison have the same total individual strength.[108] Thus, there may be ways in which coherence may still be truth-conducive after all.

Thirdly, it is critical to note that these results do not make coherence non-valuable from an epistemic point of view. It has been established that some of the coherence measures proposed in the literature are reliability-conducive in the sense that a higher degree of coherence raises the probability that the information sources are reliable.[109] It has also been argued that coherence is confirmation-conducive, ie, the coherence of a set of statements facilitates the confirmation of such statements.[110] Finally, it has been shown that, for several of the coherence measures discussed in the literature, even if coherence does not provide an infallible guide to truth, it can give us an indication of truth.[111]

Fourthly, one may argue that these results do not affect the plausibility of a coherence theory of justification because, whatever their merits, the problem of truth-conduciveness, as discussed in Bayesian epistemology, is not the same thing as the truth-connection problem addressed by epistemic coherentism. Bayesian truth-conduciveness is exclusively a property of a set of probability functions, which may be either interpreted as degrees of belief or as objective chances. In contrast, the truth-connection problem is concerned with the relationship between an individual's system of beliefs and the world. This problem calls for a theory that is able to deal with both credences and objective chances, but Bayesian epistemology cannot simultaneously entertain both a subjective and an objective interpretation of probability.[112] Thus, there are reasons to doubt that these results are relevant for the traditional epistemological concerns regarding the relationship between coherence and truth.

Last, and more radically, there seem to be good reasons to be sceptical that coherence and the problem of truth-conduciveness thereof may be analysed by using probabilistic methods. Siebel has persuasively argued that probabilistic measures are not rich enough to capture the notion of coherence. Explanatory relations, argues Siebel, are critical to coherence and, since explanation cannot be captured in purely probabilistic terms, there is no hope for the project of developing a probabilistic theory of coherence.[113] Thagard has argued that any attempt to relate coherence and truth by means of probability faces three insurmountable problems. First, neither an interpretation of probability as frequencies nor an interpretation

[108] Shogenji (1999). For a critique, see Olsson (2005: 119–23).

[109] See Olsson and Schubert (2007); Schubert (2011) and (2012a); and Schubert and Olsson (2013). *Cf* Schubert (2012b) (arguing that while coherence measures are reliability-conducive in restricted scenarios, they are not reliability-conducive in general).

[110] Dietrich and Moretti (2005) and Moretti (2007).

[111] Angere (2007) and (2008).

[112] See Wheeler (2012: 137–38).

[113] See Siebel (2005) and Siebel (2011).

of probability as subjective degrees of belief allows us to connect coherence and truth. For this connection to obtain, there must be links between coherence and probability and probability and truth. The frequentist interpretation fails in making the first link, whereas the interpretation of probability as degree of belief fails in making the second link. Secondly, the probabilistic analyses of coherence proposed thus far, have failed, on their own terms, to connect coherence and truth. Last, there are formidable difficulties involved in implementing probabilistic reasoning computationally.[114] Finally, Lycan has argued that the challenge to show that the fact that a belief coheres with others makes it more likely to be true in the sense that it makes it more probable according to Bayesianism or any other probabilistic theory begs the question. It assumes that probability theory is the fundamental norm against which the main claims of coherentism need to be tested. But this is precisely what coherentists would dispute. Every epistemology, says Lycan, takes some norm or norms as fundamental; for the coherentist, explanatory inference is basic. Probability theory is not to be accepted as a more fundamental norm. Rather, it may be viewed as a 'special purpose tool that serves the more general and fundamental norms of explanatory coherence'.[115]

To sum up, there is a number of ways in which one may question the adequacy of the project of addressing issues of coherence and truth in terms of probability as a whole as well some of the specific findings obtained by this body of literature. Thus, the impossibility results need not be taken to have conclusively proven that coherence is not truth-conducive. This said, however, there is no denying that these results show the severe difficulties inherent in connecting up coherence and truth even in restricted scenarios.

## IV. THE PROBLEM OF METAJUSTIFICATION

The foregoing discussion of the problem of how coherence can be shown to be truth-conducive suggests the following questions: (i) How should we characterize the relation between coherence and truth? In which framework, realist, anti-realist, or otherwise, do we have better prospects of satisfactorily meeting the truth objection against coherentism? (ii) All the accounts of coherence discussed so far assume that an argument to the effect that coherence is truth-conducive is required for coherentist standards of justification to be themselves justified. But, what justifies this assumption? Are there any other arguments on the basis of which coherentist standards of justification could be justified?

114 Thagard (2007b: 31–32).
115 Lycan (2012: 18).

## A. Coherence: The Way to Truth

None of the arguments for the truth-conduciveness of coherence that have been presented so far seem conclusive. On the one hand, two realist strategies can be distinguished: (i) the introduction of an externalist element in the coherentist account of justification, eg Lehrer; and (ii) the appeal to some instance of inference to the best explanation, eg BonJour and Thagard. The very same project of developing an externalist version of coherentism, on which the first strategy depends, seems to undermine the motivation of coherence theories. For, as BonJour has argued, if externalism were an option, one would not need to get into the muddy waters of coherentism, in the first place.[116] The second realist strategy does not seem to work either, since it seems viciously circular to appeal to inference to the best explanation to justify coherentist standards of justification, given that the concept of 'best explanation' crucially includes criteria of coherence.

On the other hand, non-realists' solutions to the problem of connecting truth with coherence depend on some kind of conceptual relation between truth and justification. Indeed, this line of argument does provide an answer to the question of how the truth-connection may be effected, but at the price of buying an epistemic account of truth, which is, as I have argued, problematic for various reasons.

Davidson's argument for the truth-conduciveness of coherence—which arguably overcomes the realist-anti-realist dichotomy—turns out to depend on a number of assumptions about interpretation that are highly controversial (that meaning and belief attribution are holistic and normative) and on a transcendental argument (the argument of the omniscient interpreter) the legitimacy of which is more than doubtful. Moreover, Davidson's approach presents an additional problem. Even if one accepted his views on interpretation as well as the omniscient interpreter argument, it still remains to be shown that Davidson's argument is one that shows that coherence is truth-conducive, and not one that merely shows that there is a presumption in favour of the truth of a belief that belongs to any system of beliefs. According to this reading of Davidson, it is coherence with a 'significant mass of beliefs'—in Davidson's words—that carries with it a presumption of truth. But, since for a belief to be such it must be connected in a dense pattern of belief, there is no possibility for a belief to fail to cohere with *some* belief system. Hence, it is not clear why, in this view, one should

[116] Williams also takes commitment to internalism to be essential to coherentism. In his view, externalism breaks the essential link between local and global justification, which is a basic tenet of coherence theories of justification. The reason is that local justification presupposes global justification (as the coherentist claims) only if justification requires cognitive access to the reasons on which such justification depends. See Williams (1996: 295). *Cf* Lehrer (2000a) (discussed in ch 3) as well as Goldberg (2012).

regard justification as a matter of coherence, or coherence as an indicative of truth, any more than any other property that a belief system must, according to this view, exhibit.[117]

Last, attempts to relate coherence and truth *via* the notion of probability—rather than through the concept of belief, as Davidson does—have proved unsuccessful, in light of the impossibility results that show that not even under favourable conditions does a higher degree of coherence imply a higher likelihood of truth.

That there are no conclusive arguments for the truth-conduciveness of coherence is, no wonder, a discouraging result for anyone who endorses a coherentist view of justification. Nonetheless, these results do not prevent coherentism from being a plausible theory of justification. First, it is no surprise that the coherentist efforts to conclusively refute scepticism have not been successful. After all, in this regard, other epistemic theories of justification do not seem to be better off. In addition, the legitimacy of cohererentist standards of justification, as I will argue below, does not exclusively depend on the ability to show that coherence and truth are connected in the right way. There are other reasons, besides truth-conduciveness, on the basis of which standards of justification can be justified.

### B. Metajustification without Truth

To be sure, truth is an important value in epistemology, as well as (at least in some views) in other domains, such as ethics. Nonetheless, the relevance of truth should not obscure the fact that other goals are also significant in both scientific and moral inquiry. For example, speed and efficacy are important cognitive goals, and fairness is without doubt pivotal in moral and legal justification. Hence, the metajustification of standards of justification (coherentist or otherwise) does not exclusively depend on whether those standards can be shown to be truth-conducive, but also on the extent to which these standards promote the achievement of important goals in a given domain. In this regard, coherentist criteria of justification seem to be in a reasonably good position. The coherence of our beliefs, as much as the coherence of our plans, seems to be an important condition of the efficient role that beliefs and plans play in both the theoretical and the practical domain.[118] As explained above, coherence among beliefs have been shown to be conducive to reliability as well as confirmation. It is also widely accepted that coherence is, at least, an essential ingredient of any reasonable

[117] A similar point is made by Sosa. Sosa argues that, in Davidson's theory, coherence is epistemically superfluous. In fact, Davidson's arguments, in Sosa's view, would equally uphold foundational reliability. Sosa (1986a: 396).

[118] See Harman (1980).

view of formal justice and that it is instrumental to a number of important practical goals, such as coordination or efficacy.[119]

Not only does coherence help us realize a number of epistemic and practical goals besides the (controversial) goal of truth, but there are also a number of reasons why coherentist standards of justification are attractive. Among others, coherentist standards of justification have the resources to account for the role that emotions play in both theoretical and practical reasoning;[120] these standards are also well equipped to model the dynamic and social aspects of justification;[121] and they play an important constitutive role in both individual political identity.[122]

In addition to this positive justification of coherentism, two other kinds of negative justification may be adduced. First, as long as the formidable problems of foundationalism are not solved, there are good reasons for seeking out alternative accounts of epistemic justification, such as coherence theories of justification. And secondly, provided that descriptive issues are relevant to normative matters, 'hardness arguments',[123] which are based on the idea that other types of justification, eg probabilistic reasoning, are just too difficult for us to do, can also be used for justifying coherentist criteria of justification. If, in addition, one takes into account the increasing number of empirical studies that lend support to the thesis that coherence-based patterns of inference are used in much scientific and ordinary reasoning, one has still a further reason (and one that does not depend either on the problematic truth-conduciveness of coherence) for justifying coherentist standards of justification.[124]

## V. CONCLUSIONS

One of the main objections that have been addressed against coherence theories of justification is that there does not seem to be an appropriate connection between coherence and truth. There are a number of strategies that attempt to show that this objection may be successfully met. On the realist side, some philosophers have tried to connect up coherence and truth by means of an explanatory inference (eg BonJour and Thagard), while others have effected this connection by adding an externalist dimension to coherentism (eg Lehrer). From an anti-realist framework, the argument

[119] See eg Neil MacCormick's views on justice and coherence, in ch 1. On the claim that coherence promotes a number of important values in the practical domain, see ch 7.

[120] See Thagard ((2000a: 165–223) and (2003)). See also ch 4, for a discussion of Thagard's views on emotion and coherence.

[121] On the dynamic aspects, see Haack (2000). On the social dimensions, see Mercier (2012).

[122] See Hurley (1989). See also ch 7 for a discussion of Hurley's views.

[123] See Millgram (1991).

[124] I shall give a thorough account of the reasons for coherence in ch 10.

for the truth-conduciveness of coherence depends on forging a conceptual relationship between truth and justification. These strategies, as argued, do not provide conclusive reasons for believing that beliefs accepted by virtue of their coherence are also likely to be true.

Davidson's strategy for connecting up coherence and truth does not fit well within either realism or anti-realism, but is rather grounded on a particular view about how belief, truth and meaning relate to each other. According to Davidson, from his theory of interpretation, it follows that there is a presumption in favour of the truth of a belief that coheres with a system of beliefs. The main arguments for this thesis, however, the omniscient interpreter argument and the argument from the causal dependence of belief content, as shown, are controversial for a number of reasons. Hence, while Davidson's strategy seems to circumvent the main problems besetting efforts to show that coherence leads to truth as correspondence as well as the main objections that may be raised against coherence theories of truth, it also fails to satisfactorily solve the problem of the truth-conduciveness of coherence.

Finally, recent efforts to address the problem of the connection between coherence and truth by using the tools of probabilistic theory, more specifically, Bayesianism, have shown that coherence is not truth-conducive in a *ceteris paribus* sense in restricted scenarios, where sources are assumed to be initially credible as well as independent. Even if, as argued, there are several ways in which the proponent of a coherence theory of justification may avert the threat of these results, these results show the serious difficulties involved in establishing a relation between coherence and truth.

However, I have argued that from the fact that all these attempts to relate coherence and truth face severe problems it does not follow that the case for the justification of coherentist standards of justification is doomed to failure, as the metajustification of standards of justification does not exclusively depend on their truth-conduciveness but also on the extent to which they help us realize a number of important goals other than truth. I shall aim to articulate a justification of the coherentist standards of justification which is not based exclusively on the controversial truth-conduciveness of coherence in chapter ten. But before addressing the issue of how coherentist standards of justification may themselves be justified, we still need to complete the discussion of coherence theories of justification. Until now, I have examined the role that coherence plays in justification in the theoretical domain. An analysis of the place of coherence in justification in the practical realm is still due. This will be the task for the following two chapters.

# 7

# *Practical Coherence*

THIS CHAPTER EXPLORES the role of coherence in practical reasoning. Practical reasoning is reasoning about what to do, as opposed to theoretical reasoning, the point of which is to figure out what to believe.[1] The study of practical reasoning has been a rapidly changing area of study, in which largely new views—among them, coherentist views—have been recently proposed.[2] A crucial issue in contemporary research on practical reasoning is that of determining what the right forms for practical inference are, that is to say, what inference patterns are legitimate methods for arriving at decisions, intentions to act, judgements about what to do, plans and other practical antecedents of action.[3]

The received answer to this question is instrumentalism, the view that practical inference is a kind of means-end reasoning.[4] Several problems arise from considering that means-end reasoning is the only legitimate pattern of practical inference. A main problem is that the instrumentalist account makes ultimate ends come out arbitrary and places them beyond the reach of deliberation, despite the common sense evidence that we do deliberate about ends. Several alternatives to instrumentalism have been proposed with a view to answering the question of what inference patterns other than means-ends reasoning we employ when deliberating about what to do. Some theorists have answered this question by appealing to coherence. That is, some think of practical reasoning as coherence-driven reasoning. In this view, practical inferences that lead one to increase the coherence of

[1] For the differences, similarities and relations between practical and theoretical reasoning, see Harman (1995: 77–78). See also Audi (1989: 102–06). Audi (2001) provides a systematic treatment of the structure of rationality with a particular focus on similarities and relations between theoretical and practical rationality.

[2] For an overview of the state of the field over the 1980s and 1990s, see Millgram (2001). For an overview of earlier work, see Raz (1978).

[3] Millgram (2001: 2).

[4] Hume gives an earlier expression of the instrumentalist view. For an introduction to Hume's views and the instrumentalist conception of practical reasoning, see Audi (1989) ch 2. Expected utility theory, the standard decision theory in some interpretations, is read as providing a formal expression of the instrumentalist approach, where the agent's goal is to maximize his expected utility.

one's practical commitments are legitimate, and the practical conclusions that they yield, justified.

There are several theories of practical reasoning that take coherence to be the crucial standard for assessing the legitimacy of our practical inferences. These coherence-based theories of practical reasoning share a number of important features. Most importantly, they take a holistic stance towards practical justification, denying the instrumentalist tenet that it must be grounded in desires that are beyond the scope of deliberation. Nonetheless, there are important differences among them, and thus they cannot be said to constitute a unified alternative. Coherence-based theories of practical reasoning differ in three important respects: what one's practical commitments, eg ends, norms, values, goals etc are, such that coherence with them yields practically justified conclusions; what practical coherence is supposed to consist in; and in which ways the structure of practical inference should be understood.

In this chapter, I shall examine three different coherence-based models of practical reasoning.[5] First, specificationism holds that practical reasoning consists, at least partly, in specifying ends and norms in a way that enhances coherence. Such coherence is a matter of gradations of practical conflict and mutual support among one's ends and norms. Secondly, cased-based theories claim that deliberation importantly proceeds case by case in a way that preserves coherence across analogous cases. Last, explanatory approaches to practical reasoning take practical inference to be an inference to the most coherent plan. Coherence, in this view, consists in the satisfaction of a number of positive and negative constraints that result from relations among one's goals and actions. Thus, these proposals put forward different views about what practical coherence amounts to and what kind of inference pattern best captures the way in which we deliberate about what to do.

An important question is pending in the background of this debate: why should coherence among one's practical commitments be sought in the first place? Why should such enhancement of coherence be a reason for accepting a practical conclusion? Some coherentist theorists have engaged to a limited extent in this second-order debate. In the course of reviewing the most relevant coherentist positions, I shall contrast the different strategies that these theorists have employed in order to argue for a coherence-based view of practical reasoning.

[5] For an earlier and suggestive account of the relevance of coherence in practical reasoning, the details of which I shall not deal with here, see Harman (1986: 77 and 82–84). I will also set aside some instrumentalist theories that give coherence a prominent role, such as expected utility theory and informed desires theories.

## I. SPECIFICATIONISM

### A. Specificationism, Application and Balancing

Specificationism is the view according to which practical reasoning must consist partly in specifying an agent's ends and norms. Specificationism is an alternative to the instrumentalist view that all practical reasoning is means-end reasoning. Against instrumentalism, specificationists argue that some ends, such as 'happiness', a 'good constitution of a political body', or 'to live up to my ideal of success', are just too vague and indefinite to serve as starting points for means-ends reasoning. Thus, practical reasoning must involve deliberation not only about means, but also about ends. In particular, we need to further specify the indefinite ends so that they can serve as starting points for means-ends reasoning. The early pivotal papers on specificationism were by Kolnai and Wiggins.[6] Richardson has further developed the specificationist proposal in three important respects. First, he offers a detailed definition of the operation of specification. Secondly, he advances an additional reason for specifying ends.[7] Many of our norms (or ends) conflict, but often we may remove the conflict by specifying them. Last, he addresses a crucial issue in the specificationist agenda, that of marking out what distinguishes rational specifications from irrational, or incorrect, specifications, ie the so-called 'problem of normative control'.[8] Since, in any instance of specificatory reasoning, the less definite starting points do not constrain the more specific conclusions, the question arises as to what makes some of the specifications right and others wrong.[9] Richardson has addressed this issue by invoking the notion of coherence.[10] In Richardson's view, a specification is rational to the extent that it enhances the coherence of the agent's practical commitments.[11] Thus, this version of specificationism is, in an important sense, a coherentist one.

Richardson's coherentist account of conflict resolution is meant to be an alternative to both 'deductive application' and 'balancing'. Deductive application and balancing are, in his view, the two dominant models about

[6] Wiggins (1980) and Kolnai (1978). Wiggins attributes the specificationist view to Aristotle, while Kolnai develops specificationism as an alternative to the Aristotelian view.

[7] Richardson (1994). Richardson (1990: 279–310) focuses on the specification of norms.

[8] Furthermore, Broadi has argued that specification cannot be properly understood as reasoning, given that the conclusions of such a train of thought have more content than its premises, the relation between them cannot be inferential. See Broadi (1987: 238).

[9] See Millgram (1994: 504).

[10] Millgram's suggestion that specification relies essentially on practical experience may be understood as an alternative solution to the problem of normative control. According to Millgram, practical experience may provide the propositions required for successfully building inferential links between the initial ends and their specifications. See Millgram (1997: 136–38).

[11] The coherentist aspect of Richardson's view may have an antecedent in Kolnai, who briefly mentions 'consonance' as a factor in arriving at more concrete specifications of one's ends. See Kolnai (1978).

how to bring potentially conflicting norms to bear on a concrete practical problem. In the model of application, rules reach down cases by deductive inference that subsumes the case under a rule.[12] According to the balancing model, we respond to value conflict by intuitive weighing or balancing the importance of the values or norms involved.[13] These two models seem to exhaust the possibilities for bringing norms and ends to bear on concrete practical issues. The reason for such an appearance is the claim, which is taken for granted in most of the literature on decision theory and practical reasoning, that value commensurability is a prerequisite of rational choice. The power of this idea should be located, according to Richardson, in a particular ideal of the practical system as a deductive hierarchy. In this view, practical conflicts must be settled by appeal to a principle of superior validity. If value commensurability does not obtain, and thus if there are no higher order rules that could rationally settle the conflicts, then we must fall back on intuition. Richardson argues that either way the initial set of norms and ends is held fixed and beyond the scope of deliberation, and either must contain priority rules that resolve the conflict or be supplemented by intuitive balancing to determine which norm overrides.

Richardson argues that neither of these two models is satisfactory. On the one hand, the model of application is based on a pyramidal ideal of practical theory that is unattainable. In this view, all practical justification flows, via deduction, from some general principles on the basis of which conflicts are to be adjudicated. However, he claims, the ideal of solving conflicts by appealing to a higher authority is mistaken because it jumps together two features, generality and warrant, that in fact vary independently. For example, some of the normative judgements that stand most firm are quite concrete, eg about the evil of the Holocaust. On the other hand, the balancing model is not satisfactory either for it unduly restricts the scope of rationality in practical reasoning. Intuitive weighing places the decision beyond the pale of justification, leaving the reasons for the decision unarticulated.

Fortunately, in Richardson's view, these two models are not the only alternatives available because, in contrast to what is generally assumed, commensurability is not a prerequisite of rational choice. Commensurating, argues Richardson, is not the only way to rationally systematize. In place of an ideal of practical theory as a hierarchical structure, Richardson proposes a holistic structure for practical theory. A coherence ideal is put forward by Richardson as an alternative picture of how we may systematize our

[12] An exemplar of a deductivist approach is Sidgwick (1981).

[13] According to Richardson, in teleological versions, values are balanced, as in Nagel (1979). In non-consequentialist versions, principles are balanced, as in Bradley (1927). Most influential approaches are hybrids that combine the balancing view with an appeal to elements of the model of application. Richardson critically examines Ross' account of prima facie duties as an exemplar of these models in (1990: 288–90) and (1994: 36–37).

practical commitments in a way that allows us to rationally cope with practical conflicts in the face of value incommensurability. On Richardson's proposal, when our norms conflict, instead of trying to figure out which of the norms will override or intuitively balance one against the other, we should specify them so that they cohere with each other. I shall now explain what this operation of specification amounts to and how Richardson defines the coherence standard by which we may distinguish correct specifications from incorrect specifications. I will conclude this section by presenting Richardson's arguments for the rationality of pursuing coherence among our practical norms.

## B. The Relation of Specification

As we have seen, Richardson's proposal is structured around the idea that practical reasoning must consist partly in making a norm (or an end) more specific. Specification is a relation that holds between two ends or norms, the initial norm or end and its specification.[14] The model of specification supposes that the norms to which we are committed are typically not absolute. A schematic example of a logically absolute end-norm is the following:

(i) Everything necessary to achieve end *E* is to be done.

The logically universal form of this absolute end norm is as follows:

(i') For all actions *x*, if doing *x* is necessary to achieving end *E*, then *x* is to be done.

A non-absolute norm would implicitly begin with a 'generally speaking' instead of 'always' or 'for all actions.' For example:

(i*) For most actions *x*, if doing *x* is necessary to achieving end *E*, then *x* is to be done.

For specification to be possible, it must be the case that the norms being specified are not 'absolute'. As Richardson explains, there are two possible results of an operation of specification: either the more specific norm stands alongside the initial norm or else it replaces it. In the first case, if the initial norm were absolute, then the specification would be otiose, since it would be already implied by the initial norm. For example, if we begin with 'it is always wrong to lie', then 'it is wrong to lie to someone who has the right to truth' would be redundant. In the latter case, if the more specific norm that replaces the one it specifies were absolute, the result would be an implied

[14] Richardson thinks of ends as embedding a normative element. Because of that, he shifts back and forth between speaking of ends and norms. When presenting Richardson's view, I will also indistinctively refer to the specification of either norms or ends. See Richardson (1994: 50).

exception that would be logically incompatible with the initial norm's universal command, making it difficult to see in which sense the latter norm is a specification of the original one. For example, if we begin with 'it is always wrong to lie', and we replace it for 'it is right to lie to someone who is in danger if the truth is not spoken', which is logically incompatible with the initial norm, then the initial commitments are not honoured, but set aside. Thus, the model of specification demands that one suppose that the norms and ends being specified are not logically absolute. This supposition, argues Richardson, poses no difficulty, since the norms and ends to which we are commonly committed are typically qualified, at least implicitly, by variants of 'generally' or 'for the most part'.

Before getting into the details of Richardson's definition of specification, I will introduce some of his definitions of preliminary notions. The first one is that of 'absolute counterpart'. Although the model of specification supposes that norms and ends are not absolute, Richardson finds it convenient to define the relation of specification by reference to absolute versions of these norms that can have well-defined and bivalent conditions of satisfaction. The 'absolute counterpart' of an end-norm of the form of (i*) is one that restores it to the form of (i') by replacing the hedging 'for most actions' with the absolute 'for all actions'. For example, the absolute counterpart of the end-norm 'generally, do whatever is required for moral perfection' is 'always do whatever is required for moral perfection'. The way in which the satisfaction of the absolute counterpart of an end-norm is to be understood depends, according to Richardson, on the 'type' of norm involved. That is, it depends on whether the norm at stake is an end, a permission, a requirement or a prohibition. An 'instance' of an absolute norm is an alternative action that satisfies it. For example, an instance of an end is an example of an action that achieves it, eg to cultivate one's intellectual virtues is an instance of the end of achieving moral perfection.

On the basis of these notions, Richardson defines 'specification' as follows:

End-norm *p* is a specification of end-norm *q* (or specifies *q*) if and only if:

(a) every possible instance of the absolute counterpart of *p* would count as an instance of the absolute counterpart of *q* (in other words, any act that satisfies *p*'s absolute counterpart also satisfies *q*'s absolute counterpart);
(b) *p* qualifies *q* substantively (and not just by converting universal quantifiers to existential ones) by adding clauses describing what the action or end is or where, when, why, how, by what means, by whom or to whom the action is to be done or the end is to be pursued; and
(c) none of these added clauses in *p* is substantively irrelevant to *q*.[15]

[15] Richardson (1994: 72).

This definition sets out in a relatively precise way the relation in which the specified norm stands to the initial norm. Clause (a) establishes a semantic condition of extensional narrowing. By means of this clause, Richardson enables specification to be defined in terms of the ordinary notion of containment, but without requiring that it proceed from absolute norms. This clause allows us to rule out making an exception by disjunction. That is, a norm that says 'generally speaking, when I have received great benefits from someone that were not simply my due, I am to do whatever is necessary to express my gratitude to him or her' cannot be specified to read 'generally speaking, when I have received great benefits from someone that were not simply my due, I am to do whatever is necessary either to express my gratitude to him or her or to surreptitiously aiding his or her child'. Clause (b) makes clear in what sense the operation of specification goes beyond the subset requirement of clause (a), ruling, for instance, that a move from 'torture is always wrong' to 'torture is sometimes wrong' is not a specification. This clause adds a syntactic condition of glossing the determinables, ruling that for a specification to be such it must set out substantive qualifications that add information about the scope of applicability of the norm or the nature of the act or end enjoined. For example, 'euthanasia is generally right' might be specified by 'it is generally right to shut off the respirator of a patient in an irreversible coma'. Last, clause (c) rules out some forms of specification by conjunction. For instance, it blocks taking 'to promote the health of one's patients and to write a great opera' as a specification of the end of promoting the health of one's patients, since writing an opera is irrelevant to the patient's health.[16]

The operation of specification, as defined above, aims at resolving conflicts among our ends and norms by modifying the initial ends and norms in a way that meets certain conditions. Richardson illustrates the operation of specification by means of the following example.[17] Consider a course of deliberation about whether to withhold nutrition and hydration from a severely malformed newborn so as to let him die. In this case there are at least three principles in contention: (1) a prohibition on directly killing innocent people (here, the newborn); (2) a duty to respect the reasonable choices of parents regarding their children (let us suppose that in this hypothetical case the parents want the child to die); and (3) a duty to benefit the persons over whom one has responsibility (here, from the point of view

[16] It is important to notice that Richardson plugs into the definition of specification a notion of 'substantive' relevance as opposed to 'practical' relevance. In his view, every norm may be practically relevant to every other because of the possibility of contingent conflicts between them. For instance, one might imagine a situation in which the fact that I write an opera is not practically irrelevant to my taking care of my patients, because of, for example, time constraints or scheduling conflicts.

[17] Richardson (1990: 303). For other detailed examples of specification, see Richardson ((1994: 171–74 and 212–17) and (2000: 300–02)).

of the medical personnel, the patients). The suggestion of the specification model is that we should not assume that the principles mentioned are all fixed in their content so that we must either balance one principle against the other or rank the principles in some lexical fashion that prohibits these trade-offs within certain ranges. Instead, we should revise the principles in order to resolve the conflict.

Richardson illustrates the foregoing idea in two ways, with a revision of a norm that is not itself a case of specification, and second, by a specification proper. Suppose, in a first step, that the deliberator examines her reasons for accepting (1), the prohibition on killing, and decides that it is a specification of a more general principle requiring respect for self-conscious life. Suppose also that the present case leads her to further specify (1) by reference to (3), the principle of benefit. As a result, she replaces (1) by (1'):

> It is generally wrong directly to kill innocent human beings who have attained self-consciousness, and generally wrong to kill human beings with the (genetic?) potential to develop self-consciousness who would not be better off dead, but it is not generally wrong directly to kill human beings who meet neither of these criteria.

Its explicit exception prevents (1') from being a specification proper of the original prohibition—it would be ruled out by clause (a) of the definition of specification, but it could still be defended as a specification of the underlying norm of respect for life, and as a norm that resolves many conflicts among the norms governing the treatment of defective newborns. Let us suppose, however, that the particular case at stake is one in which it does not appear that the baby would be better off dead. In these cases, there is still a clash between the revised principle (1') of respect for life and the principle (2) of parental choice. One could replace (2) by a specified principle (2') that restricts its scope of application, so as to obtain (2'): a duty to respect the reasonable choices of parents regarding their children so long as they respect the children's rights. The move from (2) to (2') would count as a proper specification. With (1') and (2') the conflict seems to be settled: there is no requirement, in this case, to respect parental choice since it would go against the child's right to life.

Therefore, Richardson's suggestion is that we resolve normative conflicts by revising norms.[18] Specification, claims Richardson, allows us to address

[18] One may question the extent to which the operation of specification actually revises the initial set of norms, or whether it merely expands such a set. As explained, Richardson distinguishes two possible outcomes of the operation of specification: either the specified norm stands alongside the original norm, or it replaces it. In the former case, it is clear that the operation of specification merely changes the set by addition. In the latter, the label of revision might be more appropriate. It is important to keep in mind, though, that specification does not result in thorough revisions of the initial set of norms, such as deleting a norm without replacing it by its specified version. Thus, the focus is more on tailoring the initial set of norms to solve concrete practical problems, than on truly modifying the norms that provide the

a problem that any theory that appeals to revision as a mode of conflict resolution must confront, to wit, the problem of what ensures that the outcome of a revision is, in any significant way, a revision or interpretation of the initial norm, and not a new norm.[19] Richardson refers to this problem as the 'question of stability',[20] to which I turn now.

## C. The Question of Stability

The model of specification is meant to provide a way for reasoning in the practical realm in a non-deductive fashion. As we have seen, Richardson claims that deductive hierarchies are not appropriate structures for practical reasoning. In his view, we need to turn to non-foundational, or holistic, structures to give an account of the way in which we may rationally solve practical conflicts. As opposed to deductive models, holistic theories of practical reasoning allow us to deal with value conflict by recommending the revision of the conflicting norms in a way that enhances coherence. Holistic proposals circumvent the problems of deductivism, but they have other problems in their turn. Most importantly, holistic models must face the problem of giving an account of what licenses us to assert that a modification of the original norm is still, in some significant sense, the same norm. That is, when norms conflict, revision seems to be called for, but the question arises as to whether in being revised these norms are really being overthrown, or set aside, instead of guiding action in any way. This 'question of stability', as Richardson calls it, is a crucial one, for it points to a core problem that coherentist models must address, to wit, the problem of how to guarantee a place for stable practical theory while allowing the thorough revisability of any norm that holism requires. In Richardson's view, this question remains unanswered by current holistic approaches to conflict resolution. While some coherentist approaches, such as Hurley's, place too much emphasis on theory to the detriment of revisability, others, such as

framework within which those problems are to be resolved. DeGrazia also seems to interpret the operation of specification as a non-revisionist one when he claims that an apt metaphor for describing the process by which norms get further specified is that of 'growth' and not one of 'revision'. The latter, he claims, would be appropriate for most common conceptions of reflective equilibrium. See DeGrazia (1992: 528).

[19] There are, claims Richardson, two kinds of interpretation: revisions that go in the direction of greater abstractness and those that go in the direction of greater concreteness. Specification is one of four modes of interpreting norms so as to make them more concrete. The other three modes are: moves that narrow without glossing, moves that gloss without narrowing, and sharpening. See Richardson (2000: 287–91).

[20] See Richardson (1990: 291).

Dewey's, allow an unrestricted scope for revisability at the cost of unduly neglecting the role of theoretical continuity in deliberation.[21]

The relation of specification, claims Richardson, provides a way to preserve theoretical continuity despite revisability by laying out conditions between the initial norm and the more specific norm that is brought to bear in practice (ie the conditions formulated in the definition of specification) which explain how the original commitments are honoured. The notion of an instance of a general norm's absolute counterpart enables one to clearly set out what has remained untouched by the process of revision. In this way, the model of specification, unlike other coherentist proposals, allows us to distinguish the 'progressive refinement of a theory that remains the same in its essentials from the mere shifting from one holistic equilibrium to another'.[22] Thus, specificationism, claims Richardson, provides an alternative to the model of application which, nonetheless, satisfactorily addresses the question of stability that remains unanswered in other holistic views by recognizing the relevance of both theory and revisability in practical reasoning.

## D. A Coherentist Standard of Practical Rationality

So far we have seen in what respects, in Richardson's view, the model of specification has advantages over the model of application as well as over other coherentist models. Now, if there were no rational constraints on specification, it would be hard to see why the specification model should be preferred to the balancing model. Richardson proposes a coherence standard for the rationality of specification. He writes, 'A specification is rationally defensible so long as it enhances the mutual support among the set of norms found acceptable upon reflection'.[23] Unlike the operation of balancing, or weighing, the ideal of 'reflective coherence' provides, claims Richardson, an alternative model for rationally settling conflicts among our norms. Richardson explicates this coherence standard as follows: 'Building coherence among one's norms and ends is a matter of finding or constructing intelligible positive connections or links or mutual support among them and of removing relations of opposition or conflict'.[24]

Hence, two elements are relevant to the coherence standard: absence of practical conflicts and mutual support. 'Practical conflicts', ie conflicts

[21] Susan Hurley presents her theory of practical reasoning in Hurley (1989). I shall examine Hurley's views in the next section of this chapter. On Dewey's view on this subject, see Dewey ((1979), (1983), and (1988)). Richardson compares these two approaches with his own (1994: 159–69).

[22] Richardson (1994: 171).

[23] Richardson (1990: 302).

[24] Richardson (1994: 144).

about what one ought to do, occur when the agent is faced with norms whose joint satisfaction is impossible. These conflicts vary in strength, which depends on gradations of necessity. Thus, the degree of practical conflict depends on the sense in which satisfying two norms is 'impossible' for an agent. Richardson proposes the following scale for the strength of practical conflicts, in order of increasing distance from true logical impossibility:[25]

(a) conceptual impossibility (eg being a married bachelor);
(b) physical impossibility (eg being in two places at the same time);
(c) impossibility given human nature;
(d) impossibility given the constraints of current technology; and
(e) improbability (of the form *p*, but probably not-*p*).

There are also other types of conflict that, though hard to place in this progression, are also relevant to the assessment of the degree of coherence among norms and ends:

(a) impossibility given time constraints;
(b) conflict in principle;
(c) conflict by tradition; and
(d) conflict given current laws and institutions.

Scheduling conflicts, commitment to conflicting principles, traditions, laws and institutions often give rise to practical conflicts.

The second notion that is crucial to the standard of coherence is that of 'mutual support'. The degree of coherence also depends on the strength of the positive connections among our normative commitments.[26] What does argumentative support amount to? Richardson holds that some kinds of mutual support are simple oppositions of the kinds of conflict already classified. For instance, to the physically impossible corresponds the physically necessary. However, in his view, other types are best examined independently from the idea of practical conflict. Richardson points out four of these:[27]

(a) Orderings of finality. Ordering one's norm as means to an end or as being sought one for the sake of another. This relation is, according to Richardson, the most important sort of connection among one's norms.
(b) Contingent synergy. Practical support can be contingent or even fortuitous, eg one can get a job offer in the same town where one's partner lives, allowing a move that serves both career and family relations.

[25] ibid, 145.
[26] On the need for this positive dimension of coherence in addition to the negative one, ie the absence of practical conflicts, see DeGrazia (1992: 529).
[27] Richardson (1994: 149).

(c) Explanatory support. Explanatory support among one's norms and ends is an essential tool for self-understanding. Explanatory relations are crucial for developing a coherent and unified conception of our practical commitments. Such a cohesive role importantly resembles the role that such relations play in relation to scientific theories.
(d) Narrative unity. Someone's ends can also cohere as elements of a life that makes sense as a story. In Richardson's view, it is unclear what narrative unity amounts to. It certainly overlaps with the notion of explanatory support. But the notion of narrative unity is also a matter of aesthetic considerations, such as balance, proportion or variety. In the same way as explanatory support, narrative unity can also contribute to one's self-conception even if from a less theoretical perspective.

Thus, in Richardson's view, practical coherence is a matter of gradations of conflict and mutual support. And it can be promoted in a variety of ways, by avoiding the different types of practical conflict and exploiting the diverse ways in which mutual support can be built. Such coherence provides the standard against which the rationality of the outcome of deliberation should be assessed. In Richardson's view, a deliberation that specifies norms (or ends) in a way that enhances the degree of practical coherence among one's normative commitments has a strong claim to rationality. I shall now examine the reasons why, according to Richardson, coherence may be taken to provide such a standard of rationality.

## E. The Value of Coherence

Why should coherence be built among our practical commitments? What is that makes coherence valuable? Richardson offers three arguments for the rationality of pursuing practical coherence, namely, the argument from coordination, the argument from happiness, and an argument to the effect that practical coherence is the central element of practical justification.[28] While the first two arguments are instrumental, and provide pragmatic reasons to build coherence among one's practical commitments, the latter argument supports the claim that coherence not only has an instrumental value, but also a regulative one.

[28] On the argument from happiness and the argument from coordination, see Richardson (1994: 152–58). On the argument to the effect that coherence is the central element of practical justification, see ibid, 174–83.

### *i. The Argument from Coordination*

Some degree of coherence is crucial for coordinating one's actions with others and with us. Bratman gives the following example:

> If I plan both to leave my car at home for Susan and also to drive my car to Tanner library, all the while knowing that I have only one car, I am unlikely to succeed in my effort at coordination.[29]

Nonetheless, he says that since these benefits must be balanced against the benefits of flexibility in one's planning, this argument supports only a moderate degree of practical coherence. If we turn from avoiding conflicts to building mutual support among one's ends and norms, the argument from coordination becomes weaker—claims Richardson. Unifying one's system of ends (or norms) is not always beneficial, for we do value diversity in our lives. In Richardson's view, the force of the argument must still be further qualified in relation to a distinction between 'coherence' and 'constancy'. Coherence, says Richardson, is the virtue of the whole system of norms at one time. In contrast, constancy is the virtue that applies to the system as it shifts through time.[30] Since constancy is also an important virtue for securing successful coordination, when assessing the pragmatic benefits of coherence, it is important that we separate out what is due to constancy. A further distinction between 'systemic coherence' and 'connectedness', claims Richardson, is also relevant here. Systemic coherence requires that all of an agent's practical commitments be mutually supportive or at least non-conflicting; when only some subsets of them are, we rather speak of mere connectedness.[31] Whereas some degree of systemic coherence is surely necessary for coordination, both intrapersonal and interpersonal, it can also certainly survive a conflict, of any degree, between any two ends or norms.[32]

### *ii. The Argument from Happiness*

Richardson claims that coherent planning is constitutively linked to the ideas of happiness and unity of the self.[33] The pursuit of happiness (and of

[29] Bratman (1987: 31).

[30] Richardson (1994: 152). The distinction between 'coherence' and 'constancy' parallels the distinction between 'synchronic coherence' and 'diachronic coherence'.

[31] ibid, 154. The distinction seems to be one between 'local' and 'global' coherence.

[32] It is doubtful that both intrapersonal and interpersonal coordination can actually survive a conflict of *any* degree between *any* two ends and norms as Richardson claims. If the conflicting ends and norms are among the highest ranked, and the conflict is of a strong degree, then one has reason to suspect that coordination may not succeed at all. It may suffice to consider the consequences for such coordination that a conflict between two constitutional norms, or a conflict between two leading principles of action, may bring about.

[33] Hurley has argued that coherence plays a constitutive role in the self-determination of unified persons, see Hurley (1989: 262). The relevance of coherence for the unity of agency has also been defended by Millgram (1997: 51).

the vague goal of the unity of the self) is greatly aided by some degree of coherence among our ends and norms. Nonetheless, Richardson claims that this argument, like the argument from coordination, only supports some degree of coherence. The reason is that a demand for strong coherence, argues Richardson, is not built into the conception that most people have of their own happiness.[34] To require that it be so is to depart too radically from our conception of happiness.

### *iii. The Argument from Justification as Mutual Support*

In addition to the two foregoing arguments, Richardson provides a non-instrumental argument for the rationality of pursuing coherence when reasoning about what to do. According to Richardson, practical justification typically depends upon mutual support, which is, as has just been explained, the core positive dimension of coherence. He writes, 'Mutual support, holistically addressed, among the commitments that stand firm on reflection, is the main positive basis of practical justification'.[35] Hence, it is rational to pursue practical coherence, for, one might say, it is rational to aim at practically justified commitments. Richardson characterizes this coherentist view of practical justification by means of the following four characteristics:[36]

#### a. Bidirectionality

Practical reasoning is 'bidirectional' because, in building justificatory connections, it works both from the more general to the more specific and also in the other direction.

#### b. Revisability

Every norm is open to revision. Justification does not take for granted that any norm or end stands firm a priori. Richardson allows for (but does not assume) the possibility that some ends are self-evident. However, the status of any given end as self-evident is subject to rebuttal by the conflicts that arise between it and other ends. When two norms or ends conflict, their claim to self-evidence may be rebutted and they can be retained only after deliberation, not simply as self-evident. Thus, when norms conflict, we have

[34] Bittner has proposed that such a strong connection between coherence and happiness does hold in Bittner (1989) ch VI. According to Bittner, only plans that are coherent with one's projected happiness are good reasons for action. For a critique to Bittner's views on coherence and happiness, see Richardson (1994: 155–56).

[35] Richardson (1994: 176).

[36] On the main characteristics of this coherence ideal see, ibid, 140–42 and 176–78.

reason to revise any of them and in any direction in order to enhance the mutual support that is required for justification.

### c. Holism

According to Richardson, justification is holistic in two related senses. To start with, by 'holism' he refers to the absence of segmentation and a mutual relevance of all members of a whole. Since any two principles can come into practical conflict, mutual support must be built between any two principles. This rules out any strong partitioning of the agent's norms into mutually irrelevant sets, so that coherence is pursued only within each part. Any practical commitment is potentially relevant to the revision of any other. In addition, the assessment of coherence requires, in the ideal, a survey of the whole system of norms.[37]

### d. Reflective Sovereignty

By 'reflective sovereignty', Richardson refers to a central feature of justification, to wit, that it 'looks to no other authority than the deliberating agent'.[38] The idea of reflective sovereignty expresses Richardson's commitment to a view of deliberation that gives an essential role to critical reflection. As opposed to the pyramidal ideal of practical theory, in which conflicts are solved by appealing to a higher authority, Richardson puts forward an ideal of deliberation as critical reflection. When deliberating, rather than appealing to some norm or end of highest authority, the deliberator retains the authority to accept or reject a revision of any of her norms or ends. Such a revision is carried out by searching for coherence among the practical commitments that stand firm for her on reflection.

According to Richardson, this idea of justification as mutual support is exemplified by Rawls' notion of reflective equilibrium.[39] Nevertheless, this notion, Richardson argues, should be modified to fully capture the prominent place that emotions and perceptions have in deliberation. Emotions and perceptions play several roles in individual deliberation. To start with, emotionally informed perceptions of the particulars of an agent's situation are crucial in deliberation. Sensitive perception is required to see what values are at stake, what problems for action one must face and what possibilities are available. Emotion often heightens and directs our attention

[37] This proposal involves a high degree of idealization and this sheds doubts as to whether it makes practical justification unattainable for human agents. As I have already noted, similar problems arise in relation to holistic models of epistemic justification. For a discussion of the problems of holism about epistemic justification, see ch 3. On the problems of holism in legal reasoning about both norms and facts, see chs 1 and 2, respectively.

[38] Richardson (1994: 177).

[39] For an extensive discussion of the method of reflective equilibrium, see ch 8.

towards the most important aspects of the deliberator's situation. For example, fear can focus our mind, helping us detect ways to escape and get out of a dangerous situation. In addition, emotions are important clues to one's normative commitments. The emotions elicited by some ethical or practical problem are essential sources of self-awareness, since they help to make us aware of what our practical commitments really are. Last, emotions are sometimes not only important for fully expressing our commitments, but they are also an input to deliberation in their own right.

Thus, Richardson argues that emotion and perception must be included in the set of items among which reflective coherence is sought. Rawls's notion of 'considered judgement' is meant to capture constraints on the inputs of reflective equilibrium. When Rawls characterizes this notion, he seems to be suggesting that emotion must be set aside for judgements to be 'considerate'. However, claims Richardson, since emotion is an important source of self-awareness, to set it aside may obstruct the proper articulation of our considered judgements. Moreover, some of them can only find an emotional expression. Richardson proposes to broaden the notion of reflective equilibrium to embrace emotionally guided perception of the particulars of the situation and emotionally guided awareness of one's normative commitments, creating what he calls 'extended reflective equilibrium'.[40] When such equilibrium is achieved, reflective coherence emerges, and the outcome of practical reasoning is properly justified.[41]

## F. Rationality, Coherence and Commensurability

As we have seen, a main problem that specificationist views face is that of normative control. To recall, the problem of normative control is that of showing what makes some ways of specifying an end or a norm right and others wrong, given that there are many ways in which one can make an abstract end or norm more concrete. Richardson's coherentist version of specificationism aims to meet this challenge by appealing to a coherence standard. An objection may be raised against this sort of response to the problem of normative control, namely, that it succeeds in addressing this problem only if coherence is treated as a commensurating standard. But Richardson's proposal, it may be argued, builds on the assumption that value commensurability must not be seen as a prerequisite of rational

[40] On the idea of extended reflective equilibrium, see Richardson (1994: 183).

[41] The need to include emotions into the base of coherence (ie the set of elements the coherence of which is relevant for justification) has also been emphasized by Thagard. See below in this chapter at III.C.

choice.[42] Therefore, he cannot take coherence to be a *commensurans* on pain of contradiction, with the result that the problem of normative control remains unsolved. Richardson formulates this objection as follows:

> The problem is that there are all too many possible paths of specification that might be taken ... What kinds of reason can be given for specifying an end one way rather than another? The objector will urge that there are only two ways: either by looking to see which one maximizes coherence or else intuitively. Either way, he concludes, my attempt to make out a method of deliberating rationally without appeal to commensurability fails. If the choice between paths is made by maximizing coherence, then rationality is achieved by treating coherence as the commensurating end. If the choice between paths is made by a situation-specific intuition, then it is not made rationally. Is there a rational basis for determining which specification should be adopted?[43]

Richardson replies to this objection by claiming that the notion of coherence has the power to guide the deliberator down one path of specification rather than another. We can compare the systemic coherence of alternative paths without a precise or quantitative measure. Richardson argues that nothing in his account commits one to the idea that coherence is to be maximized, and some elements may pull against it. In particular, one of the main features of practical justification, to wit, reflective sovereignty, provides this account with the resources for meeting the objection. It is the deliberator, claims Richardson, who must settle the limits of systematization. The agent may block systematization in the name of some consideration that demands that one sticks to one's initial commitments even if they lead one to irresolvable conflict. Richardson refers to this counterweight to coherence as 'integrity', 'constancy' or 'conservatism'.[44]

At this point, an objector might interpret Richardson's views as follows: there are two prima facie principles of practical rationality, coherence maximization and integrity, so that when coherence guides us it does so as a commensurating standard, and when it clashes with integrity, we should decide by intuitively balancing these standards against each other. Richardson claims, however, that his proposal does not amount to defence of such a position. Deliberators, he argues, must approach higher-levels conflicts, such as the conflict between coherence and integrity, as they approach more concrete ones, namely, by specifying the norms or ends involved, eg the ideals of coherence and integrity themselves. In Richardson's view, there is no paradox in supposing that the coherence standard might itself be

[42] While the specificationist model does not presuppose value commensurability, nothing in the model of specification makes it incompatible with the existence of value commensurability. See Richardson (1994: 111).

[43] ibid, 175.

[44] This objection is very similar to what Hurley calls the 'problem of the authority of theory'. I shall discuss this problem later in this chapter, at s II.E.

subjected to revision so as to enhance the coherence of the deliberator's set of commitments. Since justification can flow from the bottom up, and not only from the top down, it may be possible for the deliberator to compare the mutual support offered by each interpretation of coherence over another without begging the question. In this way, argues Richardson, the ideal of practical coherence rationally—and not simply intuitively—guides deliberation without serving as a commensurating standard.

However, doubts may be raised as to whether the foregoing response satisfactorily addresses the problem of normative control. Even if it is granted that a choice between alternative paths of specification in terms of their contributions to practical coherence does not require that coherence be quantitatively measured, it is at least doubtful that Richardson's notion of practical coherence is specific enough to ensure that these judgements are not underdetermined—which is to say that the problem of normative control is not, after all, solved. The same difficulty arises when we move to higher-level conflicts, eg conflicts between coherence and integrity. For, one may still ask: how do we choose among different interpretations of the coherence standard? What makes some specifications right and others wrong? In complex cases, these judgements also seem to be underdetermined. For coherence to exercise normative control over the results of deliberation, it must be defined in a more detailed way. Thus, a more concrete notion of coherence is required for Richardson's proposal to solve the problem of normative control.[45]

## II. COHERENTIST CASE-BASED DELIBERATION

### A. The New Casuistry

The notion of coherence also plays a pivotal role in casuistry, a method of practical reasoning which, like specificationism, has its roots in Aristotle. In the 1980s, Jonsen and Toulmin called for a revival of this method as an alternative to the principle-based paradigm according to which moral theory (or, more generally, practical theory) operates on a set of rules and principles.[46] As opposed to the 'tyranny of principles', Jonsen and Toulmin defend an approach to deliberation that emphasizes its case-based nature. In this approach, deliberation importantly proceeds case by case. Instead of taking a set of rules and principles as a starting point, they suggest

[45] Millgram has also argued that Richardson's notion of coherence is not precise enough for the purpose of separating out right from wrong specifications in Millgram (1994: 504).

[46] Gert, Culver and Clouser take Richardson's specificationism to be 'a last ditch effort' to maintain a principle-based approach to practical reasoning. See Gert, Culver and Clouser (2000: 318).

that we start by clear 'paradigm' cases. In this view, the crucial task when deliberating consists in classifying cases on the basis of their similarities and differences with these paradigms, which serve to illuminate less clear cases by using argument by analogy.[47] The notion of coherence is used in this tradition as a standard against which to check the rationality of the decisions that result from this use of the analogy. An important criterion for the rationality of these decisions, it is held, is that they cohere among themselves. A sophisticated account of case-based deliberation that gives a crucial role to the notion of coherence is that of Hurley, on whose proposal I shall focus in the next pages.[48]

## B. Motivation for a Coherence Account of Deliberation

Hurley's coherentist approach to deliberation is meant to be an alternative to subjectivism about reasons for action. 'Subjectivism', argues Hurley, results from combining two views, namely, centralism and non-cognitivism. 'Centralism' about reasons for action holds that general concepts such as 'right' and 'ought' are conceptually prior and independent of specific reason-giving concepts, such as 'just' and 'unkind'. For instance, centralism about law would hold that the general concept of law is prior to and independent of specific legal concepts and principles, as determined by various specific legal practices. Hurley takes Hart's rule of recognition to be one such concept. 'Non-cognitivism' holds that evaluative concepts do not express beliefs that may be true or false, but they serve to express attitudes, in particular, preferences. Putting these two claims together we get the subjectivist view, ie the view that preferences (that general evaluative concepts express) are prior and independent from values (or specific reason-giving concepts) and that they determine values.

This subjectivist position is, argues Hurley, problematic for several reasons.[49] In its place, she defends objectivism about reasons for action, which is the denial of subjectivism so understood. More specifically, Hurley argues for a coherentist version of objectivism according to which values and preferences are, as a constitutive matter, interdependent. The crucial problem for this view is to give an account of what this interdependence consists of. And here is where the notion of coherence gets into the

[47] See Jonsen and Toulmin (1988).

[48] Hurley exposes her account of deliberation in Hurley (1989). In the next chapter, I shall examine Goldman's method of analogy and difference, which is a case-based method of moral reasoning that also relies heavily on the notion of coherence.

[49] Hurley directs arguments against the two main components of the subjectivist view, that is, centralism and non-cognitivism. For Hurley's arguments against centralism, see Hurley (1989: 20–28). She argues against non-cognitivism in ch 9 of (1989). For Hurley's critique of the subjectivist view that preferences determine values, see (1989) ch 6.

picture. Hurley proposes that specific reasons giving practices (values) and judgements about what to do relate to each other as subject matter does to theory. Which theory? The theory, which is sought in deliberation, that best displays as coherent the relationships among those values. More precisely, Hurley's coherentist version of objectivism holds that there is a conceptual relationship between judgements about what to do and specific values. The former are a function, what Hurley calls 'the coherence function', of the latter. Now I proceed to examine in some detail how Hurley characterizes this coherentist approach to deliberation.

## C. Deliberation as Theorizing

As stated, Hurley aims at providing a coherentist account of the interdependence between conflicting values and judgements about what should be done. The fundamental claim of such a coherentist account is that the relationships in question are those of subject matter to theory. That is, a coherence account holds that practical judgements about what should be done, all things considered, are responsible to theory.[50] In particular, they are responsible to the theory that best displays coherence among the several reasons that apply to the alternatives. As she puts it:

> [W]hen we say that a particular alternative would be right, it is part of what we mean that there is some theory which is the best theory about the specific values that apply to the alternatives at hand and that this theory favors a particular alternative.[51]

That is, part of what we mean by 'right' is decision in accord to such best theory. More specifically, Hurley states her coherentist account of the relationship between specific reasons and all-things-considered reasons as follows:

> [T]o say that a certain act ought to be done is to say that it is favored by the theory, whichever it may be, that gives the best account of the relationship among the specific reasons (such as ethical values, legal doctrines, and precedents) that apply to the alternatives in question.[52]

For example, consider the following practical problem, given by Sen:[53] Annapurna wants someone to clear up the garden, and three employers—Dinu,

[50] Putnam's critique of conventionalism—which, according to Hurley, legal positivism exemplifies—provides the starting point of Hurley's account of the relationship between reasons in conflict, on the one hand, and all-things-considered judgements, on the other. See Putnam (1975) and Hurley (1989: 189–93).

[51] ibid, 12.

[52] ibid, 225.

[53] Sen (1999: 55).

Bishanno and Rogini—want very much the job. Dinu is the poorest of the three, Bishanno is the unhappiest, and getting the job would relieve him of his predicament and Rogini is debilitated from a terrible disease that could be cured if he had the money. Annapurna wonders what she really should do. Deliberation about what ought to be done in this case would involve, according to Hurley's coherentist views, the development of a theory about 'income-poverty', 'happiness' and 'quality of life', on the basis of which the deliberator, in this case, Annapurna, would determine which value has priority in the particular situation, according to the weighted and qualified principles that figure in that theory.

Hence, the relation of interdependence between specific reasons and judgements about what ought to be done, all things considered, is the relation between theory, to be built in deliberation, and subject matter, ie the reasons whose relation is to be established by the theory. Such theory is represented by what Hurley calls the 'coherence function'. This function allows us to characterize the interdependence relation in a more precise way. All-things-considered reasons are claimed to be a function of the specific reasons that conflict in a particular situation. Such a function is the outcome of the theorizing activity that deliberation amounts to, and that deliberators strive for. As Hurley puts it:

> [T]he deliberator's task is to seek the ethical, or legal, theory that best displays coherence. Another way of putting this is to say that deliberation involves a process of constructing hypotheses about the content of a coherence function, which represents the theory sought in deliberation, and which takes us from alternatives ranked by specific reasons to all-things-considered rankings.[54]

Deliberation is thus a kind of theoretical activity that aims at coherence, more precisely, at the construction of a coherence function.[55] I turn now to examine the general structure of the deliberative process that leads to the construction of the coherence function that represents the theory sought in deliberation and on which the resolution of practical problems depends.

[54] Hurley (1989: 225).

[55] Hurley emphasizes that it is important to be clear about what her coherence theory commits one to accept. This coherence account claims that to say that a certain act ought to be done is to say that the theory that best displays coherence among the values that apply to the alternatives favours that alternative. Thus, this coherence account makes, as a conceptual matter, merely an existential claim about a theory, to wit, that there is some theory (represented by the coherence function) that best displays coherence, not which one it is. The latter is a substantive issue that is to be determined a posteriori by theoretical deliberation. See Hurley (1989: 225).

## D. The Structure of the Deliberative Process

Hurley illustrates the general structure of the kind of theorizing, or deliberation, that aims at coherence by means of a legal example, namely, the conflict between the doctrine of bargained-for consideration and the doctrine of estoppel in cases of gratuitous promises that induce reasonable-to-expect reliance.[56] The problem is as follows. Suppose that a promise is made gratuitously, and the promisee relies on it to his detriment, where the promise is of a kind such that the promisor should reasonably have expected it to induce action on the part of the promisee. Now, suppose the promisee sues the promisor for failing to fulfil the promise. Is the promisor under a legal obligation to the promisee or not? The common law doctrine of consideration requires an element of bargain or exchange to be present in order for a valid and enforceable contractual relationship to arise. Since the consideration requirement is not met, the promisor seems not to be under a contractual obligation. But he has acted irresponsibly in making and then breaking a promise that he should reasonably have expected to induce reliance. This makes him a wrongdoer, and there is a principle of law, the doctrine of estoppel, that prevents a party from taking unfair advantage of a predicament in which that party's own bad behaviour has placed his adversary. This doctrine seems to support holding that the promisor is stopped from asserting that his promise is not binding. What decision as to the promisor's liability is then favoured by the theory that best displays a coherent relationship between the consideration and estoppel doctrines? How should a legal decision-maker arrive at such a theory?

We may distinguish, according to Hurley, various stages in deliberation. These different stages are represented in what Hurley calls the 'deliberative matrix'. Through the process of deliberation we fill in the matrix until it is completed, as in the figure shown below. The *first stage* of deliberation consists in specifying the problem. This involves giving a description of the alternatives available. For example:

1: gratuitous promises that induce reasonable-to-expect reliance do give rise to liability.
-1: gratuitous promises that induce reasonable-to-expect reliance do not give rise to liability.

It also involves determining which reason-giving practices bear on the alternatives in question, and how they rank them. In the example, the doctrine of consideration (C) ranks -1 above 1, and the doctrine of estoppel (E)

[56] See ibid, 203–17. For an ethical illustration see ibid, 219–22. Hurley's account of deliberation is intended to be applicable to any practical problem about conflicting ends, whether it involves the conflicting interests of a single person, or the interests of many, as in the legal and ethical realm.

ranks them the other way around.[57] What reasons bear on the alternatives and how may not be clear. It requires us to develop perceptual capacities, through experience and education, in order to illuminate what is at stake in the first place.

When the reasons that bear on the alternatives conflict, as in our case, then we must go to the *second stage* of deliberation, at which we try to articulate the principles and purposes that inform each of the relevant reason-giving practices. In our example, the policy of encouraging business (B) provides a rationale for the doctrine of consideration. Business, it is held, would be positively discouraged by the enforcement of all promises, and the requirement of consideration provides a means of selectively enforcing promises. The estoppel doctrine is a procedural manifestation of the tort principle (T) that one ought to pay for the injuries one does to another, including the losses that others suffer in reasonable reliance of one's promises.

At the *third stage*, we collect data for theorizing about the relationships between the specific reason-giving practices by looking at other cases, either actual or hypothetical, on which the principles and purposes that figure in the problem at hand also have a bearing, and on which we hold settled judgements. In the problem at stake, Hurley considers three issues. The first is whether the normal measure of contractual damage should be expectancy or reliance, the former being supported by the settled law. This is actually the solution that is favoured by both the tort principle and the policy of encouraging business. Hurley cites Fuller and Perdue who hold that a general preference for the expectancy measure has the indirect effect of protecting promises against reliance losses as well as facilitating business agreements.

Secondly, she considers the hypothetical question of whether if gratuitous promises that induce reasonable-to-expect reliance do give rise to liability, the measure of damages in these cases should be expectancy or reliance. Fuller and Perdue suggest that the weight of the policy of encouraging business in favour of the expectancy measure is negligible in these cases, since they are generally made in personal contexts removed from the systems of credit and finance on which business depends. Thus, reliance seems an appropriate measure in these cases.

[57] It is worth noticing that Hurley uses favourableness to conflicting legal doctrines, in contrast to favourableness to the plaintiff or the defendant, as the basic means of organizing the data. In Hurley's view, the doctrine-oriented method of organizing data has certain advantages over the party-oriented one. Within a narrowly limited area of law, eg trade secrets law, plaintiffs typically represent one legal doctrine and defendants another. But when one comes to generalize, plaintiffs and defendants no longer represent particular legal doctrines. By organizing cases according to legal doctrines one can bring insights about the relationships between legal doctrines from one area of law to another in which the same doctrines apply. See Hurley (1989: 416) fn 24.

Last, she considers the issue, on which there are some actual cases, of whether, in contract cases that involve deceit and in which reliance losses exceed expectancy, the measure of damages should be expectancy or reliance. In these cases, the tort principle takes priority over the policy of encouraging business despite their relevance to business dealings. In Hurley's view, there are two reasons to think that the tort principle has also a special force in the gratuitous promise cases. First, in these cases the wrongdoing is more than merely contractual, and this makes them more like cases of deceit than like cases of simple breach of contract. Secondly, if the tort principle has added force against the principle of encouraging business in cases of deceit, there is more reason to think that it enjoys also a special force in cases that are removed from business dealings. Thus, the analysis of the third issue favours a reliance measure for damages in gratuitous promises that induce reasonable-to-expect reliance.

Hurley labels and describes the alternatives presented by these three issues as follows:

*ne*: the normal measure of contractual damage is expectancy.
*nr*: the normal measure of contractual damage is reliance.
*le*: if gratuitous promises that induce reasonable-to-expect reliance do give rise to liability, then the measure of damages in such cases is expectancy.
*lr*: if gratuitous promises that induce reasonable-to-expect reliance do give rise to liability, then the measure of damages in such cases is reliance.
*de*: in contract cases that involve deceit and in which reliance losses exceed expectancy the measure of damages is expectancy.
*dr*: in contract cases that involve deceit and in which reliance losses exceed expectancy the measure of damages is reliance.

The data collected at the third stage form the basis for the theorizing that we do at the *fourth stage*, the aim of which is to construct a hypothesis about the relationships between the conflicting reasons under various types of circumstances. This hypothesis is a partial specification of the coherence function, which tells us what the relative weights of the reasons in different circumstances are. Thus, this weighing function accounts for the information represented by the settled cases. The information represented in the first kind of issues, between *ne* and *nr*, tells us nothing about the relative weights of *B* and *T*, since both of them favour *ne*. *B* and *T* do conflict in the second issue over alternatives *le* and *lr*. Since the issue is resolved in favour of *lr*, we may conclude that there are at least some circumstances under which *T* outweighs *B*. A careful examination of the alternatives *le* and *lr* reveals that they can be characterized more fully by the following propositions:

*p*: the promises these cases involve are of a kind seldom made or relied on in the course of business.
*q*: these cases involve more than merely contractual wrongdoing.

Thus, a close scrutiny of *le* and *lr* suggests the following hypothesis about the relationship between *B* and *T*: *T* outweighs *B* when *p* and *q* obtain. This hypothesis may be refined by considering the third issue, between *de* and *dr*. This issue is resolved in favour of *dr*, thus, when *q* obtains *T*'s weight relative to *B* is increased, independently of *p*. We may also wonder whether *p* has the effect of diminishing the weight of *B* independently of the fact that *q*. This is interesting for, if the two effects operate in the absence of another, the total effect when both *p* and *q* obtain may be much greater. In order to answer this question we go back to the third stage, and look for another issue in which *B* and *T* conflict, but where *p*, but not *q* obtains. Hurley suggests that we consider the issue of whether, in suits brought by foster children for breach of contract to adopt, the measure of damages is expectancy (*fe*) or reliance (*fr*). In fact, this issue is settled in some jurisdictions in favour of reliance. Thus, the working hypothesis can still be further refined: *p* does have the effect of diminishing the weight of *B* relative to *T* independently of *q*. Thus, going back and forth between stages three and four, looking for settled and hypothetical cases helps to qualify our hypothesis about how *T* and *B* relate to each other. This process of theorizing is open-ended in that someone may come up with a new case or a more subtle analysis, and our theory may have to be further refined or even abandoned.[58]

In the *fifth stage*, we work out the implications of the best theory that we have been able to construct for the issue that we have to decide. The work done so far (and reflected in the second, third, fourth, and fifth arrows of the deliberative matrix) allows us to arrive at the following partial specification of the coherence function: when *q* obtains the weight of *T* relative to *B* is augmented and when *p* obtains the weight of *B* relative to *T* is diminished. Both circumstances characterize the cases that we have to resolve, namely, cases of gratuitous promises that induce reasonable-to-expect reliance. Those cases involve other than mere contractual wrongdoing and such promises are seldom made or relied on in the course of business. Thus, claims Hurley, we decide that in these cases the tort principle, which motivates the doctrine of estoppel, outweighs the policy of encouraging business, which motivates the doctrine of consideration, and thus, that promisors in these cases should be held liable. This coherence function represents the theory that makes best sense of the relationships about specific and conflicting reasons. Such theory, Hurley claims, is not given a priori, but is constructed through the process of deliberation.

[58] Thus, this reasoning is defeasible, as coherence-driven reasoning is mostly characterized. For an analysis of the relationship between coherence and defeasibility in legal reasoning, see ch 1.

This is the deliberative matrix in which Hurley represents the foregoing deliberative process:

| *C (... B...)* | *E (... T...)* | *Resolution* |
|---|---|---|
| -1<br>1 | 1<br>-1 | 1&p&q<br>-1&p&q |
| ne<br>nr | ne<br>nr | ne<br>nr |
| le&p&q<br>lr&p&q | lr&p&q<br>lr&p&q | lr&-p&q<br>le&p&q |
| de&-p&q<br>dr&-p&q | dr&-p&q<br>de&-p&q | dr&-p&q<br>de&-p&q |
| fe&p&-q<br>dr&p&-q | fr&p&-q<br>fe&p&-q | fr&p&-q<br>fe&p&-q |

**Figure 1: The Deliberative matrix.**

### E. Reasons in Deliberation: The Problem of the Authority of Theory

According to Hurley, there are at least three kinds of reasons that are operative in a deliberative process, such as the process which the foregoing legal example illustrates, to wit, 'deductive' reasons, 'practical' reasons and 'theoretical' reasons. First, deductive reasons can be used at any point. For example, the promisor employs deductive reasoning when he argues that only if the element of bargained-for-consideration is present does contractual liability arise; the element of bargained-for consideration is not present in the case at hand; therefore, contractual liability does not arise. Secondly, practical reasons—reasons for action or decision, as opposed to reasons for belief—are at the core of the deliberative process. For example, when I recognize that the element of bargained-for consideration is not present, or that an act would violate a right, I have a practical reason. Lastly, reasons of a theoretical nature operate in the process of deliberation at each stage. These reasons are reasons for beliefs about the relationships among specific practical reasons; for example, the reasons to believe that the doctrine of consideration enjoys a priority over the doctrine of estoppel under certain circumstances.

Hurley claims that there is an interplay between our specific reasons and our theorizing about the relationships among them. This view, as Hurley explicitly says, is in accordance with Rawls' two-way technique of reflective equilibrium. In particular, this account of deliberation seeks, in Daniels' terminology, 'wide' reflective equilibrium, the kind of equilibrium that brings theories into consideration.[59] She also puts her view in relation to Dworkin's views about the interplay between legal practices and the principles that figure in legal theories as well as to Wittgenstein's remarks on justification to the effect that it is not a single action or decision that gets justified, but whole systems of action and decision. Thus, Hurley's coherentist account of deliberation is, in an important sense, a holistic one.[60]

The relationship between theoretical reasons and reasons of other kinds gives rise to the following problem, which Hurley calls 'the problem of the authority of theory'.[61] Someone could be sceptical about the authority of the theory and ask why any set of ideas, or any structure of principles, should have any special authority over our sentiments and our inclinations just because it has the structure of a theory.[62] As an objection to Hurley's coherence account, this version of scepticism questions why one ought to do the action favoured by the theory that best displays coherent relationships among the conflicting values, rather than acting on one of the conflicting reasons the theory is about.[63]

According to Hurley, 'the solution to the problem of the authority of theory is to recognize that the supposed problem arises from demanding the impossible, namely, the elimination of conflict'.[64] The sceptic about the authority of theory seems to think that a solution to the problem must be provided by yet another higher-order reason that will eliminate the conflict. But, in Hurley's view, this way of looking at the problem misconstrues the role of theories in deliberation. These theories are theories about conflicting specific values. They do not eliminate conflict, which would be an impossible task. In Hurley's view, it is a feature of our values that they may stand in ultimate conflict, and such conflict is not merely apparent, but real. Hurley claims that conflicting reasons for action are not prima facie reasons, but what she calls 'pro tanto reasons'. Prima facie reasons are reasons

[59] In ch 8 I consider in detail the distinction between narrow and wide equilibrium.

[60] Hurley's views on interpretation are broadly inspired by Davidson's holistic views on interpretation, as it is patent through the book (see, esp pt I) and as Hurley recognizes in the introduction (1989: 3). This association yields further support for the claim that Hurley's coherentism is committed to holism about values.

[61] On the problem of the authority of theory, see Hurley (1989: 196–200 and 260–63).

[62] Eg, as Hurley points out, Williams is someone who has expressed this kind of scepticism. See B Williams (1985) ch 6.

[63] Hurley (1989: 261). It is interesting to note that what Hurley calls 'the problem of the authority of theory' is similar to Richardson's problem about how to solve higher-order conflicts between coherence and what he calls 'integrity'. Their solutions to this problem are, however, quite different. Whereas, in Richardson's view, we may block theory-making and act upon one of the conflicting reasons in the name of integrity, in Hurley's account, we should keep on systematizing, as coherence is not optional but a constitutive constraint of deliberation.

[64] Hurley (1989: 262).

that may turn not to apply when we learn more about the situation, in which case they have no residual force. This interpretation of conflicting reasons goes well with what she calls an 'evidential view of conflict', where reasons are seen as pieces of evidence that ultimately allow us to explain the conflict away. In contrast to this view, Hurley argues that reasons for action may lead to ineliminable conflict. Consider, for instance, a conflict between justice and kindness. One could do the kind act because kindness requires it, even in the face of one's all-things-considered judgement that one ought to do the just act. In doing so, Hurley argues, one would be acting irrationally, but one would still be acting for a reason, namely, because of the kindness of the act. Jackson explains in a very clear way the notion of pro tanto reasons as follows:

> *Pro tanto* reasons are like forces ... A force $F_1$ acting on a particle can be such that by itself would accelerate the particle towards North. At the same time there may be another force $F_2$ which by itself would accelerate the particle towards South. Perhaps $F_1$ is greater than $F_2$ so that there is a resultant force towards North. Nevertheless, $F_2$ still exists, it explains why the particle does not accelerate more briskly towards North. The overwhelmed force is still there. Similarly, when pro tanto reasons clash, the overwhelmed reason survives.[65]

Theoretical reasons, argues Hurley, are no more insulated from conflict with other reasons than the pro tanto reasons that the theory is about are among themselves. It can be the case that an act is just but unkind; and that such an act is favoured by the best theory of justice and kindness; the act may still be unkind. Unkindness is no more cancelled out by considerations of coherence (ie theoretical reasons) than it is by considerations of justice. Nothing in the conceptual relationship between pro tanto reasons and all-things-considered reasons (that are a function of the former reasons) requires them not to conflict.[66]

Thus, theories do not eliminate conflict, neither are they supposed to do so. Rather, theories provide a way to rationally proceed in the face of conflict. But, then, one may ask, why should we seek a coherent way of resolving conflict given that it cannot be eliminated? Hurley's answer to this question brings to light her views about the value of coherence and the nature of deliberation as a theoretical activity that aims at coherence. Hurley gives coherence a constitutive role, not an epistemic one.[67] In her

[65] F Jackson (1992: 478).

[66] For a detailed account of Hurley's views on the nature of conflict and her distinction between pro tanto and prima facie reasons, see Hurley (1989) ch 7. Some legal theorists have introduced this distinction in their accounts of conflict between several moral and legal reasons in the legal context. Most importantly, the notion of a pro tanto reason plays a pivotal role in Peczenik's theory of legal argumentation. For an extensive discussion of Peczenik's weigh and balance model of legal reasoning, see ch 1.

[67] It is interesting to note that Hurley puts the distinction between the epistemic and the constitutive role of coherence in connection with Dworkin's distinction between natural and constructive models of coherence. See Hurley (1989: 422) fn 15.

view, the coherence function constitutes what should be done, rather than revealing to us what should be done. The latter view on coherence would only be appropriate if reasons for action were prima facie and conflict were merely apparent. But, as we have seen, she rejects such evidential account of conflict. Still, she argues, there is a point in searching coherence even though conflicting values retain their force in the face of contrary all-things-considered judgements, that is, even though, conflict is not explained away. The constitutive role of coherence is better understood in the context of Hurley's views on the nature of deliberation.

According to Hurley, deliberation is a kind of 'self-interpretation' and 'self-determination'. In fact, she argues that it is distinctive of persons that they are self-determining and self-interpreting agents, and thus that they engage in deliberation. Hurley follows Davidson in claiming that coherence is not optional, but that it provides a constitutive constraint on interpretation, that is, it makes interpretation, the attribution of meaning, possible.[68] Given that, according to Hurley, deliberation is a kind of interpretation (ie an interpretation the object of which is the self) coherence also plays an important role in the determination of individual identity (in individual deliberation) and in the personification of communities (in interpersonal deliberation).[69] Regarding the role of coherence in individual deliberation she writes:

> It is distinctive of persons to reflect on their own values and attitudes, and thus to arrive at judgments about [what] they should do, all things considered, and corresponding higher-order attitudes. In thus seeking coherence, they are seeking their very identities as persons, seeking to determine themselves out of the various subsystems responsive and responsible to various conflicting interests and values; in deliberating about what to do they are trying to determine who they really are. Thus, deliberation, the search for coherence, is a kind of self-interpretation and self-determination. Interpretation is guided by various constitutive constraints, among them those that constrain us to seek to understand ourselves and others as coherent, as unified persons; but the unity of persons, the coherence they seek, is not more fundamental than or prior to the familiar reason-giving practices that also inform interpretation. Both formal and substantive constraints are needed, and neither sort is derivative from the other. Personal coherence is not something that is given by experience, even at a single point in time, it's something that must be achieved. Moreover, it is fragile and sometimes fails to maintain authority over breakaway subsystems. Nevertheless, it's only against a background of

[68] For an account of the role of coherence in Davidson's theory of interpretation, see ch 6.

[69] When discussing the role of coherence in the determination of a community's identity, Hurley refers to Dworkin. Dworkin's views, as Hurley's, are broadly inspired by Davidson's theory of interpretation (for a discussion of Dworkin's views, see ch 1). It is important to notice that Hurley does not see the determination of individual identity as independent from the determination of community's identity. Rather, she defends a 'neo-classical' conception of ethics, where personality and polity are claimed to converge.

> the concern with personal coherence and the norms of pattern that embody our conception of coherence that attributions of disunity make sense. The concern with personal coherence is not something we are free to disown entirely, nor is it an appropriate object of empirical skepticism.[70]

As the passage above beautifully poses it, coherence has a constitutive role in the sense that it is a constitutive constraint on the kind of self-interpretation that deliberation amounts to. It is now clear why, even though we cannot eliminate conflict, there is a point in seeking a coherent way of proceeding in the face of such a conflict, to wit, that it is the only way that we can proceed, if we are to proceed as persons at all. Thus, a person has indeed a strong reason for acting upon the demands of the theory that best displays coherence among the conflicting reasons, as opposed to acting upon the demand of one of those reasons, namely, that in so doing he is determining who he is. And this is not a question that we, as persons, are free to be concerned with. At least, if we are to be persons at all as opposed to what Frankfurt calls 'wantons', who take their own preferences as given and have no interest in self-determination.[71] As Hurley puts it, 'for *persons*, questions about what kind of agent to be ... must arise. It cannot be a problem *that* they do, for it is a distinctive feature of personhood that they do'.[72] In fact, argues Hurley, it is not as if it were up to the deliberator to decide whether he wants to be a person (and act upon the demands of coherence) or whether he is satisfied with being merely a wanton. Any reason for a decision to become a wanton is self-defeating, for the desire to do so would be in itself a mark of personhood. Thus, the problem of the authority of theory, Hurley seems to claim, not only relies on a wrong view of conflict (as evidential) and of the nature of conflicting reasons (as prima facie), but it also poses a question that cannot intelligibly arise, once the interpretative nature of deliberation and the constitutive role of coherence are brought to light.[73]

[70] Hurley (1989: 262).

[71] See Frankfurt (1971).

[72] Hurley (1989: 263).

[73] One may wonder, however, whether Hurley satisfactorily responds to a less extreme version of the problem of authority of theory, namely, what reason do we have to act upon the demands of coherence as opposed to upon the demands of one of the conflicting reasons 'in some occasions'? In fact, it is this rather modest version of the problem that generally arises when using coherentist standards of rationality in deliberation. Judges do not generally ask themselves what reason they have for generally acting upon the demands of the interpretation that makes the best sense of the legal practice, but what reason they have for acting that way in a particular case, where reliance on one of the conflicting reasons seems to provide a better solution. And these questions do not seem to be satisfactorily addressed by Hurley's appeal to the constitutive role of coherence. The legal community's identity does not seem to be significantly diminished by one single act, anymore that a person becomes a wanton simply because he does not act, in a particular case, on the reasons provided by the theory.

## F. Coherence, Commensurability and Value Pluralism

As we have seen, Hurley's coherentist account recommends that we rationally resolve conflicts by seeking a coherent relationship among the conflicting values. Hurley considers the problem of whether such an account commits one to accepting that values are commensurable.[74] The problem is as follows. It is fundamental to any conception of rationality that a transitivity requirement be met. That is, theories sought in deliberation and represented by coherence functions must not generate intransitivities among the claims about what should be done. Such transitivity is often made out to be tantamount to the commensurability of values. As a result, commensurability seems to follow from a conception of rationality as coherence. Thus, we seem to be forced to choose between irrationalism and commensurability. Hurley argues that there are two kinds of strategies for avoiding the inference from rationality to commensurability. Either one rejects that rationality requires commensurability, and thus expands the notion of rationality so as to accommodate intransitivity, or we reject the assumption that transitivity amounts to commensurability. Hurley finds the first way of responding to this problem unattractive. In her view, no reasons have been given that are strong enough for overriding the deep sense in which intransitive judgements about what to do are irrational. Thus, she aims to resist the inference from rationality as coherence to commensurability by pursuing the latter strategy, that is, by denying that transitivity amounts to commensurability.[75]

In place of a conception of transitivity as commensurability, she defends a conception of transitivity as coherence. In her view, transitivity does not indicate a single dimension of value that underlies and commensurates conflicting values, but it is simply 'a requirement of any decent theory about the relationships among discrete conflicting values'.[76] That is, the transitivity of practical judgements reflects a feature of the theories about the relevant values, and not a common feature of these values. Why should theories be such as to generate transitive judgements? The reason is that, argues Hurley, a good theory about the relationships among values that apply to any set of alternatives must take into account the way in which

[74] Hurley (1989) ch 6, esp 256–60.

[75] It might be interesting to compare Hurley's strategy for blocking the inference from rationality to commensurability with Richardson's. In Richardson's view, there are two premises that support the conclusion that commensurability is a prerequisite of rational choice: (i) rationality requires systematization; and (ii) systematization requires commensurability. He accepts (i) but rejects (ii), replacing the idea of commensurability by the idea of coherence. Since transitivity is a basic property of systems, his strategy turns out to be similar to that of Hurley, in that both stick to an idea of rationality that requires that we give a core role to the notion of systematization. Both Hurley and Richardson opt for replacing commensurability as a criterion that allows a rational order to arise by the notion of coherence.

[76] ibid, 259.

these values apply in other settled and hypothetical cases as well. When such analysis reveals that a certain hypothesis about how values relate to each other would produce an intransitivity, we do not consider that we have already arrived at a satisfactory theory. The very point of the theorizing activity is to qualify hypotheses about how values relate to each other so as to find a coherent way to proceed in conflicting cases, a way that avoids intransitivity results. But such a theory, Hurley claims, need not necessarily commensurate those values. Neither has it to be monistic. Hurley claims that, given the constitutive role of coherence, the question of whether commensurability does obtain, or whether monism or pluralism about values is correct, is a substantive issue, the resolution of which depends on the results of theorizing or deliberation. Only if the outcome of such deliberation were a monistic theory, would coherence amount to commensurability.[77] Thus, Hurley's coherence theory is not committed to value commensurability, neither is it committed to either a monistic or a pluralistic theory of value.[78]

## G. Scepticism, Coherence and Objectivity

As explained, Hurley turns to coherence to provide an objectivist account of reasons. Hurley's coherentist version of objectivism is both non-centralist and cognitivist. First, it is non-centralist in that reasons for action and all-things-considered reasons are claimed to be interdependent. According to her coherentist account of the interdependence relation, judgements about what to do are those that are favoured by the theory that gives the best account of the relationships among specific values or reasons that apply. Second, it is cognitivist in that judgements about what to do are claimed to express beliefs that can be either true or false. In Hurley's coherentist version, those beliefs are theoretical beliefs, which may be false if (i) there is no such a theory or (ii) such a theory does not favour the alternative in question. Thus, Hurley's account of the truth conditions of judgements

[77] Nonetheless, as Jackson has pointed out, it is clear that she does not think that it is at all likely that deliberation would turn out to yield a monistic theory. F Jackson (1992: 477).

[78] It is important to note that, according to Hurley, commensurability in the sense of formal unity is perfectly compatible with value pluralism. Thus, it may still be possible to formally represent the search for coherence as the maximization of some one magnitude while claiming that such formal unity does not correspond to substantive unity, ie a monistic theory of value. A monistic theory requires, in her view, that the magnitude being maximized have an independent descriptive or explanatory content. Merely formal unity does not *per se* confer such explanatory unity on the magnitude constructed. For an illustration of how such a formal unity may be constructed, see Hurley (1989: 264–70).

about what should be done is a coherentist account.[79] It is by means of theorizing that the truth of such judgements is determined. For instance, the truth about what the law is in a particular case is determined by means of legal theorizing of the sort exemplified above. Now, the question arises as to the sense in which these judgements may be said to have a claim to objectivity and whether such a conception of objectivity provides a response to scepticism.

Hurley's views on objectivity are broadly inspired by the philosophies of Wittgenstein and Davidson. As opposed to a 'metaphysical' conception of objectivity, Hurley embraces a 'practice' view of objectivity. She writes:

> The issue of whether there are right answers to questions about what ought to be done when reasons for action conflict is not properly addressed in terms of uncashed metaphors such as those involved in denials that to-be-doneness is somehow 'out there,' part of the 'furniture of the universe.' It should rather be addressed by attending to the power, scope, and characteristics of the theorizing about reasons for action in which we engage.[80]

Thus, in her view, a coherentist claim to objectivity turns on the power and scope of the theoretical practices that lead to judgements about what ought to be done, rather than giving reign to the metaphysics of ethical or legal reality.[81] Objectivity emerges, following Wittgenstein and Davidson, in the context of such practice of theorizing (or deliberation), that is, in the context of interpretation. Constraints on interpretation are required for the attribution of mental states, such as meanings and attitudes, to be possible at all. They have, as it were, a constitutive role in relation to the contents of mental states. Since understanding is possible, these constitutive constraints do hold. Thus, the mind must not be seen as independent from the world, but it is world-laden, that is, it is 'naturalized'. In the same way, the concept of objective reasons for action emerges in the context of deliberation, as an exercise on (self) interpretation and, in so being, they are also naturalized. In order to determine the content of judgements about what to do, formal (eg consistency) and substantive constraints are required. In this sense, the content of judgements about what to do is not independent from the specific

[79] Jackson (wrongly, in my view) takes Hurley to be a moral realist. See F Jackson (1992), throughout. Nowhere does Hurley commit herself to such a view. Her view, as that of Davidson, is better regarded as one that cannot be easily placed under either the realist or the non-realist labels. For the defence of the claim that Davidson's views on truth are better interpreted as challenging the realist-anti-realist dichotomy, see ch 6.

[80] Hurley (1989: 201).

[81] This more modest view of objectivity is the kind of objectivity which, according to Hurley, Dworkin defends. In her view, Dworkin's account is a kind of coherence account, according to which the concept of law is responsible to legal, political and ethical theory. See ibid, as in index. On Dworkin's concept of objectivity, see ch 1.

reason-giving practices that they are about. Thus, the value-ladeness of these judgements is an aspect of the world-ladeness of the mind.

The rejection of the independence of mind from world, preference from value, has the effect of silencing radical external scepticism. The practice view questions the very intelligibility of this kind of scepticism, by denying the independence assumption that gives rise to the sceptical problem in the first place. Still, other sceptical challenges may be raised against the coherentist account of deliberation. Hurley takes deliberation to be, as shown, an exercise of self-interpretation and self-determination. The central role that interpretation plays in this account gives rise to two other sources of scepticism, which Hurley refers to as 'the question of overdetermination' and the 'question of indeterminacy'.[82]

The question of overdetermination asks: are the conditions imposed over a coherence function so stringent as to make it impossible, a priori, that any function satisfies them? I shall dwell on this question only very superficially but, nevertheless, it is interesting to mention it, at least, since it is a problem that most coherence theories have not even considered.[83] Arrow has shown that it is impossible for social welfare functions to meet a set of fundamental and minimal conditions of rationality while guaranteeing the transitivity of social preferences. Hurley wonders whether similar impossibility results threaten the existence of the coherence function, and concludes that they do not. The reason is that some of the formally analogous conditions to those that social welfare functions must meet cannot be reasonably imposed on coherence functions. In particular, some of these conditions include the requirement that the coherence function apply to counterevaluative alternatives, and this aspiration makes no sense from the point of view of a non-centralist account of reasons. Deliberators aim at arriving at judgements about what to do by theorizing about the relationship among the values that actually apply. Consideration of counterevaluative possibilities does not provide relevant data for such theorizing. Moreover, as non-centralism holds, there is a relation of constitutive interdependence among specific values and judgements about what should be done. Substantive constraints, ie specific values, are required for those judgements to have any

[82] In addition to these two challenges, ie overdetermination and indeterminacy, Hurley examines in detail another kind of sceptical challenge that might be posed against her coherentist view of deliberation, namely, scepticism about knowledge of all-things-considered judgements. A sceptic might argue that our beliefs about what ought to be done do not track their truth, either with respect to the existence of a best theory or with respect to the alternatives it favours, because we are bad at discovering what ought to be done, or subjected to systematic error, or deception. If this is so, the sceptic claims, then our beliefs about what ought to be done will not constitute knowledge. Hurley replies to this kind of scepticism by indicating its proper scope (ch 14) and by appealing to democratic institutions (ch 15), as a means for arriving at knowledge about what should be done when there are epistemic obstacles to the search of coherence.

[83] See Hurley (1989) ch 12 for a discussion of the issue of overdetermination.

content at all. Thus, to claim that coherence functions must be applicable to counterevaluative possibilities would be to ignore the constitutive role that substantive constraints play in any interpretative activity. We could interpret these conditions as requiring that the coherence function apply to merely counterfactual, and not to counterevaluative possibilities. But Hurley argues that this possibility is blocked because it violates a formal constraint on interpretation, namely, a requirement of supervenience according to which, in all conceptually possible worlds, if two alternatives differ in some non-evaluative characteristic, then they differ in some evaluative characteristic as well. Thus, according to Hurley, substantive and formal constraints on interpretation ensure that, a priori, coherence functions are not overdetermined.

The question of indeterminacy asks: might there always be too many eligible interpretations so that nothing determines a best theory or right interpretation? Hurley's solution to this problem also appeals to constitutive constraints on interpretation. Formal constraints (eg consistency) and substantive constraints (eg values) avert the threat of radical indeterminacy while allowing enough room for disagreement. It is crucial to notice that the threat of indeterminacy that Hurley focuses on is that of radical indeterminacy, which is based on a kind of a priori scepticism. She does not exclude the possibility of occasional, 'livable-with', a posteriori underdetermination. That is, she does not rule out the possibility that, as a result of deliberation, we arrive at two different coherence functions that are equally successful. Neither does she regard such possibility as a threat to the rationality of coherentist deliberation.[84] Still one may regard as legitimate the question of how one is supposed to choose between two different coherence functions that seem to represent equally good theories. Furthermore, as Richardson has pointed out, there seem to be no way in which we may compare two coherence functions each of them working from a different set of specific values.[85] At this stage, a version of the problem of normative control, which we were concerned with while explaining Richardson's views, seems to arise again. How do we mark off the theories that are right from those that are wrong? How do we tell coherence functions that lead to right judgements about what to do from those that do not? Given that (i) we may start from different sets of values; (ii) we may arrive at different coherence functions, even if proceeding from the same set of values; and (iii) we have not a clear idea of what coherence, beyond responsiveness to theory, is supposed to be, the problem of normative control arises in relation to Hurley's proposal in a pressing way. We need a more precise account

[84] In this respect, her view contrasts with most coherentist accounts, which have strived to rule out this type of indeterminacy. As explained in ch 3, one of the main objections against coherentism, and one that most coherence accounts have attempted to meet, is the so-called 'alternate systems objection'.

[85] Richardson (1994: 168).

of how the base of coherence—in this version of coherentism, the set of specific values—is individuated and a more concrete notion of coherence for us to be able to exercise normative control over the results of deliberation. A precise account of the notion of coherence that is relevant to practical reasoning may be found in Thagard and Millgram's work, to which I turn now.

## III. INFERENCE TO THE MOST COHERENT PLAN

### A. Calculation, Intuition and Coherence

Thagard, in collaboration with Millgram, has proposed a theory of deliberative coherence (hereinafter TDC) and its computational implementation in DECO.[86] TDC explains how decisions are made on the basis of coherence among actions and goals. This kind of coherence is relevant to practical inference, from individual decision-making to ethical, political and legal issues.[87] In this view, practical inference is inference to the most coherent plan, that is, the most coherent set of actions and goals. TDC is meant to be an alternative to classical decision theory, according to which decision makers must calculate the expected utility of alternative courses of action and pick the alternative with the highest expected value. In Thagard and Millgram's view, this theory is inadequate both as a descriptive and as a normative theory. Empirical studies have shown that basic assumptions of decision theory, eg the assumption that preferences are transitive, are often violated. In addition, if seen as a kind of instrumentalism, where the agent's goal is to maximize his expected utility, classical decision theory does not set up an adequate standard for the rationality of our decisions. The complete unrevisability of one's goals that instrumentalism advocates is 'a sign of neurosis and an unintelligent rigidity, not rationality'.[88] Similar problems arise with any view that sees decision-making as calculation-based and that takes goals (and their weights) as fixed.

As an alternative to calculation-based models, one could put forward the view that decisions should be based on what emotional reactions tell us. However, argues Thagard, intuition-based alternatives also have serious disadvantages. In contrast to calculation-based models, they do not put the decision process to the open, enabling the decision-maker and others to carefully review it, so as to make sure that no relevant alternatives have been

[86] Thagard and Millgram (1995: 441–42). Millgram and Thagard (1996) further develop the theory of deliberative coherence. See also Thagard ((2000a: 127–32) and (2012: 119–41)).

[87] Deliberative coherence is a main component of ethical coherence. I address the issue of how deliberative coherence plays out in moral reasoning in the next chapter.

[88] Millgram and Thagard (1996: 75).

neglected and that it is not based on inaccurate information. Nonetheless, intuition-based models capture an important element of decision-making, to wit, emotional judgements, which ensure that decisions take into account what one really cares about and that have an important motivational force. In order to make room for the role that emotion plays in reasoning about what to do, Thagard extends TDC by including 'emotional coherence' and its computational implementation HOTCO. Thagard claims that this model offers a synthesis of the intuition and calculation models, and helps us appreciate how calculation and intuition are crucial components in practical reasoning.[89] I shall start by explaining how, according to Thagard and Millgram, deliberative coherence should be understood. Then, I shall move to explaining Thagard's proposal for complementing TDC with a theory of emotional coherence.[90]

### B. Principles of Deliberative Coherence

As I explained in chapter four, Thagard and Verbeurgt have constructed a model of coherence as constraint satisfaction. In this model, coherence-based inference consists in dividing a set of elements into accepted and rejected in a way that maximizes the satisfaction of multiple (negative and positive) constraints. A characterization of how this type of inference works in different domains requires a further specification of both the elements involved and the constraints. In chapter four, I examined how this theory gives an account of coherence-based inferences about what to believe. Here, we shall see how the constraint satisfaction theory may be applied to inferences about what to do as well. A detailed explanation of TDC—which I briefly introduced in chapter four, is now in order. In Millgram and Thagard's theory of deliberative coherence, elements are actions and goals. They consider that distinctions between goals (and subgoals) and actions are contextual rather than intrinsic. In their view, what in one context is best described as an action, in another may be best described as a goal. For example, if my main goal is to travel from Barcelona to Melbourne, I will set myself the subgoal of getting to Barcelona's airport, but this subgoal may be also described as an action to be performed. Because of that, they refer to both actions and goals as deliberative 'factors' in decision-making. Positive and negative constraints arise from coherence and incoherence

[89] In this sense, Thagard, like Richardson, aims at finding an alternative to the view that decision-making either relies on commensurability or it must fall back on intuition and irrationality.

[90] For such an extension of the model of deliberative coherence, see Thagard (2001: 355–73).

relations among factors. Factors cohere with each other according to the following principles:

*Principle L1: Symmetry.* Coherence and incoherence are symmetrical relations: if factor (action or goal) $F_1$ coheres with factor $F_2$, then $F_2$ coheres with $F_1$.
*Principle L2: Facilitation.* Consider factors $F_1$,......., $F_n$, that together facilitate the accomplishment of factor $F_G$. Then
(a) each $F_1$ coheres with $F_G$,
(b) each $F_i$ coheres with each other $F_j$, and
(c) the greater the number of actions required, the less the coherence among the actions and goals.
*Principle L3: Incompatibility.*
(a) If two factors cannot both be performed or achieved, then they are strongly incoherent.
(b) If two factors are difficult to perform or achieve together, then they are weakly incoherent.
*Principle L4: Goal Priority.* Some goals are desirable for intrinsic or other non-coherence reasons.
*Principle L5: Judgement.* Facilitation and competition relations can depend on coherence with judgements about the acceptability of factual beliefs.
*Principle L6: Decision.* Decisions are made on the basis of an assessment of the overall coherence of a set of actions and goals.

The main positive constraint is established by facilitation relations between actions and goals, as well as relations between actions that jointly contribute to achieving the same goal. For example, if getting an article on the Islamic influence on contract law in fifteenth century Spain finished requires updating my references, a last trip to the archives and doing some editing work, all these subgoals or actions cohere among themselves, and with the basic goal of finishing my article. The third clause of the 'principle of facilitation' expresses a preference for simpler plans, so that coherence decreases as more actions are required. As Thagard and Millgram point out, TDC is ruthlessly simplified in that, among other things, it is restricted to the instrumental relation of facilitation, excluding other types of justification-bearing links between deliberative factors that, in their view, are still too controversial, for instance, specification relations, analogy or relations between values and preferences.[91] The 'principle of incompatibility' establishes a relation of incoherence between pairs of factors. Negative constraints arise from two kinds of incoherence relations, strong and weak. 'Strong incoherence' arises when two factors are completely incompatible;

[91] In this respect, Thagard and Millgram's model need not be seen as incompatible with Richardson's or Hurley's models, but as complementary. A further development of TDC could take into consideration justification-bearing links other than facilitation.

for example, I cannot be both on my way to the archives and updating my references at the office. 'Weak incoherence' arises when some factors are only moderately in conflict; eg, it is difficult, although perhaps not impossible, to finish my article while getting into town in time to go to the movies.[92] The 'principle of goal priority' acknowledges the fact that some things are simply desired for their own sakes. Nonetheless, such goals may be abandoned when they incohere with one's other goals and actions. Intrinsic desirability is held to be independent of coherence considerations. However, Thagard and Millgram suggest that priority goals may have that status in virtue of their coherence with practical commitments that are not being considered in the particular problem at hand.[93] Coherence relations, as opposed to facilitation relations, are symmetrical, as the 'principle of symmetry' states. This principle allows us to model the revision of goals that are not the means to further goals. Nonetheless, the principle of goal priority generates a de facto asymmetry, when it is computationally implemented. This is, they claim, as it should be. Priority goals do play a central role in deliberation, which is not to say that they are beyond criticism, and the sole basis for choosing action, as instrumentalism holds. The 'principle of judgement' expresses the idea that coherence between actions and goals depends on the acceptability of one's beliefs about what facilitates what, which in turn is a matter of coherence. Thus, explanatory coherence and other kinds of coherence on which epistemic justification depends are relevant to assessing the deliberative coherence to which practical justification amounts to. Finally, the 'principle of decision' states that decisions are made by assessing holistically various competing goals and actions.

The principles of deliberative coherence embody a view of practical inference and decision-making that clearly departs from the classical theory of decision-making. In the latter approach, practical inference proceeds from ends that are given to means to those ends. Thus, decision-making consists of choosing the best action to achieve a given goal. As opposed to this instrumentalist view of practical reasoning, in Millgram and Thagard's account, practical reasoning involves deliberation not only about means, but also about ends. Hence, decision-making is depicted as a coherence-driven process for evaluating and revising both actions and goals.

As is apparent, the principles of deliberative coherence have essentially the same structure as the principles of explanatory coherence, which were

[92] Richardson offers a classification of the different ways in which two propositions may be incompatible which includes finer distinctions than the broad categories (strong and weak) that Thagard and Millgram employ. Richardson's classification is based on the causes of conflict, and in that sense, it may help us detect as well as correct possible sources of incoherence. Nonetheless, in many instances, to detect simply weak and strong incoherence is probably enough for making a cursory appraisal of the coherence of our decisions.

[93] See Thagard and Millgram (1995: 443) and Millgram and Thagard (1996: 74).

introduced in chapter four.[94] Just as the acceptability of beliefs depends on their explanatory coherence with a complex set of data and hypotheses, the desirability of actions and goals is determined on the basis of judgements of deliberative coherence. If theory evaluation—theoretical inference—is seen as inference to the best explanation, decision-making is best seen, in Thagard and Millgram's words, as 'inference to the best plan'. Thus, coherence is the main factor in determining both what to believe and what to do. Likewise, the computational implementation of the theory of deliberative coherence (DECO) is constructed taking ECHO, the computational implementation of the theory of explanatory coherence, as a model.[95] In DECO, factors are represented by individual units, coherence relations by excitatory links between units and incoherence relations by inhibitory links. A special unit with a fixed initial activation level is linked to units representing intrinsically desirable goals. Activation percolates through the network starting from the special unit until the activation levels of the units stabilize. The plans whose nodes have positive activations are selected, whereas those whose nodes have near zero or negative activation are rejected. It may be the case that some units do not have either a significantly positive or negative activation or that strongly incompatible factors wind up with similar values. In these cases, coherence considerations do not settle the issue and either one has to decide on some other basis or look for other considerations with which the factors so far considered might cohere or incohere. Since DECO closely resembles ECHO I refer the reader to the details and examples that were provided in relation to the latter network.[96]

## C. Emotional Coherence in Practical Inference

Thagard claims that the theory of deliberative coherence may be extended to encompass the crucial role that emotions play in decision-making. He proposes to integrate emotional inputs with inferences based on deliberative coherence so as to yield decisions that are both emotionally marked and reasonable. The basic idea is to combine the theory of deliberative coherence with the theory of emotional coherence. As explained in chapter four,

[94] See ch 4 s III. Please notice that the theory of deliberative coherence lacks a principle analogous to the principle of analogy in the theory of explanatory coherence. As I said, Millgram and Thagard explicitly reduce positive constraints to facilitation relations. In their view, analogical relations would be, like other types of non-instrumentalist justification-bearing links, too controversial to be included.

[95] For the details of the ECHO program, see ch 4 s III.

[96] Thagard and Millgram examine in detail how DECO performs in an agenda problem and a menu-planning problem in (1996: 78–83). They consider a more ambitious problem about how a professor could decide whether to accept a job offer in the face of the considerable dislocation and loss of relations for his family that such moving would involve in Thagard and Millgram (1995: 444–49).

emotional coherence is not a different kind of coherence, but an expanded way of considering the elements and constraints that enter into a coherence calculation, eg the deliberative factors and constraints as stated by TDC.[97] Goals and actions are either accepted or rejected, depending on the degree of activation of the unit that represents them. Such a degree is interpreted as the degree of acceptability of the element. Thagard proposes that, in addition to acceptability, deliberative factors have an emotional valence, which can be positive (likability, desirability) or negative. For instance, the valence of 'happiness' for most people is highly positive, while the valence of 'pain' is highly negative. Just as elements are related to each other by positive and negative deliberative constraints, so they can also be related by positive and negative valence constraints. Some elements have intrinsic positive and negative valences, for example, happiness and pain. Other elements acquire their valences by virtue of the connections with elements with intrinsic valences. These connections can be valence constraints, or any of the constraints posited by the theory of deliberative coherence. For example, if there is a facilitation constraint between 'studying philosophy' and 'being happier' where the latter has an intrinsic positive valence, then 'studying philosophy' can acquire a positive valence. The valence of an element depends on the valences and acceptability of all the elements to which it is connected. Thagard proposes that we expand the connectionist model for representing coherence-based decision-making into one that incorporates emotional coherence. The suggestion is that we attach valences in addition to activations to the units that represent deliberative factors. In the expanded model, HOTCO, emotional decisions emerge from the spread of both activation and valences through the system.[98]

Thagard gives some reasons why this model of decision-making may be seen as being both descriptively and prescriptively adequate. First, this theory provides a psychologically realistic way of understanding the role of intuitions in decisions. It also makes more realistic demands on individuals than calculation models, which have little application in real life situations, where agents rarely know the relevant probabilities and utilities.[99] Secondly, since removing emotions from decisions is psychologically impossible, normative principles cannot require that we eliminate emotions from decisions. Last, there are some recent results in neuroscience that support the view that emotion-free decision-making would be, if possible at all,

[97] For a fuller explanation of Thagard's theory of emotional coherence and how it interacts with different kinds of coherence so as to yield epistemically justified beliefs, see ch 4. For an explanation of the place of emotional coherence in Thagard's coherentist approach to moral justification, see ch 8.

[98] For the details of HOTCO, see ch 4.

[99] See ch 2, for a discussion of the problems of probabilism.

highly defective.[100] These results, claims Thagard, provide us with further reasons for making our decisions sensitive to our emotional judgements.

In so doing, we should make sure that our decisions are based on informed intuitions, and not on quick intuitions that are the result of emotional distortions, such as intense craving.[101] In fact, argues Thagard, noticing the role of emotional coherence in decision-making enables us to expand the list of fallacies to include emotional factors of bad decision-making. I suggest that we call such common errors in reasoning 'emotional fallacies'. Intense craving, failing to perceive the emotional attitudes of others or wishful thinking would be among them. As explained in chapter four, wishful thinking has been modelled by Thagard in HOTCO2. To recall, in this network, not only can the acceptability of elements influence valences, but the influence can also go in the other direction, from valences to activations. As was shown, this computational model has proved useful for understanding biased fact-reasoning in law and science.[102] Likewise, HOTCO and HOTCO2 might shed some light on the role of emotional judgements in both good and bad practical reasoning. In the next chapter, I shall touch upon the ways in which emotional coherence interacts with other kinds of coherence to arrive at justified ethical judgements. To be sure, as Thagard recognizes, HOTCO is not a full model of emotional cognition. Neither does HOTCO2 provide a complete account of the many different ways in which emotions can result in bad practical inferences. Nonetheless, Thagard's model may be regarded as a first step towards bringing together emotive and cognitive aspects when reasoning about what to do.

## D. Why Coherence?

As explained, Thagard and Millgram claim that when revision of our motivational system is called off because there is a conflict or contradiction among goals, this revision should be such as to increase the coherence of the motivational system. But—it might be objected—there are many different ways of removing conflict, why should we follow the coherence-maximization strategy? Thagard and Millgram provide three reasons why a coherence approach to conflict resolution is attractive. First, goals that hang together are likely to be more efficient in their use of resources, and coherent plans of action are more likely to work than decisions that involve overlapping plans of action, or competing courses of action.

[100] Thagard (2000a: 212).

[101] See Thagard (2001: 366).

[102] See ch 4. There, I examine how, according to Thagard, HOTCO2 models jurors' reasoning in the controversial *OJ Simpson* case, and so illuminates the role of emotions in factual inferences in law.

Secondly, plans of action are constitutive of persons and their lives. A certain degree of coherence is necessary both to being an (unified) agent and to having a (single) life. Since the point of practical reasoning is to guide us in the decisions that shape our lives, it is desirable that it tends to increase the coherence of our system of goals. Millgram and Thagard make an important qualification to this reason for pursuing coherence. Increasing coherence, they claim, increases fragility as well. When everything fits together, finding that you are wrong in one thing has ramifications for everything you believe or desire. Thus, it is probably better if everything does not fit too tightly, so that if something goes wrong one still has other relatively independent bases (job, family, and so on) to get going on. Thus, Thagard and Millgram, like Richardson, claim that there are probably limits to the desirability of deliberative coherence.

Last, the answer to the question of why one should revise one's system of goals so as to increase coherence lies in the connections between descriptive and normative theories of rationality, on the one hand, and our actual practices, on the other. They claim that an argument in support of DECO would consist primarily in its ability to extensively reconstruct available bodies of practical inference. This task, they admit, has barely begun, because the notion of coherence that TDC embodies is still too preliminary to warrant embarking on such a project. As we have seen, there are important aspects of practical reasoning that Thagard and Millgram's theory have not yet incorporated. But the ability to reconstruct inferential practices has been proved to be an effective argument for the legitimacy of TEC and ECHO, as a theory for revising our systems of beliefs rationally. ECHO has been used descriptively, to represent actual cognitive processes that had so far resisted formalization. And it has also been used normatively, to rationally reconstruct them. Rational reconstructions of this kind are arguments for the legitimacy of the pattern of inference that ECHO represents. Similarly, a defence of the legitimacy of coherence-based inference represented in DECO could be based on an argument to the effect that (i) DECO's picture of deliberation conforms to the way in which people, who we believe are doing things right, deliberate; and (ii) it rationally reconstructs those practical inferences.

It is important to note that rational reconstructions normally require that we be able to clearly represent the patterns of inference that they deploy. In their view, logic, prior to becoming a branch of mathematics in the twentieth century, was the name for the study of forms and inference. Logic has so far provided us with the techniques for representing many patterns of inference, but there are some patterns of reasoning, eg inference to the best explanation, that have so far resisted formalization. DECO is a tool for doing logic in this old-fashioned way. It is a computational technique that aims at representing a coherence-based pattern of inference, and by so doing it helps answer the question of whether such a pattern is legitimate. If Millgram and Thagard are right, then we should expect that further experimental evidence about, for instance, how well DECO represents, among others, courts' reasonings, political scientists' reasonings and experimental subjects' reasonings would provide a way of assessing and improving TDC, and a way of showing the extent to which coherence-based patterns of practical inference may be held to be legitimate.

## IV. CONCLUSIONS

In this chapter I have examined three different proposals about the relevance of coherence for justified judgements about what to do. Richardson views coherence as the main criterion for the rationality of practical inferences, which further specify our practical commitments. For Hurley, practical reasoning is case-based reasoning. When reasoning about what to do, we examine settled and hypothetical cases, and we build up a theory—represented by a coherence function—that best displays relationships among the conflicting values that apply to the alternative courses of action and that best makes sense of the body of practice as a whole. Last, Thagard and Millgram claim practical inference to be an inference to the most coherent plan, which is the plan that best satisfies a number of positive and negative constraints.

Despite differences, there are a number of features that these proposals share. First, they are meant to be an alternative to instrumentalism. They aim at showing that, in addition to means-end reasoning, there are other kinds of legitimate practical inferences, eg operations of specification, practical analogy, or inferences that lead one to accept the decision that maximally satisfies a number of coherence constraints. Secondly, and related to the previous point, they all give a marginal role to deductive inference in practical reasoning. If practical syllogisms were the model of practical reasoning, then it would be hard to see how deliberation could be of ends. The ends (in the means-end type of practical syllogism) and the norms (in the rule-case type) which provide the major premise would be fixed and beyond deliberative revision. It is a main motivation of the coherence theories that we have examined to provide a rational procedure for addressing practical conflicts in a way that goes beyond the limited resources provided by deductive reasoning. Last, all these proposals defend holistic views of practical justification. Judgements about what to do are not justified in isolation, but their justification depends on the relations that they have with other practical commitments. In this view, no deliberative element is immune to revision. It is, in fact, these proposals' commitment to holism that makes room for the revision of goals that instrumentalism blocks.

Holism, as has been argued before, has some undesirable consequences.[103] One of them is that it makes unrealistic demands on the part of the agent.

[103] See chs 1 and 2 for the problems of holism about legal justification and chs 3 and 4 for the problems of holism about epistemic justification.

We do not seem to be capable of assessing the coherence of the whole system of attitudes, goals etc on which the justification of a judgement about what to do ultimately depends. This problem affects the coherentist theories that we have examined to different degrees. The holistic standard for the rationality of specification that Richardson demands is, most likely, impossible to achieve. Hurley restricts the kind of theorizing that deliberation involves to the values (as they play out in settled and hypothetical cases) that are relevant to the case under consideration, and this makes the problems of holism less severe, at least when compared with the kind of deliberation that an unrestricted holism would recommend. Thagard and Millgram's claim that we take some goals as priority goals may provide us with a procedure that we may reasonably impose on agents, without giving up the holistic ambitions. The desirability of these goals, in Millgram and Thagard's view, may depend on coherence considerations that are not questioned in the problem at hand. Pursuing this suggestion, we could take priority goals to be goals that are 'contextually self-justified'.[104] In this sense, even though the justification of these goals depends on the whole network of connections, we do not require that the whole network be surveyed for them to be accepted as justified in a given context of deliberation.

The coherentist alternative is attractive for a number of reasons. Firstly, it provides an alternative to instrumentalism that does not simply amount to employing our intuition. Unlike intuition-based models, coherentist theories provide us with a decision-making procedure that is open to public scrutiny and criticism. Secondly, it is important to note that, unlike other models that also aim at providing a rational decision-making procedure, coherence theories may bypass the commensurability issue. Other methods of conflict resolution, eg standard decision theory, can only work on the (controversial) assumption that values are commensurable. In contrast, if some of the arguments given in this chapter are sound, coherentist approaches may be workable whether commensurability obtains or not. These arguments show that coherentism is compatible with value pluralism. If this is so, then, the validity of claims that associate coherence accounts with monistic theories would be undermined.[105] Thirdly, the coherentist alternative is appealing because it is psychologically more realistic than competitors. Judgements of coherence can be sensibly made without knowing what the utilities of various outcomes are, or without having our practical commitments perfectly arranged into a deductive system, ready to be applied.

[104] A similar strategy was employed to account for Peczenik's claim that authority reasons have a privileged position in legal reasoning (see ch 1). On the notion of 'contextually basic belief', see ch 3.

[105] The objection against coherence theories on the grounds that they are incompatible with pluralism about value has been most forcefully stated by Raz. For a discussion of Raz's criticism, and, more generally, of the relationship between pluralism and coherence methods in law, see ch 1.

Besides, Hurley, Richardson, Millgram and Thagard have given compelling arguments for the rationality of pursuing coherence among our practical commitments.[106] The main lines of argument include: (i) coherence is constitutive of the identity of persons as rational and unified agents; (ii), closely related to (i), coherence has an instrumental value in relation to happiness; (iii) coherence promotes successful coordination; and (iv) coherent actions tend to be more effective. I shall not take a position at this stage as to whether the connection between rationality and coherence is better forged indirectly (eg via a general pragmatic argument, as Richardson does) or whether it is of a conceptual kind, ie whether it should be built into the conception of rationality (as in Hurley's theory). Here, it may suffice to point out that these arguments, taken together, give good reasons for pursuing (a certain degree of) practical coherence.

The main challenge to coherence accounts is to give a solution to the problem of normative control: does coherence allow us to distinguish correct from incorrect practical inferences? How could we rationally choose among coherent courses of action? An answer to this problem requires a notion of coherence that is precise enough for making comparative assessments of coherence. Thagard's theory of coherence as constraint satisfaction seems to me to be on the right track for giving a satisfactory answer to the problem of normative control. If, in addition, emotions can be incorporated into the model, as Thagard claims, then we have a further reason for embracing this conception of coherence. Thagard's model could provide a way to formally treat Richardson's claims about the need of extending reflective equilibrium so as to encompass the role of emotions in deliberation, or Hurley's views on the relevance of perceptual capacities and moral experience in deliberation.[107] In addition, Thagard's model may provide the framework for incorporating Hurley's and Richardson's achievements in the study of practical reasoning. One could enrich the model so as to include analogy as well as specification relations in addition to facilitation relations. Expanding the list of positive (and negative) constraints to give an account of these relations must go hand-in-hand with expanding the base of coherence, ie the set of elements that are the input to the coherence calculation. In addition to goals, actions and emotions, one should also include norms (principles and rules) as well as values and other relevant practical reasons (eg legal doctrines or precedents).[108]

[106] *Cf* Kolodny ((2007) and (2008)) (arguing that there are no rational requirements of (formal) coherence). See also Raz (2005).

[107] As will be shown in the next chapter, recent ethical theory has drawn attention to the role that emotions play in ethical judgement. In this sense, Thagard's theory of emotional coherence could be used to give a formal expression to the role of emotional attitudes, empathy etc in moral reasoning.

[108] Bench-Capon and Sartor make a similar point as regards legal reasoning. In their view, two kinds of inputs ought to be incorporated into Thagard's theory, to wit, precedents and values. See Bench-Capon and Sartor (2003).

Despite the intrinsic virtues of Thagard's model, and its capacity to absorb other theorists' theoretical achievements, there are several problems with this theory. Most importantly, it does not address the question of how the input is generated, eg how to determine one's goals, the range of relevant actions or how facilitation relations arise.[109] The problem is one that deserves serious attention. If one accepts the view that the generation of the base of coherence and the selection of its elements cannot be sharply kept as distinct, then that the model does not address the issue of how elements are generated severely diminishes the plausibility of the evaluation process that it formalizes. However, that the model lacks generation mechanisms might also be seen as pointing towards the need to include this model, and the conception of coherence it embodies, within a broader theory of practical reasoning. In this sense, coherence considerations may be regarded as crucial in a theory of practical reasoning, but they need to be properly connected with other aspects of such a theory for them to contribute effectively to the justification of our practical judgements. For instance, Millgram's view about how practical induction may lead us to adopt new goals nicely complements the theory of practical coherence. Or a well-developed theory of analogy in the practical domain may be seen as essential for establishing the positive constraints that derive from analogical relations. Thus, the problem of the input brings to light the need to insert the theory of practical coherence within a full theory of practical reasoning.[110]

The analysis of these coherence-based theories of practical reasoning has given us a sense of how (practical) coherence may be relevant to practical reasoning, like (epistemic) coherence was shown to be relevant to theoretical reasoning. In earlier chapters, epistemic coherence was seen as crucial to the justification of factual inferences in science. Let us see now what credit can be given to practical coherence in the enterprise of justifying moral beliefs.

[109] For a more detailed discussion of this problem in relation to ECHO, as well as of other problems that Thagard's model gives rise to, see ch 4.

[110] A similar conclusion was drawn with regard to epistemic coherence. See ch 3.

# 8

# *Beyond Reflective Equilibrium*

IN THIS CHAPTER, my goal is to give an account of the place of coherence in moral reasoning. In moral theory, coherence has been given a prominent role at three distinct levels. First, some have advocated a coherence method of moral inquiry. That is, some have claimed coherence to be a crucial tool for theory construction in ethics. Others have defended coherentist accounts of the justification of our moral views. From this perspective, coherence does not only help us construct a moral theory, but it also provides the standard against which such a theory must be evaluated. Still other philosophers have advocated not only a coherentist account of the criteria of justification of our moral beliefs, but also a coherentist account of their truth-conditions. Hence, in the ethical domain three main questions have been answered by appeal to coherence: a methodological question (what method should we follow to attain moral knowledge?), an epistemic question (when are our moral beliefs, judgements, principles, etc justified?) and a metaphysical one (what is the nature of moral truth?).

The methodological, epistemic and metaphysical questions have not always been clearly distinguished in the coherentist literature. Moreover, it is unclear whether some coherence theories (eg Rawls' method of reflective equilibrium) are meant to provide an answer to one or other of these issues. Some moral philosophers have even denied that coherence methods, in particular, Rawls' method of reflective equilibrium, involve any epistemic or metaethical claim. In this view, Rawls' coherence method is better located within a conception of ethics that recommends that epistemological and metaphysical questions be set aside. Ethics, it is held, is a practical discipline all the way down. From this point of view, the purpose of moral theorizing is not to provide us with a set of epistemically justified moral beliefs, and thus to bring us closer to moral truth. Instead, moral theorizing must provide us with practical solutions to practical problems. From this perspective, coherence may be seen as a pivotal tool for developing moral outlooks that help us solve these problems. Furthermore, insofar as coherence among our moral convictions is all we need for our practical purposes, we can hold these moral convictions as justified. Hence, coherence is claimed to provide a standard of practical, instead of epistemic, justification. The adequacy of epistemic standards of justification is to be assessed in relation to whether they lead us to accept as justified beliefs that are likely to be true. In contrast, the idea of justification as a practical task is independent of metaphysical considerations about whether beliefs so justified are more or less likely to be true.

Here, we seem to have two different conceptions of the task of moral philosophy. The first views moral reasoning as significantly similar to scientific reasoning. Moral judgements, in this view, enjoy a kind of objectivity that is analogous to that of empirical or theoretical judgements in the empirical sciences. In contrast, the second rejects the view that moral objectivity should be understood on the model of scientific objectivity. It starts from the idea that there is a substantial contrast between facts and norms, or values, and claims that a form of objectivity can be elaborated for the ethical side of the contrast.[1] Hence, one may address the so-called 'problem of placing ethics' by endorsing either a 'continuity' thesis or a 'discontinuity' thesis.[2] Those who accept the former tend to conceive ethics as a theoretically-oriented discipline. Those who reject it tend to think of ethics as a practically-oriented discipline. In the theoretically-oriented approach, moral reasoning aims at providing us with true and epistemically justified beliefs. In this view, moral philosophy is better conceived as a branch of epistemology, ie moral epistemology. In the practically-oriented one, the problem of moral truth is set aside, and the epistemic view of justification is replaced by a practical one. In this view, moral philosophy is first and foremost a practical discipline.

One's position concerning the way in which moral philosophy should be done has implications for one's views on coherence and its role in moral reasoning. In the theoretically-oriented approach, coherence is claimed to provide a criterion of epistemic justification. A moral belief is (epistemically) justified if belongs to a maximally coherent set of both moral and non-moral beliefs. Whereas some take such coherence to be evidence of moral truth in the sense of correspondence with an independent moral order (ie moral realism), others take such coherence to be constitutive of moral truth (ie anti-realism). In the practically-oriented approach, coherence is a pivotal tool for solving practical problems as well as a key standard for judging the correctedness of our solutions to moral problems.

In this chapter, I shall provide an account of the main coherentist theories in ethics. I shall attempt to distinguish the methodological, epistemic and metaphysical claims that are involved in the coherence theories under discussion, and explore the connections (if any) between them. I shall also examine the implications of inserting coherence methods into a conception

[1] I am disregarding here those views that claim that there is a substantial contrast between ethics and science, and that take this contrast as an argument for denying that anything like moral objectivity exists.

[2] See Darwall, Gibbard and Railton (1997: 8–9).

of moral philosophy as either a more theoretically- or practically-oriented discipline. More specifically, my aim is to examine whether adherence to coherence methods commits us to any particular view about truth and objectivity in ethics.

The structure of this chapter is as follows. First, I shall provide a brief account of the foundationalist-coherentist debate as applied to ethics.[3] Then, I will examine the most influential coherentist account of moral reasoning, to wit, Rawls' method of reflective equilibrium, as well as the main objections that have been raised against this method. Next, I will analyse three main coherentist theories of moral reasoning: DePaul's method of balance and refinement, Goldman's method of analogy and difference and Thagard's theory of ethical coherence.[4] After having reviewed the most prominent coherentist accounts in ethics, I will examine the relations between coherence, realism and anti-realism in ethics.

## I. THE METHOD OF REFLECTIVE EQUILIBRIUM

### A. Coherentism and Foundationalism in Ethics

Foundationalism and coherentism are the most influential alternative theories of the structure of ethical justification. These two theories represent the application of foundationalist and coherentist theories of the structure of empirical justification to the justification of moral beliefs. Moral foundationalism holds that one's moral belief *p* is justified just in case *p* is either (i) foundational, ie non-inferentially justified, self-justifying or immediately justified; or (ii) based on the appropriate kind of inference from foundational beliefs.[5] In contrast, a coherence theory of justification holds that one's moral belief *p* is justified insofar as *p* is part of a coherent system of beliefs.

An important attraction of the coherence theory of ethical justification is that its main competitor—ie foundationalism—faces serious objections: (i) there seem to be no uncontroversial candidates for the role of foundational beliefs; and (ii) even if there were, the foundation they would provide is too paltry to serve as the basis for non-basic justified moral beliefs.[6]

[3] For an account of the main versions of foundationalism and coherentism that have been defended in relation to the justification of empirical beliefs, see ch 3.

[4] Other coherence theories in ethics include DeMarco ((1994) and (1997)); Ellis (1992); and Engel (2012).

[5] For a clarifying discussion of the main tenets of moral foundationalism and a classification of the main types of moral foundationalism, see Timmons (1987). For a related taxonomy of foundationalist accounts of moral justification, see Hare (1996).

[6] These objections are similar to those that are addressed against foundationalism about the structure of empirical beliefs (see ch 3). However, there are some peculiarities that stem from the nature of putative foundational beliefs in the moral domain.

One account of foundational moral beliefs is suggested by an analogy with basic empirical beliefs: reliable ethical observers 'perceive', 'intuit' or 'detect' moral properties which are attached to particular acts in a way analogous to how we perceive the physical properties of objects. This account of basic moral beliefs, which characterizes some versions of intuitionism, is hard to accept.[7] Unlike ordinary perceptual judgements, we do not have a causal theory that explains the reliability of particular moral judgements. Alternatively, one could explain foundational moral beliefs in terms of self-evidence or self-warrant. However, it is difficult to give an account of self-evident beliefs that is able to provide us with a stock of beliefs adequate for supporting the edifice of moral knowledge and that does not involve a story about reliability similar to that of the former account. Hence, moral foundationalism seems to be even more problematical than its empirical counterpart.

In face of the serious objections that ethical foundationalism faces, some have turned to coherence in search of an alternative account of the structure of ethical justification.[8] The most popular version of moral coherentism is Rawls' theory of reflective equilibrium. The next section is devoted to examining this theory as well as the main objections that have been addressed against it.

## B. The Method of Reflective Equilibrium

As was originally proposed by Rawls[9] and later developed by Daniels,[10] the method of reflective equilibrium is a method for moral theory construction. According to this method, the process of developing an acceptable moral theory is a matter of shifting back and forth among our initial moral judgements and a set of moral principles, adjusting each other in the light of relevant background theories. This conception of the method of theory construction was first advocated by Goodman. Goodman described the process of bringing judgements about particular inferences and about

[7] On intuitionism, with a particular focus on the relation between this theory and foundationalism, see Brink (1989: 107–13).

[8] Further motivation to develop a coherentist account of moral justification comes from the fact that the main argument given in favour of foundationalism, ie the regress of argument, fails to provide strong support to foundationalism. The level ascent argument discussed in ch 3 to the effect that there are no basic beliefs capable of stopping the regress also questions the feasibility of foundationalist accounts of moral, rather than epistemic, justification. For a discussion of this argument in the context of ethical justification, see Brink (1989: 104–22). A variation of this argument is provided by Sayre-McCord (1996: 153–66).

[9] Rawls ((1951), (1974–75), (1999), and (2001: 29–32)).

[10] Daniels ((1980b) and (1996)).

general principles of inference into accord with each other. In the agreement thus achieved, Goodman maintained, lies all justification needed for our theories of deductive and inductive inference.[11]

We owe to Rawls the application of a modified version of Goodman's method to the ethical domain as well as the term 'reflective equilibrium', which has been used to describe the set of principles and judgements that have been brought into coherence with one another in the way that Goodman suggested. By introducing this method into moral theory, Rawls challenged the foundationalist picture of moral justification and moral theory construction that had dominated moral philosophy at least for the first half of the twentieth century. He writes: 'A conception of justice cannot be deduced from self-evident premises or conditions on principles: instead, its justification is a matter of the mutual support of many considerations, of everything fitting together into one coherent view'.[12] Rawls distinguishes between 'narrow' and 'wide' reflective equilibrium.[13] The method of narrow reflective equilibrium has us[14] begin with a set of initial moral judgements, filter this set, trying to eliminate those members which, upon reflection, seem suspect, and then in light of this new set of 'considered moral judgements', we are to propose a set of moral principles aimed at systematizing and explicating our considered moral judgements. Revising both our considered moral judgements and moral principles we eventually reach a point of 'narrow reflective equilibrium' in which both sets cohere with each other. Then, we may widen our circle of judgements by considering how well the moral principles reached in narrow reflective equilibrium fit with various background theories, and we may advance philosophical arguments intended to bring out the relative strengths and weaknesses of alternative sets of moral principles. The revision of this more enlarged set of judgements with a view to reaching maximal coherence among its members leads us to reach a point of 'wide reflective equilibrium'.

[11] Goodman (1983: 63–64).

[12] Rawls (1999: 19).

[13] The distinction between narrow and wide reflective equilibrium is implicit in Rawls (1999: 43) and explicit in Rawls (1974–75: 8). Daniels has further elaborated the distinction. See n 10 above.

[14] By 'us', I mean each of the individuals who follow the method of reflective equilibrium. The method is to be followed by an individual inquirer. For a proposal about how reflective equilibrium could operate for a community of inquirers, see Baccarini (1991). In this paper, Baccarini presents an attempt to combine the method of reflective equilibrium with Lehrer and Wagner's method of rational consensus. By combining these two methods we may achieve what Lehrer calls 'reflective consensual equilibrium'. See Lehrer (1991b). For a different proposal about how we may arrive at consensus in moral issues by following a coherence method, see Thagard (2000a) ch 7.

It is wide reflective equilibrium, as Daniels has argued, that is of interest to moral philosophy.[15] Narrow reflective equilibrium sticks to the traditional view of moral theories according to which moral theory consists of a set of moral judgements plus a set of principles that account for, or generate them. This two-tiered view reduces the range of possible theories of justification in ethics to a few unattractive alternatives. On the one hand, one may grant a privileged epistemological status either to the moral judgements (ie 'intuitions') or to the moral principles (eg calling them self-evident or a priori). But these foundationalist alternatives must face, as we have seen, severe problems. On the other hand, one could advocate a coherence view of justification, and deny that any such set enjoys a special epistemic status. However, we cannot get very far with a theory of justification that simply requires coherence among moral judgements and moral principles, especially in the face of plausible reasons for rejecting moral judgements, eg charges about bias, prejudice and historical accident. Wide reflective equilibrium reveals a greater complexity in the structure of moral theories than the traditional view. Consequently, it permits us to formulate stronger coherence constraints that may provide adequate pressure to revise our moral judgements, and so make the coherentist alternative more plausible.

The system in wide reflective equilibrium, which includes a set of considered moral judgements, a set of moral principles and a set of relevant background theories, must satisfy what Daniels calls the 'independence constraint'.[16] According to Daniels, the background theories in wide reflective equilibrium should show that our set of moral principles is more acceptable than alternative principles on grounds to some degree independent of the match between the moral principles and the set of considered moral judgements accepted in narrow reflective equilibrium. If our moral principles are not in this way independently supported, then there seems to be no gain over the support that principles would have in a corresponding narrow reflective equilibrium. Another way to raise this point, holds Daniels, is to ask how we can be sure that the moral principles that systematize our considered moral judgements are not just 'accidental generalizations' of the 'moral facts' analogous to the accidental generalizations that we want to distinguish from real scientific laws. In order to achieve independent support for the moral principles and rule out their being mere accidental generalizations, Daniels suggests that we should require that background theories be more than reformulations of the same set of considered moral

[15] Rawls has drawn an analogy between searching for moral principles in reflective equilibrium and searching a grammar in descriptive syntactics. Daniels (1980a) claimed that the analogy best holds for narrow, and not for wide reflective equilibrium. It is precisely the features of wide reflective equilibrium that distinguish it from syntactic methods that make the wide, unlike the narrow, an appropriate method for ethical justification. In contrast, Holmgren (1989) has argued that we have reasons to prefer narrow to wide reflective equilibrium.

[16] Daniels (1996: 22).

judgements. The set of considered moral judgements that constrains the background theories and the set of moral judgements that constrains the set of moral principles must be to some degree disjoint.[17]

The satisfaction of this independence constraint has two benefits. First, it may force the revision of considered judgements that otherwise would have gone unchallenged. This additional revisionary pressure is crucial for the method of equilibrium to yield justified beliefs, given that considered moral judgements have no epistemological status and are open, as we have said, to many charges about bias, prejudice or historical accident. In addition, this constraint makes sure that support for the moral principles is brought from as wide a justificatory circle as possible. This widening of the justificatory network may have, however, a drawback. A good deal of idealization is involved in characterizing the process of justification in terms of coherence among all our moral and non-moral beliefs, which, moreover, satisfies an independence constraint. This raises doubts about the adequacy of this method for justifying moral beliefs in the ordinary, non-ideal, cases.[18]

Now, what is desirable about our system of moral beliefs being in wide reflective equilibrium? Daniels holds that two roles may be ascribed to the method of reflective equilibrium, a modest role and a daring one.[19] In its 'modest' role, the method of reflective equilibrium is primarily analytic and explicative. By revealing the complex structure of our moral theories, it helps us explain central features of moral reasoning. For instance, our judgements about what is problematic, plausible and relevant in moral argument, or what constitutes evidence for and against moral judgements and principles, may be determined by the relevant background theories. In addition, it may help us locate more effectively sources of moral disagreement. We may even reduce disagreements that seem intractable at the level of moral judgements and principles to more tractable disagreements about background theories. In its 'daring' role, the method of reflective equilibrium also serves as the basis for a coherence account of moral justification. In this view, beliefs in wide reflective equilibrium are members of a maximally coherent set and are, in virtue of that membership, justified.[20]

The ascription of either a modest or a daring role to the method of reflective equilibrium determines the value that one attributes to this method.

[17] For an illustration of wide reflective equilibrium and of how it may satisfy the independence constraint, see Daniels (1980b).

[18] See Stich ((1998: 95–112) and (1990)). One may attempt to acknowledge the limits of actual agents in a way that preserves the demanding view of justification that reflective equilibrium embodies by taking reflective equilibrium to be a regulative ideal of our practices of justification. This strategy is not, however, without problems. For a critique, see Sayre-MacCord (1985).

[19] Daniels (1980b: 101–02).

[20] For a discussion of the sense in which reflective equilibrium is a method of justification, see Scanlon (2003).

When one attributes a *modest role* to the method, one sees it primarily as a *method of moral inquiry* that has an important *practical value*. When one ascribes a *daring role* to the method, one views it as a *theory of justification*, and thus as a method that has an *epistemic value*. If one accepts the former (modest) interpretation, one may consistently follow the method of reflective equilibrium while embracing a foundationalist theory of justification.[21] Under the latter (daring) interpretation, one is committed to accepting both a coherence method of moral inquiry and a coherence view of justification. This stronger interpretation is compatible with holding either a realist or an anti-realist view of moral truth. That is, one may hold that beliefs in wide reflective equilibrium are justified because they are evidence of an inquiry-independent moral truth, ie moral realism. Alternatively, one may hold that beliefs in wide reflective equilibrium are justified since they are conducive to a truth that we construct as a result of moral inquiry, ie moral anti-realism. Thus, accepting the method of reflective equilibrium as both a method of moral inquiry and a method of justification leaves open the question of whether a realist or an anti-realist conception of moral truth must be endorsed.

I will address below in detail the issue of whether we have reasons for accepting either a realist or an anti-realist interpretation of the method of reflective equilibrium.[22] Now, I shall introduce some of the main objections that have been addressed against this method. It may be useful though to keep in mind the different interpretations (realist or constructivist) of this method that might be given, for the force of these objections heavily depends on which interpretation one favours.

## C. Objections against Reflective Equilibrium

Several objections have been raised against the method of reflective equilibrium. While some of them are general objections against coherence methods, others object to particular features of the method of reflective equilibrium. I shall consider the particular objections first. These objections mostly concern the role that considered moral judgements play in this method. Daniels has provided the most articulated defence of the method of reflective equilibrium in the face of these objections. It follows both a statement of these objections as well as Daniels' reply to them.

1. *The method of reflective equilibrium, with its reliance on considered moral judgements, is really a form of moral intuitionism.*[23] Daniels has

[21] DePaul (1986) has shown that the method is compatible with foundationalism.
[22] See s V below.
[23] The charge is made by Hare (1975); Singer (1974); and Brandt (1979) ch 1.

forcefully argued that this charge is unfounded.[24] Intuitionist theories have generally been foundationalist. There are no foundationalist commitments in reflective equilibrium. No set of moral beliefs is picked out as foundational, and no especial epistemological priority is granted to considered moral judgements.

2. *The method of reflective equilibrium merely systematizes some set of moral judgements*. If considered judgements do not carry an epistemological privilege, as the reply to (1) establishes, why should we accept the moral theory that results from systematizing them? Daniels denies that wide reflective equilibrium merely systematizes some determinate set of judgements. Rather, it permits extensive revisions of these moral judgements. These judgements may be revised in light of other parts of the moral system. First, they may be revised so as to make them cohere with proposed moral principles. If the method allowed no other revision, then the charge that reflective equilibrium is covert foundationalism could be raised again. For this kind of revision is also allowed by sophisticated forms of intuitionism. However, wide reflective equilibrium goes beyond this kind of revision. Unlike the narrow variety, and unlike any kind of intuitionism, wide reflective equilibrium allows for more drastic theory-based revisions. Accepted background theories may lead us to revise the considered moral judgements. In addition, we are also forced to assess their acceptability in relation to alternative background theories, which incorporate different considered moral judgements.

3. Even if one grants that moral principles accepted in reflective equilibrium do not merely systematize our moral judgements, still the problem of why we should accept a body of principles that takes our considered moral judgements as a starting point remains. The problem is the opposite of the accusation of covert intuitionism. *Considered moral judgements, it is claimed, are not foundational enough for being a proper basis for the development of moral theory*. Brandt has raised this objection in a forceful way.[25] Brandt characterizes the method of reflective equilibrium as follows. We begin with a set of initial moral judgements. We assign them an 'initial credence' level and rule out those with a low initial credence level. Then, we propose principles and attempt to bring principles and judgements together to produce a system with the highest overall credence level. The problem, argues Brandt, is that unless there is a reason for thinking that initial credence levels correspond to credibilities, that is, that they are initially credible rather than merely initially believed, we have no reason to believe that increasing the credence level of the whole system would move us closer to moral truth.

[24] Daniels (1996: 26–27).
[25] Brandt (1979) ch 1.

Daniels provides a three-fold response to Brandt's no credibility objection. First, he claims that much of the plausibility of this objection derives from a contrast between non-moral observation reports and considered moral judgements: whereas we can tell a story about why observation reports are reliable, moral judgements seem suspect. However, we should not hold against moral judgements that they function differently from observation reports, for this is as it should be, given that they are different kinds of judgements. Secondly, the 'no credibility' criticism is at best premature, for only after we develop an acceptable moral theory in wide reflective equilibrium, will we be able to determine what kind of 'fact', if any, is involved in considered moral judgements. Thirdly, we should not deny the credibility of considered moral judgements just because there is widespread disagreement, since there is also agreement on many, and such agreement can be explained in terms of truth-conduciveness.[26]

Brandt's 'no credibility' objection is a specific application to the method of reflective equilibrium of the general objection that has been raised against coherence methods, to wit, that we have no reason to believe that these methods are truth-conducive. This complaint lies behind some familiar objections against coherence theories of justification, ie the alternative coherent systems objection and the isolation objection.[27] We may briefly formulate these general objections as follows:

4. *The truth objection*: There is no reason to suppose that maximizing coherence will lead to moral beliefs that correspond to an inquiry independent reality, unless one adopts a non-realist theory of moral truth.

5. *Isolation objection (or input objection)*: Maximizing the internal coherence of one's moral judgements with other moral and non-moral judgements does not require any input from a realm of inquiry-independent reality. Thus, there is no reason to suppose that such a system of moral beliefs is likely to be true.

6. *Alternative coherent systems objection*: Maximizing coherence does not discriminate among competing normative moral theories that are equally coherent.

Three other general objections against coherence methods have been addressed against the method of reflective equilibrium. These objections move the discussion away from the controversial metaphysical arena, and

[26] Daniels (1996).

[27] These objections have been raised against theories of both epistemic and moral justification. For an account of these objections with respect to empirical justification as well as of the main lines of response, see ch 3. I shall take up these objections in relation to moral justification in s V below.

shed some doubts on particular methodological aspects of the coherentist proposals.[28] They may be stated as follows:

7. *Conservatism.* Coherence methods of justification are conservative in the sense that they do not allow for a critical attitude towards one's own moral views. These methods, it is argued, limit moral inquiry to what people now hold.[29] Coherentists have attempted to meet this objection by invoking two features of the method of reflective equilibrium.[30] First, one could attempt to meet this objection by appealing to the thorough revisability allowed by this method. No considered judgement at any level of generality is, in principle, immune to revision. Still someone may press the point and claim that such revisability does not help us meet the objection. We revise our considered moral beliefs in light of other parts of our own system of beliefs and thus there is still no objective point from which the coherence of such system may be assessed. Ultimately, the method sanctifies our moral views, even if it allows the revision of our initial considered judgements and other parts of our initial moral system. Coherentists may reply to this stage of the objection by doubting that it is even possible to start from an external and objective point distinct from our own. The method of reflective equilibrium is conservative in the way in which moral inquiry needs to be, for one cannot start moral inquiry from scratch. A second main feature of the method is also invoked: not only does this method allow the inquirer ample opportunities to revise her considered moral judgements, moral principles and background theories, but it also directs her to consider arguments in support of and against her moral view as well as to assess its plausibility in relation to alternative moral views.

8. *Circularity.* Coherence theories of ethical justification are viciously circular. Coherentists about ethical justification have replied by rejecting the linear view of inference that gives rise to the objection in the first place. We need to distinguish two kinds of justification: systemic justification and contextual justification. Systemic justification results when we consistently require that justifying beliefs be themselves justified. Contextualist justification is incomplete, in that it does not require that all justifying beliefs be justified, but certain background beliefs are treated as justified, even though they would have to be justified at the systemic level. Inference, it is held, only appears to be linear because in normal contexts of justification we treat some beliefs as justified. But when we move from the contextual, local level of justification, to the systemic level, background beliefs are also brought into question, and their justification can only be explained

[28] On these objections, as addressed against coherence theories of legal justification, see chs 1 and 2. For these objections as they have been directed against coherence theories of epistemic justification, see ch 3.

[29] See Brandt (1979: 21–22); Hare (1981: 76); and Copp (1984).

[30] See Rawls (1974–75: 7–8). For a similar line of response, see Brink (1989: 141).

in relation to their place within our system of beliefs. At the systemic level of justification, the appearance of linearity disappears, and justification is seen as a matter of mutual support. Thus, moral coherentism can explain the importance of linearity and the inadmissibility of circular reasoning at the local level, while offering a non-linear, holistic, account of systemic justification.[31]

9. *Vagueness*. A main criticism against the method of reflective equilibrium is that it has remained vague about the nature of coherence and about how moral judgements, principles and background theories should be brought into agreement.[32] We may further elaborate this point if we consider that the term 'reflective equilibrium' suffers from the well-known 'process-product' ambiguity. On the one hand, by 'reflective equilibrium' one may refer to the process that leads one to achieve the desired equilibrium point. On the other hand, 'reflective equilibrium' may be understood as the product of such a process, namely, a system of beliefs that is in a state of equilibrium. The method of reflective equilibrium does not provide a detailed coherentist account of ethical justification, whether it is interpreted as a process or as a product. If taken as a process, several questions remain unanswered: how the descriptive question—how people do reach equilibrium—and the prescriptive one—how they should reach it—relate to each other? By which coherence-based mechanisms do moral beliefs and principles modify each other? To what extent can they be altered in the light of background theories? If taken as a product, the method of reflexive equilibrium has little content. What does it mean to say that we have achieved a state of 'reflective equilibrium'? When does a moral theory come closer than another one does to such a state? We need a concrete specification of the notion of coherence to determine which of a number of theories is most coherent and how coherence should be built.

In the following sections of this chapter I shall introduce three alternative coherence methods of moral inquiry: DePaul's method of balance and refinement, Goldman's method of analogy and difference, and Thagard's theory of ethical coherence. The primary motivation for these proposals is to develop a coherentist view of moral reasoning that successfully meets (some of) the foregoing objections and, hence, that provides a plausible alternative to ethical foundationalism.

[31] The response is the same as the one given to the objection from circularity raised against coherentist theories of empirical justification. See ch 3. For this objection in the context of ethical justification, see Brink (1989: 123–24).

[32] Thagard (2000a: 126).

## II. BALANCE AND REFINEMENT

DePaul's coherentist proposal is basically concerned with the methodological question of how we should resolve conflicts involving our moral beliefs and develop one's moral views accordingly. DePaul's coherence-based theory is not one about either justification or truth. In fact, he endorses a foundationalist epistemology and a theory of moral truth as correspondence. He is exclusively interested in advancing a coherence method of moral inquiry, to wit, the method of balance and refinement.[33] In his view, current coherence methods of moral inquiry are deficient in several respects. These problems are not peculiar to coherence methods, but they stem from the general view of moral inquiry within which these methods are located. I shall first present what, according to DePaul, is wrong with the dominant view of moral inquiry. After that, I shall examine DePaul's criticism of current coherence methods. Finally, I shall present DePaul's own proposed method as well as his argumentative strategy for defending it against competitors.

### A. Against the Intellectualist View of Moral Inquiry

DePaul claims that the view of moral inquiry that dominates current moral philosophy is inadequate. In the first place, it focuses on beliefs and neglects the role of experience in moral inquiry. In the second place, it is based on a mechanistic and scientistic view of the method of moral inquiry, which disregards the role of inquirers in coming to have an epistemically respectable moral outlook. In the third place, it is mostly concerned with systematizing our moral judgements into moral theory, instead of aiming at refining our ability to generate and improve our moral judgements. Lastly, it is exclusively based on reasoning and argument, and it neglects the relevance of reflection on real life experiences as well as experiences with film, literature and arts in general for moral inquiry.

As an alternative to this 'intellectualist' view of moral inquiry, DePaul proposes the 'method of balance and refinement'. This method incorporates much of Rawls' method of reflective equilibrium, and so leads inquirers to a systematic, coherent and *balanced* moral outlook, but goes beyond coherentism in making room for moral experience, in order to ensure that inquirers work with a *refined* faculty of moral judgement. Before discussing the method of balance and refinement, I shall introduce what DePaul calls the 'radical conception of reflective equilibrium'. The method of radical reflective equilibrium is a first step towards reconceiving moral inquiry

[33] DePaul has advanced his coherentist project in a number of works. See DePaul ((1986), (1987), (1988a), (1988b), (1988c) and (1998)). DePaul (1993) presents most of his views in a final form.

(and, more specifically, coherence methods) moving it away from the sort of intellectualist inquiry that, according to DePaul, dominates current moral epistemology.

### B. Conservative vs Radical Reflective Equilibrium

DePaul begins his task of reshaping coherence methods of moral inquiry by distinguishing between a conservative conception of Rawls' method of reflective equilibrium and a radical conception of this method.[34] According to the conservative conception, the inquirer's task is to construct a coherent system of beliefs by investigating the connections between his considered judgements, a set of moral principles and a set of background theories. When a person uncovers a conflict, she will revise the belief to which she is less strongly committed. More generally, the person aims at achieving the most coherent set of beliefs that maximizes her degree of initial commitment. Two features distinguish the conservative interpretation of reflective equilibrium: (i) the only changes that the method envisions are those that are required to make the initial system of beliefs coherent; and (ii) the outcome of this process of revision, ie the inquirer's point of reflective equilibrium, is virtually a function of the person's initial beliefs.[35]

In contrast, radical reflective equilibrium (i) allows changes that go beyond what is necessary to resolve conflicts among a person's initial beliefs; and (ii) the result of these changes are neither determined nor even constrained by the person's initial moral beliefs. In short, the method of radical reflective equilibrium makes room for 'discontinuous revisions of beliefs', that is for revisions that are not required to eliminate conflict among one's initial commitments and the outcome of which is not determined by the believer's reliance on initial credence levels. This is the kind of belief revision that is involved in what DePaul calls 'moral conversion'. For example, a person who reads Marx for the first time, and comes away from this experience as a committed Marxist, has experienced such a conversion.[36] Since moral conversions, DePaul claims, may lead inquirers to improve their moral outlooks, a method of moral inquiry must make room for this kind of discontinuous change of belief. The radical method, as opposed to the conservative one, can give an account of this kind of belief change. Hence, we have reason to prefer the radical to the conservative interpretation of the method of reflective equilibrium.

[34] DePaul (1987) introduces and defends a radical interpretation of the method of reflective equilibrium. See also DePaul (1993) ch 1.

[35] See DePaul (1993: 39).

[36] ibid, 40–41.

Further support for the radical method of reflective equilibrium comes from considering the prospects of meeting the objections that are traditionally raised against the method of reflective equilibrium. DePaul argues that a radical interpretation of the method of reflective equilibrium allows us to see most of the criticisms to this method as inappropriate. According to DePaul, the majority of those who have criticized the method of reflective equilibrium have employed some form of what he calls the 'no contact with reality' objection (ie the truth objection). A method of moral inquiry, it is held, must bring our moral beliefs into an appropriate sort of contact with moral reality. But, the objection asks, what reason can be given for thinking that the method of reflective equilibrium, can ensure this kind of contact?

More specifically, the 'no contact with reality' objection, as directed against the method of reflective equilibrium, is formulated as follows:

> A method of inquiry cannot be acceptable unless it is likely to lead inquirers to accept true theories. The method of reflective equilibrium will not lead inquirers to accept true theories unless the beliefs that guide and constrain theory construction, ie the inquirer's considered moral judgments or initial credence levels, are credible.[37]

This objection involves the following claims: (i) reflective equilibrium cannot be an adequate method of moral inquiry unless it is likely to lead to true theories; (ii) reflective equilibrium is unlikely to lead inquirers to true theories unless our considered moral judgements are credible; and (iii) the credibility of our moral beliefs has not yet been established.

According to DePaul, one might try to respond to the no contact objection by rejecting (i). Moral inquiry is directed towards a complex goal, which includes truth, but also other values. Thus, contrary to what (i) assumes, the adequacy of methods of moral inquiry does not depend exclusively on their truth-conduciveness but on how well they contribute to achieving the diverse goals of moral inquiry. Alternatively, a line of response to the no credibility objection that does not rely upon rejecting (i) opens up if we accept the radical interpretation of reflective equilibrium.[38] The method of reflective equilibrium allows for discontinuous changes of belief, and even permits that initial beliefs be abandoned wholesale, when large moral conversions occur. Thus, if the method of reflective equilibrium is interpreted radically, neither the no credibility objection, nor the attempts to meet this

[37] ibid.

[38] DePaul suggests still an additional way for meeting the no contact objection. Instead of challenging either (i) or (ii), one could attempt to undermine (iii). According to DePaul, one could employ an argument analogous to BonJour's argument for the reliability of our perceptual beliefs in order to show the credibility of our considered moral judgements. For BonJour's argument, see ch 3. For DePaul's attempt to use BonJour's argument to yield a response to the no contact objection, see (1993: 27–30). Brink uses a similar strategy for meeting this objection. On this strategy, see s V.B. of this chapter.

objection by showing that our considered moral judgements are reliable, are cogent. Under the radical interpretation, no set of beliefs serves to guide and constrain the inquirer through the process. Therefore, it cannot be an objection to the method that the beliefs that guide and constrain the process of revision, ie the initial beliefs, are not reliable. Neither does it make sense to defend the method by arguing that these initial beliefs are reliable. Since the radical method of reflective equilibrium allows for discontinuous revisions of belief, questions about the value of the method do not reduce to questions about its input, as the credibility objection assumes.

The contrast between conservative and radical reflective equilibrium allows DePaul to start reshaping the conception of moral inquiry in the following sense. To begin with, the introduction of the notion of moral conversions points towards the relevance of experience in the development of our moral outlooks. In addition, the radical interpretation of reflective equilibrium allows us to see that methods of moral inquiry are not aptly characterized as functions from input to output beliefs. Since the input does not determine the output, the method can take different persons from the same inputs to different outputs. Thus, the radical interpretation marks a significant departure from the mechanical conception of moral methodology that the conservative interpretation represents. Last, as the previous point brings to light, the conservative conception focuses on beliefs, whereas the radical conception focuses on inquirers. In the former conception, once the inquirer's initial system of beliefs is given, the moral theory that is accepted in reflective equilibrium is nearly determined. In contrast, the radical method grants a more active role to the inquirer in the process of theory construction. For he can alter at any point the structure of his system of beliefs in a way that is not determined by what he happens to believe when he first engaged in moral inquiry. As we shall see, the method of balance and refinement builds on these features of moral inquiry, to present us with a picture of moral inquiry which, DePaul claims, is far removed from the sort of inquiry that the standard view on the method of reflective equilibrium represents.

## C. Rationality and the Method of Balance and Refinement

Why should we follow DePaul's method as opposed to the more traditional coherence methods? DePaul defends his method of balance and refinement on the grounds that it does quite well in helping us achieve two cherished epistemic goods, to wit, rationality and warrant. To say that a belief is rational, holds DePaul, is to say that 'a believer has done all she can, as determined from her own point of view, to insure that the belief is true'.[39] Warrant

[39] DePaul (1993: 5).

is the 'positive epistemic status that plays the central part in distinguishing knowledge from mere true belief?[40] DePaul claims that (1) the method of balance and refinement is the only method that can guarantee rational moral beliefs; and (2) even though the method cannot guarantee warranted beliefs, it is possible for some moral inquirers to have warranted moral beliefs as a result of following the method. In this section, I shall examine DePaul's arguments for (1); the next section will discuss his arguments for (2).

DePaul argues for the claim that the method of balance and refinement is the only rational method of moral inquiry in two steps. In a first step, he rules out as irrational all methods except for the radical method of reflective equilibrium and the method of balance and refinement (i). In a second step, he eliminates as irrational the radical method of reflective equilibrium so that the method of balance and refinement remains as the only rational method (ii). Let us now see in some detail each step of DePaul's argument to the effect that balance and refinement is the only method of moral inquiry that can guarantee that one ends up with a rational system of moral beliefs.[41]

### *i. The Case for the Irrationality of Methods of Moral Inquiry other than Radical Reflective Equilibrium and the Method of Balance and Refinement*

According to DePaul, the rationality of methods of moral inquiry must be assessed in relation to two parameters: a static parameter and a dynamic one. First, we must assess whether the method leads us to accept a rational system of beliefs. Secondly, we must assess whether it recommends us to follow rational revisions of belief, that is, whether it brings us to a rational system of beliefs by following a number of steps that it is rational for us to take. The requirement that a method of moral inquiry lead to a rational system of beliefs held at a given time plays a comparatively unimportant role in DePaul's argument, since, in his view, many methods of moral inquiry satisfy this requirement. The requirement that a method of moral inquiry lead to rational revisions of belief plays the most significant role in DePaul's

[40] ibid, 5. DePaul takes warrant to play the most significant role in elevating true belief to knowledge. He does not claim though that it does convert true belief into knowledge because some other feature is required to handle Gettier-style problems, that is, cases in which a true and warranted belief fails to constitute knowledge. Even though he is aware of this possibility, DePaul ignores the Gettier problem because, in his view, this type of problem is not significant in the moral domain. See DePaul (1993: 224) fn 11.

[41] DePaul argues that methods other than radical reflective equilibrium and the method of balance and refinement are irrational in (1993) ch 3. For DePaul's argument to the effect that even reflective equilibrium falls short of rationality, and thus that the only rational method of moral inquiry is the method of balance and refinement, see DePaul (1993) ch 4.

argument, for—he claims—this requirement is met only by the radical method of reflective equilibrium and the method of balance and refinement.

Now, what does the rationality of a procedure of belief revision consist in? DePaul claims that what is rational to revise is determined by what would seem likely to be true to the person, after giving the matter some thought, where this reflection includes consideration of relevant alternatives and the acquisition of appropriate additional evidence. In light of what is involved in the rational revision of beliefs, it is apparent that the method of reflective equilibrium is a rational method, for it directs the inquirer: (i) to consider the connections among his own beliefs, alternatives to those beliefs and arguments that might be given to decide among those alternatives; and (ii) to revise according to what seems to be correct as a result of such reflection. Since the method of balance and refinement inherits all these features of radical reflective equilibrium, it is also a rational method of moral inquiry.

DePaul argues that there are no rational alternatives to the radical method of reflective equilibrium and the method of balance and refinement. A genuine alternative to the method of radical reflective equilibrium would have to issue some sort of directive requiring inquirers either to leave something out of their reflection or not to revise according to what seems to be correct upon reflection, that is, to favour some set of propositions, regardless of which beliefs the inquirer would consider more likely to be true after reflection. Clearly either directive would lead inquirers to make irrational revisions of beliefs. DePaul claims that there is another way of interpreting purported alternatives to reflective equilibrium so that they do not direct irrational revisions of beliefs. According to this interpretation, critics of reflective equilibrium are not proposing genuine alternatives to this method. But these proposals are, in fact, particular workings through this method, albeit by inquirers who are more strongly committed to certain epistemic principles or metaethical theories than to their considered moral judgements. Hence, these inquirers actually favour these principles and metaethical views as a result of following the method of reflective equilibrium, even if apparently they claim to be following an alternative method. Thus, according to DePaul, only the method of reflective equilibrium and the method of balance and refinement are rational methods. Other methods are either irrational or they are not genuine alternatives.

### *ii. The Case for the Irrationality of the Method of Radical Reflective Equilibrium*

So far, we have seen that, according to DePaul, methods other than reflective equilibrium and its successor, the method of balance and refinement, do not guarantee rational moral beliefs. Now, DePaul claims that even the method of reflective equilibrium fails to lead inquirers to accept rational beliefs, and hence, that balance and refinement is, ultimately, the only rational method of moral inquiry. The problem with reflective equilibrium is that is starts from a wrong assumption that both proponents and critics of this method, as well as defenders of alternative methods, share with regard to what is relevant to the rationality of moral inquiry. This assumption leaves experience out of what is relevant to the rationality of moral inquiry. As a result of this exclusion, DePaul claims, reflective equilibrium fails to guarantee rational moral inquiry.

DePaul refers to the experience that is relevant to moral inquiry as 'formative experience', and contrasts it with another kind of experience, to wit, 'reasoning experience'. Reasoning experience 'involves such things as constructing an argument from propositions one already believes, appreciating a counter-example to a moral principle one accepts, or seeing a proposition as obvious upon considering it'.[42] This kind of experience is the one that reflective equilibrium, and nearly every other method of moral inquiry, takes into consideration. According to DePaul, not all changes in moral views are the result of reasoning experiences. He calls experiences that alter one's moral beliefs and that do not fit the mould of either paradigm of reasoning experience, 'formative experiences'. Among these experiences, DePaul includes 'real life' experiences, such as living with a person who has a certain virtue or vice or closely interacting with people who value different things, as well as experiences with art. All these experiences have the potential for changing a person's moral views in ways that are markedly different from the kind of alterations that fall within the label of reasoning experience.[43] Unlike reasoning experiences, 'formative experiences feel more as if they influence one's faculty of moral judgment, intuition, or perception, so that one sees situations in a different way, and feels drawn to make different moral judgements or accept different moral principles'.[44]

Thus, formative experiences, in contrast to reasoning experiences, lead us to revise our moral beliefs by altering the way in which our moral faculty works. It is the relevance of this kind of experience for the rationality of our moral beliefs that reflective equilibrium, as much as any other method of moral inquiry to date, has failed to appreciate. As a result, argues DePaul, reflective equilibrium cannot prevent two forms of irrationality from arising, namely, 'naïveté' and 'corruption'.[45] The problem is as follows: there is no device in the method of reflective equilibrium that prevents a person who has a limited range of formative experience, ie a naïve person, from using

[42] DePaul (1993: 140).

[43] DePaul notes that there is a close connection between formative experiences and moral conversions. See DePaul (1993: 232) fn 12.

[44] DePaul (1993: 146).

[45] DePaul suggests that the irrationality of beliefs based on less than all evidence and beliefs based on misleading evidence provide a model for understanding the kind of irrationality that is involved in naïveté and corruption, respectively. See DePaul (1993: 165–69).

the method of reflective equilibrium to construct a moral theory around his beliefs, without adding to their base of formative experience. Such a person would have proceeded irrationally, insofar as he did not do all he could, as seen from his own perspective, to ensure the truth of his views. One could try to amend the method of reflective equilibrium and require that the inquirer, in addition to considering relevant alternatives and arguments, must also have some exposure to available experiences. However, argues DePaul, this straightforward modification of the method will not do. The problem is that some formative experiences are likely to have a negative influence on the epistemic status of a person's beliefs. DePaul suggests that we distinguish between 'enriching' and 'corrupting' experiences. Whereas the former are those that it would be best for a person to enjoy before making moral judgements, the latter corrupt, rather than inform, one's moral judgements. Amending the method of reflective equilibrium so that it requires the inquirer to expose himself to available formative experiences does not discriminate between those that enhance and those that corrupt our faculty of moral judgement.

Now, is there any way to amend the method of reflective equilibrium to obtain a method that would lead naïve inquirers to broaden their formative experience without forcing inquirers to have experiences that would corrupt their moral judgement? Such a method would have to rely in an important sense upon a distinction between enriching and corrupting experiences, so as to lead inquirers to seek the former and avoid the latter. According to DePaul, there are two possible ways in which we could draw the distinction between corrupting and enriching experiences. We could either distinguish them absolutely, or we may take this distinction to be relative to the inquirer's beliefs. Let us explore each of these possibilities. According to DePaul, we may take Aristotle as a representative of the former approach. In this approach, we should supplement the method of reflective equilibrium by identifying objectively the experiences that enhance and those that corrupt our moral faculty. However, argues DePaul, there are several problems with this option. First, the Aristotelian approach is externalist, in the sense that the necessary experiences are identified independently of the inquirer's beliefs. As a result, a method operating with this criterion would lead inquirers to behave irrationally, for it is possible that the method would direct them to acquire experiences that they take to be corrupting. In addition, this approach is not neutral among substantive moral conceptions, while, in the main, recent moral philosophy has been decidedly liberal in this respect.

The second possibility—the identification of enriching and corrupting formative experiences by reference to the inquirers' own system of beliefs—is the option that DePaul endorses. He holds this option to be more congenial to coherentist methods of moral inquiry, which are both internalist and liberal. DePaul proposes that in order to incorporate within a coherentist account the distinction between enriching and corrupting experiences, the following conditions should be added. First, as the inquirer seeks to fashion his moral and background beliefs into a coherent whole, he must consider whether the formative experience he has enjoyed is minimally broad, or skewed in some way, whether there are activities that he could engage in that are apt to broaden his range of experience, and what might be said for and against each of these activities with regard to whether they are likely to enhance or corrupt his capacity for making sensitive moral judgements. Second, the inquirer must seek out experiences and engage in these activities accordingly. That is, he must avoid those experiences that he considers upon reflection to be corrupting, and he must engage in those activities that he takes to produce formative experiences. In particular, he should seek additional experiences with literature, film and other forms of art, which he considers likely to further refine his moral judgement. Amending the method of reflective equilibrium by incorporating these two additions yields what DePaul calls the 'method of balance and refinement'.[46]

The method of balance and refinement, holds DePaul, requires naïve inquirers to think about the limited range of experience that they have enjoyed, and seek out additional experience accordingly, while it does not force inquirers to have formative experiences that they would regard as corrupting. Thus, this method, in contrast to the method of reflective equilibrium, protects inquirers against the irrationality involved in both naïveté and corruption. Of course, it does not deal with all epistemic deficiencies that are involved in these two phenomena. In particular, it would allow a naïve person who accepts rather weak epistemic standards, even after reflection, to hold the belief that additional formative experience is unnecessary. Nor would it prevent inquirers from falling into corruption unwittingly. But it does ensure that inquirers will proceed rationally. Hence, the method of balance and refinement does guarantee that we achieve a cognitive end of the utmost importance, to wit, rational belief.

The first part of DePaul's strategy for defending the method of balance and refinement, ie to show that this method ensures rational belief, is now complete. I move to the discussion of the second prong of DePaul's defence of the method of balance and refinement, which consists of showing that this method puts at least some inquirers in a favourable position to have warranted beliefs.

[46] DePaul (1993: 174).

### D. Warrant and the Method of Balance and Refinement

Does the method of balance and refinement yield warranted beliefs? DePaul argues that it cannot be established that the method of balance and refinement will guarantee inquirers warranted beliefs.[47] There is always the possibility that naïve inquirers would remain naïve, even after careful reflection. And it is always possible for inquirers to be unaware of the corrupting character of the experiences in which they engage. In these two cases, inquirers following the method of balance and refinement will not reach warranted beliefs. However, claims DePaul, these possibilities are not a decisive objection against the adequacy of the method. The demand for a method to guarantee knowledge to anyone who follows it stems from the view that the epistemic status of output beliefs must be explained exclusively in terms of features of the method. However, as has been argued, DePaul rejects this mechanistic view of the methods of moral inquiry. Instead of focusing on methods, DePaul suggests that we shift the emphasis to the individual inquirer, and holds that the epistemic status of accepted beliefs must be accounted for not only in terms of features of the method, but also in terms of features of the inquirer. Thus, instead of demanding that a method guarantee knowledge, regardless of who employs the method, we should demand that a method aid the inquirer to attain knowledge, and guarantee that it be possible for some persons (those who make the right contribution to the process) to come to have warranted beliefs. Thus, we should reformulate the question upon which the second part of the defence of the method of balance and refinement depends, and ask: is it possible for inquirers who come with the 'right frame of mind', as DePaul puts it, to reach warranted beliefs as a result of employing the method of balance and refinement?

DePaul shows that it is indeed possible for some inquirers to arrive at warranted beliefs by following the method of balance and refinement. When reflecting on how our perceptual beliefs get warranted, argues DePaul, we may come to see how balance and refinement may lead to warranted beliefs. More specifically, DePaul's proposal involves the following claims: (i) our moral faculty is analogous to our faculty of perceptual judgements; (ii) our moral beliefs are warranted in a way analogous to the way in which perceptual beliefs are warranted; and (iii) this analogy yields an account of moral naïveté, corruption and the role of literature and the arts in dealing with both phenomena. I shall now briefly explain each of these claims.

First, a word must be said about DePaul's explanation of the terms of the analogy that provides the starting point of his account of warrant. The analogy is not between moral judgements and perception of simple qualities,

[47] For DePaul's conception of warrant, see DePaul (1993: 75–91).

eg seeing that a book is red. DePaul characterizes the relevant kind of perception as follows:

> I am thinking of our capacity to make fine perceptual discriminations on the basis of a sort of complicated gestalt, where typically a person can acquire the ability to make the relevant discriminations only after a considerable amount of experience, and sometimes even training. Think, then, of the ability of connoisseurs to make fine discriminations between wines, the ability of an experienced biologist to 'see' through a microscope or, to use an example with which I am more familiar, the ability of a riding master to 'see' various things about a moving horse.[48]

Thus, DePaul's claim is that our faculty of moral judgement is analogous to our faculty for making such complex perceptual discriminations.

Secondly, just as our perceptual faculty requires perceptual experience to work properly, ie to produce warranted beliefs, does our faculty of moral judgement require moral experience to yield warranted beliefs. Such experience does not merely serve as an input to the faculty that processes this input and yields a belief as output, ie a perceptual or moral belief, but it also alters the faculty itself, so that it functions better. Since the method of balance and refinement asks the inquirer to seek out enriching experiences that improve her faculty of moral judgement, it leads to warranted beliefs, and beliefs with more warrant. According to DePaul, not all warranted moral beliefs are products of a faculty analogous to perception. Some moral beliefs are warranted in a derivative way, as a result of being related to warranted beliefs and being members of a coherent system. Since the method of balance and refinement incorporates the role that argument and systematization plays in moral theory construction, it can also account for the derivative warrant of these beliefs. Thus, the element of 'refinement' leads to beliefs that are directly warranted, and the element of 'balance' leads to beliefs that are derivatively warranted.

Last, DePaul contends that an account of the warrant of moral beliefs based on an analogy with our perceptual faculty provides an adequate explanation of naïveté, corruption, and the role of literature and the arts in moral inquiry. The problem of the naïve is that his beliefs are the products of a faculty of moral judgement that has not been used enough, or on a sufficient number of situations. As regards corruption, the problem is that the faculty of moral judgement has lost its degree of attunement as a result of the person being exposed to corrupting experiences. Literature as well as other forms of art helps relieve naïveté and keeps us away from corruption by supplying the kind of experience that is needed to develop a person's faculty of moral judgement. More specifically, it supplies additional cases on which a person can exercise his faculty of moral judgement, cases that are, moreover, sufficiently distant to minimize the effects of personal bias,

[48] DePaul (1993: 202).

and that, insofar as they are less complex than real life situations, are well-suited for training our faculty of moral judgement.

To sum up, according to DePaul, the method of balance and refinement leads some inquirers to accept warranted beliefs. In addition, as explained, it guarantees that inquirers will accept rational beliefs as a result of following the method. Given that rationality and warrant are two main goals of moral inquiry, we have good reason, claims DePaul, to be satisfied with a method that allows us to achieve this much, and thus, we have good reason for following this method.

Indeed, DePaul has formulated an interesting challenge to coherence methods of moral inquiry: if a coherence account is not to certify naïve or corrupt inquirers, it must require some measure of relevant formative experience. It is, however, controversial, whether his coherence method, ie the method of balance and refinement, succeeds in overcoming this problem. To start with, it is quite doubtful that this methodology is as morally neutral as he wants it to be.[49] DePaul's proposal seems to heavily rely on some previous view about which experiences are formative, which corrupting, and what is required for one's moral faculty to be appropriately attuned, and this sheds doubts over the purported liberal character of the theory. Besides, the role that experiences previously identified as either formative or corrupting play in this theory also compromises the commitment to internalism, which is central to coherentism.

Nonetheless, DePaul's proposal is valuable insofar as it brings to light the need to include elements other than beliefs, ie experiences, into the set that is relevant for assessing the coherence of one's moral outlook. In addition, DePaul's remarks on the importance of literature and the arts in moral inquiry suggest yet another way in which we may extend such a set. This view of moral philosophy as a discipline that requires as much argument as perception and that brings together philosophical work with art and literature has important implications for moral education.[50] Because of that, it may nicely complement those coherence theories which importantly rely on the inquirer's skills and abilities to render one's moral judgements coherent.[51] One such theory is Goldman's method of analogy and difference, which I shall discuss in the next section.

[49] See Blackburn (1988) and Timmons (1995).

[50] See Brandt (1985). Brandt argues that DePaul's views are better interpreted as views about moral education rather than as views about how moral philosophers should conduct their inquiries.

[51] As opposed to these theories, one may advance a more mechanistic view of what is involved in computing coherence such as, for instance, Thagard's computational model of ethical coherence. I shall introduce this model in s IV of this chapter.

## III. REASONING FROM ANALOGY AND DIFFERENCE

Goldman's coherentist proposal is structured around the idea that moral reasoning is at bottom case-based reasoning.[52] This conception of moral reasoning is meant to be an alternative to both rule-based moral reasoning and particularism. Rule theorists—as Goldman characterizes them—assume that moral reasoning always consists in the application of rules to particular cases.[53] In their view, only general principles can create coherence within sets of judgements.[54] As opposed to rule-based theorists, particularists deny that rules are needed in moral deliberation. According to particularism, when directly confronted with a controversial case, we perceive the morally relevant factors and how they weigh against each other in the concrete context.[55] None of these positions, argues Goldman, provides a satisfactory account of moral reasoning.[56]

As opposed to both rule-based theorists and particularists, Goldman claims that the correct answer to a controversial issue is that which is most coherent with a base of settled judgements. Coherence is a matter of the satisfaction of what Goldman calls 'the Kantian constraint'. This constraint requires that we do not judge cases differently without being able to cite a relevant (and generalizable) difference between them.[57] Hence, in Goldman's view, moral reasoning is neither a matter of applying rules nor an intuitive balancing of reasons, but rather it consists in reasoning from analogy and difference under the Kantian constraint. When such constraint is satisfied, our moral judgements are coherent, and therefore, justified.

Let us now see in detail how Goldman's method of analogy and difference works. First, I shall explain the Kantian constraint. Then, I will describe the main steps on which reasoning under this constraint consists. Last, I will examine Goldman's replies to some of the objections that might be raised against his view. Before entering into the details of Goldman's proposal, I must say a word about its intended scope of application. Goldman's theory is meant to be a theory about how to reason not only in the moral domain,

[52] Similarly, Hurley also favours a coherentist cased-based approach to practical reasoning. See ch 7.

[53] Goldman takes Hare, Schauer, and Raz to be defending the most sophisticated versions of rule-based theories. See Hare (1981); Raz (1999); and Schauer (1991).

[54] That principles create coherence among judgements is the view that, argues Goldman, both Rawls and Dworkin endorse. See Rawls (1999) and Dworkin (1986).

[55] Goldman takes Dancy to represent the particularist position he argues against; see Dancy (1993).

[56] Goldman argues against rule-based approaches to moral reasoning in AH Goldman (2002) ch 1. For his critique of moral particularism, see ibid, 150–55.

[57] In this sense, Goldman is committed to a very strong version of internalism about justification. He writes that the coherentist requirement—the Kantian constraint—requires 'not only that there be morally relevant differences for all differences in moral judgments but that evaluators have such justifying reasons and be able to produce them when their judgments are challenged'; AH Goldman (1989: 141).

but also in the legal one.[58] In Goldman's view, moral and legal reasoning are similar in structure, although the two databases from which each kind of reasoning proceeds are different.[59] In both moral and legal cases, we reason from analogy and difference to the most coherent decision with the base of settled judgements, ie moral and legal judgements, respectively. Despite the structural analogies, there is a prominent disanalogy, claims Goldman, between the two domains, namely, the principle of precedent, which requires that judges conform their decisions to earlier decisions by certain other courts. No such requirement exists in the moral realm. Except for this major difference, the structure of reasoning in the moral and legal domain is similar. While filling in the details of his proposal, Goldman focuses on moral reasoning, and so will I when explaining his views. Nonetheless, it is important to keep in mind that Goldman's theses about moral reasoning are intended to be fully applicable to legal reasoning as well.

### A. The Kantian Constraint

The Kantian constraint is a central piece of Goldman's coherentist project. Goldman's rejection of a rule-based model of practical reasoning leads him to discard the associated view that coherence of particular judgements requires that they be supported by general principles or universal rules. This is the standpoint of the most influential models of coherence both in the moral domain, eg Rawls,[60] and in the legal one, eg Dworkin.[61] Such a principled model of coherence should be replaced, in Goldman's view, by a different conception of coherence that measures coherence only among a set of particular judgements. The demand of coherence does not require that a set of particular judgements be supported by universal principles or rules, but rather that it satisfy what Goldman refers to as the 'Kantian constraint', so called because—he says—it is a 'charitable partial interpretation' of Kant's universalization requirement. Goldman states this constraint as follows: 'One must not judge a case differently from a previously settled case unless one can cite a morally relevant difference between them, a difference that can be shown to make a difference in other cases as well'.[62]

This requirement has two parts: (i) one must find a relevant difference between cases judged differently; and (ii) these differences must be relevant

[58] Goldman doubts that something similar to the reasoning structures that characterize moral and legal deliberation exists for prudential reasoning. Thus, unlike the theories surveyed in the previous chapter, ie Thagard's, Richardson's, and Hurley's theories, Goldman only gives an important role to coherence in practical reasoning about legal and moral problems.

[59] AH Goldman (1989) argues for this view. See also AH Goldman (1988a: 185–92).

[60] Goldman criticizes Rawls' model of reflective equilibrium in AH Goldman (2002: 158–61).

[61] Goldman criticizes Dworkin's views on legal coherence in AH Goldman (2002: 114–17).

[62] AH Goldman (2002: 161).

more broadly, that is, they must distinguish other cases as well. Now, what constitutes a relevant difference? Goldman claims that a difference between two cases is relevant if 'it affects the values at stake in the two cases'.[63] Relevance is, in this sense, relative to the domain of discourse, eg moral or legal. When there are no violations of this constraint, a set of judgements is coherent in that it will not both pursue and defeat the same values in the same circumstances. In Goldman's view, the latter is the sense of coherence that is relevant to the moral (and legal) realm. In this domain, coherence among moral (or legal) judgements is required because such judgements guide action, and actions aim to fulfil purposes or realize values. Goldman explains this point as follows:

> Since moral judgments guide moral actions, I must, if I am to be moral, judge two situations in the same way if I cannot distinguish them morally. Otherwise my judgments will be self-defeating in just the way that actions at cross-purposes are self-defeating. I will defeat an aim that I am committed to pursuing in just those circumstances at hand.[64]

Thus, satisfaction of the requirement ensures that one's judgements are coherent so that they can guide action in a non self-defeating way. The need to avoid self-defeating judgements is the main reason why coherence, argues Goldman, is sought in moral reasoning.

In Goldman's view, reasoning from analogy and difference under the Kantian constraint differs both from applying rules and from the kind of case-based reasoning that particularists advocate. On the one hand, this requirement is a weaker constraint on analogical reasoning than the requirement to act in accordance with strictly universal rules whenever their conditions of application obtain. On the other hand, even though the particularist position is compatible with the first clause of the constraint, particularists cannot accept its second clause, which Goldman calls the 'requirement of generality'. If, as particularists argue, context can eliminate the moral relevance of a factor or even change its valence, then it should be possible that a factor be relevant only in a single context. The ever-present possibility of nullification or reversal would prevent relevant differences from being generalized, as the Kantian constraint requires.

The aforementioned difference between the method of analogy and difference and the particularist account of moral reasoning is not, claims Goldman, a minor one. It is crucial that the Kantian constraint include the second clause for it not to be reduced to triviality. Without the requirement of generality, all sets of judgements will be coherent as long as cases differ in whatever respect someone might claim to see as relevant, eg one could distinguish abortion from infanticide by arguing that infants and foetuses

[63] ibid, 137.
[64] ibid, 162.

breathe in different ways, and that the manner of respiration is morally relevant here although nowhere else. Against particularists, Goldman argues that the requirement of generality must be accepted for a number of reasons. To start with, the requirement that relevant factors not be unique to a particular context is part of the normative conventions we adopt to settle disputes peacefully. Only generalized factors are allowed to function as reasons in moral argument. In addition, the idea that there could be a property that makes a unique thing valuable presupposes an untenable realist view about values. Things that we value are things that satisfy our needs or that we have learned to value. In both cases, these sources of value recur, or we would not have learned, adopted or continued to value them. Last, in order to avoid comparative injustice we need to obey the generality requirement. Thus, a demand for fairness, which is central in the moral domain, prevents us from taking factors to be relevant only in a unique context.

### B. Goldman's Method of Analogy and Difference

As we have seen, in moral (and legal) reasoning, the goal is to find the solution of a controversial case that is most coherent with the database of settled judgements, ie where such coherence amounts to the satisfaction of the two-fold Kantian constraint. But, how does one proceed to arrive at such decision? According to Goldman, moral (and legal) reasoning is a process that consists of the following four steps.[65] First, we must specify those factors or values that are morally relevant in a case. This identification requires both information about the context and empathetic identification with the interests of the individuals affected. We must know which alternative actions are available, how they are likely to realize or frustrate the competing values at stake and how the individuals involved are likely to feel and react to our possible actions. Consider, to take one of Goldman's examples, the issue of passive euthanasia. In this case, we must identify the competing values at stake from the patient's side, eg life versus avoidance of suffering and freedom of choice, and from the doctor's side, eg the possible effects on medical practices of allowing death versus blocking informed patient choice. In so doing, some factual information is relevant, such as information about how rational patients in terminal conditions are, or how legalized euthanasia in other societies has affected the medical profession.

Secondly, once agreement on what the relevant values at stake are is reached, one should also seek agreement on what their ordering is in the present context. This requires that we look to previously settled cases in

[65] Goldman reviews the steps that moral reasoning without rules involves in AH Goldman (2002: 169–75).

which priorities among those values are determined in a way that is acceptable to those who are engaged in moral deliberation. Here, we must identify either real or hypothetical situations in which similar interests compete but where our judgements are more confident than in the case at hand. For example, in the case of passive euthanasia, we could take the right of patients to refuse medical treatment in other contexts as a paradigm case.

The third step is to seek disanalogies between the context at issue and these less problematic cases to determine whether these disanalogies are morally relevant, that is, whether they affect the values at stake. To continue with the example of passive euthanasia, if one were to take the opponents of the patient choice's point of view, one could see the imminent threat of death as a relevant difference between passive euthanasia and other medical situations. For Goldman, the accurate identification of differences is as crucial to coherence as the recognition of analogies. To judge cases differently without being able to cite a relevant difference produces as much incoherence as judging in the same way when there is a difference that is morally relevant. And just as we should try to avoid over-assimilation when morally deliberating, we should also try to avoid over-complication or false distinctions.

Last, in a critical spirit, we must attempt to find further similar cases in which our judgements may come down on the other side. This step naturally follows the third, since finding disanalogies to proposed cases leads one to seek closer analogies. For example, in light of the difference between the right of patients to refuse medical treatment in contexts in which there is no imminent death threat and passive euthanasia, one could think of the right of doctors to intervene in order to prevent attempts at suicide from succeeding.

In Goldman's view, this thorough search for similarities and differences requires some skills that exceed those involved in applying rules for solving a particular moral problem. Moral knowledge, argues Goldman, requires much more than knowledge of a set of rules, it consists in 'knowing how to act consistently with coherent orderings of norms or competing values as expressed in settled judgements in a large variety of cases or contexts'.[66] Such knowledge is brought to bear on present problematic cases through an appreciation of both similarities and differences. This requires that the moral agent employ some skills that, Goldman explains, are not unlike those of a good lawyer or doctor, to wit, the ability to empathize with various interests, the ability to think of and imagine morally charged situations that are analogous to the case at hand and the ability to identify morally relevant properties. These skills develop only on the basis of a sufficiently broad first-hand and second-hand experience of the right kind. The right

[66] ibid, 172.

kind of experience is the one that 'sensitizes us to the feelings and interests of all involved, and that reveals similarities and differences that reflect that sensitivity better than our prior frameworks'.[67] Thus, Goldman takes this sensitizing kind experience to play a crucial role in moral reasoning.[68]

### C. Some Objections against Goldman's Method

Goldman considers some of the objections that may be raised against his account of moral reasoning.[69] Here, I shall briefly consider these objections as well as Goldman's reply to them. Whereas some of these objections question particular aspects of Goldman's theory, others are typically raised against coherentist methods in ethics.[70] Thus, an examination of them will not only allow us to identify the main problems in Goldman's argument but also to assess whether his theory has the resources for meeting the traditional objections against coherentism in ethics.

The first objection arises from Goldman's description of moral knowledge and reasoning skills. It might be objected that this description ties moral capacities too closely to cognitive skills. Correct moral judgement—it might be argued—crucially depends on good character, and is not so much a matter of searching complex analogies; otherwise, how could relatively unsophisticated people so often be able to do the right thing? Goldman replies to this objection by pointing at the role that emotions play in his theory of moral reasoning. Affective capacities, eg empathetic identification, are crucial for generating the proper inputs. Nonetheless, he does reject the view according to which, when facing a moral problem, we should trust to gut feelings rather than to the outcome of complex reasoning.[71] In his view, gut feelings and immediate perceptions are often based on misleading similarities, and are not a suitable move in dispute-resolution, which is a central function of moral systems.

The second objection derives from Dancy's particularism, and it concerns the move from settled cases to controversial ones. Dancy argues that we cannot assimilate the judgement of the case at hand to that of settled cases without knowing which properties are relevant in the controversial case. The problem is that, in order to know this, we must already know how to judge the case at hand. Thus, settled cases are of no use for judging

[67] ibid, 183.

[68] As we have seen, other authors, most importantly DePaul, have also vindicated the role of both first-hand and second-hand experience in moral reasoning. See s II above.

[69] AH Goldman ((2002: 175–83) and (1988: 192–212)).

[70] For a list of these objections, see s I.C above in this chapter.

[71] Goldman refers to Stuart Hampshire as a proponent of this view; see Hampshire (1983: 105–10).

controversial cases.[72] In Goldman's view, this objection begs the question. One cannot know which properties are relevant prior to judging a case, only if one accepts—as particularists do—that a property may be relevant in a particular context and nowhere else. But this is precisely what Goldman denies. In his view, we can know that if a property is not generally relevant, then it is not relevant in the case at hand either. Hence, we can decide whether a property is relevant in the present case prior to deciding that case. And in the absence of relevant differences, we may assimilate the problematic case to the settled one. Thus, Dancy's objection would only apply if his particularist framework were already accepted.

The third objection asks whether the method of analogy and difference is useful when facing genuine novelty. The question arises as to whether there will always be settled judgements from which to reason by analogy in a genuinely novel case. In Goldman's view, this does not pose a problem for his method of reasoning because, at some level of generality, there will always be similar values and interests that have competed in the past. For example, even though internet invasions of privacy were, at some point, a new kind of threat, their wrongness can be seen as deriving from more traditional forms of invading privacy. Thus, we should always be able to find paradigms from which to reason.[73]

The next objections are among those that are traditionally raised against coherentist methods in ethics. The fourth objection questions the status of settled cases. The charge is that such judgements represent only established intuitions, eg social and personal prejudices. Coherence with such judgements will be only as worthy as they are, which is—the objector claims—not much.[74] In Goldman's view, we can provide our set of settled judgements with better credentials than those that the objector claims them to have. To start with, the set of judgements from which we must reason are subjected to fully informed reflection. Then, while proceeding from this informed input in accordance with the method of analogy and difference, we may find that some apparent settled judgements are incoherent with others. Thus, a test of 'narrow coherence', eg coherence between controversial judgements and analogous settled judgements, may rule out some of these initially apt judgements as incoherent. In addition, claims Goldman, informed judgements must not only cohere with one another, but our set of judgements must also satisfy some coherence requirements as a whole. That is, they should also satisfactorily pass a test of 'broad coherence', ie coherence between moral frameworks and extra-moral constraints, ie facts and experience, the social

[72] Dancy (1985b: 146–47).

[73] The problem here is to successfully reply to this objection while avoiding falling into the risk of overassimilation that Goldman warns us against.

[74] This is the so-called 'credibility objection'. See ss I.C, II.B and V.A of this chapter for different responses to this objection.

aims of moral systems and psychological facts.[75] These tests of narrow and broad coherence may lead to calling into question previously settled cases, and ensure that we get a fully coherent and informed set of settled judgements as opposed to a set that only has dubious credentials.

Appeal to broad coherence is also meant to provide an answer to a related objection, to wit, the 'alternative coherent systems objection'. To recall, the problem is that, faced with several moral frameworks that are equally coherent, one cannot justify, by the coherentist standards, a commitment to any of them.[76] The alternative coherent systems objection raises the question of justification at a global level in a clear and pressing way. In Goldman's view, this question would admit of a straightforward answer if one accepted moral realism, that is, the view that there are moral properties such that correspondence with them renders moral judgements true.[77] The global justification of one's commitment to a set of values and judgements would then differ from the local justification of particular moral beliefs only in scope. In both cases, the goal would be to arrive at beliefs that correspond to real moral properties. However, for reasons that will be explained below, Goldman rejects the realist view, and so needs to look for a different answer to the question of global justification. The answer is provided, claims Goldman, by the notion of broad coherence. We can assess moral systems according to criteria of coherence with a set of extra-moral standards. Still, as Goldman recognizes, these criteria will not single out a unique moral framework. Nonetheless, argues Goldman, even if choices among systems that pass all tests of broad coherence cannot be justified on the basis of these criteria, this does not pose a problem for a couple of reasons. To start with, once moral realism is not accepted, there need not be a uniquely true moral system. In addition, even if some choices are groundless, from the point of view of individuals who are situated in a particular historical and social context, such choices, even when reflective and conscious, need not be seen that way.

Last, Goldman's theory faces the charge of conservatism that is traditionally raised against coherence views of justification. In particular, it might be objected that the method of analogy and difference is too conservative in that it always requires that new issues be settled by assimilation to previously decided cases. With regard to law, Goldman claims that institutional reasons justify the conservatism inherent to the principle of precedent. Concerning ethics, Goldman replies to this objection by claiming that no

[75] Goldman sometimes refers to the distinction narrow/broad coherence as internal/external coherence. The latter terms are employed by De George. De George distinguishes between the coherence of elements of an ethical theory with each other, ie 'internal coherence', and the coherence of an ethical theory with 'our moral and general experience, knowledge and beliefs', ie 'external coherence'. See De George (1990: 39) and Magnell (1994: 469 and 465–66).

[76] See s I.C above.

[77] On moral realism, see s V.A of this chapter.

moral judgement is immune to revision, and thus, that paradigms may also be changed in the course of reasoning. Experience, in his view, plays a crucial role in bringing about these revisions, as it can teach us that differences that were thought to be relevant do not generalize, or that cases regarded as analogous are relevantly different. We may change our paradigms in light of judgements that arise from experience, provided that it is of the right kind. When such novel experience gives rise to judgements that are seen to be in conflict with those that were previously settled, we may restore coherence by revising the latter.

Goldman's responses bring to light again the need for coherentism to make room for emotions and experience in moral reasoning. Taking into account the role of both emotions and experience may help us to meet some of the traditional objections against coherentism. In this respect, it is important to emphasize the important role that empathy plays in moral reasoning, which Goldman rightly incorporates into his theory. Thus, we find in Goldman's theory interesting suggestions in relation to how we could expand coherence methods so as to embrace factors such as emotions, empathetic understanding, and moral experience. However, there is, I believe, a fundamental problem with Goldman's case-based coherentism as a whole. There is no reason why we should restrict the elements the coherence of which is relevant to moral justification to particular moral judgements. Neither is there any reason why we should restrict coherence relations to analogical relations. Moreover, such a restrictive view significantly diminishes the coherentists' chances of successfully meeting the standard objections. For example, the prospects of meeting the alternative coherent systems objection are bleak if one endorses such a narrow view of what ethical coherence amounts to. For, surely, there could be several sets of moral beliefs that enjoy the same degree of the sort of analogical coherence that Goldman envisions. A richer and more complex account of both the elements of coherence and the kind of coherence relations that are relevant in moral deliberation is put forward by Thagard's theory, to which I turn now.

## IV. ETHICAL COHERENCE AS CONSTRAINT SATISFACTION

Thagard's constraint satisfaction approach to coherence is an ambitious project with a wide range of applications. In chapter four, I examined how Thagard's theory accounts for epistemic justification; to recall, according to this theory, epistemic justification results from the interaction of several kinds of coherence—ie deductive, perceptual, conceptual, analogical and explanatory. And, in chapter seven, I examined the theory of deliberative coherence developed by Thagard in collaboration with Millgram. Thagard claims that his theory of coherence may provide an account of ethical justification as well. Ethical justification, in his view, results from the interaction of deductive, analogical, explanatory and deliberative coherence. Hence, like epistemic justification, ethical justification involves the interaction of several kinds of coherence, with the major addition of deliberative coherence.

My discussion of Thagard's theory of ethical coherence will proceed as follows. First, I shall give an account of the kinds of coherence that, according to Thagard, contribute to moral justification. This theory, like Thagard's theory of epistemic coherence, is naturalistic in that it tries to answer questions about the methods we should use to reach moral beliefs by using knowledge about the ways in which people actually reason about moral issues.[78] Then, I shall present Thagard's coherentist account of the process of moral reasoning and discuss some of the problems that arise from studying this process from the perspective of a naturalized moral epistemology. In the process of moral reasoning, emotions play a critical role. As explained in earlier chapters, Thagard has developed a theory of emotional coherence that is meant to capture the emotional components of our reasoning processes. I will conclude my discussion of Thagard's approach to ethical coherence by describing how his theory of emotional coherence may be put to work to give an account of the emotional aspects of moral judgement.

## A. A Multicoherence Theory of Ethical Judgements

As argued above, one of the main problems of coherence theories of moral reasoning is that they have remained vague about the nature of coherence. In particular, the key notion of current coherentist approaches to ethics, to wit, 'reflective equilibrium', is hopelessly imprecise. How the state of equilibrium is to be characterized as well as how such a state is reached remains poorly specified. Thagard's theory of ethical coherence aims at providing a clear definition of this notion. Thagard holds that the justification of ethical judgements and ethical principles can be accomplished by taking into account four kinds of coherence: deductive, explanatory, analogical and deliberative coherence.[79] He writes:

> Reflective equilibrium requires integrated assessment of deductive coherence (fit between principles and judgments), explanatory coherence (fit of principles and judgments with empirical hypotheses), deliberative coherence (fit of judgments

[78] Thus, Thagard's theory may be located within the framework of 'metaethical' naturalism rather than 'normative' ethical naturalism. The latter, as opposed to the former, 'attempts to answer questions about what to do ... by using knowledge of how we actually behave'. See May, Friedman and Clark (1996: 3).

[79] For the development of this theory, see Thagard (1998) and (2000a) ch 5.

with goals) and analogical coherence (fit of judgments with other judgments in similar cases).[80]

I shall now describe the contribution of each kind of coherence to ethical justification. This requires that one indicate the kinds of elements and constraints that are relevant to ethical conclusions. To illustrate such contribution, I will use Thagard's case study: capital punishment.[81] In Toronto, in 1995, Paul Bernardo was convicted for sexual torture and murder of two women. Canadian Law does not admit capital punishment, and he was sentenced to life prison. Some people who had long argued against capital punishment felt strongly inclined to judge that execution in this case would nevertheless be appropriate. In Thagard's view, the constraint satisfaction theory of ethical justification can show how the incoherence of such views can be overcome.

i. *Deductive coherence*. For this kind of coherence as applied to ethics, the elements are propositions, including both general ethical principles and particular judgements. The main positive constraint derives from a relation of entailment, eg the principle that capital punishment is wrong entails that Paul Bernardo should not be executed. Negative constraints arise because of contradictions between propositions, eg capital punishment is wrong and capital punishment is right.
ii. *Explanatory coherence*. Ethics requires attention to this kind of coherence whenever ethical decisions depend in part on the evaluation of empirical hypotheses, as is frequently the case. For example, one common argument for capital punishment is that it is a deterrent to future crimes, which depends on the empirical hypothesis that having capital punishment reduces crimes. Evaluation of this hypothesis requires evaluation of evidence, such as the comparison of crime rates in countries or states with and without death penalty. Explanatory and deductive coherence are interconnected whenever the entailment relation depends on empirical hypotheses. For example, someone might argue that killing innocent people is wrong, and since capital punishment sometimes kills innocent people, it is also wrong. This entailment depends on the empirical hypothesis that innocent people are sometimes executed.
iii. *Deliberative coherence*. This type of coherence is relevant to ethical decisions that take into account the consequences of actions. For example, someone might argue that executing Bernardo will be much cheaper than imprisoning him for life, and thus that execution facilitates the goal of saving Canadian taxpayers money. As opposed to individual decision-making, goals in ethical decisions must be the objective interests

[80] Thagard (2000a: 406).

[81] Thagard has also illustrated his theory of coherence, although in much less detail, with debates on abortion. See Thagard (1998: 415–17) and (2000a: 144–48).

of all concerned. Deliberative coherence depends in part on explanatory coherence, since the judgement that an action facilitates a goal depends on the plausibility of a causal hypothesis, which is a matter of explanatory coherence. In addition, questions about what constitutes an objective interest are also tied with empirical hypotheses about the nature of human beings and their societies. For example, the families of Paul Bernardo's victims may want to see him killed, but whether execution would bring them some relief is an empirical question to be addressed on the basis of its explanatory coherence with psychological evidence.

iv. *Analogical coherence.* As has been explained before, the establishment of correspondences is a constraint satisfaction problem, in which positive constraints are based on similarity, structure, and purpose. In the case of ethical deliberations, the purpose is to transfer the moral judgement about a source analogue (an accepted case) to a target analogue (a contested case).[82] For example, if capital punishment is relevantly similar to killing a defenceless victim, an act that is obviously wrong, then capital punishment is also wrong. Analogical coherence can help establish the deductive and deliberative coherence of an ethical decision. For example, the analogy between killing a defenceless victim and the state executing a prisoner can help establish the deductive conclusion that Bernardo should not be executed.

In Thagard's view, this multicoherence theory of ethics shows how the traditional conflict between Kantian ethics and consequentialist ethical views can be overcome. Each approach to ethical justification identifies one kind of coherence, deductive and deliberative coherence, respectively. Both can be smoothly integrated—he claims—into the theory of ethical coherence as constraint satisfaction.[83] Thagard has run a computer simulation using three programs, ie ECHO, ACME and DECO, together to produce a common network. These programs implement the theory of explanatory coherence, the theory of analogical coherence and the theory of deliberative coherence, respectively. Figure 1 shows the constraint network for the case under discussion. Again, solid lines are positive constraints and dotted lines are negative constraints:[84]

[82] See ch 4.

[83] *Cf* Guarini (2007) (arguing that the most that follows from Thagard's theory is that some weight must be given to both Kantian and utilitarian types of considerations, but that the theory does not help overcome the debate between Kantianism and consecuentialism as it is unclear how much weight must be assigned to each of the different kinds of coherence).

[84] Thagard (1998: 416).

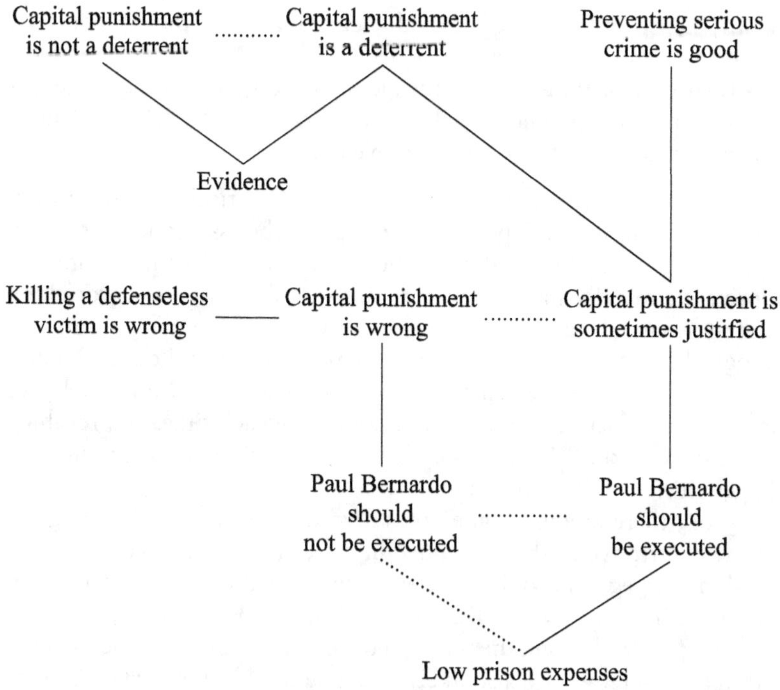


**Figure 1: Constraint Satisfaction Network for the Capital Punishment Example.**

## B. The Process of Moral Reasoning: The Descriptive and Normative

Thagard claims that, from the perspective of this theory, reaching an ethical decision is a complex process that involves the following steps:[85]

1. Identify deductive elements (principles, judgements) and positive and negative constraints among them.
2. Identify deliberative elements (actions, goals) and positive and negative constraints among them.
3. Identify explanatory elements (hypotheses, evidence) and positive and negative constraints among them.
4. Identify constraints linking the explanatory elements with deductive and deliberative elements.
5. Identify analogical elements (mapping hypotheses) and positive and negative constraints among them.

[85] ibid, 413.

6. Identify constraints linking the analogical elements with the deductive, deliberative and explanatory elements.
7. Finally, use algorithms to maximize coherence by accepting some elements and rejecting others in the way that approximately maximizes satisfaction of the positive and negative constraints.

This theory of ethical coherence is intended to be 'biscriptive', ie it is meant to be both descriptive and prescriptive.[86] Nonetheless, argues Thagard, several problems must be faced in relation to both the descriptive and the prescriptive claims. To start with, according to Thagard, this procedure, although normatively appealing, is probably too demanding given our psychological resources.[87] Our working memory is too limited to simultaneously entertain all the elements and constraints at once. More likely, we alternate between focusing on a kind of coherence each time, and reaching a tentative conclusion.[88] Thus, instead of reaching a global maximum, we usually get stuck at a local maximum.

In addition, there are also some normative worries. First, says Thagard, linking the descriptive to the normative in ethics is more problematic than in other domains, eg philosophy of science, since we do not have recognized inferential experts such as, say, Darwin or Einstein. However, I believe that the problem goes far beyond the purported lack of recognized experts in the moral domain. Here, we are also likely to encounter all standard objections to naturalized moral epistemology. The most familiar objection is that the subject of moral epistemology cannot be naturalized since so doing would mean that it is no longer normative, and thus, remove a defining, indeed critical, feature of moral epistemology. Ethics, it is claimed, attempts to tell people what they ought to do, and not merely what they do. The same objection is raised against naturalized epistemology. This approach, it is argued, undermines the normative status of epistemology. However, the objection appears to intensify in the moral case.[89] Secondly, the question arises as to whether the coherentist method yields judgements that are objectively right. Thagard's response is that we should be obliged to take into consideration all issues that are deemed as relevant. In his view, because ethical reasoning is often social, attention to current debates allows us to identify the relevant elements and constraints. He compares the requirement of taking into account a broad range of considerations that are brought to bear on ethical issues in public debate to the requirement in epistemology that anyone evaluating a hypothesis should take into account the full range of empirical evidence and alternative hypotheses. Hence, Thagard's suggestion seems to

[86] Thagard (1998: 417).
[87] On this problem, see Guarini (2007: 34–42).
[88] This is argued by Hoadley, Ranney and Shank (1994).
[89] Campbell and Hunter (2000: 5–6).

be that we should be satisfied with this sense of objectivity in the ethical domain, just as we are in the scientific one. Thirdly, it is a difficult issue to figure out the weights that are to be assigned to the constraints. Thagard points out that we can only hope that, once the discussion establishes a common set of constraints, coherence algorithms can yield consensus.[90] And last, there is the danger that deliberative coherence will have an undesirable effect on explanatory coherence. Normatively, we want explanatory coherence to affect deliberative coherence and not vice versa.[91]

Despite these problems, Thagard claims that his theory of moral reasoning is normatively adequate since it can handle the complexity of moral reasoning, it avoids the problems of foundationalist approaches to ethics, and it is based on a precise and computable notion of coherence, as opposed to alternative coherentist moral epistemologies. A further advantage—he claims—is that this computational theory of ethical coherence can be easily complemented with a theory of emotional coherence. Thus, it can smoothly and rigorously integrate the emotional component into a coherence model of moral reasoning.

### C. Emotional Coherence and Ethical Coherence

In chapter four, I introduced Thagard's theory of emotional coherence. I have already showed how this theory interacts with other kinds of coherence to arrive at epistemically justified beliefs (in chapter four) as well as justified decisions (in chapter seven). Here, I would like to examine the relevance of Thagard's theory of emotional coherence for ethical judgements. Ethical judgements usually involve a strong emotional component. Thagard claims that the theory of emotional coherence, by integrating emotional inputs with coherence-based ethical inference, may help bring together the cognitive and emotional aspects of moral reasoning.

In addition, the theory of emotional coherence may help to explain some psychological phenomena that have a pivotal importance in moral reasoning. One such phenomenon is 'empathy'. According to Barnes and Thagard, 'empathy is a kind of emotional analogy, in which a person *A* constructs an emotional image of person *B* by mapping *B*'s situation onto a similar situation previously experienced emotionally by *A*'.[92] Thus, in this kind of

[90] Most coherence models focus exclusively on the coherence of an individual's set of moral beliefs. In contrast, Thagard develops an account of how the achievement of a coherent system of beliefs is a social process as well as an individual one. For Thagard's model of consensus, see Thagard (2000a) ch 7.

[91] On Thagard and Millgram's views on the relation between explanatory and deliberative coherence, see ch 7.

[92] Barnes and Thagard (1997), quoted in Thagard (2000a: 183).

analogy, what is mapped is not propositional information, but a feeling or an image of a feeling.

Thagard gives the following example of empathy:

> When new graduate students arrive from overseas, they are often overwhelmed by arriving in a very different country and university and by having to work in English, if that is not their native language. My best shot at understanding their mental state comes from remembering my own disorientation when I went to study in Cambridge, England, in 1971. Everything seemed different and odd: the colleges, the town, the people, the food, the money, etc. Despite having minor language difficulties, it was months before I felt I knew what I was doing. Because foreign students' situations are relevantly similar to mine many years ago, I can project my remembered emotional state of bewilderment and anxiety onto them, using my imagination to amplify its intensity because of greater cultural and linguistic differences that they may face.[93]

As this example clearly illustrates, achieving empathetic understanding may require more than simply retrieving an emotionally charged source analogue to map onto a given target. One may need to generate a source analogue (England-only-worse analog). Then, one establishes a correspondence between my imagined situation and yours (the target analog), and ascribes an emotional valence to your situation that is similar to the emotional valence that I ascribe to mine. The theory of emotional coherence suggests the following procedure for how to achieve empathetic understanding:[94]

1. take what you know of P's personality and situation, and use explanatory and other kinds of coherence to make inferences about it that supplement the given information;
2. use analogical coherence to retrieve a similar situation from your own experience;
3. enhance the retrieved situation so as to bring it closer to P's;
4. use coherence-based inferences and emotional coherence to generate a valence for your constructed situation;
5. project this valence onto P as representing P's likely emotional state in that situation.

Thus, a full range of coherence inferences are involved in reaching empathetic understanding; most importantly, analogical inferences which transfer emotional valences. Such transfers are implemented by HOTCO, in the form of positive and negative valences.[95] Hence, Thagard's multicoherence theory of ethics, together with the theory of emotional coherence, as implemented by HOTCO, gives an account of both the cognitive and emotional aspects of moral reasoning. Of course, interaction of these two aspects does

[93] ibid.
[94] ibid, 186.
[95] See ch 4.

not necessarily result in better moral judgements. There are cases in which emotional coherence may be in conflict with the other kinds of coherence that are involved in ethical judgement. For instance, social prejudice based on negative stereotypes may lead to wrong judgements. Thus, emotional coherence may bring about normatively inappropriate judgements. Yet, emotion-free ethical judgement is also likely to be highly defective. Thus, what is needed is an account of the important role that emotions play in our process of moral belief formation that acknowledges the fact that emotions, though necessary, may also bias and distort judgement. Computationally, Thagard's theory tries to deal with some of the negative impact of emotions on ethical judgement by allowing activations to influence values, but not the other way around. Even if this theory is limited in that it does not deal with the full range of emotions, as well as with the different ways in which emotions may undermine our moral judgements, it is an important step towards integrating and formalizing the cognitive and emotional components of moral reasoning.

We have now completed the survey of the main coherence theories in ethics. In the next section, I shall consider the implications of coherence methods of moral inquiry for a conception of moral truth and moral objectivity.

## V. COHERENCE, TRUTH AND OBJECTIVITY IN ETHICS

### A. Moral Realism, Moral Anti-Realism and Coherence

There are two main views on what moral truth and objectivity amounts to: the realist and the anti-realist view. These views are analogous to the realist and anti-realist conceptions of the truth of empirical statements discussed in chapter six. Realism in ethics is the view that there is a moral reality whose existence and nature is largely independent of our moral theories and moral beliefs. In this view, moral truth is a matter of moral beliefs corresponding to inquiry-independent moral facts.[96] In contrast to moral realism, anti-realist views deny the existence of moral facts and properties that are independent of our moral theories and beliefs. We can distinguish relativist and non-relativist forms of anti-realism. As opposed to non-relativist versions, relativist forms of anti-realism hold that there are a plurality of moral facts, each constituted by different bodies of beliefs. The most important

[96] Naturalist and non-naturalist versions of moral realism may be distinguished. As opposed to British moral realism, American moral realism in the last decades has been naturalistic. For defences of naturalistic moral realism, see Brink (1989); Boyd (1997); Railton (1986); and Sturgeon (1985). For a systematic presentation of British moral realism, see Platts (1979) ch 10. For a contrast between the naturalistic and the non-naturalistic versions of moral realism, see Arrington (1989) ch 4.

non-relativist version of anti-realism is constructivism.[97] In this view, there is a single set of moral facts that is constituted by our moral beliefs in some favourable or idealized epistemic conditions.[98] Particularly, constructivists hold that the existence and nature of moral properties depends to a large extent on our best methods of inquiry. Moral truth is, on this view, a result of these methods; we construct, rather than discover, moral properties and facts through these methods.

What are the implications of embracing a coherence method of moral inquiry for issues about objectivity and truth in ethics? Does coherentism commit us to accepting either realism or anti-realism about moral truth? If the latter, does it involve a commitment to relativism? These questions have been traditionally put as an objection against coherence theories of justification in ethics. As we saw in earlier chapters, one of the main objections that has been directed against coherence theories of epistemic justification is the so-called 'truth objection'. To recall, the truth objection says that coherentist conditions of justification cannot be shown to be truth-conducive unless truth is constructed along non-realist lines.[99] An analogous objection is addressed against coherence theories of moral justification. According to this objection, in order to ensure that some appropriate connection obtains between moral beliefs held as justified and the goal of truth, the moral coherentist must accept constructivism (or some other anti-realist view on moral truth).

Critics pressing this objection often appeal to the 'input or isolation objection' and the 'alternative coherent systems objection'.[100] According to the moral version of the 'input (or isolation) objection', maximizing the internal coherence of one's moral judgements with other moral and non-moral judgements does not require any input from a realm of inquiry-independent moral properties and facts. Thus, nothing guarantees that a coherent system of moral beliefs, though justified, is not completely isolated from the moral world that the realist envisions. According to the moral version of the 'many alternative coherent systems objection', maximizing coherence among our moral judgements does not discriminate among competing moral systems that are equally coherent. But two incompatible systems of moral beliefs cannot both correspond to the evidence-independent moral properties and facts. Together these two objections support the truth objection, ie that a

[97] *Cf* Brink (1989: 20) (identifying constructivism with idealism and distinguishing between relativist and non-relativist forms of constructivism).

[98] See Rawls (1980); Putnam ((1981) and (1987)); and Nino (1989). On Rawls' version of constructivism, see Hill (1989). On Putnam's constructivism, see Timmons (1991).

[99] On this objection, as applied to coherence theories of epistemic justification, see chs 3 and 6.

[100] See ch 3 for a discussion of the input or isolation objection as well as of the many alternative coherent systems objections as they apply to coherentist theories of epistemic justification.

coherence theory for the justification of our moral beliefs cannot be shown to be truth-conducive unless truth is constructed along non-realist lines.

If the truth objection is successful, then accepting coherence theories of justification in ethics involves a commitment to anti-realism. Just whether this should necessarily be seen as an objection, depends on whether one finds constructivism (or some other anti-realist view) a compelling view about moral truth. In this respect, the situation in ethics differs from epistemology, in that anti-realists view of moral truth are regarded by many as more attractive than anti-realist accounts of the truth conditions of empirical judgements. Here, I shall not try to assess the merits of either moral realism or constructivism. Rather, my aim is to examine the prospects of combining realism and coherence theories of moral justification, on the one hand, and anti-realism and coherence views on moral justification, on the other hand. I start with the arguments in favour and against realist interpretations of the method of reflective equilibrium.

## B. The Realist Interpretation of the Method of Reflective Equilibrium

According to the realist interpretation of reflective equilibrium, the results of reflective equilibrium provide evidence of inquiry-independent moral truths. The plausibility of this view is generally taken to depend on the further claim that considered moral judgements provide generally reliable information about inquiry-independent moral properties and facts. An account of the reliability of considered moral judgements would provide an answer to the three main objections that have been raised against realist coherentism: the input objection, the alternative coherent systems objection and the truth objection. First, an account of the reliability of considered moral judgements would provide an answer to the input objection, for these judgements would secure that moral beliefs that we hold in reflective equilibrium are not isolated from the realm of objective moral properties and facts. Secondly, one could deal with the alternative coherent systems objections by requiring that the justified moral theory (the theory that we accept in reflective equilibrium) cohere with these 'input' judgements. The satisfaction of this requirement would severely constrain the choice among alternative moral theories, and thus reduce the worries about many alternative but equally coherent systems. Last, if considered moral judgements are generally reliable, then one can hope to design a positive argument to the effect that coherence with these judgements is evidence of truths about an objective moral reality. Daniels[101] and Brink[102] have provided the most

[101] Daniels (1996: 33–40).
[102] Brink (1989: 122–44).

articulated defences of realist coherentism. Both of them represent two different strategies for meeting the foregoing objections.[103] I shall start with Daniels' reply to these objections.

Daniels denies that reflective equilibrium need be viewed as constitutive of moral truth, as convergence in wide reflective equilibrium may be evidence of moral truth.[104] In Daniels' view—as we saw before—there is no need to assume at the current stage of moral inquiry the burden of providing an account of the reliability of our moral judgements. Such an account, he argues, is surely needed. But he suggests that we wait until convergence is obtained to provide the required account of the reliability of our moral judgements. The method of reflective equilibrium, holds Daniels, may greatly aid to bring about this convergence. Specifically, it may lead to a better understanding of the sources of moral agreement and disagreement. In addition, it may make disagreement more tractable by reducing moral disagreements to more resoluble disagreements in relevant background theory. Daniels' 'wait and see' strategy can be read as proposing that we first address the alternative coherent systems objection, and strive for convergence, and then that we address the input objection.

Daniels' response to the alternative and input objections has been harshly criticized in the literature. First, critics have questioned that we have any reason to be optimistic about the prospects of convergence. The method has been used already by many for some time without producing any significant convergence.[105] In addition, there are no compelling reasons for thinking that wide reflective equilibrium is much better off in bringing about convergence than narrow reflective equilibrium, given that background theories depend, for their justification, on considered moral judgements.[106] Secondly, critics have argued that, even if such convergence took place, it would not help make the case for a realist construal of the method of reflective equilibrium. The reason is that an account of the reliability of considered moral judgements given *after* convergence is achieved does not help to answer the input objection.[107] If we want to preserve the crucial role of considered moral judgements in the selection and testing of moral theories then the reliability of these judgements ought to be independent of the particular theory which is selected by this method. If we wait until a moral theory is selected, and then use that very theory to explain the reliability of

[103] For an excellent discussion of recent defences of realist coherentism in ethics, see Timmons (1990).

[104] A stronger thesis is defended by Holmgren, who claims that reflective equilibrium needs to be viewed as presupposing objective moral truths that are independent of our moral beliefs. See Holmgren (1987).

[105] DePaul (1993: 51–55).

[106] Timmons (1990: 106).

[107] Timmons (1990: 107).

the considered judgements that were used in the selection process, we can suspect that the methodology is as objective as the realist wants it to be.

As opposed to Daniels' strategy, Brink's strategy can be read as a proposal to deal first with the input objection, and then with the alternative coherent systems objection.[108] Brink's account of the reliability of moral judgements relies on the important role that second-order beliefs play in coherentism.[109] These beliefs, argues Brink, establish a set of reliability conditions, which are themselves guided by considerations of coherence. In his view, coherence with a set of 'considered moral beliefs', ie beliefs that are reliably formed, can be evidence of objective moral truth. This set of reliable moral judgements thus secures that beliefs justified through reflective equilibrium are not severed from an objective realm of moral properties and facts. Once the input (or isolation) objection is met, one could also reduce worries about the alternative coherent systems objection. For coherence with this set of judgements is a reasonable constraint that may help select among competing moral systems.

Brink's strategy has also been criticized on several grounds. To start with, it is by no means clear that any of our moral judgements is the result of any causal interplay with objective moral properties. In this respect, moral beliefs markedly differ from empirical beliefs. For our epistemic access to an inquiry-independent-reality via observational beliefs is far less problematical than the idea that some judgements provide us with epistemic access to objective moral properties.[110] Thus, we need a reason for thinking that considered moral judgements do represent an input from putative moral properties. And secondly, there is interpersonal variation in people's considered moral beliefs. This variation sheds further doubts about the supposition that these judgements provide us with access to moral properties and facts.

So much for the realist replies to the input and alternative coherent systems objections. Now, what about the truth objection? Daniels has offered an indirect argument to the effect that holding agreement in wide reflective equilibrium is evidence of realist moral truth. Consider, first, an argument of the following form:

(1) in a given area of inquiry, the methods used are successful in the sense that they produce convergence and a growth of knowledge;
(2) the only plausible account of the success of these methods is that they lead us to better and better approximations of truths of the kind relevant to the inquiry;
(3) therefore, we should adopt a realist account of the relevant objects of inquiry.[111]

[108] Brink (1989: 130–32).
[109] Brink's account of the reliability of moral judgements is similar to BonJour's account of the reliability of perceptual judgements, which was discussed in ch 3.
[110] *Cf* Boyd (1997). For a critique of Boyd's proposal, see Timmons (1990: 115–22).
[111] Daniels (1996: 37).

Arguments of this form have been advanced to defend realism with regard to theoretical terms in the empirical sciences.[112] Daniels' suggestion is that an argument similar to the argument for scientific realism may be used for defending that there is an evidential relation between agreement in wide equilibrium and objective moral truth. He writes:

> Suppose that coherence constraints in wide equilibrium turn out to be consensus producing. Then, since these constraints are similar to their analogous in science in other respects, they may also be evidential. That is, we have some reason to think that wide reflective equilibrium involves methods that will lead us to objective moral truths if there are any.[113]

Thus, Daniels claims that the only plausible account of the success of the method of reflective equilibrium, ie the fact that it produces convergence, is that it leads us to objective moral truths, if there are any. The problem with this argument is that, as I have already said, there are several reasons for questioning the prospects of convergence. Besides, an account of the reliability of moral judgements is needed for running an argument for moral realism analogous to the argument for scientific realism, which depends, in its turn, on some reliability account of observation statements. Hence, Daniels' argument for the truth-conduciveness of coherence crucially depends on a plausible story about the reliability of moral judgements, which is so far unavailable.

Brink does not spell out explicitly a positive argument for the truth-conduciveness of coherence among our moral judgements. However, his discussion of coherence and realism as regards empirical beliefs as well his use of BonJour's coherentist theory of epistemic justification for developing a version of moral realism gives us a hint about how his argument would proceed.[114] Presumably, his view would be that the best explanation of coherence *cum* stability of a set of moral judgements that includes a number of second-order beliefs about the reliability of moral beliefs is that it brings us closer to moral truth. Of course, the problems that I have already noted in relation to Brink's account of the reliability of moral judgements will carry over this response to the truth-connection.

Thus, none of the arguments for meeting the isolation, input and truth objection within a moral realist framework is conclusive. This should not surprise us since attempts to meet these objections in the less muddy waters of empirical knowledge were also shown to be inconclusive.[115] Let us now examine the non-realist strategies for establishing the adequacy of coherence methods of moral inquiry.

[112] See ch 4, s I.B.
[113] ibid, 38.
[114] Brink (1989: 125–30).
[115] See ch 6 s IV.

## C. The Constructivist Interpretation of Reflective Equilibrium

According to the constructivist interpretation of reflective equilibrium, the result of this method does not provide evidence of inquiry-independent moral truths.[116] Then, what relation holds between the results of the method of reflective equilibrium (or any other coherence method), under a constructivist interpretation, and moral truth? The answer to this question depends on what constructivism is. However, just how constructivism may be characterized is far from clear.[117] For our purposes, it is important to distinguish two main construals of constructivism.[118] Under one interpretation, constructivism holds an anti-realist view of moral truth, ie moral truth is not independent of our practices of inquiry.[119] Under another interpretation, it can be seen as embodying a different view of what doing moral philosophy means. In this view, moral theory construction is not an epistemic, but rather, a practical task. Moral philosophy does not have truth as its target, but it is directed towards achieving a practical aim, ie the design of a public conception of justice. In this view, talk about moral truth is irrelevant to the purposes of moral theorizing. We may refer to these two interpretations of constructivism as 'metaphysical' and 'political' constructivism, respectively.[120]

These two interpretations lead to a different understanding of the disagreement between moral realism and constructivism. In the first (metaphysical) interpretation, moral realists and constructivists differ in their views on the nature of moral truth. Whereas moral realists hold a realist view of moral truth, constructivists hold an anti-realist view of moral truth. But both share an understanding of moral philosophy as moral epistemology as well as a view of the method of reflective equilibrium as a theory of epistemic justification, and both take truth-conduciveness to provide the criterion of adequacy for standards of justification.

Under the second (political) interpretation, the locus of disagreement between moral realists and constructivists is not the nature of truth, but

[116] For a defence of this interpretation, see Dworkin (1977: 161–68). For a critique of Dworkin's arguments to the effect that a constructive model best supports the method of reflective equilibrium, see Holmgren (1987).

[117] For an informative discussion of the main features of constructivism and a taxonomy of constructivist views, see Street (2008) and (2010). See also Lenman and Shemmer (2012b: 1–6).

[118] Another important distinction is the distinction between global vs local constructivism. The former, unlike the latter, applies to the whole normative domain. Rawls' constructivism is of local variety as is concerned with questions of political justice. See Lenman and Shemmer (2012a).

[119] See Putnam (1981); Habermas (1994); and Nino (1988).

[120] The reference to Rawls' title 'Justice as Fairness: Political not Metaphysical' is obvious. To these kinds of constructivism, Brink adds a third interpretation of constructivism, as developed by Rawls, to wit, 'epistemological' constructivism; see Brink (1989: 303–10).

the general conception of moral philosophy. On this interpretation, where moral realists and constructivists really differ is not on the issue of whether truth is realist or anti-realist, but on whether moral philosophy should be concerned with such an issue in the first place. What is wrong with the moral realist point of view, the constructivist says, is not so much its acceptance of a realist view of truth, as it is the fact that they view moral philosophy as a branch of epistemology. As opposed to this view, moral philosophy, the constructivist holds, is a practical subject. On this view, the method of reflective equilibrium has mainly a heuristic value, rather than an epistemic one, and its adequacy should not be assessed in terms of truth-conduciveness, but it depends on how well it helps bring about the practical aims that moral philosophers strive to achieve.[121]

Which constructivist model—metaphysical or political—best supports Rawls' coherence method? Rawls' views evolved and changed in the course of his writings. Thus, when addressing the issue of whether Rawls' views involve a commitment to anti-realism or whether they represent a conception of moral philosophy that remains agnostic with regard to metaphysical issues, we should keep in mind that the answer may depend on which of Rawls' writings one takes into account. It is, I believe, reasonably clear, that Rawls' views in 'Justice as Fairness: Political not Metaphysical', as well as in 'The Idea of an Overlapping Consensus', support only a political constructivist reading. However, it is a controversial issue whether his earlier writings support readings other than the political constructivist one. It is not my aim here to engage in an exegesis of Rawls' writings; but, in order to clarify Rawls' views on coherence and truth, it is important to examine some anti-realist interpretations of his writings. Nino and Brink have proposed such interpretations. Both are very careful in restricting their conclusions to some of Rawls' works, in particular, to *A Theory of Justice* and 'Kantian Constructivism in Moral Theory', respectively.

Nino has defended an anti-realist interpretation of Rawls' metaethical views as presented in *A Theory of Justice*.[122] Nino contends that Rawls' theory involves the following characterization of moral truth:

> [A] moral judgment is true when it derives from a principle that would be accepted in the original position, that is, when it derives from a general, universal, public, or final principle that would be accepted under conditions of impartiality, rationality, knowledge of relevant facts ...[123]

In his view, the method of reflective equilibrium would be a method that provides us with epistemic access to moral truth conceived in this way.

[121] For this way of drawing the contrast between moral realism and constructivism, see Korsgaard (2003).

[122] See Nino (1988) and (1989) ch 5.

[123] Nino (1988: 91). My translation.

Thus, Nino claims that the results of the method of reflective equilibrium are not constitutive of moral truth, but that moral truth amounts to acceptability under some ideal conditions, as specified in the original position.

Brink has defended the view according to which 'Kantian Constructivism in Moral Theory' could be read as containing a commitment to anti-realism. On this interpretation, Rawls would be committed to the metaethical view according to which 'moral truth is constituted by our moral beliefs, in particular, by our ideals of the person'.[124] Thus, Rawls' purported anti-realism, in Brink's interpretation, is closely linked to the ideals of the person, rather than to the original position, as Nino claims. According to Brink, it is coherence with a set of moral beliefs about persons (the ideals of the person) that constitutes moral truth, and not acceptance under ideal conditions (the original position). However, even if the difference is an important one, we should not overdraw the contrast. For the original position is a device by which Rawls represents the basic features of the Kantian conception of the person. Hence, the characteristics of the procedure depend ultimately on the characteristics of the ideal of the person that is accepted.[125]

Now, whether or not Nino and Brink are right in interpreting Rawls' views (as presented in *A Theory of Justice* and 'Kantian Constructivism in Moral Theory') as involving a commitment to anti-realism, I believe that there is no room for this interpretation as far as Rawls' later writings are concerned. An interpretation of 'Kantian Constructivism in Moral Theory' as involving a commitment to political constructivism is indeed very plausible, and such a commitment is even explicit in 'Justice as Fairness: Political not Metaphysical'. Rawls' commitment to a political version of constructivism is a centrepiece of the thesis defended in 'The Idea of an Overlapping Consensus'. As explained, two main tenets distinguish political constructivism from metaphysical versions of constructivism. First, political constructivism is claimed to be neutral about metaethical views. And secondly, it implies a conception of moral philosophy as a practical and political discipline, as opposed to one that has an epistemic nature. Both of these claims find their most explicit statement and defence in Rawls' writings.

Rawls argued for the first tenet of political constructivism—the claim of independence—as early as in 'The Independence of Moral Theory'.[126] There, he claimed that moral theory is independent from other parts of philosophy, in particular from the theory of meaning, the philosophy of mind and most importantly for our purposes, metaphysics and epistemology. The independence of moral theory from epistemology arises from the fact that the procedure for moral theory construction, namely, the method of reflective equilibrium, does not presuppose the existence of objective

[124] Brink (1989: 305).
[125] See Hill (1989: 755–56).
[126] Rawls (1974–75).

moral truths. And he suggests that we 'suspend consideration' of the notion of moral truth, and aim, instead, at further developing moral theory. Provisionally, he writes, 'we may bracket the problem of moral truth and turn to moral theory'.[127] Many years later, he still reiterates the independence claim, 'a public conception of justice should be, so far as possible, independent of controversial philosophical and religious doctrines'.[128] Rawls writes:

> Thus, in what I have called 'Kantian constructivism' we try to avoid the problem of truth and the controversy between realism and subjectivism about the status of moral and political values. This form of constructivism neither asserts nor denies these doctrines ... The hope is that, by this method of avoidance, as we might call it, existing differences between contending political views can at least be moderated, even if not entirely removed, and that social cooperation on the basis of mutual respect can be maintained.[129]

A moral theory that proceeds by following a 'method of avoidance' looks indeed very different from the kind of moral philosophy that commits one to a particular view about truth, and that takes the search for truth as its main aim. Instead, political constructivism is based on a conception of moral philosophy as a practical and political subject. Rawls states the second main tenet of political constructivism as follows:

> the aim of justice as fairness as a political conception is practical, not metaphysical or epistemological. That is, it presents itself not as a conception of justice that is true, but one that can serve as a basis of informed and willing political agreement between citizens viewed as free and equal persons.[130]

Thus, on Rawls' view, principles of justice are reasonable (or unreasonable) rather than true (or false). The principles that are accepted in reflective equilibrium are not moral truths, but political principles that reasonable adherents of different moral perspectives can agree upon.[131]

Now, how does constructivism help us solve the problem that we are concerned with, namely, the problem of showing coherence methods to be truth-conducive? Do we have any reason to believe that beliefs accepted in reflective equilibrium, eg Rawls's two principles of justice, are likely to be true? Let us start first with metaphysical constructivism. Metaphysical constructivism claims that the results of the method of reflective equilibrium are constitutive of moral truth. Thus, the problem of the truth-conduciveness of coherence is solved by forging a conceptual relation between justified beliefs (under some ideal conditions) and true beliefs. This solution to

[127] ibid, 7.
[128] Rawls (1985: 223). The same point is expressed in Rawls (1988: 8).
[129] Rawls (1985: 230–31). See also Rawls (1988: 13).
[130] Rawls (1985: 230).
[131] Rawls (1980: 564). See also Rawls (1988: 15).

the problem inherits all the problems of anti-realists views, in ethics and everywhere else.[132] Most importantly, by conflating truth with justification, it is unclear the sense in which truth can be seen as providing the objective element that knowledge, in this case, ethical knowledge, requires. As a result, doubts may be raised as to whether, at the end, they lead us to a kind of relativism. The details of the different theories are, nonetheless, crucial for assessing their success in securing a kind of moral objectivity and conjuring the ghost of moral relativism away.

The strategy of political constructivism for solving the problem of the truth-conduciveness of coherence consists in refusing to address this problem. It neither asserts nor denies that there are objective moral truths. It takes no stance either on whether the method of reflective equilibrium is truth-conducive. Instead, it brackets these metaphysical issues and seeks to justify the method from a practical point of view. The realist aims to show that moral judgements are reliable and, thus, that coherence with them is truth-conducive. For the political constructivists, the problem of the reliability of our considered moral judgements does not even arise. For they are not regarded as indicative of correspondence with an objective realm of moral properties and facts, but as stipulated points to work from in constructing a suitable public conception of justice. Thus, the problem of the truth-conduciveness of coherence is, like the problem of the nature of moral truth and moral facts, one that we should avoid. Once we reconceive the task of moral philosophy as a practical discipline and not as a theoretical one, the pressure to provide an answer to the problem of coherence and truth evaporates. The search for truth is better replaced by the search of a moral theory that provides a solution to the problem of justice. If the method of reflective equilibrium helps us solve this problem, then we are justified in following this method. We need no justification other than this for accepting the method of reflective equilibrium.

This solution to the problem of the truth-conduciveness of coherence makes the charge of relativism even more pressing than the solution embraced by metaphysical constructivism, for principles of justice are now seen, as Hill puts it, as a 'pragmatic compromise designed for current political purposes',[133] and not even as a working approximation to moral truth. A conception of justice is justified only insofar as it provides a public basis of political agreement. According to Rawls, this aim can only be achieved if 'it provides a reasonable way of shaping into one coherent view the deeper basis of agreement embedded in the public political culture of a constitutional regime and acceptable to its most firmly held convictions'.[134] On this view, justification 'must always proceed from some consensus, from

[132] See ch 6, for an analysis of the main objections against anti-realism.
[133] Hill (1989: 752).
[134] Rawls (1985: 229).

premises that others publicly recognize as true, or better, publicly recognize as acceptable to us for the purposes of establishing a working agreement on the fundamental questions of political justice'.[135] In short, moral objectivity, Rawls claims, 'is to be understood in terms of a suitably constructed point of view'.[136]

Therefore, in political constructivism, truth is replaced by a practical view of justification as coherence with a set of shared convictions. Objectivity is thereby relative to the 'overlapping consensus' that can be found in a particular society. This shift of focus from a view of moral justification as an epistemic ideal to justification as a practical task, which moves the late Rawls away from other forms of constructivism, also brings him closer to a position that may lend itself to some form of relativism.[137] I turn now to examine some coherence theories that are, more radically, straightforwardly committed to some version of moral relativism.

## D. Coherentist Relativism

The most elaborated and explicit statement of a coherentist version of relativism is provided by Goldman. Before getting into the details of Goldman's proposal, I shall very briefly locate moral relativism in relation to both realist and constructivist views. Relativism differs from both moral realism and constructivism in that it denies that moral judgements are universal. Instead, moral standards, relativists claim, depend on the customs and principles that govern a particular society. Relativism also differs from the foregoing views in that it denies that moral judgements are objective in the sense that they correspond to an evidence-independent reality (moral realism) or that they would be agreed upon under suitably defined conditions or by agents who enjoy a number of idealized features (constructivism). However, unlike traditional relativism, most current forms of relativism are not subjectivist either. That is, they do not interpret moral judgements as expressing or being based upon the subjective states of mind of individuals. Arrington characterizes moral relativism as 'nonobjective' to account for the fact that relativists

> often picture moral judgments as describing, as depending on their justification, or as being the response to moral customs or rules that are independent of how the individuals making these judgments actually believe or feel about the subject matter of these judgments.[138]

[135] ibid. Rawls develops and defends the idea that justification proceeds from some consensus to be found in the fundamental political ideas that we seem to share through a public political culture in Rawls (1988).

[136] Rawls (1980: 519).

[137] Habermas (1994: 28–29).

[138] Arrington (1989: 1970).

Thus, relativists hold that it is a perfectly objective matter whether or not an act accords with the rules of an individual or a group. Current versions of relativism are cognitivist. They do not deny that moral judgements have truth-values, what they deny is that moral judgements must be true or false for all persons. Relativism claims that the truth of a moral judgement is relative to the set of beliefs, customs, conventions, and rules of a social group or individual.[139] When coherence provides the criterion for identifying the set of beliefs, customs, etc relevant to determine the truth-value of moral judgements, we get a coherentist version of relativism. That is, 'coherentist relativism' claims that a moral judgement is true if it belongs to a maximally coherent set of moral judgements shared in the relevant social group.[140]

Let us now unfold the details of the coherentist relativist position defended by Goldman.[141] According to Goldman, moral reasoning and moral truth are best understood by using legal knowledge as a model.[142] Such analogy between the ethical and the legal domain leads Goldman to defend a theory of moral truth according to which 'the truth of moral judgements lies in their coherence within a moral framework'.[143] This view of moral truth, argues Goldman, parallels the concept of truth that operates in the legal domain. He writes:

> Legal arguments are purely coherentist, and the truth of statements such as 'x is liable' lies in their coherence with other judgments of the same sort, not in correspondence to a reality independent of anyone's recognition of it. The truth of a proposition of law consists in that proposition's being more analogous to those in the previously settled body of law than is its denial.[144]

Thus, the coherence of a judgement with a set of settled judgements determines its truth in both ethics and law. As explained above, according to Goldman, a moral (or legal) judgement will be coherent with a set of settled cases, if it cannot be differentiated from the closest analogous case in that base but can be relevantly distinguished from every case judged differently. Goldman's version of the coherence theory of truth is relativist, in that a

[139] Two main non-subjectivist and cognitivist versions of relativism are put forward by Harman and Wong. See Harman (1979) and Wong (1984). For a discussion of Harman's and Wong's views, see Arrington (1989) ch 5. For a discussion of relativism in connection to the notion of 'moral explanations', see Harman and Thomson (1996). On Harman's view on this issue, see Railton (1998).

[140] See eg Ryan (2000). For a coherence theory of truth that relativizes moral truth to an (idealized) normative system, see Dorsey (2006).

[141] For Goldman's views on truth and coherence, see AH Goldman ((1988a) ch V, (1990), (1988b) and (2002: 156–58)).

[142] As opposed to using empirical knowledge as a model -as moral realism does. For Goldman's critique to moral realism, see AH Goldman (1988a), especially, ch IV. See also AH Goldman ((1990: 176–79) and (2002: 156–58)).

[143] AH Goldman (1988a: 134).

[144] AH Goldman (1989: 139).

moral (or legal) judgement that coheres with the evaluator's set of accepted settled judgements will be true relative to such set, but it differs from other forms of relativism where truth conditions are a matter of coherence with the set of accepted rules (mores or conventions). Goldman gives two main arguments in support of his relativist version of the coherence theory of moral truth, to wit, the argument from scepticism and the argument from disagreement.

The first argument purports to show that coherentist relativism allows us to defeat the moral sceptic. Against scepticism, Goldman argues that we have good reasons for calling judgements that result from reasoning from analogy and difference under the coherence constraint, true. As he puts it:

> We call such judgments true, first, to contrast them with mere prejudices, guesses, or judgments that result from errors in reasoning; second, to identify them as results of sound inferences; and third, to distinguish them from justified beliefs that are not really coherent.[145]

Thus, according to Goldman, judgements that cohere with a set of settled judgements deserve the title of truth since they enjoy some of the characteristics that are typical of true beliefs. Most importantly, they are different from merely justified beliefs. An evaluator is justified in believing those judgements that seem to her on reflection to better cohere with her settled database. But those judgements will be true, and not merely justified, only if they do cohere with such a base.[146] Truth of this coherence variety, argues Goldman, generates knowledge and suffices to defeat the sceptic.[147]

Doubts may be raised as to whether Goldman's theory succeeds in meeting the challenge of moral scepticism. To start with, as Steup has claimed, the outcome of the reasoning process that Goldman advocates cannot reasonably be identified with truth. Consider arch-criminals who believe that it is permissible to harm people but not to harm members of their own gang. Surely, argues Steup, such a gang is in principle capable of reasoning so as to meet the required constraints. And if they do, we must consider their moral beliefs true, which is a consequence hard to digest. In addition, Goldman's theory implies that for any moral judgement $p$ there is a subject $A$ who knows $p$ to be true and a subject $B$ who knows $p$ to be false. For example, we know the judgement 'The arch-criminals are doing something wrong' to be true, and they know it to be false. Every moral judgement is true in relation to some system, eg the arch-criminal's system, and false

[145] AH Goldman (1988a: 197).

[146] The question arises as to how such judgements of coherence, detached from the evaluator's points of view, are to be carried out. From which perspective is the coherence of such judgements to be assessed so that they can be properly said to be true?

[147] Goldman defends an explanationist account of knowledge according to which knowledge is belief that is best explained by reference to its truth. For Goldman's explanationist view of knowledge, see AH Goldman (1988a) esp 2–12.

in relation to another system, eg our system. In terms of knowledge, the statement under discussion is known to be both true and false.[148] As Steup claims, it is difficult to see how this obscure conception of knowledge may be able to meet the sceptical challenge.

Goldman's second argument for this version of the coherence theory of truth is that it allows us to find peaceful and cooperative ways of overcoming disagreement. According to Goldman, all moral disagreement is, in principle, resolvable as long as those who participate in the debate are willing to reason from their shared database to the most coherent conclusion.[149] This argument has also been seen as problematic. Again, the source of trouble is the relativist component of Goldman's coherence theory of truth. Baccarini has held that the prospects of finding peaceful solutions to moral problems, if relativism is connected with coherentism in the way in which Goldman connects them, are meagre. Every group in a moral debate is likely to remain closed inside its moral beliefs.[150] Moreover, one might say that they will be justified in so doing, because such beliefs would be, by the standards set by the theory, true. Thus, within such a relativist framework, one may at least doubt that participants will be willing to reason from a shared set of judgements as the method of analogy and difference requires them to do.

Thus, none of Goldman's arguments conclusively supports his version of coherentist relativism. This, together with the longstanding criticisms that have been traditionally raised against relativism,[151] makes this solution to the problem of connecting up coherence and moral truth, at least until more plausible arguments for coherentist relativism are put forward, quite unattractive.

## VI. CONCLUSIONS

This chapter has discussed coherentist approaches to moral reasoning. I have started this discussion by arguing that in order to explore the role of coherence in ethics we had better keep methodological, epistemological and metaphysical questions as distinct. Coherence has been claimed to play a prominent role at all three levels. One may use a coherence method of moral inquiry without endorsing either a coherence theory of justification or a coherence theory of truth (eg DePaul). And one can endorse a coherence method and a coherence theory of justification, while rejecting a coherence theory of truth (eg Brink).

[148] See Steup (1991: 186–87).

[149] AH Goldman (2002: 162).

[150] Baccarini (1997: 191).

[151] For a statement and discussion of the main objections against moral relativism, see Arrington (1989: 200ff).

I have claimed that the coherence theory of moral justification is a promising alternative to foundationalism. Foundationalism in ethics is fraught with severe problems. Most importantly, it confronts the same problem that, as argued in chapter three, besets foundationalist views of the structure of empirical justification, ie there are no plausible candidates for basic beliefs that can both stop the regress and provide the justification for all non-basic beliefs. Moreover, foundationalism about ethical justification seems to be even more problematical than foundationalism about empirical justification for thus far we lack a convincing account of the purported reliability of basic moral beliefs.

Coherentism about moral justification also has its share of problems. The coherence theory of justification in ethics faces the traditional objections that have been raised against coherence theories of justification in general, to wit, (i) vagueness, (ii) conservatism, (iii) circularity, (iv) the alternative coherent systems objection, (v) the isolation or input objection and (vi) the truth objection. Two strategies, I have argued, may be helpful in meeting these objections: first, it is necessary to elaborate a complex and precise notion of ethical coherence; and, secondly, there is a need to develop a proper understanding of the relation between coherence and moral truth as well as of the relevance of the latter for the justification of coherence methods and coherence standards of justification in ethics.

With regard to the problem of defining a workable account of coherence for ethics, I have argued that a concept of coherence in ethics must give a precise account of the elements (the base) that enter into coherence relations as well as of the kind of relations that increase the degree of coherence of the relevant set of elements. As far as the base of coherence is concerned, there is a common trend in current moral philosophy towards expanding it so as to include elements other than moral judgements, principles and background theories. Most importantly, emotions and experience have been claimed to play a prominent role when assessing the coherence of moral views. With regard to the kind of relations that contribute to coherence, we may also favour a liberal policy. There is no reason why one should restrict coherence relations to analogical relations (as Goldman does). We rather include a full range of inferential relations such as deduction, analogy or explanatory relations (as Thagard suggests).

As to the problem of connecting coherence and truth in ethics, it is critical to note that, as argued, a coherence theory of justification does not commit one to any metaphysical view. There are different strategies for approaching the problem of coherence and moral truth. On the one hand, one may embrace a metaphysical constructivist view and claim that a conceptual relation holds between coherence (under some ideal conditions) and moral truth. Alternatively, and less plausibly, one can contend (as Goldman does) that a conceptual relation holds between the coherence of a set of beliefs within a current framework and moral truth. On the other hand, one can be a realist and attempt to bridge the gap between coherence and moral truth, understood as a property of moral facts that are independent from our beliefs and methods of inquiry. The most plausible realist argument appeals to an inference to the best explanation (eg Daniels and Brink). The best explanation, it is claimed, of the convergence and stability of moral views that includes a sufficient number of reliable moral beliefs is that they are likely to (approximately) correspond to an independent moral reality. However, these strategies need to be complemented with an account of the reliability of moral judgements, which is thus far unavailable.[152]

All the foregoing views are direct responses to the question of how coherence in ethics may be shown to be truth-conducive. But one may also doubt whether a satisfactory answer to this question is, after all, required for a thorough defence of coherence methods and coherence theories of justification in ethics. One may claim that epistemic values other than truth are crucial for assessing the adequacy of our moral standards (as DePaul contends). Moreover, one could even question that epistemic values (truth included) are the target of ethics. Instead, one could argue that practical values are crucial in moral theorizing (eg Rawls). One may bring here a number of different arguments, depending on one's views about what the practical aims that ethics must help one achieve are. For instance, Rawls defends the view according to which a conception of political justice must establish the terms of agreement among free, equal and cooperating persons, and thus coherence standards are justified as long as they help us bring this aim about. Hence, just as was concluded, in chapter six, that one may successfully address the problem of the metajustification of coherence standards of justification in the factual domain without getting into the complex issue of the nature of empirical truth, we may also conclude here that one may succeed in dealing with the problem of justifying coherentism about justification in the ethical domain without getting into the even less firm arena of moral truth. In addressing the problem of how coherence methods and coherence theories of justification may be themselves justified, we do well, I believe, in following Rawls' 'avoidance method'. Even more so if, as it seems, we can reasonably defend coherence views on non-metaphysical grounds.

[152] One could also question the same terms of the realist-antirealist debate and provide an answer to the problem of the truth-conduciveness of coherence that does not fit into either the realist or the anti-realist camps—as Davidson does in relation to coherence and truth in the empirical domain (see ch 6). I suggested earlier that Hurley's writings might be interpreted as defending such a strategy (see ch 7).

# 9

# *Discourse Coherence*

LEGAL REASONING INVOLVES the justification of both factual and normative conclusions. Thus, in order to give a full account of the role that coherence plays in legal reasoning, it is necessary to gain a good understanding of the place of coherence within a theory of epistemic as well as practical justification. With this purpose in mind, in the previous chapters I have analysed the notions of epistemic coherence and practical coherence, and the role that they play in the justification of factual and normative statements, respectively. Ultimately, the goal—which I shall address in the next (and last) chapter—is to examine how the insights on practical and epistemic coherence that we have gained through this interdisciplinary analysis may be brought together to give an account of the nature of legal coherence and its role in reasoning about both facts and norms. But before we are ready to undertake this task, there is still another domain which we should examine, to wit, the domain of interpretation. Legal reasoning, as is well known, has an interpretative nature: interpretative arguments are essential to the justification of legal conclusions. Hence, in order to develop a coherentist model of legal reasoning, it seems necessary to examine in some detail the role that coherence plays in interpretation. This is what I purport to do in this chapter. This will be our last step in this long journey back to the legal realm.

There are several kinds of interpretation, depending on the object of the interpretative activity.[1] In a very broad sense, interpretation refers to any attribution of meaning, whether linguistic or non-linguistic. Thus, one can speak of the interpretation of a work of art, the interpretation of social behaviour or the interpretation of cultural forms. In a second, more restricted, sense, one could speak of interpretation as the assignment of meaning to any written or spoken language or to any discourse. Last, in a strict sense, by interpretation one may refer to the assignment of meaning to texts that pose particularly difficult problems of interpretation, such as literary and legal texts.

Coherence has been claimed to be a relevant concept for understanding all three kinds of interpretation. First, regarding the interpretation of

[1] On the classification of kinds of interpretation according to the object of interpretation, see Wroblewski ((1985: 21ff) and (1992: 87ff)). On Wroblewski's classification, see Lifante (1999: 28–30).

non-linguistic objects, arguments from coherence have been found to be crucial for artistic interpretation as well as for the interpretation of social behaviour.[2] Secondly, several approaches to discourse interpretation are coherence-based, eg the analysis of discourse in terms of mental models or coherence relations, heuristic and intentional approaches to discourse coherence and topic-oriented theories of discourse.[3] Last, arguments from coherence have been claimed to be pivotal in the interpretation of literary[4] and legal texts.[5]

A complete account of coherence theories of interpretation would require us to engage in the daunting task of examining the role of coherence in all these different kinds of interpretation. In this chapter, I will focus exclusively on the analysis of coherence in relation to one of the several kinds of interpretation that have been just distinguished, namely, the interpretation of discourse. First, I will attempt to clarify the notion of discourse coherence by contrasting it with other related notions that also play a prominent role in discourse theory, such as cohesion, interpretability or plausibility. Next, I will briefly introduce the main coherentist approaches to discourse interpretation. All these theories endorse the view according to which the coherence of discourse is not exclusively a linguistic phenomenon, but also a matter of inferring from non-linguistic knowledge. The relevance of inference and background knowledge to discourse coherence will be examined in the following section. Then, I will assess the plausibility of coherence-based theories vis-à-vis the main alternative account of discourse interpretation, to wit, the relevance theory. Last, I shall conclude with some remarks on the nature of discourse coherence, the relation between coherence and context in interpretation and the main implications of coherence accounts of interpretation for views on interpretation and rationality.

## I. THE NOTION OF COHERENCE IN DISCOURSE THEORY

Several approaches to discourse view coherence as the key notion for understanding discourse interpretation. But, what is coherence? Coherence is a matter of 'making sense'; a discourse is coherent if it 'makes sense as a

[2] For the relevance of coherence in relation to the interpretation of works of art, see Goodman (1985) and Aschenbrenner (1985). For a coherentist analysis of the interpretation of multimodal discourse, ie discourse that combines texts with pictures or audio-visuals in general, see Bandyopadhyay (1995).

[3] For an overview of coherentist approaches to discourse, see Hellman (1995: 190–202) and Kehler (2004). Coherence also plays a prominent role in holistic theories of language interpretation—as explained in detail in ch 6.

[4] In relation to the role of coherence in the interpretation of literary texts, see Wales (1998); Perry (1979: 35–61); Dasenbrock (1993); Kris and Kaplan (1964); Robey (1986: 82–85); and Juhl (1980: 6–9).

[5] For a discussion of the place of coherence in legal interpretation, see ch 1.

whole'. Speakers have intuitions about whether a discourse or a segment of a discourse is coherent or incoherent, or whether it is more or less coherent than another. More specifically, speakers have two different kinds of intuitions: they make judgements of 'local coherence' as well as 'global coherence.' That is, speakers have local intuitions about when two adjacent discourse segments are related and global intuitions about when a discourse hangs together as a whole.[6] To explain these intuitions, however, it does not suffice to define coherence as 'making sense.' Thus, the first problem for coherence theories is to give a technical definition of coherence. A first step towards explaining the notion of coherence consists in distinguishing it from other concepts of discourse theory with which it is closely related, such as cohesion, appropriateness, consistency, plausibility, and comprehensibility.[7]

## A. Coherence and Cohesion

Cohesion refers to the surface grammatical and lexical continuity of a text. Halliday and Hasan describe it as follows: 'Cohesion is part of the system of the language. The potential for cohesion lies in the systematic resources of reference, ellipsis and so on that are built into the language itself'.[8]

The following examples illustrate several types of cohesive factors. In (1) there is a lexical repetition as a cohesive device; (2) is an example of coreference; in (3) we have an anaphoric relationship between 'his' and 'he'; and (4) illustrates a case of cohesion by ellipsis:[9]

(1) There was a big *mushroom* growing near her ... She stretched herself up on a tiptoe and peeped over the edge of the *mushroom*.
(2) *Several people* approached. *They* seemed angry.
(3) There was $4 in *his* wallet. So *he* hadn't spent all the money.
(4) John isn't *tall*, nor is ∧ Susan.

[6] The difference between local and global coherence is a commonplace in the literature on discourse interpretation. See Reinhart (1980: 163); Hobbs and Agar (1985: 8); Van Dijk (1977: 95); Conte (1988: 88) fn 6; and Glanzberg (2002: 356–58). As we have seen, the distinction between global and local coherence is also an important one in coherentist approaches to justification; see chs 1 and 2 for the relevance of this distinction to coherence theories of legal justification, and ch 3 for its role in a coherence theory of epistemic justification.

[7] The distinctions between central terms in discourse theory such as coherence, cohesion, connexity, text, grammaticality, acceptability, interpretability, understandability and plausibility have very much changed over the history of discourse theory. For a very clarifying essay on the use of these terms, see Enkvist (1989).

[8] Halliday and Hasan (1976: 5).

[9] Example (1) is from *Alice in Wonderland*, quoted in Halliday and Hasan (1976: 268); example (2) is found in Crystal (1989: 118); example (3) is taken from Blakemore (1988: 231); and example (4) is from Blass (1990: 15).

It is generally agreed that whereas cohesion is formal connectivity, coherence is connectivity at a deeper semantic-pragmatic level.[10] The problem is to determine the contribution of cohesive devices to coherence. Surely, cohesion is not a sufficient condition for coherence, for there are discourses that are perfectly well connected, from a formal point of view, and therefore, cohesive, which are, nonetheless, incoherent, such as:

(5) Elysées was black. Black English has been widely discussed. The discussions between the presidents ended last week. A week has seven days. Every day I feed my cat. Cat has four legs. The cat is on the mat. Mat has three letters.[11]

Such discourses are only apparently coherent, as Enkvist says, they are 'pseudo-coherent'.[12] It is also a controversial issue whether cohesion is a necessary condition for coherence. Thus, three positions may be distinguished as regards the relation between cohesion and coherence:

(i) Cohesion is a necessary and sufficient condition for coherence;
(ii) Cohesion is a necessary but not a sufficient condition for coherence;
(iii) Cohesion is neither a necessary nor a sufficient condition for coherence.

The first position is untenable, as texts such as (5) shows. The third position is the one that is mostly held in the recent literature. In support of this position, it is argued that there are discourses that, although not cohesive, are perfectly coherent. For example:

(6) (A) Where can I get a good meal around here?
(B) I am afraid I'm a in a bit of a hurry.[13]

Against this analysis, those who defend the second position claim that texts such as (6) although understandable, are not coherent. There is a need, they argue, to distinguish coherence from broader notions such as 'meaningfulness' or 'interpretability'. Let us now examine the relation between coherence and these other notions in discourse theory.

[10] Hatakeyama, Petöfi and Sözer (1985) have added 'connexity' to the dichotomy coherence/cohesion. The terminology is quite confusing, as there is no consistent usage in the literature. According to Enkvist (1989), connexity would be the sum total of cohesion (formal connections in the text) and coherence (linking mechanisms that manifest themselves through semantic relations and inference). Others take it that connexity means 'connectedness' by means of linguistic structures, while coherence is 'connectedness' by means of background knowledge (Linfellner-Rupertsberger (1989)). In this view, the difference between connexity and cohesion would be as follows: connexity refers to formal relations between elements in a text, while cohesion refers to thematic and semantic relations in the text (Conte (1989b: 274)). Thus, connectedness would be an all-embracing concept which has manifold aspects: coherence, cohesion and connexity (Vitacolona (1992-93: 260–62)). In general, the distinction that is taken to be the most relevant one in most of the literature is that between cohesion and coherence. Here, I shall examine the relation between coherence and cohesion, without putting even more terms in play, such as connexity or connectedness.

[11] Enkvist (1977: 111).

[12] ibid, 107.

[13] Blass (1990: 16). For other examples, see Giora (2013) and (2014).

### B. Coherence and Other Related Notions

Granted that cohesion does not amount to coherence, what else is required for text coherence? What is the relation between our intuitions of coherence and our intuitions of when a text is pragmatically acceptable, plausible, consistent or comprehensible? Do we require that a text be, for instance, consistent, in order to consider it coherent? A difficult issue for coherence theories is that of determining the relation between coherence as a technical notion and other related concepts like pragmatic acceptability, or appropriateness, plausibility, consistency and understandability. Let us examine, first, the relationship between intuitions of pragmatic acceptability and coherence. For example, consider (7):

(7) I have spent the last two years in the Ivory Coast, which is very pleasant. It has plenty of exotic fruits and the people have been very kind.[14]

Indeed, example (7) would be inappropriate as an answer to an immigration form where I am asked to state where I have spent the last two years. But is it incoherent? On the one hand, it would be hard to say that it is not coherent. Hence, it seems that our intuitions about coherence and our intuitions about what is appropriate to say in a particular context are distinct. Surely, these intuitions are related: it is more difficult to make a coherent interpretation of a discourse that violates societal conventions. That is to say, it should be more difficult to attribute a set of intentions and goals to the speaker in the light of which a coherent interpretation of the discourse can be achieved, if these conventions are not observed. But this difficulty does not undermine, one may argue, the relevance of the distinction between coherence and appropriateness or pragmatic acceptability.

On the other hand, it does not seem satisfactory either to label texts such as (7) as coherent. One may argue that the relation between a text and the context of the utterance is a decisive factor of coherence. This relation is seriously disturbed in this case, and thus, it could be argued, this prevents the text from being coherent. Reinhart has argued for such a view. According to Reinhart, a text is coherent if it satisfies three conditions: connectedness (or cohesion), consistency and relevance. In Reinhart's view, the condition of relevance consists of both semantic and pragmatic conditions, where the latter concern the relations between the sentences and the context of utterance. In this view, pragmatic appropriateness is a condition of coherence. Accordingly, in this view, texts such as (7) should be considered as incoherent. Enkvist has argued for a similar view, 'full coherence presupposes that syntax, semantics, and pragmatics are in order'.[15] Texts need to be, he claims, 'pragmatically coherent' in order to be fully coherent.

[14] Example discussed by Blass (1990: 19).
[15] Enkvist (1977: 113).

Another concept that is bounded up with coherence is that of consistency. Consistency, in Reinhart's words, is a semantic condition that requires that all sentences in a text be true in the same state of affairs (given our common assumptions about the world).[16] For instance, the following text is inconsistent:

(8) Paul is a vegetarian. He eats meet every day.[17]

But, is this text coherent? As said before, according to Reinhart, consistency is a condition of coherence. In this view, (8) would be incoherent, given that it is inconsistent. A similar conclusion would be drawn by Enkvist. In his view, contradictions such as that of (8) make sentences refer to incompatible worlds, with the result that the text becomes 'pragmatically unacceptable'. The mental models approach to discourse, which will be discussed in detail below, also takes consistency to be condition of coherence.[18] In contrast, others defend the view according to which inconsistency does not result necessarily in incoherence. For instance, Charolles claims that whether (8) is coherent depends on whether the reader succeeds in making sense of it as a whole, as in (9):

(9) that he claims to be a vegetarian (because he is a snob, or he wants to stand out), but that in actual fact, he eats meat seven days a week.[19]

Conte even argues that consistency, far from being a condition of coherence, has coherence as its condition of possibility. She claims that while consistency is a contingent *qualitas* of the text, coherence is a constitutive property of a text, that is, it is the *quidditas* of the text. In this sense, inconsistency does not exclude but includes (presupposes) coherence.[20]

Similar problems arise when we examine the relation between coherence and plausibility. Consider the following examples:

(10) Clare Russell came into the *Clarion* office on the following morning, feeling tired and depressed. She went straight to her room, took off her hat, toughed her face with a powder puff and sat down at her desk. Her mail was spread out neatly, her blotter was snowy and her inkwell was filled. But she didn't feel like work ... she drank her inkwell.

(11) The old woman was buried in her native village. She is dying of pneumonia.[21]

[16] Reinhart (1980: 1640). For a notion of consistency in the framework of dynamic semantics, see Groendendijk, Stokhof and Veltman (1996: 192).

[17] This example is taken from Charolles (1983: 94).

[18] See Johnson-Laird (1983: 371).

[19] ibid, 94.

[20] Conte (1988: 30).

[21] Examples taken from Van Dijk (1977: 82 and 99), respectively.

According to some linguists, texts that describe a totally bizarre sequence of events such as (10) and (11) are incoherent.[22] In contrast, according to others, one needs to clearly distinguish discourse coherence from plausibility. For example, Morgan and Green argue that discourses like (10) and (11), although implausible, are perfectly coherent reports of strange goings-on. As they put it, 'the fact that they are strange is a matter of our beliefs about the world, not of textual coherence'.[23] In spite of the differences between coherence and plausibility, the latter, it is argued, is extremely relevant to our judgements of coherence. For instance, as Johnson-Laird and Freedman have shown, it is more difficult to arrive at a coherent interpretation of an implausible discourse.[24] The reason why this is so is that (as will be explained below) in order to build up a coherent interpretation of discourse we make inferences from our world-knowledge. Stereotypical knowledge is easily accessible. Thus, when the knowledge required to make a coherent interpretation of a discourse deviates from our common assumptions about the world, we should encounter more difficulties in retrieving the relevant information. As a result, it will be more difficult to understand the text, that is, to make sense of it. Hence, the plausibility of the events described in a text affects its comprehensibility. But, does comprehensibility, or interpretability, amount to coherence? This leads us to the relation between the last pair of concepts that I shall examine here, that is, the relation between comprehensibility and coherence.

The way in which one understands the relation between coherence and understandability/interpretability/comprehensibility is crucial for a theory of coherence, for it determines the scope of this theory. Hobbs has argued that the notion of understandability is broader than the notion of coherence, since there are discourses, such as (12), that are understandable, even though they are not coherent, given that the individual sentences are understandable only in themselves and they contribute nothing to each other.[25]

(12) Jimmy Carter proposed a massive energy program. He used to cultivate peanuts.

Similarly, Reinhart argues that we should carefully distinguish between the set of coherent texts and the set of comprehensible texts. She writes:

> An analysis of text-coherence which does not make this distinction between coherence (a type of well-formedness) and comprehensibility will not be a theory ... since there are hardly any known limits on what the human mind can understand, given the appropriate amount of effort, imagination and patience, such an analysis

[22] See Van Dijk (1977: 99) and Enkvist (1977: 111–12).

[23] Green and Morgan (1981: 173).

[24] Some empirical studies have shown that the plausibility of a story affects its comprehensibility and its memorability. See Johnson-Laird (1983: 375ff).

[25] Hobbs (1983: 34).

> would have to wind up stating that any string of sentences forms a coherent text, a statement for which, of course, we need no theory at all.[26]

From this perspective, it follows that discourses such as (12), although perfectly comprehensible, are incoherent. However, as Reinhart recognizes, it may be hard to accept the label 'incoherent' for such perfectly understandable texts. To avoid this result, Reinhart has introduced a distinction between 'explicit coherence' and 'implicit coherence'. As opposed to explicit coherence, implicit coherence refers to those cases in which, since there are no formal links, the interpreter is obliged to use special procedures for imposing coherence.[27] In this approach, a theory of coherence would have two components: a specification of the conditions of (explicit) coherence and a specification of the procedures for imposing coherence on those texts that are not explicitly coherent.

This view on the relation between coherence and comprehensibility could presumably be expanded in order to give an account of the relations between coherence and the other notions that we have examined so far. In this approach, texts such as those discussed above, ie texts that are understandable but that lack cohesive markers, and texts that are pragmatically inappropriate, inconsistent, loosely connected or highly implausible, would be 'implicitly coherent', in that their coherence would result only from the application of special procedures that impose coherence. For instance, the interpretation of

(8) Peter is vegetarian. He eats meat every day.

As

(9) that he claims to be a vegetarian (because he is a snob, or he wants to stand out), but that in actual fact he eats meat seven days a week.

requires that the reader supply the missing steps so as to restore the consistency of the text. This text will not be 'explicitly' coherent, but only 'implicitly' so. In this view, non-coherent texts only comprise 'those rare cases in which no procedure can impose any kind of derived coherence'.[28]

Enkvist pursues a strategy similar to Reinhart's.[29] His strategy is interesting in that he approaches the problem of the place of coherence in discourse theory by analysing the notion of incoherence rather than the notion of coherence as such. In his view, incoherence may result either from syntactic evidence of non-coherence or from pragmatic evidence of non-coherence. The former is related to Reinhart's condition of cohesion, except that for Enkvist it does not suffice for incoherence that there is no formal connectivity,

[26] Reinhart (1980: 162).
[27] ibid, 163.
[28] ibid.
[29] See Enkvist (1977).

but it is also required that there *is* evidence of non-connectivity. The latter refers to Reinhart's relevance and consistency conditions, but again a positive breach of these conditions is required for incoherence. In cases in which there is neither direct evidence of non-connectivity nor direct evidence of connectivity, whether the text is coherent or not will depend on whether the interpreter succeeds in finding it so. Like Reinhart, Enkvist claims that texts will be incoherent only if they defy all attempts to find its parts interlinked in some way. Other distinctions related to the implicit/explicit distinction are also proposed in the literature. Conte distinguishes between coherence *a parte obiecti*, that is the coherence of a text, and coherence *a parte subiecti*, or coherence for a reader.[30] From this point of view, one may either study the conditions on which the coherence of a text depends (coherence *a parte obiecti*) or the procedures by which the interpreter construes coherence (coherence *a parte subiecti*). Similarly, Givón distinguishes between 'coherence in text' and 'coherence in mind'.[31]

Hence, two main views on the relation between coherence and other concepts in discourse theory with which it is closely connected may be distinguished. On the one hand, some discourse theorists keep these concepts as distinct (even if they recognize that there are some important connections between them). On the other hand, others take (at least) some of these concepts to express conditions of coherence. In this view, one may further distinguish between different kinds of coherence, depending on whether the text structure fulfils some of these conditions, or whether, instead, the interpreter is required to build or impose coherence. Which stance one takes on the relation between coherence and the other notions that we have examined here is of the utmost relevance for determining the appropriate goals and scope of a theory of discourse coherence. From the former perspective, a theory of discourse coherence has to specify what, beyond cohesion, contributes to the coherence of a text, in a way that does not blur the claimed distinctions between coherence, pragmatic acceptability, consistency, plausibility and comprehensibility. From the latter perspective, a theory of discourse coherence must specify the conditions of coherence broadly understood as well as the procedures by which interpreters succeed in making sense of a text when it fails to exhibit some of the required conditions. With all these distinctions in mind, I proceed now to examine the main theories on discourse coherence that have been proposed in the literature.

[30] Conte ((1988: 29 and 79); (1989a: 276 and 280); and (1989b: 272–74)).
[31] Givón (1995).

## II. THEORIES OF DISCOURSE COHERENCE

In the previous section, I have analysed the notion of coherence by distinguishing it from other concepts of discourse theory. Now, how may a notion of discourse coherence be positively defined? The following proposals may be distinguished: the coherence relations approach, topic-based theories of coherence, accounts of coherence in terms of mental models, the intentional approach and the heuristic approach. These theories, as we will see, give different accounts of the conditions of text coherence as well as of its role in the interpretation of discourse.

### A. Topic-based Theories of Coherence

According to this approach, coherence is a matter of 'aboutness'. A text is coherent if it can be interpreted as predicating something *about* a discourse topic.[32] 'Discourse topic' is understood, in largely intuitive terms, as the proposition, preferably made explicit, which a whole set of propositions is about. Thus, it functions as the point in reference to which all-incoming propositions are assessed. Giora defines discourse coherence as follows:

An informative discourse is well-formed if and only if it:

a. conforms to the Relevance Requirement in that all its propositions are conceived of as related to a discourse topic proposition;
b. conforms to the Graded Informativeness Condition, which requires that each proposition be more (or at least not less) informative than the one that precedes it in relation to the discourse topic; and
c. marks any deviation from Relevance and Graded Informativeness by an explicit marker, eg 'by the way', 'after all'.[33]

For example, (13) is incoherent because it is irrelevant, ie at least one of its propositions cannot be interpreted as being about the given discourse topic (ie Ronit) and there is no connector that marks the digression.

(13) Ronit is never home nowadays because she lives near school. School, you know, is the centre of the kid's social life. Uri has missed school a lot this year. He never shows up at tennis, either.[34]

In addition to obeying the Relevance and Graded Informativeness requirements, there is, argues Giora, another factor that affects the degree of coherence, namely, degree of meaning salience.[35] A meaning is salient if it is

[32] See Van Dijk (1977) ch IV; Giora ((1985a), (1985b), (1985c) and (1997)); and Glanzberg (2002).
[33] Giora (1997: 22).
[34] Giora (1985b: 703).
[35] See Giora (2014).

coded in the mental lexicon; it is non-salient if it is not coded but its decoding relies on derivational procedures. Whereas a salient meaning is accessed automatically, a non-salient interpretation requires more processing effort. Novelty, claims Giora, hampers coherence: the higher the degree of meaning salience, the higher the degree of discourse coherence.

To sum up, according to this approach to coherence, the crucial notion is that of 'topic'. Both global and local coherence are explained in terms of this notion. From a global perspective, what makes a discourse hang together is a hierarchical structure of discourse topics. Two adjacent sentences will be locally coherent if they are related via a governing discourse topic. This approach to discourse coherence is intuitively appealing. However, there is a main problem with this approach: its reliance on an unanalysed notion of discourse topic. Despite the fact that this notion has received a lot of attention, there is no accepted definition of discourse topic on which this approach to discourse coherence can rely.[36] I shall describe now an approach to discourse coherence that does not depend on the controversial notion of discourse topic, namely, the coherence relations theory.

## B. Coherence Relations Approach to Discourse

According to coherence relations theories, discourse coherence should be analysed in terms of a set of relations, such as 'justification', 'cause', 'evidence', which bind discourse segments together and the identification of which is crucial for understanding a text.[37] For example, Hobbs argues that (14) is intuitively coherent because the two discourse segments are linked by an 'explanation relation':

(14) He was in a foul humour because he had not slept well that night.[38]

In the following text, the coherence relation between the two discourse units is that of 'evidence', since the second part provides evidence for the claim put forward in the first part:

(15) Smith seems to have a new girlfriend. He's been paying a lot of visits to New York lately.[39]

There is no agreement in the literature on the number or the taxonomy of the relations that are necessary for coherence. Hobbs classifies coherence

[36] On the notion of topic, see Reinhart (1981: 53–93). For an overview of diverse approaches to the notion of topic, see Brown and Yule (1983) ch 3; Schlobinski and Schütze-Coburn (1992); and McNally (1998).

[37] See Hobbs (1983); Mann and Thompson (1986); Noorman, Sanders and Spooren (1992) and (1993); Sanders and Spooren (1999); Sanders (1997); and Bateman and Rondhuis (1997).

[38] This example is a modified version of one given by Hobbs (1983: 48).

[39] Mann and Thompson (1986: 61).

relations into four basic types (which are divided in their turn in several subtypes) according to their communicative function.[40] Mann and Thompson discuss 15 kinds of coherence relations.[41] Sanders, Spooren and Norman propose a taxonomy that classifies coherence relations in terms of four cognitive primitives: basic operation (additive and causal relations), source of coherence (semantic and pragmatic), order of segments (basic and non-basic) and polarity (positive and negative).[42]

All these approaches claim that the recognition of different coherence relations is pivotal for the interpretation of discourse. Such recognition is sometimes facilitated by the use of discourse markers, such as 'but', 'therefore' or 'so', that make explicit the coherence relation that holds between segments, eg 'because' in (14).[43] However, these relations are often left implicit in the text, eg (15). In this case, the hearer/reader must infer them in order to arrive at a coherent interpretation of the discourse. In contrast to topic-based theories of coherence, both global and local coherence are explained by appealing to the notion of 'coherence relation', instead of that of 'discourse topic'. First, global coherence results from the hierarchical structure of coherence relations. Secondly, two segments are locally coherent if they are linked by a coherence relation. This approach to discourse coherence brings to light the relevance of the several kinds of inferential connections that are involved in interpretation. However, it is a main shortcoming of this theory that it does not provide an accepted framework for the definition and classification of these relations. Now, I turn to examine an approach to discourse coherence that relies on a very different understanding of the way in which inferential connections are drawn when interpreting discourse, to wit, the theory of mental models.

## C. Mental Models of Discourse

The modern formulation of the concept of mental model is due to Kenneth Craik. In *The Nature of Explanation*, he argued that human beings translate external events into internal models and reason by manipulating these symbolic representations.[44] From Craik onwards, the notion of mental model has stimulated research in linguistics and cognitive science.

[40] Hobbs (1983).

[41] Mann and Thompson (1986).

[42] Noorman, Sanders, and Spooren (1992).

[43] According to the coherence relations approach, discourse markers are primarily linguistic devices that may be used to make explicit the coherence relations that hold between discourse segments. See Risselada and Spooren (1998). For a critique of the coherence relations approach to discourse markers from the point of view of relevance theory, see Rouchota (1998); Unger (1996); and Moeschler (1989).

[44] Craik (1943).

Explanations of visual perception, comprehension of discourse, reasoning and the representation of knowledge have invoked hypotheses of mental models.[45] According to the mental models theory of discourse, there are two levels of representation of discourse: the propositional representation, close to the linguistic form, and the mental model, which is analogous to that of the corresponding state of affairs of the world.[46] Whereas the linguistic representation captures the meaning of discourse, the mental model represents its reference, that is, the situation that the discourse describes. For example, a mental model of the assertion 'I [Philip] sold my car to Stuart for a hundred pounds' would be:[47]

| (16) | Phil -----> car | Phil -----> £100 |
|---|---|---|
| | Stuart -----> £100 | Stuart -----> car |

The coherence of a discourse, on this view, depends on the ability to construct of mental model of the discourse. As Johnson-Laird puts it, 'a necessary and sufficient condition for discourse to be coherent, as opposed to a random sequence of sentences, is that it is possible to construct a single mental model from it'.[48]

The possibility of constructing a single mental model depends on the principal factors of 'co-reference' and 'consistency'. That is, each sentence in a discourse must refer, either implicitly or explicitly, to an entity referred to, or introduced, in another sentence. In addition, the properties and relations ascribed to referents must be consistent, that is, compatible with each another and free from contradiction. For example, consider (17):

(17) Ann is a teacher.

A discourse model for (17) would be as follows:

| Discourse model | | Background knowledge |
|---|---|---|
| Ann | = | teacher |
| | | teacher |
| | | . . . |
| | | teacher |

The reason for the incoherence of discourse (18) is that there is no unique token for a teacher in the current discourse model, and thus, it is not

[45] For a brief and extremely clear introduction to the theory of mental models, see Johnson-Laird (1990: 470–99). For a detailed statement of the theory of mental models, see Johnson-Laird (1983).

[46] On the mental models approach to discourse, see Johnson-Laird (1983) chs 7, 14 and 15; Garnham, Oakhill, and Johnson-Laird (1982); Garnham (1987); Rickheit and Habel (1999); and Garnham and Oakhill (1996).

[47] Johnson-Laird (1983: 418).

[48] ibid, 370.

possible to establish the referential link required for building up the mental model of the discourse.[49]

(18) Ann is a teacher. The teacher caught a bus.

The role of background knowledge is also claimed to be critical in the interpretation of discourse. For example, consider (19):

(19) The cup was in front of the fork. It was full of milk.[50]

The reader knows that 'it' refers to 'the cup' (and not to 'the fork') from a combination of the information that is explicit in the text and background knowledge. Mental models are constructed not only on the basis of the meaning of sentences, but also on the basis of inferences from general knowledge—which is also represented in mental models—and from specific knowledge of the linguistic context. Thus, in this approach, both linguistic and non-linguistic factors have a bearing on judgements of global and local coherence. Only if these factors can be integrated in a single mental model, is a discourse globally coherent. Similarly, it is claimed that the local coherence between two text segments arises indirectly from the fact that they describe events that are so related in the world that the mental model of the discourse describes, instead of depending on the establishment of a coherence relation between text-segments.

## D. The Intentional Approach

According to some proposals, acts, intentions and goals are the backbone of a theory of discourse. From this point of view, coherence is mainly the outcome of the interpreter's ability to infer the speaker's intentions, goals and purposes on the basis of the observed acts, most importantly, speech acts.[51] This is the stance that Grosz and Sidner take. In their view, the answer to the question of what makes a discourse coherent lies in the concept of discourse intention. From this perspective, the recognition of the producer's intention with the discourse, at both the local and global levels, amounts to recognizing the purpose of the discourse. It is the recognition of this purpose, they claim, that plays a primary role in defining discourse coherence. As Grosz and Sidner put it, 'a discourse is coherent only when its discourse purpose is shared by all participants and when each utterance

[49] ibid, 382.

[50] Example discussed by Garnham and Oakhill (1996: 321).

[51] Even if speech acts are extremely important in discourse interpretation, acts that do not involve speech at all are also taken to be relevant to discourse interpretation (eg gesturing, glancing, staring, etc). On the relevance of speech theory to discourse coherence, see Brown and Yule (1983: 231–33).

of the discourse contributes to achieving this purpose', where such purpose is to be identified with the speaker's intentions.[52]

Morgan and Green have also advocated the view according to which one should approach the problem of defining discourse coherence within a theory of discourse that puts acts, goals and intentions at the forefront. Besides these notions, the notion of 'plan' plays, in their view, a crucial role in discourse theory and discourse coherence. They claim that discourse production is the pursuit of goals by performing acts of various sorts. These acts and goals are hierarchically related. They propose that we call the resulting structure 'plan'. Assigning a text structure to a discourse amounts, at least in part, to inferring such a plan. The proper approach to coherence, in their view, is to be found in matters of author's goals, plans and intentions. Discourse coherence is a function of the degree to which it is possible to form consistent hypotheses about the author's goals, plans, and intentions from reading/hearing the text. This approach to discourse coherence, they claim, is based on a 'simple but pervasive human ability: the ability to interpret the actions of other people by forming complex hypotheses about goals, plans and intentions that underlie acts'.[53] That there is a tight link between coherence and general interpretative skills is also a basic tenet of the last approach to discourse coherence that I shall consider here: the heuristic approach.

## E. The Heuristic Approach

The main tenet of the 'heuristic' approach is that coherence is primarily a principle that guides and regulates interpretation, as opposed to a property of a text.[54] More specifically, the heuristic approach to discourse coherence may be characterized by means of the following claims: (i) coherence is not typically a linguistic problem but a general principle in the interpretation of all human actions; (ii) the starting point of any interpretation is an 'assumption of coherence', ie the assumption that the actions form a coherent whole, which applies as well to the interpretation of discourse in that the interpreter starts from the assumption that the discourse is coherent;[55]

[52] Grosz and Sidner (1986: 202).

[53] Green and Morgan (1981: 175).

[54] There are various alternative labels in the literature that refer to a number of similar views on coherence, to wit, 'interpretative coherence', 'hermeneutic understanding of coherence' and 'procedural approach'. For defences of a heuristic approach to discourse coherence, see Charolles ((1983), (1985) and (1989)); Neubauer (1983); Hatakeyama, Petöfi, and Sözer (1985); and Petöfi (1985).

[55] Several authors have emphasized the presumption of coherence (or assumption of coherence) in the coherence-based literature on discourse interpretation. See Brown and Yule (1983: 224); Enkvist (1985: 234); Charolles (1983: 77); and Bublitz and Lenk (1999). Roberts and Kreuz (1993) have even argued, on the basis of an analysis of non-standard discourse, that an assumption of coherence is the only necessary and sufficient mechanism required for judgements of coherence.

(iii) the interpreter starts the process of interpretation with a disposition to construct coherence, to look for coherence and to find a coherent interpretation of any discourse as much as of any other object of interpretation;[56] (iv) in order to construe coherence, the interpreter will not only use linguistic knowledge, but inferences from other types of knowledge are also claimed to be crucial in the process. The last three aspects of interpretation—the assumption of coherence, the disposition to look for coherence, and the reader's inferential work—are closely intertwined. As Conte puts it, 'it is because the interpreter is looking for coherence, and because he expects to find meaningfulness, that he activates his systems of knowledge. It is for this reason that he draws inferences, fills in gaps, in order to construct coherence'.[57] Thus, the assumption of coherence and the disposition to find coherence explain why the interpreter engages in the inferential work that is taken to be crucial to interpretation; (v) interpretation is seen primarily as a dynamic and dialectic process in which the interpreter (the subject) interacts with the object of interpretation in order to achieve the desired result, ie a coherent interpretation; and last, (vi) the main problem of a theory of discourse coherence is not that of giving an account of conditions of coherence, but that of explaining how interpreters succeed in their constructive effort, that is, in arriving at a coherent interpretation.

There are different accounts of the process whereby the receiver interprets a discourse with a view to making it coherent. Here, I shall briefly introduce Conte's account of the interpreter's strategies for building coherence in a particular form of interpretation, which she refers to as 'reinterpretation'. In her view, cases of reinterpretation bring to light the extent to which interpretation is a constructive process that is regulated by a principle of coherence. Reinterpretation occurs when the interpreter, in order to attribute meaning to a text, is required to interpret again a preceding part of a text already interpreted. The interpretation of a part of a text may be incompatible with the interpretation of the following parts. In this case, the interpretative hypothesis of the interpreter may be changed in various ways. She may change the partition of the text in different parts (phrase, statement etc); the categories that are assigned to parts of the text (ie noun, verb, etc); the kind of statements that are involved (ie imperative, declarative, etc); the kind of illocutory force of a statement (descriptive, prescriptive); or the properties of the discourse reference. The following example, discussed by Ziff, illustrates one of these cases of reinterpretation—the second one, that is, change of categories:

(20) I watched her duck when they were throwing rotten eggs.[58]

[56] See Conte (1988: 80).
[57] Conte (1989a: 280).
[58] Ziff (1984: 38).

At first, the interpreter will take 'duck' as a verb; but when the discourse continues with:

(21) It swam out to the middle of the lake.

'duck' must be reinterpreted as a noun. That is, in the text:

(22) I watched her duck when they were throwing rotten eggs. It swam out to the middle of the lake.

'duck', originally interpreted as a verb, is reinterpreted as a noun (and 'her', which is first interpreted as a pronoun, is reinterpreted as a possessive), for otherwise one would not be able to identify the referent of the expression 'it' for which 'her duck' is an anaphoric substitute. It is in the interest of coherence that reinterpretations, such as the foregoing one, are made.

Conte views the process of interpretation as a kind of problem-solving. According to this conception of the process of interpretation, the text is best seen, in Conte's words, as 'a set of instructions' that guide the interpreter to solve the problem of interpreting the text in a coherent way. For instance, referential terms (which are the most important cohesive markers) give the interpreter instructions for identifying a referent. But these instructions may not suffice. It may be necessary to use other instructions that are closely intertwined with the interpreter's knowledge about the world. In order to achieve coherence, the interpreter needs to draw inferences. Sometimes the accepted interpretation will have to be revised in light of the successive parts of the text, as is the case in instances of reinterpretation. It is the interpreter, in his quest for coherence, who searches and, ultimately, constructs an interpretation that, like solving a puzzle, makes all elements fit together.[59]

As we have seen, in the heuristic approach, discourse coherence is first and foremost coherence for an interpreter, coherence *a parte subiecti,* as opposed to coherence of a text. The process of interpretation is a dynamic and dialectical process in which the interpreter, who expects and aims at coherence, works out a coherent interpretation of the text. In order to construct such an interpretation, the interpreter relies not only on linguistic knowledge, but also, crucially, on background knowledge. The view that discourse coherence is not a purely linguistic phenomenon, but that it is primarily a function of whether the interpreter draws the required inferences from non-linguistic knowledge, is also endorsed, to varying degrees, by the diverse views on discourse coherence examined in this section. Despite the many differences that distinguish the theories of discourse coherence that we have examined so far, they all take discourse coherence to be, at least in part, a matter of inference and background knowledge. The interpretation of a text in terms of a unitary discourse topic, its representation by means of

[59] Conte (1988: 91).

a single mental model, the recognition of implicit coherence relations, and the identification of the goals, purposes, and plans of the producer all crucially involve inferences from different bodies of non-linguistic knowledge. Hence, the relation between discourse coherence, inference, and knowledge is a pivotal issue in all the literature on discourse coherence. To this topic I turn now my attention.

## III. COHERENCE, KNOWLEDGE AND INFERENCE

### A. Kinds of Knowledge

A variety of kinds of knowledge and abilities interact to enable discourse interpretation. In the literature, there are different proposals with regard to which kinds of knowledge are relevant to discourse interpretation, how they may be classified, as well as their relative importance for the interpretation of discourse.[60] I shall group some of the systems of knowledge that have been taken to be crucial for the interpretation of discourse into three main types: linguistic knowledge, knowledge of the world and discourse-knowledge.[61]

(i) *Linguistic knowledge*. This includes, at least, the following subsystems of knowledge: knowledge of language, ie roughly, knowledge of the phonology, syntax, morphology and semantics of a language; knowledge about the use of language, ie knowledge of the principles and social conventions that regulate the use of the forms provided by the grammar of the language to achieve goals; and knowledge about communication, which includes knowledge of conversational principles, such as Grice's cooperative principle and its corollary maxims.[62]

(ii) *Knowledge of the world*, which includes encyclopaedic knowledge, that is, background knowledge and general knowledge of the way the world is; expert knowledge, which plays a critical role in the interpretation of different types of texts, eg scientific knowledge is required for the interpretation of scientific texts;[63] and knowledge of values, ie knowledge about the social system of values.[64]

[60] See Green and Morgan (1981: 177–180) and Viehweger (1989).

[61] These systems of 'knowledge' do not refer, as in philosophy, to 'true justified belief'. Particularly, it is not assumed that the bodies of belief that enter in discourse interpretation are true. In this respect, the discourse theorist's usage of 'knowledge' is very different from the philosophical usage.

[62] For Grice's principle and maxims, see Grice (1975).

[63] On the relevance of expert knowledge to the coherence of scientific texts, see Lundquist (1989).

[64] The relevance of knowledge of values for discourse coherence has been pointed out by Conte. See Conte (1988: 80).

(iii) *Discourse-knowledge.* Coherence attribution not only relies on linguistic knowledge and world-knowledge, but also on knowledge about discourse, more specifically, about discourse classification.[65] Speakers have an intuitive knowledge about kinds of discourse, such as 'conversation', 'dialogue', 'narrative text', 'poem', 'philosophical essay', 'legal text' etc. Coherence conditions are not the same for a literary discourse, a philosophical one, or a conversation.[66] Thus, the interpreter's attribution of coherence/incoherence crucially depends on whether, in addition to other systems of knowledge, she also activates the body of knowledge concerning the type of discourse to which the text in question belongs, ie 'discourse frames'.

These systems of knowledge (linguistic knowledge, world-knowledge, and discourse-knowledge) provide a stock of premises that interpreters may use in order to draw the inferences necessary to establish the coherence of a text. Let us now examine the relevance of the inferential process for achieving coherence.

## B. Coherence and Inference

Discourse coherence is, at least in part, a matter of inference. In order to make a coherent interpretation of a discourse, the receiver has to make the relevant inferential connections. If these inferences are not drawn, the relevant connections cannot be made, and thus, the text will be incoherent for the reader.[67] For example, consider (23):

(23) Are you going to play tennis? It's snowing in Tibet.[68]

In his discussion of this example, Ziff writes:

> The evident incoherence of this discourse will disappear if one is warranted, perhaps by background information, in construing it as essentially enthymematic in form; perhaps the respondent is a Tibetan Buddhist and it is known that if it is snowing in Tibet, he does not play tennis; in which case the discourse can be seen as exemplifying *modus ponens*, albeit in suppressed form, and so as coherent.[69]

[65] Mignolo (1989).

[66] The specific conditions of coherence of some types of discourse have been extensively studied. Conversational coherence and narrative coherence are surely amongst those that have received more attention in the literature. On conversational coherence, see Craig and Tracy (1983). On narrative coherence, see Samet and Shank (1984). On coherence in argumentative texts, see Moeschler (1989). For a comparison between coherence structures in written and spoken texts, see Tannen (1984).

[67] See Enkvist (1985: 239) and Samet and Shank (1984: 62).

[68] See Ziff (1984: 39).

[69] ibid.

Thus, the interpreter searches for a context of assumptions that allows her to interpret a text as coherent. The linguistic data provide an initial context. Then, this context is 'expanded' so as to include the information (most importantly world-knowledge and discourse-knowledge) that is necessary to make a coherent interpretation. The process whereby one 'expands' the context to include the missing information that is needed to make a coherent interpretation is an inferential one.[70] Hence, an important step towards better understanding discourse coherence is to analyse the inferential processes that underlies coherence construction in discourse interpretation.[71]

There are several proposals for classifying the inferences that lead to coherence in discourse interpretation. Enkvist has distinguished the following types: existential, categorial, referential, inferences concerned with states and processual.[72] For instance, (24) illustrates an 'existential inference', in which we infer the existence of something (sparking-plugs) not expressly stated or introduced from the existence of something else (the engine). In this text, a 'has-relation', eg the engine has plugs, has to be inferred by the addressee in order to interpret it:

(24) The engine stopped. The plugs were wet.

Categorial inferences consist in the establishment of 'is-relations', that is, the assignment of members to categories. Referential inferences occur when we assign referents through inference. Inferences concerned with states provide us with certain information about the mental and physical conditions of the actors referred in a discourse. Last, processual inferences allow us to bridge the gap between two or more states explicitly described in the text.

As regards narrative texts, Warren, Nicholas, and Trabasso have proposed to classify inferences into three types: informational, logical and evaluative. In their view, understanding a text requires knowledge of the answers to a set of who, what, where and when questions. Arriving at answers to these questions is accomplished by making 'informational' inferences. 'Logical' inferences are drawn to make causal connections between events or actions in a text. Last, 'evaluative' (or 'elaborative') inferences

[70] See Brown and Yule (1983: 50–58).

[71] The inferential processes involved in discourse interpretation are non-demonstrative and global. See Sperber and Wilson (1986: 65). There are diverse views about how a theory of the inferential processes involved in discourse interpretation should be developed. Some claim that deduction plays a crucial role in these processes (Sperber and Wilson (1986) ch 2), while others give it a marginal role (Brown and Yule (1983: 33ff and 256ff)). Yet others take these inferences to be, for the most part, explanatory inferences. See Back and Harnish (1979: 92–93) and Dascal (1977: 322). From the perspective of AI, see Hobbs, Stickel, Appelt and Martin (1993). From the perspective of semiotics, see Eco (1990: 155–56 and 229–56). In contrast, Johnson-Laird claims that there are no rules of inference properly speaking involved in these processes (1983) ch. 6. Some have even denied the possibility of developing a theory of the kind of inferences involved in central processes: see Fodor ((1983: 129ff) and (2000) ch 3).

[72] See Enkvist (1985: 234–48).

provide answers to why and how questions with regard to some action or event described in the text.[73]

Another classification of inference types has been proposed by Van de Velde. He distinguishes four types of inferences: syntactic, ILRRR (which stands for 'internal lexicon and the cognitively reflected representation of reality') inferences, semantic-logical inferences and action-oriented inferences.[74] 'Syntactic' inferences handle the grammatical information of a text by relying on the receiver's linguistic knowledge. 'ILRRR' inferences are grounded on knowledge about the meanings of words. 'Semantic-logical' inferences allow the reader to connect parts of text on the basis of the rules of logic. Last, 'action-oriented' inferences contribute to the identification of causality relations, the intentions of the agents, temporal order of actions or events described in the text and the hypothetical reconstruction of actions that are not explicitly described in the text.

Not only there is no agreement about what a classification of these inferences should look like, but it is even controversial whether we should consider the reconstruction of all the 'missing links' required for interpretation as instances of inferences. For example, Brown and Yule speak of 'automatic' and 'non-automatic' connections, where the former category refers to those connections that are made between elements in a text via pre-existing knowledge. According to Brown and Yule, these connections, such as the one illustrated in (24), should not count as inferences. The same goes for the 'informational inferences' and 'logical inferences' proposed by Warren, Nicholas and Trabasso, as long as they are automatically made. Presumably, Brown and Yule would also refuse to describe Van de Velde's syntactic inferences and semantic-logical inferences as inferences. Inferences, in their view, would only be those connections that require interpretative work on the reader's side. For example, as opposed to (24), the interpretation of (25) would involve an inference, the conclusion of which is c:

(25) a. Mary got some picnic supplies.
b. The beer was warm.
c. The picnic supplies mentioned included some beer.

Furthermore, Brown and Yule notice that the identification of a connection as automatic or non-automatic cannot be made independently of the person considering the text. That is, for some people 'beer' is an automatic component of a 'picnic supply', and so they do not have to draw any inferences for establishing c. For other people, such a connection is not automatic, and

[73] See Warren, Nicholas and Trabasso (1979). For an analysis of causal inferences during comprehension, see Trabasso and Suhn (1993). For a criticism of this taxonomic approach, see Brown and Yule (1983: 269) and Van Dijk (1981: 140–48).

[74] See Van de Velde ((1984), (1989a) and (1989b)).

they will have to draw an inference in order to interpret the text. Regardless of the many difficulties that the articulation of a theory of textual inference faces, discourse interpretation cannot be explained without appealing to those inferences. Only by drawing inferences from different bodies of knowledge can the receiver arrive at a coherent interpretation of a text. Thus, a theory of discourse coherence crucially depends on the development of a theory of the inferences that are necessary for interpreting a text.

A main problem that the development of such a theory of inference faces is that of identifying the premises that are employed in discourse interpretation. As has been explained before, the context in which the coherence of a text can be assessed is built up by making inferences from the text, from discourse-knowledge, and from world-knowledge. Thus, the interpretation is a product of an interplay between linguistic, discursive and non-linguistic knowledge. But now, the question arises: What world-knowledge? For any discourse can trigger numerous inferences. By combining linguistic knowledge, discourse-knowledge and world-knowledge we can get far too many alternative interpretations. Even from a small number of inferences, the set of possible continuations grows very quickly, and so we easily run into a 'problem of combinatorial explosion'.[75] Thus, we need some way to direct the inference process so that only relevant paths are pursued. Several knowledge-structures have been claimed to be crucial for cutting this problem down to size: scripts, plans and goals, frames, scenarios and schemata.[76] I turn now to examine how these knowledge-structures direct the inferential process that leads to the interpretation of discourse.

## C. Knowledge-Structures

Cognitive scientists and AI researchers have postulated different sorts of structures for representing the world-knowledge that is used as the basis for the interpretation of discourse.[77] One way of representing background

[75] Samet and Schank (1984: 71).

[76] For an overview on the role of these different knowledge-structures in the interpretation of discourse, see Brown and Yule (1983: 236–56).

[77] Like discourse theorists, when AI researchers speak of 'knowledge-structures' or 'world-knowledge' they do not assume that the representations in question are veridical or justified. This usage contrasts sharply with the use of the term in philosophy, where questions of knowledge are tightly connected with justification and truth. When AI researchers (and discourse theorists) refer to knowledge, in philosophical usage, they would be more properly speaking about belief. However, as Thagard (1984) has argued, the replacement of 'belief structures' by 'knowledge-structures' is not unproblematic either, given that beliefs are usually taken to be atomistic and propositional and it is a matter of debate whether representational schemes should be so. Thus, there does not seem to be a good candidate for substituting the, by now, well-established use of 'knowledge-structures'.

knowledge is found in Minsky's notion of 'frame'.[78] Minsky proposes that our knowledge is stored in memory in the form of data structures—frames—which represent stereotyped situations. Frames are used in the following way: 'When one encounters a new situation ... one selects from memory a structure called *Frame*. This is a remembered framework to be adapted to fit reality by changing details as necessary'.[79]

The basic structure of a frame contains labelled slots that can be filled with expressions, which can be other frames. For example, in a frame representing 'house', there will be slots labelled 'kitchen', 'bathroom' and so on. A particular house mentioned in a text will be treated as an instance of the house frame, and can be represented by filling the slots with the particular features of the individual house together with some default values that are assigned by the frame. In this approach, a text will activate several frames that will, in their turn, provide the necessary background for interpreting it.

Another notion that has been used for representing background knowledge is the notion of 'schema'. Schemata are data structures which represent generic concepts stored in memory. They are very similar to frames. They also have variables that can be associated with different aspects of the environment in different instantiations of the schema, and they provide default values for variables whose values have not been yet observed. They are also like frames in that they can be embedded, one within another. For example, the schema for the concept 'buy' will have the variables 'purchaser', 'seller', 'money', 'merchandise' and 'bargaining' (which are in their turn subschemata), together with associated knowledge about these variables, eg that the purchaser and the seller are people.

The main difference between frames and schemata is that the latter have an active dimension: they are developed and refined during the process of interpretation. In order to explain this active feature of schemata, Rumelhart draws an analogy between schemata and theories:

> The process of comprehension is very much like the process of constructing a theory, testing it against the data currently available, and as more data become available, specifying the theory further, that is, refining the default values ... If the account becomes sufficiently strained, it is given up and a new one constructed, or alternatively, if a new theory presents itself that obviously gives a more cogent account, the old one can be dropped and the new one accepted.[80]

Hence, in this account, the process of interpretation is best understood as one in which the schemata that are activated while reading a text are evaluated, refined and/or discarded.

[78] Minsky (1975).
[79] ibid, 212.
[80] Rumelhart (1980: 44).

As regards the interpretation of narrative texts, 'scripts', 'plans' and 'goals' have proved to be particularly useful for representing background knowledge.[81] In particular, Samet and Schank have claimed these knowledge-structures to be central for judgements of narrative coherence.[82] A script is a packet of information that contains representations of a set of events types that typically occur together in a more or less fixed order. For instance, the 'restaurant script' is arranged in the form of a series of scenes: the entering scene, the ordering scene, the paying scene and so on. When we hear or read a story about a restaurant, we do not have to make low-level inferences about what restaurants are for, what the consequences of entering in such a place are etc. Our restaurant script is activated and serves as a skeleton conceptualization whose slots only need to be filled in. For example, consider (26):

(26) Larry went into a restaurant. The baked salmon sounded good and he ordered it.[83]

According to Samet and Schank, there are several readings of (26) that are not even entertained: that the bake salmons sang well and Larry therefore decided to eat one, or that there is one specific salmon that appealed to Larry (as opposed to a certain type of dish). The reason why this is so is that the restaurant script, once it is activated, provides a key as to what inferences paths are worth pursuing.

In addition to scripts, Samet and Shank claim that plans and goals are particularly relevant for explaining how we make a coherent interpretation of a narrative text. Plans and goals are data structures that connect some of the specific events described as actions taken in pursuit of an end state. That is, when presented with texts such as (27), the reader constructs a representation of the character's goal, what plans are used to achieve those goals, and how the various goals interact. What controls this inferential process is the set of expectations that are triggered by pre-computed plans for frequently occurring goals.

(27) Thelma was hungry. She looked for the Michelin Guide, and eventually ended up at Lutece's.

The process of interpretation of (27) is then explained as follows: hearing that Thelma is hungry leads to a particular goal-ascription, eg to be in a state of non-hunger, and once a goal has been hypothesized, subsequent event descriptions are interpreted as referring to implementations of a plan to reach this goal.[84]

[81] See Shank and Abelson (1977).
[82] See Samet and Shank (1984).
[83] ibid, 68.
[84] ibid, 75.

These several knowledge-structures (frames, schemata, scripts, plans and goals) provide an explanation of how world-knowledge interacts with linguistic knowledge so as to enable a coherent interpretation of a text. As argued, the main problem that an account of the contribution of world-knowledge to discourse interpretation faces is that of determining the relevant representation of knowledge that is required for discourse interpretation. Knowledge-structures help cut down the size of the problem by directing the inferential process through the relevant paths. They do not provide a solution to the problem, since many schemata, frames or scripts can be activated by a single text. To be sure, other constraints on the use of world-knowledge are needed if the inferential process is not to get out of hand. In addition, these knowledge-structures play a limited role in interpretation, since they do not help readers or hearers deal with non-stereotypical situations.[85] Notwithstanding their limitations, they help to explain how readers are able to make the inferences needed to arrive at a coherent interpretation of a text.

## IV. A RELEVANCE CRITIQUE TO COHERENCE THEORIES OF DISCOURSE

The diverse coherence-based approaches to discourse interpretation that we have examined so far have been sharply criticized by relevance theorists. According to relevance approaches to discourse, it is relevance, and not coherence, that is the basic notion in a theory of discourse interpretation. In their view, coherence is only a derivative notion that must be understood within the framework of a relevance theory of discourse. In order to assess the force of the critique of relevance theorists to coherentist approaches to discourse interpretation, I will proceed as follows. First, I shall very briefly review the core theses of relevance theory. Next, I will examine the main objections that relevance theorists have addressed against coherence theories of discourse. Then, I will explain relevance theorists' conception of coherence. I shall conclude this section by claiming that, although relevance approaches to discourse have rightly pointed out some of the shortcomings of current coherence-based theories of discourse, they have failed to show that a theory of discourse interpretation can dispense with the notion of discourse coherence.

[85] See Brown and Yule (1983: 250).

## A. The Relevance Theory of Discourse Interpretation

In their splendid book *Relevance: Communication and Cognition,* Dan Sperber and Deirdre Wilson set out the main theses of the relevance theory of discourse interpretation.[86] This theory develops from a basic assumption about human cognition, to wit, the claim that human cognition tends to be geared to the maximization of relevance. The notion of relevance is defined in terms of 'cognitive effects' and 'processing effort'. That is, when processing information, people generally aim to bring about the greatest improvement of their overall representation of the world—the greater 'contextual effects'—for the least cost in processing.

Contextual effects are achieved when newly presented information interacts with a context of existing assumptions in one of three ways: by strengthening an existing assumption, by contradicting and eliminating an existing assumption or by combining with an existing assumption to yield a contextual implication. The greater the contextual effects, the greater the relevance. However, the computation of contextual effects costs some mental effort. This effort depends on three factors: the linguistic complexity of the utterance, the accessibility of the context and the inferential effort needed to compute the contextual effects of the utterance in the chosen context. Each increment in processing effort detracts from overall relevance, so that the smaller the processing effort, the greater its relevance. The following example illustrates the notion of relevance that is proposed in this framework.[87] Consider a context consisting of assumptions (28a–c):

(28) (a) People who are getting married should consult a doctor about possible hereditary risks to their children.
(b) Two people both of whom have thalassemia should be warned against having children.
(c) Susan has thalassemia.

Consider now (29) and (30):

(29) Susan, who has thalassemia, is getting married to Bill.
(30) Bill, who has thalassemia, is getting married to Susan.

Both have some contextual effect in context (28). In particular, both carry the contextual implication (31):

(31) Susan and Bill should consult a doctor about possible hereditary risks.

However, (30) has also the contextual implication (32), which (29) lacks:

(32) Susan and Bill should be warned against having children.

[86] See Sperber and Wilson (1986). Multiple reviews of *Relevance* appeared in *Behavioral and Brain Sciences*, no 10 (4), 1987, and *Mind and Language*, no 4, 1989.

[87] See Sperber and Wilson (1986: 125–27).

Hence, (30) is more relevant than (29). To illustrate how relevance is affected by the processing effort, compare (30) with (33):

(33) Bill, who has thalassemia, is getting married to Susan, and 1967 was a great year for French Wines.

When (30) and (33) are processed in the context (28), they have the same contextual effects: the extra-information conveyed by (33) is unrelated to the context and has no contextual effect whatsoever. However, this information requires some processing effort. Thus, (33) is less relevant than (30), which achieves the same contextual effects with a smaller processing effort.

According to relevance theory, there is a single criterion that governs the interpretation of discourse: the 'principle of relevance'. According to this principle, every act of communication communicates a presumption of its own optimal relevance. Sperber and Wilson define 'optimal relevance' as follows:

An utterance on a given interpretation is optimally relevant if and only if:

(a) it achieves enough effects to be worth the addressee's attention;
(b) it puts the hearer to no gratuitous effort in achieving those effects.

This criterion of interpretation is claimed to be powerful enough to exclude all but at most a single possible interpretation, among the several interpretations that are compatible with the linguistic data. These interpretations, it is claimed, are not equally accessible to the hearer. Hence, as follows from clause (b) of the definition, the first interpretation tested and found consistent with the principle of relevance is the only interpretation consistent with such a principle. How is such an interpretation arrived at?

According to relevance theory, the hearer starts with a small initial context, eg the context of the previous utterances. Then, she computes the contextual effects of the utterance in this context: if these are not enough to make the utterance worth her attention, she expands the context, getting more effects, and repeats this process until she has enough effects to make the utterance optimally relevant in a way the speaker could have foreseen. Thus, it is an essential feature of this account of interpretation that the context is not given, but has to be constructed as part of the interpretation process under the guidance of the principle of relevance. It is failure to see that this is so that makes coherence theories untenable—so the argument goes—as theories of discourse interpretation. I shall now examine the main objections that relevance theorists have addressed against coherence theories of discourse.

## B. Some Problems with the Coherence Approach to Discourse

In a number of works, the relevance theorists Blakemore, Blass, Sperber and Wilson have formulated several arguments against the various coherence-based approaches to discourse that have been presented before. More specifically, they have focused on topic-based theories of discourse and coherence relations approach, with some remarks on the mental models theory.[88] Nonetheless, they intend their critique to have force against all versions of the coherence theory.

### *i. The Relevance Critique to Topic-based Theories of Discourse Coherence*

Three main criticisms have been raised against topic-oriented theories of discourse interpretation. First, it has been argued that the notion of topic is neither necessary nor sufficient for well-formedness. There are well-formed conversations that are not approachable in terms of topic. For example, Blass argues that although (34) does not exhibit topic-continuity, it is clearly appropriate.

(34) a. What are you doing after eight o'clock?
b. Marceline: Let's talk about business.

Second, relevance theorists have claimed that the identification of topic depends not only on the content, as coherence theories seem to imply, but also on the context. Thus, the notions of 'topic' and 'aboutness', which topic-oriented theories of coherence appeal to, have to be explained in contextual terms. Some proponents of topic-oriented theories of discourse have been aware of this fact. For example, Van Dijk points out that a topic can only be identified given certain items of world-knowledge.[89] The problem is to give an account of how hearers/readers select from their total knowledge chunks the particular information that they bring to bear on the interpretation process. Since the context is not given, but chosen, we need some kind of constraint on context selection; and, it is claimed, no theory of coherence has given an account of how such a selection should be made. Relevance theorists claim that it is a criterion of relevance that determines how the right context is chosen, and, thus, whether a discourse exhibits topic unity, that is, coherence. Hence, ultimately, topic-relevance, as a condition of coherence, is derivable from the relevance theory of discourse interpretation.[90]

Last, and closely related to the previous point, Wilson has claimed that consistency with the principle of relevance sheds more light on our intuitions of acceptability/unacceptability than appeal to local or global

[88] See Blakemore (1988) and (2003); Blass (1990) and (1993); D Wilson (1998); Wilson and Matsui (1998).

[89] See Van Dijk (1977: 93ff).

[90] That topic-relevance is a derivative notion of relevance, as understood by Sperber and Wilson, is argued in Sperber and Wilson (1986: 216–17).

coherence, as these notions are understood in a topic-oriented framework. Moreover, Wilson claims that intuitions of local and global coherence may be straightforwardly captured by using the machinery of relevance theory.[91] Hence, coherence is a notion that a theory of discourse can dispense with. She illustrates her claims by means of the following examples.

(35) Bill, who has thalassemia, is getting married to Susan, and 1967 was a great year for French wines.

(36) Bill, who has thalassemia, is getting married to Susan. Both he and Susan told me that 1967 was a great year for French wines.

Wilson points out that, in many circumstances, these discourses are both irrelevant and unacceptable. Their unacceptability—so her argument goes—has to do with wasted effort in processing them, and not with the fact that their segments are unrelated. One can think of contexts in which these segments would be intuitively related, and still, they will be judged as unacceptable and irrelevant, eg (37).

(37) a. When people get married, it's usual to give a present.
b. A crate of wine is a suitable wedding present.
c. The best present is one that pleases the recipient.

In this context, the discourse segments of (35) and (36) would be intuitively related. However, they will be unacceptable. She argues that relevance can explain both intuitions. On the one hand, a discourse like (35) or (36) will be intuitively related because the interpretation of the first segment makes a difference to the relevance of the second: that is, different effects are achieved when the second segment is processed in the initial context than when it is processed in the initial context supplemented by the interpretation of the first segment. On the other hand, these discourses are unacceptable because they are inconsistent with the principle of relevance: the information that Bill has thalassemia is irrelevant in this context.

Wilson claims, along the same lines, that intuitions of global coherence are also better explained within a relevance framework than within a topic-based theory. What is crucial to judgements of acceptability—argues Wilson—is the contextual information, and not the discourse topic. The comprehensibility or incomprehensibility of a text depends on whether the required contextual information is accessible, rather than on the existence of a discourse topic. Topics are important to comprehension only to the extent that they make such information accessible. But a text would be equally comprehensible if the required contextual information were made accessible in some other way. Hence, Wilson concludes, topic-relevance, as

[91] For an argument to the effect that relevance theory cannot account for the speaker's intuitions of coherence, see Giora (1997). For a reply, see D Wilson (1998). For Giora's reply see, Giora (1998).

a condition of coherence, is a derivative notion, that has to be explained in the context of the relevance theory of discourse interpretation.

### *ii. The Relevance Critique to the Coherence Relations Approach to Discourse Coherence*

Relevance theorists have argued that discourse interpretation cannot be explained either in terms of coherence relations. They give three reasons for their claim. First, if utterance interpretation merely consisted in the discovery of coherence relations among the sentences in the text, then, single-clause utterances and discourse-initial utterances would not be interpretable at all. For example, the discourse of (38), discussed by Blakemore, does not exhibit any coherence relation, but it would be perfectly interpretable, and appropriate, in some contexts.

(38) Trespassers will be prosecuted.

Secondly, coherence relations are neither necessary nor sufficient for textuality. That coherence relations are not even necessary for textuality is claimed on the basis of examples like (39), in which each of the sentences stands in a coherence relation with the preceding one and yet the result is non-sense.

(39) Amos, a blue-eyed Friesian, who has a sister in Kenya, went there on safari. One of the elephants was just about to give birth and stepped on a blade of grass when Amos decided to eat a mango. There are onions, mangoes and bowls from China in the markets of Kenya. Enamel bowls have pretty patterns but are more expensive than clay pots. Amos enjoys watching Kenyan women carry pots in their heads.

Coherence relations are not sufficient for textuality either. If they were sufficient, we would not be able to distinguish (40), which is well formed, from (41), which is not, even though both exhibit what Hobbs calls an 'elaboration relation'.[92]

(40) Help. Help.
(41) A box of cornflakes. A box of cornflakes, please. A box of cornflakes, please ...

As Blass points out, it is possible to think of a context in which both (40) and (41) would be appropriate. However, the reason for the repetition would be apparent only in the circumstances in which the text is produced. Hence, it cannot be explained on the basis of coherence alone. What these examples show is that in order to give an adequate account of appropriateness and inappropriateness we must turn to context.

[92] Examples (44) and (45) are discussed by Blass (1990: 18–19).

The relevance of context for judgements of acceptability, as opposed to their explanation in terms of coherence relations, is corroborated by examples like (42). In this example, we have a text that exhibits a coherence relation—the second sentence is 'an elaboration' of the first one, according to Hobbs' taxonomy. Such a text—it is argued—can be appropriate in a context and inappropriate in another. While it is appropriate as part of an autobiography, it is inappropriate as part of a curriculum vitae.

(42) I was born in Lower Hutt, New Zealand. It used to be a dormitory suburb of Wellington, but is now a busy town with high-rise office blocks.[93]

Last, it is argued that referential ambiguity cannot be accounted for on a coherence-based approach, for there are contexts in which the intended interpretation is not the one that maintains the coherence with the preceding text, such as (43).

(43) A: What did Susan say?
B: You've dropped your purse.

Example (43) has two possible interpretations: it could be either a report of Susan's assertion or an assertion by B that A has dropped his pursue. Only the first interpretation maintains coherence relations, but this utterance would be often intended and successfully understood as conveying the alternative interpretation. Hence, coherence relations do not provide a satisfactory criterion of evaluation of discourse interpretations.

### *iii. The Relevance Critique and the Mental Models Theory of Discourse Coherence*

The relevance critique to the mental models theory of discourse interpretation bears again on the notion of context. Johnson-Laird argues that mental models are only partially derived from what is semantically encoded because hearers need to use contextual assumptions to construct a coherent mental model. For relevance theorists, this view of the role of context in interpretation is fundamentally misguided. The role of context is not that of merely helping the reader/hearer to establish coherence relations in the mental model of discourse any more than it is to establish coherence relations between segments of a text. In contrast, it is argued, the choice of context and, hence, the interpretation of discourse, is determined by the aim of achieving relevance.[94]

Thus, as has been shown, relevance theorists claim that whether a discourse makes sense cannot be explained in terms of topic-continuity. Neither can it be understood—they argue—by appeal to coherence relations

[93] Blakemore (1988: 234).

[94] See Blass (1993: 92) and Blakemore (1988: 232).

or mental models. Then, how should we explain the speaker's intuitions of coherence? I turn now to examine the notion of discourse coherence that is proposed by relevance theorists.

### C. The Notion of Coherence in Relevance Theory

According to the relevance theory what 'making sense' involves is the recognition of relevance between texts and contexts. A text is coherent if the set of contextual assumptions used in the interpretation of an utterance are made available by the preceding discourse. If the preceding discourse does not make contextual assumptions accessible for a new utterance, then, the hearer will not be able to see any connection, and the discourse will seem incoherent.[95] For example, in this approach, what makes (34) intuitively connected is that, despite the fact that there are no coherence relations linking the sentences, and despite the apparent disparity of topic, the hearer needs to make crucial use of the information derived from the interpretation of the first sentence. In contrast, examples such as (44) are intuitively unconnected because the information made accessible by (44A) makes no contribution to the context in which (44B) is processed.

(44) A: Tomatoes have been cheap this year, haven't they?
B: Look who's coming.

Hence, it is argued, the coherence of a discourse is a by-product of its relevance: the result of the hearer's search for relevance. When discourse is perceived as connected, those intuitions can be illuminated by a relevance framework. In cases in which discourse, although appropriate, is perceived as lacking connectedness, those intuitions of unacceptability and unconnectedness are also explained by appeal to the principle of relevance. What guides discourse interpretation is the presumption of relevance, and not an assumption of coherence. Discourse is interpreted as being connected only when the hearer finds that this is the most relevant way of interpreting it. It is thus, relevance, and not coherence, they claim, that is the principle that explains discourse interpretation.

[95] See Blakemore (1988: 241–42).

## D. The Relevance Critique to Coherence Theories of Discourse Examined

The foregoing criticisms to the diverse coherence-based theories of discourse may be summarized in the following three arguments:

(i) *Coherence is neither necessary nor sufficient for the well-formedness of discourse.* Relevance theory explains intuitions of acceptability better than the coherence theory does. There are perfectly acceptable texts, which are nonetheless incoherent. By the same token, there are some coherent discourses that are, however, unacceptable.

(ii) *Coherence-based theories do not give a right account of the role of context in interpretation.* Relevant theorists argue that coherence-based theories underestimate the role that contextual factors and inferential processes play in discourse interpretation. The view according to which there are only a few gaps in the text that the hearer can fill by applying some coherence-based strategy is fundamentally distorted. The role of context in comprehension is more fundamental than the gap-filling talk may suggest. The problem with coherence-based approaches is that they look for connections primarily at the level of content and thus miss the real factors that account for discourse connectivity. As Blass puts it, 'What is lacking in these approaches is an adequate notion of context, and the relation between text and context'.[96]

(iii) *Coherence is not the main criterion of discourse interpretation, but it is just a derivative notion.* What guides the process of interpretation is not the search for coherence, but the search for relevance. Principles of coherence are used in this process only as a result of the hearer/reader search for the interpretation that yields more contextual effects with less processing effort. In addition, the criterion of evaluation of interpretations is not coherence, but consistency with the principle of relevance. For only this criterion singles out one interpretation among the several interpretations that are compatible with the linguistic data. Thus, the process and the product of interpretation must be explained not in a coherentist framework, but rather in a relevance-based one.

These arguments raise exceedingly important issues about the nature of interpretation and the notion of coherence to which it is bound, to wit, the relation between coherence and judgements of intelligibility and acceptability; the relation between context and coherence; and the relation between

[96] Blass (1990: 19–20).

coherence and rationality in discourse interpretation. Let me briefly consider the bearing of the foregoing arguments on these three controversial issues.

First, as we have seen, a main strategy for arguing against coherence theories has been to present examples in which our intuitions of acceptability/appropriateness and intelligibility differ from our intuitions about the degree of connectivity of the discourse. However, one may wonder why these cases are supposed to be counter-examples to a coherentist account of discourse. To start with, coherence theories have not claimed that only coherence can explain discourse interpretation. Thus, nothing prevents a particular discourse from being interpreted on the basis of non-coherentist criteria, eg to keep one's wallet under control, in example (43). The problem is, however, to give a satisfactory account of the limits of coherence in the interpretation of discourse and of how criteria of coherence are related to other criteria of interpretation.

In addition, there is no reason why the most coherent discourse should also be the most appropriate one, or the most acceptable. It is one thing for a discourse to make sense, and a different one, is for it to be appropriate in a particular context. Moreover, as we have seen, it is a controversial issue whether coherence should be straightforwardly equated with comprehensibility. On the contrary, as has been suggested, the understandability of a discourse is a much broader notion than that of coherence.[97] Surely, there are interesting connections between both notions. It is a main objective of a theory of coherence to give an account of how these notions relate to each other.

Secondly, relevance theorists have highlighted the extent to which discourse coherence depends on contextual factors. Coherence theorists have been aware of this fact to varying degrees, and some of them have emphasized the role that context plays in our judgements of coherence. As we have seen, virtually all discourse theorists claim that the reader needs to make inferences from non-linguistic knowledge to arrive at any interpretation at all, let alone, a coherent one. However, there are some problems with the coherentist account of how world-knowledge interacts with linguistic knowledge in discourse interpretation. To start with, there is no unitary and complete account of the nature and kinds of inferences that lead interpreters to build a context in which the coherence of a text can be assessed. Besides, coherence theories still owe us a good explanation of how readers select the relevant extra-linguistic knowledge that is necessary to reach a coherent interpretation of a text. This is a reason, I believe, not to abandon coherence theories but to make the notion of context a central part of a theory of discourse coherence. That is, a theory of discourse coherence must be complemented with a theory of context-construction and context-selection.

[97] See Hobbs (1983: 33–34) and Reinhart (1980: 161–62).

To be sure, relevance theory can provide extremely valuable insights into how such a theory may be developed.

Last, one may wonder why, given that coherentist approaches to discourse interpretation do not provide a satisfactory account of context, as opposed to relevance theories, and once it has been recognized that such an account is crucial in a theory of discourse interpretation, one should still insist in making coherence a central notion in discourse interpretation. The reason why this is so is related to some assumptions about the ultimate goals of the interpretative activity as well as about the nature of interpretation. At bottom, the choice between a relevance-based framework and a coherence-based one is a choice about what concept of rationality we take to lie behind the activity of interpretation. From the point of view of relevance theory, the ultimate goal of cognition is the efficient processing of information. Thus, the model of rationality-efficiency is the one upon which the concept of interpretation is modelled.

As opposed to this view of cognition and communication, one can see cognition as an activity that is directed towards the goal of achieving understanding. As Moravcsik has argued, humans should be seen as '*homo explanans* and not primarily as mere information processors'.[98] It is because we seek understanding that we engage in the activity of interpretation in the first place. From this point of view, the rationality-efficiency model is not appropriate for explaining the nature of interpretation. Relevance, defined in terms of cognitive effects and processing effort, cannot be the only principle that guides interpretation.[99] Surely, in some contexts of interpretation, it suffices to arrive at an interpretation that allows us to improve our representation of the world for the least processing effort. But in many cases, we do not stop the process of interpretation at this point. That is, we do not regard relevance (in Sperber and Wilson's sense) as the ultimate criterion of evaluation of interpretations. At least, this is surely the case for conscious processes of textual interpretation to which the relevance principle is also intended to be applied.[100]

Hence, it is because a main goal of interpretation is to seek understanding and explanation, and not simply to process information as efficiently as possible, that a theory of discourse should give a prominent place to the notion of coherence, given that this notion, as many have argued, is closely

[98] Moravcsik (1990: 213).

[99] Several authors have criticized Sperber and Wilson's notion of relevance on the grounds that it is unduly restrictive. See Goroayska and Lindsay (1993); Berg (1991); Walker (1989b); and Cummings (1998).

[100] See Sperber and Wilson (1986: 75).

bound to those of explanation[101] and understanding.[102] Still, it is necessary to clarify which notion of coherence should function as a criterion of interpretation as well as how contextual factors should be incorporated into a coherentist theory of interpretation. It also remains to be explained how the notion of discourse rationality from which discourse coherence stems should be characterized. In short, the relevance critique to the coherence theory does not show the untenability of the coherentist framework, but it does indicate some of the problems that a theory of discourse coherence needs to confront for it to be a plausible theory of discourse interpretation. I shall conclude this chapter by examining the extent to which the coherence theories of discourse examined above have the resources for successfully addressing these problems.

## V. COHERENCE, CONTEXT AND RATIONALITY

The relevance critique to coherence theories of discourse brings to light some issues that a theory of discourse coherence has to address. In light of this critique, we may conclude that a coherence-based account of discourse interpretation needs to give an answer to the following questions:

1. What is discourse coherence? What are the criteria that an interpretation should meet in order to be coherent? To ascertain these criteria, it will have to be determined how cohesion, consistency, and the several kinds of semantic and pragmatic connectivity that contribute to coherence relate to each other. In so doing, the relation between coherence and other notions of discourse theory, such as plausibility, appropriateness, or intelligibility, needs to be examined and clarified.
2. How does the process of interpretation work in a coherentist framework, namely, how does the interpreter manage to understand a text in a coherent way? The ability to construct and select an appropriate context is pivotal for the success of the interpretative activity. In such a process of contextualization two notions seem to be crucial: inference and relevance. Thus, a coherentist account of interpretation will have to explain how these notions relate to each other.
3. Why should coherence play such a relevant role in a theory of interpretation? A coherence-based theory of discourse must give an

[101] That coherence is a notion closely related to that of explanation has been a central tenet of the theories of explanatory coherence; see ch 4. For the relation between explanation, understanding and coherence, and their connection with the goal of cognition, see Moravcsik (1990: 205–12).

[102] For some philosophical analyses of the relation between coherence and understanding, see Cooper (1994a) and Österman (2001). On the relation between coherence and understanding in the context of discourse theory, see Bókay (1989).

account of the relation between coherence and rationality in discourse interpretation.

Now, do current coherence theories of discourse interpretation provide a satisfactory answer to these questions? Let us take up each of these questions in turn.

## A. The Notion of Discourse Coherence Revisited

In the previous sections, I have examined different approaches to the problem of defining the notion of discourse coherence. This problem has been addressed by (i) distinguishing coherence from other notions, such as cohesion, appropriateness, plausibility or understandability; (ii) examining different views on the sources of coherence in discourse; and (iii) distinguishing several types of coherence that are relevant to discourse interpretation. By addressing these issues, current coherence theories go a long way towards meeting the challenge of developing an adequate notion of coherence. In what follows, I shall argue that further insights into the nature of discourse coherence may be achieved if we approach the problem of providing a technical notion of coherence by analysing the notion of 'incoherence'. This strategy is suggested, but not fully developed, in the coherentist literature. In addition, I shall claim that the different views on discourse coherence, and some of the kinds of discourse coherence that are distinguished in the literature, properly construed, should not be seen as alternative theories of discourse coherence, but as complementary views that focus on partial aspects of discourse coherence. Hence, a full account of discourse coherence would require the integration of these different dimensions into a unified theory.

### *i. On Coherence, Cohesion and Other Notions*

As argued, most discourse theorists agree that cohesion does not amount to coherence, even if they disagree on the extent to which cohesion is necessary for coherence. Whereas some claim that a text may be coherent even if it is not cohesive, others contend that cohesion is a necessary feature of coherence (at least of 'explicit coherence'). An interesting approach to this problem may be that of focusing on the relevance of cohesive marks of 'incoherence'. From this point of view, marks of no-cohesion result in incoherence or at least impair text coherence. For instance, Enkvist gives the following example of syntactic evidence of non-coherence:

(45) Susie went to London. Peter had known him for a long time.[103]

[103] Enkvist (1977: 115).

'Susie' and 'him' disagree in gender. If we replace 'him' by 'her', the coherence of the text is restored. The relationship between coherence and other notions such as consistency or plausibility is also clarified if we consider how they bear on judgements of incoherence. Consider:

(46) I have a blue-eyed wife. She has brown eyes.[104]

(47) Q: Are there any interesting paintings here?
A: The use of oblique angles, it keeps the walls from falling over us.[105]

Lack of consistency (46) or plausibility (47) seriously impairs the coherence of a text. When explicit evidence of connectivity or non-connectivity is lacking, it is the interpreter who needs to interpret the message so as to make it coherent. Thus, texts which lack explicit coherence may be shown to be 'implicitly coherent', through the application of special procedures by the interpreter.

The analysis of the relationship between coherence and other related notions in discourse theory brings to light two important features of coherence: (i) coherence is a gradual notion;[106] and (ii) there is a variety of sources of coherence. On one extreme of the scale, we have those rare texts on which almost no procedure can impose any kind of coherence. The foregoing examples may be taken to illustrate this extreme of the scale. On the other extreme, we have those texts in which the syntax, the semantics, and the pragmatics are in order. In between the extremes, we have those texts which exhibit different degrees of coherence depending on whether there is lack of cohesion (or even evidence of non-cohesion), or whether some semantic or pragmatic condition is violated. In these cases, the coherence of the text will depend on whether the interpreter manages to interpret it in a way that makes sense. From this point of view, as stated above, there are two main objectives for a theory of coherence. First, it should identify the sources of coherence, that is, the syntactic, semantic and pragmatic means on which the degree of coherence of a text depends. And second, it should give an account of the interpretative procedures that restore or establish the coherence of a text.

### *ii. Sources of Coherence*

As regards the first objective for a theory of discourse coherence—the identification of sources of coherence—in earlier sections we have reviewed a number of different views on what, beyond cohesion, constitutes discourse coherence. Different theorists present their views as if they were

[104] ibid, 121.

[105] Glanzberg (2002: 364).

[106] For a number of papers that address the scalar or gradual nature of coherence, see Bublitz, Lenk and Ventola (1999).

in opposition with one another. However, there seems to be no need to choose among the different theories of discourse coherence that are proposed in the literature. These theories may be rather seen as complementary. Each of these theories may be viewed as focusing on one of the different factors that contribute to discourse coherence. Mental models and topic-based theories focus on semantic sources of coherence. Relational approaches of coherence identify semantic and pragmatic means of coherence construction. The intentional approach focuses on pragmatic sources. The same may be said of the heuristic approach, even if there is an important distinction between this approach and the intentional one. While the intentional approach focuses on the producer's point of view, the heuristic approach focuses on the interpreter's point of view, more precisely, on how the interpreter interacts with the object—the message—of interpretation. Again, a consideration of cases of incoherence may shed light on what the primary means for coherence are.

Two main kinds of incoherence may be distinguished, to wit, 'semantic' and 'pragmatic' incoherence. The former has to do with the relevance of the discourse to the achievement of certain goals. The latter concerns the relevance of the propositions to each other in the discourse, and its characterization involves reference to 'aboutness', meaning relations, entailment etc.[107] That is to say, a discourse may be incoherent either because it fails to comply with some semantic condition or because it fails to make sense in the light of a postulated set of goals and intentions. Margolis has proposed to consider yet another type of incoherence:

> [I]ncoherence in the lives of human beings appears as a breach in rational forms of behavior or production relative to normal or characteristic human interests; but irrationality or incoherence sometimes appears, in a deeper sense, in departures from normal human interests, regardless of the conditional coherence of behavior relative to deeply deviant actual interests.[108]

Thus, following Margolis, we may say that a discourse is incoherent if it only makes sense in the light of a set of purposes or goals that depart too radically from characteristic human objectives.

One could describe the latter type of incoherence by distinguishing between 'internal' and 'external' coherence, so that these deviant discourses would be internally coherent but incoherent from an external perspective. The distinction between internal and external coherence is quite close to a classification of types of connectivity that have been proposed by Samet and Shank. Samet and Shank argue that we can distinguish between the internal connectivity of the hearer's representation of the text and the integratibility of this unified representation into the hearer's pre-existing

[107] See Dascal (1977: 313).
[108] Margolis (1984: 22).

conceptual framework. In the latter case, the connection is *external* to the representation: it holds between the hearer's representation and his world-knowledge. They write:

> This distinction is reflected in the difference between (1) the condition in which a person's pronouncements are so obscure or confused that we have no real idea of what he is trying to say; and (2) instances where we can determine what the message is, but where the message makes no sense from our point of view ... Real understanding involves both interdependent processes.[109]

A distinction between 'descriptive understanding' and 'explanatory understanding', proposed by Cooper, may help to clarify the breach of coherence that is involved in discourses that, although internally coherent, fail to be externally coherent.[110] While 'descriptive understanding' refers to understanding-what, and involves finding the most adequate description of the phenomenon in question, 'explanatory understanding' refers to understanding-why, and involves finding the best explanation of the phenomenon at issue. Lack of external coherence—we may say—deprives the interpreter of the latter, but not of the former kind of understanding. That there is no real understanding when the second condition that Samet and Shank mention is not met may also be illuminated if we consider an essential feature of understanding, to wit, that understanding is not an absolute concept, but that it depends on a point of view. As Cooper has suggested, 'intelligibility' and 'unintelligibility' are relative, never absolute. 'A phenomenon—he writes—is intelligible or unintelligible relative to a given point of view, or body of beliefs or knowledge'.[111] Similarly, the coherence of a discourse also requires a point of view. When the reader fails to identify a point of view from which the message makes sense, the coherence of the message is impaired, even if he does understand what the message is about (that is, even if he has descriptive understanding).

### *iii. Kinds of Coherence*

As explained when discussing the theories of discourse coherence, different kinds of coherence are relevant to discourse interpretation. First, we may make a distinction between local and global coherence, depending on whether judgements of coherence refer to parts of a text or to the text as a whole. Secondly, we may tell apart syntactic, semantic, and pragmatic coherence, depending on what the sources that contribute to coherence are. Thirdly, we may differentiate between internal and external coherence, depending on whether one focuses on the text, or one goes beyond the text

109 Samet and Shank (1984: 59).
110 Cooper (1994a: 11–12).
111 Cooper (1994a: 13).

so as to make it fit with a broader system of thought and action. Another important distinction is that between coherence *a parte obiecti* and coherence *a parte subiecti*. This distinction points towards two different perspectives from which discourse coherence may be studied. One may study discourse coherence by analysing the coherence of a text. This amounts to studying the text from the point of view of the producer, who has a number of resources available to make a text coherent. Alternatively, one may study discourse coherence from the point of view of the interpreter, who in an 'effort after meaning'[112] makes use of the explicit marks of coherence in the text, and sometimes, puts a number of interpretative procedures at work to arrive at a coherent interpretation of a text. A complete understanding of discourse coherence requires both perspectives. Or rather, it requires that we view coherence as the result of a collaborative effort between the producer and the receptor of the text.[113] Again, it is apparent that only a theory of coherence that gives an account of both the textual mechanisms of coherence used by the producer and the interpretative mechanisms of coherence used by the interpreter can provide us with valuable insights as to what determines our judgements of discourse coherence. We have already seen the various mechanisms that determine the coherence of a text; let us now examine the second kind of mechanisms, ie the interpretative mechanisms.

### B. Discourse Coherence and Context

What, according to coherence theories, is the nature of the procedures by which readers make a coherent interpretation of a text? As some have implicitly suggested, and others have explicitly argued for, the key to coherence is context. From this perspective, the procedure whereby discourse coherence is construed or restored is one of contextualization. Margolis writes:

> Context is the clue, however. Faced with an apparently non-coherent (not obviously coherent or incoherent) array of human thought and behavior or work, we search for a plausible or likely context of human purposes within which a given set of dreams, thoughts, plans, endeavors, theories, stories, paintings, statements, utterances, fears, commitments, hopes, or the like may be shown to be relevantly coherent or incoherent.[114]

[112] Bartlett (1932) (1995: 227).

[113] For an number of papers that address the extent to which discourse coherence is the result of a collaborative effort between the writer/speaker and the reader/hearer, see Bublitz, Lenk, and Ventola (1999) s I; and Gernsbacher and Givón (1995).

[114] Margolis (1984: 23).

In this process, inferences, as we have seen, are crucial. The reader's inferential process allows her to make judgements of coherence by providing her with a context in which the coherence of the discourse may be assessed.

As explained above, a taxonomic approach to the problem of the relation between coherence and inference has been the dominant one in the literature. However, there are reasons to doubt the adequacy of this approach. To start with, there is no single taxonomy that is generally accepted. And most of the classifications available in the literature, as we have seen, are neither exclusive, nor exhaustive. In addition, this state of affairs may not simply be a contingent fact about the present state of research, as it is not even clear that a taxonomic approach is feasible at all.[115] Margolis writes:

> It must be emphasized that there is no antecedent table of human contexts supplied with appropriate criteria of application that can be assigned to particular (provisionally) non-coherent phenomena such that, by applying them, we may straightforwardly settle the question of their coherence or incoherence ... Perhaps the most powerful generalization that can be offered about querying coherence in particular contexts are these: (a) human utterances and acts are not even intelligible if taken atomistically, without reference to internal relations of rationality; and (b) there is no single, real, total system of such relations open to discovery, applicable to the canons of scientific grammar, scientific psychology, or the like, capable of confirming or disconfirming neutral judgments of coherence.[116]

Hence, there are reasons to doubt the adequacy of a taxonomic approach to the study of inference and coherence. Nonetheless, such an analysis may prove to be useful insofar as it 'illustrates' the kinds of inferences that interpreters perform when searching for coherence.

These inferences, as shown, rely on different kinds of non-linguistic knowledge. More specifically, the premises of these inferences are drawn from various types of knowledge of discourse and world-knowledge. As has been argued, different knowledge-structures are claimed to play an important role in directing the inferential process that leads to the interpretation of discourse. Despite their relevance, these knowledge-structures fail to constrain the inferential process in a satisfactory way. First, these structures are meant to store exclusively stereotypical knowledge, and non-stereotypical knowledge is often necessary to properly arrive at a coherent interpretation of a text.

In addition, any text may activate several knowledge-structures, and thus, it may trigger different inferences. How do we decide which inferential path we should follow? The main problem is that of determining the relevant partial representation that is needed to make a coherent interpretation. That is, the problem is that of selecting one context among the possible contexts

[115] See Brown and Yule (1983: 269).
[116] Margolis (1984: 22–23).

within which a given discourse may be shown to be coherent. It is in relation with this problem that relevance theories claim to have an advantage over coherence theories. In their view, as we have seen, the reader selects the context in which the utterance may be shown to be optimally relevant. That is, the hearer selects the minimal context that would be enough to make the utterance worth his attention. In this view, the process of interpretation has an 'inbuilt stopping place': the first interpretation that is found to be consistent with the principle of relevance is the one that should be attributed to the speaker. In contrast, it seems that coherence theories are committed to claiming that interpreters should search for the context that maximizes coherence. But if so, the problem arises as to when interpreters should stop the interpretation process. When is an interpretation coherent enough? As opposed to the relevance theory, there is no a ready answer to this question within a coherence theory. Even if there is no clear-cut solution to this problem, we may find in the coherentist literature some useful suggestions in this regard.

First, a criterion of economy, like in relevance theory, is proposed by coherence theorists as well. In this sense, Enkvist claims that we should assume the principle, stated by Joos, that the 'least meaning is the best meaning'. In terms of inferencing, this means that 'we adopt the most likely minimum of available inferences or chains of inferences'.[117] A related principle is proposed by Brown and Yule: the 'principle of local interpretation'. This principle instructs the reader not to construct a context any larger than he needs to arrive at an interpretation.[118] Secondly, a 'principle of analogy' also restricts the task of context-construction. Brown and Yule explain: 'an individual's experience of past events of a similar kind will equip him with expectations, hypotheses, about what are likely to be relevant aspects of context'.[119] In this way, the receiver is constrained in his interpretation by past experience of similar discourses, by analogy with previous similar texts. Last, the stopping place of the process of interpretation also depends on the receptor and on the situation. Enkvist writes: 'A doctor responsible for a patient will contemplate a symptom more thoroughly than a doctor off duty, and an ignorant layman's inferences would be likely to be fewer in number and scope'.[120] What Enkvist seems to have in mind here is that the interests and purposes of the interpreter are critical for determining whether the degree of coherence achieved by processing a text in the constructed context is adequate.

Other factors also seem to be relevant here. For instance, the kind of interpretative activity may also impose time limits that reduce the range of possible interpretations which may be considered, eg utterance

[117] Enkvist (1985: 245).
[118] Brown and Yule (1983: 59).
[119] ibid, 61.
[120] Enkvist (1985: 244).

comprehension in everyday conversation operates with smaller time frames than, say, a theological interpretation of a religious text. In addition, there is still another way in which the kind of interpretative activity constrains the search for coherence. Every type of interpretation imposes a characteristic set of objectives the identification of which dramatically reduces the directions in which the coherence of the discourse is to be sought. The interpreter will look for the most coherent interpretation among the set of contexts that allows him to interpret the discourse as oriented towards the realization of these purposes.

In short, we seem to stop our quest for coherence when we have reached, as Beaugrande and Dressler put it, a 'threshold of termination', ie 'where the comprehension and integration of the text is deemed as satisfactory'.[121] And the determination of this 'threshold of termination' is a matter of a number of different factors, such as economic needs, the goals and interests of the reader and a number of constraints imposed by the kind of interpretative activity that one is engaged in. All these factors determine the 'depth of processing',[122] ie how much interpretative work the reader is likely to undertake—how deep the processing task will get—in order to arrive at a coherent interpretation of a text. Different degrees of coherence—which result from the different extent to which the problem of interpretation is fathomed—may be deemed as satisfactory in a particular situation of interpretation.

Now, given the multifarious dimensions of discourse coherence and the indeterminate contours of the procedure by which interpreters contextualize a text so as to make it coherent, why should coherence have such a prominent place in discourse theory? Should not we give up the study of the conditions of text coherence and the procedures for imposing coherence, and try to explicate discourse interpretation in terms of more precisely defined notions? It is, I would argue, a commitment to a certain view about the rationality of discourse that provides the answer to these questions. To my knowledge, the issue has not been considered explicitly in the coherentist literature on discourse interpretation. Nonetheless, there are several suggestions that help us reconstruct the picture of rationality that lies behind the coherentist view of discourse interpretation.

## C. Coherence and Rationality in Discourse Interpretation

A conception of interpretation as a rational practice underwrites approaches to discourse interpretation in which the notion of coherence plays a prominent

[121] De Beaugrande and Dressler (1981: 43).
[122] Brown and Yule (1983: 266).

role. In the interpretation of discourse thus conceived, coherence ought to play a critical role, given the intimate link that exists between the notion of coherence and that of rationality. The connection between coherence and rationality may be claimed to be a constitutive one. As Margolis puts it, 'incoherence is breach or violation of whatever is constitutive of the rational organization of human thought and action'. [123] Thus, coherence may be held to be not merely relevant to discourse interpretation, but rather a constitutive constraint of the rationality of discourse.

It is in light of this link between coherence and rationality that we may better understand some of the core tenets of the coherentist approach to discourse interpretation. In this approach, as has been explained, the interpreter starts with the presumption that discourse is coherent. This presumption of coherence may be now seen as stemming from a general presumption of rationality: addresses presume discourses to be coherent because they are produced by rational speakers.[124] Another pivotal element of the coherentist approach to discourse interpretation, to wit, the claim that the addressee's role is to look for the most coherent interpretation of a discourse, may also be viewed as rooted in a presumption of rationality, in this case, in the presumption that hearers/readers are, as much as speakers, rational agents. The rational way of dealing with incoherence is, as Ziff puts it, 'to attempt to eliminate it, and failing at that to live with it, contain it, insofar as possible'.[125] Thus, rational speakers will communicate in a way that helps readers preserve the assumption of coherence and rational interpreters will strive to iron discrepancies out and find a coherent interpretation of the discourse. This is, precisely, what coherence theories expect producers and receptors to do.[126]

From this account of the presumption of coherence and the disposition to create coherence emerges a view of interpretation that has a strong normative component. Both speakers and addresses, as rational agents, are 'responsible' for the success of the interpretative process. In fact, a language of 'duties' has been used in the literature in connection with discourse

[123] Margolis (1984: 16).

[124] See Charolles (1983: 75).

[125] See Ziff (1984: 41).

[126] Of course, this is not to say that all discourse is coherent. The presumption of coherence can be shown not to hold. The reader may be unable to preserve this presumption, ie no coherent interpretation can be made of the discourse. This may be due to failure of communication or lack of rationality, either on the speaker's or on the interpreter's side. On the one hand, it may be that the presumption cannot be preserved because the speaker has failed in his task of formulating his message in a way that it can be given a coherent interpretation or the reader has not succeeded in the interpretative task. On the other hand, the presumption may have to be given up because either the speaker or the hearer is not behaving rationally. This is actually what happens in cases of non-standard discourse, such as schizophrenic discourse. See Roberts and Kreuz (1993: 456–58).

coherence.[127] Given this understanding of interpretation as normative, it does not suffice that a theory of discourse interpretation be descriptively adequate, that is, that it accurately account for our practices of discourse interpretation, but it has to be normatively adequate as well, ie it has to set up appropriate standards for assessing whether a particular interpretation is justified.

Coherence theories of discourse interpretation seem to score reasonably well in both the descriptive and the normative dimensions. From a descriptive point of view, coherence seems to be a general principle of interpretation: from visual data to human actions.[128] We seem to be 'biased' towards coherence, as Ziff says, 'We humans are fanciers, connoisseurs, of coherence: I do not know why, but we are; there is no doubt about it; coherence catches our eye, fixes our attention, focuses our mind'.[129] The interpretation of discourse, as much as the interpretation of any other object, seems also to be governed by coherence-considerations. Thus, a theory of discourse interpretation must give a prominent role to coherence if it is to be descriptively adequate, just as coherence-based theories to discourse do.

This is not to say that coherence is all that there is to discourse interpretation. As argued before, relevance theory is wanting in that it endorses a reductive view of rationality as well as of the purposes of communication, which lead it to erect the presumption of relevance as the only principle that governs discourse interpretation. It is crucial that a coherence-based theory of discourse interpretation does not fall prey to the same objection. Just as we are not merely information processors, and our only goal in communication is not to process the maximum amount of information as economically as possible, we do not simply have 'understanding' as the only goal of our interpretative practices.[130] Hence, for a coherence theory of discourse interpretation to be descriptively adequate, it should make room for factors other than coherence which also enter in the process of interpretation.

From a normative perspective, a coherence theory of discourse interpretation would be adequate only if there is a reason to think that coherence provides appropriate standards for the justification of interpretation. There are several problems that await further research and the solution of which will be decisive for assessing whether coherence theories of discourse

[127] See Wales (1998: 134) who speaks of coherence as a 'duty of the author' and a 'duty of the reader'.

[128] In relation to coherence as a general principle in the interpretation of human actions, see Charolles (1983: 71–74) and Thagard (2000a). For a discussion of the social dimensions of coherence-based interpretation, see Mercier (2012).

[129] See Ziff (1984: 34).

[130] For instance, as some studies have shown, people use language that hampers coherence and that interferes with comprehension in order to produce aesthetic effects. See Giora, Kotler, Shuval and Fein (forthcoming). Coherence is also breached to convey emotions and to advance social goals (see Giora (2014)).

interpretation are normatively adequate. First, much more needs to be said about the view of rationality that is bound up with the notion of discourse coherence. Secondly, it is necessary to give some reasons why this conception of rationality should be preferred to alternative views of rationality, which are also claimed to govern discourse interpretation.[131] Thirdly, it has to be shown that the coherentist standards of discourse interpretation are reasonably objective.

The need for a coherence theory of discourse interpretation to address the issue of objectivity is all the more pressing in light of some developments on the coherentist literature on discourse theory. Bublitz writes:

> We are witnessing a trend in the field of discourse and text analysis which is moving away from reducing coherence to a product of (formally represented) cohesion and/or (semantically established) connectivity. Instead, there is an attempt to reach a more user and context-oriented interpretative understanding which is more interactively negotiated and is less dependent on the language of the text itself.[132]

To be sure, insofar as this move towards a more interpreter-oriented and context-dependent notion of coherence is a move away from 'reducing' coherence to a formal product it is a move in the right direction. The problem arises when this perspective is taken to be the only legitimate perspective, that is to say, when it is claimed to replace any other perspective of analysis. And this is the implication of some studies that present the different views on coherence as irreconcilable perspectives.[133]

This approach to discourse coherence not only gives rise to an undue restriction of potentially illuminating lines of research, but it also makes a problem that is latent in most coherentist approaches to discourse more severe. The problem is that of avoiding that a coherence-based theory of discourse ends up legitimizing any interpretation, as long as it is—by the interpreter's lights—coherent. To start with, there may be many alternative and equally coherent interpretations that one may reasonably make, which leave us then with no criteria for selecting one of them in a non-arbitrary way.[134] In addition, a coherence theory may also end up validating a purported interpretation of a text, as long as it is coherent, even if there is no significant way in which one may consider such an interpretation a possible

[131] For instance, Grice's conversational maxims are reformulated by Kasher as maxims that follow from a Rationality Principle. See Kasher ((1976) and (1982)). And Sperber and Wilson's principle of relevance, as we have seen, is of a piece with a particular view of the kind of rationality that is operative in discourse interpretation. For an analysis of the relation between Grice's, Kasher's, and Sperber and Wilson's criteria of rationality, see Ziv (1988).

[132] Bublitz (1999: 2).

[133] The title of Givón's article 'Coherence in Mind *vs.* Coherence in Text' is very telling in this regard. Emphasis added. See Givón (1995).

[134] This is the interpretative version of a longstanding objection against coherence theories of justification, to wit, the alternative coherent systems objection. On this objection, see ch 3.

interpretation of the text.[135] Trabasso, Suhn and Payton write: 'The experience of event relatedness suggests that coherence is a highly subjective and intuitive concept, that it exists in the mind of the beholder, and that it is largely a matter of personal judgment'.[136] If discourse coherence is exclusively seen as a mental phenomenon, as these authors contend, then, the coherence theory of discourse interpretation deprives us of any objective standard against which the validity of an interpretation may be assessed.

Despite the subjectivist trend that characterizes some contemporary approaches to discourse coherence, nothing impedes the development of a coherentist and objectivist theory of discourse interpretation. For instance, Van de Velde has claimed that a theory of the inferences that readers make for construing the coherence of a text may help the task of providing criteria for 'rationalizing' and 'desubjectivizing' the interpretative activity. The different rules that govern these inferences control the way in which receivers, in their quest for coherence, may add information to the verbal text which is in no way suggested or sanctioned by it.[137] There are also, as argued, some factors that constrain the construction of the context in which the coherence of discourse may be assessed. And textual mechanisms of coherence put some constraints to the activity of interpretation as well.

In fact, paradoxically, coherence theories of interpretation have been put forward as alternatives to subjective views on the nature of interpretation in domains other than discourse theory. For instance, in Zima's reading, Eco's theory of literary interpretation can be described as a dialectic between freedom of interpretation and fidelity of the structured context of the message.[138] It is, argues Zima, in this view of interpretation as a dialectic between determinacy and indeterminacy, the limits of interpretation and the limits of interpretative freedom, that the notion of 'interpretative coherence' plays a crucial role.[139] A holistic theory of interpretation, more specifically, Davidson's theory, has also been used for elaborating a critique of reader-oriented literary theory, such as Fish's theory, as well as an alternative to deconstructionist theories.[140] And Dworkin's coherentist theory of interpretation has been taken to provide a defence of objectivism about, in this case, legal interpretation.[141] Hence, in light of these developments, it

[135] This is the interpretative version of the so-called 'isolation objection'. On this objection, see ch 3. An interpretative version of this objection, as it applies against Dworkin's theory of legal interpretation, was examined in ch 1.

[136] Trabasso, Suhn and Payton (1995: 189). Jucker (1999) seems to be quite sympathetic to this view.

[137] Van de Velde (1989b: 556).

[138] See Eco (1990).

[139] Zima (1999: 127–28).

[140] See Dasenbrock (1993), esp introduction and essays 1 and 2.

[141] On Dworkin's theory of interpretation, see ch 1.

seems that the prospects of articulating theories of discourse coherence that do not result in naked subjectivism are good.[142]

## VI. CONCLUSIONS

This chapter has discussed the current state of the coherence theory of discourse interpretation. The literature on discourse coherence comes from a number of different linguistic traditions and different disciplines: text-linguistics (studies on cohesion, topic-based theories and hermeneutic approaches to coherence), discourse processing (coherence relations approach), cognitive science (mental models of discourse and relevance theory), artificial intelligence (work on knowledge-structures) and pragmatics (intentional approach).

The findings of the survey and discussion of this literature conducted in this chapter may be succinctly summarized in the following points: (i) discourse coherence is a gradual notion. We gain understanding of the notion of coherence by viewing it as a scalar notion that goes from incoherence to coherence; (ii) several kinds of coherence are relevant to discourse interpretation: local/global, internal/external, *a parte obiecti* and *a parte subiecti* and implicit/explicit, are some important distinctions; (iii) there are various sources of coherence: syntactic, semantic and pragmatic. The different theories of coherence defended in the literature are best seen as complementary in that they provide valuable insights as to how some of these various factors contribute to coherence; (iv) both the producer and the receptor play a significant role in coherence construction; (v) a theory of discourse coherence has two components: a theory of the conditions of text coherence and a theory of the procedures for arriving at a coherent interpretation of a text; (vi) the procedure whereby coherence is constructed is first and foremost one of contextualization, in which inferences from non-linguistic knowledge play a prominent role; (vii) several factors direct and constraint this inferential process—knowledge-structures and discursive frames, economic principles, principles of analogy, the goals of communication and the interests of the receptor are amongst the most relevant factors; (viii) coherence is a constitutive property of the rationality of discourse, where such rationality should not be equated with efficiency in information processing; (ix) an assumption of coherence and a drive towards coherence

[142] A further question concerns the issue of whether a coherence theory of discourse interpretation is committed to a coherentist account of the truth of interpretative claims and, if this is so, what the credentials of such theory are. For an argument against a coherence theory of truth for interpretative claims in the context of literature, see Currie (1991). On the role of coherence in holistic theories of interpretation and on the relevance of these theories for the debate over the nature of truth, see ch 6.

is crucial in discourse interpretation; (x) a coherence theory of discourse is not committed to subjectivism about discourse interpretation.

Despite the substantial amount of research on coherence and discourse interpretation that has been undertaken in the last decades, there are still many problems that remain open in the current state of the theory of discourse coherence. First, a better understanding of the notion of coherence and of the ways in which various kinds of coherence contribute to the coherence of discourse is required. Secondly, several questions need to be addressed in order to give an account of the role and place of arguments from coherence in discourse interpretation. Most importantly, the process of contextualization and inference that leads to discourse coherence needs to be further understood. Last, several questions concerning the normative standing of a coherentist approach to discourse interpretation await further research.

Notwithstanding these problems, it does not seem that a theory of discourse interpretation can dispense with a notion of discourse coherence, particularly in light of the close link that exists between this notion and the notion of discourse rationality. To be sure, discourse coherence is not as clear-cut a concept as Sperber and Wilson's relevance is, neither is it of a piece with a view of discourse rationality that is neatly defined in terms of maximum information for the minimum processing effort. But, paraphrasing Moravski, to refuse to include the notion of discourse coherence in a theory of discourse interpretation on the grounds that, as of now, it is not as susceptible of analytic description as other more clear-cut notions would be to put the cart before the horse. The issue is rather: can we really have an adequate account of interpretation as related to the use and understanding of discourse without this notion?[143] In this chapter, I hope to have shown that we cannot. In the next (and last) chapter, I shall try to show something that, perhaps, some readers might be less inclined to concede: that we cannot give either an adequate account of legal reasoning and legal interpretation without the notion of coherence, despite the many problems that, as we have seen, this notion faces in all the domains studied so far.

[143] Moravcsik (1990: 213–14).

# Part III

# Coherence and Reason in Law

# 10

# *A Coherence Theory of Legal Reasoning*

THE PREVIOUS CHAPTERS have analysed the coherence theory from a number of different perspectives. I have first examined the current state of the coherence theory in law. Then, I have explored how the notion of coherence contributes to justification in various domains other than law. The scope of this investigation has been quite broad covering epistemic justification, the justification of scientific beliefs, the justification of belief changes, practical justification, moral justification and the justification of interpretative beliefs. The guiding idea has been that an analysis of coherence in a number of different justificatory contexts will shed some light on the elusive notion of coherence and the role that it plays in the justification of legal decisions.[1]

As we have seen, the notion of coherence figures prominently in current theories of justification of both evidentiary and normative judgments in law. However, a number of important issues remain open in the current state of the coherence theory of law. Most importantly, coherence theories of legal justification are vulnerable to a number of serious objections. In this interdisciplinary journey, it has been my aim to explore which tools are available in reflections about coherence and justification in different domains for improving upon the coherence theory in law. We are back now, after this long detour, in Law's land. I suggest that we walk along the same path again by revisiting the problems of the coherence theory in law; rethinking what coherence theories of justification in domains other than law have to offer; and investigating the main lines along which the coherence theory of legal justification may be constructed. These are the aims that I intend to accomplish in this (last) chapter.

[1] The whole 'interdisciplinary' strategy is wrongheaded if Daya is correct that: 'There is no unitary "coherence" as many have supposed. Rather there are "coherences" each of a distinct type belonging to realms autonomous and independent in their nature'. (1960: 204). *Pace* Daya, I hope that the reader would be persuaded by now that there is a commonality in the structure of coherentist justification, the motivation driving the proposal of coherence theories and the challenges facing coherentism across disciplines, so that the attempt to apply some of the insights gained in the course of studying coherence in domains other than law to develop a theory of legal coherence is not futile.

The structure of this chapter is as follows. First, I shall recapitulate the main problems of the coherence theory in law. Then, I shall identify the most important elements of the coherence theories that I have surveyed in previous chapters, and bring to light some of the insights that might help us sketch a model of coherence for law that overcomes these problems. Next, I will elaborate the principal elements of a coherence theory of legal reasoning. This theory, I shall argue, is in a better position to deal with some of the main objections that may be addressed against coherence theories in law. I will then examine the view of justification on which this model relies and contrast it with the picture of justification that is assumed by the standard theory of legal reasoning. I shall conclude by pointing out some of the problems of the coherence-based model defended here, the exploration of which opens up—I shall suggest—interesting avenues for future research.

## I. REDRAWING A MAP OF PROBLEMS

In chapters one and two, I have examined in detail a number of coherence theories of legal justification of normative propositions as well as some prominent coherence-based approaches to legal reasoning about evidence. The joint study of coherence theories of legal reasoning about both disputed questions of fact and disputed questions of law has revealed that the problems that confront the coherence theory of legal justification of factual propositions and the coherence theory of legal justification of normative propositions are similar in structure. I identify five problem areas in the current state of the coherence theory of law. The problems are the following:

### A. What is Legal Coherence?

Many theories of legal justification of both conclusions about disputed questions of fact and conclusions about disputed questions of law give coherence a momentous role in legal justification. However, these theories leave the notion of coherence mostly undefined. The notion of normative coherence that figures in coherentist accounts of legal justification is very vague. It is reasonably clear that this notion needs to be distinguished from consistency and that it is crucially linked to the idea of legal principle. But beyond this, little more is said about what makes a set of norms coherent or more coherent than alternatives. An important effort to determine precisely what coherence (as distinct from mere consistency) requires is that of Alexy and Peczenik. However, as argued, their account of the criteria of coherence still remains too vague for the purposes of legal justification insofar as it fails to determine how the different criteria of coherence should be balanced against each other in order to arrive at a coherent judgement.

Coherence-based theories of fact-reasoning in law also rely on an unspecified notion of coherence. Evidence scholars appeal to the notion of coherence as a key standard for determining the 'goodness' of a particular explanation of the facts under dispute or for comparing the relative plausibility of alternative explanations. However, they fail to provide an articulated account of the notion of coherence that is relevant to the justification of conclusions about disputed questions of fact. In addition, most evidence scholars, like legal semioticians, legal theorists and legal psychologists, take 'narrative coherence' to be the kind of coherence that is at work in legal reasoning about facts. This notion of coherence is not only left poorly specified, but it also has a limited scope of application in that it can only be used in those cases in which the representation of evidence bears a narrative structure. A notable exception to this state of affairs is Simon and collaborators' work on coherence-based reasoning. Simon has worked out a notion of coherence as constraint satisfaction for fact-reasoning in law which is very precise and applicable to cases that do not involve the construction and comparison of alternative narratives. However, Simon's model is meant to be a descriptive model of legal decision-making about facts, rather than a model for the justification of conclusions about disputed questions of fact. Hence, a precise account of the concept of legal coherence is missing in current theories of legal justification of both normative and factual propositions.

## B. Holistic Tendencies

A main problem for coherence theories in law is that they have an unrestricted commitment to holism about justification. Coherentist theories of the justification of normative propositions in law endorse the view according to which it is the *whole* system of beliefs about the law and political morality that confers justification. This unrestrained holistic tendency is clearly exemplified by Dworkin's influential coherence model, by Peczenik's weigh and balance theory as well as by Hage's integrative version of legal coherence. Similarly, coherence-based approaches to the justification of factual conclusions in law take the legal decision-maker's *whole* system of beliefs to be the justification-conferring system. In this view, legal decisions about facts result from the interaction between the evidence at trial and the decision-maker's knowledge about the world.

Holism about justification is highly problematic for a number of reasons. First, it is psychologically implausible: computations of 'global' coherence are beyond the memory resources and cognitive capacities of legal decision-makers. Secondly, it is descriptively inadequate, for legal decision-makers do not typically bring to bear all their beliefs when solving a particular legal case. And last, it is normatively troubling, because it makes the justification of any particular decision defeasible on the grounds of the incoherence of any area of a belief system, even if it is very distant from the belief whose justification is at stake. Furthermore, one may legitimately question the assumption that any area of an agent's belief system (even if it is 'in the near neighbourhood') should be relevant to the assessment of the justificatory status of any belief about what the law is or what the facts under dispute are. In the normative domain, doubts may be raised about whether the coherence (or incoherence) of some subset of moral beliefs should have any bearing on the justification of a legal (rather than a moral) decision. In the factual domain, this worry gives rise to what I have called the 'dangers of the case-as-a-whole'. The problem is that the holistic approach allows decisions to be made on beliefs other than those which the decision-maker is warranted in asserting on the basis of the proofs at trial. Beliefs about character-traits, group identity, prejudices, stereotypes and other irrelevant considerations can be used by decision-makers following a holistic approach. These dangers are quite real, as Simon and collaborators have empirically shown, and a holistic approach to fact-reasoning propitiates, rather than contains, the tendency to base one's decisions about facts in beliefs extraneous to the relevant evidence at trial.

## C. Some Problems of the Structure of Coherentist Justification

Coherentist accounts of legal justification about both facts and norms face two main methodological problems, to wit, the problem of circularity and the problem of conservatism. Coherentism seems to involve a vicious circularity in that it licenses an inference from *p* to *q*, and then from *q* to *p*. When reasoning about norms, the coherence theory leads one to justify the acceptance of a particular legal principle on the grounds that it best coheres with a set of legal rules, while making the justification of this set depend on its coherence with the very same legal principle. When reasoning about facts, the coherence theory licenses an inference from a belief in a particular piece of evidence to a belief in a particular hypothesis, while holding the belief in this hypothesis justified by virtue of its coherence with the very same piece of evidence that prompted us to entertain this hypothesis in the first place.

Coherentist inference in law may not only be objected to on the grounds of vicious circularity, but it also seems to be unduly conservative. Coherence theories of legal justification have a built-in conservative tendency insofar as they make the justification of new elements depend on their coherence with a pre-existing structure. This conservative bent is an obstacle to normative change and legal innovation and, in morally deficient legal systems, it leads to committing new injustices in the name of coherence with a settled body of law. In the factual domain, the conservatism inherent in coherence theories of legal justification leads legal decision-makers to interpret incoming evidence so as to make it fit with previously formulated hypotheses and, in the worst scenario, it may even conduce them to blatantly disregard new evidence on the grounds of its incoherence with accepted hypotheses.

Thus, current coherence theories of justification of conclusions about both facts and law should face the challenge of showing how a coherence account of legal inference may be articulated in a way that avoids vicious circularity and undesirable conservative implications.

### D. How to Reason when Seeking Coherence in Law?

Current coherence theories of reasoning about both facts and law are incomplete in that they fail to provide an account of the coherence-based patterns of reasoning that lead legal decision-makers to construct and select the best interpretation of the facts under dispute or the relevant body of legal norms. Coherence theories urge legal agents to decide on the guilt/innocence of the defendant on the grounds of the story that makes best sense of the evidence as a whole, and to determine the best legal ruling based on the most coherent interpretation of the whole body of beliefs about the law and political morality. However, without any further clarification of how we have to proceed in order to construct and select the most coherent interpretation of both the law and the facts relevant to the case at stake, this advice amounts to little more than a recommendation to simply decide on the grounds of what 'intuitively' seems more coherent. In short, a coherence-based model of legal reasoning that lacks a detailed account of the inference patterns that lie behind coherence-based legal decision-making cannot be properly distinguished from intuition-based models. Thus, it is necessary to specify clearly the mechanisms whereby legal decision-makers reach the most coherent decision for coherentism to provide a plausible theory of legal justification.

### E. Why does Coherence Justify in Law?

An intriguing question lurking behind the debate about the role of coherence in legal justification about both disputed questions of fact and disputed questions of law is why coherence should have any justificatory force at all in the legal setting. That giving a justificatory role to coherence in law might be problematic and in need of justification becomes clear as soon as one notices three main problems that shadow any attempt to provide an account of legal justification in terms of coherence, and which current coherence theories in law have so far failed to successfully address.

First, current coherence theories of legal justification are vulnerable to a version of the problem of 'isolation' or the 'input' problem. As regards fact-reasoning in law, the problem is that coherence theories fail to ensure that the evidence at trial plays the role that it ought to play in the construction and selection of the best theory of the case. With regard to normative reasoning in law, the objection is that coherence theories do not guarantee that reasons from authority play the role that they should in the construction and selection of the best theory of the law. The worry in both cases is that one may achieve coherence between one's beliefs (about the facts under dispute and about what the law is in a particular case) by disregarding the input (the evidence at trial and reasons from authority) which ensures contact with reality (the relevant facts and the relevant authoritative legal materials). As a result, legal decision-makers may be justified (by the coherentist standards) in deciding on the basis of theories of the case and theories of the law that are utterly severed from what the facts really are and what the law is.

Secondly, the coherence theory of justification fails to guide legal decision-makers whenever there are several alternative interpretations of the facts under dispute and the relevant norms that are equally coherent. Coherence alone does not allow legal decision-makers to pick as justified one particular factual hypothesis or one particular interpretative hypothesis about what the law requires among a set of equally coherent hypotheses. Thus, in the event of 'coherence ties', or when faced with 'legal dilemmas', the coherence theory of justification gives rise to indeterminacy about what the facts of the case are or what the law is.

Last, coherence theories of legal justification do not provide us with any reason to believe that accepting beliefs by virtue of their coherence leads legal decision-makers to accept beliefs that are likely to be true (or correct). For the coherence theory to be a plausible candidate for a correct theory of legal justification it is necessary to show that coherence and truth (or correctness) are connected in the right way. That is, an argument is required to the effect that accepting the most coherent explanation of the facts under dispute and the most coherent interpretation of the relevant legal materials is likely to yield true (or correct) beliefs about what the facts of the case are and what the law requires in the particular case.

In an important sense, the last problem is the primary one, for, arguably, a solution to this problem would place the coherence theory in a much better position to provide a solution to the other two problems. Therefore, the key issue that needs to be addressed is that of showing that justification as coherence is truth-conducive (or that it leads to correctedness). Even though in the current state of the coherence theory this issue has been dealt with to some extent, there is still no satisfactory answer to the question of why accepting as justified beliefs by virtue of their coherence is likely to lead us to accept beliefs about the facts under dispute and beliefs about what the law is that are likely to be true (or correct). Thus, the coherence theory needs to be complemented with an account of how coherentist standards of legal justification connect up with truth (and correctness). More generally, what is missing in the current state of the coherence theory is a thorough account of why coherentist standards of legal justification are themselves justified—their truth-conduciveness (or correctness-conduciveness) being one standard against which the justification of coherentist standards of justification may be measured but by no means, as I will argue later, the only way in which the justificatory value of coherence may be defended.

Indeed, the foregoing problems need to be taken seriously. However, they do not call into question the viability of the coherentist project, but rather, they set up an agenda of research. As argued, these problems are not distinctive of the legal versions of the coherence theory (although, undoubtedly, the details of the problems are) but analogous problems affect coherence theories of justification in domains other than law. The suggestion—to repeat—is that an analysis of the role that coherence plays in a variety of justificatory contexts may prove to be useful in devising some strategies for improving upon the current state of the coherence theory in law. In earlier chapters (chapters three through nine), I have undertaken the task of examining the most relevant coherentist proposals in a number of different fields. Let us now point out the main lessons that we have learned about coherence along this interdisciplinary journey.

## II. THE BUILDING BLOCKS OF THE COHERENCE THEORY

The main motivation for undertaking an analysis of coherence theories in a variety of disciplines has been that of improving upon current coherence theories of legal reasoning. However, the task of showing how the insights that we have gained from this analysis may help us advance a coherence theory of legal justification which is in a better position to overcome the problems affecting current versions of coherentism in law is still due. The study of coherence theories in different realms furnishes us, I shall claim, with the building blocks of such a coherence theory. There follows an account of the main things to take away from this interdisciplinary inquiry.

### A. Views on Coherence

In previous chapters, I have examined different views on epistemic coherence, practical coherence, ethical coherence and discourse coherence. This interdisciplinary approach to the notion of coherence has given us—I hope—a better understanding of this slippery concept. Among the many different conceptions of coherence that have been proposed in diverse domains, I find Thagard's conception of coherence as constraint satisfaction particularly attractive for a number of reasons.[2] First, this conception of coherence—unlike most notions of coherence—is a very precise one. Secondly, Thagard's abstract characterization of coherence has the virtue of being applicable to many different domains, and more importantly for our purposes, to both evidential and normative reasoning. Thirdly, the constraint satisfaction approach to coherence is in a better position than alternative theories to meet some of the traditional objections that have been raised against coherentism. Fourthly, not only is it appealing from a normative point of view, but it also has a better claim to psychological plausibility than competing conceptions. And last, unlike other conceptions of coherence, this theory of coherence can be easily extended so as to account for the role that emotions play in reasoning. Thus, one of the main ideas that I shall take away from the interdisciplinary analysis undertaken above is the view of coherence as constraint satisfaction.

## B. Context and Coherence

A recurrent theme in coherence theories across domains is the recognition that context is the key to coherence. As argued, contextualism about epistemic justification provides us with a third theory of epistemic justification that avoids the problems deriving from foundationalism's commitment to atomism about justification as well as the problems deriving from coherentism's commitment to holism about justification.[3] Foundationalists claim that justification is transferred from one belief to another, until we reach basic beliefs which are self-justified. The problem, though, as we saw, is that the very notion of 'basic belief' is highly problematical. In place of this linear view of justification, coherentists claim that justification is holistic in that it is the whole system of beliefs that confers justification. However, as argued, this commitment to holism is the source of a number of serious problems. The contextualist solution takes it that the unit of justification is neither a single belief nor the whole system of beliefs, but a relevant subset of beliefs the identification of which is a matter of context. It is coherence with this relevant set of beliefs that confers justification. Just as contextualism seems to be a promising alternative to both foundationalism and coherentism about epistemic justification, an analogous version of contextualism about moral rather than epistemic justification also seems to be a very attractive alternative to both coherentism and foundationalism in ethics.[4]

[2] See ch 4.
[3] See ch 3.
[4] See ch 8.

The need for wedding coherentism and contextualism is not only apparent when justifying beliefs and actions, but also with regard to issues of interpretation. As argued, we should give relevance theorists credit for having pointed out a main shortcoming in coherence theories of discourse interpretation of all varieties, namely, that they neglect the crucial role that context plays in discourse interpretation. The interpreter's task is best seen as that of seeking out a context within which the coherence/incoherence of a discourse may be assessed. Thus, coherence theories of discourse interpretation need to pay careful attention to context if they are to provide us with a plausible alternative to the relevance theory.[5]

Hence, the analysis of a variety of coherence theories leaves us the main contextualist insight that coherentist standards of justification and interpretation are context-dependent. Any theory of coherence needs to account for the fact that our judgements of coherence, and thus our judgements about which beliefs, actions, plans, interpretations etc are justified, are sensitive to context.

## C. Coherence-based Reasoning as Explanatory Reasoning

A main problem for all the coherence theories that I have examined in earlier chapters is that of specifying the inference-patterns that lie behind coherence-based reasoning. As explained, with regard to normative reasoning in law, coherence theories are defended as a main alternative to rule-based approaches.[6] And concerning legal reasoning about facts, coherence theories are proposed as alternatives to probability models.[7] The problem is that these coherence theories lack an account of the legitimate reasoning patterns that lead to action and belief that is on an equal footing to those of rival accounts. While competing accounts of normative and factual inference in law are solidly grounded in deductive and inductive logic, respectively, we still lack a good account of coherence-based legal inference. An analogous problem was encountered again and again in almost all coherence theories examined in disciplines other than law. A major challenge to coherence theories of epistemic justification is that of specifying how a holistic view of inference could be conceptualized.[8] Similarly, a central problem for coherentist methods in ethics and practical reasoning is to explain the mysterious inferential processes which lead to the desired equilibrium.[9] And it is also a main shortcoming of coherence-based theories of discourse that they fail

[5] See ch 9.
[6] See ch 1.
[7] See ch 2.
[8] See ch 3.
[9] See chs 7 and 8.

to provide an account of how interpreters infer from linguistic knowledge, discourse-knowledge and world-knowledge to arrive at the most coherent interpretation.[10] The inner workings of the kind of global computations which coherence theories require seem to be so far inscrutable.

It is mainly among advocates of coherence theories of theory choice in science that we may find a solution to the problem of conceptualizing coherence-based inference.[11] In contrast to probabilistic approaches to theory choice in science, coherence-based theories seem to be based on unduly vague accounts of scientific inference. However, this is only apparently so. To recall, explanationists are committed to the view that 'inference to the best explanation' is the kind of inference that best captures much scientific reasoning. And, as argued, this kind of inference is, at bottom, a coherence-enhancing inference. Furthermore, explanationist accounts of scientific inference may be articulated in as much detail as the probabilistic ones. Computational implementations of these accounts have been developed which are comparable to the probabilistic networks that simulate probabilistic approaches to scientific inference. Moreover, the comparison is favourable in terms of efficacy, computational cost etc to the explanationist views.[12] Thus, the suggestion to take away is that coherence-based inference in science, as much as everywhere else, may be described as an explanatory kind of inference. We have the tools of abductive reasoning to elaborate a solid account of the kinds of inferences which—according to coherentism- lead to justified beliefs and actions.

## D. Making it Coherent

How do we make our beliefs coherent? Which are mechanisms whereby we may make our moral principles, background theories and particular moral judgements hang together? By what means may we modify our interpretative beliefs so that they make sense as a whole? What are the processes that lead us to make our plans and actions coherent with each other? These questions remain unanswered in most coherence theories. Yet these are important questions for anyone interested in developing a coherence theory that gives concrete guidance to its users. 'Make it cohere' does not seem to be enough as a recommendation to an agent who seeks justified empirical beliefs, moral beliefs or interpretative beliefs, or who aims at undertaking justified actions. The formal work that has been done in the area of belief revision comes to the rescue here.[13] Belief revision formalisms provide

[10] See ch 9.
[11] See ch 4.
[12] See Thagard ((2000a) ch 8, (2000b) and (2004)).
[13] See ch 5.

a reasonably detailed account of coherence-making mechanisms. The classification of three main operations whereby coherence is established (to recall, contraction, expansion and revision) is, I believe, of the utmost importance for articulating a coherence theory of justification that has the capacity to guide agents in forming justified beliefs and regulate their actions. Thus, coherentist approaches to belief revision furnish us with the tools necessary to give a detailed account of the process whereby we may render our beliefs, actions, plans etc coherent.

## E. A Plural Defence of the Value of Coherence

A recurrent objection against coherence theories of justification in all domains is that we have no reason to believe that coherence and truth connect up in the right way. Indeed, through the course of the study of coherence theories of justification in a variety of disciplines, I have found no conclusive argument to the effect that coherence is truth-conducive. There are, to be sure, interesting strategies that purport to show that coherentist standards of justification are connected with truth. But, as we have seen, each of these strategies comes with its own set of problems.[14]

Despite the fact that the relationship between coherence and truth is highly problematical, the study of coherence theories also suggests that the relevance of the much discussed problem of the truth-connection might have been overstated. Both critics and advocates of the coherence theory take it that a solution to the problem of the truth-conduciveness of coherence is a condition *sine qua non* coherence theories of justification are a non-starter. The assumption is that standards of justification should be shown to be truth-conducive in order for them to be plausible accounts of justification at all. Coherence theories of justification are then found wanting insofar as they fail to conclusively satisfy the truth condition. However, in the bulk of the literature on coherentism, there are also some suggestions that lead to question the assumption that lies at the centre of the discussion on coherentism, to repeat, that the validity of standards of justification depends on their truth-conduciveness. The basic idea is that, contrary to what is generally assumed, standards of justification may be shown to be legitimate on grounds other than their truth-conduciveness, and, more specifically, that we may have reason to value coherence-based standards of justification even if there is no conclusive argument to the effect that they are linked with truth.

To start with, several proponents of coherence theories have argued that even though truth is a momentous value in both the theoretical and

[14] See ch 6.

the practical domain, there is a plurality of cognitive and practical ends.[15] Thus, coherence is to be valued as long as it helps us to achieve a variety of cognitive and practical goals. For example, DePaul argues that a coherence method for moral inquiry may be justified insofar as it leads us to accept rational and warranted beliefs, even if it cannot be shown to be truth-conducive.[16] Olsson and Schubert have defended that coherence is epistemically valuable insofar as it is reliability-conducive.[17] And most proponents of coherence-based theories of practical reasoning defend the value of coherence on the grounds that it contributes to realize a number of practical goals, such as coordination or efficacy.[18]

In addition, in both the discussion of epistemic and practical coherence, there are defences of coherence that appeal to its constitutive value. To recall, Harman claims coherence to be constitutive of the notion of belief.[19] According to Davidson, membership to a coherent body of beliefs is also constitutive of the very same concept of belief.[20] In the practical domain, it may suffice to recall here Hurley's discussion of the constitutive value of coherence in individual and community identity, or Millgram and Thagard's views on the relevance of coherence for unified agency.[21]

Thus, one may defend standards of justification and, more specifically, coherence-based standards of justification, on grounds other than their truth-conduciveness. This is not to deny that truth is a value of the utmost importance for finding our way in both the empirical and the practical world. The value of truth is surely a central one, but from this it does not follow that it is possible—or desirable—to reduce the rich variety of our cognitive and practical goals to one single value. The discussion of coherence theories leaves us the important insight that there are reasons why coherence may be valued in both the theoretical and the practical domain in addition to its controversial truth-conduciveness.

### F. Coherence and Reasoning about Ends

Another important idea to take away from the discussion of coherence theories reviewed in earlier chapters is the claim that coherence methods

[15] By 'truth' in the practical domain I refer to traditional views of moral truth as correspondence with an independent moral reality, as well as to properties such as 'correctness', for those who feel less inclined to use the word 'truth' regarding moral statements.

[16] See ch 8.

[17] See ch 6.

[18] See ch 7.

[19] See ch 4.

[20] See ch 6.

[21] See ch 7.

provide us with a way for reasoning about ends.[22] That is to say, not only do coherence-based theories guide us on how to reason from means to ends (truth being an important one, but by no means the only end we are interested in achieving when reasoning about what to believe and what to do), but also in reasoning about how we may best achieve a number of competing (and sometimes conflicting) ends. This makes coherence—as I will argue later—a valuable tool for reasoning in the legal context, given the variety of values and goals that legal systems aim to advance.

## G. Coherence, Rationality and Responsibility

A main idea to preserve from the discussion of coherence theories is that standards of epistemic responsibility are crucial to justification and, more specifically, to coherentist justification. In a nutshell, a central component of a coherence theory of justification is an account of epistemic responsibility. Let me explain.

In order to accept as justified a belief, an action, an interpretation, or any other element, by virtue of its coherence, we need to generate a pool of plausible alternatives and then choose the most coherent one among them. We have seen at several places that this is the basic mechanism whereby judgements of coherence are made.[23] Under this view, how well we perform when generating and evaluating alternatives is relevant to determining how much reason we have for accepting as justified an alternative on the grounds that it is the most coherent one available. Thus, whether an agent is justified in accepting a belief, an action, an interpretation etc partly depends on whether she has considered all the relevant alternatives and assessed their relative coherence in the proper way. Responsible epistemic behaviour in inquiry and deliberation turns out to be crucial for coherentist justification.

Even if, to my knowledge, a responsibilist *cum* coherentist theory of justification is still to be worked out in detail, the suggestion that epistemic responsibility is an important concept in a coherence theory may be found in some of the coherentist literature. BonJour has argued that epistemic responsibility is at the core of the notion of epistemic justification.[24] Lehrer has similarly contended that trustworthiness, which is the keystone of his coherence theory of justification, is a matter of intellectual virtue.[25] In addition, some proponents of coherence theories of moral justification as well as practical deliberation have emphasized the relevance of features of the agent that are necessary for responsible epistemic behaviour to attributions

[22] See ch 7.
[23] See esp ch 4.
[24] See BonJour (1985: 8).
[25] See Lehrer ((2000b: 648–50) and (2001)).

of justified belief. For instance, DePaul has argued for the need to develop a refined faculty of moral judgement in order to make a proper use of coherence methods of moral inquiry.[26] Goldman has claimed that, for the coherence-based method of analogy and difference to yield justified beliefs, it is crucial that the moral reasoner employ some skills, such as the ability to empathize with various interests, the ability to think and imagine situations that are analogous to the case at hand, or the ability to discriminate morally relevant properties.[27] And Hurley has argued that case-based deliberation crucially requires that the agent engages distinctive imaginative capacities, sensibilities and insight.[28] As regards discourse interpretation, standards of responsibility were also shown to be pivotal for successfully arriving at a coherent interpretation and—as stated earlier—some discourse theorists have even talked of coherence in terms of 'duties' of the interpreter and the producer.[29]

In short, judgements of epistemic responsibility have a bearing on judgements of coherence, and thus, on attributions of justified belief. The relationship between epistemic responsibility and coherentist justification is one that any theory of coherence must give an account of.

## H. Coherence and Agency

Another thesis that the analysis of coherence theories of justification in a variety of domains brings to light is that coherentism is a theory of justification in which the agent occupies a central place. As explained, in discourse theory, there is an important distinction between coherence *a parte obiecti* and coherence *a parte subiecti*, that is, between the coherence of a text as such and the coherence that the interpreter brings to a text.[30] It is, arguably, the presence of the latter kind of coherence that accounts for judgements of discourse coherence. Coherence, in this view, is the result of the effort of the interpreter: it is not a given property of a text, but it has to be built in the course of interpretation. Thus, a coherentist theory of discourse interpretation is inextricably linked with an agent point of view.

This point applies to coherence theories across the board. While earlier proponents of coherence theories of justification defined coherence exclusively in logical terms, as a property of sets of sentences, contemporary versions of coherentism have recognized the important role that epistemic

[26] ibid.
[27] See ch 8.
[28] See ch 7.
[29] See ch 9.
[30] See ch 9.

agents play in rendering their system of beliefs coherent.[31] Likewise, rather than considering coherence as a given property of practical or moral systems, contemporary theories of practical and moral coherence focus on coherence as something that the deliberator constructs through the process of justification.[32] Similarly, in law, as opposed to more traditional approaches that study coherence as a feature of legal systems, the focus has shifted to the analysis of the ways in which legal decision-makers bring coherence about.[33] Thus, a lesson to be drawn from the analysis of coherence theories in a variety of domains is the relevance of the contribution of the subject to judgements of coherence and, thus, justification.

## I. Coherentism and Naturalism

The examination of coherence theories that have been proposed in diverse disciplines shows that these theories have a good deal of psychological plausibility. Coherence seems to be hardwired in our psychological structure.[34] This gives coherentism a distinctive advantage over competing accounts of justification and makes it of a piece with the naturalistic project of developing theories of rationality that have the resources to guide and thereby ameliorate our practices of justification. Even though the natural tendency towards coherence is, from a naturalistic perspective, a reason for adhering to coherence theories, it is also—as shown—the source of one of the main problems of coherentism, namely, the risk of 'fabricating' of coherence.[35] As explained, empirical studies indicate a proclivity to construct coherence in the course of decision-making in objectionable ways. Thus, the analysis of coherence theories across domains shows that coherentism is well-aligned with naturalism, but it also makes patent the need to develop a theory of coherence that is not only psychologically plausible but also normatively attractive.

## J. Coherence and Anti-Formalism

In the different fields in which coherence theories have been proposed, and which have been examined in previous chapters, coherence theories have been advanced as an anti-formalist alternative to scepticism. Thus, a similar motivation drives coherence theories in different domains. In epistemology,

[31] See ch 3.
[32] See chs 7 and 8.
[33] See ch 1.
[34] See esp ch 2.
[35] See esp ch 2.

coherentism has been claimed to provide a non-foundational response to the problem of scepticism.[36] Similarly, coherence theories in ethics aim at providing a solution to the regress problem alternative to the traditional, foundationalist, one.[37] Coherentist approaches to practical reasoning are meant to be an alternative to both formal models of practical inference (ie deductive models and, more recently, expected utility models) and intuition-based models of decision-making.[38] In philosophy of science, coherentism also provides a middle-way between formalist approaches to the problem of theory-choice (eg Bayesianism) and sceptical ones.[39] Similarly, in discourse theory, coherentism has been advanced as an alternative to formal models of discourse rationality, such as the cost-benefit model endorsed by relevance theorists, and sceptical, subjectivist, approaches to discourse interpretation.[40] Coherence theories of law and adjudication seek to provide a non-sceptical alternative to the foundationalist view of legal justification embodied in formal positivism. And, in the context of evidential reasoning in law, the aim of coherence theories is to deliver a non-sceptical alternative to Bayesian models of legal proof.

Thus, coherentist proposals across domains result from a firm conviction that formal models of rationality, ie models that derive criteria of rationality from formal theories such as deductive logic, probability theory etc, cannot be appropriately applied in a number of domains.[41] This, however, does not mean that one should give victory to the sceptic who claims that we cannot have knowledge in those domains. Rather, the difficulties facing the development of formal approaches to rationality in a number of fields make it patent that there is a need to develop broader models of rationality that have the resources to give an account of our practices of justification. Coherence theories aim to satisfy this need by providing a middle way between formal theories of rationality and sceptical views. The examination of coherence theories in different fields suggests that the success—and shortcomings—of the coherentist project should be assessed in the light of this objective.

The foregoing coherentist ideas provide us with the main guidelines for constructing a coherence-based model of legal reasoning. Now, I propose that we put these tools to use in order to construct such a model. The coherence model of legal justification that I shall articulate in the next sections has the following elements: (i) an account of legal coherence in terms of constraint satisfaction; (ii) a view of coherence-based legal inference as

[36] See ch 3.
[37] See ch 8.
[38] See ch 7.
[39] See ch 4.
[40] See ch 9.
[41] These models are what Stein calls the 'standard theory of rationality'; see E Stein (1996).

inference to the best explanation; (iii) a view of legal justification as optimal coherence; and (iv) a contextualized account of the coherentist standards of legal justification. I proceed now to examine each of these elements in detail.

## III. LEGAL COHERENCE AS CONSTRAINT SATISFACTION

The first element of the coherence-based account of legal reasoning that I intend to develop in this chapter is a conception of legal coherence as constraint satisfaction. There are some important, albeit limited, attempts to apply this notion of coherence to the legal domain. Simon has showed that a notion of coherence as constraint satisfaction best characterizes appellate judicial legal decision-making as well as legal decision-making at trial.[42] However, Simon's theory is exclusively an empirical theory, and not a normative approach. In contrast, Thagard has claimed the theory of coherence as constraint satisfaction to be a normative theory of reasoning.[43] Nonetheless, he has developed legal applications of the theory exclusively in the context of legal fact-finding. In addition, these applications are quite limited, in that they do not incorporate important factors that enter in jurors' reasoning, such as the relevance of consequences or the standards of proof. Constraint satisfaction models of coherence have also been applied to model some particular aspects of normative reasoning in law.[44] Even though these attempts illuminate important dimensions of legal reasoning, they do not provide a complete theory of legal coherence in terms of constraint satisfaction. Thagard's theory of coherence as constraint satisfaction, I would argue, suitably modified and extended, provides the framework for developing such a theory.[45]

I have described in detail Thagard's theory in earlier chapters, but it may be handy to have here a brief statement of the main thrust of the theory.[46] To recall, Thagard claims that coherence is a matter of maximizing the satisfaction of a number of positive and negative constraints among a set of given elements. To achieve coherence, we divide up a set of elements into

[42] See ch 2.

[43] See ch 4.

[44] See Bench-Capon and Sartor (2001b); Joseph and Prakken (2009); Araszkiewicz ((2010a), (2010b), (2012) and (2013)); Araszkiewicz and Šavelka (2012); and Šavelka (2013). See also Robbennolt et al (2010), for a constraint-satisfaction model of how judges make decisions to maximize the satisfaction of their varying goals, that is, to achieve deliberative coherence.

[45] Hage (2013) argues, to the contrary, that constraint satisfaction approaches to legal coherence are not attractive ways to model legal coherence insofar as they are forms of 'narrow' coherentism, which he rejects in favour of 'integrated' coherentism.

[46] See ch 4.

two disjoint subsets A—which contains accepted elements—and R—which contains rejected elements—by taking into account the coherence and incoherence relations that hold between pairs of elements of the given set. For example, if a hypothesis $h_1$ explains a piece of evidence $e_1$, then we want to ensure that if $h_1$ is accepted, so is $e_1$. And if $h_1$ contradicts $h_2$, then we want to make sure that if $h_1$ is accepted, then $h_2$ is rejected. Thus, the coherence problem is that of dividing a set of elements into A and R in a way that best satisfies the positive (coherence relations) and negative (incoherence relations) constraints. This abstract characterization of coherence is applicable to a wide variety of problems. The solution of a coherence problem involves the interaction of different kinds of coherence, with different kinds of elements and constraints. Thus, a particular application of the abstract characterization of coherence as constraint satisfaction requires the specification of the kinds of coherence involved as well as the elements and constraints that are relevant in a particular domain.

As explained, Thagard has developed a number of applications of this theory.[47] Two such applications are particularly relevant for our purposes, namely, the description of both epistemic justification and ethical justification as coherence problems.[48] My claim is that these applications provide the base upon which a theory of coherence as constraint satisfaction for legal reasoning may be modelled. More specifically, we may develop a concept of coherence for the justification of conclusions about disputed questions of fact on the basis of Thagard's model of epistemic coherence, and a theory of coherence for the justification of conclusions about disputed questions of law on the basis of Thagard's theory of ethical coherence. In what follows, I shall suggest some lines along which a constraint satisfaction approach to legal coherence may be constructed. I start by sketching a notion of coherence as constraint satisfaction that is operative in legal reasoning about facts, and that I shall refer to as 'factual coherence'. Then, I move to working out a notion of coherence as constraint satisfaction that is appropriate for legal reasoning about norms, and that I shall refer to as 'normative coherence'. I conclude this section by examining the 'deep structure' that, under the approach of coherence as constraint satisfaction, legal inference about both facts and norms shares.

### A. Factual Coherence

An account of the justification of factual claims in law in terms of coherence as constraint satisfaction can be modelled, as I have just suggested,

[47] See chs 4, 7 and 8.
[48] See chs 4 and 8.

after Thagard's theory of epistemic justification. As explained in chapter four, on Thagard's account, epistemic justification requires the interaction of five kinds of coherence: explanatory, analogical, deductive, perceptual and conceptual. Each of these kinds of coherence is further specified by means of a set of principles, which state the relevant elements and constraints. To recall, according to the principles of explanatory coherence, which is the most important contributor to epistemic justification, explanatory coherence is a symmetrical relation between hypotheses and evidence within a set (E1). It arises out of relations of explanation and analogical relations between evidence and hypotheses (E2, E3). Relations of contradiction and competition give rise to incoherence (E5, E6). And the acceptability of a proposition is claimed to be a matter of its coherence with the rest of propositions within a set (E7), some of which enjoy, nonetheless, a degree of acceptability on their own (E4). The problem of epistemic justification is that of determining how we may come to accept (as justified) some elements and reject (as unjustified) others in a way that maximizes the satisfaction of a number of positive and negative constraints as established by the principles of the foregoing kinds of coherence.

Thagard's theory of epistemic justification can be profitably used to analyse the issue of the justification of conclusions about disputed questions of fact. However, some modifications at all three levels—that is, the kinds of coherence involved, the constraints and the relevant elements—need to be introduced in order to account for the specificities of reasoning about evidence in the legal context. Among others, the following salient differences must be taken into account:

i. Reasoning about evidence in law takes place within an institutional framework that is designed to advance a number of different goals. Fact-finding accuracy is, to be sure, a momentous value in our legal systems. However, the law is interested in advancing values other than truth. Rules of evidence and procedure are in place to ensure that the complex set of values that law is meant to protect is realized. Two such normative standards are particularly important, to wit, the standards of proof and the presumption of innocence.[49] The evaluation of the explanatory coherence of alternative explanations of the facts under dispute is carried

[49] The presumption of innocence, the standard of proof and admissibility rules are, in most legal systems, the most important constraints which define the normative institutional framework within which the explanatory evaluation of hypotheses about the events being litigated proceeds. There are, however, other rules of evidence and procedure—as well as constitutional doctrines—that might further constrain coherentist reasoning in forensic contexts. eg in some legal systems there are corroboration rules, which would prevent the acceptance of an element unless another one is also accepted. Or, for another example, some legal systems have rules of weight, which may assign some priority to some elements, in addition to the priority given to propositions describing evidence as well as to innocence hypotheses, in the coherence calculation.

out within a normative framework that requires a sceptical stance towards the guilt-hypothesis: this hypothesis may be accepted only if belief in this hypothesis satisfies the applicable standard, for instance, if it is 'beyond a reasonable doubt', and provided that the presumption of innocence is rebutted. Thus, these normative standards have a crucial bearing on the evaluation of alternative explanatory hypotheses and ought to be incorporated within a coherence-based theory of reasoning about facts. I suggest that these standards may be treated as constituting 'institutional' constraints that must be satisfied when maximizing coherence. Specifically, the reasonable doubt standard requires that the guilt hypothesis be accepted only if its degree of justification is sufficiently high to meet the standard and the presumption of innocence demands that hypotheses compatible with innocence be given priority in being accepted.[50]

ii. Not only does the institutional dimension of legal argumentation give rise to a number of additional constraints, but it also puts some limits to the kind of elements that may be included within the coherence calculation. The law of evidence makes inadmissible evidence that would be deemed as relevant were we able to pursue inquiry free from institutional boundaries. For instance, in common law systems, evidence whose probative value is outweighed by its prejudicial effect is inadmissible and, in most legal systems, relevant evidence illegally obtained is ruled out as inadmissible. In the context of a coherence theory of factual reasoning for law, this means that there is a limit to the kind of elements that can enter into the base of coherence. Thus, only some subset of the evidence available enjoys the kind of data priority that the theory of explanatory coherence grants.

iii. Last, another important difference between reasoning about evidence in law and reasoning about evidence in other contexts is that fact-reasoning in law is, ultimately, a piece of an instance of practical reasoning.[51] We form beliefs about the guilt or innocence of the defendant upon which a decision about whether to convict or acquit is then based. The reasoning that leads to the acceptance of a belief about guilt or innocence provides the factual premise of a practical syllogism which is, ultimately, the basis for the decision. From this point of view,

[50] Thagard has also suggested that reasonable doubt might be viewed as an additional constraint on the maximization of coherence. In this view, this constraint would require that the hypothesis concerning guilt be substantially more plausible than those concerning innocence; see Thagard (2006: 366). As for the presumption of innocence, Thagard has suggested that one could modify ECHO, the computational implementation of the theory of explanatory coherence, in several ways so as to account for it. My suggestion, as shown below, is to modify instead the principles of explanatory coherence, more specifically, the principle of data priority.

[51] See Twinning (2006: 318).

> fact-finding should be located, in the legal context, within a theory of practical reasoning. From a constraint satisfaction framework, the natural way to place the practical considerations that are relevant to reasoning about evidence in law is in a theory of deliberative coherence. As we saw in chapter seven, Thagard has developed, in collaboration with Millgram, an account of practical inference as inference to the most coherent plan, that is, to the plan that best satisfies a number of positive and negative constraints among a set of actions and goals, as established by the principles of deliberative coherence. The suggestion is that, in addition to the kinds of coherence which are involved in assessing the justification of epistemic claims, there is one more kind of coherence that is relevant to the justification of factual claims in law, to wit, deliberative coherence.[52]

The conception of factual coherence that results from introducing the foregoing modifications may be stated as follows:

> *Factual Coherence.* Factual coherence involves the integrated assessment of explanatory coherence (fit between hypotheses and the evidence at trial); analogical coherence (fit between mapping hypotheses); conceptual coherence (fit between concepts); perceptual coherence (fit of visual interpretations and non-verbal representations); deductive coherence (fit between general principles and particular judgements); and deliberative coherence (fit between deliberative factors and the goals of adjudication).

Indeed 'analogical coherence' plays a prominent role in fact-reasoning in law. As Hastie and Pennington have shown, some kinds of analogy are relevant to jurors' reasoning processes, such as the analogy to the self.[53] 'Conceptual coherence' is also pivotal in fact-reasoning in law. This kind of coherence is critical in applying stereotypes, which is, arguably, an important part of reasoning about evidence in law.[54] While reasoning about evidence is certainly non-deductive, there is no denying that deduction has a role to play when drawing conclusions about disputed questions of fact. Thus, 'deductive coherence' is at the very least one of the kinds of coherence that is relevant for the justification of factual conclusions in law. 'Perceptual coherence' is required to give an account of the fact-finders' reasoning processes that involve non-verbal representations. Some of the factual inferences in law are best understood as 'visual' abductions, that is, abductions that use pictorial or other iconic representations. For instance,

[52] Arguably, deliberative coherence is relevant to the justification of any factual claim, whether in law or in any other domain, if, as some philosophers have persuasively argued, the epistemic justification of a belief does not only depend on epistemic factors but also on pragmatic ones. See Fantl and McGrath ((2002), (2009) and (2011)); Hookway (1990: 139); Stanley (2005); and Hawthorne and Stanley (2008: 571).

[53] See ch 2.

[54] See Thagard and Kunda (1998).

a picture of the scene of a crime may suggest a likely narrative about how the events took place.[55] 'Deliberative coherence' plays a role in determining which decision about the events at trial is best in light of the several goals that the legal system is meant to serve. Last, 'explanatory coherence' is, like in epistemic justification, the most important kind of coherence in a theory of fact-reasoning in law.

As argued, some of the principles of explanatory coherence need to be modified so as to account for some features specific to factual reasoning in law. More specifically, the principles of explanatory coherence should be revised (revisions in italics) to read as follows:

> Principle E1: Symmetry. Explanatory coherence is a symmetrical relation, unlike, say conditional probability. That is, two propositions *p* and *q* cohere with each other equally.
> Principle E2: Explanation. (1) A hypothesis coheres with what it explains which can be either evidence or another hypothesis; (2) hypotheses that together explain some other proposition cohere with each other; and (3) the more hypotheses it takes to explain something, the lower the degree of coherence.
> Principle E3: Analogy. Similar hypotheses that explain similar pieces of evidence cohere.
> *Principle E4: Priority. (a) Propositions that describe admissible evidence at trial have a degree of acceptability on their own; (b) factual hypotheses that are compatible with innocence have a degree of acceptability on their own.*
> Principle E5: Contradiction. Contradictory propositions are incoherent with each other.
> Principle E6: Competition. If *p* and *q* both explain a proposition and if *p* and *q* are not explanatorily connected, then *p* and *q* are incoherent with each other (*p* and *q* are explanatorily connected if one explains the other or if together they explain something).
> *Principle E7: Acceptance. (a) The acceptability of a proposition in a system of propositions (ie a theory of the case) depends on its coherence with them; (b) the guilt hypothesis may be accepted only if it is justified to a degree sufficient to satisfy the applicable standard of proof.*

The revised version of Principle E4 is both narrower and broader than the original one. It is narrower, as only some of the propositions that describe the results of observations, ie those that describe admissible evidence at trial, enjoy a degree of priority. And it is also broader, for it is not only evidence propositions that should be given priority in the legal context, but hypotheses compatible with innocence also have a degree of acceptability

[55] On visual abduction, see Thagard and Shelley (1997).

on their own. The proposed version of Principle E7 significantly restricts the propositions that may be accepted on grounds of their coherence to those that meet the applicable standard of proof.

Let me illustrate how the revised version of the theory of explanatory coherence would apply to law by means of an example, the *R v Angela Cannings* case.[56] Angela Cannings was the mother of four children, Gemma, Jason, Jade and Matthew. Three of these children (Gemma, Jason and Matthew) died in infancy. She was charged with the murder of both of her sons, Jason and Matthew. The charge for the murder of her first child, Gemma, did not proceed. Three of the children, including the daughter who survived, Jade, had suffered an acute or apparent life threatening event (ALTE). All the ALTEs and the deaths occurred when the babies were in sole care of the mother. The Crown alleged that the defendant had smothered both her sons, intending to kill them by obstructing their upper airways. To support that allegation it was suggested that the death of Gemma and each of the ALTEs suffered by the other children were also the result of smothering by the defendant and that these actions formed part of an 'overall pattern'. The defendant, a woman described by hospital staff as a loving mother, denied harming any of her children. Her case was that the deaths were natural, if unexplained, incidents to be classified as sudden infant death syndrome (SIDS). The Crown adduced expert evidence as to the extreme rarity of three infant SIDS in one family, which suggested that smothering was the most likely diagnosis. There was no medical evidence that Mrs Cannings had any personality disorder or psychiatric condition. Nevertheless, as was accepted without hesitation by Dr Johnson, an expert witness, parents who appear to be affectionate and caring towards their children do sometimes kill them. Expert medical witnesses on behalf of the defendant supported the claim that three unexplained infant deaths in the same family do not, however, inexorably lead to the conclusion that they must have resulted from unnatural causes.

On 16 April 2002 in the Crown Court at Winchester, the defendant was convicted of murdering both her sons. On appeal the convictions were quashed. Significant new evidence was presented before the Court. After the trial, further investigation was carried out into the Cannings' extended family which revealed further infant deaths. One of these deaths was particularly relevant to the case. Unbeknown to the defendant at trial, she had a half-sister, who following these convictions made herself known to her solicitors. She had three children, two of whom suffered ALTEs. This, according to the Court, supported the view that there might well be a genetic cause for the deaths of the Cannings' children. A substantial body of medical research, not before the jury, and received by the Court of Appeals

[56] *R v Cannings* [2004] EWCA Crim 1.

in evidence, further fortified the analysis that there was a reasonable possibility that the deaths of these children could be natural, even if, at the present stage of the research, unexplained. If, to the contrary, the appellant had indeed killed her children—as the jury found that she had, the logical approach to her repeated pregnancies would have been that she was having babies to kill them. That, said the Court, predicated an extraordinary state of mind contradicted by the uncontested evidence about the love and care Mrs Cannings bestowed to her children.

The hypothesis that Angela Cannings killed her babies explains the evidence that the babies are dead, so the hypothesis and the evidence cohere with each other, as Principle E2, explanation, states. Although the relation between the *explanans* and the *explanadum* is asymmetrical, with hypotheses explaining evidence but not vice versa, the coherence relation between them is symmetrical, as Principle E1, symmetry, establishes. Thus, if the hypothesis that Angela Cannings killed her babies coheres with the evidence that the babies are dead, then that evidence and the guilt hypothesis also cohere. Principle E2 also allows the possibility of hypotheses explaining each other, as when the hypothesis that Angela Cannings was the murderer is explained by the hypothesis that only apparently was she a loving mother. This principle also says that hypotheses that together explain some other proposition cohere with each other. For example, the hypothesis that the testimony of hospital staff saying that there was no evidence of ill-treatment or lack of care is true and the hypothesis that there was a genetic condition in the Cannings family, together explain the evidence that the babies showed no sign of physical interference, and thus cohere with each other. The last part of Principle E2 says that the more hypotheses it takes to explain something, the lower the degree of coherence. For example, the hypothesis that Angela Cannings orchestrated but did not commit the murders requires multiple hypotheses that lack simplicity. Principle E3, analogy, states that similar hypotheses that explain similar pieces of evidence cohere. For example, if Angela Cannings had a past history of violent acts towards her children, then these cases would provide analogies that make the hypothesis that the deaths of the babies resulted from deliberate infliction of harm more plausible. The first part of Principle E4 says that propositions that describe evidence, eg the absence of any evidence of psychical violence in the post mortem medical examinations, have a degree of acceptability on their own, that is, that they have a priority in being accepted. The second part of this principle establishes that propositions that would imply the innocence of Angela Cannings also enjoy a degree of acceptability on their own. According to Principle E5, contradictory propositions, for example, the hypothesis that the infant deaths were natural and the hypothesis that they were unnatural, are incoherent with each other. Incoherence relations may also be established between two hypotheses if they are in competition—as Principle E6 says. Two hypotheses compete with each other if they both explain a proposition but are not explanatorily connected. For instance, the hypothesis that Jason and Matthew had a genetic defect and the hypothesis that they were killed compete with each other even though these are not contradictory, for it is logically possible that both children had a genetic defect, but that they were smothered. Since both hypotheses explain the evidence of the infant deaths, but neither one explains the other nor do they together explain the evidence, they are incoherent with each other. Last, the first part of Principle E7 says that the acceptability of any proposition (eg that the Angela Cannings children had a genetic defect) depends on its coherence with the rest of elements to which it belongs, while the second requires that the guilt hypothesis (ie that Angela Cannings killed her babies) be accepted only if it satisfies the applicable standard of proof.

To conclude, in order to apply Thagard's coherence-based theory of epistemic justification to give an account of the justification of conclusions about disputed questions of fact it is necessary to add new constraints, ie institutional constraints, to modify some of the constraints imposed by the theory, eg the principle of data priority, in order to limit the set of elements whose coherence is relevant to justification as well as to include another kind of coherence, ie deliberative coherence. These modifications, I would argue, bring the model of coherence as constraint satisfaction closer to capturing the complexities of legal reasoning about facts. Having shown how a theory of factual coherence may be modelled on the basis of Thagard's constraint satisfaction approach to coherence, I turn now to examine how this framework can be applied to elaborate a notion of coherence for the justification of normative conclusions in law.

### B. Normative Coherence

A theory of normative coherence as constraint satisfaction may be modelled, as suggested, after Thagard's theory of ethical coherence. To recall, according to Thagard, moral justification requires the interaction of four kinds of coherence: deductive, explanatory, analogical and deliberative coherence.[57] Under this view, the justification of a moral judgement depends upon the satisfaction of a number of positive and negative constraints within a given set of elements as established by the principles of the foregoing kinds of coherence. Several changes need to be introduced in order to give an account of the kind of coherence that is relevant to the justification of conclusions of disputed questions of law.

i. First, analogical coherence and deductive coherence refer to the fit of particular moral judgements with other judgements in similar cases,

[57] See ch 8.

and the fit between general moral principles and particular moral judgements, respectively. Legal versions of these kinds of coherence, ie versions of coherence in which the relevant elements are legal judgments and principles rather than moral ones, need to be developed and incorporated within a theory of normative coherence.

ii. Secondly, the theory of deliberative coherence, in which elements are only actions and goals and constraints are restricted to relations of facilitation and incompatibility, has to be enriched to give an account of the variety of considerations which enter into legal deliberation.

iii. Last, normative reasoning in law, unlike moral reasoning, is an interpretative form of reasoning.[58] Thus, one must crucially add yet another kind of coherence, to wit, 'interpretative coherence', which is the most important contributor to the legal justification of normative conclusions.

The conception of normative coherence as constraint satisfaction that results from introducing these modifications may be stated as follows:

> *Normative Coherence.* Normative coherence requires the integrated assessment of deductive coherence (fit between legal principles, rules and judgments), explanatory coherence (fit of legal principles, rules and judgments with empirical hypotheses), deliberative coherence (fit of legal principles, rules and judgments with the legal system's goals and values), analogical coherence (fit of legal judgments with other judgments in similar cases) and interpretative coherence (fit of interpretative hypotheses with legal principles, rules and judgments).

Let us briefly see the contribution of each of these kinds of coherence to legal justification. 'Deductive coherence' is, of course, relevant to the justification of conclusions about disputed questions of law. For this kind of coherence as applied to law, the elements are legal norms (ie general principles of law and legal rules) and particular legal judgments. The main positive constraint is a relation of entailment and the most important negative constraint is contradiction.[59] For instance, there is a positive constraint between the legal principle that prohibits discrimination against women and the rule that prohibits that different salaries be paid to men and women in retribution for the same work; and there is a negative constraint between two legal rules which contradict each other, such as the rule that establishes mandatory retirement at age 65 and the rule that establishes

[58] On the role of interpretation in coherence-based legal reasoning, see J Dickson, 'Interpretation and Coherence in Legal Reasoning', *The Stanford Encyclopedia of Philosophy* (Spring 2010 edn), EN Zalta (ed), http://plato.stanford.edu/archives/spr2010/entries/legal-reas-interpret/.

[59] Deductive constraints may be established between legal principles and legal rules; legal rules and particular legal judgments; legal rules; legal principles; and legal principles and legal judgments; see Araszkiewicz (2010a: 177).

mandatory retirement at age 70. It is this kind of coherence upon which earlier coherence theories of law focused.[60]

The relevance of 'analogical coherence' for legal justification cannot be overstated. As we saw, some authors, such as Goldman, have even gone as far as to define legal coherence exclusively in analogical terms.[61] More moderately, analogical relations play a most prominent role in some coherence-based theories of legal reasoning, such as Hurley's.[62] In analogical coherence as applied to law, the elements are hypotheses about what features of the target analogue (the case to be decided) map to what features of the source analogue (the settled body of precedent). In analogical coherence, to recall, positive constraints arise from visual and semantic similarity, purpose and structure, while negative constraints occur between hypotheses that represent incompatible mappings. In law, a further source of positive (and negative) constraints would be axiological similarities (and differences). For example, mapping hypotheses that connect precedents that protect related values cohere with each other.

'Explanatory coherence' plays a role in legal reasoning about rules because, like in ethics, legal decisions often depend in part on the evaluation of empirical hypotheses. For example, the US Supreme Court decision, *Roper v Simmons*, declaring it unconstitutional to sentence anyone to death for a crime that he or she committed when younger than 18 was based, partly, on the empirical hypothesis that the development of the human brain is such that juveniles' capacity to foresee the consequences of their acts is seriously underdeveloped.[63] Such an empirical hypothesis is to be evaluated, like any other empirical hypothesis, by maximizing the coherence of positive and negative constraints (as established by the theory of explanatory coherence) among the set of competing hypotheses and relevant evidence.

'Deliberative coherence' is relevant to legal inference as much as it is to any other kind of practical inference. To recall, in the theory of deliberative coherence, as developed by Thagard and Millgram, elements are actions and goals, the main positive constraint is established by facilitation relations and the main negative constraint is established by relations of incompatibility. It is necessary to further develop Thagard and Millgram's account of deliberative coherence for it to be able to capture the different factors that enter into legal deliberation. I already suggested (in chapter seven) some ways in which the theory of deliberative coherence could be expanded. To start with, within the set of deliberative factors one should include, in addition to actions and goals, norms (principles and rules) as well as values and preferences and other relevant practical reasons (eg legal

[60] See Pastore (1991).
[61] See ch 8.
[62] See ch 7.
[63] *Roper v Simmons*, 543 U.S. 551 (2005).

doctrines and precedents). In addition, the set of positive constraints should be expanded so as to include relations of coherence other than facilitation, such as relations of analogy and specification. As for negative constraints, it is also necessary to include a richer set of incoherence relations, besides relations of incompatibility. As I suggested in chapter seven, Richardson's account of practical conflict may be useful for identifying the different sources of practical incoherence, and thus for formulating a set of principles that establish the various ways in which negative constraints may arise among deliberative factors.

Last, what I have referred to as 'interpretative coherence' is the most important contributor to the justification of conclusions about disputed questions of law. Legal interpretation may be construed as a coherence problem. As explained, in order to show that a particular problem is a coherence problem it is necessary to specify the relevant elements and constraints, to provide an interpretation of acceptance and rejection, and to show that the solution to the problem does in fact involve the satisfaction of the specified constraints. How should we go about showing that legal interpretation may be described in terms of coherence as constraint satisfaction? To start with, I suggest that we use Thagard's theory of explanatory coherence as a model for construing the skeleton of a theory of interpretative coherence.

In interpretative coherence, elements are interpretative hypotheses and 'normative elements', which include rules and principles embedded in the relevant case law and statutory law as well as settled legal judgments.[64] Interpretative hypotheses and normative elements play a role in interpretative coherence analogous to the role that empirical hypotheses and evidence, respectively, play in explanatory coherence. Under this view, rules and principles provide evidence or support a particular interpretative hypothesis—similar to the way in which observations provide evidence for a particular explanatory hypothesis. Positive and negative constraints—coherence and incoherence relations—are established among interpretative hypotheses and normative elements according to a set of principles which mimic the principles of explanatory coherence: symmetry, explanation, analogy, data priority, contradiction, competition and acceptance.

The principles of interpretative coherence read as follows:

Principle I1: Symmetry. Interpretative coherence is a symmetrical relation. That is, two propositions $p$ and $q$ cohere with each other equally.

Principle I2: Explanation. (a) An interpretative hypothesis coheres with what it explains which can be either normative elements or another

[64] As Araszkiewicz has suggested, work concerning types of legal norms may be extremely useful in devising a more nuanced account of the elements that should figure in a constraint satisfaction approach to coherence. See Araszkiewicz (2013: 239).

hypothesis; (b) interpretative hypotheses that together explain some other proposition cohere with each other; and (c) the more interpretative hypotheses it takes to explain something, the lower the degree of coherence.

Principle I3: Analogy. Similar interpretative hypotheses that explain similar normative elements cohere.

Principle I4: Data priority. Propositions that describe reasons from authority have a degree of acceptability on their own.

Principle I5: Contradiction. Contradictory propositions are incoherent with each other.

Principle I6: Competition. If *p* and *q* both explain a proposition and if *p* and *q* are not explanatorily connected, then *p* and *q* are incoherent with each other (*p* and *q* are explanatorily connected if one explains the other or if together they explain something).

Principle I7: Acceptance. The acceptability of a proposition in a system of propositions depends on its coherence with them.

Let us illustrate the foregoing principles of interpretative coherence by means of an example, to wit, the *Sweet v Parsley* case.[65] Miss Sweet, a school teacher in Oxford, was tenant of a farmhouse outside Oxford. She sub-let all rooms in the farmhouse except for one, which she kept for herself, to other persons, with the kitchen and the rest of the house retained for common use. She visited occasionally the house to stay overnight, collect the rent and check that the house was in good condition. The police discovered that residents in the house were smoking cannabis and charged Miss Sweet for managing premises used for the purpose of smoking cannabis, contrary to the Dangerous Drugs Act 1965, more specifically, section 5 (b) of the Act, which provided that

> If a person is concerned in the management of any premises used for any such purpose as aforesaid ['the purposes of smoking cannabis or cannabis resin or of dealing in cannabis or cannabis resin']; he shall be guilty of an offence against this Act.

The trial court found as a fact that Miss Sweet 'had no knowledge whatsoever that the house was being used for the purposes of smoking cannabis or cannabis resin'. Nevertheless, the Court convicted her because in its opinion the Act implied absolute liability, that is to say, liability without regard to a person's intention or knowledge as to the purpose in question, provided she or he was actually concerned in the management of the relevant premises, as Miss Sweet indubitably was. At the first level of appeal this view was upheld but, on the final appeal to the House of Lords, this interpretation

[65] [1968] 2 All ER 337 (CCA); [1970] AC 132, [1969] 1 AUR 347 (HL). This case is also discussed in N MacCormick (2005: 196–99).

was rejected in favour of an interpretation according to which the offence of being concerned with the management of premises used for the purpose of smoking cannabis does require guilty knowledge or intention in the 'purpose' in question.

The House of Lords gave the following reasons in favour of allowing the appeal and quashing the conviction. First, it said that there was an ambiguity in the act, for the 'purpose' could be interpreted as 'the purpose of the smoker' or 'the purpose of the management'. Both interpretations were found to be consistent with the Act. Secondly, however, it stated that the consequences of holding that the smoker's purpose suffices are unacceptable, as it would mean that any person concerned in the management of any premises would be required to exercise complete supervision over all persons who enter the premises and would be guilty of an offence if, unknown to him, someone smoked cannabis eluding even the most sophisticated measures of supervision. Thirdly, reference was made to previous and analogous legislation which dealt with other 'anti-social' activities, such as the keeping of brothels, opium 'dens' and gaming houses, none of which created offences of strict or absolute liability. Fourthly, reference was made to the earlier decision of *Warner v Metropolitan Police Commissioner* from which there could be extracted a principle concerning the differentiation of offences of absolute liability from those requiring *mens rea*. According to this principle, where conviction does not carry a moral stigma, liability may be strict or absolute; where offences do carry some stigma, *mens rea* ought to be required. Finally, the principle of interpretation that 'if a penal provision is reasonably capable of two interpretations, that interpretation which is most favourable to the accused must be adopted' completed the justification of the decision.

As said before, in interpretative coherence, elements are interpretative hypotheses and normative elements. In this case, two main interpretative hypotheses may be distinguished:

> H1: The offence of 'being concerned in the management of any premises used for any such purpose' requires guilty knowledge or intention of participation in the 'purpose' in question.
> H2: The offence of 'being concerned in the management of any premises used for any such purpose' does not require guilty knowledge or intention of participation in the 'purpose' in question.

The relevant normative elements include the principle of interpretation mentioned above, legislation of other 'anti-social' activities and the judgment in the *Warner v Metropolitan Police Commissioner* case.[66] According

[66] The consequentialist argument used by the House of Lords to the effect that holding that the smoker's purpose suffices for conviction has unacceptable implications is an argument that pertains to considerations of deliberative coherence (to recall, fit between legal judgments

to the 'principle of symmetry', interpretative coherence is a symmetric relation. For example, H1 and the judgment in the *Warner* case cohere with each other equally. The 'principle of explanation', as applied to the problem of legal interpretation, says that an interpretative hypothesis coheres with what it explains; that interpretative hypotheses that together explain some other proposition cohere with each other; and that the more hypotheses it takes to explain something, the lower the degree of coherence. For instance, H1 coheres with other interpretative hypotheses it helps explain, such as the hypothesis (H4) that the purpose in question should be that of the management, as well as with the set of normative elements (for instance, earlier legislation and the judgment in the *Warner* case) it explains;[67] H1 and H4 which together explain legislation analogous to the Dangerous Drugs Act cohere with each other; and 'simplicity' is in theory construction in law, as much as it is in theory construction in science, a cognitive virtue that enhances coherence. The 'principle of analogy' establishes that similar interpretative hypotheses that explain similar normative elements cohere with each other. For instance, H1, which is advanced to explain the actual case concerning cannabis consumption regulated by the Dangerous Drugs Act of 1965, coheres with the interpretative hypothesis that the earlier Dangerous Drugs Act of 1920 did not create offences of strict or absolute liability insofar as both explain relevantly similar cases. A version of the 'principle of data priority' for legal interpretation recognizes the priority that reasons from authority enjoy in legal reasoning by establishing that propositions that describe authoritative reasons (for instance, the proposition describing the judgment reached in the *Warner* case or the proposition describing section 5 of the statute in question) have a degree of acceptability on their own. The 'principle of contradiction' says that contradictory propositions are incoherent with each other. For instance, H1 and H2 are incoherent with each other. Contradiction in interpretative coherence cannot be restricted to logical inconsistency, but it refers also to axiological contradiction—which would arise if, for example, some statutes concerning anti-social conduct were interpreted in a way that gives the value of public safety a priority over the conviction of an innocent person, ie as offences of absolute liability, whereas other statutes were interpreted so that the injustice of convicting an innocent person is taken to outweigh the value of public safety, ie as offences requiring *mens rea*. Incoherence also arises

and the legal system's goals and values) rather than interpretative coherence. It is, however, an argument that may be reconstructed in coherentist terms. *Cf* N MacCormick (2005: 198) (restricting arguments from coherence to those arguments that appeal to fit with anti-social legislation as well as with the earlier decision in *Warner v Metropolitan Police Commissioner*).

[67] Of course, it is required to articulate a notion of explanation that is appropriate to the context of reasoning about norms in law. For a proposal about how this might be done, see Bench-Capon and Sartor (2001a).

when two interpretative hypotheses, which are not explanatorily connected, explain a proposition, as the 'principle of competition' states. For example, the hypothesis that section 5 (b) creates an absolute defence because, unlike other sections of the Act, it does not explicitly require *mens rea* (as it was concluded at the first level of Appeals) and the hypothesis that whenever a section is silent as to *mens rea* there is a presumption that we must read in words appropriate to require *mens rea* (as it was established on the appeal to the House of Lords) are incoherent with each other given that both seek to explain the wording of section 5 (b) but are not explanatorily related. Last, according to the 'principle of acceptance', the acceptability of a proposition in a system of propositions depends on its coherence with them. Thus, the acceptance of H1 depends on its coherence with other interpretative hypotheses (H4 and H5) and the relevant set of normative elements, ie the principles of interpretation mentioned above, the *Warner* case, and the Dangerous Drugs Act.[68]

## C. A Unified View of Legal Inference

The foregoing analysis of legal coherence as constraint satisfaction suggests a unified view of legal inference. Both factual coherence and normative coherence share a common structure, even if the relevant constraints and elements, as well as the kinds of coherence involved, vary depending on whether it is the justification of a normative or factual conclusion that is at stake. When reasoning about both facts and norms in law we should accept as justified the beliefs about the facts under dispute and about what the law requires that belong to the subset A that results from dividing up a set of elements into accepted (A) and rejected (R) in a way that maximizes coherence. Thus, the application of the constraint satisfaction approach to coherence to law allows us to see the common pattern that lies behind coherence-based legal inferences as well as to give a unified account of the conditions under which beliefs about both the law and the facts are justified.

[68] As explained, Thagard has implemented the theories of different kinds of coherence by means of a number of connectionist programs. See ch 4 for a description of ECHO, the program that implements the theory of explanatory coherence, and ch 7 for a description of DECO, the program that implements practical coherence. For a description of ACME, the program that implements the theory of analogical coherence, see Holyoak and Thagard (1989). It would also be desirable to develop computational implementations of the theory of interpretative coherence to analyse legal cases that involve difficult problems of interpretation. The networks that would result from such implementation could also be represented by constraint networks built by analogy with the networks that Thagard employs to represent other coherence problems. As is well known, there have been several important efforts in legal scholarship to represent problems of interpretation (see eg Toulmin (2003) and Atienza (1991)). Connectionist networks, I would suggest, may provide an easy and friendly way to represent problems of legal interpretation.

Now, how do we get to subset A? How do we determine which conclusions about either the facts or the law should be accepted as justified? The process of coherence maximization, I would argue, is best viewed as an inference to the best explanation, in which we generate a number of candidate hypotheses, and select, among them, the one that coheres best. Under this view, when reasoning about both disputed questions of law and disputed questions of fact, we produce a number of plausible interpretative and factual hypotheses, respectively, and accept as justified the one that maximizes coherence. More interestingly, we may view coherence-based inference in law as an 'inference to the best theory': when reasoning about both facts and law, we infer the theory of the case and the theory of the law (that is, the theory about what the facts under dispute are and the theory about what the law requires) that best satisfies a number of positive and negative constraints.[69] A coherence-based approach to legal inference thus brings to light the relevant role that theories play in legal deliberation.[70] The next section examines in detail this view of coherence-based legal inference as an explanatory kind of inference.

## IV. INFERENCE TO THE BEST LEGAL EXPLANATION

The second element of the proposed version of legal coherentism is an account of coherence-driven legal inference as an inference to the best explanation. To be sure, that inference to the best explanation is crucial in legal reasoning is not new. Some scholars have argued for the importance of abduction in fact-reasoning in law, and others have even claimed that abduction is the main form of reasoning about evidence in law.[71] However, the vast majority of legal scholars who have claimed that abduction occupies a prominent role in a theory of legal reasoning about evidence have viewed it exclusively as a mechanism of discovery.[72] To recall, there are

[69] See Kuipers (2003).

[70] Several authors have emphasized the role that theories play in legal deliberation. Twining has argued for the relevance of theories of the case in reasoning about evidence in law (see Twining (2006) esp ch 8). Hurley has claimed that legal deliberation aims at developing the theory that best displays as coherent the relationship among the legal doctrines and precedents that apply to the alternatives in question (Hurley (1989) esp ch 11). It is a main tenet of Dworkin's theory of adjudication that there is no firm line that divides jurisprudence and adjudication: both involve the construction of an interpretative theory that best explains and justifies the law as a whole (Dworkin: 1986). And, in the field of AI, Bench-Capon and Sartor have argued that case-based reasoning in law consists in constructing a theory, using it to explain cases, and evaluating competing theories so as to adjudicate between them; see Bench-Capon and Sartor ((2001a) and (2003)).

[71] See Schum ((1986), (2001) ch 9 and (2002)); Josephson and Josephson (1994); Josephson (2002); and Walton (2002) esp xv, 43, 105 and 213.

[72] See eg Schum's landmark work on abduction in law.

two main views about abduction.[73] According to a weak version, the scope of abduction is restricted to the discovery of hypotheses. In contrast, the strong version claims that abduction is a pattern of reasoning that leads to both the generation *and* evaluation of hypotheses. Thus, it has been the weak rather than the strong version of abduction that has been mostly embraced by legal scholars.[74]

Instead, I shall argue here for the applicability of a strong version of abduction to legal reasoning. That is, my claim is that abduction (properly construed as inference to the best explanation) is a method of evaluation as well as a method of generation of factual hypotheses in the legal context. Among legal scholars, a main reason for advocating a weak, instead of a strong, version of abduction as inference to the best explanation is the purported lack of any criterion for determining what the 'best' explanation is.[75] Here, I shall argue that it is coherence standards (more specifically, those embodied in the view of coherence as constraint satisfaction that I have examined in the previous section) that provide us with such criteria of evaluation.

While abduction has been discussed to some extent in evidence scholarship, the possibilities of using a model of inference to the best explanation to give an account of the inference pattern that leads to the acceptance of a particular interpretative hypothesis in law remain largely unexplored.[76] Hence, a full model of inference to the best explanation in law, one that gives an account of the significance of this kind of inference in the generation and the justification of both factual and interpretative hypotheses in law is still lacking. Needless to say, I cannot provide such a model here, but in what follows I shall suggest some lines along which such a model may be developed.

## A. The Structure of Explanatory Inference in Law

I have claimed that we arrive at the decision about what the law requires or what the facts under dispute at trial are that is justified by virtue of its coherence by means of an inference to the best explanation. Of course,

[73] See ch 4.

[74] But see Abimbola (2001); Pardo and Allen (2008); and Pardo (2013) for an application of inference to the best explanation (IBE) to factual inference in law. Explanationist accounts of factual inference in law have been defended in the field of AI (see Josephson and Josephson (1994)); philosophy (see Thagard ((1989), (2004) and (2006))); logic (see Woods (2010)) and argumentation theory (see Walton (2002)).

[75] See eg Schum (2002: 318).

[76] For some accounts of the role of abduction in normative reasoning in law, see McJohn (1993); Brewer (1996); Bonorino (1993); Bourcier (1999); Papaux (1999); Walton (2002), esp. ch 5; and Maranhão ((2011) and (2012b)).

there is more to inference in law than inference to the best explanation, eg deduction plays a role in legal justification. But the point is that, while seeking coherence in law, we employ a distinct form of inference, that is, an explanatory kind of inference. Given that much legal inference is coherence-driven, inference to the best explanation is ubiquitous in the legal context. We may thus learn a great deal about legal inference—more specifically about the kind of inference whereby we construe coherence in the course of legal decision-making—by examining what a model of inference to the best explanation has to offer.

Now, what is the structure of explanatory inference? Lipton has elaborated a detailed account of the structure of inferences to the best explanation according to which the mechanism we use to settle on which explanation to infer has two stages, to wit, a process of generation and a process of selection.[77] Lipton's idea is that we infer to the best explanation by first generating a short list of plausible candidates, and then by selecting the best from that list. We never begin with a 'full menu', as Lipton puts it, of all possible explanations, for this would be too large to generate and handle. Yet, the set of explanations that we consider is not generated randomly. Instead, he argues, we use some sort of shortlist mechanism whereby we generate a small number of live candidates, from which we then choose. From this point of view, inference to the best explanation includes 'two-filters', one that selects the plausible candidates and another that selects from among them. There is, however, I would argue, an intermediate stage that is exceedingly important, to wit, a 'context of pursuit', in which working hypotheses are subjected to a preliminary assessment and developed in further detail.[78] Under this view, it is clear that inference to the best explanation is primarily an eliminative method, for an explanation emerges as best by a process whereby one eliminates alternative explanations.[79] And, from this description of the mechanics of inference to the best explanation it is also plain that inference to the best explanation is an ampliative (defeasible or non-monotonic) form of inference, given that, of course, it is always possible to discover an even better explanation which defeats the hypothesis that has been chosen as best.[80]

The foregoing analysis of the structure and nature of inference to the best explanation has important consequences for legal inference, if, as I have claimed, the latter is an instance of the former. To start with, it follows from the foregoing analysis that an inference to the best explanation of the facts under dispute at trial and an inference to the best interpretative hypothesis

[77] See Lipton (2004: 148–51).

[78] The label 'context of pursuit' is Laudan's (1977: 110). On this context, see Sintonen and Kikeri (2004: 214–18).

[79] Psillos (2007).

[80] See Psillos (2002: 622).

about what the law requires in a particular case is an eliminative and defeasible type of inference. And secondly, under a model of inference to the best explanation, legal inference consists of three stages. Legal decision-makers infer the best explanatory or interpretative hypothesis in law by first constructing a set of plausible candidates, then by revising them with a view to making them as good as they can be and, finally, by choosing the best from this set—the candidate, I shall argue, that best satisfies the coherence standards. Let us now see in some detail the three main stages that may be distinguished in coherence-based reasoning in law.

### B. Discovering Explanations

To start with, legal decision-makers need to generate a limited pool of alternatives from which coherence-based reasoning may then proceed. How do legal decision-makers come up with a set of plausible alternatives? Little is known about how we come up with novel factual or interpretative hypotheses and how we ascertain which of these hypotheses is worth being seriously considered.[81] Of course, I do not attempt to give an answer to the question of how legal decision-makers manage to come up with a relatively narrow set of promising alternatives. However, I would like to note that coherence considerations play a role here, as much as they do in the process of selection. Coherence contributes to the generation of a relevant set of elements in different ways.

First, coherence enters implicitly in the process of generation via background knowledge.[82] The judgement of plausibility upon which the generation of a restricted number of candidates hinges on depends heavily on background knowledge. Our background beliefs—we take it—indicate which hypotheses one ought to seriously consider. Thus, coherence with background beliefs helps us narrow down the range of plausible candidates to a manageable size. For instance, when reasoning about evidence in law, beliefs about how crimes are usually committed play a prevalent role, so that decision-makers tend to include within the set of hypotheses to be considered those hypotheses which cohere with those beliefs. Similarly, when reasoning about norms in law, background knowledge about precedents and settled principles is also crucial in determining which interpretative hypotheses are plausible enough to make it to the second filter. Hypotheses

[81] It was not until the 1980s that there was a certain revival of interest in the topic of discovery in philosophy of science. See Nickles (1980) and (1985); Kelly (1987); Lugg (1985); H. A. Simon (1973); Kantorovich (1993); Meheus and Nickles (1999); Aliseda (2004) and (2006); and Magnani (2009). In the last decades, work in AI has also contributed significantly to the study of discovery issues. See Langley, HA Simon, Bradshaw and Zytkow (1987); Shrager and Langley (1990); and HA Simon (1998).

[82] Lipton (2004: 150–51).

which, if accepted, would require us to reject (on grounds of incoherence) much of our empirical beliefs or our beliefs about the law are not merely discarded but are not even considered.

This tendency to generate hypotheses that cohere with our background beliefs is quite risky. The role that coherence—via background knowledge—plays in the generation stage is a double-edged sword. On the one hand, it focuses inquiry, by avoiding waste of time and effort in formulating and discarding crazy hypotheses that nobody could genuinely consider. To state the obvious, no serious lawyer would say that the crime was committed by an unnatural force because we most firmly believe that crimes are 'usually' committed by humans.[83] And no judge would say that a given problem of interpretation ought to be solved as the principle that nothing prevents one from benefiting from one's own wrongdoing dictates, which clearly conflicts with our most entrenched convictions about the law. But, on the other hand, the role that coherence with background knowledge plays in the process of generation has also its negative side. Favouring hypotheses that cohere with our background empirical beliefs might prevent us from considering hypotheses which, rare as they might be, are best supported by the evidence we have in the particular case. And a tendency to generate hypotheses that cohere with our background normative beliefs may also hinder normative change. Here, we face the recalcitrant problem of conservatism which seems to undermine coherence methods, and to which I shall return later.[84]

Secondly, coherence also enters into the process of generation through a number of marshalling mechanisms. The success that we enjoy in generating important new hypotheses and discovering new evidence depends to a great extent upon how well we have marshalled or organized the evidence we have.[85] Marshalling methods stimulate asking the right questions without which we stand little chance of generating fruitful possibilities. Some important marshalling strategies such as 'scenarios', 'schemata' and 'theories of the case' are coherence-oriented. Thus, coherence pushes us towards productive investigative paths by contributing to the effective marshalling of the ideas and evidence that we have.

Thirdly, the generation of new elements is sometimes driven by an effort after coherence. Successful inquiry is first and foremost an exercise of interrogation.[86] The search for coherence motivates the formulation of a

[83] As one of the Grimm brothers said in the film *The Grimm Brothers*. Of course, the important proviso 'in our culture in the twenty-first century' is missing here. IBE is, as I said before, a highly contextual kind of inference insofar as it depends on substantive background beliefs which vary with context; see ch 4.

[84] See s VII below.

[85] See Tillers and Schum (1991); Schum and Tillers (1991); and Schum ((1999) and (2001: 489–504)).

[86] Sintonen and Kikeri (2004: 227–33).

set of questions which importantly aid the aim of inquiry. Asking what data would cohere with a particular hypothesis, or what hypothesis could make sense of some data we have is an effective way of identifying relevant evidence as well as coming up with innovative hypotheses. It is important to notice here that formulating promising hypotheses and discovering relevant evidence goes hand-in-hand in the process of inquiry. On the one hand, by supposing that one factual hypothesis is true, we can work out what further evidence might be relevant. Or we may notice the relevance of a particular body of precedent for a given problem of interpretation by considering, for the purposes of inquiry, that one interpretative hypothesis is correct. On the other hand, we may come up with a new factual hypothesis by supposing what would, if true, explain a particular piece of evidence we have. Similarly, we may articulate a novel interpretative hypothesis by searching for an overarching principle which, if correct, could make sense of a set of apparently conflicting rules. Thus, there is a feedback between hypothesis formation and data acquisition in actual legal inquiry, and coherence seems to significantly contribute to this feedback.

Last, *in*coherence is also a driving force in inquiry. Emotional reactions, such as surprise or anxiety, that signal incoherence may trigger hypotheses formation. That is, sometimes the generation of new elements is prompted by failure to achieve an interpretation that adequately satisfies the criteria of coherence.[87] In the context of law, we may say that the anxiety produced by the fact that a guilt-hypothesis fails to make full sense of the available evidence may motivate the search for an alternative hypothesis (which might, in turn, suggest the relevance of additional evidence) that is compatible with a story of innocence. Or incongruity of the so far best solution to an interpretative problem in law with one's firm convictions about what the main values which the legal system is meant to protect are may be accompanied by a lively sense of non-conformity that might trigger the search for an alternative interpretation (and for normative materials that might support the new interpretative hypothesis).

In short, in the process of discovery, legal decision-makers identify a 'base' of coherence, that is, the set of elements over which the coherence calculation proceeds, which provides the basis for constructing a 'contrast set', that is, a set of competing alternatives. But the task is not over once we have a reasonable pool of alternatives, for it is necessary to make those alternatives the best that they can be, in order to ensure a fair comparison of their relative degree of coherence. Hence, the best case should be made for each of the alternatives under consideration before picking one of them (in the selection stage) as best, which is the goal to be accomplished at the second stage of explanatory inference, ie the context of pursuit.

[87] Thagard (2000a: 67).

## C. The Context of Pursuit

How do we build up a contrast set that contains a set of alternatives that are as coherent as they can be? What are the mechanisms available for so doing? Here, belief revision operations are, I think, extremely helpful. As explained in chapter five, belief revision operations are designed for modelling what is involved in rational belief change. The guiding idea is that coherence (variously understood) provides the standard against which the rationality of the outcome of a process of belief change (the output system of beliefs) is to be determined. Belief revision operations explicate what is required for changing our system of beliefs rationally (that is, for maximizing its coherence). The suggestion is that we may employ the different coherence-making mechanisms formalized by the belief revision literature in order to clarify what is involved in maximizing the coherence of the several alternatives under consideration, ie the theories about what the law requires in a particular case or about what the facts at trial are.[88]

To recall, there are two main strategies whereby one may build coherence among one's beliefs: subtractive and additive. While the former construes coherence by subtracting a belief (or more) from an incoherent set, the latter consists of adding one (or more) beliefs to an incoherent set in order to make it coherent. To these subtractive and additive strategies, we should add yet one more way in which the coherence of a particular set (a decision alternative) might be enhanced, and which I shall refer to, borrowing Conte's term, as 'reinterpretation'.[89] Often, we remove the incoherencies in our belief systems by changing (rather than by deleting) one (or more) elements within the system.

These three operations may significantly help legal decision-makers enhance the coherence of the different alternatives under consideration.[90] Legal decision-makers may use 'subtractive' strategies to augment the coherence of a decision alternative. For instance, one may determine that one should reject a particular piece of evidence on the grounds of its incoherence with one of the proposed hypotheses; or rule out a precedent as mistaken because it conflicts with the principles upon which one of the decision

[88] I have examined the relevance of belief revision formalisms to explanatory reasoning in law in Amaya (2007). On the connection between belief revision and abduction, see Aliseda (2006) ch 8 and Olsson (1997c).

[89] See Conte (1988: 85–86). According to Conte, we may render a discourse coherent through a particular kind of interpretation, which she refers to as 'reinterpretation'. Reinterpretation occurs when the interpreter, in order to attribute meaning to a text, is required to make a second interpretation of a preceding part of a text that has already been interpreted. For a fuller account of how the process of reinterpretation, as described by Conte, works, see ch 9.

[90] *Cf* Maranhão (2011) (arguing that there are two main operations whereby coherence is constructed in the context of legal reasoning—about disputed questions of law, namely, conservative contraction and conservative expansion).

alternatives relies. The 'additive' strategy is also useful. For example, one may increase the coherence of a particular interpretation of the facts under dispute by adding a testimony that lends support to such an interpretation; or one may enhance the coherence of a particular interpretation of the normative materials by citing a precedent which lends support to such an interpretative hypothesis. Last, the 'reinterpretative' strategy is, indeed, very common in legal decision-making. For instance, one may reinterpret a piece of evidence which apparently conflicts with the factual hypothesis that one is arguing for so that it supports the hypothesis; or one may reinterpret a body of precedent with a view to showing that it coheres with one's proposed decision.

These belief revision operations are effective strategies for rendering each of the decision alternatives under consideration as coherent as they can be. Not only are they appealing, from a normative standpoint, but they also characterize quite well the kind of operations performed by legal decision-makers when searching for the most coherent arrangement of the different elements that enter into their decisions. Simon has persuasively shown that legal decision-makers restructure the legal materials so as to build up a coherent mental model of the decision task by means of what he refers to as 'gate-keeping', 'bolstering' and 'rule-selecting'.[91] These three operations correspond, he says, with most typologies offered by cognitive consistency theorists, to wit, changing elements, adding new elements and decreasing the importance of dissonant elements. There is substantial psychological evidence that we use these kind of operations for enhancing the coherence (or reducing the incoherence) among our beliefs. These kinds of operations closely resemble the kind of operations that belief revision formalisms advocate. Thus, these operations not only provide a useful classification of the strategies that legal decision-makers have at their disposal for enhancing the coherence of each of the alternatives, but they also accurately describe the processes whereby we construe coherence in the course of decision-making (as much in law as everywhere else).

There are, however, some dangers involved in employing these different coherence-making mechanisms. While it seems necessary, in order to ensure a fair evaluation of the different alternatives, that each of the alternatives be shown to be as coherent as it can be, it cannot be denied that there is always the possibility that the process whereby the coherence of each of these alternatives is maximized is performed in such a way as to ensure that one of the decision alternatives ends up being later selected. That is, there is always the risk that one uses these different mechanisms for inflating the degree of coherence of one's preferred alternative and deflating the degree of coherence of the competing alternatives. In fact, this is what happens,

[91] D Simon (1998: 85ff).

according to Simon, in the course of legal decision-making.[92] One might then make it the case that while rendering each of the decision alternatives the most coherent it can be, one's preferred alternative is shown to be more coherent than it actually is, and competing alternatives are rendered in fact less coherent than they could have been shown to be. This, of course, would result in a biased, rather than a fair, evaluation of the alternatives. We might be so wired—as Simon and collaborators' psychological research shows—that such manipulations of the decision alternatives are an essential part of what is involved, as a matter of fact, in effective decision-making. But while to some extent these manipulations might be indispensable for reaching a decision at all, it does still seem possible—and indeed, desirable—to keep these psychological tendencies from running wild. Complementing—in the way that I shall suggest later—a theory of coherence-based reasoning with a theory of epistemic responsibility might be a way of exploiting the drive towards coherence which—as empirical studies show—guides our decision-processes, while avoiding the dangers inherent in coherence-based reasoning.

### D. Selecting the Best Explanation

Inference to the best explanation has us select, among a set of plausible candidates, the candidate that is best. But, one may ask, what is meant by 'best'? By 'best' explanation we may understand, as some prominent advocates of inference to the best explanation have suggested, the explanation that best coheres.[93] That is, criteria of coherence provide us with the standards of evaluation against which we may determine which one among a number of alternative explanations is best.[94] As I have argued before, the most plausible account that we have of the notion of coherence is Thagard's theory of coherence as constraint satisfaction, upon which a theory of legal coherence may be developed. Thus, the suggestion is that, in law, the 'best'

[92] See ch 2.

[93] See Psillos (2002: 616 and 619); Thagard and Shelley (1997); Harman ((1980), (1986) and (1995)); and Lycan (1988). Lipton claims that inference to the best explanation should be understood as inference to the 'loveliest' explanation, that is, to the explanation that would, if true, provide the most understanding (2004: 59). Given the close link that exists between understanding and coherence, characterizing inference to the best explanation as inference to the loveliest explanation so understood comes very close to claiming that the best explanation is the most coherent one. As argued, understanding something is, in an important sense, coming to see how it coheres with our system of beliefs. From this point of view, the explanation that provides most understanding is the explanation that would, if true, make the incorporation of the *explanandum* into our system of beliefs the most coherent one. On the relation between coherence and understanding, see ch 9.

[94] *Cf* Schiavello (2011) (arguing that a coherentist interpretation of inference to the best explanation in law only allows us to identify a subset of acceptable explanations, from which legal decision-makers may choose based on subjective preferences and values).

of the 'inference to the best explanation' slogan is the explanation that best satisfies a number of coherence constraints, as stated by the principles of factual and normative coherence.[95]

## E. A Procedure for Coherence-driven Legal Inference

Let us recapitulate. The process of coherence-maximization in the context of legal reasoning about both conclusions about facts and conclusions about law is an explanatory inference which may be described as follows:

1. The *specification of a base of coherence*, that is, the set of factual or interpretative hypotheses and relevant evidence over which the coherence calculation proceeds.
2. The *construction of a contrast set* that contains a number of alternative theories of the case or theories about what the law requires from which the most coherent one is to be selected.
3. The *pursuit* of the alternative theories of the case or theories about what the law requires by means of a number of coherence-making mechanisms.
4. The *evaluation* of the coherence of the alternative theories of the case or theories about what the law requires against the criteria of factual and normative coherence.
5. The *selection as justified* of the most coherent of the alternative theories of the case or the theories about what the law requires, that is, the theory that best satisfies the criteria of factual or normative coherence.

Thus, the result of this process of coherence-maximization is the selection as justified of the theory about what the facts are or what the law requires that best coheres. Three important characteristics of the foregoing description of the process of coherence-maximization should be noted. First, this account of legal inference does not assume that the base of coherence remains fixed during the process of coherence-maximization. Rather, the base of coherence is transitory and may be modified in the course of legal decision-making. The pursuit of the alternative theories of the case requires us to modify the base of coherence in several ways, by adding new elements, eliminating some of the elements or changing their interpretation.

[95] This coherentist interpretation of best is not uncontroversial. Alternatively, one could understand 'best' as the 'likeliest' or 'more probable'. Most importantly, there are some attempts to cast IBE into a Bayesian framework. On this view, the best explanation is the explanation that has a higher posterior probability as determined by Bayes theorem. It has also suggested that we may equate the best explanation with the hypothesis that enjoys a higher likelihood (see Niiniluoto (2003)). For a critique of Bayesian interpretations of IBE, see Lipton (2004) and Psillos ((2004) and (2007)).

This squares well with the dynamics of legal inquiry, for typically evidence and hypotheses become available sequentially in the course of legal inquiry.

Secondly, coherence is not computed at once among all the evidence and hypotheses, but is constructed incrementally, by focusing on subsets of elements (ie the theories of the case or the theories of the law) at a time. On this view, legal decision-makers work with a 'travelling focus of attention' concentrating on some alternatives and then on others.[96] This local approach to coherence-building seems psychologically more realistic than a global approach, for limitations of memory and attention make it unlikely that we are able to consider at once all the coherence relations that hold among the whole set of elements.

Last, the different stages of coherence-based inference are distinguished here for the sake of clarity, but in real instances of reasoning, legal decision-makers move back and forth between stages. If they are not satisfied with any of the alternatives being evaluated, they may strive to find out additional evidence or they may seek out alternative hypotheses in the course of deliberation. New evidence may also prompt the reconsideration of a hypothesis that was discarded before in the process of coherence construction. Thus, the proposed account of coherence-driven legal reasoning brings to light the extent to which discovery and justification go hand-in-hand in the course of legal decision-making.

Let me illustrate this explanationist approach to legal inference in terms of an example already introduced, ie the *R v Angela Cannings* case.[97] The *first* stage is to specify the base of coherence. This involves specifying the set of hypotheses and evidence over which the coherence calculation is performed, eg $H_1$ Angela Cannings killed her babies; $H_2$ Jason and Matthew's deaths were natural; $H_3$ Jason and Matthew were killed by someone else; $H_4$ Angela Cannings was a loving mother; $H_5$ There is a genetic defect in the Cannings family, and so on.

At the *second* stage, the trier of fact specifies the set of theories of the case. Absent evidence that indicated the possibility that the babies might have been deliberately harmed by someone other than their mother, two theories of the case were considered. The first one, ie 'the Angela Cannings-did-it' theory, takes Lady Bracknell's approach as its starting point: 'to lose one baby is a misfortune, two carelessness, three murder'.[98] On this theory, the extreme rarity of three unexplained infant deaths in the same family grounds a powerful inference that deaths must have resulted from deliberate harm. The baby boys were smothered by someone who *appears* to be an affectionate mother and these deaths were related to a 'pattern' of events in the family. The second theory of the case, ie 'the natural deaths'

[96] See Hoadley, Ranney and Schank (1994) and D Simon (1998: 80–81).
[97] See s III.A.
[98] See Wilde (2008).

theory, proceeds on the basis that the fact that there are unexplained deaths in our current state of knowledge does not exclude that there is a reasonable possibility that the deaths may be natural. Furthermore, it does not make sense to think that she had murdered her babies, for that would entail that she was becoming repeatedly pregnant with the sole purpose of killing the babies after they were born. Given that Angela Cannings was a loving mother and that there was no evidence that she had any personality disorder or psychiatric condition, the conclusion that she killed her babies does not seem cogent.

The construction of the theories of the case involves determining the coherence and incoherence relations that hold between the different elements, ie evidence and hypotheses. In order to do so, it is necessary to consider which evidence is explained by which hypothesis, whether there are any explanatory connections between competing hypotheses, whether there are relevant analogies at work or whether there are any contradictions between propositions describing evidence or hypotheses. For example, the hypothesis that Angela Cannings killed her babies coheres with expert evidence as to the rarity of three infant deaths in one family. And the hypothesis that there was a genetic defect in the Cannings family coheres with the hypothesis that the deaths were natural, as both are explanatorily related. By the end of this process, the fact-finder would have constructed a number of theories of the case, each of which contains several hypotheses and evidence that cohere with each other, ie the 'Angela Cannings-did-it' and the 'natural deaths theory', in this case.

At the *third* stage the theories of the case under consideration are refined and revised with a view to making them the best that they can be. As argued earlier, there are three main strategies whereby coherence may be enhanced: additive, subtractive and reinterpretative. For example, the fact that there was a third death in the family may be reinterpreted, in light of evidence of the possible existence of a genetic defect in the Cannings extended family, as evidence that lends support to the hypothesis that the babies' deaths were natural, rather than as evidence of guilt. As a result of this reinterpretation, the degree of coherence of the natural deaths theory is enhanced. Or adding the belief that women who appear to be affectionate mothers sometimes kill their children increases the coherence of the Angela Cannings-did-it theory, by ironing out a possible inconsistency between the hypothesis that the babies were deliberately harmed and evidence that the babies were loved and cared for by their parents. This process of pursuit ensures that each competing theory of the case is developed and seriously considered before one takes any decision as to which of them is explanatorily best.

At the *fourth* stage, the fact-finder assesses the coherence of the alternative theories of the case by examining the extent to which they satisfy the coherence constraints. She will have to consider whether the guilt theory explains the evidence at trial or whether, to the contrary, the natural deaths theory better explains the evidence available. She will also consider which of the theories is simpler and examine whether they fit with background knowledge about analogous cases. Sources of incoherence, that is, inconsistencies and incompatibilities, will have to be identified as well. In the explanatory evaluation of the theories of the case, the fact-finder will have to give a priority both to the evidence admitted at trial as well as to the hypotheses that are compatible with innocence. The outcome of this evaluation is to arrive at comparative judgements of explanatory coherence. While, as was stated earlier, the someone-else-did-it theory lacks evidential support, the Angela Cannings-did-it theory and the natural deaths theory both explain a substantial part of the evidence admitted at trial.

Finally, at the *fifth* stage, the most coherent theory of the case is selected, provided that its degree of justification (on this account, its degree of coherence) is high enough to satisfy the applicable standard of proof. In this case, I would argue that, as the Court of Appeals held, the acceptance of the Angela-did-it theory was not justified. First, there existed a coherent theory of innocence compatible with the evidence at trial. Most importantly, the body of expert evidence showed that, while three deaths in the same family was very rare indeed, there was a reasonable possibility that the deaths were natural. Secondly, some subset of the evidence is best explained by the innocence hypothesis, ie evidence that Angela Cannings cared for and loved her children. While that evidence was also consistent with a guilt hypothesis (it is possible to be both a loving mother and a baby killer), the innocence hypothesis coheres with it in a way that the guilt hypothesis does not. In light of these reasons, a coherence analysis would not sanction the acceptance of the guilt hypothesis. On appeal, this analysis was further fortified by the introduction of new evidence (expert evidence as well as evidence of other unexplained deaths in the Cannings extended family) that significantly increased the degree of coherence of the natural deaths theory. Thus, the conclusion of this piece of explanatory reasoning is that the natural deaths theory is the most coherent theory and thus should be accepted as justified.

Similarly, we may reconstruct the Court's reasoning in the *Sweet v Parsley* case discussed earlier in terms of the five-step procedure described above. In this case, two theories of the law were considered: the 'absolute liability' theory and the '*mens rea*' theory, with the latter theory being accepted as justified on grounds of its coherence with the relevant body of case law, statutory law and established principles of common law. Hence, the explanationist approach advanced here shows that legal inference about both facts and norms share one and the same structure.

### F. The Coherence Bias

The version of explanatory coherentism articulated above faces the following problem: there are cases in which the theory that best satisfies the criteria of factual or normative coherence is nonetheless intuitively unjustified. In other words, doubts may be raised as to whether satisfaction of the criteria of coherence is sufficient for justification. Two kinds of problem-cases may be distinguished:

i. *Problems with the base of coherence.* These are cases in which the input to coherence-based reasoning, that is, the set of relevant evidence and hypotheses over which the calculation of coherence proceeds, is the result of defective inquiry. In cases of this sort, a theory of the case that best satisfies the criteria of coherence does so only because the legal decision-maker has taken into account a less comprehensive body of evidence and hypotheses than the set that would have resulted if he had inquired properly about the case.

To start with, legal decision-makers may ignore relevant evidence. For example, they may select evidence on the basis of how well it fits their working hypothesis. In fact, problems of biased selection of evidence are, as some studies have shown, recurrent in both police investigations and judicial fact-finding.[99] Furthermore, research into memory suggests that memory for information congruent with prior beliefs is better than memory for information irrelevant to prior beliefs; there is also evidence that people tend to drive their attention to encode information consistent with their expectations and are prone to seek information that supports rather than disconfirms their beliefs. This 'confirmation bias' may distort the generation of the base of coherence, which would, right from the beginning, be biased towards one of the alternative theories being considered.[100]

For example, in the *R v Angela Cannings* case, a juror who, right from the beginning of the trial, firmly believes that the defendant is guilty, may ignore or suppress incoming expert evidence that shows that there is a reasonable possibility that the deaths may be natural. In a similar fashion, a judge in the *Sweet v Parsley* case may selectively choose among the relevant precedents those earlier decisions that support her claim that absolute liability is appropriate, even for offences carrying moral stigma, and purposefully disregard authorities which may cast doubt upon this proposition. Once one misconstrues the base of coherence in this way, the guilt hypothesis emerges, in both cases, as the most coherent—indeed, the only coherent—hypothesis.

[99] See Wagenaar, Van Koppen and Crombag (1993) ch 11.
[100] On the confirmation bias, see Mercier and Sperber (2011: 63–66).

Difficulties may also arise regarding the construction of the contrast set. Lack of imagination, prejudice, excessive reliance on the parties' configuration of alternatives or professional routines—in the case of judicial reasoning—may lead legal decision-makers to ignore relevant alternatives. On the coherence-based account of legal inference outlined above, legal inference in law works by exclusion. One theory is accepted as justified on the grounds that it is the best of a set of available alternatives on a test of coherence. But then unless the legal decision-maker has a reason to believe that she has ruled out the relevant alternatives to her claim about what the facts are or what the law requires, belief in the best explanatory or interpretative hypothesis fails to be justified. To be sure, inferring to the best of a 'bad lot' cannot yield justified beliefs.[101] At the very least, a relevant set of alternative theories needs to be considered for conclusions of inference to the best explanation to be justified.

To continue with our examples, a juror owing to extreme repulsion at the thought of a mother killing her offspring may fail to give due consideration to the possibility—the seriousness of which is indicated by the evidence available—that the defendant may be guilty and faced with what seem to him to be the only possible explanations of the deaths of the children—either they were killed by someone other than their mother or their deaths were natural—settles on the natural deaths explanation as the most coherent explanation of the events being litigated. A juror that reasoned from such a defective contrast set would be intuitively unjustified in believing in the innocence hypothesis, despite the fact that this is the most coherent explanation of those considered.[102]

Similarly, a judge obsessed with the prevention of cannabis consumption may fail to give the hypothesis that *mens rea* ought to be required a hearing, and, overemphasizing the state interest in convicting the guilty in these cases, may end up accepting as justified the hypothesis that the offence of 'being concerned in the management of any premises used for any such purpose' does not require guilty knowledge or intention of participation in the 'purpose' in question on the grounds that it is the only coherent interpretative hypothesis. Such an acceptance would be, however, intuitively unjustified despite it being, by the interpreter's lights, the only coherent hypothesis.

ii. *Problems with the coherence calculation.* There are cases in which a theory of the case or the law satisfies the criteria of factual or normative

[101] This is the so-called 'objection from the bad lot' or 'problem of underconsideration' raised by Van Fraassen against models of inference to the best explanation in science; see ch 4. For a detailed discussion of this problem and its relevance to legal fact-finding, see Amaya (2009).

[102] As I will argue below, such belief would be, nonetheless, justified iff it could be accepted as such by an epistemically responsible fact-finder. An important distinction needs to be made between the conditions under which a fact-finder is justified in believing that $p$ and the conditions under which the belief that $p$ is justified.

coherence but the reason why it does so traces back to certain defects in the way in which the legal decision-maker performs the coherence calculation. In these cases, the reasoning is defective for reasons that do not have to do with the input to such a process (ie the evidence and hypotheses) but rather with the quality of the process as such. Legal decision-makers may attempt to maximize coherence by inflating some alternatives while deflating others. In fact, as we saw, there is substantial evidence that shows that this 'coherence bias' is at work in the evaluation of hypotheses in the legal context. In the process of legal decision-making, subjects restructure the diverse and conflicting considerations that provide equivocal support for different decision alternatives until they reach a representation in which the chosen alternative is supported by strong considerations and the rejected one is supported by weak considerations. Once the decision alternatives have been manipulated in such a way, the evaluation of those alternatives is already skewed towards one's preferred alternative.[103]

To illustrate, a fact-finder may believe that Angela Cannings is guilty and misrepresent some aspects of the evidence available that would support the innocence hypothesis. For example, she may downplay the relevance of evidence that she was a loving mother, shed doubts over the reliability of expert evidence that indicates that there is a reasonable possibility that the deaths be natural, while wholeheartedly accepting expert evidence as to the rarity of three deaths occurring in the same family etc. As a result, the theory of the case entailing guilt will enjoy a high degree of coherence, and, to be sure, a much higher degree than the natural deaths theory. It seems, however, that there is a strong sense in which such a belief in the guilt of the defendant would be unjustified.

The same kind of problem arises in the context of reasoning about norms, rather than facts. For instance, a judge may insist on artfully distinguishing cannabis consumption from other 'anti-social' activities such as opium consumption, which are offences that explicitly require *mens rea*; she may overlook the relevance of precedents establishing that *mens rea* is an essential ingredient of every offence; and she may stubbornly stick to the view that the absence of the word 'knowingly' in the statute provides conclusive evidence that an offence of absolute liability has been created, sparing herself the trouble of examining the relevant body of case law and common law principles. The outcome of such a defective reasoning process would surely be that the 'absolute liability' theory enjoys a much higher degree of coherence than the '*mens rea*' theory, contrary to what would have been the case had she analysed the relevant body of law in a diligent and open-minded manner.

[103] See ch 2.

In all of these cases, there does not seem to be sufficient reason to accept as justified the outcome of the process of a coherence-driven inference. The theory that best satisfies the criteria of coherence seems, however, intuitively unjustified, as it satisfies the criteria better than alternative theories only because the legal decision-makers has reasoned about the case in a defective way. In the first kind of cases, legal decision-makers ignore disconfirming evidence or alternative hypotheses, ie they ignore potential defeaters to the claim that a given hypothesis is best. In the second kind of cases, legal fact-finders distort the evaluation of the evidence and hypotheses that threaten to defeat their claim. In both cases, the satisfaction of the criteria of coherence does not seem to be sufficient for justification. It is not only that legal decision-makers are to be blamed for inquiring and deliberating about the case in a defective way, but the justificatory status of the theories that result from such processes of inquiry and deliberation is undermined. To start with, the coherence that results from reasoning from a defective base by distorting the deliberation factors does not seem to be epistemically valuable. There does not seem to be anything especially worthy about believing a theory about what the facts are or what the law requires by virtue of its coherence, when such coherence is but the product of one's cognitive failure. Besides, even if one might attribute some merit to having a coherent system of beliefs, even in cases in which such coherence results from objectionable epistemic behaviour, there is a straightforward sense in which belief in such theories is unjustified: for, had the legal decision-maker been conscientious in forming his belief, he would not have accepted such a theory on the grounds that it coheres best. In other words, there seems to be a clear sense in which the legal decision-maker ought not to believe the way he does.[104]

This problem is not unique to the version of legal coherentism proposed here, but it is a serious problem to any coherence theory of justification. One may reach coherence—however such notion might be defined—by reasoning from a defective base or one may construct coherence over the course of decision-making in a biased way and the resulting system of beliefs seems unjustified, despite it enjoying a high degree of coherence. The coherence theory of justification needs to be modified in order to block ascriptions of justified belief in cases in which coherence-based inference is vitiated in some of these ways. The suggestion is that there is a need to impose a further condition on the process of coherence maximization for it to be justification-conferring, namely, it has to be such that an 'epistemically responsible' agent could have reached such a conclusion in

[104] See Baehr (2009: 549–52).

like circumstances.[105] Coherence irrespective of the process whereby it may be reached does not yield justification: a belief is justified only if it could be the outcome of epistemically responsible coherence-based reasoning.[106] In short, coherentism needs to be wedded to a 'responsibilist' account of justification.[107] That is to say, epistemic responsibility is a crucial component of a coherence theory of justification.[108] An account of what epistemic responsibility requires in legal contexts is the third main element of the coherence theory of legal reasoning, to which I turn now.

## V. LEGAL JUSTIFICATION BY OPTIMAL COHERENCE

In the previous sections, I have argued that one is justified in accepting an interpretative hypothesis or a factual hypothesis if it belongs to the subset A which results from partitioning a set S into accepted and rejected elements in a way that maximizes coherence. I have suggested that we may understand the process whereby we divide a set of elements into 'accepted' and

[105] Similarly, Baehr has argued that evidentialism needs to be modified by incorporating a condition according to which 'justification supervenes on a belief that fits a person's evidence only if this person has exercised certain intellectual *virtues* in the formation and maintenance of this belief' (Baehr (2008: 484–85)). BonJour's account of a priori justification also endorses a similar responsibility-based constraint according to which a person is a priori justified in believing a given claim just in case he has rational insight into the necessity of this claim provided that such insight has been arrived at on the basis of 'reasonably careful reflection', which is incompatible, argues BonJour, with dogmatism, bias and other intellectual vices; see BonJour (1998a: 110–15). Interestingly, Khalifa has provided a defence of inference to the best explanation (against the argument from the bad lot) that also amounts to imposing a responsibilist constraint on explanatory inference: if a scientist responsibly infers a hypothesis via IBE, then he has good reason to take that hypothesis to be true; see Khalifa (2010).

[106] It might be argued that supplementing coherence with an additional condition that makes epistemically responsible behaviour necessary for justification makes the requirement of coherence superfluous, for coherence would typically be one of the epistemic virtues that make an agent epistemically responsible. It does not: justification, on the proposed account, is still a matter of coherence—while not any kind of coherence will do, it is still coherence, of the right sort, that confers justification. Considerations of epistemic responsibility constrain the process whereby justified beliefs may be reached, but it is not that the resulting beliefs are justified because of the virtues of the agents, but what makes them justified are virtue-independent reasons, that is, reasons from coherence. The proposed responsibilist version of coherentism should thus be distinguished from pure responsibilist epistemologies that seek to analyse justification exclusively in virtue terms and that make justification-conferring properties, such as coherence, derivative of virtues; see Amaya (2013: 22–24).

[107] On the notion of epistemic responsibility and its relation to justification, see among others Alston ((1989) and (2005)); Montmarquet (1993); Goldman (1988); Heil (1983) and (1992); Kornblith (1983); Steup (1999b); and Foley and Wolterstorff's contributions to Steup and Sosa (2005).

[108] *Cf* Schiavello (2011) (arguing that the distinction between the coherence that is the product of epistemically responsible behaviour and that which is the product of prejudice and bias is linked to a strong objectivist position that is incompatible with the claim that coherence is constructed rather than found in the process of interpretation). For a reply, see Amaya (2011c).

'rejected' by virtue of their coherence as an inference to the best explanation. Coherence-driven reasoning is, first and foremost, an explanatory kind of reasoning. When we seek the most coherent account of the facts under dispute or of a body of norms we need to generate a number of alternative explanations and then choose the most coherent of them. As explained, a problem with this explanatory account of coherence-based inference is that it may yield beliefs which, while coherent, are intuitively unjustified. I have suggested that bringing the notion of 'epistemic responsibility' into the picture may help us to solve what I have referred to as the 'coherence bias'. In this section, I would like to further explore this suggestion. The thesis that I shall argue for may be succinctly stated as follows: an interpretative/factual hypothesis in law is justified if it belongs to A *and* A is optimally coherent. A subset A is 'optimally coherent' if it could be the result of epistemically responsible coherence-based reasoning. On this view, legal justification results from optimal coherence.

### A. Virtues, Duties and Epistemic Responsibility

What is it is for a legal decision-maker to behave in an epistemically responsible way? Two main accounts of epistemic responsibility may be distinguished: a 'deontic' approach and an 'aretaic' approach. Under a deontic-approach, epistemic responsibility is a matter of duty-fulfilment. One is epistemically responsible to the extent that one complies with one's epistemological duties, such as the duty to believe as the evidence dictates or the duty to seek out more evidence about propositions that are less than certain on one's evidence.[109] According to the aretaic conception of epistemic responsibility, one is epistemically responsible insofar as one properly exercises a number of intellectual virtues, such as diligence, courage to face criticism, perseverance in following a line of inquiry or open-mindedness.[110] Epistemically responsible action amounts, in this approach, to intellectually virtuous behaviour.

Initially, a deontic approach to the epistemic responsibility of legal decision-makers seems more adequate than an aretaic one, for the law aims

[109] The most influential contemporary statement of such a view is by Chisholm (1977). For an account of epistemological duties see Feldman ((1988) and (2002)). For a discussion of the epistemological duty to seek more evidence, see Hall and Johnson (1998).

[110] The most influential statements of 'virtue responsibilism' include Montmarquet (1993) and Code (1987). For a discussion of this trend in virtue epistemology, see Axtell (1997) and J Greco and J Turri, 'Virtue Epistemology', *The Stanford Encyclopedia of Philosophy* (Winter 2011 edn), EN Zalta (ed), http://plato.stanford.edu/archives/win2011/entries/epistemology-virtue/.

There are different views in the literature about which traits of character count as intellectual virtues, and how to best classify them. See among others Montmarquet (1987); Cooper (1994b); and Roberts and Woods (2007).

at requiring standards of conduct that are minimally acceptable, rather than at setting up ideal models of conduct. We may distinguish, following Fuller, between two kinds of morality: the 'morality of aspiration' and the 'morality of duty'. While the former is 'the morality of the Good life, of excellence, of the fullest realization of human powers', the latter 'lays down the basic rules without which an ordered society is impossible'.[111] It is the morality of duty, rather than the morality of aspiration, says Fuller, that provides us with 'workable standards of judgment in law'.[112] For, 'there is no way open to us by which we can compel a man to live the life of reason. We can only seek to exclude from this life the grosser and more obvious manifestations of chance and irrationality'.[113] Thus, given law's aim of ordering social life and the limits of what can be achieved by legal means, it seems that we must turn to deontic concepts in order to provide an account of the standards of epistemic responsibility that should govern legal decision-making.

However, there are some reasons why, I would argue, an aretaic approach to legal decision-maker's epistemic responsibility is preferable. First, virtue concepts have the advantage of greater richness than deontic concepts. Bernard Williams' well-known distinction between 'thin' and 'thick' concepts is to the point here.[114] Unlike deontic concepts, virtue concepts are 'thick' in Williams's sense and they convey not merely a negative or positive epistemic evaluation, but indicate the way in which the epistemic agent acted properly or improperly. Secondly, a virtue approach does not (implausibly) reduce good epistemic practice to rule-following. Just as there does not seem to be any complete set of rules sufficient to give a determinate answer to the question of what one should do in a particular situation of moral choice, epistemic evaluation does not seem to be strictly rule-governed either. Third, virtue approaches to epistemology are in a better position than deontological ones to give an account of epistemic values such as wisdom, insight or understanding, which are surely critical in the context of legal decision-making. Last, virtue epistemology allows us to put forward an ideal of the legal agent according to which legal decision-makers do not merely aspire to avoid prohibited epistemic conduct, but they aim to engage in epistemically valuable conduct. Thus, an aretaic approach to epistemology has some distinctive advantages over a deontic one.[115] In light of these reasons, virtue epistemology,

[111] See Fuller (1969: 5).
[112] Fuller (1969: 9).
[113] ibid.
[114] B Williams ((1985: 128–30, 140–42, and 150–52).
[115] See Zagzebski (1996: 15–29), for an interesting discussion of some advantages of virtue theories in both epistemology and ethics.

I would argue, provides us with an adequate framework for analysing the standards of epistemic responsibility of legal decision-makers.[116]

This is not to say that duties are irrelevant for determining whether a legal decision-maker has behaved in an epistemically responsible way. It is unnecessary, I believe, to make an explicit reference to the notion of duty when defining the standards of epistemic responsibility because it goes without saying that an epistemically virtuous agent would, in most cases, comply impeccably with her epistemic duties—although, given that she is a virtuous agent, she will know, when, in light of the particular circumstances of the case, the applicability of the rule that imposes duties should be, exceptionally, called into question. In this sense, the language of duties is redundant.[117] But from this it does not follow that duties cannot play any significant role in a virtue-based theory of epistemic responsibility. A distinction, by Michelon, between 'strong' and 'weak' versions of virtue theory is helpful for clarifying the sense in which there is room for duties within an aretaic approach to the standards of epistemic responsibility.[118] According to the 'strong version', virtue theory is incompatible with assigning any value to the concept of duty. In contrast, the 'weak' version of virtue theory claims that, while deontic concepts are derivative from virtue concepts, it is nonetheless useful to identify and use the relevant set of epistemological duties. The version defended here is weak in this sense. Notions of duty may play several important roles in an aretaic theory of epistemic responsibility for legal decision-makers. First, they might help legal decision-makers identify the kind of epistemic behaviour that they are expected to exhibit. Second, when epistemic duties are stated in legal rules, they importantly constrain legal decision-makers' epistemic behaviour, for fidelity to law is, to be sure, a core virtue in any plausible account of virtuous behaviour in the context of legal reasoning. Last, the language of duties may also positively contribute to the process whereby legal decision-makers acquire

[116] Alternatively, one could endorse an irenic approach to the standards of epistemic responsibility, which combines deontic and aretaic elements. On this view, legal decision-makers are epistemically responsible to the extent that they both comply with certain epistemological duties and exercise a number of intellectual virtues. I have defended such a view before (see Amaya ((2011a) and (2013))). Or one could also make virtues derivative of duties. One way this could be done is by appealing to a duty to 'behave in ways that will maximize the person's number of true beliefs and minimize that person's number of false beliefs' (Feldman (2002: 372)). On this view, epistemic duties are expanded so as to include behaviours that have a long-term effect on the character of beliefs. These behaviours include, most importantly, one would say, the cultivation and exercise of intellectual virtues.

[117] See Statman (1997: 6).

[118] See Michelon (2011a). The distinction between weak and strong versions of virtue theory is similar to the distinction between reductionist versions of virtue theory and replacement versions (Watson: 1997). Louden (1997) has argued against the thesis of the explanatory primacy of virtue that underscores both versions of virtue theory, ie the claim that right action should be explained in virtue terms, and argued that notions of virtue should be combined with irreducible notions of duty.

the intellectual virtues. Hence, by explaining the standards of epistemic responsibility that ought to govern legal decision-making in aretaic terms, I do not intend to deny the central role that epistemic duties may play in a theory of legal justification.[119]

## B. Responsibilism: Causal and Counterfactual

I have argued that virtue-based standards of epistemic responsibility ought to figure in the coherentist analysis of legal justification. Now, it is critical to note that the responsibilist account of legal justification proposed here is 'counterfactual' rather than 'causal'. A causal version would say that a legal decision is justified if it is the outcome of epistemically responsible coherence-based reasoning. In contrast, the counterfactual version states that a decision is justified if it *could* be the outcome of epistemically responsible coherence-based reasoning. Thus, the counterfactual version allows for the possibility that a legal decision be justified, provided that an epistemically responsible legal decision-maker could have accepted it as justified, even if it results from an irresponsible process of coherence maximization.[120] This is important if we want to preserve, as we most certainly should, the crucial distinction between 'normative' reasons and 'explanatory' reasons, that is to say, the distinction between the reasons that support a decision and the reasons that explain why a particular decision was taken.[121] That a right legal decision was taken for the wrong reasons does not in the least reduce its correctness. For instance, a legal decision to provide compensation for physical injury caused by driving under the influence of alcohol might be correct even if the decision itself was motivated by the judge's disgust at alcohol consumption rather than by a careful assessment of the facts of the case and the applicable rules. Of course, a judge who takes the right decision for the wrong reasons is not praiseworthy for doing it. Indeed, a judge who takes a decision based on revulsion at the defendant deserves criticism. But this does not imply in any way the incorrectness of the decision, which might well be justified, in light of the evidence available and the principles regulating compensation for physical injury.

This does not amount to saying that it is indifferent whether legal decision-makers take their decisions for the right reasons. To be sure, there is something amiss in a right legal decision which has been taken for the wrong reasons. We expect legal decision-makers to be properly motivated, and it is certainly desirable that the justifications they offer for their decisions are not merely a rationalization aimed at making them publicly

[119] On the role of rules in a virtue approach to legal reasoning, see Amaya (2011b).
[120] See Amaya (2011a).
[121] See N MacCormick (2008: 6–12).

acceptable. But from this it does not follow that the normative and the explanatory reasons for a legal decision are indistinguishable. The rightness of a legal decision is a function of the former, but not of the latter. The causal version, however, makes the justification of a legal decision (wrongly) depend on the psychological process whereby such a decision was taken.[122] Thus, this theory fails to distinguish the conditions under which a legal decision is justified from the conditions under which a legal decision-maker is justified in taking a decision.

To sum up, I have argued that legal justification is a matter of optimal coherence. That is, a belief about the facts under dispute or about the law is justified if it could be the result of epistemically responsible coherence-based reasoning. On this approach to the justification of evidentiary and normative judgments in law, justification is the product of the effort of the decision-maker who strives after coherence in an epistemically responsible way. But, one may ask, how much evidence seeking is necessary for epistemically responsible legal decision-making? How many alternatives are relevant and ought to be properly considered in the legal setting? And when is the best alternative good enough for the purposes of legal justification? Without an answer to these questions the proposed account of legal justification remains hopelessly vague. The suggestion that I want to pursue is that due attention to context gives us an answer to the foregoing questions. What qualifies as epistemically responsible behaviour, and thus, the severity of our standards of legal justification, depends in an important sense, I shall argue, on a number of contextual factors. Thus, the claim is that contextual factors determine the appropriate level of care, and thus, determine whether one is justified in accepting a particular factual or interpretative hypothesis as the basis of one's legal decision. A defence of this claim is the target of the next section.

## VI. COHERENCE IN CONTEXT

So far I have explored in some detail three main components of the coherence theory of legal justification I am arguing for, to wit, a conception of legal coherence as constraint satisfaction, a description of the dynamics of legal justification in terms of inference to the best explanation and a view of legal justification as optimal coherence, which required unfolding an account of epistemic responsibility for legal decision-makers. In sum, I have claimed that a belief about what the law requires on a particular issue and what the facts under dispute are in a particular case is justified if it could be the outcome of epistemically responsible coherence-based reasoning.

122 For a defence of the view that legal justification does not merely demand deciding *in accordance with* virtue, but rather it requires deciding *from* virtue, see Solum (2003).

A main issue that needs to be considered at this point is that of spelling out the conditions under which the coherentist standard of justification that I have articulated above is satisfied. In other words, until now I have been concerned with identifying the relevant standard of legal justification, but I have not dealt with the issue of how severe this standard should be. In this section, I propose to address the issue of what counts as an adequate justification under the coherentist view. There are three dimensions along which coherence-based standards of legal justification may be raised or lowered, to wit, the threshold of coherence required for justification; the conditions for membership of the contrast set; and the size of the base of coherence. Thus, fixing the severity of the coherentist standards of legal justification requires that the following questions be addressed: (i) What are the minimal conditions that need to be met in order to satisfy the coherentist standards of legal justification? That is, when is the most coherent of a number of alternatives good enough for the purposes of legal justification? (ii) How many alternatives do legal decision-makers need to check in order to live up to the standards of epistemic responsibility the satisfaction of which is a condition of legal justification? and (iii) How broad should the base of coherence be so that coherence with it yields legal justification?

I would like to suggest that taking due notice of 'context', in the way recommended by contextualist theories of epistemic justification, is a successful strategy for answering the foregoing questions. As explained in chapter three, the key contextualist insight is that the severity of the standards of justification varies with context. Contextualism is neutral as to the analysis of justification. There is, thus, room for a 'contextualized' version of different accounts of justification. A contextualized version of the coherentist standard of legal justification that I have proposed would state that the threshold of coherence, the constitution of the contrast set and the size of the base of coherence shift with context. Let us now see specifically which features of context are relevant for the justification of normative and evidentiary judgments in law and how they fix the severity of coherentist standards of justification.

## A. The Context of Legal Justification

The following contextual factors, I would argue, have a bearing on legal justification—this list is intended to be merely indicative, rather than exhaustive.[123]

[123] For some attempts in the direction of providing a precise account of the contextual factors that are relevant to justification, see Dretske (1981: 373ff); Lewis (1996); and M Williams (2001: 159–74). For a discussion of a number of alternative ways in which the notion of relevance may be understood, see Vogel (1999: 163–68) and Sosa (2004).

i. *The stakes.* Importance plays a chief role in fixing the severity of the standards of justification. When the costs of being wrong are very high, a stricter standard of justification is in order.[124] For instance, in most legal systems, the standards of justification are raised in cases that involve serious criminal offences.

ii. *The role.* Expertise and one's occupation also determine the 'level of scrutiny', as Fogelin likes to put it, which is appropriate in a particular context of justification.[125] For example, the range of alternative explanations that ought to be considered in constitutional adjudication is much broader than the set of alternatives that is necessary to examine at trial level. Whereas a lower court may properly ignore some interpretative possibilities that require a substantial revision of the settled interpretation of a body of precedent, considering such possibilities is appropriate and indeed required for justification in the context of constitutional adjudication.

iii. *Goals.* There are various goals that might be relevant in a particular context of legal justification and relative to which a particular decision or belief might be properly characterized as justified.[126] For instance, a non-guilty verdict may be justified in light of the goals of adjudication (which provide the rationale for rules that make inadmissible what would otherwise be relevant evidence), while a belief in the guilt of the defendant might well be justified in a context in which, unlike the legal one, the only goal were the acquisition of true beliefs.

iv. *Resources.* The level of scrutiny that is reasonable in a particular context depends on the resources available. For example, time severely constrains the range of relevant alternatives that judges may consider when solving a particular case, unlike the range of alternatives that it may be possible to consider in the context of legal or moral theorizing.

v. *Methodological constraints.* Standards of justification are importantly affected by the kind of inquiry that we are engaged in. What is at stake here, as Williams puts it, is not so much the 'level' of scrutiny as the 'angle' of scrutiny. He writes: 'Within the practice of doing history, we can be more or less strict in our standards of evidence. But some questions have to be set aside for us to think historically at all'.[127] Similarly, the fact that a question of *legal* justification is being raised constrains the range of alternatives that ought to be seriously considered. The following example by Sinnott-Armstrong vividly illustrates

[124] The relevance of the importance of being right about a certain matter for the severity of the standards of justification has been often pointed out in the contextualist literature; see Timmons (1999: 211); Annis (1978: 215); Fogelin (2000: 48); Lewis (1996: 556); and M Williams (2001: 161). *Cf* Dretske (1981: 375).

[125] Fogelin (2003: 102).

[126] See Timmons (1999: 192–93).

[127] M Williams (2001: 160). See also M Williams (2000: 84).

the point: 'Suppose that a desperate defence attorney argues, 'Perhaps we are all deceived by a demon'. Surely the judge and jury could attend to this statement and yet properly ignore it by not letting it affect their belief in the defendant's guilt'.[128] While the possibility that we are all deceived by a demon is surely a relevant possibility that ought to be taken seriously in the context of epistemological inquiry, it can be properly ignored in the forensic context.

vi. *Dialectical features.* Justificatory practices take place in a dialectical context that constrains what may be taken for granted and what, to the contrary, is a relevant alternative that needs to be ruled out for one's claim to be justified. The fact of mentioning or raising a possible defeator triggers a higher level of scrutiny. For example, an expert testimony may not be taken at face value as soon as doubts are raised about the credibility of the expert. The extent to which dialectical features of the context are relevant for setting the severity of the standards of justification is a controversial issue. According to some philosophers, mentioning a possible defeater to one's claim, no matter how remote, raises the standards of justification.[129] More plausibly, other philosophers hold that only those alternatives which we have some reason to believe that they obtain or at least some positive reason to doubt that are false are relevant in a particular context.[130]

The foregoing contextual factors constrain the degree of coherence that may be required for legal justification, the number of alternatives that one must consider in order to be justified, as well as the size of the justificatory set. In this way, context helps to fix what counts as justified by the coherentist standards of legal justification. Contextual mechanisms set the severity of these standards by both raising and lowering these standards as appropriate in a particular context.[131] On the one hand, features of the context impose a 'lower limit' to what we may count as coherent and, thus, as legally justified. On the other hand, contextual features also impose an 'upper limit' to how much coherence is required for legal justification, how many alternatives are relevant and how many elements ought to be included in the base of coherence. Hence, it is crucial to notice that context does not only help us to ensure that we do not *under*consider alternatives, but

[128] Sinnott-Armstrong (2002: 76).

[129] See eg Lewis (1996: 559).

[130] This view has its roots in Peirce's writings, and it also enjoys some popularity now, particularly among the advocates of 'inferential' views of contextualism; see Annis (1978: 214) and M Williams (2001: 161).

[131] It is worth noticing that, as DeRose says, contextualists have concentrated 'on discerning the mechanisms by which epistemic standards are raised ... and have not worried much about how standards can be lowered' (2004: 8).

also that we do not *over*consider alternatives.[132] A contextualist approach secures that we do no less but also no more than what is required for justification in a particular context.

## B. Contextualizing the Coherentist Standards of Justification

I turn now to examine how taking context into account can help us tackle the issues that the coherentist account of legal justification that I sketched above prompt us to consider, to recall, what counts as coherent enough for the purposes of legal justification; what are the members of the contrast set—that is, the set of alternatives such that inferring to the most coherent of them yields legal justification; and, how the base of coherence is individuated. I shall refer to these problems as the 'problem of minimal coherence', the 'problem of the contrast set' and the 'problem of the base', respectively.

### *i. The Problem of Minimal Coherence*

On a contextualist approach to the standards of coherentist justification, the degree of coherence that is sufficient for legal justification depends on context. As a matter of fact, the contextualist insight that the threshold of justification is context-dependent is already deeply embedded in the legal culture. Consider, for example, the standards of proof. The threshold of justification of decisions in civil proceedings is typically lower than what is required for justification in a criminal proceeding. Furthermore, the severity of the standards of justification also varies with the seriousness of the

[132] Now, while the reasons for ensuring that we do not underconsider alternatives are pretty obvious, it may not be immediately clear why we should be concerned with not overconsidering alternatives. The rationale which explains why overconsideration should be a problem is, I would suggest, an economic one. Given our limited cognitive resources, as well as time constraints, we have an interest in avoiding doing extra work which is not needed for the justificatory task at hand. These constraints are particularly visible in the context of legal justification, in which time limits are stricter than in other kinds of inquiry, and in which there is a clear interest in maximizing the use of the institutional resources available. Fogelin has also considered the economic dimension of the standards of epistemic justification when he speaks of 'epistemic transaction costs', ie costs which are involved in raising a level of scrutiny. These costs, he says, like most costs, we prefer not to incur and thus, he recommends, we should not raise the level of scrutiny in the absence of a particular reason to do so (see Fogelin (2003: 123–24)).

In addition, it could be argued that, given that standards of justification are context-bound, there is a sense in which, setting aside economic considerations, not every raise of the standards may be seen as 'reasonable'. That is, even if we had unlimited resources, it seems unreasonable to require that the hypothesis that, for instance, we are all brains in a vat, be ruled out for a belief about the identity of the perpetrator in a criminal trial to be justified. DeRose briefly comments upon the view (which he rejects) according to which there are some reasonable standards for evaluating epistemic claims in a particular conversational context in (2004: 13).

criminal offence.[133] This legal practice may be easily explained within a contextualist framework. The importance of being right and the costs of being wrong have a momentous influence in setting the threshold of justification. Under a coherentist approach to justification, this means that the threshold-setting mechanisms that determine what is minimally coherent are context-dependent. A particular account of the facts under dispute may be coherent enough to justify finding for the plaintiff in a civil case, while it falls below the threshold of coherence required to find against the defendant in a criminal case—as it was the case, for example, in the OJ Simpson trials, discussed in chapter four.

### *ii. The Problem of the Contrast Set*

The contrast set from which coherence reasoning proceeds is also a matter that depends on features of the context. For instance, dialectical constraints shape the contrast set by making some alternatives salient and making it proper for the legal decision-maker to exclude some alternatives from consideration. Consider again the testimony of John in a case of murder, reported in chapter three. To recall, John takes the witness stand and testifies that he saw Alice killing George. The possibility that John was hallucinating that Alice killed George is a possibility that the fact-finder may indeed properly exclude from the contrast set. However, once the defence attorney claims that, at the moment of the crime, John was under the effects of a drug which may cause hallucinations as a side-effect, this possibility becomes a relevant possibility—as long as there is some positive reason to believe that it might obtain—that needs to be included within the contrast set. An analogous point may be made with regard to the constitution of the contrast set in legal reasoning about norms. Interpretative possibilities that are excluded from consideration in a particular context of justification may become relevant—and thus part of the contrast set—by way of being proposed by one of the parties.

### *iii. The Problem of the Base*

The domain within which coherence ought to be sought is also dependent on contextual factors. For instance, at trial level, it may be sufficient for a base to be justification-conferring that it include the relevant precedents and statutes which belong to the same area of the law as the case under consideration. But in the kind of hard cases which typically face higher courts, and the decision of which is likely to severely affect the parties involved in ways that cannot be remedied later in the process, the domain

[133] See Lillquist (2002–03: 85).

within which coherence ought to be sought needs to be expanded. That is to say, the base of coherence broadens as the stakes of the case go higher. Contextual factors also contribute to the constitution of the base by requiring that some elements be included and that they be attributed a special weight in the coherence calculation. For instance, as argued before, reasons from authority enjoy a privilege status within the set of elements from which coherentist reasoning proceeds in the context of legal justification. Methodological constraints explain why this should be so. Not to give a special weight to these reasons would amount to changing the nature of the inquiry altogether. As Peczenik succinctly puts it, the relevance of reasons from authority is taken for granted as soon as one decides to argue from the legal point of view, that is, to be engaged in *legal* reasoning as opposed to other kinds of reasoning.[134]

To sum up, it is a main contextualist tenet that the severity of standards of justification varies with context. Coherentist standards of legal justification may be raised or lowered in three ways: by lowering or raising the degree of coherence that is required for justification; by expanding or contracting the range of relevant alternatives; and by augmenting or reducing the size of the base of coherence. Contextual features—I have argued—help fix the threshold of coherence, the criteria for membership of the contrast set and the domain of coherence. The contextualization of the coherentist standards of justification is the fourth—and last—of the main components of the coherence theory of legal justification proposed here. We are now in a position to provide a succinct statement of the main tenet of this theory:

> A belief about the law or the facts is justified if and only if it is optimally coherent, that is to say, if it is a belief that an epistemically responsible legal decision-maker might hold by virtue of its coherence in like circumstances.

I proceed now to examine how this model deals with some of the objections which, I have argued, saddle current coherence theories of legal justification.

## VII. THE PROBLEMS OF COHERENTISM REVISITED

I have identified earlier in this chapter five problem areas for current coherence-based accounts of legal reasoning. How does the model of coherence that I have articulated above deal with these problems? As I argued before, these problems are but particular applications to the legal context of traditional objections that have been raised against coherence theories of justification which have a longer ancestry, such as coherence theories of epistemic justification. With the aid of what we have learned in the process of surveying the coherence theories of justification that have been proposed

[134] Peczenik (1992: 147).

in domains other than law, let us now examine the prospects of meeting these objections for the proposed coherence theory of legal justification.

### A. The Problem of Vagueness

Unlike other coherentist theories of legal justification, the model that I have articulated above is based on a precise notion of coherence as constraint satisfaction. In contrast to the notion of narrative coherence upon which coherentist approaches to evidential reasoning in law rely, a notion of factual coherence as constraint satisfaction provides a set of clear criteria against which the relative coherence of alternative theories of the case may be measured. Theories of normative coherence, as much as coherence-based theories of fact reasoning in law, rely on notions of coherence that are poorly specified. The notion of normative coherence as constraint satisfaction puts a remedy to this state of affairs by setting up a number of principles for comparing and evaluating the different theories of law that compete for providing a solution to a particular legal problem.[135]

### B. Two Challenges to the Structure of Coherentist Justification: Circularity and Conservatism

There are two main problems that a coherence-based account of legal inference gives rise to: the problem of circularity and the problem of conservatism. A coherence-based theory of legal reasoning—such as the one articulated above—needs to show that coherence-based inference is not viciously circular and that it is not inherently conservative. Let us take up each of these challenges in turn.

The problem of circularity only arises if one accepts a linear account of inference according to which justification involves a chain of beliefs along which justification is transferred from one element to another one down the chain. But there is no reason why a coherence theory of legal justification should burden itself with such a view. As I argued in chapter three, advocates of coherence theories of epistemic justification have shown that once we replace a linear view of inference with a holistic one, the circularity involved in coherentism may be shown to be benign. The model proposed rests on such a holistic view of inference in that—as the principle of acceptability says—the justificatory status of any element depends on its coherence with the rest of the elements in the set. In addition, the model assumes that relations of coherence are symmetrical, and thus that two

[135] *Cf* Pethick (2014: 131–35) (arguing that the constraint satisfaction approach to legal coherence developed here does not overcome the problem of vagueness insofar as it fails to distinguish between the intension and the extension of coherence).

elements which cohere with one another are mutually interdependent, not that one is inferred from the other. In this way, a theory of legal coherence as constraint satisfaction avoids the problem of circularity that is endemic to coherence theories in law.[136] The theory does not justify the acceptance of a particular principle on the grounds that it coheres best with a set of rules, and then justifies a decision based on one of these rules because it coheres best with this very same principle. The theory does not license either an inference from a piece of evidence to the hypothesis that best explains it, and then an inference from that hypothesis to the very same piece of evidence on the grounds that it is best explained by this hypothesis. Rather, the theory shows how the acceptance of interpretative and factual hypotheses, normative elements and evidence depends on their coherence with the rest of the elements, and how explanatory hypotheses and evidence, on the one hand, and interpretative hypotheses and normative elements, on the other, mutually support each other.

This theory of legal coherence also allows us to put worries about conservatism to rest. In the context of fact-reasoning in law, the risk is that, while seeking coherence, legal fact-finders may not give evidence its due: they may reinterpret evidence so that it best coheres with the factual hypothesis that is being favoured, or even blatantly disregard evidence that does not fit with such a hypothesis. However, this risk is averted because, as the principle of data priority states, the model gives priority to the evidence at trial over the rest of the elements which enter into the coherence calculation. It is, of course, still possible that evidence be discarded, if doing so maximizes the coherence of the whole set. But this is as it should be: after all, there are occasionally good reasons for doubting the reliability of the evidence offered at trial. However, the theory of coherence ensures that, unless coherence overwhelmingly requires the rejection of evidence, evidence at trial will be accepted and, thus, that it will have a momentous role in determining which hypothesis about the facts under dispute we may accept as justified. In the context of normative reasoning, this theory gives priority to propositions that describe reasons from authority. In so doing—it might be argued—it sanctions a conservative tendency and prevents genuine normative change. Let me make two comments by way of a reply. To be sure, coherence-based reasoning is conservative in that it makes fit with the body of authoritative materials an important condition of justification. Now, it is a distinctive feature of legal reasoning that reasons from authority enjoy a privileged status. Indeed, to give priority to reasons from authority is part and parcel of what it means to be engaged in 'legal' reasoning in the first place. Thus, it cannot be a problem for a coherence theory that it recognize the prominent role that such reasons play when justifying normative conclusions in

[136] *Cf* Redondo (2011).

law. But, of course, it is also desirable that a theory of reasoning allow for normative change when necessary. The theory of coherence does recognize this need in that it permits that reasons from authority be rejected when doing so significantly increases the coherence of the overall set of reasons. Thus, this theory exhibits a moderate kind of conservatism which is, I believe, a distinctive characteristic of our practices of legal justification.

## C. The Problems of Holism

I argued before that the holistic commitment of coherence theories in law gives rise to serious problems. More specifically, it threatens the descriptive adequacy of coherence theories of legal reasoning; sheds doubts over their psychological plausibility; and undermines their normative force.[137] The coherence theory that I have articulated above overcomes these problems by embracing a contextualist approach to the standards of legal justification. Under this view, the set of beliefs over which the coherence calculation proceeds is not taken to be the whole system of one's beliefs, but rather a subset that is shown to be relevant in the particular context. Features of the context—such as the costs of being wrong, one's institutional role, or the resources available—determine the appropriate size of the domain within which coherence is to be sought in a particular instance of legal justification. This contextual strategy for individuating the base of coherence, brings the model of coherence closer to what legal decision-makers are able to achieve, given their cognitive resources; improves the descriptive adequacy of the theory of coherence in that it better portrays the reasoning processes whereby justified decisions are reached in the legal context; and, last, dissipates some of the normative worries that have been raised against coherence models in law, insofar as it makes the justification of any belief about the law or the facts depend exclusively on the coherence of a relevant subset of beliefs.

## D. What is Coherence-based Inference?

One of the main elements of the model of coherence for law that I have argued for before is a view of coherence-based legal inference as an inference to the best explanation. Under this view, legal decision-makers generate a number of plausible candidates (theories of the case and theories of the law) and then select, among them, the one that best satisfies the coherence

[137] For a discussion of these problems in the context of epistemic reasoning, see ch 3.

standards.[138] While, to be sure, there is much more work to be done to elucidate the mechanics of explanatory inference (and much more needs to be said about how inferences to the best explanation confer warrant upon their conclusions), the model of inference to the best explanation provides a detailed enough description of the way in which coherence-driven inference in law works. Thus, the reasoning processes whereby we seek coherence in law no longer seem mysterious, but particular instances of recognizable patterns of explanatory reasoning. As a result, the purported advantage of probabilistic views of factual inference in law and of rule-based accounts of legal reasoning about disputed questions of law over coherence-based models on the grounds that the latter lack a clear view of the inference patterns that lead to justified legal conclusions evaporates.

### E. The Value of Coherence

A defence of a coherence-based account of legal inference must give an answer to the question of why coherence should be sought after in the legal context in the first place. Given the problems concerning the relationship between coherence and truth, it cannot be taken for granted that coherence is a value that should be pursued when reasoning in law. Quite the contrary. If—as is generally assumed—a defence of the justificatory force of coherence requires an argument to the effect that coherence is truth-conducive, and given that no conclusive argument of this sort seems to be within sight, the question of why we should accept conclusions in law by virtue of their coherence is a pressing one. The problem of truth and related problems—to recall, the problem of coherence ties and the problem of isolation—need to be addressed before certifying the viability of a coherence theory of legal reasoning. Tackling these issues requires us to engage in a second-order debate: the problems do not concern the definition of justification in terms of coherence, but they derive from a demand for reasons why coherentist standards of legal justification should be accepted in the first place. The next section attempts to satisfy this demand by suggesting some ways in which the value of coherence in law may be defended.

## VIII. THE REASONS FOR COHERENCE

Why does coherence justify in law? Why should one endorse a coherentist standard for the justification of normative and factual propositions in law? The adequacy of coherentist standards of justification is often called into

[138] *Cf* Redondo (2011) (arguing that explanatory coherentism fails to describe accurately the legal inferential practice). For a reply, see Amaya (2011c).

question by raising doubts about their truth-conduciveness. The strategy of the critic of coherence methods is as follows: it is first claimed that a defence of a theory of justification must show that accepting beliefs as justified according to the theory leads one to accept beliefs which are likely to be true; next, it is argued that it has not been shown that coherence and truth are related in a proper way; hence, it is concluded, a defence of the coherentist standards of justification is doomed to failure. As I argued in chapters six and eight, this strategy does not succeed in undermining the coherentist project because a thorough defence of the viability of a theory of justification does not depend—as the critic assumes—on showing the theory to be truth-conducive. While, to be sure, truth-conduciveness is a crucial standard for assessing the adequacy of a theory of justification, there are also other criteria that are relevant for evaluating a particular theory of justification. For one, even if truth is a momentous value when reasoning about both what to believe and what to do, we are also interested in achieving, in our reasonings, values other than truth, and, as long as this is so, the adequacy of a theory of justification will depend on how well it helps us realize the complex set of goals—truth included—that we aim at advancing in a particular domain. In what follows I shall suggest some lines of argument for supporting a coherence theory of justification for law.

### A. The Argument from Anti-Foundationalism

The first reason for endorsing a coherentist standard for legal justification is a negative one, to wit, the enormous difficulties that the foundationalist view of justification encounters. As has been shown in earlier chapters, foundationalist theories of both moral and epistemic justification face severe objections. Similarly, the foundationalist view of justification that characterizes strong versions of legal positivism is in a serious predicament. And the failure of foundationalist epistemologies carries over foundationalist approaches to evidence and proof in law as well. The problems that foundationalism in its many varieties and in different domains faces make the coherentist alternative initially attractive, even if, of course, a full defence of coherentism requires that some positive reasons be given for its desirability.

### B. Coherence and Emotion

Reasoning about both what to do and what to believe is a hot cognitive process as much in law as in any other domain. In this work, I have not examined in detail the issue of the role of emotions in legal reasoning about both facts and norms. However, at various points in previous chapters,

I have emphasized the emotional side of practical and theoretical judgements as well as the importance of emotions in legal reasoning.[139] A complete theory of legal reasoning, I have argued, needs to give an account of the role that emotions play in reasoning about both disputed questions of fact and disputed questions of law. As has been explained, some advocates of coherence theories have shown how emotions may be incorporated within their theories.[140] Most prominently, Thagard has articulated in detail a coherence theory for the justification of empirical and ethical judgements that integrates the role that cognition and emotion play in forming and justifying empirical and moral beliefs.[141] Recently, some recent studies have shown that coherence-based reasoning can be extended to encompass hot cognitions.[142] Because relations of coherence (and incoherence) are not restricted to propositional elements, and because judgements of coherence (and incoherence) are sensitive to emotional responses, a coherence theory is better located than alternative theories to give an account of the role that emotions play in justification. This gives an important advantage to coherence theories of legal justification over alternative views of justification which are less easily amendable to make room for the 'hot' components of legal reasoning.

### C. The Argument from Psychological Plausibility

Our cognitive equipment is geared towards coherence. There is substantial psychological evidence that shows the relevance of coherence in our reasoning processes, some of which I have reviewed in previous chapters.[143] Empirical studies strongly suggest that that we find explanatory thinking natural: explanatory considerations are the engine that drives much inference in ordinary life.[144] Moravski has persuasively argued that cognition can be viewed as an activity that is directed towards the goal of achieving understanding, and that humans may be seen, in an important sense, as *homo explanans*.[145] Simon and collaborators have shown that complex decision tasks, such as judicial reasoning as well as reasoning about evidence, are carried out by building up coherence among a number of

[139] See chs 4, 7 and 9.

[140] See eg Richardson's theory of practical reasoning and DePaul's theory of moral reasoning in chs 7 and 8, respectively.

[141] See chs 4 and 8.

[142] Simon, Stenstrom and Read (forthcoming).

[143] See especially ch 2.

[144] Lipton has interpreted Kahneman and Tversky's well-known results as indicating the presence of a strong proclivity to explanatory thinking, see Lipton (2004: 108–13).

[145] See Moravcsik (1990: 213).

decision factors.[146] In the context of legal fact-finding, these results support previous work by Hastie and Pennington that showed the relevance of coherence standards in jurors' reasonings.[147] That coherence plays an important role in the formation and evaluation of factual hypotheses in law has also been shown, in the context of criminal law, by Wagenaar and collaborators.[148] All the foregoing studies—among others—provide the coherence theory of justification with a solid empirical basis. Despite the fact that, as I have argued, some concerns may be raised, given our cognitive limitations, about the feasibility of the process of coherentist justification as is portrayed in some coherence theories, the coherence theory of justification has a strong claim to psychological plausibility. The fact that this is so is an important reason for preferring a coherence theory of legal reasoning over competing views on reasoning which have been shown to fare badly as descriptions of our inferential practices such as, for instance, Bayesianism. First, from the perspective of naturalism, it is a requirement of any theory of justification that it does not set up normative standards that we are not even able to approximate. Facts about how we reason have a bearing—under this view—on questions about how we ought to reason. The coherence theory of legal reasoning seems to satisfactorily meet this naturalistic constraint. Secondly, a theory of legal reasoning is expected to guide legal decision-makers in realizing their task. The coherence theory, insofar as it builds upon legal decision-makers' natural reasoning processes, seems more apt to perform this guiding role. Thus, the psychological plausibility of the coherence theory of legal justification is an important reason for endorsing this theory.

### D. The Argument from the Dynamics of Justification

It is an advantage of the coherence theory that, unlike other models of justification, it has the resources to give an account of the dynamic aspects of justification.[149] In earlier chapters, we have seen how coherence accounts of justification allow us to model major conceptual changes, such as those involved in scientific revolutions, as well as piecemeal revisions in one's system of beliefs, like those formalized by belief revision theories.[150] As opposed to the static view of justification that the foundationalist model of justification assumes, coherence theories are congenial to a dynamic view of justification. In law, questions about how legal decision-makers

[146] See ch 2.
[147] See ch 2.
[148] See ch 2.
[149] See Haack (2000).
[150] See chs 4 and 5.

evaluate incoming new evidence and change their explanatory account of the facts under dispute accordingly, and issues about how they assess the relative goodness of alternative interpretations about what the law requires in the particular case and integrate them into their accepted views about the law are, indeed, important questions. These questions, I submit, may be profitably addressed within the framework of a coherence theory of legal justification.

### E. The Epistemic Value of Coherence

To be sure, even if, as I have said, a defence of a method of justification does not depend exclusively on having conclusive reasons for its truth-conduciveness, still, an argument to the effect that justified beliefs, according to the method, are also likely to be true is an important part of such a defence. How does the coherence theory of justification fare with regard to the goal of truth? As we have seen, none of the arguments that have been designed to show that coherence and truth are related in the right way have succeeded in putting worries about the truth-conduciveness of coherence to rest. However, the case for the truth-conduciveness of coherence is not hopeless.

The first thing to note is that foundationalism has not been able either to meet the sceptical challenge that, for all we know, our body of justified beliefs might well turn out to be comprehensibly false. In this sense, coherentism is not worse off than its main competitor. Secondly, it is important to notice that coherence-based reasoning is a defeasible form of inference. Thus, by its nature, it is not a form of inference that is guaranteed to yield true beliefs. To require that it be shown that by accepting beliefs on grounds of their coherence we can be sure to accept beliefs which are also likely to be true is to ignore the defeasible character of coherence-based inference. Thirdly, given Hume's problem, we are deprived of any reason—it may be claimed—for taking coherence-based inference to be truth-topic. For an argument to the effect that coherence-based inference—as a kind of non-deductive inference—is truth-conducive would be a non-deductive argument, and therefore would beg the question. However, this is hardly a distinctive problem for coherentism. The project of grounding the edifice of knowledge on a set of secure beliefs from which the rest of the beliefs flow deductively is not viable. Appealing to non-deductive methods in order to justify our beliefs is, thus, unavoidable. Of course, in the absence of a response to Hume's problem, coherence methods cannot be ensured to yield true beliefs, but neither can any other theory of justification that resorts—as cannot be otherwise—to non-demonstrative or defeasible forms of reasoning. Now, against this background, I want to argue that, leaving radical sceptical worries aside, the prospects of showing that coherence is properly connected with truth are reasonably good.

In earlier chapters, we have seen that there is an array of different strategies for showing that coherence among empirical beliefs connects up with truth as correspondence in the right way.[151] These strategies provide a useful starting point for mounting an argument to the effect that accepting factual propositions in law by virtue of their coherence is likely to advance the goal of truth. The problem of the truth-conduciveness of coherence is much less acute in the normative domain than in the factual one, given that non-realist accounts of the truth of normative propositions are generally viewed as more plausible than non-realist accounts of the truth of empirical propositions, and that coherentist theories of justification are less problematically combined with non-realist views of truth, than with views of truth as correspondence. Similarly, in law, the task of showing coherence to be truth-conducive is less cumbersome in the context of reasoning about normative conclusions than in the context of reasoning about facts. The problem of coherence and truth is particularly recalcitrant if truth is understood along realist lines, but a realist construal of the truth of propositions of law is highly implausible. Thus, the problems deriving from connecting up coherence with truth do not, in principle, put any serious obstacle to analysing the justification of normative conclusions in law in terms of coherence.

In short, while it cannot be shown that endorsing a coherence theory for the justification of factual and normative propositions in law will never misguide us, for it may certainly lead us to accept beliefs about the facts and the law as justified which are, nevertheless, false or incorrect, there are still good reasons for supporting the desirability of such methods from the perspective of advancing the goal of truth in law. In addition, it is critical to note that the discussion of coherence theories conducted in earlier chapters has brought to light that there are several reasons why coherence is epistemically valuable regardless of their truth-conduciveness. As some proponents of probabilistic approaches to coherence have shown, coherence is conducive to reliability and confirmation and it has an important heuristic value.[152] Coherence has also been claimed to be intrinsically linked to the value of understanding.[153] Thus, there are a number of important epistemic reasons to seek coherence when reasoning in the legal context.

[151] We may bridge the gap between coherence and truth by appealing to an inference to the best explanation, as BonJour and Thagard do, by introducing an externalist element in a coherentist epistemology, as Lehrer suggests, or by forging a conceptual link between coherence and truth via the concept of belief, à la Davidson. For a discussion of these strategies, see chs 3, 4 and 6.

[152] See ch 6.

[153] See ch 9.

## F. The Practical Value of Coherence

Legal institutions are designed to advance a number of different goals, and coherence—I shall argue—is a valuable tool for realizing some of these goals. As some advocates of coherentist approaches to practical reasoning have shown, coherence promotes successful coordination and effectiveness.[154] In the legal context, some degree of coherence is also crucial for coordinating actions, and actions which cohere with each other tend to be more effective as well. Law is a collective enterprise, and legal decision-makers are more likely to succeed in their efforts at coordination if the decisions they make are part of a coherent plan of action. Similarly, law's project of regulating and transforming social life is more likely to work if it embodies a coherent plan than if it involves overlapping goals and conflicting courses of action. Thus, coherence has practical benefits as much in law as in any other practical domain. In addition, coherence aids the realization of values that are distinctive to the legal context. Coherence is instrumental to the value of legal certainty.[155] Among other ways in which coherence promotes legal certainty is by facilitating knowledge of the law, for a coherent body of norms is more easily remembered and understood. And coherence also promotes the efficacy of the legal system, for a coherent body of norms is also easier to be applied and followed.[156] Besides, a certain degree of coherence in legal decision-making at both the legislative and the judicial level is also pivotal for securing the social stability that the law aims to preserve.[157] Thus, there are valuable practical reasons for pursuing coherence in the course of legal decision-making.[158]

## G. The Argument from the Social Function of Coherence

Several researchers in cognitive psychology have argued that coherence has an important social function. People who are not coherent are poorly perceived by others. In contrast, the coherence in one's statements makes it more likely that they will be accepted by others, ie coherence is positively correlated with consensuality. This significantly increases people's confidence, for when people think that their statements are likely to be shared by others, attitude certainty and strength increase. Thus, we have important

[154] See ch 7.

[155] See Pino (1998) s 4 and Moral (2003: 320).

[156] In this sense, we may say that coherence promotes both the 'efficacy' of the legal system (the degree of application of the law) as well as the 'effectiveness' of the legal system (the extent to which the law succeeds in bringing about its goals).

[157] Alexy and Peczenik (1990: 145).

[158] *Cf* McGarry (2013).

incentives to 'look' coherent.[159] More specifically, there is evidence that indicates that coherence evaluation, ie when we represent the coherence of different mental states and draw inferences from it, serves two interrelated functions. First, the evaluation of the coherence of other people's statements is used for 'epistemic vigilance', ie to detect whether there is anything wrong with someone else's statements. And, secondly, given that communicated information is tested by reference to its coherence, we turn coherence evaluation mechanisms on ourselves in order to be perceived as being right.[160]

Now, the social aims of coherence evaluation suggest another important set of reasons for pursuing coherence in legal reasoning: coherence in legal decision-making increases the public acceptability of the decisions;[161] it has a positive impact in the citizens' confidence in the legal system; and it critically contributes to building consensus around issues which are, at times, fairly divisive, as it occurs when courts have to adjudicate in cases that involve matters of fundamental principle. Thus, there are important social benefits associated to the coherence of legal decisions.

## H. The Argument from Conflict Resolution

Law is a complex institution directed towards solving conflict through argumentative means.[162] Conflicts of values are pervasive in law. How to address these conflicts by the force of reason? How may we rationally proceed when the different values that the law aims to protect come into conflict? As I argued when discussing coherence theories of practical reasoning, coherence is of a piece with a non-instrumentalist view of practical reasoning according to which we may rationally deliberate about ends, and not merely about what the best means to achieve some fixed ends are. Some of the coherence-theories of practical inference surveyed in chapter seven provide illuminating accounts of how a coherentist approach to justification guides agents on how to deliberate about what the best course of action in light of a set of conflicting ends is. In law, coherence is also a most valuable guide to deciding among competing decisions about the law and about the facts under dispute in cases of value-conflict. Richardson's coherentist version of specificationism provides us with a fruitful way of addressing

[159] See Kurzban and Aktipis (2007).

[160] See Mercier (2012).

[161] *Cf* Simon and Scurich (2011) (showing that judicial decisions accompanied by monolithic reasoning—multiple one-sided reasoning—are judged as less acceptable than decisions accompanied by multiple two-sided reasoning). It is unclear, however, whether Simon and Scurich's results shed doubts over the persuasive value of coherence. As argued, coherence reasoning—and theorizing—rather than explaining conflict away, provides a way to proceed in the face of conflict. Thus, coherence reasoning need not be monolithic, but it is compatible with admitting to good reasons of both sides.

[162] See Atienza (2006: 59).

normative conflict in law. When two norms or values come into conflict, legal decision-makers may rationally deal with this conflict by specifying them in a way that enhances coherence. And Hurley's view that, when deliberating in the practical domain, judgements about what one should do, all-things-considered, are determined by the most coherent theory of the different values which apply is also extremely useful for understanding how a coherence theory would help deliberate about ends in the legal context. It follows from Hurley's account of deliberation that, when faced with conflict, legal decision-makers ought to take the decision, among competing courses of action, that is dictated by the theory that makes the best sense of the relationships among the conflicting reasons. Therefore, it is not as if, for example, faced with a conflict between legal certainty and justice, at some point a legal decision-maker merely chooses to decide on the basis of either one or the other. Rather, she is to take the decision which is favoured by the best theory that she has been able to construct while deliberating about how the conflicting values at stake are related to one another.

Thus, not only does coherence help us realize truth and other values in law, as I have argued above, but it also helps us reason about how to weigh and balance these values when they come into conflict in a legal case. That is, coherence is not merely instrumental to the ends that the law aims at promoting, but it crucially helps us deliberate about these very ends. In so doing, it expands the space of reason in law by providing a method for reasoning about ends in law, and not only for rationally assessing which, among competing courses of action, is best in promoting a given set of goals that are placed beyond the pale of deliberation. The ability of coherence-based theories to provide guidance about how to deliberate about ends, and thus, to realize law's function of resolving conflict by argumentative means, provides a strong reason in support of legal coherentism.

## I. The Constitutive Value of Coherence

The foregoing considerations about the pervasiveness of conflict in law lead us to consider yet another reason for pursuing legal coherence, namely, its constitutive value. Coherence plays a constitutive role in individual identity and political identity. A certain degree of coherence in individual and collective deliberation is necessary to be both a unified agent and part of a distinctive political community.[163] One may ask: in the face of conflict, why

[163] That coherence has a constitutive value in individual identity has been argued by Richardson, Thagard and Millgram, and, most extensively, by Hurley (see ch 7). I have argued that coherence plays a constitutive role in political communities in Dworkin's theory in ch 1. See also Michelon ((2011b) (arguing that the value of coherence may be grounded in a narrative conception of human life)).

shouldn't one decide upon one of the conflicting values, as opposed to strive after coherence? The reason why this is so is that by deliberating about the values and goals in conflict when deciding a particular issue legal agents are determining their own identity as members of a political community. Individual identity and group identity are not fixed—as Hurley brilliantly argued- but they are the result of self-interpretation.[164] Legal decision-makers are not free to disregard a concern for coherence because in so doing they would be refusing to determine their own identity as members of the political community to which they belong. The constitutive dimension of coherence in individual self-determination and group self-determination gives us a foundational reason for valuing coherence as a guiding standard in legal decision-making.

The preceding arguments, taken together, strongly support the case for pursuing (a certain degree) of coherence in the course of legal reasoning.[165] To be sure, a theory of coherence in law (as much as in any other domain) faces its own set of problems which provides a countervailing set of reasons that militate against legal coherentism. However, while the arguments against coherentism need to be taken seriously, they do not succeed in undermining legal coherentism. I have shown how the proposed version of the coherence theory of legal justification may overcome the problems of coherentism or, at least, mitigate the force of the objections that have been raised against it. Thus, I hope to have shown that, given the reasons that support the coherence theory in law, and given that—as argued—the problems of legal coherentism are not intractable, a theory of legal justification—such as the one proposed—which gives a prominent role to reasons from coherence is on the right track. Before putting an end to this book, I would still like to deal with a last issue, to wit, I want to have a look beyond the restricted domain of the coherence theory in law to the general theory of legal reasoning and rationality to which it pertains. More specifically, I would like to explore the implications of the proposed coherence theory of legal justification for the standard theory of legal reasoning.

## IX. COHERENCE, LEGAL REASONING AND LEGAL THEORY

In the foregoing sections, I have articulated and defended a coherence theory of legal justification. This theory puts forward a picture of legal justification that has the following prominent features. First, legal justification

164 See Hurley (1989).

165 It is critical to note that a certain dose of 'incoherence' is also valuable. The value of incoherence may be recognized from within a coherentist framework—as some proponents of coherentist approaches to practical reasoning have done (see ch 7). For an argument to the effect that some degree of incoherence may also be beneficial in the context of legal reasoning, see Lariguet (2011). On some of the benefits associated to incoherence, see also Haack (2004).

is, under this account, *non-foundationalist* in that it denies that there is any set of propositions which provide the foundation upon which the justification of the rest of factual and normative propositions in law lies. Secondly, this theory embodies a *contextualist* view of legal justification according to which standards for the justification of conclusions about either disputed questions of law or disputed questions of fact are context-dependent. Thirdly, the theory of coherence proposed puts forward a *responsibilist* account of legal justification. Under this view, the standards of behaviour that regulate inquiry and deliberation in the legal context have a bearing on the justificatory status of the resulting legal decisions. Fourthly, this model advocates a *naturalistic* approach to legal justification, that is, it relies on a view about the relationship between normative and descriptive issues according to which facts about how legal decision-makers reason are relevant for answering questions about how they should reason. Fifthly, it takes *explanatory reasoning* to be the main kind of reasoning in the justification of conclusions about disputed questions of fact and disputed questions of law. Last, this version of coherentism rests on a *non-instrumentalist* view of legal reasoning according to which deliberation in the legal context is also of ends.

The picture of legal justification that the coherence theory of justification advances leads us to question some of the assumptions that characterize standard approaches to legal reasoning. In what follows, I shall briefly examine the extent to which the proposed model of justification departs from the picture of justification that is assumed in most current work on legal reasoning and whether it leads us to revise or rethink some of the assumptions upon which the standard view about legal reasoning relies.

### A. Legal Reasoning without Foundations

Coherence theories are non-foundationalist in that they reject that there is any set of either factual or normative propositions that provide the basis upon which the justification of the rest of factual and normative propositions in law depends. In this sense, as argued before, coherentist approaches to legal reasoning are alternatives to formal positivist approaches to reasoning about norms in law and to probabilistic approaches to reasoning about evidence in law, insofar as both of these rely on a foundationalist epistemology.

As opposed to coherentism, foundationalism is based on a linear view of inference according to which there are some basic elements (reasons from authority, when reasoning about norms, and propositions that describe evidence, when reasoning about facts) upon which the chains of justification are based. In contrast, in the holistic view of inference, which coherentism advocates, the justification of any element is a matter of its coherence with the rest of members of the system to which it belongs. It is a problem of this view of justification, as noted, that it may not give reasons from authority (when reasoning about norms) and evidence (when reasoning about facts) the role that they ought to play in legal justification. Is 'isolation' from what the law—as authoritatively enacted—requires and from what the facts under dispute really are the price of coherence? Does the rejection of foundationalism inevitably lead to severing legal justification from reality in this way? The proposed coherence theory of justification depicts the problem of legal justification as a 'discriminating problem' and, in so doing, it distinguishes itself from other coherentist accounts of legal justification and overcomes the threat of isolation.

As explained in chapter four, three kinds of coherence problems may be distinguished: 'pure' coherence problems, which do not favour any elements as worthy of acceptance; 'foundational' coherence problems, which favour a set of elements for acceptance as self-justified; and 'discriminating' coherence problems, which favour a set of elements for acceptance, even if ultimately such an acceptance depends on their coherence with all other elements. In the model of legal justification articulated above, by virtue of the 'principle of data priority', reasons from authority and propositions describing evidence at trial have a degree of acceptability on their own, even if their acceptance will still depend on their coherence with the rest of elements. In this way, this coherentist theory of legal justification departs from foundationalist accounts in that coherence is, ultimately, the source of legal justification, but it also diverges from other coherence theories, such as Dworkin's, which conceptualize legal justification as a 'pure' coherence problem, rather than as a 'discriminating' one. In so doing, it gives reasons from authority and evidence their due in legal justification. It could be objected that introducing the principle of data priority makes the theory, after all, a foundationalist one.[166] However, as argued before, this principle does not sneak a foundationalist element in the theory because the justification of the elements which—according to the principle—enjoy priority depends, as much as the justification of any other element, on their coherence with the rest of elements.[167] In addition, the principle of data priority does not distort the coherentist nature of the model proposed insofar as a justification of this principle by virtue of its coherence is readily available: such a principle is justified because it coheres best with second-order beliefs about the weight that some kinds of elements—propositions that describe authoritative acts and propositions that describe evidence—have in justification in the legal context.

[166] See Lariguet (2011).
[167] See ch 4.

## B. A Contextualist Picture of Legal Justification

In current work on legal justification, it is a commonplace that standards for the justification of conclusions about disputed questions of law and disputed questions of fact are context-invariant. Under this view, features of the context, such as the relevant goals, time constraints or the stakes, are not relevant for assessing whether a particular conclusion in law is justified. To be sure, even if the conditions under which such conclusions are justified are assumed to be independent of context in most work on legal reasoning, the contextualist approach is not a newcomer in the legal literature. There are some scholars—such as Peczenik—who have drawn attention to the significance of context in legal justification and, more generally, in legal reasoning.[168] And, some evidence scholars have argued for the relevance of contextualism about epistemic justification for a theory of fact-finding in law.[169] However, a full contextualist theory of legal justification has not been developed yet. The version of coherentism proposed attempts to incorporate the contextualist insight that standards of justification are context-bound within a theory of legal justification. In so doing, it builds upon the contextualist elements that exist in the literature, and deviates from much work on legal reasoning that assumes that the conditions under which propositions of law and propositions of fact in law are justified are the same across contexts.

## C. Responsibilism about Legal Justification

The standard view on legal reasoning assumes that the standards governing the behaviour of legal decision-makers have no bearing on the issue of whether conclusions about either disputed questions of law or disputed questions of fact are justified. The discussion of the duties which legal decision-makers ought to comply with and the study of the features that mark off virtuous behaviour in the legal context have been relegated to the context of developing codes of professional conduct. The literature on professional ethics and the literature on legal reasoning have thus been viewed as two disconnected bodies of literature. Whereas both consequentialist and Kantian ethics have played a prominent role in legal theory, virtue ethics has received comparatively much less attention. 'Virtue jurisprudence' is still a pretty much underdeveloped theoretical option.[170] The few attempts

[168] See ch 1.

[169] Golanski (2000–01).

[170] For collections of essays in virtue jurisprudence, see Solum and Farrelly (2008) and Amaya and Ho (2012a). For a discussion of the current state of the studies on virtue and law, see Amaya and Ho (2012b).

to date to give an account of legal justification by using virtue ethics have been mostly concerned with the justification of normative conclusions in law.[171] Thus far, the relevance of virtue theory for the epistemology of legal proof has only begun to be explored.[172] In contrast, the coherence model that I have argued for is based on the assumption that standards of epistemic responsibility are inextricably linked with standards of legal justification of both factual and normative propositions, where such standards are defined in terms of virtues and, derivatively, of duties. In this sense, this model explores the relevance of virtue theory to issues of justification of normative and factual conclusions in law. Thus, an account of the virtues and duties of legal decision-makers is shown to be not merely the appropriate subject of professional ethics, but a substantial part of a theory of legal justification.

## D. Explanatory Reasoning in Law

Under the view of legal reasoning that the coherence model underwrites, explanatory inference has a central role in arriving at justified conclusions about both facts and law. With regard to reasoning about disputed questions of fact, this explanationist approach to factual inference provides an alternative to the highly problematical probabilistic model and shows how explanatory inference is not only at work in the context of discovery—as is assumed by most evidence scholars—but also in the context of justification. In addition, the proposed explanatory model brings to light the relevance of explanatory inference to the justification of normative propositions in law, which has been largely sidestepped in standard theories of legal reasoning.

One important consequence of endorsing an explanationist approach to legal inference has to do with the question of what the proper subject of a theory of legal reasoning is. Theories of legal reasoning traditionally deal with questions related to the justification of normative conclusions in law. This focus is limited in two respects: it places issues pertaining to the context of discovery beyond the scope of application of the theory and it neglects the study of fact-reasoning in law. An explanatory view of legal inference shows how the study of legal reasoning should not be limited in this way. First, inference to the best explanation is an inference pattern that operates both in the context of discovery and in the context of justification. Thus, it challenges the assumption that characterizes most current work on legal reasoning according to which issues of discovery and issues of

[171] See Solum (2003) and Amaya ((2011b) and (2012)).
[172] See Amaya (2008); (Ho (2008) and (2012)); and Schauer (2012).

justification should be kept as distinct.[173] Under a view of legal inference as inference to the best explanation, both questions of justification and questions of discovery are at the centre of a theory of legal reasoning.

Secondly, inference to the best explanation is meant to be a pattern of inference that captures the reasoning processes that lead to justified conclusions about both factual and normative propositions in law. Hence, a model of inference to the best explanation brings to light the structural parallelisms that exist between factual inference in law and inference about norms in law, and paves the way for a unitary treatment of both. Under this view, the study of the reasoning processes that lead to the formation and evaluation of factual hypotheses in law are as much the concern of a theory of legal reasoning as is the study of the reasoning processes whereby hypotheses about what the law requires are formulated and assessed.

## E. Jurisprudence Naturalized

Theories of legal reasoning have been mostly concerned, as I have just said, with the study of issues pertaining to the context of justification, and they have taken questions about the context of discovery to be beyond the scope of application of the theory. The reason why this has been so can be traced back to deeply entrenched views about how philosophy and psychology and, more broadly, the normative and the descriptive, are related to each other. The shared view has it that philosophy and psychology are neatly separated disciplines: while the former is a normative enterprise, the latter is a descriptive one. It is then assumed that the study of the context of discovery is psychologists' business, while the study of the context of justification is the main concern of legal philosophers.[174] It is worth saying that this clear separation between philosophy and psychology, and this description of the proper domain of application of psychological and philosophical theories, respectively, is of a quite recent vintage. Before the start of the twentieth century, and the advent of analytic philosophy, the study of the mind and human behaviour was a central concern of philosophers. Now, with the emergence of the cognitive sciences, the many interconnections between philosophy and psychology have been reestablished, and the standard view about the relationship between the

[173] Even if some legal theories insist in that there is no sharp distinction between the context of discovery and the context of justification, still the focus, with few exceptions is on justification; see B Anderson (1996) and Haltutten (2000).

[174] Legal realists, however, were indeed particularly interested in the psychology of legal reasoning. In contrast, a focus on the context of justification characterizes most legal positivist approaches to legal reasoning.

normative and the descriptive, the context of discovery and the context of justification, has been reexamined.

In this context, a trend towards naturalizing philosophy has been a main development in different branches of philosophy such as epistemology, philosophy of science and ethics.[175] The main tenet of naturalism, to recall, is that philosophy is continuous with science so that empirical work has an important bearing on how the normative problems which are the main concern of philosophy should be addressed. In law, however, the naturalist trend has not taken off. With few exceptions, it continues to be assumed, among legal scholars, that issues about the psychology of legal decision-making are not relevant for answering questions about the justification of legal decisions.[176] Thus, a strict is/ought distinction still characterizes most work in legal reasoning.

In contrast, the model of coherence proposed has been articulated and defended from within a naturalistic framework which rejects that any sharp distinction be drawn between theories about how legal decision-makers reason and theories about how they ought to reason. To start with, in the course of discussing and evaluating the current state of the coherence theory in law, the psychological plausibility of current theories of legal reasoning has been viewed as a main criterion for assessing their adequacy. That competing models of evidential reasoning, such as Bayesianism, impose forms of reasoning that are alien to legal decision-makers' natural reasoning processes has been taken to be a main argument against these models. Likewise, the fact that some coherentist theories of legal reasoning, like Dworkin's, disown the naturalistic constraint that 'ought implies can' has been claimed to be a strong reason that militates against these theories. That empirical work supports holistic approaches to evidence and proof as well as coherence-based approaches to legal reasoning at appellate level has also been considered as a main argument in support of a coherence theory of legal reasoning.

The proposed coherence model puts forward a view of legal reasoning which, in the spirit of naturalism, takes due notice of legal decision-makers' cognitive endowment. First, this model is based upon a view of coherence as constraint satisfaction which, as has been shown, has a strong claim to psychological plausibility. It also endorses a contextualist approach to the problem of individuating the base of coherence which is responsive to the cognitive abilities and memory resources of legal decision-makers.

[175] See chs 3, 4 and 8.

[176] See Leiter (1998) and B Leiter, 'Naturalism in Legal Philosophy', *The Stanford Encyclopedia of Philosophy* (Fall 2012 edition), EN Zalta (ed), http://plato.stanford.edu/archives/fall2012/entries/lawphil-naturalism/. Leiter, together with Allen, has also applied a naturalistic approach to analyse evidentiary issues; see Allen and Leiter ((2001) and (2003)). For critiques to this approach, see Nance (2001) and Redmayne (2003).

This model is thus of a piece with a 'naturalized' jurisprudence—still to be developed—which would be more in tune with current philosophical work in areas other than law, and that would bring to light the relevance of psychological literature to the theory of legal reasoning.

### F. Value Pluralism and the Limits of Reason in Law

The coherence theory proposed embraces a non-instrumentalist view of legal reasoning. Under this view, means-ends reasoning is not the only legitimate form of legal reasoning, but deliberation in law is also about ends. Law is responsive to a plurality of values that are likely to come into conflict. The instrumentalist account of legal reasoning makes the value choices which are necessarily involved in legal reasoning come out arbitrarily. In contrast, according to non-instrumentalism, it is part and parcel of legal reasoning to deliberate about the different values which apply to a particular case so as to proceed rationally in the face of conflict. Coherence-based reasoning is—I have argued—a most important kind of inference for deliberating about ends in the forensic context. In this way, value pluralism in law, far from being a reason that militates against the adequacy of coherence theories of legal reasoning, provides the rationale for such methods. It is because there is conflict of values in law that we need patterns of inference other than means-ends reasoning, most importantly, coherence-based reasoning, to decide rationally, rather than arbitrarily, when conflict arises. Thus, this model, by focusing on coherence-driven inference as an important kind of non-instrumentalist inference, is meant to contribute to the study of the reasoning patterns whereby we deliberate about ends in law.[177] More broadly, a coherence theory such as the one proposed is expected to be a part of a view of legal rationality that expands the scope of reason in law by placing ends within the reach of deliberation.

## X. CONCLUSIONS

This book has scrutinized the concept of coherence from a variety of perspectives. After examining the current state of the coherence theory in law, I have explored the role that coherence plays in theoretical and practical reasoning in different domains. I have first examined the place of coherence within theories of epistemic justification, and how it relates to the main cognitive goal of truth. Then, I have focused on the role that coherentist

[177] The model of balancing is, probably, the most important approach to the study of legal reasoning about ends. See Alexy (2003).

standards play in theory choice in science and in small-scale belief changes such as those formalized by theories of belief revision. Next, I have considered the relevance of coherence for a theory of practical reasoning as well as the importance of coherence in moral deliberation. And last, I have examined the significance of coherence as a principle that guides discourse interpretation.

I have then tried to bring the insights learned along the way together in a coherence theory of legal reasoning. This theory—I have argued- has four main elements: a notion of legal coherence as constraint satisfaction, a view of coherence-based legal inference as inference to the best explanation, a conception of legal justification as optimal coherence, and the idea that coherentist standards of justification are context-dependent. According to this theory, a belief about the law or the facts under dispute is justified if and only if it could be the outcome of a piece of coherence-based reasoning performed by a similarly circumstanced epistemically responsible legal decision-maker. Coherence-based legal inference, under this view, has an explanatory structure: it consists first in generating a shortlist of plausible candidates from which one then infers to the best, ie the theory about either the case or the law that best satisfies the criteria of factual and normative coherence.

This theory is grounded on a view of legal justification that is non-foundationalist, naturalistic, explanationist, responsibilist, contextualist and non-instrumental. The proposed coherence model of justification is of a piece with a theory of legal reasoning according to which the justification of any element depends upon its relations with the rest of the elements; that takes the project of ameliorating the legal practice seriously by grounding prescriptions about how legal decision-makers ought to reason in facts about how they reason; that claims that explanatory merit is pivotal for assessments of justification, and thus, of coherence; that contends that standards of justification are responsibility-oriented and context-dependent; and that has the ambition to regulate both means-ends reasoning as well as reasoning about ends.

The theory of optimal coherence has some advantages over other coherentist approaches to legal reasoning. First, it has a wider scope of application in that it is meant to be applicable to reasoning about both disputed questions of fact and disputed questions of law. The study of the role that coherence plays in the justification of conclusions about disputed questions of fact has been largely neglected in the literature on legal reasoning, which has dealt mainly with issues related to the justification of conclusions about disputed questions of law. Issues of coherence and justification of factual propositions in law have been addressed to some extent by evidence scholars and legal psychologists. Holistic theories of evidence and proof and narrative approaches to fact-reasoning—I have argued—significantly advance the case for coherentism in the context of factual reasoning in law, although they fall short of providing a well-rounded coherence-based theory. It has been my aim to bring together the literature on legal reasoning and the literature on evidence law in order to have a complete picture of the current state of the coherence theory in law and to give a unified account of the role that coherence plays in legal reasoning about both facts and norms. A number of serious objections threaten the plausibility of coherence theories in law. While by no means do I claim to have solved the problems of legal coherentism, the coherence model—as argued—does much by way of meeting these objections. That there is but a tenuous connection between coherence and truth (or correctness) is thought to be a most forceful objection against coherence theories of justification. I have shown that the objection is less compelling than it might appear because, first, the case for the truth-conduciveness of coherence is far from being hopeless, and, secondly, there are a number of strong reasons that support the view that coherence should be endorsed with justificatory force in law.

Of course, coherentism is not the panacea for the problem of analysing legal justification, and while the version of coherentism proposed has some reasons to recommend it, it also faces many problems. Let me briefly mention some of the main difficulties that the proposed theory encounters. First, all the problems of the theory of coherence as constraint satisfaction are inherited by the proposed model of coherence. The problem of the input is as severe in law as in any other domain. When does an interpretative hypothesis explain the relevant precedents? When does a piece of information provide evidence for an explanatory hypothesis? What are the conditions under which two explanatory hypotheses are analogous? Too much needs to be known and too many difficult issues need to be settled before one is ready to perform the coherence calculation. In addition, while I have modified in some respects Thagard's proposal so as to bring it more in line with what legal decision-makers can attain, much more remains to be done before we can certify the psychological plausibility of the proposed model. And what has been said about the process whereby legal decision-makers generate the relevant elements does not even scratch the surface of the mechanics of discovery in law. The analysis of the process of generation needs to be incorporated within a complete coherence theory of legal reasoning. The problem of how to put together the different kinds of coherence that are relevant to justification in a particular domain also arises here. I have contended that the justification of conclusions about disputed questions of law requires the integrated assessment of explanatory, deductive, analogical, interpretative and deliberative coherence, and that the justification of conclusions about disputed questions of fact involves the combination of explanatory, perceptual, deductive, analogical, conceptual and deliberative coherence. It is necessary to give a more detailed account of how these kinds of coherence interact in order to give an optimal solution to a legal problem.[178]

Secondly, I have only sketched a model of inference to the best explanation for law. Much more needs to be said about the stage of discovery which this kind of inference involves. It would also be desirable to have a full-blown theory of 'legal explanation'; particularly, an analysis of the notion of explanation that figures in normative reasoning in law is most necessary. I have suggested that appealing to epistemic responsibility may provide a solution to what is, to my mind, the most serious problem that an explanatory version of coherentism faces, to wit, the coherence bias. Still, complementing explanatory coherentism with a theory of epistemic responsibility does not put all worries about the legitimacy of inference to the best explanation to rest for, one may ask, what reason do we have to take the best alternative, that is, under this view, the most coherent one, as justified? A lot more needs to be said about how inferences to the best explanation confer warrant upon their conclusions in the legal context. Some recent attempts to discuss the problem of the legitimacy of inference to the best explanation within Pollock's framework for the analysis of defeasible reasoning are very promising.[179] If so, further work on the issue of how inference to the best explanation in law is justification-conferring is likely to intertwine in exciting ways with current work on defeasible reasoning in law.[180]

Thirdly, I have argued for the relevance of standards of epistemic responsibility for attributions of justified belief in law. However, the relationship between epistemic responsibility and justification is quite complex, and I have not even attempted to deal with the many problems that a responsibilist view of legal justification gives rise to. First, doubts may be raised about whether epistemic responsibility is a necessary condition for legal justification. One might think of Stella, who is a lucky but inconsiderate and reckless judge. She has the gift of coherence: she hits upon the most coherent decision, but, not having reflected in the course of decision-making, she is unable to give any reasons for her decision. The decision just happens to be the right one by mere luck. Is Stella's decision justified? There is a sense in which, one might say, Stella's decision is justified, even though it is the outcome of epistemically irresponsible behaviour. Secondly, one may question whether epistemic responsibility is a sufficient condition for justification. Consider Alison, who is an extremely cautious and hard-worker, but short-sighted judge. Despite the fact that she has done all that it can be expected of her, she fails to take due notice of relevant evidence, does not succeed

[178] See Araskiewicz (2013), for a discussion of different challenges facing the development of a constraint satisfaction approach to legal coherence.

[179] See Psillos (2002).

[180] See eg Ferrer and Ratti (2012).

in thinking up promising alternatives, and fails to appreciate the bearing of available evidence on the competing hypotheses under consideration. Something is epistemically amiss in Alison's decision, despite all her good efforts. Her decision is the outcome of an epistemically responsible—but deficient—cognitive process which, one may argue, fails to yield justification.

One could address these cases in which, purportedly, epistemic responsibility and justification come apart by distinguishing between 'subjective' and 'objective' conceptions of justification. From this perspective, Stella's decision is subjectively unjustified, but objectively justified, and Alison's is objectively unjustified, even if it is subjectively justified. Alternatively, one may want to distinguish, as I have suggested above, between a belief being justified and a person being justified in holding a belief. On this view, Stella would be unjustified in making her decision, even if the decision itself would be justified. And Alison would be justified in making her decision, which is nonetheless unjustified. Still, one may even deny that justification and epistemic responsibility are linked in the way in which a responsibilist view of justification has it, and claim that they are rather different kinds of epistemic appraisal. A further question would then be whether both kinds of epistemic appraisals are relevant in law, or whether instead we should be concerned exclusively with the justificatory status of the decision and leave the purported responsibility/irresponsibility of legal decision-makers to legal decision-makers' own business. At bottom, the issue is mainly whether standards of epistemic responsibility hook up with truth/correctness in the right way. If epistemically responsible behaviour were shown to be truth-conducive, there would be no point in distinguishing subjective from objective justification, or the justificatory status of a decision from a legal decision-maker being justified in taking such a decision. Cases of epistemic luck and incompetence could be then addressed within a framework that shows how good epistemic behaviour conduces to right decisions. Insofar as this framework is missing, Stella and Alison would continue to pose serious problems to any theory, such as the one proposed here, which endorses a responsibilist view of legal justification.

Fourthly, contextualism about justification leads—it may be argued—to forms of relativism or scepticism that are unacceptable. Indeed, there are different forms of contextualism, some of which are dangerously close to relativist views. By endorsing the view that the justificatory status of a legal decision depends on context, one is open to the charge of relativism that is addressed against, at least, some versions of contextualism. Just whether a contextualist position has the resources for meeting the objection from relativism mainly depends upon how the context that is taken to be relevant to legal justification is identified. Much more needs to be said about which features of the context have a bearing on judgements of coherence, and how contexts are individualized in a particular instance of justification, for a contextualized version of the coherence theory to be free of relativist or sceptical suspicions.

Fifthly, worries may be raised about whether one can endorse a naturalistic theory of legal justification while preserving its normative dimension. The charge that naturalism is incompatible with the normativity of a theory of justification has been raised against naturalistic approaches to epistemology and ethics, and it applies equally to any project that attempts to naturalize jurisprudence. There are, however, many different kinds of naturalism, and the objection that naturalism is at odds with the normativity of the theory of justification has a different force against the different versions of naturalism. It has to be shown how it is possible to carry out the naturalistic program within jurisprudence in a way that preserves the crucial normative dimension of the theory of legal justification.

Last, it might be argued that the model of legal justification proposed here assumes an over-intellectualized view of legal decision-making in that it gives too much importance to legal decision-makers' epistemic virtues and intellectual abilities. But, what is the bearing of these epistemic capacities on practical judgements? To what extent are practical abilities such as sensitivity to detail, or the ability to appreciate the moral relevance of features in a particular situation, parasitic on epistemic capacities? In order to sustain the claim that the proposed model does give to epistemic capacities their just due in legal decision-making, it would be necessary to clarify the issue of how moral and epistemic abilities contribute to sound legal judgment, and more specifically, how the moral duties and virtues, and the epistemic duties and virtues of legal decision-makers, if distinct, are related to each other.

The foregoing problems pose serious challenges to the coherence theory of legal reasoning that has been proposed in this book. I cannot offer here a careful formulation of these problems, nor can I attempt to answer them. I have merely indicated some questions that a thorough development and defence of the proposed model would prompt one to consider. However important it is for this model of coherence to have an answer to these questions, it is crucial to notice that these problems are linked to broader issues such as the relationship between contextualism and relativism in law; the implications of naturalism for the normativity of legal theory; the defeasible nature of explanatory reasoning etc which we cannot expect this model of coherence—or any other model—to solve. Indeed, it would be unfair to charge any coherence theory with the task of providing adequate solutions to the diverse and difficult issues with which the notion of coherence is intertwined. What these problems make clear, in my view, is the need for a theory of coherence to be located within a broader theory of legal reasoning that successfully deals with these questions.[181] The foregoing list of problems brings to light the need to incorporate some concepts in legal

[181] The coherence theory is an important piece of a theory of legal rationality, but there is more to rationality in law than coherence. *Cf* Atienza (2011) (arguing that the theory of legal coherence defended in this work is so broad that it ends up being identified with that of rationality). On this point, see Amaya (2011c).

theory—such as 'epistemic virtue' or 'legal explanation'—which have not been central in most legal theorizing; the need to address some issues—like discovery in legal decision-making, or explanatory reasoning in law—which have not been traditionally the focus of the theory of legal reasoning; and the need to reconsider some of the assumptions—as the 'divorce' between the psychology of legal decision-making and normative questions in law, or the separation between the context of discovery and the context of justification—which characterize the standard view on legal reasoning. In this sense, these problems, I believe, point towards potentially interesting avenues for future research in both the coherence theory in law as well as, more generally, the theory of legal reasoning.

# References


——— 'Approaches du Discours de la Preuve en Droit', *International Journal for the Semiotics of Law,* vol I (3), 1988, and vol II (4), 1989.

Abimbola, Kola (2002) 'Abductive Reasoning in Law: Taxonomy and Inference to the Best Explanation' in M MacCrimmon and P Tillers (eds), *The Dynamics of Judicial Proof: Computation, Logic, and Common Sense* (Heidelberg, Physica-Verlag).

Abrams, K and Keren H (2010) 'Who is Afraid of Law and the Emotions?' 94 *Minnesota Law Review.*

Abu-Hareira, M (1986) 'An Early Holistic Conception of Judicial Fact-Finding' 79 *Juridical Review.*

Aitken, CGG (1995) *Statistics and the Evaluation of Evidence for Forensic Scientists* (Chichester, John Wiley and Sons).

Akiba, K (2000) 'Shogenji's Probabilistic Measure of Coherence is Incoherent' 60 *Analysis.*

Alchourrón, C and Makinson, D (1985) 'On the Logic of Theory Change: Safe Contraction' 44 *Studia Logica.*

_____, Gärdenfors, P and Makinson, D (1985) 'On the Logic of Theory Change: Partial Meet Contraction and Revision Functions' 50 *Journal of Symbolic Logic.*

Alcoff, L (1996) *New Versions of the Coherence Theory* (Ithaca, Cornell University Press).

——— (2001) 'The Case of Coherence' in M Lynch (ed), *The Nature of Truth* (Cambridge, MIT Press).

Alexander, L and Kress, K (1995) 'Against Legal Principles' in A Marmor (ed), *Law and Interpretation* (Oxford, Clarendon Press).

Alexy, R (1998) 'Coherence and Argumentation or the Genuine Twin Criterialess Super Criterion' in A Aarnio et al (eds), *On Coherence Theory in Law* (Lund, Juristförlager i Lund).

_____ (2003) 'On Balancing and Subsumption: A Structural Comparison' 16 *Ratio Iuris.*

_____ and Peczenik, A (1990) 'The Concept of Coherence and its Significance for Discursive Rationality' 3 *Ratio Iuris.*

Aliseda, A (1997) 'A Unified Framework for Abductive and Inductive Reasoning in Philosophy and AI' in PA Flach and AC Kakas (eds), *Proceedings of the IJCAI's 97 Workshop on Abduction and Induction in Artificial Intelligence* (Department of Computer Science, University of Bristol).

_____ (2004) 'Logics in Scientific Discovery' 9 *Foundations of Science.*

_____ (2006) *Abductive Reasoning: Logical Investigations into Discovery and Explanation* (Dordrecht, Springer).

Allen, RJ (1986) 'A Reconceptualization of Civil Trials' 66 *Boston University Law Review.*

_____ (1991) 'The Nature of Juridical Proof' 13 *Cardozo Law Review.*

_____ (1994) 'Factual Ambiguity and a Theory of Evidence' 58 *Northwestern University Law Review.*

_____ (1997a) 'Rationality, Algorithms, and Juridical Proof: A Preliminary Inquiry' 1 *International Journal of Evidence and Proof.*

_____ (1997b) 'Reasoning and its Foundation: Some Responses' 1 *International Journal of Evidence and Proof.*

_____ (2000) 'Clarifying the Burden of Persuasion and Bayesian Decision Rules: a Response to Professor Kaye' 4 *The International Journal of Evidence and Proof.*

_____ (2005) 'The Narrative Fallacy, the Relative Plausibility Theory, and a Theory of the Trial' 3 *International Commentary on Evidence.*

_____ et al (1994–95) 'Probability and Proof in *State v. Skipper*: An Internet Exchange' 35 *Jurimetrics.*

_____ and Leiter, B (2001) 'Naturalized Epistemology and the Law of Evidence' 87 *Virginia Law Review.*

——— and ——— (2003) 'Naturalized Epistemology and the Law of Evidence: Reply to Redmayne' 4 *Michigan State Law Review.*

——— and Redmayne, M (eds) (1997) 'Bayesianism and Juridical Proof' 1 *International Journal of Evidence and Proof.* Special issue.

_____ and Stein, A (2013) 'Evidence, Probability, and the Burden of Proof' 55 *Arizona Law Review.*

Alonso, JP (2006) *Interpretación de las normas y derecho penal* (Buenos Aires, Editores del Puerto).

Alston, W (1971) 'Varieties of Privileged Access' 8 *American Philosophical Quarterly.*

——— (1976) 'Two Types of Foundationalism' 8 *The Journal of Philosophy.*

——— (1989) *Epistemic Justification* (Ithaca, Cornell University Press).

——— (1998) 'Foundationalism' in E Sosa and J Dancy (eds), *In Companion to Epistemology* (Oxford, Basil Blackwell).

——— (2005) *Beyond 'Justification': Dimensions of Epistemic Evaluation* (Ithaca, Cornell University Press).

Amaya, A (2007) 'Formal Models of Coherence and Legal Epistemology' 15 *Artificial Intelligence and Law.*

_____ (2008) 'Justification, Coherence, and Epistemic Responsibility' 5 *Episteme: A Journal of Social Epistemology.*

_____ (2009) 'Inference to the Best Legal Explanation' in H Kaptein, H Prakken and B Verheij (eds), *Legal Evidence and Proof: Statistics, Stories, Logic* (Aldershot, Ashgate).

_____ (2011a) 'Legal Justification by Optimal Coherence' 24 *Ratio Iuris.*

_____ (2011b) 'Virtue and Reason in Law' in M del Mar (ed), *New Waves in the Philosophy of Law* (New York, Palgrave-MacMillan).

_____ (2011c) 'Coherencia, justificación y derecho: respuesta a los participantes' X *Discusiones.*

_____ (2012) 'The Role of Virtue in Legal Justification' in A Amaya and HL Ho (eds), *Law, Virtue and Justice* (Oxford, Hart Publishing).

_____ (2013) 'Coherence, Evidence, and Legal Proof' 19 *Legal Theory.*

_____ and Ho, HL (2012a) *Law, Virtue and Justice* (Oxford, Hart Publishing).

_____ and _____ (2012b) 'Of Law, Virtue, and Justice' in A Amaya and HL Ho (eds) *Law, Virtue and Justice* (Oxford, Hart Publishing).

Anderson, B (1996) *'Discovery' in Legal Decision-Making* (Dordrecht, Kluwer).
Anderson, D (1986) 'The Evolution of Peirce's Concept of Abduction' 22 *Transactions of the Charles S. Peirce Society.*
Anderson, TJ (1995) 'On Generalizations I: A Preliminary Exploration' 40 *South Texas Law Review.*
Angere, S (2007) 'The Defeasible Nature of Coherentist Justification' 157 *Synthese.*
______ (2008) 'Coherence as Heuristic' 117 *Mind.*
Annis, DB (1978) 'A Contextualist Theory of Epistemic Justification' 15 *American Philosophical Quarterly.*
Araszkiewicz, M (2010a) 'The Concept of Coherence in Legal Argumentation in the Context of European Private Law and Europeanization of National Private Law: A Theoretical Study' PhD Diss, Jagiellonian University, Kraków.
______ (2010b) 'Balancing of Legal Principles and Constraint Satisfaction' in RGF Winkels (ed), *Legal Knowledge and Information Systems* (Amsterdam, IOS).
______ (2012) 'Coherence-Based Account of the Doctrine of Consistent Interpretation' in M Palmirani et al (eds), *AI Approaches to the Complexity of Legal Systems* (Berlin, Springer).
______ (2013) 'Limits of Constraint Satisfaction Theory of Coherence as a Theory of (Legal) Reasoning' in M Araszkiewicz and J Šavelka (eds), *Coherence: Insights from Philosophy, Jurisprudence, and Artificial Intelligence* (Dordrecht, Springer).
______ and Savelka, J (2012) 'Two Methods for Representing Judicial Reasoning in the Framework of Coherence as Constraint Satisfaction' in K Atkinson (ed), *Legal Knowledge and Information Systems.* JURIX: the Twenty-Fourth Annual Conference (Amsterdam, IOS Press).
Armstrong, DM (1973) *Belief, Truth, and Knowledge* (London, Cambridge University Press).
Arrington, RL (1989) *Rationalism, Realism and Relativism: Perspectives in Contemporary Philosophy* (Ithaca, Cornell University Press).
Aschenbrenner, K (1985) *The Concept of Coherence in Art* (Dordrecht, Kluwer).
Atienza, M (1991) *Las Razones del Derecho* (Madrid, Centro de Estudios Constitucionales).
——— (2006) *El Derecho como argumentación* (Barcelona, Ariel).
______ (2011) '¿Coherencia o racionalidad?' X *Discusiones.*
______ and Ruiz, J (1998) *A Theory of Legal Sentences* (Dordrecht, Kluwer).
Audi, R (1988) 'Foundationalism, Coherentism, and Epistemological Dogmatism' 2 *Philosophical Perspectives.*
——— (1989) *Practical Reasoning* (London, Routledge).
——— (1998) *Epistemology* (London, Routledge).
——— (2001) *The Architecture of Reason* (Oxford, Oxford University Press).
Aune, B (1967) *Knowledge, Mind, and Nature* (New York, Random House).
Axtell, G (1997) 'Recent Work on Virtue Epistemology' 34 *American Philosophical Quarterly.*
Ayer, AJ (1955) *Foundations of Empirical Knowledge* (New York, St Martin's Press).
Baccarini, E (1991) 'Rational Consensus and Coherence Methods in Ethics' 40 *Grazer Philosophische Studien.* Special issue.
——— (1997) 'Morality by Coherence' 18 *Acta Analytica.*
Back, K and Harnish, R (1979) *Linguistic Communication and Speech Acts* (Cambridge, MIT Press).

Baehr, J (2008) 'Four Varieties of Character-Based Virtue Epistemology' 46 *The Southern Journal of Philosophy.*

______ (2009) 'Evidentialism, Vice, and Virtue' LXXVIII *Philosophy and Phenomenological Research.*

Bandes, SA (ed) (1999) *The Passions of Law* (New York, New York University Press).

Bandyopadhyay, S (1995) 'Characterizing Coherence in Multimodal Discourse' in D Andler et al (eds), *Facets of Rationality* (New Delhi-London, Sage Publications).

Bankowski, Z (1990) 'The Jury and Reality' in P Nerhot (ed), *Law, Interpretation, and Reality: Essays in Epistemology, Hermeneutics, and Jurisprudence* (Dordrecht, Kluwer).

Bartelborth, T (1996) 'Scientific Explanation' in W Balzer and CU Moulines (eds), *Structuralist Theory of Science: Focal Issues, New Results* (Berlin, deGruyter).

——— (1999) 'Coherence and Explanation' 50 *Erkenntnis.*

Bartlett, FC (1932) (1995) *Remembering: A Study in Experimental and Social Psychology* (Cambridge, Cambridge University Press).

Barnes, A and Thagard, P (1997) 'Empathy and Analogy' 36 *Dialogue: Canadian Philosophical Review.*

Barnes, E (1995) 'Inference to the Loveliest Explanation' 103 *Synthese.*

Bateman, JA and Rondhuis, KJ (1997) 'Coherence Relations: Towards a General Specification' 24 *Discourse Processes.*

Bayón, JC (2001) 'Why is Legal Reasoning Defeasible?' in A Soeteman (ed), *Pluralism and Law* (Dordrecht, Kluwer).

Bench-Capon, T and Sartor, G (2001a) 'Theory Based Explanation of Case Law Domains' in *Artificial Intelligence, Proceedings of the Eighth International Conference on Artificial Intelligence and Law* (New York, ACM Press).

______ and ______ (2001b) 'A Quantitative Approach to Theory Coherence' in B Verheij et al (eds) *Legal Knowledge and Information Systems.* JURIX 2001: The Fourteenth Annual Conference (Amsterdam, IOS).

——— and ——— (2003) 'A Model of Legal Reasoning with Cases Incorporating Theories and Values' in 'AI and Law' 150 *Artificial Intelligence.* Special Issue.

Bender, J (ed) (1989a) *The Current State of the Coherence Theory: Critical Essays on the Epistemic Theories of Keith Lehrer and Laurence BonJour, with Replies* (Dordrecht, Kluwer).

—— (1989b) 'Coherence, Justification, and Knowledge: The Current Debate' in J Bender (ed), *The Current State of the Coherence Theory: Critical Essays on the Epistemic Theories of Keith Lehrer and Laurence BonJour, with Replies* (Dordrecht, Kluwer).

Ben-Menahem, Y (1990) 'The Inference to the Best Explanation' 33 *Erkenntnis.*

Bennett, WL and Feldman, MS (1981) *Reconstructing Reality in the Courtroom: Justice and Judgment in American Culture* (New Brunswick, Rutgers University Press).

Berg, J (1991) 'The Relevant Relevance' 16 *Journal of Pragmatics.*

Bertea, S (2005a) 'The Arguments from Coherence: Analysis and Evaluation' 25 *Oxford Journal of Legal Studies.*

——— (2005b) 'Does Arguing from Coherence Make Sense' 19 *Argumentation.*

Betz, G (2012) 'Justifying Inference to the Best Explanation as a Practical Meta-Syllogism on Dialectical Structures' 31 *Synthese.*

Bex, FJ (2011) *Arguments, Stories and Criminal Evidence: A Formal Hybrid Theory* (Dordrecht, Springer).
——— et al (2010) 'A Hybrid Formal Theory of Arguments, Stories, and Criminal Evidence' 18 *Artificial Intelligence and Law.*
——— and Verheij, B (2012) 'Solving a Murder Case by Asking Critical Questions: An Approach to Fact-Finding in Terms of Argumentation and Story Schemes' 26 *Argumentation.*
_____ and _____ (2013) 'Legal Stories and the Process of Proof' 21 *Artificial Intelligence and Law.*
Bilgrami, A (1994) *Belief and Meaning* (Oxford, Blackwell).
Bilz, K (2010) 'We Don't Want to Hear it: Psychology, Literature, and the Narrative Model of Judging' *University of Illinois Law Review.*
Bittner, R (1989) *What Reason Demands* (Cambridge, Cambridge University Press).
Bix, B (2003) *Jurisprudence: Theory and Context*, 3rd edn (London, Sweet and Maxwell).
Blackburn, SW (1984) *Spreading the World* (Oxford, Clarendon Press).
——— (1988) 'On the Very Idea of Formative Experience: DePaul's Challenge to Coherence Theories in Ethics' 49 *Philosophy and Phenomenological Research.*
Blakemore, D (1988) 'The Organization of Discourse' in FJ Newmeyer (ed), *Linguistics: The Cambridge Survey*, vol 4 (Cambridge, Cambridge University Press).
_____ (2003) 'Discourse and Relevance Theory' in D Schiffrin, D Tannen and HE Hamilton (eds), *The Handbook of Discourse Analysis* (Malden, Wiley-Blackwell).
Blanshard, B (1939) *The Nature of Thought* (London, Allen & Unwin).
——— (2001) 'Coherence as the Nature of Truth' in M Lynch (ed), *The Nature of Truth* (Cambridge, MIT).
Blass, R (1990) *Relevance Relations in Discourse* (Cambridge, Cambridge University Press).
——— (1993) 'Are There Logical Relations in a Text?' 90 *Lingua.*
Block, N (1986) 'Advertisement for a Semantics for Psychology' 10 *Midwest Studies in Philosophy.*
——— (1995) 'An Argument for Holism' 14 *Proceedings for the Aristotelian Society.*
——— (1998) 'Holism, Mental and Semantic' in E Craig (ed), *The Routledge Encyclopedia of Philosophy* (London, Routledge).
Bobbio, N (1971) 'Le bon legislateur' in H Hubien (ed), *Le Raisonnement juridique* (Brussels, Bruylant).
Bochman, A (1999) 'A Foundational Theory of Belief and Belief Change' 108 *Artificial Intelligence.*
——— (2000) 'A Foundationalist View of the AGM Theory of Belief Change' 116 *Artificial Intelligence.*
——— (2002) 'Entrenchment versus Dependence: Coherence and Foundations in Belief Change' 116 *Journal of Logic, Language and Information.*
Bogdan, RJ (ed) (1981) *Keith Lehrer* (Dordrecht, Reidel).
Bogen, J (1989) 'Coherence and Science' in J Bender (ed), *The Current State of the Coherence Theory: Critical Essays on the Epistemic Theories of Keith Lehrer and Laurence BonJour, with Replies* (Dordrecht, Kluwer).
Bókay, A (1989) 'Understanding, Text, and Coherence' in ME Conte, JS Pëtofi and E Sözer (eds), *Text and Discourse Connectedness* (Amsterdam, John Benjamins).

BonJour, L (1976) 'The Coherence Theory of Empirical Knowledge' 30 *Philosophical Studies.*

——— (1978) 'Can Empirical Knowledge have a Foundation?' 15 *American Philosophical Quarterly.*

——— (1980) 'Externalist Theories of Empirical Knowledge' 5 *Midwest Studies in Philosophy.*

——— (1985) *The Structure of Empirical Knowledge* (Cambridge, Cambridge University Press).

——— (1988) 'Reply to Moser' 48 *Analysis.*

——— (1989) 'Replies and Clarifications' in J Bender (ed), *The Current State of the Coherence Theory: Critical Essays on the Epistemic Theories of Keith Lehrer and Laurence BonJour, with Replies* (Dordrecht, Kluwer).

——— (1994) 'Fumerton on Incoherence Theories' 19 *Journal of Philosophical Research.*

——— (1997) 'Haack on Justification and Experience' 122 *Synthese.*

——— (1998a) *In Defense of Pure Reason* (Cambridge, Cambridge University Press).

——— (1998b) 'Internalism/Externalism' in J Dancy and E Sosa (eds), *A Companion to Epistemology* (Malden, Blackwell).

——— (1999a) 'The Dialectic of Foundationalism and Coherentism' in J Greco and E Sosa (eds), *The Blackwell Guide to Epistemology* (Oxford, Blackwell).

——— (1999b) 'Foundationalism and the External World' 13 *Philosophical Perspectives.*

_____ (2001) 'Toward a Defense of Empirical Foundationalism' in M DePaul (ed), *Resurrecting Old-Fashioned Foundationalism* (Lanham, Rowman and Littlefield).

Bonorino, P (1993) 'Sobre la abducción' 14 *Doxa: Cuadernos de Filosofía del Derecho.*

Bornstein, BH and Wiener, RL (eds) (2006) 'Special Issue on Emotion in Legal Judgment and Decision Making' 30 *Law and Human Behavior.*

_____ (eds) (2010) *Emotion and the Law: Psychological Perspectives* (New York, Springer).

Bosanquet, B (1920) *Implication and Linear Inference* (London, MacMillan).

Bourcier, D (1999) 'Interprétation et abduction: La science du droit est-elle concernée par la sérenpidité?' 42 *Revue Interdisciplinaire d'Etudes Juridiques.*

Bovens, L and Hartmann, S (2003a) 'Solving the Riddle of Coherence' 112 *Mind.*

_____ and _____ (2003b) *Bayesian Epistemology* (Oxford: Oxford University Press).

_____ and Olsson, EJ (2002) 'Believing More, Risking Less: On Coherence, Truth, and Non-Trivial Extensions' 57 *Erkenntnis.*

Boyd, R (1985) 'Lex Oranti est Lex Credendi' in P Churchland and C Hooker (eds), *Images of Science* (Chicago, University of Chicago Press).

——— (1997) 'How to be a Moral Realist?' in S Darwall, A Gibbard and P Railton (eds), *Moral Discourse and Practice* (Oxford, Oxford University Press).

Bradley, FH (1914) *Essays on Truth and Reality* (Oxford, Oxford University Press).

——— (1927) 'My Station and its Duties' *Ethical Studies* (Oxford, Clarendon Press).

Brandl, J Gombocz, WL and Piller, C (eds) (1991) 'Metamind, Knowledge and Coherence: Essays on the Philosophy of Keith Lehrer' 40 *Grazer Philosophische Studien.* Special issue.

Brandom, R (1994) *Making it Explicit* (Cambridge, Harvard University Press).
Brandt, RB (1979) *A Theory of the Good and the Right* (Oxford, Oxford University Press).
——— (1985) 'Moral Theory and Moral Education' 85 *The Journal of Philosophy*.
Bratman, ME (1987) *Intention, Plans, and Practical Reasoning* (Cambridge, Harvard University Press).
_____ (1992) 'Practical Reasoning and Acceptance in Context' 101 *Mind*.
Brendel, E (1999) 'Coherence Theory of Knowledge: A Gradational Account' 50 *Erkenntnis*.
Brewer, S (1996) 'Exemplary Reasoning' 109 *Harvard Law Review*.
Brink, D (1988) 'Legal Theory Legal Interpretation, and Judicial Review' 17 *Philosophy and Public Affairs*.
——— (1989) *Moral Realism and the Foundations of Ethics* (Cambridge, Cambridge University Press).
Broadi, SW (1987) 'The Problem of Practical Intellect in Aristotle's Ethics' in J Cleary (ed), *Proceedings of the Boston Area Colloquium in Ancient Philosophy*, vol 3 (Lanham, University Press of America).
Brown, G and Yule G (1983) *Discourse Analysis* (Cambridge, Cambridge University Press).
Brown HI (1994) 'Reason, Judgment, and Bayes's Law' 61 *Philosophy of Science*.
Bruecker, AL (1986) 'Charity and Skepticism' 67 *Pacific Philosophical Quarterly*.
——— (1988) 'Problems with Internalist Coherentism' 58 *Philosophical Studies*.
Bublitz, W (1999) 'Introduction: Views of Coherence' in W Bublitz, U Lenk and E Ventola (eds), *Coherence in Spoken and Written Discourse* (Amsterdam, John Benjamins).
——— and Lenk, U (1999) 'Disturbed Coherence: "Fill Me In"' in W Bublitz, U Lenk and E Ventola (eds), *Coherence in Spoken and Written Discourse* (Amsterdam, John Benjamins).
———, Lenk U and Ventola W (eds) (1999) *Coherence in Spoken and Written Discourse* (Amsterdam, John Benjamins).
Burley, J (ed) (2004) *Dworkin and His Critics: With Replies by Dworkin* (Malden, Willey Blackwell).
Byrne, M (1995) 'The Convergence of Explanatory Coherence and the Story Model: A Case Study in Juror Decision' in *Proceedings of the Seventeenth Annual Conference of the Cognitive Science Society* (Hillsdale, Lawrence Erlbaum Associates).
Callen, CR (1982) 'Notes on a Grand Illusion: Some Limits on the Use of Bayesian Theory in Evidence Law' 57 *Indiana Law Journal*.
_____ (1991) 'Cognitive Science, Bayesian Norms and Rules of Evidence' 154 *Journal of the Royal Statistical Society*.
——— et al (2003) 'Visions of Rationality in Evidence Law', Symposium *Michigan State Law Review*.
Campbell, R and Hunter, B (eds) (2000) 'Introduction' to 'Moral Epistemology Naturalized' Suppl 26 *Canadian Journal of Philosophy*.
Campos, GC (2011) 'On the Distinction between Peirce's Abduction and Lipton's Inference to the Best Explanation' 180 *Synthese*.
Cantwell, J (1999) 'Static Justification and the Dynamics of Belief' 50 *Erkenntnis*.
——— (2001) 'Two Notions of Epistemic Entrenchment' in M Williams and H Rott (eds), *Frontiers in Belief Revision* (Dordrecht, Kluwer).

Carriquiry, AL (1997) 'Bayesian Decision-Making: Impossible Task?' 1 *The International Journal of Evidence and Proof.*
——— and Allen, RJ (1997) 'Factual Ambiguity and a Theory of Evidence Reconsidered: A Dialogue between a Statistician and a Law Professor' 31 *Israel Law Review.*
Chang, R (ed) (1997) *Incommensurability, Incomparability and Practical Reason* (Cambridge, Harvard University Press).
Charolles, M (1983) 'Coherence as a Principle in the Interpretation of Discourse' 3 *Text.*
——— (1985) 'Text Connexity, Text Coherence, and Text Interpretation' in E Sözer (ed), *Text Connexity, Text Coherence: Aspects, Methods, Results* (Hamburg, Buske).
——— (1989) 'Text Coherence and Text Interpretation Processing' in ME Conte, JS Petöfi and E Sözer (eds), *Text and Discourse Connectedness* (Amsterdam, John Benjamins).
Cherniak, C (1986) *Minimal Rationality* (Cambridge, MIT).
Chisholm, RM (1977) *Theory of Knowledge*, 2nd edn (Englewood Cliffs, Prentice-Hall).
——— (1982) *The Foundations of Knowing* (Minneapolis, University of Minnesota Press).
Clark, R (1988) 'Vicious Infinite Regress Arguments' 2 *Philosophical Perspectives.*
Code, L (1987) *Epistemic Responsibility* (Hanover, University Press of New England).
Cohen, LJ (1977) *The Probable and the Provable* (Oxford, Clarendon Press).
——— (1980) 'The Logic of Proof' *Criminal Law Review.*
——— (1987) 'On Analyzing the Standards of Forensic Evidence: A Reply to Schoeman' 54 *Philosophy of Science.*
Cohen, M (ed) (1983) *Ronald Dworkin and Contemporary Jurisprudence* (Totowa, Rowman and Allanheld).
Cohen, S (1984) 'Justification and Truth' 46 *Philosophical Studies.*
______ (1992) *An Essay on Belief and Acceptance* (Oxford, Clarendon Press).
——— (1999) 'Lehrer on Coherence and Self-Trust' 59 *Philosophy and Phenomenological Research.*
Coleman, J (1982) 'Negative and Positive Positivism' 11 *Journal of Legal Studies.*
______ (1987) (ed) 'Dworkin's Law's Empire' 6 *Law and Philosophy.* Special Issue.
——— (1998) 'Incorporationism, Conventionality and the Practical Difference Thesis' 4 *Legal Theory.*
——— (2001) *The Practice of Principle* (New York, Oxford University Press).
——— and Leiter B (1993) 'Determinacy, Objectivity and Authority' 142 *University of Pennsylvania Law Review.*
Comanducci, P and Guastini R (1987) *L'analisi del ragionamento giuridico* (Turin, Giappichelli).
Conte, ME (1988) *Condizioni di coerenza: ricerche di linguistica testuale* (Florence, La Nuova Italia).
——— (1989a) 'Coherence in Interpretation' in W Heydrich, F Neubauer, JS Petröfi and E Sözer (eds), *Connexity and Coherence: Analysis of Text and Discourse* (Berlin, DeGruyter).

——— (1989b) 'Coesione testuale: recenti ricerche italiane' in ME Conte (ed), *La linguistica testuale* (Milan, Feltrinelli).

Cooper, D (1985–86) 'Anthropology and Translation' 86 *Aristotelian Society Proceedings.*

Cooper, N (1994a) 'Understanding' Suppl 68 *Proceedings of the Aristotelian Society.*

——— (1994b) 'The Intellectual Virtues' 69 *Philosophy.*

Copp, D (1984) 'Considered Moral Judgments and Moral Justification: Conservatism in Moral Theory' in D Coop and D Zimmerman (eds), *Morality, Reason and Truth* (Totowa, Rowman and Littlefield).

Corfield, D and Williamson, J (eds) (2001) *Foundations of Bayesianism* (Dordrecht, Kluwer).

Craig, E (2000) 'Response to Lehrer' 60 *Philosophy and Phenomenological Research.*

Craig, RT (1990) 'Davidson and the Sceptic: The Thumbnail Version' 50 *Analysis.*

——— and Tracy, D (eds) (1983) *Conversational Coherence* (London, Sage).

Craik, K (1943) *The Nature of Explanation* (Cambridge, Cambridge University Press).

Cresto, E (2010) 'Belief and Contextual Acceptance' 177 *Synthese.*

Cross, CB (1999) 'Coherence and Truth Conducive Justification' 59 *Analysis.*

Crystal, D (ed) (1989) *The Cambridge Encyclopedia of Language* (Cambridge, Cambridge University Press).

Cullison, AD (1970) 'Identification by Probabilities and Trial by Arithmetic' 6 *Houston Law Review.*

Cummings, L (1998) 'The Scientific Reductionism of Relevance Theory: The Lesson from Logical Positivism' 29 *Journal of Pragmatics.*

Currie, G (1991) 'Interpreting Fictions' in R Freedman and L Reinhart (eds), *On Literary Theory and Philosophy* (London, MacMillan).

Dalmiya, V (1990) 'Coherence, Truth and the "Omniscient Interpreter"' 40 *The Philosophical Quarterly.*

Damasio, AR (1994) *Descartes's Error* (New York, Putnam's Sons).

Damaška, M (1990) 'Atomistic and Holistic Evaluation of Evidence: A Comparative View' in SD Clark (ed), *Comparative and Private International Law* (Berlin, Duncker and Humblot).

——— (1998) 'Truth in Adjudication' 49 *Hastings Law Journal.*

Damnjanovic, N and Candlish, S (2013) 'The Myth of the Coherence Theory of Truth' in M Textor (ed), *Judgment and Truth in Early Analytic Philosophy and Phenomenology* (Hampshire, Palgrave MacMillan).

Dancy, J (1984) 'On Coherent Theories of Justification: Can an Empiricist be a Coherentist?' 21 *American Philosophical Quarterly.*

——— (1985a) *An Introduction to Contemporary Epistemology* (Oxford, Blackwell).

——— (1985b) 'The Role of Imaginary Cases in Ethics' 66 *Pacific Philosophical Quarterly.*

——— (1993) *Moral Reasons* (Oxford, Blackwell).

Daniels, N (1980a) 'On Some Methods of Ethics and Linguistics' 37 *Philosophical Studies.*

——— (1980b) 'Reflective Equilibrium and Archimedean Points' 10 *Canadian Journal of Philosophy.*

——— (1996) 'Wide Reflective Equilibrium and Theory Acceptance in Ethics' in *Justice and Justification: Reflective Equilibrium in Theory and Practice* (Cambridge, Cambridge University Press).

Darwall, S Gilbbard, A and Railton, P (1997) 'Toward *Fin de Siècle* Ethics: Some Trends' in S Darwall, S Gilbbard and P Railton (eds), *Moral Discourse and Practice: Some Philosophical Approaches* (New York, Oxford University Press).

Dascal, M (1977) 'Conversational Relevance' 1 *Journal of Pragmatics.*

Dasenbrock, RW (1993) *Literary Theory After Davidson* (University Park Pennsylvania, Pennsylvania State University Press).

David, M (1991) 'On the Roles of Trustworthiness and Acceptance' 40 *Grazer Philosophische Studien.* Special issue.

Davidson, D (1984) *Inquiries into Truth and Interpretation* (Oxford, Oxford University Press).

——— (1990) 'The Structure and Content of Truth' 87 *The Journal of Philosophy.*

——— (1999) 'Reply to AC Genova' in LE Hahn (ed), *The Philosophy of Donald Davidson* (Chicago, Open Court).

——— (2001a) *Subjective, Intersubjective, Objective* (Oxford, Oxford University Press).

——— (2001b) *Essays in Actions and Events* (Oxford, Oxford University Press).

Davis, WA and Bender, J (1989) 'Fundamental Troubles with the Coherence Theory' in J Bender (ed), *The Current State of the Coherence Theory: Critical Essays on the Epistemic Theories of Keith Lehrer and Laurence BonJour, with Replies* (Dordrecht, Kluwer).

Dawes, GW (2013) 'Belief is not the Issue: A Defense of Inference to the Best Explanation' 26 *Ratio.*

Dawid, AP (2002) 'Bayes's Theorem and the Weighting of Evidence by Juries' in R Swinburne (ed), *Bayes's Theorem* (Oxford, Oxford University Press).

Day, T (1989) 'Circularity, Non-Linear Justification, and Holistic Coherentism' in J Bender (ed), *The Current State of the Coherence Theory: Critical Essays on the Epistemic Theories of Keith Lehrer and Laurence BonJour, with Replies* (Dordrecht, Kluwer).

——— and Kincaid, H (1994) 'Putting Inference to the Best Explanation in its Place' 98 *Synthese.*

Daya (1960) 'Types of Coherence' 10 *The Philosophical Quarterly.*

De Beaugrande, R and Dressler, W (1981) *Text, Discourse, and Process* (New Jersey, Norwood).

De George, RT (1990) 'Ethics and Coherence' 64 *Proceedings of the American Philosophical Association.*

DeGrazia, D (1992) 'Moving Forward in Bioethical Theory: Theories Cases, and Specified Principlism' 17 *The Journal of Medicine and Philosophy.*

DeMarco, JP (1994) *A Coherence Theory in Ethics* (Amsterdam, Rodopi).

_____ (1997) 'Coherence and Applied Ethics' 14 *Journal of Applied Philosophy.*

den Boer, M (1995) Review of *Anchored Narratives,* by WA Wagenaar, PJ Van Koppen and HFM Crombag 8 *International Journal for the Semiotics of Law.*

Dennett, D (1981) 'Intentional Systems' in *Brainstorms* (Cambridge, MIT).

——— (1990) 'The Interpretation of Texts, People, and other Artifacts' Suppl 1 *Philosophy and Phenomenological Research.*

DePaul, M (1986) 'Reflective Equilibrium and Foundationalism' 23 *American Philosophical Quarterly.*

——— (1987) 'Two Conceptions of Coherence Methods' 96 *Mind.*

——— (1988a) 'Argument and Perception: The Role of Literature in Moral Inquiry' 85 *The Journal of Philosophy.*

——— (1988b) 'Naiveté and Corruption in Moral Inquiry' 48 *Philosophy and Phenomenological Research.*

——— (1988c) 'The Problem of the Criterion and Coherence Methods in Ethics' 18 *Canadian Journal of Philosophy.*

——— (1993) *Balance and Refinement: Beyond Coherence Methods of Moral Inquiry* (London, Routledge).

——— (1998) 'Why Bother with Reflective Equilibrium?' in RM DePaul and W Ramsey (eds), *Rethinking Intuition: The Psychology of Intuition and its Role in Philosophical Inquiry* (Lanham, Rowman and Littlefield).

——— (ed) (2001) *Resurrecting Old-Fashioned Foundationalism* (Lanham, Rowman and Littlefield).

DeRose, K (1999) 'Contextualism: An Explanation and Defense' in J Greco and E Sosa (eds), *The Blackwell Guide to Epistemology* (Malden, Blackwell).

——— (2004) 'Single Scoreboard Semantics' 119 *Philosophical Studies.*

——— (2009) *The Case for Contextualism: Knowledge, Skepticism, and Context,* vol 1 (Oxford, Clarendon Press).

Dershowitz, AM (1996) *Reasonable Doubts: The Criminal Justice System and the O.J. Simpson Case* (New York, Simon and Schuster).

Dewey, J (1979) 'The Logic of Judgments of Practice' in JA Boydston (ed), *The Middle Works, 1899-1924,* vol 8 (Carbondale, Southern Illinois University Press).

——— 'Human Nature and Conduct' in JA Boydston (ed), *The Middle Works, 1899-1924,* vol 14 (Carbondale, Southern Illinois University Press).

——— (1988) 'Theory of Valuation' in JA Boydston (ed), *The Later Works, 1925-1953,* vol 13 (Carbondale, Southern Illinois University Press).

Dietrich, E (1989) 'Is Thagard's Theory of Explanatory Coherence the New Logical Positivism?' Open Peer Commentary on 'Explanatory Coherence' by P Thagard 12 *Behavioral and Brain Sciences.*

Dietrich, F and Moretti, L (2005) 'On Coherent Sets and the Transmission of Confirmation' 72 *Philosophy of Science.*

Donnelly, P (1997) 'Approximation, Comparison and Bayesian Reasoning in Juridical Proof' 1 *The International Journal of Evidence and Proof.*

Dorsey, D (2006) 'A Coherence Theory of Truth in Ethics' 127 *Philosophical Studies.*

Douven, I (1999) 'Inference to the Best Explanation Made Coherent' 66 *Philosophy of Science.*

——— and Meijs, W (2007) 'Measuring Coherence' 156 *Synthese.*

Doyle, J (1992) 'Reason Maintenance and Belief Revision: Foundations vs. Coherence Theories' in P Gärdenfors (ed), *Belief Revision* (Cambridge, Cambridge University Press).

Dretske, F (1981) 'The Pragmatic Dimension of Knowledge' 40 *Philosophical Studies.*

Dummett, M (1978) *Truth and Other Enigmas* (Cambridge, Harvard University Press).

——— (2001) 'Truth' in M Lynch (ed), *The Nature of Truth* (Cambridge, MIT).

Duran, J (1986) 'A Contextualist Modification of Cornman' 16 *Philosophia.*
——— (1993) 'Naturalizing Lehrer's Coherentism' 22 *Philosophical Papers.*
Dworkin, R (1972) 'No Right Answer?' in PMS Hacker and J Raz (eds), *Law, Morality and Society* (Oxford, Clarendon Press).
——— (1977) *Taking Rights Seriously* (Cambridge, Harvard University Press).
——— (1983a) 'A Reply by Ronald Dworkin' in M Cohen (ed), *Ronald Dworkin and Contemporary Jurisprudence* (Totowa, Rowman and Littlefield).
——— (1983b) 'My Reply to Stanley Fish (and Walter Benn Michaels): Please Don't Talk About Objectivity Any More' in WJT Mitchell (ed), *The Politics of Interpretation* (London, University of Chicago Press).
——— (1985) *A Matter of Principle* (Cambridge, Harvard University Press).
——— (1986) *Law's Empire* (London, Fontana).
——— (1993) 'Natural Law Revisited' in J Arthur and WH Shaw (eds), *Readings in the Philosophy of Law* (New Jersey, Prentice Hall).
——— (1994) 'Law, Philosophy, and Interpretation' 80 *Archiv für Rechts und Sozialphilosophie.*
——— (1996) 'Objectivity and Truth: You'd Better Believe it' 25 *Philosophy and Public Affairs.*
——— (2002) 'Thirty Years On' Review of *The Practice of Principle*, by J Coleman 15 *Harvard Law Review.*
——— (2011) *Justice for Hedgehogs* (Cambridge, Harvard University Press).
Earman, J (1992) *Bayes or Bust? A Critical Examination of Bayesian Confirmation Theory* (Cambridge, MIT Press).
Eco, U (1990) *I limiti dell' interpretazione* (Milan, Bompiani). Translated as *The Limits of Interpretation* (Bloomington, Indiana University Press, 1994).
Edmunson, WA (1996) 'The Antinomy of Coherence and Determinancy' 82 *Iowa Law Review.*
Eggleston, R (1983) *Proof and Probability,* 2nd edn (London, Weindenfield and Nicolson).
Elgin, C (1997) *Between the Absolute and the Arbitrary* (Ithaca, Cornell University Press).
Eliasmith, C and Thagard, P (1997) 'Waves, Particles, and Explanatory Coherence' 48 *The British Journal for the Philosophy of Science.*
Ellis, RE (1992) *Coherence and Verification in Ethics* (Lanham, University Press of America).
Endicott, T (1998) 'Herbert Hart and the Semantic Sting' 4 *Legal Theory.*
Engel, M (2012) 'Coherentism and the Epistemic Justification of Moral Beliefs: A Case Study in How to Do Practical Ethics without Appeal to a Moral Theory' 50 *The Southern Journal of Philosophy.*
Engel, P (ed) (2000) *Believing and Accepting* (Dordrecht, Kluwer).
Enkvist, NE (1977) 'Coherence, Pseudo-Coherence and Non-Coherence' in J Östman (ed), *Cohesion and Semantics* (Åbo, Publications of the Research Institute of the Åbo Foundation).
——— (1985) 'Coherence and Inference' in U Pieper and G Stickel (eds), *Studia Linguistica Diachronica et Synchronica* (Berlin, Mouton de Gruyter).
——— (1989) 'From Text to Interpretability: A Contribution to Discussion of Basic Terms in Text Linguistics' in W Heydrich, F Neubauer, J Petöfi and E Sözer (eds), *Connexity and Coherence: Analysis of Text and Discourse* (Berlin, De Gruyter).

Ennis, RH (1968) 'Enumerative Induction and Best Explanation' 65 *The Journal of Philosophy*.
Evnine, S (1991) *Donald Davidson* (Stanford, Stanford University Press).
Falappa, M, Kern-Isberner, G and Simari, G (2009) 'Belief Revision and Argumentation Theory' in G Simari and I Rahwan (eds), *Argumentation in Artificial Intelligence* (Dordrecht, Springer).
Fales, E (1996) *A Defense of the Given* (Lanham, Rowman and Littlefield).
Fantl, J and McGrath, M (2002) 'Evidence, Pragmatics, and Justification' 111 *The Philosophical Review*.
—— (2009) *Knowledge in an Uncertain World* (Oxford, Oxford University Press).
—— (2011) 'Pragmatic Encroachment' in S Bernecker and D Pritchard (eds), *The Routledge Companion to Epistemology* (London, Routledge).
Feder, E (1992) 'Semantic Fields and the Individuation of Content' in A Lehrer and E Feder (eds), *Frames, Fields and Contrasts: New Essays on Semantic and Lexical Organization* (Hillsdale, Erlbaum).
Feldman, R (1988) 'Epistemic Obligations' 2 *Philosophical Perspectives*.
—— (1989) 'Lehrer's Coherence Theory of Knowledge' in J Bender (ed), *The Current State of the Coherence Theory: Critical Essays on the Epistemic Theories of Keith Lehrer and Laurence BonJour, with Replies* (Dordrecht, Kluwer).
—— (2002) 'Epistemological Duties' in P Moser (ed), *The Oxford Handbook of Epistemology* (Oxford, Oxford University Press).
—— (2005) 'Justification Is Internal' in M Steup and E Sosa (eds), *Contemporary Debates in Epistemology* (Malden, Blackwell).
Fermé, E and Hansson, SO (2011) 'AGM 25 Years: Twenty-Five Years of Research in Belief Change' 40 *Journal of Philosophical Logic*.
Ferrer, J and Ratti, GB (eds) (2012) *The Logic of Legal Requirements: Essays on Defeasibility* (Oxford, Oxford University Press).
Festa, R, Aliseda, A and Peijnenburg, J (eds), (2005) *Confirmation, Empirical Progress and Truth Approximation* (Amsterdam, Rodopi).
Feteris, E (1999) *Fundamentals of Legal Argumentation: A Survey of Theories on the Justification of Judicial Decisions* (Dordrecht, Kluwer).
Fienberg, SE (1997) 'Theories of Legal Evidence: What Properties Should They Ideally Possess and When Are They Informative?' 1 *The International Journal of Evidence and Proof*.
Finkelstein, MO and Fairley WB (1970) 'A Bayesian Approach to Identification Evidence?' 83 *Harvard Law Review*.
Finnis, J (1987) 'On Reason and Authority in Law's Empire' 6 *Law and Philosophy*.
—— (1992) 'Natural Law and Legal Reasoning' in R George (ed), *Natural Law Theory* (Oxford, Clarendon Press).
Firth, R (1973) 'Coherence, Certainty and Epistemic Priority' in R Chisholm and R Swartz (eds), *Empirical Knowledge* (Englewood Cliffs, PrenticeHall).
Fish, S (1982) 'Working on the Chain Gang' 60 *Texas Law Review*.
—— (1983) 'Wrong Again' 60 *Texas Law Review*.
—— (1987) 'Still Wrong after All these Years' 6 *Law and Philosophy*.
Fitelson, B (2003) 'A Probabilistic Theory of Coherence' 63 *Analysis*.
Flach, PA and Kakas, AC (2001) 'Abduction and Inductive Reasoning: Background Issues' in PA Flach and AC Kakas (eds), *Abduction and Induction* (Dordrecht, Kluwer).

Fodor, J (1983) *The Modularity of Mind* (Cambridge, MIT Press).
——— (2000) *The Mind doesn't Work that Way* (Cambridge, MIT Press).
——— and Lepore, E (1992) *Holism: A Shopper's Guide* (Oxford, Blackwell).
Fogelin, RJ (2000) 'Contextualism and Externalism: Trading in One Form of Skepticism for Another' in E Sosa and E Villanueva (eds), 'Skepticism' 10 *Philosophical Issues*. Special issue.
——— (2003) *Walking the Tightrope of Reason: The Precarious Life of a Rational Animal* (New York, Oxford University Press).
Foley, R (1993) *Working without a Net: A Study of Egocentric Epistemology* (New York, Oxford University Press).
——— and Fumerton, R (1985) 'Davidson's Theism?' 48 *Philosophical Studies*.
Frankfurt, H (1971) 'Freedom of the Will and the Concept of Person' 68 *Journal of Philosophy*.
Friedman, RD (1992) 'Infinite Strands, Infinitesimally Thin: Story Telling, Bayesianism, Hearsay, and other Evidence' 14 *Cardozo Law Review*.
______ (1996) 'Assessing Evidence' 94 *Michigan Law Review*.
______ (1997a) 'Answering the Bayesioskeptical Challenge' 1 *The International Journal of Evidence and Proof*.
______ (1997b) 'Towards a (Bayesian) Convergence?' 1 *The International Journal of Evidence and Proof*.
Fritzman, J (1992) 'Against Coherence' 29 *American Philosophical Quarterly*.
Fuhrmann, A (1991) 'Theory Contraction though Base Contraction' 20 *Journal of Philosophical Logic*.
______ (1997) *An Essay on Contraction*. Studies in Logic, Language, and Information (Stanford, CSLI Publications).
Fuller, LL (1969), *The Morality of Law*, rev edn (New Haven, Yale University Press).
Fumerton, R (1980) 'Induction and Reasoning to the Best Explanation' 47 *Philosophy of Science*.
______ (1988) 'The Internalism/ Externalism Controversy' 2 *Philosophical Perspectives*.
______ (1992) 'Skepticism and Reasoning to the Explanation' 2 *Philosophical Issues*.
______ (1994) 'The Incoherence of Coherence Theories' 19 *Journal of Philosophical Research*.
______ (1999) 'A Critique of Coherentism' in L Pojman (ed), *The Theory of Knowledge: Classical and Contemporary Readings*, 2nd edn (Belmont, Wadsworth).
Galavotti, MC (1988) 'Rationality and Probability' in *Reason in Law* (Milan, A Giuffrè).
Galliers, JR (1992) 'Autonomous Belief Revision and Communication' in P Gärdenfors (ed), *Belief Revision* (Cambridge, Cambridge University Press).
Gärderfors, P (1988) *Knowledge in Flux* (Cambridge, MIT Press).
——— (1990) 'The Dynamics of Belief Systems: Foundations vs. Coherence Theories' 172 *Revue International de Philosophie*. Reprinted in P Gärderfors, (2005) *The Dynamics of Thought* (Dordrecht, Springer).
——— (2003) 'Belief Revision: An Introduction' in P Gärdenfors (ed), *Belief Revision* (Cambridge, Cambridge University Press).

——— and Makinson, D (1988) 'Revisions of Knowledge Systems Using Epistemic Entrenchment' in M Vardi (ed), *Theoretical Aspects of Reasoning about Knowledge* (Los Altos, Morgan Kaufman).

——— and Rott, H (1995) 'Belief Revision' in DM Gabbay, CJ Hogger and JA Robinson (eds), *Handbook of Logic in Artificial Intelligence and Logic Programming*, vol 4 (Oxford, Oxford University Press).

Garnham, A (1987) *Mental Models as Representations of Discourse and Text* (Chichester, Ellis Horwood).

——— and Oakhill, J (1996) 'The Mental Models Theory of Language Comprehension' in BD Britton and AC Graesser (eds), *Models of Understanding* (Mahwah, Erlbaun).

——— Oakhill, JV and Johnson-Laird, PN (1982) 'Referential Continuity and the Coherence of Discourse' 1 *Cognition*.

Gastwirth, JL (2000) *Statistical Science in the Courtroom* (New York, Springer-Verlag).

Gelfert, A (2010) 'Reconsidering the Role of Inference to the Best Explanation in the Epistemology of Testimony' 41 *Studies in History and Philosophy of Science*.

Genova, AC (1999) 'The Very Idea of Massive Truth' in LE Hahn (ed), *The Philosophy of Donald Davidson* (Chicago, Open Court).

Gernsbacher, MA and Givón, T (eds) (1995) *Coherence in Spontaneous Text* (Amsterdam, John Benjamins).

Gert, B Cluver, CM and Clouser KD (2000) 'Common Morality vs. Specified Principlism: Reply to Richardson' 25 *Journal of Medicine and Philosophy*.

Gianformaggio, L (1990) 'Legal Certainty, Coherence and Consensus: Variations on a Theme by MacCormick' in P Nerhot (ed), *Law, Interpretation, and Reality: Essays in Epistemology, Hermeneutics, and Jurisprudence* (Dordrecht, Kluwer).

Ginet, C (2005) 'Infinitism Is not the Solution to the Regress Problem' in M Steup and E Sosa (eds) *Contemporary Debates in Epistemology* (Malden, Blackwell).

Giora, R (1985a) 'A Text-Based Analysis of Non-Narrative Discourse' 12 *Theoretical Linguistics*.

——— (1985b) 'Notes Towards a Theory of Text Coherence' 6 *Poetics Today*.

——— (1985c) 'On the Informativeness Requirement' 12 *Journal of Pragmatics*.

——— (1997) 'Discourse Coherence and the Theory of Relevance: Stumbling Blocks in Search of a Unified Theory' 27 *Journal of Pragmatics*.

——— (1998) 'Discourse Coherence is an Independent Notion: A Reply to Deirdre Wilson' 29 *Journal of Pragmatics*.

_____ (2013) 'Cohesion' in G Khan (ed), *Encyclopedia of Hebrew Language and Linguistics* (Boston, Brill).

_____ (2014) 'Cognitive and Social Aspects of Coherence' in TM Holtgraves (ed) *Oxford Handbook of Language and Social Psychology* (New York, Oxford University Press).

_____Giora, R, Kotler, N, Shuval, N, and Fein, O (forthcoming) 'Know Hope: Metaphor, Coherence, Optimal Innovation and Pleasure' in G Brône, K Feyaerts and T Veale (eds), *Cognitive Linguistics Meets Humor Research: Current Trends and New Developments* (Berlin/New York, Mouton de Gruyter).

Givón, T (1995) 'Coherence in Text vs. Coherence in Mind' in MA Gernsbacher and T Givón (Amsterdam, John Benjamins).

Glanzberg, M (2002) 'Context and Discourse' 17 *Mind and Language*.

_____ (2013) 'Truth' in E Lepore and K Ludwig *A Companion to Donald Davidson* (Malden, Blackwell).
Glass, A (1988) 'Dworkin, Fish and Legal Practice' 19 *Rechtstheorie.*
Glass, DH (2007) 'Coherence Measures and Inference to the Best Explanation' 157 *Synthese.*
_____ (2012) 'Inference to the Best Explanation: Does it Track Truth?' 185 *Synthese.*
Godfrey-Smith, P (2003) *Theory and Reality: An Introduction to the Philosophy of Science* (Chicago, Chicago University Press).
Golanski, A (2000–01) 'Why Legal Scholar's Get *Daubert* Wrong: A Contextualist Explanation of Law's Epistemology' 22 *Whittier Law Review.*
Goldberg, S (2012) 'A Reliabilist Foundationalist Coherentism' 77 *Erkenntnis.*
Goldman, A (1976) 'Discrimination and Perceptual Knowledge' 73 *The Journal of Philosophy.*
——— (1979) 'What is Justified Belief?' in G Pappas (ed), *Justification and Knowledge* (Dordrecht, Reidel).
——— (1986) *Epistemology and Cognition* (Cambridge, Harvard University Press).
——— (1988) 'Strong and Weak Justification' 2 *Philosophical Perspectives.*
——— (1989) 'BonJour's Structure of Empirical Knowledge' in J Bender (ed), *The Current State of the Coherence Theory: Critical Essays on the Epistemic Theories of Keith Lehrer and Lawrence BonJour, with Replies* (Dordrecht, Kluwer).
_____ (2000) 'What is Justified Belief?' in E Sosa and J Kim (eds), *Epistemology: An Anthology* (Blackwell, Malden).
——— (2002) 'Quasi-Objective Bayesianism and Legal Evidence' 42 *Jurimetrics.*
Goldman, AH (1988a) *Moral Knowledge* (London, Routledge).
——— (1988b) 'Global Moral Commitment' 25 *American Philosophical Quarterly.*
——— (1989) 'Legal Reasoning as a Model for Moral Reasoning' 8 *Law and Philosophy.*
——— (1990) 'Skepticism about Goodness and Rightness' Suppl 29 *The Southern Journal of Philosophy.*
_____ (2002) *Practical Rules: When we Need them and when we Don't* (Cambridge, Cambridge University Press).
Goodman, N (1978) *Ways of World-Making* (Indianapolis, Hackett).
——— (1983) *Fact, Fiction and Forecast*, 4th edn (Cambridge, Harvard University Press).
——— (1985) *Languages of Art* (Indianapolis, Bobbs-Merrill).
Goroayska, B and Lindsay, R (1993) 'The Roots of Relevance' 19 *Journal of Pragmatics.*
Greco, J (1993) Review of *The Current State of the Coherence Theory*, edited by J Bender 27 *Noûs.*
_____ (2005) 'Justification Is not Internal' in M Steup and E Sosa (eds), *Contemporary Debates in Epistemology* (Malden: Blackwell).
Green, GM and Morgan, JL (1981) 'Pragmatics, Grammar, and Discourse' in P Cole (ed), *Radical Pragmatics* (New York, Academic Press).
Grice, P (1975) 'Logic and Conversation' in P Cole and J Morgan (eds), *Syntax and Semantics*, vol 3, *Speech Acts* (New York, Academic Press).
Groendendijk, J Stokhof, M and Veltman, F (1996) 'Coreference and Modality' in S Lappin (ed), *The Handbook of Contemporary Semantic Theory* (Oxford, Blackwell).

Grosz, BJ and Sidner, CL (1986) 'Attention Intention and the Structure of Discourse' 12 *Computational Linguistics*.

Grundmann, T (1999) 'BonJour's Self-Defeating Argument for Coherentism' 50 *Erkenntnis*.

Guarini, M (2007) 'Computation, Coherence, and Ethical Reasoning' 17 *Minds and Machines*.

Guest, S (2012) *Ronald Dworkin*, 3rd edn (Stanford, Stanford University Press).

Günther, K (1989) 'A Normative Conception of Coherence for a Discursive Theory of Legal Justication' 2 *Ratio Iuris*.

______ (1993) *The Sense of Appropriateness: Application Discourses in Morality and Law* (Albany, State University of New York Press).

______ (1995) 'Legal Adjudication and Democracy' 3 *European Journal of Philosophy*.

Haack, S (1993) *Evidence and Inquiry: Towards Reconstruction in Epistemology* (Oxford, Blackwell).

______ (1997) 'Précis of *Evidence and Inquiry: Towards Reconstruction in Epistemology*' 112 *Synthese*.

______ (2000) 'A Foundherentist Theory of Empirical Justification' in E Sosa and J Kim (eds), *Epistemology: An Anthology* (Malden, Blackwell).

______ (2004) 'Coherence, Consistency, Congruity, Cohesiveness &c.: Remain Calm! Don't Go Overboard!' 35 *New Literary History*.

______ (2012) 'The Embedded Epistemologist: Dispatches from the Legal Front' 25 *Ratio Iuris*.

Haakonssen, K (1981) 'The Limits of Reason and the Infinity of Argument' 67 *Archiv für Rechts und Sozialphilosophie*.

Habermas, J (1994) *Justification and Application: Remarks on Discourse Ethics* (Cambridge, MIT Press).

______ (1996) *Between Facts and Norms* (Cambridge, MIT Press).

Hacking, I (2001) *An Introduction to Probability and Inductive Logic* (Cambridge, Cambridge University Press).

Hage, JC (2001) 'Formalizing Legal Coherence' in *Proceedings of the 8th International Conference on Artificial Intelligence and Law* (New York, ACM).

______ (2003) 'Law and Defeasibility' 11 *Artificial Intelligence and Law*.

______ (2004) 'Law and Coherence' 17 *Ratio Iuris*.

______ (2005) *Studies in Legal Logic* (Berlin, Springer).

______ (2013) 'Three Kinds of Coherentism' in M Araszkiewicz and J Šavelka (eds), *Coherence: Insights from Philosophy, Jurisprudence and Artificial Intelligence* (Dordrecht, Springer).

______ and Peczenik, A (2000) 'Law, Morals, and Defeasibility' 13 *Ratio Iuris*.

Hájek, A and Hartmann, S (2010) 'Bayesian Epistemology' in J Dancy, E Sosa and M Steup (eds), *A Companion to Epistemology*, 2nd edn (Malden, Wiley-Blackwell).

Halbach, V (1999) 'On Lehrer's Principle of Trustworthiness' 50 *Erkenntnis*.

Hall, RJ and Johnson, CR (1998) 'The Epistemic Duty to Seek More Evidence' 35 *American Philosophical Quarterly*.

Halliday, MAK and Hasan, R (1976) *Cohesion in English* (London, Longman).

Haltutten, R (2000) 'Justification as a Process of Discovery' 13 *Ratio Iuris*.

Hampshire, S (1983) *Morality and Conflict* (Cambridge, Harvard University Press).

Hanen, M (1983) 'Justification as Coherence' in MA Stewart (ed), *Law, Morality, and Rights* (Kluwer, Dordrecht).

Hanson, N (1961) 'Is there a Logic of Discovery?' in H Feigl and G Maxwell (eds), *Current Issues in the Philosophy of Science* (New York, Holt, Rinehart, and Winston).

Hansson, SO (1994a) 'Taking Belief Bases Seriously' in D Prawitz and D Westertål (eds), *Logic and Philosophy of Science in Uppsala* (Dordrecht, Kluwer).

_____ (1994b) 'Kernel Contraction' 59 *Journal of Symbolic Logic.*

_____ (1996a) 'Knowledge-Level Analysis of Belief Base Operations' 82 *Artificial Intelligence.*

_____ (1996b) 'Extending Rabinowicz' Account of Stability' in S Lindström, R Sliwinski and J Östergerg (eds), *Odds and Ends: Philosophical Essays Dedicated to Wlodek Rabinowicz* (Uppsala, Dept of Philosophy, Uppsala University).

_____ (1997a) 'What's New Isn't Always Best' 63 *Theoria.*

_____ (1997b) 'Semi-Revision' 7 *Journal of Applied Non-Classical Logic.*

_____ (1999a) *A Textbook of Belief Dynamics: Theory Change and Database Updating* (Dordrecht, Kluwer).

_____ (1999b) 'A Survey of Non-Prioritized Belief Revision' in V Halbach and EJ Olsson (eds), 'Coherence and the Dynamics of Belief' 50 *Erkenntnis.* Special issue.

_____ (2003) 'Ten Philosophical Problems in Belief Revision' 13 *Journal of Logic and Computation.*

_____ (2006) 'Coherence in Epistemology and Belief Revision' 128 *Philosophical Studies.*

_____ and Olsson, EJ (1999) 'Providing Foundations for Coherentism' in V Halbach and EJ Olsson (eds), 'Coherence and the Dynamics of Belief' 50 *Erkenntnis.* Special issue.

_____ and Wassermann, R (2002) 'Local Change' 70 *Studia Logica.*

Hare, RM (1975) 'Rawls' Theory of Justice' in N Daniels (ed), *Reading Rawls: Critical Studies on Rawls' A Theory of Justice* (New York, Basic Books).

_____ (1981) *Moral Thinking* (Oxford, Clarendon).

_____ (1996) 'Foundationalism and Coherentism in Ethics' in W Sinnott-Armstrong and M Timmons (eds), *Moral Knowledge* (Oxford, Oxford University Press).

Harker, J (1984) 'Can There be an Infinite Regress of Justified Beliefs?' 62 *Australasian Journal of Philosophy.*

Harman, G (1965) 'Inference to the Best Explanation' 74 *The Philosophical Review.*

_____ (1968) 'Enumerative Induction and Inference to the Best Explanation' 65 *The Journal of Philosophy.*

_____ (1973) *Thought* (Princeton, Princeton University Press).

_____ (1979) *The Nature of Morality* (Oxford, Oxford University Press).

_____ (1980) 'Reasoning and Explanatory Coherence' 17 *American Philosophical Quarterly.*

_____ (1986) *Change in View: Principles of Reasoning* (Cambridge, MIT Press).

_____ (1995) 'Rationality' in E Smith and E Osherson (eds), *An Invitation to Cognitive Science*, vol 3 (Cambridge, MIT Press).

_____ (2004) 'Practical Aspects of Theoretical Reasoning' in AR Mele and P Rawling (eds), *The Oxford Handbook of Rationality* (New York, Oxford University Press).

_____ and Thomson, J (1996) *Moral Relativism and Moral Objectivity* (Cambridge, Blackwell).

Harper, W L (1976) 'Rational Conceptual Change' PSA 1976, vol 2 (East Lansing, Philosophy of Science Association).

Hastie, R (2008) 'What's the Story: Explanations and Narratives in Civil Jury Decisions' in BH Bornstein et al (eds), *Civil Juries and Civil Justice* (New York, Springer).

_____ and Pennington, N (1986) 'Evidence Evaluation in Complex Decision-Making' 51 *Journal of Personality and Social Psychology.*

_____ and _____ (1991) 'A Cognitive Theory of Juror Decision-Making: The Story Model' 13 *Cardozo Law Review.*

_____ and _____ (1992) 'Explaining the Evidence: Tests of the Story Model for Juror Decision-Making' 62 *Journal of Personality and Social Psychology.*

_____ and _____ (1993a) 'Reasoning in Explanation-Based Decision-Making' 49 *Cognition.*

_____ and _____ (1993b) 'The Story Model' in R Hastie (ed), *Inside the Juror: The Psychology of Juror Decision-Making* (Cambridge, Cambridge University Press).

_____ and _____ (1996) 'The O.J. Simpson Stories: Behavioral Scientists' Reflections on the People of the State of California V. Orenthal James Simpson' 67 *University of Colorado Law Review.*

_____ and _____ (2000) 'Explanation-Based Decision-Making' in T Connolly, HR Arkes and KH Hammond (eds), *Judgment and Decision-Making: An Interdisciplinary Reader*, 2nd edn (Cambridge, Cambridge University Press).

_____ and _____ (2003) 'The Story Model for Juror Decision-Making' in DD Koski and MJ Sacks (eds), *The Jury Trial in Criminal Justice* (Durham, Carolina Academic Press).

Hatakeyama, K, Petöfi J and Sözer, E (1985) 'Text, Connexity, Cohesion, Coherence' in E Sözer (ed), *Text Connexity, Text Coherence: Aspects, Methods, Results* (Hamburg, Buske).

Hawthorne, J and Stanley, J (2008) 'Knowledge and Action' 105 *The Journal of Philosophy.*

Heath, J (1997) 'Foundationalism and Practical Reason' 106 *Mind.*

Heil, J (1983) 'Believing what One Ought' 80 *The Journal of Philosophy.*

_____ (1992) 'Believing Reasonably' 26 *Nous.*

Hellman, C (1995) 'The Notion of Coherence in Discourse' in G Rickheit and C Habel (eds), *Focus and Coherence in Discourse Processing* (Berlin, DeGruyter).

Hempel, C (1934–35) 'On the Logical Positivist's Theory of Truth' 2 *Analysis.*

Henderson, DK (1994) 'Epistemic Competence and Contextualist Epistemology: Why Contextualism is Not Just the Poor Person's Coherentism' 91 *The Journal of Philosophy.*

Hendricks, FV and Faye, J (1999) 'Abducting Explanation' in L Magnani, NJ Nersessian and P Thagard (eds), *Model-Based Reasoning in Scientific Discovery* (New York, Kluwer/Plenum).

Hershovitz, S (ed) (2008) *Exploring Law's Empire: The Jurisprudence of Ronald Dworkin* (Oxford, Oxford University Press).

Hill, T (1989) 'Kantian Constructivism in Ethics' 99 *Ethics.*

Himma, KE (2002) 'Ambiguously Stung' 8 *Legal Theory.*

Hintikka, J (1998) 'What is Abduction? The Fundamental Problem of Contemporary Epistemology' 34 *Transactions of the Charles S. Peirce Society.*
Ho, HL (2008), *A Philosophy of Evidence Law: Justice in the Search for Truth* (Oxford, Oxford University Press).
______ (2012) 'Virtuous Deliberation on the Criminal Verdict' in A Amaya and HL Ho (eds), *Virtue, Law and Justice* (Oxford, Hart Publishing).
Hoadley, CM, Ranney, M and Schank, P (1994) 'WanderECHO: A Connectionist Simulation of Limited Coherence' in E Ram and K Eiselt (eds), *Proceedings of the Sixteenth Annual Conference of the Cognitive Science Society* (Hillsdale, Lawrence Erlbaum Associates).
Hobbs, JR (1983) 'Why is Discourse Coherent?' in F Neubauer (ed), *Coherence in Natural Language Texts* (Hamburg, Buske).
______ and Agar, MH (1985) 'The Coherence of Incoherent Discourse' 4 *Journal of Language and Social Psychology.*
______, Stickel, M, Appelt, D and Martin, P (1993) 'Interpretation as Abduction' 63 *Artificial Intelligence.*
Hodgson, D (1993) 'Probability: the Logic of the Law—A Response' 13 *Oxford Journal of Legal Studies.*
Hoffmaster, B (1980) 'A Holistic Approach to Judicial Justification' 15 *Erkenntnis.*
Holmgren, M (1987) 'Wide Reflective Equilibrium and Objective Moral Truth' 18 *Metaphilosophy.*
______ (1989) 'The Wide and Narrow Reflective Equilibrium' 19 *Canadian Journal of Philosophy.*
______ and Simon, D (1999) 'Bidirectional Reasoning in Decision-Making by Constraint Satisfaction' 128 *Journal of Experimental Psychology: General.*
______ and Thagard, P (1989) 'Analogical Mapping by Constraint Satisfaction' 13 *Cognitive Science.*
______ and Thagard, P (1995) *Mental Leaps: Analogy in Creative Thought* (Cambridge, MIT Press).
Honeyball, S and Walter, J (1998) *Integrity, Community, and Interpretation* (Dartmouth, Ashgate).
Hookway, C (1990) *Scepticism* (London and New York, Routledge).
Horwich, P (1990) *Truth* (Oxford, Blackwell).
Howson, C (1995) 'Theories of Probability' 46 *The British Journal for the Philosophy of Science.*
______ and Urbach, P (1993) *Scientific Reasoning: The Bayesian Approach* (Chicago, Open Court).
Huemer, M (1997) 'Probability and Coherence Justification' XXXV *The Southern Journal of Philosophy.*
______ (2007) 'Weak Bayesian Coherentism' 157 *Synthese.*
______ (2011) 'Does Probability Theory Refute Coherentism?' 108 *The Journal of Philosophy.*
Hurley, SL (1989) *Natural Reasons: Personality and Polity* (Oxford, Oxford University Press).
______ (1990) 'Coherence, Hypothetical Cases and Precedent' 10 *Oxford Journal of Legal Studies.*
Hursthouse, R (1999) *On Virtue Ethics* (Oxford, Oxford University Press).
Iranzo, V (2001) 'Bad Lots, Best Explanations' 33 *Crítica.*

_____ (2007) 'Abduction and Inference to the Best Explanation' 60 *Theoria*.

_____ (2008) 'Bayesianism and Inference to the Best Explanation' 61 *Theoria*.

Jackson, B (1985) *Semiotics and Legal Theory* (London, Routledge and Kegan Paul).

_____ (1988a) *Law, Fact, and Narrative Coherence* (Merseyside, Deborah Charles Publications).

_____ (1988b) 'Narrative Models in Legal Proof' 1 *International Journal for the Semiotics of Law*.

_____ (1991) 'Semiotic Scepticism: A Response to Neil MacCormick' 4 *International Journal for the Semiotics of Law*.

_____ (1992) 'MacCormick on Logical Justification in Easy Cases: A Semiotic Critique' 5 *International Journal of the Semiotics of Law*.

_____ (1995) *Making Sense in Law: Linguistic, Psychological, and Semiotic Perspectives* (Liverpool, Deborah Charles Publications).

_____ (1996a) *Making Sense in Jurisprudence* (Liverpool, Deborah Charles Publications).

_____ (1996b) '"Anchored Narratives" and the Interface of Law, Psychology and Semiotics' Review of *Anchored Narratives*, by WA Wagenaar, PJ Van Koppen and HFM Crombag 1 *Legal and Criminological Psychology*.

Jackson, F (1992) 'Critical Notice. S. L. Hurley, Natural Reasons: Personality and Polity' 70 *Australasian Journal of Philosophy*.

Jackson, JD (1990) 'Law, Fact, and Narrative Coherence: A Deep Look at Court Adjudication' 3 *International Journal for the Semiotics of Law*.

_____ and Doran, S (1995) *Judge without Jury: Diplock Trials in the Adversary System* (Oxford, Clarendon Press).

Joachim, HH (1906) *The Nature of Truth* (Oxford, Oxford University Press).

Johnson-Laird, PN (1983) *Mental Models: Towards a Cognitive Science of Language, Inference, and Consciousness* (Cambridge, Harvard University Press).

_____ (1990) 'Mental Models' in MI Posner (ed), *Foundations of Cognitive Science* (Cambridge, MIT Press).

Jonsen, AR and Toulmin, S (1988) *The Abuse of Casuistry: A History of Moral Reasoning* (Berkeley, University of California Press).

Joseph, S and Prakken, H (2009) 'Coherence-driven Argumentation to Norm Consensus' *Proceedings of the 12th International Conference on Artificial Intelligence and Law* (New York, ACM).

Josephson, JR (1994) 'Conceptual Analysis of Abduction' in JR Josephson and S Josephson (eds), *Abductive Inference: Computation, Philosophy, Technology* (Cambridge, Cambridge University Press).

_____ (1998) 'Abduction-Prediction Model of Scientific Inference Reflected in a Prototype System for Model-Based Diagnosis' 61 *Philosophica*.

_____ (2000) 'Smart Inductive Generalizations are Abductions' in PA Flach and AC Kakas (eds), *Abduction and Induction: Essays on their Relation and Integration* (Dordrecht, Kluwer).

_____ (2002) 'On the Proof Dynamics of Inference to the Best Explanation' in M MacCrimmon and P Tillers (eds), *The Dynamics of Judicial Proof* (Heidelberg, Physica-Verlag).

_____ and S Josephson (eds) (1994), *Abductive Inference: Computation, Philosophy, Technology* (Cambridge, Cambridge University Press).

Joyce, JM (2004) 'Bayesianism' in AR Mele and P Rawling (eds), *The Oxford Handbook of Rationality* (New York, Oxford University Press).

Jucker, AH (1999) Review of *Coherence in Spontaneous Text*, edited by MA Gernbascher and T Givón 27 *Journal of Pragmatics.*

Juhl, PD (1980) *Interpretation: An Essay in the Philosophy of Literary Criticism* (Princeton, Princeton University Press).

Kadane, JB and Schum, DA (1996) *A Probabilistic Analysis of the Sacco and Vanzetti Evidence* (New York, John Wiley and Sons).

Kantorovich, A (1993) *Scientific Discovery* (New York, State University of New York).

Kapitan, T (1992) 'Peirce and the Autonomy of Abductive Reasoning' 37 *Erkenntnis.*

_____ (1997) 'Peirce and the Structure of Abductive Inference' in N Hauser, DD Roberts and JV Evra (eds), *Studies in the Logic of Charles Sanders Peirce* (Bloomington, Indiana University Press).

Kasher, A (1976) 'Conversational Maxims and Rationality' in A Kasher (ed), *Language in Focus: Foundations, Methods, and Systems* (Dordrecht, Reidel).

_____ (1982) 'Gricean Inference Revisited' 29 *Philosophica.*

Kaye, DH (1988) 'Do We Need a Calculus of Weigh to Understand Proof Beyond Reasonable Doubt?' in P Tillers and E Green (eds), *Probability and Inference in the Law of Evidence: The Uses and Limits of Bayesianism* (Boston, Reidel).

_____ (1997) 'Statistical Decision Theory and the Burdens of Persuasion: Completeness, Generality and Utility' 1 *The International Journal of Evidence and Proof.*

_____ (1999) 'Clarifying the Burden of Persuasion: What Bayesian Decision Rules Do and Do not Do' 3 *International Journal of Evidence and Proof.*

Kehler, A (2004) 'Discourse Coherence' in L Horn and G Ward (eds), *The Handbook of Pragmatics* (Malden, Blackwell).

Kelly, KT (1987) 'The Logic of Discovery' 54 *Philosophy of Science.*

Kennedy, D (1997) *A Critique of Adjudication (fin de siècle)* (Cambridge, Harvard University Press).

Khalifa, K (2010) 'Default Privilege and Bad Lots: Underconsideration and Explanatory Inference' 24 *International Studies in the Philosophy of Science.*

Kim, K (1993) 'Internalism and Externalism in Epistemology' 30 *American Philosophical Quarterly.*

Kitcher, P (1992) 'The Naturalists Return' 101 *The Philosophical Review.*

_____ and Salmon, WC (eds) (1989) *Scientific Explanation* Minnesota Studies in the Philosophy of Science 13 (Minneapolis, University of Minnesota Press).

Klayman, J and Hogarth, RM (1989) 'Does ECHO Explain Explanation?' Open Peer Commentary on 'Explanatory Coherence' by P Thagard' 12 *Behavioral and Brain Sciences.*

Klein, P (1986) 'Radical Interpretation and Global Skepticism' in E Lepore (ed), *Truth and Interpretation: Perspectives on the Philosophy of Donald Davidson* (Oxford, Blackwell).

_____ (2005) 'Infinitism is the Solution to the Regress Problem' in M Steup and E Sosa (eds), *Contemporary Debates in Epistemology* (Malden, Blackwell).

_____ and Warfield, TA (1994) 'What Price Coherence?' 54 *Analysis.*

Koehler, JJ (1992) 'Probabilities in the Courtroom: An Evaluation of the Objections and Policies' in DK Kagohiro and WS Laufer (eds), *Handbook of Psychology and Law* (New York, Springer-Verlag).

Kolnai, A (1978) 'Deliberation is of Ends' in *Ethics, Value, and Reality* (Indianapolis, Hackett).

Kolodny, N (2007) 'How does Coherence Matter?' CVII *Proceedings of the Aristotelian Society.*

_____ (2008) 'Why Be Disposed to be Coherent?' 118 *Ethics.*

Kornblith, H (1983) 'Justified Belief and Epistemically Responsible Action' 92 *The Philosophical Review.*

_____ (1989) 'The Unattainability of Coherence' in Hackett (ed), *The Current State of the Coherence Theory: Critical Essays on the Epistemic Theories of Keith Lehrer and Laurence BonJour, with Replies* (Dordrecht, Kluwer).

_____ (1993) *Naturalizing Epistemology* (Cambridge, MIT Press).

_____ (ed) (2001) *Epistemology: Internalism and Externalism* (Malden, Blackwell).

Korsgaard, C (2003) 'Realism and Constructivism in the Twentieth Century Moral Philosophy' APA Centennial Supplement *The Journal of Philosophical Research.*

Kress, K (1984) 'Legal Reasoning and Coherence Theories: Dworkin's Right Thesis, Retroactivity, and the Linear Order of Decisions' 72 *California Law Review.*

_____ (1994) 'Coherence and Formalism' 16 *Harvard Journal of Law and Public Policy.*

_____ (1996) 'Coherence' in D Patterson (ed), *A Companion to Philosophy of Law and Legal Theory* (Cambridge, Blackwell).

Kris, E and Kaplan, A (1964) 'Aesthetic Ambiguity' in WE Kennick (ed), *Art and Philosophy* (New York, St. Martin's Press).

Kuipers, TAF (2000) *From Instrumentalism to Constructive Realism: On Some Relations between Confirmation, Empirical Progress and Truth Approximation* (Dordrecht, Kluwer).

_____ (2003) 'Inference to the Best Theory, rather than Inference to the Best Explanation' in F Stadler (ed), *Institute of Vienna Circle Yearbook* 10 (Kluwer, Dordrecht).

Kunda, Z (1999) *Social Cognition* (Cambridge, MIT Press).

_____ and Thagard, P (1996) 'Forming Impressions from Stereotypes, Traits, and Behaviours: A Parallel-Constraint Satisfaction Theory' 103 *Psychological Review.*

Kurzban, R and Aktipis, CA (2007) 'Modularity and the Social Mind: Are Psychologists Too Self-ish? 11 *Personality and Social Psychology Review.*

Kvanvig, J (1997) 'A Defense of Coherentism' 22 *Journal of Philosophical Research.*

_____ (2012) 'Coherentism and Justified Inconsistent Beliefs: A Solution' 50 *Philosophy and Phenomenological Research.*

La Rue, LH (1992) 'Stories Versus Theories at the Cardozo Evidence Conference: It's Just Another Metaphor to Me' 14 *Cardozo Law Review.*

Ladyman, J, Douven, I, Horsten, L and Van Fraassen, B (1997) 'A Defence of Van Fraassen's Critique of Abductive Inference: Reply to Psillos' 47 *The Philosophical Quarterly.*

Lance, M (2000) 'The Best is the Enemy of the Good: Bayesian Epistemology as a Case Study of Unhelpful Idealization' 71 *Ponzan Studies in the Philosophy of Science and the Humanities.*

Langley, P, Simon, HA, Bradshaw, GL and Zytkow, JM (1987) *Scientific Discovery: Computational Explorations of the Creative Process* (Cambridge, MIT Press).

Lariguet, G (2011) 'Todo lo que usted quería saber sobre la coherencia y no se atrevió a preguntarle a Amalia Amaya' X *Discusiones*.

Laudan, L (1977) *Progress and its Problems: Towards a Theory of Scientific Growth* (Berkeley and Los Angeles, University of California Press).

______ (2003) 'Is Reasonable Doubt Reasonable?' 9 *Legal Theory*.

Ledwon, L (2003) 'The Poetics of Evidence: Some Applications from Law & Literature' 21 *Quinnipiac Law Review*.

Lehrer, K (1974) *Knowledge* (Oxford, Clarendon Press).

______ (1979) 'The Gettier Problem and the Analysis of Knowledge' in G S Pappas (ed), *Justification and Knowledge* (Dordrecht, Reidel).

______ (1982) 'Knowledge, Truth, and Ontology' in W Leinfellner, E Kraemer and J Schank (eds), *Language and Ontology: Proceedings of the 6th International Wittgenstein Symposium* (Vienna, Hölder-Pichler-Tempsky).

______ (1983) 'Belief, Acceptance, and Cognition' in H Parret (ed), *On Believing* (Berlin, DeGruyter).

______ (1986a) 'Rationality and Trustworthiness' 8-9 *Protosoziologie*.

______ (1986b) 'The Coherence Theory of Knowledge' 14 *Philosophical Topics*.

______ (1988) 'Metaknowledge: Undefeated Justification' 74 *Synthese*.

______ (1989) 'Coherence and the Truth Connection: A Reply to my Critics' in J Bender (ed), *The Current State of the Coherence Theory: Critical Essays on the Epistemic Theories of Keith Lehrer and Laurence BonJour, with Replies* (Dordrecht, Kluwer).

______ (1990) *Metamind* (Oxford, Clarendon Press).

______ (1991a) 'Reply to Christian Piller' 40 *Grazer Philosophische Studien*. Special issue.

______ (1991b) 'Reply to Elvio Baccarini' 40 *Grazer Philosophische Studien*. Special issue.

______ (1991c) 'Reply to Marian David' 40 *Grazer Philosophische Studien*. Special issue.

______ (1997) *Self-Trust: A Study of Reason, Knowledge, and Autonomy* (Oxford, Clarendon Press).

______ (1999) 'Justification, Coherence, and Knowledge' 50 *Erkenntnis*.

______ (2000a) *Theory of Knowledge*, 2nd edn (Boulder, Westview Press).

______ (2000b) 'Discursive Knowledge' 60 *Philosophy and Phenomenological Research*.

______ (2000c) 'Acceptance and Belief Revisited' in P Engel (ed), *Believing and Accepting* (Dordrecht: Kluwer).

______ (2001) 'The Virtue of Knowledge' in A Fariweather and L Zagzbeski (eds) *Virtue Epistemology: Essays on Epistemic Virtue and Responsibility* (New York, Oxford University Press).

______ (2005) 'Coherence and the Truth Connection' 63 *Erkenntnis*.

______ and Cohen, S (1983) 'Justification, Truth, and Coherence' 55 *Synthese*.

Leiter, B (1998) 'Naturalism and Naturalized Jurisprudence' in B Bix (ed), *Analyzing Law: New Essays in Legal Theory* (Oxford, Clarendon Press).

______ (2001) 'Objectivity, Morality, and Adjudication' in B Leiter (ed), *Objectivity in Law and Morals* (Cambridge, Cambridge University Press).

Lemos, N (1989) 'Epistemic Priority and Coherence' in J Bender (ed), *The Current State of the Coherence Theory: Critical Essays on the Epistemic Theories of Keith Lehrer and Laurence BonJour, with Replies* (Dordrecht, Kluwer).

Lempert, R (1986) 'The New Evidence Scholarship: Analyzing the Process of Proof' 66 *Boston University Law Review.*

______ (1997) 'Of Flutes, Oboes and the *As If* World of Evidence Law' 1 *The International Journal of Evidence and Proof.*

Lenman, J and Shemmer, Y (2012a) 'Introduction' in J Lenman and Y Shemmer (eds), *Constructivism in Practical Philosophy* (Oxford, Oxford University Press).

______ (eds) (2012b) *Constructivism in Practical Philosophy* (Oxford, Oxford University Press).

Lenoble, J (1998) 'La théorie de la coherence narrative en droit' 33 *Archives de Philosophie du droit.*

Levenbaum, B (1984) 'Coherence in Legal Reasoning' 3 *Law and Philosophy.*

Levi, I (1977) 'Subjunctives, Dispositions, and Chances' 34 *Synthese.*

______ (1991) *The Fixation of Belief and its Undoing: Changing Beliefs through Inquiry* (Cambridge, Cambridge University Press).

Lewis, CI (1946) *An Analysis of Knowledge and Valuation* (La Salle, Open Court).

______ (1980) 'Veridical Hallucination and Prosthetic Vision' 58 *Australasian Journal of Philosophy.*

______ (1983) 'Radical Interpretation' in *Philosophical Papers*, vol 1 (Oxford, Oxford University Press).

______ (1996) 'Elusive Knowledge' 74 *Australasian Journal of Philosophy.*

Lifante, I (1999) *La interpretación jurídica en la teoría del Derecho contemporánea* (Madrid, Centro de Estudios Políticos y Constitucionales).

Ligertwood, A (1997) 'Bayesians and the World Out There' 1 *International Journal of Evidence and Proof.*

Lillquist, E (2002–03) 'Recasting Reasonable Doubt: Decision Theory and the Virtues of Variability' 36 *University of California Davis Law Review.*

Linfellner-Rupertsberger, E (1989) 'Connexity, Coherence, and the Semantic Net' in ME Conte, JS Petöfi and E Sözer (eds), *Text and Discourse Connectedness* (Amsterdam, John Benjamins).

Lipton, P (1993) 'Is the Best Good Enough?' 93 *Proceedings of the Aristotelian Society.*

______ (2000) 'Inference to the Best Explanation' in W Newton-Smith (ed), *A Companion to the Philosophy of Science* (Malden, Blackwell).

______ (2001) 'Is Explanation a Guide to Inference? A Reply to Wesley C. Salmon' in G Hon and SS Rakover (eds), *Explanation: Theoretical Approaches and Applications* (Dordrecht, Kluwer).

______ (2004) *Inference to the Best Explanation*, 2nd edn (London and New York, Routledge, 1st edn (1991).

______ (2007) 'Alien Abduction: Inference to the Best Explanation and the Management of Testimony' 4 *Episteme.*

Louden, RB (1997) 'On Some Vices of Virtue Ethics' in R Crisp and M Slote (eds) *Virtue Ethics* (Oxford, Oxford University Press).

Lugg, A (1985) 'The Process of Discovery' 52 *Philosophy of Science.*

Lundquist, L (1989) 'Coherence in Scientific Texts' in W Heydrich, W Heydrich, F Neubauer, J Petöfi and E Sözer (eds), *Connexity and Coherence: Analysis of Text and Discourse* (Berlin, DeGruyter).

Lycan, WG (1988) *Judgment and Justification* (New York, Cambridge University Press).

______ (1989) 'Explanationism, ECHO, and the Connectionist Paradigm' Open Peer Commentary on 'Explanatory Coherence' by P Thagard 12 *Behavioral and Brain Sciences*.

______ (1996) 'Plantinga and Coherentisms' in JL Kvanvig (ed), *Warrant and Contemporary Epistemology: Essays in Honor of Plantinga's Theory of Knowledge* (Lanham, Rowman and Littlefield).

______ (2012) 'Explanationist Rebuttals (Coherentism Defended Again)' 50 *The Southern Journal of Philosophy*.

Lynch, D (2001) 'Introduction: The Mystery of Truth' in D Lynch (ed) *The Nature of Truth* (Cambridge, MIT).

Lynch, MP (ed) (1998) 'Real Knowing: Situating Social Epistemology' 12 *Social Epistemology*. Special Issue.

MacCormick, N (1980) 'The Coherence of a Case and the Reasonableness of Doubt' 2 *Liverpool Law Review*.

______ (1981) 'The Limits of Reason: A Reply to Dr. Knud Haakonssen' 67 *Archiv für Rechts und Sozialphilosophie*.

______ (1982) 'The Nature of Legal Reasoning: A Brief Replay' 2 *Legal Studies*.

______ (1983) 'Dworkin as a Pre-Benthamite' in M Cohen (ed), *Ronald Dworkin and Contemporary Jurisprudence* (Totowa, Rowman and Allanheld).

______ (1984) 'Coherence in Legal Justification' in A Peczenik, L Lindahl and B van Roermund (eds), *Theory of Legal Science* (Dordrecht, Reidel). A revised version was published in W Krawietz et al (eds), (1984) *Theorie der Normen. Festgabe für Ota Weinberger zum* (Berlin, Duncker and Humblot).

______ (1985) 'The Limits of Rationality in Legal Reasoning' 11 *Rechstheorie*.

______ (1991) 'Notes on Narrativity and the Normative Syllogism' 4 *International Journal for the Semiotics of Law*.

______ (1992) 'A Deductivist Rejoinder to a Semiotic Critique' 5 *International Journal of the Semiotics of Law*.

______ (1993) 'Argumentation and Interpretation in Law' 6 *Ratio Iuris*.

______ (1994) *Legal Reasoning and Legal Theory* (Oxford, Clarendon Press).

______ (1995) 'Defeasibility in Law and Logic' in Z Bankowski et al (eds), *Informatics and the Foundations of Legal Reasoning* (Dordrecht, Kluwer).

______ (1999) 'My Philosophy of Law' in LJ Wintgens (ed), *The Law in Philosophical Perspectives* (Dordrecht, Kluwer).

______ (2005) *Rhetoric and the Rule of Law: A Theory of Legal Reasoning* (Oxford, Oxford University Press).

______ (2008) *Practical Reason in Law and Morality* (Oxford, Oxford University Press).

______ and Summers, RS (1991) 'Interpretation and Justification' in N MacCormick and RS Summers (eds), *Interpreting Statutes: A Comparative Study* (Aldershot, Dartmouth).

MacCormick, PJ (1996) *Starmaking: Realism, Anti-Realism, Irrealism* (Cambridge, MIT Press).

Mackie, J (1983) 'The Third Theory of the Law' in M Cohen (ed), *Ronald Dworkin and Contemporary Jurisprudence* (Totowa, Rowman and Allanheld).

Mackonis, A (2013) 'Inference to the Best Explanation, Coherence and other Explanatory Virtues' 190 *Synthese*.

Magnani, L (2001) *Abduction, Reason, and Science* (Dordrecht, Kluwer).

_____ (2009) *Abductive Cognition: The Epistemological and Eco-Cognitive Dimensions of Hypothetical Reasoning* (Dordrecht, Springer-Verlag).

Magnell, T (1994) 'Dialogue. The Place of Coherence and Moral Rules in Ethics: Richard De George and Bernard Gert' 28 *The Journal of Value Inquiry.*

Makinson, DC (2005) *Bridges from Classical to NonMonotonic Logic* (London, College Publications).

_____ and Gärdenfors, P (1991) 'Relations between the Logic of Theory Change and Nonmonotonic Logic' in A Fuhrmann and Morreau, M (eds), *The Logic of Theory Change* (Berlin, Springer-Verlag).

Malpas, JE (1992) *Donald Davidson and the Mirror of Meaning: Holism, Truth, Interpretation* (Cambridge, Cambridge University Press).

Maniaci, G (2008) *Razionalità ed equilibrio riflessivo nell' argomentazione giudiziale* (Turin, Giappichelli).

Mann, W and Thompson, S (1986) 'Relational Propositions in Discourse' 9 *Discourse Processes.*

Manning, R (1994) 'Justified Acceptance, Information, and Knowledge' 25 *The Philosophical Forum.*

Maranhão, J (2009) 'Conservative Contraction' in W Carnielli, ME Coniglio, IM Loffredo D'Ottaviano (eds) *The Many Sides of Logic* (London, College Publications).

_____ (2011) 'Coherencia en el Derecho: conservadurismo y fidelidad a la base de las reglas' X *Discusiones.*

_____ (2012a) 'Defeasibility, Contributory Conditionals, and Refinement of Legal Systems' in J Ferrer and G Ratti (eds), *The Logic of Legal Requirements: Essays on Defeasibility* (Oxford, Oxford University Press).

_____ (2012b) *Positivismo jurídico lógico-inclusivo* (São Paolo, Marcial Pons).

_____ (2013) *Estudos sobre lógica e direito* (São Paolo, Marcial Pons).

Mares, ED (2002) 'A Paraconsistent Theory of Belief Revision' 56 *Erkenntnis.*

Margolis, J (1984) 'The Locus of Coherence' 7 *Linguistics and Philosophy.*

Markman, AB (2002) 'Can't We all Just Get Along?' Review of *Coherence in Thought and Action,* by P Thagard 11 *Metascience.*

Marmor, A (1991) 'Coherence, Holism, and Interpretation: The Epistemic Foundations of Dworkin's Legal Theory' 10 *Law and Philosophy.*

_____ (1992) *Interpretation and Legal Theory* (Oxford, Clarendon Press).

Mattey, GJ (1989) 'Personal Coherence, Objectivity and Reliability' in J Bender (ed), *The Current State of the Coherence Theory: Critical Essays on the Epistemic Theories of Keith Lehrer and Laurence BonJour, with Replies* (Dordrecht, Kluwer).

May, L, Friedman, M and Clark, A (1996) 'Introduction' in L May, M Friedman and A Clark (eds), *Mind and Morals: Essays on Cognitive Science and Ethics* (Cambridge, MIT Press).

McAuliff, BD, Nemeth, RJ, Borstein, BH and Penrod, SD (2003) 'Jury Decision-Making in the Twenty-First Century: Confronting Science and Technology in Court' in D Carson and R Bull (eds), *Handbook of Psychology in Legal Contexts,* 2nd edn (Chichester, John Wiley and Sons, Ltd.).

McCauley, R (1989) 'Acceptability, Analogy, and the Acceptability of Analogies' Open Peer Commentary on 'Explanatory Coherence' by P Thagard 12 *Behavioral and Brain Sciences.*

McGarry, J (2013) 'The Possibility and Value of Coherence' 34 *Liverpool Law Review*.

McGinn, C (1986) 'Radical Interpretation and Epistemology' in E Lepore (ed), *Truth and Interpretation: Perspectives on the Philosophy of Donald Davidson* (Oxford, Blackwell).

McJohn, SM (1993) 'On Uberty: Legal Reasoning by Analogy and Peirce's Theory of Abduction' 29 *Willamette Law Review*.

McNally, L (1998) 'On Recent Formal Analysis of Topic' in J Ginzburg, Z Khasidashvili, C Vogel, JJ Lévy and E Vallduví (eds), *The Tbilisi Symposium on Logic, Language, and Computation* (Stanford, CSLI).

Meheus, J and Nickles, T (1999) 'Scientific Discovery and Creativity: Methodological Approaches' 4 *Foundations of Science*.

Meijs, W (2007) 'A Corrective to Bovens and Hartmann's Measure of Coherence' 133 *Philosophical Studies*.

_____ and Douven, I (2005) 'Bovens and Hartmann on Coherence' 113 *Mind*.

_____ and _____ (2007) 'On the Alleged Impossibility of Coherence' 157 *Synthese*.

Menashe, D and Shamash, HE (2005) 'Pass the Sirens By: Further Thoughts on Narrative and Admissibility Rules' 5 *International Commentary on Evidence*.

Mercier, H (2012) 'The Social Functions of Explicit Coherence Evaluation' 11 *Mind and Society*.

_____ and Sperber, D (2011) 'Why Do Humans Reason? Arguments for an Argumentative Theory' 34 *Behavioral and Brain Sciences*.

Merricks, T (1995) 'On Behalf of the Coherentist' 55 *Analysis*.

Michaels, WB (1983) 'Is There a Politics of Interpretation?' in WJT Mitchell (ed), *The Politics of Interpretation* (Chicago, University of Chicago Press).

Michelon, C (2011a) 'Las razones de la coherencia' X *Discusiones*.

_____ (2011b) 'Princípios e Coerência na Argumentação Jurídica' in C Barbieri and RP Macedo Jr (eds), *Direito e Interpretação: Racionalidade e Instituições* (São Paolo, Saraiva).

Michon, JA (1997) 'The Time Has Come to Put this Debate Aside and Move on to Other Matters' 1 *International Journal of Evidence and Proof*.

Mignolo, WD (1989) 'Semiosis, Coherence, and Universes of Meaning' in ME Conte, JS Petöfi, and E Sözer (eds), *Text and Discourse Connectedness* (Amsterdam, John Benjamins).

Miller, D (1974) 'Popper's Qualitative Theory of Verisimilitude' 25 *The British Journal for the Philosophy of Science*.

Miller, L and Read, S (1991) 'On the Coherence of Mental Models of Persons and Relationships' in G Fletcher and F Finchman (eds), *Cognition in Close Relationships* (Hillsdale, Erlbaum).

Millgram, E (1991) 'Harman's Hardness Arguments' 72 *Pacific Philosophical Journal*.

_____ (1994) Review of *Practical Reasoning about Final Ends*, by HS Richardson 105 *Mind*.

_____ (1997) *Practical Induction* (Cambridge, Harvard University Press).

_____ (2000) 'Coherence: The Prize of the Ticket' 97 *The Journal of Philosophy*.

_____ (2001) 'Practical Reasoning: The Current State of Play' in E Millgram (ed), *Varieties of Practical Inference* (Cambridge, MIT Press).

______ (ed) (2001) *Varieties of Practical Inference* (Cambridge, MIT Press).
______ and Thagard, P (1996) 'Deliberative Coherence' 108 *Synthese.*
Minnameier, G (2004) 'Peirce-Suit of Truth—Why Inference to the Best Explanation and Abduction Ought not to be Confused' 60 *Erkenntnis.*
Minsky, M (1975) 'A Framework for Representing Knowledge' in PH Winston (ed), *The Psychology of Computer Vision* (New York, McGraw Hill).
Mnookin, J (2013) 'Atomism, Holism, and the Judicial Assessment of Evidence' 60 *UCLA Law Review.*
Moeschler, J (1989) 'Pragmatic Connectives, Argumentative Coherence and Relevance' 3 *Argumentation.*
Montmarquet, J (1987) 'Epistemic Virtue' 96 *Mind.*
______ (1993) *Epistemic Virtue and Doxastic Responsibility* (Lanham, Rowman and Littlefield).
Moore, M (1985) 'A Natural Law Theory of Interpretation' 85 *California Law Review.*
______ (1987) 'Metaphysics, Epistemology, and Legal Theory' 60 *Southern California Law Review.*
______ (2004) *Objectivity in Ethics and Law* (Dartmouth, Ashgate).
Moral, L (2003) 'A Modest Notion of Coherence in Legal Reasoning: A Model for the European Court of Justice' 16 *Ratio Iuris.*
Moravcsik, JME (1990) *Thought and Language* (London and New York, Routledge).
Moretti, L (2007) 'Ways in which Coherence is Confirmation Conducive' 157 *Synthese.*
Moser, PK (1985) *Empirical Justification* (Dordrecht and Boston, Reidel).
______ (1986) Review of *The Structure of Empirical Knowledge*, by L BonJour 47 *Philosophy and Phenomenological Research.*
______ (1988) 'Internalism and Coherentism: A Dilemma' 48 *Analysis.*
______ (1989) 'Lehrer's Coherentism and the Isolation Objection' in J Bender (ed), *The Current State of the Coherence Theory: Critical Essays on the Epistemic Theories of Keith Lehrer and Laurence BonJour, with Replies* (Dordrecht, Kluwer).
Nagel, T (1979) 'The Fragmentation of Value' in *Mortal Questions* (Cambridge, Cambridge University Press).
Nance, DA (2001) 'Naturalized Epistemology and the Critique of Evidence Theory' 87 *Virginia Law Review.*
Nayak, AC, Nelson, P and Polansky, H (1996) 'Belief Change as Change in Epistemic Entrenchment' 109 *Synthese.*
Nerhot, P (1990) 'Interpretation and Legal Science' in P Nerhot (ed), *Law, Interpretation, and Reality: Essays in Epistemology, Hermeneutics, and Jurisprudence* (Dordrecht, Kluwer).
Nesson, C (1979) 'Reasonable Doubt and Permissive Inferences: The Value of Complexity' 92 *Harvard Law Review.*
______ (1985) 'The Evidence of the Event? On Judicial Proof and the Acceptability of Verdicts' 98 *Harvard Law Review.*
______ (1986) 'Agent Orange Meets Blue Bus: Fact-Finding at the Frontier of Knowledge' 66 *Boston University Law Review.*
Neubauer, F (ed) (1983) *Coherence in Natural Language Texts* (Hamburg, Buske).

Neurath, O (1959) 'Protocol Sentences' in AJ Ayer (ed), *Logical Positivism* (New York, The Free Press).
Newton-Smith, WH (2000) 'Explanation' in WH Newton-Smith (ed), *A Companion to the Philosophy of Science* (Malden, Blackwell).
Nickles, T (ed) (1980) *Scientific Discovery, Logic, and Rationality* (Dordrecht, Reidel).
______ (1985) 'Beyond Divorce: Current Status of the Discovery Debate' 52 *Philosophy of Science.*
Nicolson, D (1994) 'Truth, Reason, and Justice: Epistemology and Politics in Evidence Discourse' 57 *Modern Law Review.*
Niiniluoto, I (1999) 'Defending Abduction' 66 *Philosophy of Science.*
______ (2003) 'Truth-Seeking by Abduction' in F Stadler (ed), 10 *Institute of Vienna Circle Yearbook* (Kluwer, Dordrecht).
Nine, C and Lehrer, K (2001) 'The Functional Role of Acceptance in Lehrer's Theory of Knowledge' 32 *The Philosophical Forum.*
Nino, CS (1988) 'Constructivismo epistemológico: entre Habermas y Rawls' 5 *Doxa: Cuadernos de Filosofía del Derecho.*
______ (1989) *El Constructivismo Ético* (Madrid, Centro de Estudios Constitucionales).
Noorman, L, Sanders, T and Spooren, W (1992) 'Toward a Taxonomy of Coherence Relations' 15 *Discourse Processes.*
______, ______ and ______ (1993) 'Coherence Relations in a Cognitive Theory of Discourse Representation' 4 *Cognitive Linguistics.*
Norris, C (1999) 'Truth, Interpretation, and the Web of Belief: Some Problems with Meaning-Holism' 11 *Philosophical Writings.*
Nozick, R (1981) *Philosophical Explanations* (Cambridge, Harvard University Press).
______ (1993) *The Nature of Rationality* (Princeton, Princeton University Press).
Oakley, J and Cocking, D (2001) *Virtue Ethics and Professional Roles* (Cambridge, Cambridge University Press).
Oaksford, M and Chater, N (2007) *Bayesian Rationality: The Probabilistic Approach to Human Reasoning* (New York: Oxford University Press).
Olsson, EJ (1997a) 'A Coherence Interpretation of Semi-Revision' 63 *Theoria.*
______ (1997b) 'Coherence and the Modularity of Mind' 75 *Australasian Journal of Philosophy.*
______ (1997c) 'Coherence: Studies in Epistemology and Belief Revision' (Uppsala, Comprehensive Summaries of Uppsala Dissertations).
______ (1998) 'Making Beliefs Coherent' 7 *Journal of Logic, Language, and Information.*
______ (1999) 'Cohering With' 50 *Erkenntnis.*
______ (2001) 'Why Coherence is not Truth-Conducive? 61 *Analysis.*
______ (2002) 'What is the Problem of Coherence and Truth?' 99 *The Journal of Philosophy.*
______ (ed) (2003) *The Epistemology of Keith Lehrer* (Dordrecht, Kluwer).
______ (2005) *Against Coherence: Truth, Probability, and Justification* (Oxford, Oxford University Press).
______ and Enqvist, S (eds) (2011) *Belief Revision Meets Philosophy of Science* (Berlin, Springer).

______and Schubert, S (2007) 'Reliability Conducive Measures of Coherence' 157 *Synthese*.

Ost, F (1985) 'La légitimité dans le discours juridique: Cohérence, performance, consensus ou dissensus?' in N MacCormick, S Panou and L Lombardi (eds), *Conditions of Validity and Cognition in Modern Legal Thought* (Stuttgart, Franz Steiner Verlang).

Österman, B (2001) 'Is There a General Theory of Understanding?' 69 *Acta Philosophica Fennica*.

Paavola, S (2006) 'Hanssonian and Harmanian Abduction as Models of Discovery' 20 *International Studies in the Philosophy of Science*.

Pagin, P (2013) 'Radical Interpretation and the Principle of Charity' in E Lepore and K Ludwig, *A Companion to Donald Davidson* (Malden, Blackwell).

Papaux, A (1999) 'Hermenéutique juridique, qualification et abduction' 42 *Revue Interdisciplinaire d'Études Juridiques*.

Papinau, D (1993) *Philosophical Naturalism* (Oxford, Basil Blackwell).

Pardo, MS (2000) 'Juridical Proof, Evidence, and Pragmatic Meaning: Toward Evidentiary Holism' 95 *Northwestern University Law Review*.

______ (2013) 'The Nature and Purpose of Evidence Theory' 66 *Vanderbilt Law Review*.

______ and Allen RJ (2008) 'Juridical Proof and the Best Explanation' 27 *Law and Philosophy*.

Park, C (1990–91) 'Evidence Scholarship, Old and New' 75 *Minnesota Law Review*.

______ and Saks, MJ (2006) 'Evidence Scholarship Reconsidered: Results of the Interdisciplinary Turn' 46 *Boston College Law Review*.

______ et al (2010) 'Bayes Wars Redivivus—An Exchange' 8 *International Commentary on Evidence*.

Pastore, B (1991) 'Sistemi Normativi e Coerenza' in L Gianformaggio (ed), *Sistemi normativi statici e dinamici* (Turin, Giappichelli).

Patterson, D (1996) *Law and Truth* (Oxford, Oxford University Press).

Peczenik, A (1989) *On Law and Reason* (Dordrecht, Kluwer).

______ (1990) 'Coherence, Truth, and Rightness in the Law' in P Nerhot (ed), *Law, Interpretation, and Reality: Essays in Epistemology, Hermeneutics, and Jurisprudence* (Dordrecht, Kluwer).

______ (1992) 'Weighing Values' 14 *International Journal for the Semiotics of Law*.

______ (1994) 'Law, Morality, Coherence and Truth' 7 *Ratio Iuris*.

______ (1995) 'Argumentation in Ethics, Legal Dogmatics, and Legal Practice' 9 *Argumentation*.

______ (1997a) 'Jumps and Logic in the Law' in H Prakken and G Sartor (eds), *Logical Models of Legal Argumentation* (Dordrecht, Kluwer).

______ (1997b) 'The Passion for Reason: Some Remarks on Coherence in the Law' in E Garzón Valdés, W Krawietz, GH von Wright and R Zimmerling (eds), *Normative Systems in Legal and Moral Theory* (Berlin, Ducker and Humblot).

______ (1998a) 'A Coherence Theory of Juristic Knowledge' in A Aarnio et al (eds), *On Coherence Theory of Law* (Lund, Juristförlager i Lund).

______ (1998b) 'Second Thoughts on Coherence and Juristic Knowledge' in A Aarnio et al (eds), *On Coherence Theory of Law* (Lund, Juristförlager i Lund).

______ (1999) 'The Passion for Reason' in LJ Wintgens (ed), *The Law in Philosophical Perspectives* (Dordrecht, Kluwer).

______ (2000a) 'Certainty or Coherence?' in W Krawietz et al (eds), *The Reasonable as Rational? On Legal Argumentation and Justification. Festschrift for Aulis Aarnio* (Berlin, Duncker and Humblot).

______ (2000b) 'Scientia Iuris–An Unsolved Philosophical Problem' 2 *Ethical Theory and Moral Practice.*

______ (2004) 'Can Philosophy Help Legal Doctrine?' 17 *Ratio Iuris.*

______ (2009) *On Law and Reason*, 2nd edn (Dordrecht, Springer).

______ and Hage, JC (2004) 'Legal Knowledge of What?' 13 *Ratio Iuris.*

Peirce, CS (1932–58) *Collected Papers of Charles Sanders Peirce* in P Weiss, C Hartshorne and AW Burk (eds), (Cambridge, Harvard University Press).

Peng, PCH and Keane, M (1989) 'Explanatory Coherence as a Psychological Theory, Open Peer Commentary on 'Explanatory Coherence' by P Thagard 12 *Behavioral and Brain Sciences.*

Peng, Y and Reggia, J (1990) *Abductive Inference Models for Diagnostic Problem Solving* (New York, Springer-Verlag).

Peppas, P (2008) 'Belief Revision' in F van Harmelen, V Lifschitz and B Porter (eds) *Handbook of Knowledge Representation* (Amsterdam, Elsevier).

Pérez-Bermejo, JM (2006) *Coherencia y sistema jurídico* (Madrid-Barcelona, Marcial Pons).

______ (2007) 'Alcune osservazioni sul valore della coerenza nei sistemi giuridici' 7 *Diritto e Questioni Pubbliche.*

______ (2013) 'Coherence: An Outline in Six Metaphors' in M Araszkiewicz and J Šavelka (eds), *Coherence, Insights from Philosophy, Jurisprudence, and Artificial Intelligence* (Dordrecht, Springer).

Perry, M (1979) 'Literary Dynamics: How the Order of a Text Creates its Meanings' 1 *Poetics Today.*

Peterson, P (1989) 'How Reasonable is Lehrer's Coherence Theory? Beats me' in J Bender (ed), *The Current State of the Coherence Theory: Critical Essays on the Epistemic Theories of Keith Lehrer and Laurence BonJour, with Replies* (Dordrecht, Kluwer).

Pethick, S (2008) 'Solving the Impossible: The Puzzle of Coherence, Consistency and Law' 59 *Northern Ireland Legal Quarterly.*

______ (2014) 'On the Entanglement of Coherence' 27 *Ratio Iuris.*

Petöfi, J (1985) 'Procedural Aspects of Text Interpretation: Interaction between Text and Interpreter in the Meaning-Constitutive Interpretation' in E Sözer (ed), *Text Connexity, Text Coherence: Aspects, Methods, Results* (Hamburg, Buske).

Piller, C (1991) 'On Keith Lehrer's Belief in Acceptance' in J Brandl, WL Gombocz and C Piller (eds), 'Metamind, Knowledge, and Coherence: Essays in the Philosophy of Keith Lehrer' 40 *Grazer Philosophische Studien.* Special issue.

Pino, G (1998) 'Coerenza e verità nell'argomentazione giuridica. Alcune riflessioni' 1 *Rivista Internazionale di Filosofia del Diritto.*

Pintore, A (2000) *Law Without Truth* (Liverpool, Deborah and Charles Publications).

Pitt, J (1988) *Theories of Explanation* (New York, Oxford University Press).

Plantinga, A (1993) *Warrant: The Current Debate* (Oxford, Oxford University Press).

Platts, M (1979) *Ways of Meaning* (London, Routledge).

Pollock, J (1974) *Knowledge and Justification* (Princeton, Princeton University Press).

______ (1984) 'Reliability and Justified Belief' 14 *Canadian Journal of Philosophy.*

______ (1986) *Contemporary Theories of Knowledge* (Totowa, Rowman and Littlefield).

Pollock, J and Gillies, AS (2000) 'Belief Revision and Epistemology' 122 *Synthese.*

Poston, T (ed) (2012) 'Epistemic Coherentism' 50 *Southern Journal of Philosophy.* Special issue.

Prakken, H (1997) *Logical Tools for Modeling Legal Argument: A Study of Defeasible Reasoning in Law* (Dordrecht, Kluwer).

______ and Sartor, G (2004) 'The Three Faces of Defeasibility in Law' 17 *Ratio Iuris.*

Pryor, J (2001) 'Highlights of Recent Epistemology' 52 *The British Journal for the Philosophy of Science.*

Psillos, S (1996) 'On Van Fraassen's Critique of Abductive Reasoning' 46 *The Philosophical Quarterly.*

______ (1997) 'How Not to Defend Constructive Empiricism: A Rejoinder' 47 *The Philosophical Quarterly.*

______ (2001) 'Abduction: Between Conceptual Richness and Computational Complexity' in PA Flach and AC Kakas (eds), *Abduction and Induction: Essays on their Relation and Integration* (Dordrecht, Kluwer).

______ (2002) 'Simply the Best: A Case for Abduction' in AC Kakas and F Sadri (eds), *Computational Logic* (Berlin, Springer-Verlag).

______ (2004) 'Inference to the Best Explanation and Bayesianism' in F Stadler (ed), *Institute of Vienna Circle Yearbook* 10 (Kluwer, Dordrecht).

______ (2007) 'The Fine Structure of Inference to the Best Explanation' 74 *Philosophy and Phenomenological Research.*

Puntel, LB (1998) 'Is Truth Ideal Coherence?' in A Wüstehube and M Quante (eds), *Pragmatic Idealism: Critical Essays on Nicholas Rescher's System of Pragmatic Idealism* (Amsterdam, Rodopi).

Putnam, H (1975) 'The Refutation of Conventionalism' in *Mind, Language and Reality,* Philosophical Papers, vol 2 (Cambridge, Cambridge University Press).

______ (1978) *Meaning and the Moral Sciences* (London, Hutchinson).

______ (1981) *Reason, Truth and History* (Cambridge, Harvard University Press).

______ (1987) *The Many Faces of Realism* (La Salle, Open Court).

Quine, WVO (1953) 'Two Dogmas of Empiricism' in *From a Logical Point of View* (Cambridge, Harvard University Press).

______ (1960) *Word and Object* (Cambridge, MIT Press).

______ (1969) *Ontological Relativity and Other Essays* (New York, Columbia University Press).

Quinton, A (1973) *The Nature of Things* (London, Routledge).

Rabinowicz, W (1989) 'Stable and Retrievable Operations' 56 *Philosophy of Science.*

______ (1996) 'Stable Revision, or Is Preservation Worth Preserving?' in A Fuhrmann and H Rott (eds), *Logic, Action, and Information* (Berlin, DeGruyter).

______ (1998) 'Peczenik's Passionate Reason' in A Aarnio et al (eds), *On Coherence Theory of Law* (Lund, Juristsförlaget i Lund).

Railton, P (1998) 'Moral Explanation and Moral Objectivity' 58 *Philosophy and Phenomenological Research.*

______ (1986) 'Moral Realism' 95 *Philosophical Review*. Reprinted in S Darwall, A Gibbard and P Railton (eds), (1997) *Moral Discourse and Practice* (Oxford, Oxford University Press).

Ramsey, FP (1926) 'Truth and Probability' in DH Mellor (ed), *Philosophical Papers* (New York, Cambridge University Press, 1990).

Ranney, M (1991) 'Explorations in Explanatory Coherence' in E Bar-On, E Eylon and Z Schertz (eds), *Designing Intelligent Learning Environments* (Norwood, Ablex).

Rasmussen, SA (1987) 'The Intelligibility of Abortive Omniscience' 37 *Philosophical Quarterly*.

Ratti, GB (2007) 'La coerentizzazione dei sistemi giuridici' 7 *Diritto e Questioni Pubbliche*.

Rawling, P (1999) 'Reasonable Doubt and the Presumption of Innocence: The Case of the Bayesian Juror' 18 *Topoi*.

Rawls, J (1951) 'Outline for a Decision Procedure in Ethics' 60 *The Philosophical Review*.

______ (1974–75) 'The Independence of Moral Theory' 48 *Proceedings and Addresses of the American Philosophical Association*.

______ (1980) 'Kantian Constructivism in Moral Theory' 77 *The Journal of Philosophy*.

______ (1985) 'Justice as Fairness: Political not Metaphysical' 14 *Philosophy and Public Affairs*.

______ (1988) 'The Idea of an Overlapping Consensus' 7 *Oxford Journal of Legal Studies*.

______ (1999) *A Theory of Justice*, rev edn (Cambridge, Harvard University Press).

______ (2001) *Justice as Fairness: A Restatement* (Cambridge, Harvard University Press).

Raz, J (ed) (1978) *Practical Reasoning* (Oxford, Oxford University Press).

______ (1979) *The Authority of Law: Essays on Law and Morality* (Oxford, Clarendon Press).

______ (1985) 'Authority, Law, and Morality' 68 *The Monist*.

______ (1986a) 'Dworkin: A New Link in the Chain' 74 *California Law Review*.

______ (1986b) *The Morality of Freedom* (Oxford, Clarendon Press).

______ (1992) 'The Relevance of Coherence' 72 *Boston University Law Review*.

______ (1999) *Practical Reason and Norms* (Oxford, Oxford University Press).

______ (2004) 'Speaking with One Voice: On Dworkinian Integrity and Coherence' in Burley, J (ed), *Dworkin and His Critics: With Replies by Dworkin* (Malden, Willey Blackwell).

______ (2005) 'The Myth of Instrumental Rationality' 1 *Journal of Ethics and Social Philosophy*.

Read S, Snow C and Simon D (2003) 'Constraint Satisfaction Processes in Social Reasoning' in R Alterman and D Kirsch (eds), *Proceedings of the 25th Annual Conference of the Cognitive Science Society* (Mahwah, Earlbaum).

Redmayne, M (1997) 'Presenting Probabilities in Court: The DNA Experience' 1 *The International Journal of Evidence and Proof*.

______ (1998) 'Bayesianism and Proof' in M Freeman and H Reece (eds), *Science in Court* (Aldershot, Ashgate).

______ (2003) 'Rationality, Naturalism, and Evidence Law' 4 *Michigan State Law Review*.

Redondo, MC (2011) 'Decidir en modo justificado: una explicación coherentista' X *Discusiones*.
Reichenbach, H (1938) *Experience and Prediction* (Chicago, Chicago University Press).
Reinhart, T (1980) 'Conditions for Text Coherence' 1 *Poetics Today*.
_____ (1981) 'Pragmatics and Linguistics: An Analysis of Sentence Topics' 27 *Philosophica*.
Rescher, N (1973) *The Coherence Theory of Truth* (Oxford, Clarendon Press).
_____ (1978) *Peirce's Philosophy of Science* (Notre Dame, University of Notre Dame Press).
_____ (1979) *Cognitive Systematization: A Systems-Theoretic Approach to a Coherentist Theory of Knowledge* (Lanham, Rowman and Littlefield).
_____ (1985) 'Truth as Ideal Coherence' 38 *Review of Metaphysics*.
Rescorla, M (2013) 'Rationality as a Constitutive Ideal' in E Lepore and K Ludwig, *A Companion to Donald Davidson* (Malden, Blackwell).
Richardson, HS (1990) 'Specifying Norms as a Way to Resolve Concrete Ethical Problems' 19 *Philosophy and Public Affairs*.
_____ (1994) *Practical Reasoning about Final Ends* (Cambridge, Cambridge University Press).
_____ (2000) 'Specifying, Balancing, and Interpreting Bioethical Principles' 25 *Journal of Medicine and Philosophy*.
Richmond, A (1999) 'Between Abduction and the Deep Blue Sea' 49 *The Philosophical Quarterly*.
Rickheit, G and Habel, C (eds) (1999) *Mental Models in Discourse Processing and Reasoning* (Amsterdam, Elsevier).
Ripstein, A (2007) *Ronald Dworkin* (Cambridge, Cambridge University Press).
Risjord, M (1993) 'Wittgenstein's Woodcutters: The Problem of Apparent Irrationality' 30 *American Philosophical Quarterly*.
Risselada, R and Spooren, W (eds) (1998) 'Discourse Markers and Coherence Relations' 30 *Journal of Pragmatics*.
Robbennolt, JK, MacCoun, RJ, and Darley, JM (2010) 'Multiple Constraint Satisfaction in Judging' in D Klein and G Mitchell (eds) *The Psychology of Judicial Decision Making* (Oxford, New York).
Roberts, RC and Woods, JW (2007), *Intellectual Virtues: An Essay in Regulative Epistemology* (Oxford, Oxford University Press).
Roberts, RM and Kreuz, RJ (1993) 'Non-Standard Discourse and its Coherence' 16 *Discourse Processes*.
Robertson, B and Vignaux, GA (1993) 'Probability–The Logic of the Law' 13 *Oxford Journal of Legal Studies*.
_____ and _____ (1995) *Interpreting Evidence* (Chichester, John Wiley and Sons).
_____ and _____ (1997) 'An Enthusiastic Response to Allen's 12 Problems' 1 *The International Journal of Evidence and Proof*.
Robey, D (1986) 'Anglo-American New Criticism' in A Jefferson and D Robey (eds), *Modern Literary Theory* (London, Batsford).
Roche, W (2011) 'Coherentism and Inconsistency' 27 *Southwest Philosophy Review*.
_____ (2012) 'Witness Agreement and the Truth-Conduciveness of Coherentist Justification' 50 *The Southern Journal of Philosophy*.

______ (2013) 'Coherence and Probability: A Probabilistic Account of Coherence' in M Araszkiewicz and J Šavelka (eds) *Coherence: Insights from Philosophy, Jurisprudence, and Artificial Intelligence* (Dordrecht, Springer).

Rodriguez-Blanco, V (2001) 'A Revision of the Constitutive and Epistemic Coherence Theories in Law' 14 *Ratio Iuris*.

Rorty, R (1979) *The Mirror of Nature* (Princeton, Princeton University Press).

______ (1986) 'Pragmatism, Davidson and Truth' in E Lepore (ed), *Truth and Interpretation: Perspectives on the Philosophy of Donald Davidson* (Oxford, Blackwell).

Rosati, CS (2004) 'Some Puzzles about Objectivity of Law' 23 *Law and Philosophy*.

Ross, L and Anderson, CA (1982) 'Shortcomings in the Attribution Process: Origins and Maintenance of Erroneous Social Assessments' in D Kahneman, P Slovic and A Tversky (eds), *Judgment under Uncertainty: Heuristics and Biases* (Cambridge, Cambridge University Press).

Rott, H (1992a) 'Modeling for Belief Change: Prioritization and Entrenchment' 58 *Theoria*.

______ (1992b) 'Preferential Belief Change Using Generalized Epistemic Entrenchment' 1 *Journal of Logic, Language and Information*.

______ (1999) 'Coherence and Conservatism in the Dynamics of Belief' 50 *Erkenntnis*.

______ (2000) 'Two Dogmas of Belief Revision' 97 *The Journal of Philosophy*.

______ (2001) *Change, Choice, and Inference: A Study of Belief Revision and Nonmonotonic Inference* (Oxford, Oxford University Press).

______ and Pagnuco, M (2000) 'Severe Withdrawal (and Recovery)' 28 *Journal of Philosophical Logic*.

Rott, M (1986) 'Davidson and Social Science' in E Lepore (ed), *Truth and Interpretation: Perspectives on the Philosophy of Donald Davidson* (Oxford, Blackwell).

Rouchota, W (1998) 'Connectives, Coherence and Relevance' in V Rouchota and AH Jucker (eds), *Current Issues in Relevance Theory* (Amsterdam, John Benjamins).

Ruben, D (1993) *Explanation* (Oxford, Oxford University Press).

Rumelhart, DE (1980) 'Schemata: The Building Blocks of Cognition' in RJ Spiro, BC Bruce and WF Brewer (eds), *Theoretical Issues in Reading Comprehension* (Hillsdale, Erlbaum).

Russell, B (1906–07) 'On the Nature of Truth' 7 *Proceedings of the Aristotelian Society*.

______ (1912) *The Problems of Philosophy* (Oxford, Oxford University Press).

Ryan, JA (2000) 'Coherentist Naturalism in Ethics' 25 *Journal of Philosophical Research*.

Sacks, MJ and Thompson, WC (2003) 'Assessing Evidence: Proving Facts' in D Carson and R Bull (eds), *Handbook of Psychology in Legal Contexts*, 2nd edn (Chichester, John Wiley and Sons Ltd).

Salmon, WC (1990) *Four Decades of Scientific Explanation* (Minneapolis, University of Minnesota Press).

______ (2001a) 'Explanation and Confirmation: A Bayesian Critique of Inference to the Best Explanation' in G Hon and S Rakover (eds), *Explanation: Theoretical Approaches and Applications* (Dordrecht, Kluwer).

(2001b) 'Reflections of a Bashful Bayesian: A Reply to Peter Lipton' in G Hon and SS Rakover (eds), *Explanation: Theoretical Approaches and Applications* (Dordrecht, Kluwer).

Samet, J and Schank, R (1984) 'Coherence and Connectivity' 7 *Linguistics and Philosophy*.

Sanders, T (1997) 'Semantic and Pragmatic Sources of Coherence: On the Categorization of Coherence Relations in Context' 24 *Discourse Processes*.

_____ and Spooren, W (1999) 'Communicative Intentions and Coherence Relations' in W Bublitz, U Lenk and E Ventola (eds), *Coherence in Spoken and Written Discourse* (Amsterdam, John Benjamins).

Sartor, G (1995) 'Defeasibility in Legal Reasoning' in Z Bankowski et al (eds), *Informatics and the Foundations of Legal Reasoning* (Dordrecht, Kluwer).

Sartorious, R (1968) 'The Justification of the Judicial Decision' 78 *Ethics*.

_____ (1971) 'Social Policy and Judicial Legislation' 8 *American Philosophical Quarterly*.

Šavelka, J (2013) 'Coherence as Constraint Satisfaction: Judicial Reasoning Support Mechanism' in M Araszkiewicz and J Šavelka (eds) *Coherence: Insights from Philosophy, Jurisprudence, and Artificial Intelligence* (Dordrecht, Springer).

Sayre-MacCord, G (1985) 'Coherence and Models for Moral Theorizing' 66 *Pacific Philosophical Quarterly*.

_____ (1996) 'Coherentist Epistemology and Moral Theory' in W Sinnott-Armstrong and M Timmons (eds), *Moral Knowledge* (Oxford, Oxford University Press).

Scanlon, TM (2003) 'Rawls on Justification' in S Freeman (ed), *The Cambridge Companion to Rawls* (Cambridge, Cambridge University Press).

Schauer, F (1986–87) 'The Jurisprudence of Reasons' 85 *Michigan Law Review*.

_____ (1991) *Playing by the Rules: A Philosophical Examination of Rule-Based Decision-Making in Law and in Life* (Oxford, Clarendon Press).

_____ (1998) 'On the Supposed Defeasibility of Legal Rules' 51 *Current Legal Problems*.

_____ (2003) *Profiles, Probabilities, and Stereotypes* (Cambridge, Harvard University Press).

_____ (2012) 'Must Virtue be Particular?' in A Amaya and HL Ho (eds), *Law, Virtue and Justice* (Oxford, Hart Publishing).

Schiavello, A (2001) 'On "Coherence" and "Law": An Analysis of Different Models' 14 *Ratio Iuris*.

_____ (2011) 'Tre Osservazioni su 'Diez tesis acerca de la coherencia en el Derecho'' X *Discusiones*.

_____ (2013) 'The Third Theory of Legal Objectivity' in M Araszkiewicz and J Šavelka (eds), *Coherence, Insights from Philosophy, Jurisprudence, and Artificial Intelligence* (Dordrecht, Springer).

Schimtt, F (2004), 'Epistemology and Cognitive Science' in I Niiniluoto, M Sintonen and J Wolenski (eds), *Handbook of Epistemology* (Dordrecht, Kluwer).

Schlobinski, P and Schütze-Coburn, S (1992) 'On the Topic of Topic and Topic Continuity' 30 *Linguistics*.

Schoeman, F (1987) 'Cohen on Inductive Probability and the Law of Evidence' 54 *Philosophy of Science*.

Schröter, MW (2006) 'European Legal Reasoning: A Coherence-Based Approach' 92 *Archiv für Rechts und Sozialphilosophie*.

Schubert, S (2011) 'Coherence and Reliability: The Case of Overlapping Testimonies' 74 *Erkenntnis.*

——— (2012a) 'Coherence Reasoning and Reliability: A Defense of Shogenji's Measure' 187 *Synthese.*

_____ (2012b) 'Is Coherence Conducive to Reliability?' 187 *Synthese.*

_____ and Olsson, EJ (2012) 'On the Coherence of Higher Order Beliefs' 50 *The Southern Journal of Philosophy.*

_____ (2013) 'Coherence and Reliability in Judicial Reasoning' in M Araszkiewicz and J Šavelka (eds) *Coherence: Insights from Philosophy, Jurisprudence, and Artificial Intelligence* (Dordrecht, Springer).

Schum, DA (1986) 'Probability and the Processes of Discovery, Proof, and Choice' 66 *Boston University Law Review.*

_____ (1999) 'Marshalling Thoughts and Evidence during Fact Investigation' 40 *South Texas Law Review.*

_____ (2001) *The Evidential Foundations of Probabilistic Reasoning* (Evanston, Northwestern University Press).

_____ (2002) 'Species of Abductive Reasoning in Fact Investigation in Law' in M MacCrimmon and P Tillers (eds), *The Dynamics of Judicial Proof: Computation, Logic and Common Sense* (Heildelberg, Springer-Verlag).

_____ and Tillers, P (1991) 'Marshalling Evidence for Adversary Litigation' 12 *Cardozo Law Review.*

Schupbach, JN (2008) 'On the Alleged Impossibility of Bayesian Coherentism' 141 *Philosophical Studies.*

_____ (2011) 62 'New Hope for Shogenji's Coherence Measure' *The British Journal of Philosophy of Science.*

Schurz, G (2008) 'Patterns of Abduction' 164 *Synthese.*

Schweizer, M (2014) 'Comparing Holistic and Atomistic Evaluation of Evidence' 13 *Law, Probability and Risk.*

Sebeok, A and Eco, U (1983) *The Sign of Three: Dupin, Holmes, and Peirce* (Bloomington, Indiana University Press).

Seigel, ML (1994) 'A Pragmatic Critique of Modern Evidence Scholarship' 88 *Northwestern University Law Review.*

Sellars, W (1956) 'Empiricism and the Philosophy of Mind' 1 *Minnesota Studies in the Philosophy of Science.*

_____ (1963) *Science, Perception, and Reality* (New York, Humanities Press).

Sen, A (1999) *Development as Freedom* (New York, Knopf).

Shaffer, MJ (2002) 'Coherence, Justification, and the AGM Theory of Belief Revision' in Y Bouchard (ed), *Perspectives on Coherentism* (Aylmer, Editions du Scribe).

Shank, RC and Abelson, RP (1977) *Scripts, Plans, Goals and Understanding: An Inquiry into Human Knowledge-Structures* (Hillsdale, Erlbaum).

Shelley, J (1985) 'Interpretation in Law: the Fish-Dworkin Debate' 73 *California Law Review.*

Sherman, N (1989) *The Fabric of Character: Aristotle's Theory of Virtue* (New York, Oxford University Press).

Shiner, RA (1988) 'Adjudication, Coherence and Moral Value' in AF Bayefsky (ed), *Legal Theory Meets Legal Practice* (Edmonton, Academic Printing).

Shogenji, T (1999) 'Is Coherence Truth-Conducive?' 59 *Analysis.*

_____ (2001) 'The Role of Coherence in Epistemic Justification' 79 *Australasian Journal of Philosophy*.

_____ (2005) 'Justification from Scratch' 125 *Philosophical Studies*.

Shrager, J and Langley, P (eds) (1990) *Computational Models of Scientific Discovery and Theory Formation* (San Mateo, Morgan Kauffman).

Sidgwick, H (1981) *The Methods of Ethics* (Indianapolis, Hackett Pub Co).

Siebel, M (2004) 'On Fitelson's Measure of Coherence' 64 *Analysis*.

_____ (2005) 'Against Probabilistic Measures of Coherence' 63 *Erkenntnis*.

_____ (2011) 'Why Explanation and thus Coherence cannot be reduced to Probability' 71 *Analysis*.

_____ and Wolff, W (2008) 'Equivalent Testimonies as a Touchstone of Coherence' 161 *Synthese*.

Silvers, S (1989) 'Coherence, Observation, and the Justification of Empirical Belief' in J Bender (ed), *The Current State of the Coherence Theory* (Dordrecht, Kluwer).

Simmonds, NE (1987) 'Imperial Visions and Mundane Practices' 46 *Cambridge Law Journal*.

Simon, D (1998) 'A Psychological Model of Judicial Decision-Making' 30 *Rutgers Law Journal*.

_____ (2002) 'Freedom and Constraint in Adjudication: A Look though the Lens of Cognitive Psychology' 67 *Brooklyn Law Review*.

_____ (2004) 'A Third View of the Black Box: Cognitive Coherence in Legal Decision-Making' 71 *The University of Chicago Law Review*.

_____ (2011) 'The Limited Diagnosticity of Criminal Trials' 64 *Vanderbilt Law Review*.

_____ (2012) *In Doubt: The Psychology of the Criminal Justice Process* (Cambridge, Harvard University Press).

_____ et al (2000) 'The Emergence of Coherence Over the Course of Decision-Making' 27 *Journal of Experimental Psychology: Learning, Memory and Cognition*.

_____ and Holyoak, KJ (2002) 'Structural Dynamics of Cognition: From Consistency Theories to Constraint Satisfaction' 6 *Personality and Social Psychology Review*.

_____, Snow, J and Read, S (2004) 'The Redux of Cognitive Consistency Theories: Evidence Judgments by Constraint Satisfaction' 86 *Journal of Personality and Social Psychology*.

_____ and Scurich, N (2011) (eds) 'Lay Judgments of Judicial Decision Making' 8 *Journal of Empirical Legal Studies*.

_____, Stenstrom, D and Read SJ (forthcoming) 'The Coherence Effect: Blending Cognition and Emotion'.

Simon, HA (1973) 'Does Scientific Discovery Have a Logic?' 40 *Philosophy of Science*. Reprinted in (1977) 'Models of Discovery' 54 *Boston Studies in the Philosophy of Science* and in H Keuth (ed), (1998) *Karl Popper* (Berlin, Akademie Verlag).

_____ (1998) 'Discovering Explanations' 8 *Minds and Machines*.

Singer, P (1974) 'Sidgwick and Reflective Equilibrium' 58 *Monist*.

Sinnott-Armstrong, W (2002) 'What's in a Contrast Class?' 62 *Analysis*.

Sintonen, M and Kikeri, M (2004) 'Scientific Discovery' in I Niiniluoto, M Sintonen and J Wolenski (eds) *Handbook of Epistemology* (Dordrecht, Kluwer).

Sloman, SA (1994) 'When Explanations Compete: the Role of Explanatory Coherence on Judgments of Likelihood' 53 *Cognition*.

Smart, JJ (1999) 'Correspondence, Coherence, and Realism' in LE Hahn (ed), *The Philosophy of Donald Davidson* (Chicago, Open Court).

Solum, LB (2003) 'Virtue Jurisprudence: A Virtue-Centred Theory of Judging' in M Brady and D Pritchard (eds), *Moral and Epistemic Virtues* (Malden, Blackwell).

____ and Farrelly, C (2008) *Virtue Jurisprudence* (New York, Palgrave MacMillan).

Sosa, E (1980) 'The Raft and the Pyramid: Coherence vs. Foundations in the Theory of Knowledge' 5 *Midwest Studies in Philosophy*. Reprinted in *Knowledge in Perspective: Selected Essays in Epistemology* (Cambridge, Cambridge University Press, 1991).

______ (1986a) '"Circular" Coherence and "Absurd" Foundations' in E Lepore (ed), *Truth and Interpretation: Perspectives on the Philosophy of Donald Davidson* (Oxford, Blackwell).

______ (2004) 'Relevant Alternatives, Contextualism Included' 119 *Philosophical Studies*.

Sperber, D and Wilson, D (1986) *Relevance: Communication and Cognition* (Oxford, Blackwell).

Stalnaker, R (1984) *Inquiry* (Cambridge, MIT Press).

Stanley, J (2005) *Knowledge and Practical Interests* (Oxford, Oxford University Press).

Stark, S (2001) 'Virtue and Emotion' 35 *Noûs*.

Statman, D (1997) 'Introduction to Virtue Ethics' in D Statman (ed), *Virtue Ethics: A Critical Reader*, (Edinburgh, Edinburgh University Press).

Stavropoulos, N (1996) *Objectivity in Law* (Oxford, Clarendon Press).

Stein, A (1996) 'The Refoundation of Evidence Law' 9 *Canadian Journal of Law and Jurisprudence*.

______ (1997a) 'Judicial Fact-finding and Bayesian Method: the Case for Deeper Skepticism about their Combination' 1 *The International Journal of Evidence and Proof*.

______ (1997b) 'Bayesioskepticism Justified' 1 *The International Journal of Evidence and Proof*.

Stein, E (1996) *Without Good Reason: The Rationality Debate in Philosophy and Cognitive Science* (Oxford, Oxford University Press).

Stern, R (2004) 'Coherence as a Test for Truth' LXIX *Philosophy and Phenomenological Research*.

Steup, M (1989) 'BonJour's Anti-Foundationalist Argument' in J Bender (ed), *The Current State of the Coherence Theory: Critical Essays on the Epistemic Theories of Keith Lehrer and Laurence BonJour, with Replies* (Dordrecht, Kluwer).

______ (1991) 'Moral Truth and Coherence: Comments on Goldman' 29 *Southern Journal of Philosophy*.

______ (1999a) 'A Defense of Internalism' in L Pojman (ed), *Theory of Knowledge: Classical and Contemporary Readings*, 2nd edn (Belmont, Wadsworth).

______ (ed) (1999b) *Knowledge, Truth, and Duty: Essays on Epistemic Justification, Responsibility, and Virtue* (Oxford, Oxford University Press).

______ and Sosa, E (eds) (2005) *Contemporary Debates in Epistemology* (Malden, Blackwell).

Stich, S (1990) *The Fragmentation of Reason* (Cambridge, MIT Press).

______ (1998) 'Reflective Equilibrium, Analytic Epistemology and the Problem of Cognitive Diversity' in M DePaul and W Ramsey (eds), *Rethinking Intuition* (Lanham, Rowman and Littlefield).

Street, S (2008) 'Constructivism about Reasons' in R Shafer-Landau, *Oxford Studies in Metaethics*, vol 3 (Oxford, Oxford University Press).

______ (2010) 'What is Constructivism in Ethics and Metaethics?' 5 *Philosophy Compass*.

Sturgeon, N (1985) 'Moral Explanations' in D Copp and D Zimmerman (eds), *Morality, Reason and Truth* (Totowa, Rowman and Allenheld).

Summers, R (1999) 'Formal Legal Truth and Substantive Truth in Judicial Fact-finding—Their Justified Divergence in Some Particular Cases' 18 *Law and Philosophy*.

Swain, M (1989) 'BonJour's Coherence Theory' in J Bender (ed), *The Current State of the Coherence Theory: Critical Essays on the Epistemic Theories of Keith Lehrer and Laurence BonJour, with Replies* (Dordrecht, Kluwer).

Swiburne, R (ed) (2002) *Bayes's Theorem* (New York, Oxford University Press).

Tannen, D (ed) (1984) *Coherence in Spoken and Written Discourse* (Ablex, Norwood).

Taroni, F et al (2006) *Bayesian Networks and Probabilistic Inference in Forensic Science* (Chichester, John Wiley).

Taruffo, M (1992) *La Prova dei Fatti Giuridici* (Milan, Giuffrè).

______ (2003) 'Rethinking the Standards of Proof' 51 *American Journal of Comparative Law*.

Tennant, N (2012) *Changes of Mind: An Essay on Rational Belief Revision* (Oxford, Oxford University Press).

Tersman, F (1992) 'Coherence and Disagreement' 65 *Philosophical Studies*.

Thagard, P (1978) 'The Best Explanation: Criteria for Theory Choice' 75 *Journal of Philosophy*.

______ (1984) 'Frames, Knowledge and Inference' 61 *Synthese*.

______ (1988) *Computational Philosophy of Science* (Cambridge, MIT Press).

______ (1989) 'Explanatory Coherence' 12 *Behavioral and Brain Sciences*.

______ (1991) 'The Dinosaur Debate: Explanatory Coherence and the Problem of Competing Hypotheses' in J Pollock and R Cummins (eds), *Philosophy and AI: Essays in the Interface* (Cambridge, MIT Press).

______ (1992a) *Conceptual Revolutions* (Princeton, Princeton University Press).

______ (1992b) 'Adversarial Problem Solving: Modelling an Opponent Using Explanatory Coherence' 16 *Cognitive Science*.

______ (1997) 'Coherent and Creative Conceptual Combinations' in TB Ward, SM Smith and J Vaid (eds), *Creative Thought: An Investigation of Conceptual Structures and Processes* (Washington, American Psychological Association).

______ (1998) 'Ethical Coherence' 11 *Philosophical Psychology*.

______ (2000a) *Coherence in Thought and Action* (Cambridge, MIT Press).

______ (2000b) 'Probabilistic Networks and Explanatory Coherence' 1 *Cognitive Science Quarterly*.

______ (2001) 'How to Make Decisions: Coherence, Emotion, and Practical Inference' in E Millgram (ed), *Varieties of Practical Reasoning* (Cambridge, MIT Press).

______ (2002) 'The Passionate Scientist: Emotion in Scientific Cognition' in P Carruthers, S Stich and M Siegel (eds), *The Cognitive Basis of Science* (Cambridge, Cambridge University Press).

______ (2003) 'Why wasn't O.J. Convicted? Emotional Coherence in Legal Inference' 17 *Cognition and Emotion*.

______ (2004) 'Causal Inference in Legal Decision-Making: Explanatory Coherence vs. Bayesian Networks' 18 *Applied Artificial Intelligence*.

______ (2006) *Hot Thought: Mechanisms and Applications of Emotional Cognition* (Cambridge, MIT).

______ (2007a) 'Coherence, Truth, and the Development of Scientific Knowledge' 74 *Philosophy of Science*.

______ (2007b) 'Abductive Inference: From Philosophical Analysis to Neural Mechanisms' in A Feeney and E Heit (eds), *Inductive Reasoning: Experimental, Developmental, and Computational Approaches* (Cambridge, Cambridge University Press).

______ (2012) 'Coherence: The Price is Right' 50 *The Southern Journal of Philosophy*.

______, Eliasmith, C, Rusnock P and Shelley, C (2002) 'Knowledge and Coherence' in R Elio (ed), *Common Sense, Reasoning, and Rationality* (New York, Oxford University Press).

______ and Kunda, Z (1998) 'Making Sense of People' in SJ Read and LC Miller (eds) *Connectionist Models of Social Reasoning and Social Behavior* (Mahwah, Lawrence Earlbaum).

______ and Millgram, E (1995) 'Inference to the Best Plan: A Coherence Theory of Decision' in R Ashwin and DB Leake (eds), *Goal Driven Learning* (Cambridge, MIT).

______ and Shelley, C (1997) 'Abductive Reasoning: Logic, Visual Thinking and Coherence' in ML Dalla Chiara, K Doets, D Mundici and J van Benthem (eds), *Logic and Scientific Methods* (Dordrecht, Kluwer).

______ and Verbeurgt, K (1998) 'Coherence as Constraint Satisfaction' 22 *Cognitive Science*.

Tillers, P (1986a) 'Mapping Inferential Domains' 66 *Boston University Law Review*.

______ (1986b) 'Introduction to Symposium on Probability and Inference in the Law of Evidence' 66 *Boston University Law Review*.

______ (1989) 'Webs of Things in the Mind: A New Science of Evidence' 87 *Michigan Law Review*.

______ (2011) 'Trial by Mathematics—Reconsidered' 10 *Law, Probability, and Risk*.

______ et al (1991) 'Symposium: Decision and Inference in Litigation' 13 *Cardozo Law Review*.

______ and Green, ED (eds) (1988) *Probability and Inference in the Law of Evidence* (Dordrecht, Kluwer).

______ and Schum, DA (1991) 'A Theory of Preliminary Fact Investigation' 24 *UC Davis Law Review*.

Timmons, M (1987) 'Foundationalism and the Structure of Ethical Justification' 97 *Ethics*.

______ (1990) 'On the Epistemic Status of Considered Moral Judgments' 29 *The Southern Journal of Philosophy*.

______ (1991) 'Putnam's Moral Objectivism' 34 *Erkenntnis*.

______ (1993) 'Moral Justification in Context' 76 *The Monist*.

______ (1995) Review of *Balance and Refinement: Beyond Coherence Methods of Moral Inquiry*, by M DePaul 105 *Ethics*.

——— (1999) *Morality without Foundations: A Defense of Ethical Contextualism* (New York, Oxford University Press).

Toombs, E (2003) 'Harmony, Explanatory Coherence, and the Debate between the Reticular Theory and the Neuron Theory of Nerve Cell Structure: ECHO's Resolution of a Quiet Revolution' 34 *Studies in History and Philosophy of Biological and Biomedical Science.*

Toulmin, SE (2003) *The Uses of Argument* (Cambridge, Cambridge University Press).

Trabasso, T and Suhn, S (1993) 'Understanding Text: Achieving Explanatory Coherence Through On-Line Inferences and Mental Operations in Working Memory' 16 *Discourse Processes.*

———, Suhn, S and Payton, P (1995) 'Explanatory Coherence in Understanding and Talking about Events' in MA Gernbascher and T Givón (eds), *Coherence in Spontaneous Text* (Amsterdam, John Benjamins).

Tramel, P (2008) 'Haack's Foundherentism is a Foundationalism' 160 *Synthese.*

Tribe, L (1971) 'Trial by Mathematics: Precision and Ritual in the Legal Process' 84 *Harvard Law Review.*

Triplett, T (1990) 'Recent Work on Foundationalism' 27 *American Philosophical Quarterly.*

Tuomela, R (2000) 'Belief versus Acceptance' 2 *Philosophical Explorations.*

Twining, W (1985) *Theories of Evidence: Bentham and Wigmore* (Stanford, Stanford University Press).

——— (1986) 'The Boston Symposium: A Comment' 66 *Boston University Law Review.*

——— (1991) 'The New Evidence Scholarship' 13 *Cardozo Law Review.*

——— (1992) 'Debating Probabilities' in W Twining and A Stein (eds), *Evidence and Proof* (New York, New York University Press).

——— (1997) 'Recent Trends in Evidence Scholarship' in JF Nijboer and JM Reijntjes (eds), *Proceedings of the First World Conference on New Trends in Criminal Investigation and Evidence* (Lelystad, Open University of the Netherlands).

——— (1999a) 'Narrative and Generalizations in Argumentation about Questions of Fact' 40 *South Texas Law Review.*

——— (1999b) 'Necessary but Dangerous: Generalizations and Narrative in Argumentation about 'Facts' in Criminal Process?' in M Malsch and JF Nijboer (eds), *Complex Cases: Perspectives on the Netherlands Criminal Justice System* (Amsterdam, Thela Thesis).

——— (2002) *The Great Juristic Bazaar* (Dartmouth, Ashgate).

——— (2003) 'Evidence as a Multidisciplinary Subject' 2 *Law, Probability and Risk.*

——— (2006) *Rethinking Evidence: Exploratory Essays*, 2nd edn (Cambridge, Cambridge University Press).

——— and Stein, A (eds) (1992) 'Introduction' in W Twining and A Stein (eds), *Evidence and Proof* (New York, New York University Press).

Unger, C (1996) 'The Scope of Discourse Connectives: Implications for Discourse Organization' 32 *Journal of Linguistics.*

Van Cleve, J (2011) 'Can Coherence Generate Warrant Ex Nihilo? Probability and the Logic of Concurring Witnesses' LXXXII *Philosophy and Phenomenological Research.*

Van de Velde, RG (1984) 'Inferences and Coherence in Text Interpretation' in E Sözer (ed), *Text Connexity, Text Coherence* (Hamburg, Buske).
_____ (1989a) 'Man, Verbal Text, Inferencing, and Coherence' in W Heydrich, F Neubauer, J Petöfi and E Sözer (eds), *Connexity and Coherence: Analysis of Text and Discourse* (Berlin, DeGruyter).
_____ (1989b) 'The Role of Inferences in Text Organization' in ME Conte, JS Petöfi and E Sözer (eds) *Text and Discourse Connectedness* (Amsterdam, John Benjamins).
Van Dijk, TA (1977) *Text and Context* (London, Longman).
___ (1981) Review of *Discourse Production and Comprehension*, edited by RO Freedle 17 *Journal of Linguistics.*
Van Dunné, JM (1996) 'Narrative Coherence and its Function in Judicial Decision Making and Legislation' 44 *The American Journal of Comparative Law.*
_____ (1998) 'Normative and Narrative Coherence in Legal Decision Making' 69 *Archiv für Rechts und Sozialphilosophie.*
Van Fraassen, BC (1989) *Laws and Symmetry* (Oxford, Clarendon Press).
_____ (2002) *The Empirical Stance* (New Haven, Yale University Press).
Van Roermund, B (1988) 'On "Narrative Coherence" in Legal Contexts' in C Faralli and E Pattaro (eds), *Reason in Law* (Milan, Giuffré).
_____ (1990) 'Narrative Coherence and the Guises of Legalism' in P Nerhot (ed), *Law, Interpretation, and Reality: Essays in Epistemology, Hermeneutics, and Jurisprudence* (Dordrecht, Kluwer).
_____ (1997) *Law, Narrative and Reality: An Essay in Intercepting Politics* (Dordrecht, Kluwer).
Viehweger, D (1989) 'Coherence-Interaction of Modules' in W Heydrich, F Neubauer, J Petöfi and E Sözer (eds), *Connexity and Coherence: Analysis of Text and Discourse* (Berlin, DeGruyter).
Villa, V (1990) 'Normative Coherence and Epistemological Presuppositions of Justification' in P Nerhot (ed), *Law, Interpretation and Reality: Essays in Epistemology, Hermeneutics and Jurisprudence* (Dordrecht, Kluwer).
Vitacolona, L (1992–93) Review of *Connexity and Coherence*, edited by W Heydrich, F Neubauer, JS Pëtofi and E Sözer 21–22 *Literary Semantics.*
Vogel, J (1999) 'The New Relevant Alternatives Theory' 13 *Philosophical Perspectives.*
Wacks, R (1984) 'Judges and Injustice' 101 *South African Law Journal.*
Wagenaar, WA (1996) 'Anchored Narratives: A Theory of Judicial Reasoning and its Consequences' in G Davies, S Lloyd-Bostock, M McMurran and C Wilson (eds), *Psychology, Law and Criminal Justice* (Berlin, Walter de Gruyter).
———, Van Koppen, PJ and Crombag, HFM (1993) *Anchored Narratives: The Psychology of Criminal Evidence* (New York, St Martin's Press).
Waldron, J (2008) 'Did Dworkin ever Answer the Crits?' in S Hershovitz (ed) *Exploring Law's Empire: The Jurisprudence of Ronald Dworkin* (2008).
Wales, K (1998) 'Cohesion and Coherence in Literature' in JL Mey (ed), *Concise Encyclopedia of Pragmatics* (New York, Elsevier).
Walker, RCS (1989a) *The Coherence Theory of Truth: Realism, Anti-Realism, Idealism* (London, Routledge).
_____ (1989b) Review of *Relevance: Communication and Cognition*, by D Sperber and D Wilson 4 *Mind and Language.*

Walton, D (2002) *Legal Argumentation and Evidence* (Pennsylvania, Pennsylvania State University Press).
Warren, WH, Nicholas, DW and Trabasso, T (1979) 'Event Chains and Inferences in Understanding Narratives' in RO Freedle (ed), *New Directions in Discourse Processing* (Norwood, Ablex).
Wassermann, R (1999a) 'Resource Bounded Belief Revision' 50 *Erkenntnis*.
______ (1999b) Resource-Bounded Belief Revision. ILLC Dissertation Series (Amsterdam, Institute for Logic, Language and Computation).
Wasserstron, RA (1961) *The Judicial Decision: Toward a Theory of Legal Justification* (Stanford, Stanford University Press).
Watson, G (1997) 'On the Primacy of Character' in D Statman (ed), *Virtue Ethics* (Edinburgh, Edinburgh University Press).
Weinrib, EJ (1988) 'Legal Formalism: On the Immanent Rationality of Law' 97 *Yale Law Journal*.
____ (1994) 'The Jurisprudence of Legal Formalism' 16 *Harvard Journal of Law and Public Policy*.
Weintraub, R (2013) 'Induction and Inference to the Best Explanation' 166 *Philosophical Studies*.
Weisberg, J (2009) 'Locating IBE in the Bayesian Framework' 167 *Synthese*.
Wheeler, G (2012) 'Explaining the Limits of Olsson's Impossibility Result' 50 *The Southern Journal of Philosophy*.
Wiggins, D (1980) 'Deliberation and Practical Reasoning' in A Rorty (ed) *Essays on Aristotle's Ethics* (Berkeley, University of California Press).
Wigmore, JH (1983) *Evidence in Trials at Common Law* by P Tillers (Rev) (Boston, Little Brown and Company).
Wilde, O (2008) *The Importance of Being Ernest* (Oxford, Oxford University Press).
Williams, B (1985) *Ethics and the Limits of Philosophy* (Cambridge, Harvard University Press).
Williams, G (1979) 'The Mathematics of Proof' *Criminal Law Review*.
______ (1980) 'A Short Rejoinder' *Criminal Law Review*.
Williams, M (1980) 'Coherence, Justification and Truth' 34 *Review of Metaphysics*.
______ (1996) *Unnatural Doubts: Epistemological Realism and the Basis of Scepticism*, rev edn (Princeton, Princeton University Press). First published by Blackwell (1991).
______ (1999) *Groundless Belief: An Essay on the Possibility of Epistemology*, 2nd edn (Princeton, Princeton University Press).
______ (2000) 'Is Contextualism Statable?' in E Sosa and E Villanueva (eds), 'Skepticism' 10 *Philosophical Issues*.
______ (2001) *Problems of Knowledge: A Critical Introduction to Epistemology* (Oxford, Oxford University Press).
Williams, PM (1980) 'Bayesian Conditionalisation and the Principle of Minimum Information' 31 *The British Journal for the Philosophy of Science*.
Wilson, A (1982) 'The Nature of Legal Reasoning: a Commentary with Special Reference to Professor MacCormick's Legal Theory' 2 *Legal Studies*.
Wilson, D (1998) 'Discourse, Coherence and Relevance: A Reply to Rachel Giora' 29 *Journal of Pragmatics*.
______ and Matsui, T (1998) 'Recent Approaches to Bridging: Truth, Coherence, Relevance' 10 *UCL Working Papers in Linguistics*.

Wintgens, L (1992) 'Some Critical Comments on Coherence in Law' in B Brouwer et al (eds), *Coherence and Conflict in Law*. Proceedings of the 3rd Benelux-Scandinavian Symposium in Legal Theory (Dordrecht, Kluwer).

_____ (1993) 'Coherence of the Law' 79 *Archiv für Rechts und Sozialphilosophie*.

_____ (2000) 'On Coherence and Consistency' in W Krawietz et al (eds), *The Reasonable as Rational? On Legal Argumentation and Justification. Festschrift for Aulis Aarnio* (Berlin, Duncker and Humblot).

_____ (2012) *Legisprudence: Practical Reason in Legislation* (Farnham/Burlington, Ashgate).

Wong, D (1984) *Moral Relativity* (Berkeley, University of California Press).

Woods, J (2010) 'Abduction and Proof: A Criminal Paradox' in DM Gabbay et al (eds), *Approaches to Legal Rationality* (Dordrecht, Springer).

Wright, C (1995) 'Truth and Coherence' Critical study of *The Coherence Theory of Truth* by RCS Walker 103 *Synthese*.

Wroblewski, J (1985) *Constitución y teoría de la interpretación jurídica* (Madrid, Civitas).

_____ (1992) *The Judicial Application of Law* (Dordrecht, Kluwer).

Young, JO (1995) *Global Anti-Realism* (Aldershot, Avebury).

_____ (2001) 'A Defense of the Coherence Theory of Truth' 26 *The Journal of Philosophical Research*.

Zaccaria, G (1990) 'Hermeneutics and Narrative Comprehension' in P Nerhot (ed), *Law, Interpretation and Reality: Essays in Epistemology, Hermeneutics and Jurisprudence* (Dordrecht, Kluwer).

_____ (1995) 'Dimensioni dell'ermeneutica e interpretazione giuridica' 72 *Rivista internazionale di filosofia del diritto*.

Zagzebski, L (1996) *Virtues of the Mind: An Inquiry into the Nature of Virtue and the Ethical Foundations of Knowledge* (Cambridge, Cambridge University Press).

Ziff, P (1984) 'Coherence' 7 *Linguistics and Philosophy*.

Zima, PV (1999) *The Philosophy of Modern Literary Theory* (London, Athlone Press).

Ziv, Y (1988) 'On the Rationality of "Relevance" and the Relevance of "Rationality"' 12 *Journal of Pragmatics*.

Zuckerman, A (1986) 'Law, Fact or Justice' 66 *Boston University Law Review*.

Zynda, L (1996) 'Coherence as an Ideal of Rationality' 109 *Synthese*.

# Index

*Note*: Author names are indexed only where there is significant discussion or frequent citation.

www.ingramcontent.com/pod-product-compliance
Lightning Source LLC
LaVergne TN
LVHW052207200926
848481LV00001B/51